IN THE LIGHT
OF THE WORD

Previously Published in
The American Society of Missiology Series

Protestant Pioneers in Korea, Everett Nichols Hunt, Jr.

Catholic Politics in China and Korea, Eric O. Hanson

From the Rising of the Sun, James M. Phillips

Meaning Across Cultures, Eugene A. Nida and William D. Reyburn

The Island Churches of the Pacific, Charles W. Forman

Henry Venn, Wilbert Shenk

No Other Name? Paul F. Knitter

Toward a New Age in Christian Theology, Richard Henry Drummond

The Expectation of the Poor, Guillermo Cook

Eastern Orthodox Mission Theology Today, James J. Stamoolis

Confucius, the Buddha, and the Christ, Ralph Covell

The Church and Cultures, Louis J. Luzbetak

Translating the Message, Lamin Sanneh

An African Tree of Life, Thomas G. Christensen

Missions and Money, Jonathan J. Bonk

Transforming Mission, David J. Bosch

Bread for the Journey, Anthony J. Gittins

New Face of the Church in Latin America, Guillermo Cook

Mission Legacies, edited by Gerald H. Anderson, Robert T. Coote, Norman A. Horner, and James M. Phillips

Classic Texts in Mission and World Christianity, edited by Norman E. Thomas

Christian Mission: A Case Study Approach, Alan Neely

Understanding Spiritual Power: A Forgotten Dimension of Cross-Cultural Mission and Ministry, Marguerite G. Kraft

Missiological Education for the 21st Century: The Book, the Circle and the Sandals, edited by J. Dudley Woodberry, Charles Van Engen, and Edgar J. Elliston

Dictionary of Mission: Theology, History, Perspectives, edited by Karl Müller, Theo Sundermeier, Stephen B. Bevans, and Richard H. Bliese

Earthen Vessels and Transcendent Power: American Presbyterians in China, 1837–1952, G. Thompson Brown

The Missionary Movement in American Catholic History, 1820–1980, Angelyn Dries

Mission in the New Testament: An Evangelical Approach, edited by William J. Larkin, Jr., and Joel W. Williams

Changing Frontiers of Mission, Wilbert Shenk

American Society of Missiology Series, No. 29

IN THE LIGHT
OF THE WORD

Divine Word Missionaries of North America

Ernest Brandewie

ORBIS BOOKS

Maryknoll, New York 10545

The Catholic Foreign Mission Society of America (Maryknoll) recruits and trains people for overseas missionary service. Through Orbis Books, Maryknoll aims to foster the international dialogue that is essential to mission. The books published, however, reflect the opinions of their authors and are not meant to represent the official position of the society. To obtain more information about Maryknoll and Orbis Books, please visit our website at www.maryknoll.org.

Library of Congress Cataloging-in-Publication Data

Library of Congress Cataloging-in-Publication Data

Brandewie, Ernest.
    In the light of the Word : Divine Word Missionaries of North America / Ernest Brandewie.
        p. cm. — (American Society of Missiology series; no. 29
    Includes bibliographical references and index.
    ISBN 1-57075-232-X
    1. Society of the Divine Word—United States—History. 2. Society of the Divine Word—Canada—History. I. Title. II. Series.

BV2300.S6 B73 2000
271'.79—dc21

                                                        00-040637

Leader:
May the darkness of sin
and the night of unbelief
vanish before the light of the Word
and the Spirit of grace.

Community:
And may the heart of Jesus
live in the hearts of all. Amen.[1]

In the Light of the Word
is published to commemorate
the one-hundredth anniversary
of the establishment of the
Society of the Divine Word
at Techny, Illinois.
1900-2000

---

1. Traditional prayer used by the members of the Society of the Divine Word at the conclusion of community exercises, classes, meals and other occasions.

Contents

Preface to the ASM Series   ix

Preface   xi

A Word on Sources   xv

Acknowledgments   xvii

PART ONE
FOUNDATION AND MATURATION

1. From Germany to America   3
   The Earliest Years

2. The Move West   29
   The Foundation in Shermerville Becomes Techny

3. Opening the Techny Mission Seminary   56
   The Early Years, 1906–1932

4. Maturing as a Missionary Community   82
   World War II through Vatican Council II, 1932–1970

5. Animating the Mission Cause, 1901–1970   111
   Utilizing the Media and Popular Movements

6. Formation of SVD Missionary Priests   127
   Continuity and Change, 1909–1960

7. The Brothers' Life and Formation   159
   Faithful Servants and Master Craftsmen, 1895–1960

8. The Second Vatican Council and Its Impact   169
   Changes in Religious Life and Missionary Formation, 1958–1970

PART TWO
APOSTOLATES OF DIVINE WORD MISSIONARIES
AT HOME AND ABROAD

9. Staffing African-American Parishes   179
    The SVD's Most Radical Venture in America

10. Saint Augustine's Seminary   206
    The First Seminary for African Americans

11. China   249
    Rural Missions and an Urban University

12. New Guinea   279
    The Land That History Found

13. The Philippines   312
    Strengthening a Church through Education

14. Ghana   326
    Return to Africa

15. Divine Word Missionaries of North America in Transition   343
    From the 1970s to the 1990s

Bibliography   361

Appendix   369

Index   397

Preface to the ASM Series

The purpose of the ASM (American Society of Missiology) Series is to publish—without regard for disciplinary, national, or denominational boundaries—scholarly works of high quality and wide interest on missiological themes from the entire spectrum of scholarly pursuits relevant to Christian mission, which is always the focus of books in the Series.

By *mission* is meant the effort to effect passage over the boundary between faith in Jesus Christ and its absence. In this understanding of mission, the basic functions of Christian proclamation, dialogue, witness, service, worship, liberation, and nurture are of special concern. And in that context questions arise, including, How does the transition from one cultural context to another influence the shape and interaction between these dynamic functions, especially in regard to the cultural and religious plurality that comprises the global context of Christian mission?

The promotion of scholarly dialogue among missiologists, and among missiologists and scholars in other fields of inquiry, may involve the publication of views that some missiologists cannot accept and with which members of the Editorial Committee do not agree. Manuscripts published in the Series reflect the opinions of their authors and are not understood to represent the position of the American Society of Missiology or of the Editorial Committee. Selection is guided by such criteria as intrinsic worth, readability, and accessibility to a range of interested persons and not merely to experts or specialists.

The ASM Series, in collaboration with Orbis Books, seeks to publish scholarly works of high merit and wide interest on numerous aspects of missiology—the study of mission. Able presentations on new and creative approaches to the practice and understanding of mission will receive close attention.

The ASM Series Editorial Committee
Jonathan J. Bonk
Angelyn Dries, O.S.F.
Scott W. Sunquist

Preface

Few of us reach the age of one hundred. In the light of eternity a hundred years, even a thousand years, as the Scriptures tell us, is but the blink of an eye in the mind of God. In the life of an institution, a centennial is a good time for reflection, a time to reach back to still perceptible but rapidly fading beginnings. Such is the intent of this history of the Society of the Divine Word in North America. That society is popularly known as the "SVD" for the first letters of its official Latin name, *Societas Verbi Divini*, and the individuals who belonged to the Society as "SVDs." In the year 2000 it celebrates the hundredth anniversary of the founding of its first seminary in North America for training missionary priests.

Looking back over a hundred years of SVD history for me has been somewhat like looking at old photographs of distant ancestors. I was a candidate for the Society from 1945 to 1951 and a member of it from 1951 to 1972. Its history is inextricably part of mine. I worked as one of its missioners in two of the countries to which chapters are devoted below. I did anthropological fieldwork in Papua New Guinea from 1963 to 1965, and I taught at the University of San Carlos in the Philippines from 1966 to 1972. The photos in the family album have faded and turned up at the edges. The faces staring so solemnly out have blurred. The scenes in which they stand, often stilted and formal, often seem strange. Yet there is no question that they are family, though many belong to a generation I only knew by story.

I have written this book because I believe the history of the institution that is the Society of the Divine Word is important. Although the North American segment of the SVD has never been more than a minority, its role in the history of the whole society has been important. And as the SVD has grown to become the sole major order of men to have grown in the years since the Second Vatican Council, it may be of interest to tell the tale of at least one part of that society. As Filipinos, Vietnamese, Ghanaians, Melanesians, Indians, and a new generation of North Americans take over the projects and missions founded by another generation of North American SVDs, it seems important to tell the tale of the first generations.

This book is partly the story of institutions, but more properly the story of individuals and groups of individuals who made specific decisions according to their best lights at given times. Thus their personalities enter this history. Having made the choice to examine individuals, however, I was immediately faced with whom to include and whom to leave out. The history of the Society of the Divine Word in North America and the missionaries it sent abroad would not be not complete without the work, sacrifice, and prayers of *all* its members, including—and perhaps especially—those whom the historian is most likely to overlook, because their lives seem so ordinary. Yet they were the majority and to highlight the work of the prominent few is not to belittle the contributions of anyone else.

When writing the history of a religious congregation, one immediately runs into the value and practice of prayer and of the importance of God's will and the need to search this out. These are the realms of faith, sacrifice, and grace. None of them is empirical, yet each has observable consequences. The conviction that one is doing God's will gives courage and strength to carry on. It motivates one to the point of commitment to what may seem foolhardiness to others. I hope this book does justice to that invisible dimension. It cannot be ignored in a history such as this. To do so would be an injustice to every SVD who ever worked in North America or anywhere else, to every priest or brother who stayed the course at their trade or profession. Many never left the United States to work among persons of other religious ways, let alone instructed, preached to, or baptized such into the church. Nevertheless, my research drove home constantly the point that all considered themselves to be missionaries. The example of St. Therese of Lisieux was often held up as relevant. A young, attractive, talented French girl joins a cloistered convent at the age of fifteen, dies of consumption in the same convent at the age of twenty-four, and is proclaimed Patroness of the Foreign Missions a year after she was canonized a saint in 1925—without ever leaving her Carmelite convent in Lisieux.

ORGANIZATION OF THE BOOK

Part one of this story describes the origins and growth of the Society, especially that of St. Mary's Seminary in Techny, Illinois. Part one proceeds primarily in a chronological fashion. Nevertheless, it became necessary to draw materials together on several specific topics and treat them as subject areas rather than as a part of the chronological history of the Society. A case could be made for inserting much of this material in the chronological history that comprises chapters one through four. On balance though, three subject areas merited special attention. They became chapter five on the role of the press and of Society members in founding the Catholic Students Mission Crusade, and chapters six and seven on the formation and education of those bound for the missionary priesthood and those bound for the missionary brotherhood.

Part two deals with the direct apostolates of Divine Word Missionaries of North America. The words "of North America" in the subtitle were chosen advisedly to make it clear that this history is about the work of Divine Word Missionaries in North America, of many nationalities, as well as those trained in North America and sent overseas to make a contribution to the international work of the Society of the Divine Word.

A case can be made that placing chapters nine and ten—on work among African Americans in parishes and on founding the first seminary for African Americans—in part two gives the impression that the black apostolate was not integral to the growth of the Society in North America. That is not the intent. Indeed, as I went deeper into my research, the conviction became stronger that this work is perhaps the one the Divine Word Missionaries of North America—whites, blacks, and browns—can deservedly take the greatest pride in. Nevertheless, the close junction between parish apostolate and the St. Augustine's Seminary in Bay St. Louis, Mississippi, justifies putting both the intra-Society history and the parish history together in part two. In reading chapters one through five, however, the reader should be aware from the start that he or she has not gotten the full picture of what happened in North America until chapters nine and ten are read.

Certain topics and themes recur throughout the history. It is useful to mention some of these here to alert the reader what to expect. The first is the importance of Father Arnold Janssen both for establishing the work and setting the tone of much that happened in the history of his Society in North America.

The second is the emerging international nature of the Society as a whole and within North America. Indeed, this multiethnic character has proven to be one of its most characteristic marks. It was the challenge of dealing with issues presented in the growth of the American branch of the SVD that pushed forward this charism and forced the SVD to adapt a multinational, multicultural identity in its missions. In North America, beginning with the first class of seminarians at Techny, this pattern began. Till then—although its first house was in Holland—the SVD was a European missionary order with a strong German majority. Its emerging international and multiethnic character was most publicly and formally recognized with the founding of a seminary for African Americans at a time when virtually no other congregation or diocese would accept them as candidates for membership or ordination. It is now one of the proudest marks of the SVD worldwide, where it strives to have its members work in multinational communities to witness the multicultural character of the church and the gospel in a way quite different from the pattern of national provinces of international communities staffing missions.

A third characteristic is the way individuals in the Society have taken initiatives to move into new apostolates, to start new journals, and initiate new enterprises both in the missions or in the homeland. Nor is it a question of just a few doing this. Brothers and priests, even seminarians, from the beginning looked for new and better ways of doing their work.

THE DATES OF THIS HISTORY

This history proper stops around the middle of the 1970s. There is a final chapter that outlines major happenings that have occurred since then, down to the date when my writing and research stopped. As the book will show, the general chapter of the year 1968 elected the first American as Society superior general in the person of Father John Musinsky. His election was an important landmark in the SVD's international history and also a mark of the North American provinces' maturation. The 1970s were characterized by the effort to update and rewrite the SVD constitutions and also to deepen its inner, spiritual renewal. Musinsky was one of the leading figures in this updating. To go into all this, however, would require another volume and still not be satisfactory, since the changes begun then are still underway, and one of the rules of history writing is that a generation or more must intervene before historians can even be sure what major trends were underway. In addition, most archives, including the SVD's, are cautious about allowing researchers delve into events as recent as the mid-1970s. Thus the decision was reached to terminate the history in the early years of the Musinsky generalate.

A WORD ON STYLE

English is notorious among those who have learned it as a second language for its contradictory rules in areas such as spelling and capitalization of words. As an international community, the English-speaking SVD has absorbed the conventions of German-speakers and the usages of Latin, Spanish, and Italian, since so much of its correspondence is or was done in these languages. In this volume I have endeavored to follow the rules of the *University of Chicago Manual of Style*, which favors a minimum of capitalization. This may seem strange to readers who expect to see terms such as "church" or "superior general" capitalized more often than they are here, but the *Manual* is the style guide of my publisher and brings some order in the variations one finds in SVD publications. I have not changed capitalization and punctuation in direct quotations, however, preferring to let the original writer or speaker say what he or she wants in the way they prefer, even when terms like "heathen" will cause contemporary sensitivities to bristle. I have also refrained from use of the pedantic "sic" to call attention to errors in such speech.

Finally, if I followed convention by using "SVD" behind the name of every priest or brother spoken about in this volume (for example, "Brother Patrick Hogan, SVD"), it would have become tedious. I trust that the context will make it clear in the pages that follow when a Divine Word priest or brother is being referred to.

A Word on Sources

The volume you hold is an edited version of a much longer manuscript that is available at the SVD archives in Techny, Illinois, and in Rome, as well as at several other mission study centers and universities, including the Day Mission Library at Yale University; the Center for the Study of Christianity in the Non-Western World at the University of Edinburgh; the Henry Martyn Mission Library at the University of Cambridge; the Speer Library at Princeton Theological Seminary; the Missionswissenschaftliches Institut Library of the Society of the Divine Word at Sankt Augustin, Germany; and the Urbaniana University Library, Rome. The manuscript version is more fully referenced with notes to sources in original materials than the published volume. This book is designed with the ordinary reader in mind. Rather than give endless references, I have tried to give the date of correspondence and reports and an indication of where they may be found. Those interested in reading the originals will have sufficient information to track them down, but this volume is not burdened with references that are not important to the ordinary reader.

A few words must be said here about the major sources used in this book. The notes and bibliographies indicate many sources. Here I wish to single out a few that have been especially important.

Josef Alt's collection of the letters of Father Janssen sent to North America was extremely useful, especially for the early years. I had finished my work in the period covered by Alt before his book was translated into English, however, and the translations of letters from Father Janssen that you find here are my own.[1] Included in the footnotes of this collection were enough of the questions and responses of the recipients of these letters to make a coherent account possible.

Next to be mentioned is Father Markert's journalistic account of the early years in America. Unfortunately, all of the sources on which this was based were burned in a fire at the Techny press in 1960. Markert's account fills in the picture of many events in the early years, events in which he himself was an active participant.

The third important source is the *Chronologium* put together by Father William Bonner. In preparation for the 100th Jubilee of the Society in North America, Bonner mined the archives both of the generalate in Rome and of Techny for letters and other documents that he strung together day by day, month by month, year by year. Bonner's work was especially helpful for the sections of this history dealing with the apostolate to and by African Americans.

---

1. For the published translation, see Josef Alt, ed., *Arnold Janssen, SVD: Letters to the United States of America*, trans. Robert Pung and Peter Spring (Nettetal, Germany: Steyler Verlag, 1998).

Also useful in bringing matters touching on the African-American apostolate into order is Archbishop Michael Meier's 1961 Ph.D. dissertation dealing with St. Augustine's Seminary at Bay St. Louis, Mississippi, especially for the material in the Roman archives he analyzed and quoted.

The reader will find John Donaghey's name recurring frequently in these pages, giving character vignettes portraying the lives of the generation that came to the United States from Germany in the earliest years through the 1920s. Father Donaghey taught philosophy at Techny, Conesus, and Epworth. As an educator, Donaghey became more than a teacher; he was, with Edward Norton and Charles Malin, one of the men who led the SVD to accept accreditation and to adapt American educational conventions to the needs of religious missionary formation in the 1960s and 1970s. When he left his educational ministries, he served as provincial superior at Techny for a virtually unprecedented three terms, or nine years. His provincial administration occurred precisely when many SVD stalwarts were making their paschal *transitus* to eternal life. To him fell the task of researching and writing the death notices and eulogies that provided a treasure trove of insights into the personalities and work of many of the men discussed in these pages. These frank and honest, yet caring and loving obituaries and eulogies are to be found in the Techny archives.

The archives of the SVD generalate in Rome and in Steyl in the Netherlands, as well as the archives of Techny, Bay St. Louis, and Riverside, California, also proved useful. Magazines published by the SVD in America over the years, too numerous to mention, memoirs written by various people, obituaries, personnel files have stimulated me in various ways and directions and are part of what I have drawn on in my writing.

Finally, unless otherwise noted, translations from German are mine.

Acknowledgments

First I wish to thank all those who made this history possible by their work. Their names will become known as you move into this book. Many of them left written records behind. I want to thank also the least of the priests and brothers among whom few are remembered today, the "least of the brethren" who are surely remembered by God, perhaps even as the greatest and the first. Without their persevering work, there simply would be no SVD history in North America to write about.

Next I thank all those whose memories I have picked in conversation. So many were willing to share their thoughts and experiences. Sometimes they did so formally, more often in informal conversations. To mention all these by name runs the risk of leaving many deserving people out, but the list is long. Some have died in the course of my writing. I hope I have remembered all of their words accurately. At another level, I need to say that in the choice of persons, projects, and events that are mentioned and not mentioned, I tried to be as inclusive as possible. Numerous persons deserving of mention, however, have been left out, and I regret it. The version of my work you have in your hand is about half the size of the manuscript I originally prepared. To make a book of reasonable size, my publisher rationed the number of words and many important persons, events, and projects were dropped.

All chapters were sent to people around the world who had special expertise, first-hand knowledge, or particular interest in the topic of a given chapter or chapters. They read and reflected upon them, and returned their critiques and ideas. I read all these responses carefully. In some cases it meant dropping and rewriting whole sections. Many, indeed most, wanted more material added to the parts they had read. All were constructive in their comments and oftentimes flattering in the approval they expressed. My thanks to all of these readers for the time they took in reading and responding. The final product is much better for it. Whatever mistakes, omissions, and awkwardness of expression mar the final version are to be laid at my doorstep.

My advisory committee deserves special thanks. This committee started out with Father Robert Flinn as chairman and Fathers Thomas Krosnicki and Louis Luzbetak as members. With Father Flinn's untimely death, Father Krosnicki became chairman and Father John Donaghey was added as Flinn's replacement. Krosnicki, in addition to his advice and encouragement, took care of all the details that went into this final product. Donaghey, too, always had telling comments to make. But special thanks are due to Father Luzbetak, who read and reread this manuscript as different versions appeared. To each he responded at length and in writing. But our work together went further than that as we spent many hours together discussing issues that developed as the research and writing progressed. The shape of this book, the choice of topics to include, decisions on what to leave out or play down, owe Louis Luzbetak a great debt. We sometimes ended up agreeing to disagree, but never stopped being friends. I hope he is satisfied with the final result.

Two more people deserve special mention. First of all, thanks to the archivist at Techny, Father Robert Myers, who ended up taking a special interest in this book and saw it through from beginning to end. In somewhat the same way, I owe Father Bernard Fisher special mention and thanks. He has been collecting materials on the SVD in his retirement at East Troy, Wisconsin, making available the results for his confreres and accumulating a rich store of information, all of which he generously shared with me and allowed me to take home whatever would be useful.

I dare not leave Dr. William Burrows, a former member of the Society of the Divine Word and managing editor of Orbis Books, off the list of those to whom I owe a great debt of gratitude. He put many hours into reducing the size of my very long manuscript, yet he maintained continuity. The pieces he added to achieve this, as well as sections he inserted here and there to put events and ideas in context were well chosen. His work has definitely made for a better book.

Finally, I owe my wife, Pilar, the greatest debt of gratitude of all, not just for reading and commenting on the entire manuscript, but also for taking care of all the details that saved me from the distractions and disruptions of daily living, all so that I could concentrate on this history. Without her encouragement all along the way, I would literally never have been able to finish this book.

PART ONE

FOUNDATION AND MATURATION

1

From Germany to America

The Earliest Years

On the deck of the latest steamer to arrive in Hoboken, New Jersey, from Bremen in Germany stood a young man of thirty-eight, excited to be finally in America, a goal he had been working to reach for over two years. Joseph Meyer was one of the millions of Germans who had made this same journey to America, among them many of his own relatives and village mates. He did not come, as others did, to escape harsh political conditions or to look for better economic opportunities. Nor was he seeking relief from religious persecution, much less for the mere adventure of coming to America. He came to sell German-language magazines for the religious congregation to which he belonged. Brother Wendelinus or Wendelin, as he was called in religious life, was the first member of the Society of the Divine Word to come to North America. As this young SVD took his first anxious step off the gangplank on 15 October 1895, there was no way he could have predicted the outcome and result of his arrival.

THE SOCIETY AND ITS FOUNDER

The arrival of the Society in North America could hardly have been more modest, but to understand what would follow, the reader must go back to the beginnings of the Society of the Divine Word and its founder, Arnold Janssen. From the beginning of the SVD in North America the effort was to imitate the success of the founder. It is all the more necessary to talk about the spirit, mission charism, and spirituality of Father Janssen, because he was still alive and directing the Society when Brother Wendelin was sent to America. Indeed, Janssen must be acknowledged to be the prime force behind the foundation of the Society's branch in North America. From 1895 until his death in 1909, twenty priests, forty brothers, and fifty-three sisters received their appointment directly from Father Janssen. Indeed, many of those who came after this first wave knew him from their seminary days or their years of training as brothers.

Below we briefly trace Father Janssen's life. For those seeking more, a defini-
tive biography was written by Father Fritz Bornemann in 1969 and an English version appeared in 1975. A briefer "character" biography by Father Jakob Reuter
was published in German in 1994 and is very helpful.

Arnold Janssen, the second of eleven children, was born on 5 November 1837.
Three of his siblings died in infancy. He was born in Goch, an old town situated
in the flat land west of the lower Rhine River, less than a mile from the Dutch border. Arnold came from a very pious family background; both his father and mother
were openly and publicly prayerful people. Not one, but three of their children
went into religious life. It is clear that Arnold imbibed much of the spirituality of
his parents, especially his father's. Devotion to the Holy Trinity, and especially to
the Holy Spirit and the Word Incarnate, would become the core of the SVD's spirituality. The prologue of the Gospel of John was a favorite reading and source of
meditation for Arnold's father and the source of the name Janssen would give his
missionary society.

From Münster, where he began his preparation for the priesthood, he transferred
to the University of Bonn, then back to Münster for theology. Along the way he
received his teacher's certificate for all levels in mathematics, physics, mineral-
ogy, botany, zoology, chemistry, and religion, while his certificate in languages
was restricted to lower class levels. Because he attended lectures in theology during his university studies in Bonn, he was able to finish his immediate preparation
for the priesthood in four semesters, after which he was ordained for the Diocese
of Münster on 15 August 1861. He was a few months shy of twenty-four.

For the next twelve years Janssen taught in a small public school in a small out-
of-the-way town called Bocholt. Its citizens were more interested in preparing their
children for work in industry than having them learn Latin and Greek. He was conscientious, stern, and demanding of his students, and not particularly well liked by
them, according to Bornemann's biography.

Janssen's position in Bocholt was a position of respect and security, which also
paid quite well, and he could have spent the rest of his life in this work. A crucial
step on the road to the foundation of the Society of the Divine Word was taken during this period when he became interested in the Apostleship of Prayer movement.
Father Janssen wrote a small pamphlet on devotion to the Sacred Heart of Jesus.
It contained prayers of petition to be given to anyone joining the Apostleship of
Prayer. The first run of 5,000 copies was sold out in less than a year. He then had
a second edition of 15,000 copies printed and began to foster the Apostleship of
Prayer among his friends and family and anybody else he could contact, enlisting
some 600 new members in the first year alone.

In 1869, Janssen became diocesan director of the Apostleship of Prayer League
and during school holidays traveled all over the diocese promoting this apostolate.
During one Easter vacation alone he personally visited 169 parishes in the diocese,
a feat made more difficult for him because he found it hard to deal with strangers.
At this time he was thirty-two years of age. During this period, he learned that there
was a great spiritual hunger among the people and a market for spiritual reading
material, and that personal contacts were an excellent way to make people aware
of these materials and to purchase them.

Another characteristic of the future founder was his growing awareness of the power of prayer. This became the topic of his presentation before the participants at the *Katholikentag* (a form of Catholic rally) held in Düsseldorf in 1869. Father Janssen, who was no great orator, spoke as official representative of the Apostolate of Prayer League, and he did not think small. The power of prayer would call down the grace of God on all nations. By prayer, he said, "England, ancient, proud, globe-encompassing England, could once again become a youthful Catholic nation, zealous and saved again in the renewed possession of the truth. How that would change the face of the world."

In the years before his decision to give up teaching to work full time for the Apostleship, Janssen wrote several books of prayers he had composed. These went into printings of ten and fifteen thousand copies and more, and were sent to Austria and Switzerland as well. This period in his life is important also because it gave him the insight to realize what a market there was for such printed materials. So when he started the *Kleine Herz Jesu Bote* ("The Little Messenger of the Heart of Jesus") in 1874, he knew he would gain subscribers. In 1873 he became chaplain to the Ursuline Sisters in Kempen. With minimal duties in their school, he was free to devote much more of his time to the Apostleship of Prayer. The first issue of his new magazine was advertised in Catholic newspapers and journals, after which he also sent samples to all the people, priests, teachers, and nuns he had met on his journeys on behalf of the Apostleship of Prayer, all of whose addresses he had meticulously kept. Eventually he had 3,000 firm subscribers, paid off his bills, and still had money left over. He also received donations for the missions, which he put into an interest-bearing account.

Very quickly the focus of the magazine changed to a concentration almost exclusively on foreign missions. The insight grew that materials dealing with the foreign missions were of great interest. Growing too was his realization that Catholic Germany had little concrete involvement in mission. Father Janssen began to concentrate in his magazine on what were called in German the *Heidenmissionen*, missions to the "heathen," a term a later age would find offensive. He observed with pain that Germany had no mission-sending society preparing German youth for work in the missions, though other nations had mission societies. To this theme he returned repeatedly in his magazine. He asked his readers to pray for the foundation of a German mission-sending society. In the June 1874 issue of the *Sacred Heart Messenger*, Janssen wrote:

Is there not one among you in the whole of Germany who feels called to devote himself to the missionary cause?

What would happen if German priests were to work together to organize a German mission seminary in a safe place? Such a venture, as this writer knows for certain, is in line with the wishes of the Propagation of the Faith in Rome, and even more so, with the express wish of the Holy Father himself.

Belgium, Ireland, Italy and France all have mission seminaries. There are four in Italy and five in Paris; yet Germany, this large country with so many devout Catholic families, does not have even one unless we consider North

America as a mission country and look upon the American college in Münster [founded to send priests to work among German emigrants in America] as a mission seminary. We believe that something can and should be done about this. We would be prepared, in as far as we can do so, to arrange a meeting of like-minded persons.

During this period, he read one day in the newspaper that a Bishop Timoleone Raimondi, Vicar Apostolic of Hong Kong, would be in Neuwerk, near Kempen. Janssen decided to make an appointment to interview him for a piece in his magazine. Bishop Raimondi made two points in urging Janssen himself to found the seminary. First, he told him that the task of working in the home country for the foreign missions was a vocation also. The second point was to suggest that, although Janssen may have to begin with priests and seminarians, he should also plan to begin with a Latin School for boys who otherwise might not be able to follow a call to the foreign missions for lack of funds. "Found one yourself," was the recommendation of Bishop Raimondi, and upon reflection and prayer, Father Janssen took this as the call of God's will and proceeded with vigor.

The times were right. First, Janssen was beginning his work at a time of intense German national growth and prosperity under Bismarck. Germany had become politically unified and had fought successful wars against Austria and France. At the same time, Germany was industrializing and increasing its wealth and power rapidly and visibly. True, there were recessions and setbacks, but the general progression was up until, by the end of the century, Germany was the wealthiest and strongest country in Europe.

During these same years Germany had sent millions of its sons and daughters to North and South America and extended its empire to parts of Africa, among them Togoland on the Gold Coast of Africa, to Kaiser Wilhelmsland, the New Guinea part of present-day Papua New Guinea, and to China. All these were potential mission lands and of great interest to Arnold Janssen. In time, he was able to send missionaries to all of these lands and establish their work on a firm footing because of the disposable income industrialization had put into the hands of the working people who were supporting him.

Important also for Arnold Janssen's work was the religious revival that occurred in Germany after the 1850s. Partially stemming from the turmoil resulting from the revolutions of 1848 and the impact that industrialization had brought to Catholic regions of Germany, the revival itself was broad and deep. People were moving from the rural areas into the cities of the rapidly developing Ruhr area and from the East to the West. The guild system was beginning to break down and the working men in factories and mines became a prominent force. Various associations sprang up to deal with the rootlessness all this change caused. Priests were involved in these associations, which soon took on a political cast. Because the clergy were well educated and politically engaged, they were respected and, as directors of sodalities, soon became politically important also. As one priest noted in 1861: "It can be said in praise of the current generation that divine services are zealously attended, the Holy Sacraments eagerly and frequently received, and religious instruction and edification in printed and spoken form almost greedily snapped up."

But the German state's attitude toward the church was not all positive, as exemplified in the *Kulturkampf* that Bismarck stirred up against the Catholic Church. Bismarck's vigorous reaction to the church, an overreaction as it turned out and as he later came to realize himself, was partly triggered by the proclamation of Pius IX of the doctrine of papal infallibility during the First Vatican Council on 18 July 1870. Whatever one makes of the doctrine's inner merits, from the beginning it became loaded with political overtones, since by it the pope intended to give the church a focus of unity against the forces threatening it. Bismarck feared encirclement. He had trouble with his Catholic Polish subjects to the East in Silesia, who wanted their own language and schools. He had fought and beaten Catholic Austria and France. If his own Catholic subjects joined with these other countries, Prussia would be effectively encircled. So, with his majority in the German *Reichstag*, or parliament, he began to write and promulgate the May Laws. For Arnold Janssen, the most important of these laws decreed that seminaries were to be closed, and no new ones could be opened. If priests left their parish, they could not be replaced. But the more the government enforced its laws, the more vigorous the Catholic priests and laity became, and the more they celebrated Rome and the pope.

How did all this affect Janssen's plans? First, he had to begin his mission seminary "for Germans" outside Germany. His first foundation and the motherhouse of the SVD was located just across the German border, in Steyl, Netherlands, in the province of Limburg, a few short kilometers from the German city of Kaldenkirchen. As yet having no members of his own society to serve as teachers in the seminary nor brothers to work in his press, Janssen sought to use some of the many priests who were unable to get teaching positions in Germany to help the fledgling seminary, and they did. He also hoped to enlist many German priests and seminarians for the mission cause, so he made several long trips to seminaries and colleges to recruit missionaries, but in this he was generally disappointed. Only three men initially responded, two of whom left him over the issue whether the new foundation would be a religious order under the vows of poverty, celibacy, and obedience, or an institute of diocesan priests united by a promise to work in the missions. This latter arrangement was actually the way mission societies had been organized in France and Italy. Arnold Janssen insisted on a community bound by the three religious vows.

Father Janssen's idea of a mission-sending society of priests and brothers did not spring full-blown and totally decided from the very beginning. The same can be said of the two congregations of sisters that he founded later. Initially, for example, he had no intention of joining priests and brothers in one society. It was not long, however, after he had opened the mission house at Steyl that he thought seriously about a brotherhood, and then partly because some of the workers he had assembled to take care of the many tasks that had to be done, especially at the printing press, wanted to affiliate more closely with the new Society. In 1878 he accepted the first two brother novices into his Society and on 23 May 1881, Mercolinus Elskemper took his vows as the first brother-member of the Society of the Divine Word. It was only in 1885, as a result of the first general chapter called for this very purpose, that both priests and brothers took the same three vows of poverty, celibacy, and obedience according to the constitutions that were also drafted at this chapter. The first constitution to be submitted to Roman authorities was written in 1898.

On 8 September 1875, Father Janssen finally opened his mission seminary in a small tavern in Steyl. When the word got around that a mission seminary was actually open and running, candidates for membership began to pour in so fast he could hardly keep up. He tried to build for the future, but when a building was finished the future was already upon him, and another wing had to be put up. Already in 1875, Janssen added to the small inn to accommodate the first students who entered. He had to put up a new building in 1876 and another in 1878, 1879, and in 1880.

Was the founder aware of the influence of all these events and currents in the larger society that seemed to be so favorable for the successful opening of a German mission seminary? I believe he was. He insisted repeatedly that the times, the circumstances, and the conditions under which one worked were major indicators of God's will. On 1 July 1898 he writes, "I only draw conclusions from these things and conditions. God is the one who prepares the things and conditions." It was his standard operating procedure. Once he had come to the conclusion that the times were ripe to begin something, this goal directed everything he did. He had the knack of immersing himself in the details of his enterprises without getting bogged down in them. All the detailed work he dealt with every day remained focused on the goal and somehow remained directed to it. This takes more than dogged perseverance and hard work. This requires insight and, let me say it, genius. Arnold Janssen might not have been a great singer or a spell-binding speaker, but he knew what he wanted. Better, in Arnold Janssen's way of thinking, he knew what *God* wanted. He went about doing this with great attention to detail, never wavering.

It was a difficult and confused beginning. Two of the four original members, or cofounders, left before the first year was up; only two remained, Father Janssen and seminarian John Baptist Anzer, who later became the first SVD bishop in China. But soon two seminarians from Münster also joined—John Janssen, the founder's younger brother, and his classmate, Hermann Wegener. The three seminarians were ordained in the summer of 1876 and were immediately put to work teaching in the Latin School. There were now 15 students spread over four years. In 1877 there were 33; in 1878, 48; and by the end of 1879, 96 students had entered, in spite of the fact that Janssen was very strict regarding those he accepted. There was no looking back. The Society continued to grow and expand to other countries, also to North America.

ARNOLD JANSSEN'S SPIRITUAL LEGACY

There were two facets in Arnold Janssen, one reflecting the popular piety of his day, the second reflecting the founder's devotion to God as triune. We shall explore both, but it is important to remember, in speaking of the popular piety that so marked his communities' devotional life, that contemplation and adoration of God as triune were the core of his life of prayer, particularly as he matured.

The primary reason why Arnold Janssen founded his Society of the Divine Word was to make sure that the Word of God would be brought to the whole world, according to Christ's final great command to go into the whole world and proclaim the good news to all creation (Mark 16:15), to make disciples of all the nations, baptizing them in the name of the Father, and of the Son, and of the Holy Spirit (Matthew 28:19). Primarily for this purpose, Janssen believed, Christ sent his Holy Spirit on those he had chosen to begin this work (Acts 1:8), which, it seems, is to go on to the ends of the earth and to the end of time. This was the goal and purpose of the Society and is why the spirituality he bequeathed to his Society becomes important.

Janssen's spirituality was intimately tied to popular German piety and to what is called the *devotio moderna* ("modern devotion"), an attempt to inject concreteness, emotion, and personal piety into the lives of ordinary Catholics. *Devotio moderna* was marked by devotions to the Sacred Heart of Jesus, angels, the Blessed Virgin, and saints in novenas and triduums, long prayers recited in common at night and in the morning. Father Janssen himself composed many prayers. He was quite good at this, and the prayers he composed were often published and used by many. As expressions of this, he recommended many patron saints to his spiritual sons in the constitutions of the Society.

Because the Eucharist rendered God's son present, and God was viewed primarily in his divinity and kingship, Christ in the Blessed Sacrament was approached with an exceedingly great reverence, He (always in capital letters) "up there" in the tabernacle; we, poor, sinful, unworthy creatures "down here," with the emphasis clearly on the sinfulness. Visits to the Blessed Sacrament, exposition of the Blessed Sacrament, often during Mass itself, followed by solemn benediction with much burning of incense, were frequent.

The core of Arnold Janssen's spirituality, to which he devoted himself more and more as he got older, and which he repeatedly told his confreres to adopt, was mainline, scriptural, and solid in every way. That these two forms of piety were present in the same person may seem difficult to understand, but his spirituality was primarily trinitarian. This core spirituality, as it was developed by the founder, explored and explained in his various writings and conferences, in the early constitutions, in many of the prayers he composed, in the letters he wrote, even in his ordinary conversations, was also *mission oriented*. It flowed from his contemplation of the Trinity, the core belief of the church and the primary truth that Janssen believed Jesus Christ had come to reveal to the world. Christ, for Janssen, came to make it possible for us to share in the life of this triune God. For Arnold Janssen, the life of the Trinity, therefore, is a life of love. And it is the notion of love that makes the Trinity necessary. In the thought of Hugh of St. Victor, perfect love, the kind that characterizes God, must go beyond self-love, and does so in the form of the Second Person, the Word. It was this Word, and the words of this Word, whom Janssen's sons and daughters were to make known to all nations, indeed to all creation, as Christ himself had commanded. And it was the Holy Spirit, promised by Christ the Word himself, who would work with Janssen's sons and daughters to carry out this trinitarian mission through all time.

One of Janssen's great gifts lay in his attempts to find practical ways to bring these devotions to bear on the lives of his members and to contribute to their ability to live continuously in the presence of God. He himself attempted to live and work in the presence of God. It is perhaps better to summarize Janssen's spirituality by saying that he believed God lived and worked in him. It was his task in prayer to become mindful of God's presence throughout his working day. Aware of his own and our tendencies to be forgetful of God, Janssen also introduced the "Quarterly Hour Prayer" in the three congregations he founded. On the quarter hour, a bell would ring throughout the house, classrooms, and workshops. When it rang, all were to stop what they were doing and recite the following prayer, which was led by an appointed individual:

Leader: I believe in you, O my God,
Response: Because you are the Eternal Truth.
Leader: I hope in you, O my God,
Response: Because you are infinitely merciful, faithful and almighty.
Leader: With my whole heart I love you, O my God, and am sorry for having offended you,
Response: Because you are ineffably good and lovable.
Leader: Out of love for me you are present in the Blessed Sacrament.
Response: Therefore I long for you, O my dearest Jesus.
Leader: Send me from the Father the Holy Spirit with his seven gifts,
Response: That I may glorify God in all things. Amen.

These prayers do not ask for anything particular for the individual. Rather, they call to mind the attributes of God and the corresponding attitudes and virtues that we should cultivate as a result: faith, hope, love, and the desire to do all for the glory of God. Such attitudes, he felt, were essential for life in community and as missionaries. Any study of the SVD in North America needs to recount that by the time Janssen sent his first man to the United States, he had weathered nearly twenty years as the head of the Society. In North America, perhaps as much as on mission fields, the Society would learn how necessary was a spirit of perseverance in essentials, along with flexibility in adapting to new cultures.

BROTHER WENDELIN IN AMERICA

We left the first Divine Word Missionary to North America about to step off the gangplank on 15 October 1895. The decision to send missionaries to the United States does not appear to have occupied an important place in Arnold Janssen's thoughts and deliberations at this time. His congregation had grown rapidly, so fast in fact that he had all he could do to put up buildings fast enough to accommodate all the candidates pouring in. In these first twenty years, he had opened missions where he was sending his priests and brothers. China was the first, to be succeeded by Togo in West Africa and Mozambique in East Africa, Kaiser Wilhelmsland (Northeast New Guinea), as well as Argentina, Ecuador, and Brazil in South America. His presses were humming and paying for much of this expansion, but money was always scarce. He was also occupied with the congregation of sisters he had recently founded, on 8 December 1889, the Congregation of the Missionary Sisters Servants of the Holy Spirit. And no one in the congregation *De Propaganda Fide* in Rome (the pope's curial office for mission affairs) nor from the United States itself had invited him to send missionaries to America.

The idea emerged, it appears, because of the need for funds and the possibility that Germans in the United States might want to purchase the books, pamphlets, and magazines that were a large source of the SVD's funds. Father Blum, the general procurator (the name given treasurers and fund raisers) and the priest in charge of the press and the brothers, wrote the founder on 12 July 1893:

> Should we perhaps think about opening a market in North America and should I start preparing for this possibility? I don't think it would do any harm, but it would mean that a Brother would have to go over there and arrange a place where books and magazines might be stored.

As a consequence both of miscalculation on the part of the press and the shortfall of money that people were experiencing, at the end of 1894 Steyl had several thousand copies of its fund-raising *St. Michaelskalendar* ("St. Michael's Calendar") remaining from a printing of 310,000. The *St. Michaelskalendar* was actually a rather substantial book, resembling an almanac, the first twenty pages or so of which contained a calendar that included all kinds of information for every day of the year. This was followed by articles on the missions and on topics of general interest. There was also a section on the family or on prayer. It was illustrated with pictures and became a very popular book, published annually. It was suggested that it was possible to remove the 1895 calendar from the remainders, bind in the 1896 calendar with the 1895 contents, and sell the remainders in America to the five million Germans who had migrated there. "Money," the founder was told by Frau Huch, who had made the suggestion, "is so plentiful over there, and easier to make than over here, but maybe the dangers are too great. The Brothers would have to be really solid and have some kind of support."

In the meantime, unaware of this proposal, Brother Wendelin asked Father Janssen to send him to America. He was somewhat familiar with America because four of his father's brothers and sisters were in America. Brother Wendelin was born in 1857 in Duppach. Trained as an elementary school teacher, he worked for a time in a government school. In 1877, at the age of thirty, he decided to join the Steyl missionaries as a brother, that is to say, as one who takes the three vows of poverty, chastity, and obedience and devotes his life to the work of the community (without being ordained to the priesthood). Outgoing, pleasant, with a good sense of humor and an easy way with people, Wendelin was assigned to the press as a *Reisebruder* ("traveling Brother"), one of a band of brothers who traveled throughout German-speaking Europe selling the magazines and books that the Steyl press was producing, as a way of making the new mission congregation known. These magazines were also intended to develop mission interest among their readers, to get them to pray and sacrifice for the missions as well, and to stir up vocations for the missions. These *Reisebruder* had a great positive impact on the early growth and development of the Society, especially in Germany.

With so many relatives in America, Brother Wendelin had thought of migrating to America himself even before he had entered Steyl. Often during recreation with the other brothers he would talk about America and about going there. One day, as Wendelin later told the story, another brother told him, "If you are so full of interest in America, why don't you have yourself sent there?" This gave him the impetus to ask Father Blum what he thought about this idea. Shortly afterward, Father Blum told Wendelin that Father Janssen viewed the plan favorably, which encouraged Brother Wendelin to approach the founder himself, who repeated that he thought the idea of going to America was a good one, but such an important undertaking had to be carefully considered. Then for two years, nothing happened. One day before leaving on a trip to sell more magazines, Wendelin reported to Father Janssen, who asked him, "What about your trip to America?" Later that summer, Brother Wendelin returned from one of his trips with pneumonia and while convalescing at Steyl he asked the general if he could study English, just in case he was sent to America. Janssen said yes and assigned one of the priests to teach him in the summer of 1895.

Why did Arnold Janssen take two years before he returned to the idea of sending some of his missionaries to North America? Knowing how he operated, it is hard to think he had just forgotten about the whole project. There is no evidence, however, one way or the other. He was certainly busy with other matters, but it seems, from what happened subsequently, that something else was involved. Father Janssen, apparently, could not get a handle on America. As Father Markert, who knew Janssen during his seminary days, notes:

> One cannot help but think that the whole America idea was a problem for him, something of an enigma. He was not acquainted enough with all that went by the name of America. It was too much of an unknown quantity for him. As a consequence, he hesitated to come to a definite decision which he knew might involve far-reaching consequences.[1]

At this point suffice it to say that Janssen came to realize that the United States was too rich, too powerful, too big, and too dynamic to be disregarded. There were also too many Germans there to be ignored by a German mission society founded "by Germans for Germans." They had been part of one of the largest migrations in human history. To look at ship manifests in the years between 1850 and 1914 is to see the names of huge numbers of solid German emigrants. In contrast to the Irish, who were also arriving in large numbers at the same time, these manifests show they were often tradesmen. Written neatly beside the names are their trades—type founder, printer, carpenter, butcher, wheelwright. When Brother Wendelin arrived, they had already made their mark on the interior of the new nation in states such

---

1. As I mentioned in "A Word on Sources," Father Francis Markert's name will appear frequently in this history. Important in his own right as one of the early German priests assigned to North America, he also began work on a history of the Society in his adopted homeland. The version of events we have in this citation, as is the case with many of the letters quoted in this book, as well as many accounts of early events, come directly from Markert. And because many of the original records were burned in the Techny press fire of 1960, Markert's writings are often the only source extant.

as Indiana, Illinois, Wisconsin, and Iowa. Settling together in both rural and urban communities, and sometimes hindered by their accents, they had not achieved political prominence in the way the Irish would, but they were parts of strong, prosperous communities, and they had both children and money to give to their church.

After two years of seeming neglect of the United States, one of Janssen's former pupils from Steyl came back for a visit. Father Hubertus William Joistens was born in Düsseldorf in 1868 and after leaving Steyl he found his way to St. Meinrad's Seminary in southern Indiana, where he was ordained in 1891 for the Diocese of Marquette in Michigan. He returned to Germany and visited Steyl. They talked much about America and Janssen wrote down two pages of information about America. In note form they included:

> Germans esp. in Ohio, Pennsylvania, Illinois, St. Louis, Wisconsin. German Bishops. Wigger, Bi. in New Jersey, very zealous. Kaatzer Archb. of Milwaukee, Wisc . . . Fihen [meaning Feehan] Jol. Archb. of Chicago, well-disposed to Germans, does not yet have a seminary.

In the Jubilee Book published in 1900 to commemorate the twenty-fifth anniversary of the Society's founding, two reasons were given for going to the United States. First of all, the United States was becoming too important to ignore. Second, and more specifically, Janssen wanted his Society to make contact with the zealous Catholic Germans who had already migrated to America. How this latter goal was to be achieved and connection maintained was not specified, but from his reflections and research on America at this time, the idea of developing a market for his magazines did not seem to be uppermost in his mind. On 3 September 1895, immediately after Joistens's visit, Janssen announced that he would send Brother Wendelin to America. Brother Wendelin had barely a month to get ready. The founder asked all the priests, brothers, sisters, and students at Steyl to turn in the names and addresses of relatives and friends in America, while Janssen himself arranged with the mother general of the Sisters of St. Francis of the Poor from Aachen, Germany, for a place where Wendelin could stay until he could settle somewhere on his own. Their order ran hospitals in New York and Hoboken. The mother general also arranged, through the sisters in New York, to have someone meet Brother Wendelin at the pier. To be sure he could be recognized, he was to put a big white piece of paper in his hat.

Together with the founder, Brother Wendelin drafted a letter of introduction. After the third careful revision, the text, originally written in German but preserved by Father Markert in English, went as follows:

To Whom It May Concern:
In those parts of Germany with a Catholic population, the *St. Michaels-kalendar* ["St. Michael's Almanac"], a well known and much liked story book, as well as two monthly magazines, *Stadt Gottes* ["City of God"] and the *Kleine Herz Jesu Bote* ["Little Messenger of the Sacred Heart"], have become family friends in numerous households. The home of these publications is the Mission House in Steyl near Kaldenkirchen, Rhineland. The

Society was founded September 8, 1875, with such a humble beginning that very few gave it much hope of surviving. Despite all this, it showed a continued growth to such an extent that the Steyl Society of the Divine Word, under the evident blessing of the Lord who can "create children of Israel out of stone," expanded rapidly. Many students entered and the constantly growing number of priests, Brothers and mission houses made it possible to accept the considerable number of mission fields in which the Society is now active.

Due to the strenuous nature of the mission work the Society is compelled to look for candidates, especially from those parts of the population in which the youth are brought up in simple conditions and are used to hardships. This has opened the way to the priesthood to many young men who because of poverty and similar circumstances would not have been able to pursue the long years of study for the priesthood. Others who got their start with us were able to finish their studies elsewhere. A number of these men are now active in North America, but consider the Steyl Mission House as their father's home, to which they owe the help that enabled them to enter the priesthood they now exercise in the United States.

Thus, by the working of Divine Providence, we are already in contact with North America. We may be pardoned, therefore, if we try to hold on to this thread woven by God's hand, in order to come to still closer and to have more intimate contact with that distant part of the Church.

German publishers of Catholic Almanacs and magazines have established branches in North America over the past several years. There should be no objection, then, to our undertaking, especially since we will thereby be enabled to create in North America a greater amount of help for mission work.

For this reason I have sent our Brother Wendelin, Joseph Meyer, a former school teacher in German public schools, to North America to take the preparatory steps for the realization of our plan. I kindly ask you to favor him with that confidence which a good man deserves who works for God's own cause. I wish to assure you of my own heartiest thanks for whatever assistance you will be good enough to lend him.

Steyl on the feast of St. Michael [29 September] 1895
Arnold Janssen
Superior General of the Society of the Divine Word.

By 3 October 1895, everything was ready for departure. Wendelin did not receive a mission cross, as did those who were later sent to America; what he was doing was considered an extension of what he was already doing in Germany, namely, selling magazines. Using the horse-drawn rail car, he was escorted by Janssen and a few brothers to Venlo, where he caught a train to Bremen, the port from where many Germans before him had started their journey to America. As Markert records his words:

The trip was generally uneventful. One of his traveling companions, a

Protestant German-American originally from Brandenburg, asked Wendelin what he intended to do in America. When he learned that he was going to sell magazines, he tried to dissuade Wendelin, telling him it would be a waste of time and money. Better to go into the grocery business. On October 15, after a ten day voyage, his ship docked in Hoboken. The day had come; his dreams were coming true as he nervously waited his turn down the gangplank. I shall let him tell of his first hours in the New World himself. It is a humorous story, which at the time must have been harrowing.

Before our steamer was fully docked, a crowd of people shouted greetings to the arriving passengers. I knew none was meant for me, since I had no friends to welcome me. Still I had hoped that the Sisters at St. Francis Hospital, where I was to live for the first few days, would send somebody to receive and help me when landing. Evidently, nobody had come. After looking and waiting for a long time, I disembarked, trying to make the best of a bad situation. However, I had only myself to blame. At the very beginning of my American career, I made a bad mistake. I acted too European. It had been arranged in the correspondence with the Sisters that I should make myself recognizable by wearing a piece of paper in my hat. I took it off very soon because I thought it looked silly that a man of my age and dignity should go around with a piece of paper in his hat. But the good man from the hospital was not looking for a man with dignity but for one with a piece of paper in his hat. And he looked in vain. When he eventually located me in the section where the baggage and passengers were lined up according to alphabetical order, his patience with the "greenhorn" had already grown thin, and instead of a hearty welcome to the New World, I received a sound bawling out. "Where in thunder have you been? Why didn't you have the paper in your hat as you were told?" I confessed that I had removed it because I thought it too conspicuous. "But how in all the world should I recognize you in this crowd?" I did not know.

He was in bad humor and pressed for the necessary inspection of my baggage by the revenue men. More trouble. One of my boxes was secured by iron bands. It took a man with special tools to open it. When one was found, he started working on it but unfortunately cut his hand very badly and began to bleed profusely. He expressed himself in a dock-hand's language, which, though I could not understand it, I instinctively felt was not fit to be heard by angels or men.

This did nothing for the disposition of the man who was to take care of me. And that was not the end of it. I had neglected to exchange part of my German money on the steamer, and so had no American money to pay the dock laborer and the duty collectors. There was nothing left for my guide but to dig in his own pocket and advance me the necessary money. He was not in very good a mood as we tried to reach the Lackawanna Ferry for New York as I was the last passenger off the steamer. Lack of money again became a problem. Once more he advanced money for the fare. His temperature had continued to rise. He made me feel so ashamed that I simply trotted behind him like a severely scolded little dog. But we were not through. I looked at my shoes and realized that I could not desecrate the Metropolis of America by making my entry in the gray shoes I had. They needed a shine. A bootblack on the ferry could furnish the needed shine provided I had the money to pay for it. Of course I did not. I figured that my reputation was in shambles anyway and that things could not get any worse if I asked my guide for a nickel. By now he was used to hand-outs. I took his nickel and the first class shine raised my morale considerably, and I was able to enter New York with raised head. Without another word, my guide brought me to Leo House where I exchanged my German money for American dollars. I was able to pay my debts. The added gratuity raised his estimation of me. From then on he became very friendly and communicative, and eventually we became good friends.

America did not live up to all Wendelin's expectations. The streets were not paved with gold, and money did not grow on trees; not every uncle was rich. But it still was the land of unlimited possibilities, of wide-open spaces, a land of opportunity and plenty for those willing to work. The lone SVD, facing his task of representing the Society in America, was actually quite suited for his work. Through his relatives, he was already somewhat familiar with America. Although still in temporary vows, he was a committed member of the SVD. From his own extensive *Reisebruder* experience, he was accustomed to being self-sufficient in strange surroundings. He was patient, outgoing and pleasant, approachable, and made friends easily. He was also bright and well educated, capable of making acute observations and doing the research Janssen required. He was also able to present his findings clearly in writing, and, as a former school teacher, Janssen judged he would be able to learn English quickly.

Quite naturally, Brother Wendelin quickly made friends among the Germans. Albert Marschall, the engineer at St. Francis Hospital where Wendelin was staying, took him to a meeting of the Kolping Society. Once a month was family night for this society, so very quickly Brother's circle of acquaintances and friends increased. Later in life he says of these meetings: "The hours which I spent among these excellent men form some of the most pleasant memories I have of those years." He also began to sell subscriptions to these people. Two very special friends, Frank Heinemann and his family and Joseph Schaefer, were especially close and remained good benefactors of the Society for years to come. Not only was Wendelin open and approachable, quick to make friends, he was also loyal to the friends he made.

But he needed to learn English; he needed a teacher. He found a room close to the hospital where he had stayed when he first came to America and where he continued to take his meals. Here he also found a teacher, whose name was Motz, who was also connected with the Kolping Society. Wendelin even went to night school.

Brother Wendelin soon decided to make his first long business trip, to Rochester, New York; he had many addresses of friends and relatives of SVDs who lived in Rochester. Bishop John Baptist Anzer, for example, had many friends and relatives in Rochester, and elsewhere in America, whom Wendelin was able to visit. Before he went, he sent the following letter, plus the circulars he had brought with him from Steyl, to all the people whose addresses he had brought with him:

New York, January 12, 1896

To Whom It May Concern:

You have been recommended to me by friends in the homeland. I would have considered it a special pleasure to pay you a personal visit, but for the present, I am restrained by my efforts to study English. I take this opportunity to announce my arrival in the United States. Hopefully, I will be able to visit you in the course of this year.

The purpose of my visit here is explained in the attached circular which I enclose for your kind perusal. Just recently I received a shipment of books, magazines and almanacs. Despite the urgent needs of our mission institutions, I am prevented from doing much for the propagation of this mission literature. That is why I beg you to come to my aid. You will render a very important service to the work of the propagation of the faith if you will be kind enough to assist me in my work. Likewise you will give your friends an opportunity to perform some good works and provide them with some really wholesome reading matter at a very moderate price.

I can especially recommend our *St. Michaelskalendar* which I mail for 25 cents postpaid, and the *Stadt Gottes* for the year 1895, beautifully bound for $1.50. The *Stadt Gottes*, rich in contents and beautifully illustrated, is the lowest priced and most universally read magazine of all Catholic publications in Germany.

I take the liberty to mail you a sample copy of the *St. Michaelskalendar* and I enclose a return envelope with my address.

Thanking you in advance for your kindness, I remain devotedly yours,

Brother Wendelin (Joseph Meyer)
122 — 2nd Ave.
New York City

Soon, with Mr. Schaefer helping him by storing and even mailing his books when he was on his travels, Wendelin journeyed to Buffalo, Cleveland, Philadelphia, and to Atlantic City. Everywhere he was successful. Steyl had sent 10,000 copies of the 1897 almanac (for sale during 1896). Wendelin figured he would be able to sell between 15,000 and 25,000 the following year. He contacted a Franciscan friar, Bonaventure Hammer, to translate the 1898 edition of *St. Michaelskalendar*, and the press at Steyl printed 15,000 copies. Thus he concluded that there was a good-sized market for Catholic reading materials slanted toward the missions and developing mission awareness in America, just as there had been in Germany when the founder began his apostolate of the press.

His success was such that Wendelin needed a bigger place and he needed help. His correspondence and the amount of materials sold and shipped were accelerating so fast that he could not keep up. All the while, he was also carrying out the mandate of the founder to look for a place where the Society could buy property to make a permanent foundation. In examining the correspondence about what kind of property he should find, it becomes obvious from the founder's responses that there was no clarity yet on what he wanted the Society to do and become in America. And when Arnold Janssen lacked a clear idea, he did not believe God's will was yet manifest. That meant further delay, more prayer, more study and research until he could come to a clear decision. It had always worked before, and it would work again this time; of that he was sure. God had proven him correct in this approach so often before; he wasn't going to change his method now.

In a letter of 17 January 1896, Janssen had promised to send Brother Homobonus (literally, "good man"), who had gone by the name Joseph Stiller before entering the SVD. Born in Neudorf in Prague on 21 May 1866, Homobonus was nine years younger than Wendelin. He, too, worked as a *Reisebruder* in Germany before he was sent to America. At this time he, too, was still in temporary vows. The founder wrote, "Since we have no priest available to send at this time, it was agreed that we would send Brother Homobonus as your partner in your work as well as in your worries."

In the same letter the founder told him he should look for a place to rent before Homobonus was sent, which he hoped to do as early as February. In fact, Brother Homobonus did not leave until July. He recounts his arrival in New York and his first weeks with Wendelin.

> I had informed Brother Wendelin of the date of my arrival, but I looked in vain for him. He had not expected the ship to dock as late in the evening as ten o'clock, so he waited until next morning. I spent another night on board and had plenty of time to study New York's skyline, making all kinds of good resolutions for my future stay in this new field of mission labor. When Brother Wendelin arrived at nine o'clock in the morning, we had a joyful "Wiedersehen." He saw to it that I got a good breakfast at the Leo House. There I experienced for the first time what it means to be in a strange land whose language was unknown to me. One of Brother Wendelin's questions was how much money I had with me. When he heard that I had about $500.00, he suggested that we buy a small house organ which was agreeable to me. Then came the question about our "residence." Brother Wendelin, after a fruitless search of a whole week, had been able to rent a dwelling place at 75 Harmon Street in Jersey City, N.J.
>
> Never before had I seen so much dirt everywhere [as in this newly rented residence]. We went about for a whole week cleaning in the thorough Steyl manner, sparing neither soap nor water. After that, our little convent had a different face. It had five rooms and a store-room which we changed into a bedroom for a young fellow we took in to teach us English. The rent was $22.00 a month. We "lived very happily thereafter," but not for long. We saw what little money we had dwindle like the snow before the sun. How to remedy the situation?
>
> We decided to regularly visit the Kolping Society in New York where Brother Wendelin was known and where we always found people who had an understanding interest in our mission. Then Father Bruder of the German St. Joseph's Church in New York was won over for our cause, and

he announced our work and needs together with a request to his people to pay us a visit occasionally. From then on we had numerous visitors who never left the house without leaving a souvenir behind in the form of dollar bills. There were Sundays when more than $100.00 was given us as donations. There were especially several well-to-do ladies from Brooklyn who showed themselves very generous. After the first half year, we had over $1,000.00 in the bank.

The two got along very well together. Brother Wendelin called himself "house father and bread winner" while Homobonus was "Minister of Internal Affairs." Father Markert, quoting and paraphrasing Wendelin's memoirs, says that Homobonus took very good care of the various housekeeping duties, but his culinary efficiency was still experimental. Only after several months did he have a dozen or so menus that were all "well done." Homobonus sympathized with Brother Wendelin who had to be the guinea pig for his culinary experiments. He related that Brother Wendelin stood next to him at times in the kitchen, watching him prepare the meals and would wistfully sigh: "Oh, my mother could make this and that so tastefully." When he asked him how his mother prepared this or that, he had to confess, "Of course, I don't know."

Something of the character of the two brothers, their ability to make and keep good friends, their cheerfulness, their knack of making good things happen out of nothing are revealed in their memoirs. Brother Homobonus describes their first Christmas together in America:

One day before Christmas, good Father Kuhnünch, chaplain at St. Mary's Hospital in Hoboken, paid us a visit. He had come to bless our dwelling place. While he was doing so, we heard a knock at the door. Visitors at such an inopportune time. He insisted on opening the door. There stood eleven ladies who asked him whether two Brothers from Holland lived here. He said, "Yes, two Brothers live here, but they are not to marry." The ladies laughed, assuring him that they had not come for that purpose. Then Father admitted them. Most of these ladies were Bavarian like Father, and we had a strong suspicion that he had much to do with this visit.

The ladies made it clear they had also come for a bite to eat. I went through agonies when I realized I had fourteen people to feed and only three or four knives, forks, spoons and cups. A lady, a Mrs. Kosmann who became one of our very helpful friends, said, "Brother, let me see what you have in your kitchen." I had to open my small shelf and they laughed some more when they saw how little I had. Mrs. Kosmann said, "Brother, we suspected that it would be like this so we brought our own dinner along. For once you will have a real dinner." Turning to her companions she commanded, "Now, ladies, unpack what you brought along." We had the surprise of our life. What came out of their packages and baskets looked more like a banquet. Nothing was forgotten, even the salt and pepper shaker were there. We still had no table to accommodate so many. This did not discourage these resourceful good Samaritans. Before I knew it, they had pushed our book shipment boxes together, had them covered with a table cloth, and presto, there was a table. Since these boxes were of different heights, the improvised table looked like the back of a camel. We had only three or four chairs, but the stairway had ten steps, one for each of the diners. Before these good ladies took leave, they left souvenirs in the form of pictures of George Washington, commonly called dollar bills. In this way the good Lord very convincingly took care of us.

Our first Christmas together in America had to be celebrated in proper form. Brother Wendelin decided we should have a small Christmas tree. We had our much used house organ and we had two strong voices. Brother Wendelin sang tenor while I sang bass. We invited a few friends, among them our grocery man on the corner. As far as we could figure out, he was a fallen away Catholic and his wife belonged to the holy rollers. They were certainly very good to us and treated us more as members of their family than customers. They were so touched by our little Christmas celebration that they asked us to repeat it for them in their own home. Brother Wendelin played his violin while I sang all the German *Weinachtslieder* ["Christmas songs"] I knew. This in a completely American surrounding. I knew only a few English words and said ever so many times, "Yes" and "No," not knowing whether it fit the question or the conversation. Still we had gained some more friends.

Not everything, of course, was so easy. Homobonus contracted malaria. He had come in July 1896, and Jersey City was surrounded by swamps with lots of mosquitos. By 20 August he was already ill, probably with his first bout of malaria. When the doctor finally diagnosed the illness, he advised him to return to Europe, warning that otherwise he would not live more than a year. Another doctor gave him two years. Their good friend Schaefer sent him to a sanatorium in Denville, New Jersey, for a Kneipp cure, which was a popular German treatment using water baths. Something must have worked. Homobonus did not return to Europe but lived in America until his death in 1951 at the age of 85.

Nor were they always well received on their selling tours. Let Homobonus tell the story of his visit to German Benedictines in Newark, New Jersey, in his own words.

When the brother porter opened the door, he gave me a rather strange look when I told him that I was a brother from Steyl. He bid me to step in the parlor while he called Father Prior, who appeared presently. No sooner had I told him that I was brother from Steyl and tried to tell him about Steyl and our Society than there was lightning and thunder in the room. Father Prior, a native of Bavaria, addressed me in his fully natural Bavarian way, "Now stop. You are a swindler; you get out of here quicker than you came in. If you hesitate for one moment, I will call the police. You certainly are a swindler of the worst kind. Why the very name you give yourself shows how cunning you are. Calling yourself Homobonus, a 'good man,' while you are the worst rascal. Don't you ever dare to show up where I can lay eyes on you."

But what had been such a bad start led eventually to a hearty friendship between us and the good Benedictines.

It was later learned that a few days before the appearance of Brother Homobonus, a man dressed as a priest had come to the door, claiming to be a priest from Steyl. He said Mass and tried to collect money for the mission in China.

The issue of where to live was again looming on the horizon. May 1 was fast approaching, their lease was running out, and they had either to renew or see their house rented to someone else. The question whether to buy or to rent was still there. If they were given permission to buy, that would mean a definite decision had been made regarding the work of the SVD in North America. Father Janssen, however, was not ready yet to make this decision in the spring of 1897. The will of God was not yet clear to him. The situation was about to change with the arrival of the next group of Divine Word missionaries to North America, consisting of two priests, John Baptist Peil and Joseph Fischer, and another brother, Michael Fecken, whose Christian name by birth was Emil.

THE ARRIVAL OF JOHN BAPTIST PEIL
AND THE MILTON INTERLUDE

The decision to send more people to America, among them a priest, was made in Steyl in September 1896, when the councilors voted unanimously to establish the SVD in North America. After considering Fathers John Baptist Peil and Joseph Reinke, the decision was made to send Peil instead, chiefly because Reinke's health was considered weak. But even after the decision was made, a year would intervene before Father Peil arrived. An examination of the correspondence between Wendelin and Janssen during this period makes it clear that Janssen was searching for something he could not quite put his finger on. Wendelin would answer one set of questions, only to receive another and then another. Was it because Janssen was dealing with a brother and not a priest? It would seem not. When Father Peil arrived, to be sure, he was named superior, but Janssen's incessant search for still more information did not cease. It also seems that Brother Wendelin was never enthusiastic about settling down in the New York or New Jersey area. From the beginning, according to Bornemann, he had the idea that it would be better to settle further west, perhaps in St. Louis.

A new chapter for the SVD in North America begins with the appointment on 10 May 1897, of Father John Baptist Peil to America, which may be called "the Milton interlude." When Father Peil and his two fellow SVDs arrived on 27 September 1897. the community numbered five, and all of them deserve to be called pioneers, but Peil, more than anyone else, deserves the title of "Founder of the SVD in North America." He has been unduly neglected.

John Baptist Peil was 24 years old when he entered Steyl in 1880. He was ordained in 1890. After several years as prefect of students at Steyl he was assigned to St. Gabriel's in Austria as house treasurer from Easter 1895 till his assignment to the United States in 1897. In that position, Father Peil had to know about finances, the ins and outs of construction, keeping books, and begging for money. St. Gabriel's was the major seminary for the whole Society at this time and rivaled the mother-house at Steyl both in size and complexity. He was hard-working and full of ideas. He enjoyed robust health and would not hesitate to make decisions. As would be seen, he was also able to persevere at a project until it was completed. And he thought big.

Early on he anticipated that Janssen would send some of the sisters from the two congregations he had founded to North America. Working with youth would be their first apostolate. German immigrants could be their second activity, he writes, saying it was another possible project that Father Janssen had talked about. This was, indeed, a necessary field for activity. Nevertheless Peil also writes: "Meanwhile we do not want to make too many definite plans, but rather leave it to the Holy Ghost to determine our future." It is certainly clear from his very first letter that Peil felt he had a mandate to get things moving in America and would quickly make recommendations for approval by the superior general in Steyl. He was sent as the superior and upon his arrival began to act like one.

When the three newcomers arrived, Brothers Wendelin and Homobonus and the pastors of Hoboken and West Hoboken, who had been so helpful to Brother Wendelin when he had first arrived, were there to greet them. The brothers were overjoyed. They had a religious community. And the responsibilities of looking for a place to live, deciding what kind of work to do beyond selling subscriptions to magazines, and the extra time-consuming task of supplying Arnold Janssen with the information he required were off their shoulders.

On the day after his arrival, Father Fischer wrote to the founder:

> What a joy our arrival brought to the two good Brothers your Reverence can well imagine, especially to Brother Wendelin. He evidently has labored hard in his magazine selling, and thus he does not look good at all, though his beard partly hides his sickly looks. Nevertheless, he seemingly always has been, and still is, of good mood.
>
> Yesterday was a nice day when we entered our new home. A very excellent Heinemann family had a reception prepared for us that first evening. They welcomed us while the twelve-year old daughter recited a very touching poem and handed Father Rector a bouquet of flowers.

The girl who recited the poem was named Pauline and, as Sister Maria, was to become the first American member of the Congregation of the Missionary Sisters Servants of the Holy Spirit.

Two weeks after this, Peil writes in terms that will foreshadow his own and other German SVDs' difficulties in adapting to the new land while not alarming their fellow Germans in Europe: "With regard to the spiritual life here everything is in good order. The Brothers have preserved their good spirit. It is apparent that God's help was with them. Brother Wendelin has become a full-fledged American without the less desirable traits."

These five were first in a long line of priests and brothers to come to the United States from Europe. Up until Janssen's death in 1909, forty brothers and twenty priests had been sent. During that same time, he also assigned fifty-three Missionary Sisters Servants of the Holy Spirit to the United States.

John Baptist Peil was not one to let grass grow under his feet. It seems he rarely had a second thought about any ideas that he had, and he also had the energy to carry them out. The small group of three had stepped off the boat in Hoboken on 27 September 1897. On 15 October 1897, despite all the letters that had flowed between Janssen and Wendelin on possible sites in New York and New Jersey for relocation, some of which Father Janssen had not yet even rejected, Peil decided to move to Milton, Pennsylvania, a small town sixty miles north of Harrisburg. He urged the founder to give his permission for this transfer. Janssen received Peil's letter on 28 October 1897. He sent the letter immediately to his council and on the afternoon the next day they met and decided that Father Peil could provisionally accept the offer of Milton. That same day Janssen sent a letter of confirmation spelling out the provisions and telling Peil that he was not happy with the speed and pressure he had put on him and his council. This should not be done in the future "unless it is absolutely necessary."

How did this major development take place so quickly? Its origins lie in a trip by Brother Wendelin to Philadelphia, where he had become acquainted with two German priests, Theodore and Hubert Hammeke, brothers. (Their uncle was Father Francis Xavier Nies, a Divine Word missionary to China who was murdered with Father Richard Henle, another SVD, during anti-foreign disturbances there in 1887. Father Nies had another brother in the SVD, Brother Raphael.) Theodore was exceptionally helpful to Brother Wendelin, introducing him personally to every German pastor in the city. Knowing that the SVDs were still looking for a place, Father Hammeke suggested the name of Father Anthony Kaul as someone who might be of help. He lived in Lancaster, Pennsylvania, which was in the Harrisburg Diocese, to whose bishop, Thomas McGovern, Father Kaul happened to be very close. Brother Wendelin reported this to Father Peil in October 1897. Peil immediately wrote to Father Kaul on 8 October and received an answer three days later: "In reply to your inquiry about locating in our Diocese I believe there is a favorable opening, and would respectfully suggest that you would call in person upon our good Bishop, but stopping first to see me, when we can talk the matter over, and I give you such information which may serve you when you meet the Bishop."

Father Peil had to send Brother Wendelin to do the preliminary negotiating, because he did not speak much English yet, and the bishop was Irish and did not speak German. Brother Wendelin first called on Father Kaul, who received him kindly, after which they both went to meet with Bishop McGovern. Because he needed priests badly, the bishop was willing to accept the Society of the Divine Word into his diocese. He also had a definite plan. The Society should begin an industrial training school for boys. This school would be built and maintained by the Society, in return for which the bishop would give them a 200 acre farm four miles south of Milton on which to build the school. At the same time he would turn the parish of Milton over to them. In his later years Brother Wendelin writes about this visit in his memoirs:

> This Bishop described to me in as witty, joking and drastic a manner the value and benefits of the farm as I had never dreamed to hear from a church dignitary. "Why, Brother," he said, "you go up to Milton and take hold of

that farm and you will make a lot of money. You can raise chickens, and they will lay piles of eggs. Some years ago eggs were imported from Europe and our chickens went on strike. But when McKinley became president he put a tariff on the eggs, and now our chickens lay eggs to their utmost capacity."

The bishop was a good salesman as he tried to convince the SVDs that they were getting a good deal. Brother Wendelin went to Milton, inspected the town and the farm, and brought back to New Jersey, together with a favorable report, samples of the corn grown there, 600 grains to an ear, and apples so plentiful that they were left to rot on the ground. To be sure, there were not many Catholics in the area. Milton had 7,000 inhabitants but only 150 Catholics. And Montandon, where the farm was located, had only 574 residents. Here there were only five Catholic families. Father Peil then went to Milton himself on an inspection visit.

All this was done in record time. On 19 October, eight days after receiving Father Kaul's letter—and after a trip to Lancaster and two trips to Milton—Peil sent his own report to Steyl and urged that a contract be drawn up as soon as possible.

Peil now had "provisional" approval to proceed, which for him seemed to mean something more like "full steam ahead." He began to think in terms of an orphanage attached to an industrial school, to be followed by one also for girls, a hospital, and an old folks' home. In a letter of 13 January 1898, Father Peil explained to Steyl that he would have everything put in his own name and, unless he heard otherwise at the earliest opportunity, that he would assume he had permission to buy whatever was necessary, provided he could pay for it himself. He had three houses in mind and had four thousand dollars to pay for them. In a letter of 29 November 1897, he also mentioned the case of a former pastor of Milton, dead now for many years. This priest had prophesied that the parish of Milton would someday be taken over by a religious congregation and then the whole region would become Catholic again. The bishop's secretary was the source for the story, Peil said, adding that he himself does not believe this should influence the decision to turn the parish over to the SVD.

Based on the "provisional" permission to take over the Milton parish, and with Bishop McGovern's approval, the small group got ready to move everything from New Jersey to Milton, where the plan was to stay in the rectory with the resident pastor, Father Breckel. Father Peil was confident that he would receive permission to carry out all his ideas once they were settled in Milton. And in the meantime he had added several more projects to the list. They included: founding and running a diocesan seminary at Harrisburg; opening a college, although he did realize this would have to wait a few years, because it would require many good teachers who would have to know English well; and a press, so the almanacs and magazines they planned to publish in English could be done on the spot.

Letters from Steyl kept urging patience. On 2 November 1897, Father Blum, the founder's trusted confidante—who, in addition to all his other duties, oversaw all contracts the Society entered into on a worldwide basis—wrote a letter that reflected the mind of Arnold Janssen:

Undoubtedly you have received the two letters and the telegram of Father General. I believe you are too much in a hurry. This is *not* a good thing. One or two months delay would not make any difference there. Father Superior has written you everything rather extensively, on the same day on which your letter arrived, despite the fact that the Chapter is in session. You see from this how much we here have your affairs at heart. To my mind it is a necessity that you do not go any further than accept the offer provisionally. Why bind yourself right away before you know the whole matter sufficiently? The Bishop certainly cannot object to this *Festina lente, carissime!* ["Make haste slowly, dearest one!"] When it is found advisable to print the English Almanac, you can have it printed by a printer there. Pustet [a large German publishing house] does it this way. It is not an easy thing to create a press so quickly, and just for an Almanac. We cannot give you the necessary Brothers either.

On 25 November 1897, Peil and Fischer arrived in Milton. They were followed the next day by the three brothers and a railroad car full of furniture, books, magazines, and almanacs. Father Fischer soon went on extended parish work while he was learning English, and seems to have learned the language quickly. Father Peil was also absent for long periods of time helping out in parishes, but with all the business and work as superior on his hands, Peil did not have the time to master English well. When Fischer wrote that he would preach his first English sermon on Christmas Eve, Peil would not be outdone. He felt good about his preaching effort, until at breakfast one day an old woman stepped into the room and in a most frank manner said, "Father, I wish you would not try to preach in English any more. It was awful the way you did it, and the people laughed and made fun of you." Having delivered her message, she turned and left Father Peil rather bewildered and with much less self-satisfaction. He could only mutter, "And an old woman has to tell me that!"

In the meantime, Father Peil was busily at work looking at different properties which he might purchase for the purposes he envisioned. At the same time, to legalize everything, he and Bishop McGovern drew up a contract that he sent to Steyl for final approval. By now events were moving much too fast for Father Janssen. Point three of the contract stated that the transfer of property and the parish assignment would be "in perpetuity." That was totally unacceptable to Janssen and his entire council as well. The contract was rejected. Peil was devastated—temporarily—and the rest of the small SVD community was getting nervous about the grandeur of his vision.

All Father Peil's great plans were put on hold and caution became the order of the day. The move to Milton itself was not rejected, as Peil first thought, but matters could not be decided "in perpetuity" at such an early stage. This, Janssen thought, would bind the Society too soon and too definitively. Janssen once again began to ask for more details and he made it clear that he did not want Peil hiding things from him or springing new and unrevealed dimensions of projects on him.

The gist of the final decision, communicated in a letter from Steyl dated 27 February 1898, had been to give permission to take over the parish for a limited time, from one to three years, and to establish the orphan asylum in a rented house.

They should put the idea of a contract off for a year, until the bishop and the SVD got to know each other better. In the meantime, Peil could get a better sense of conditions in North America in general and especially of the area around Milton. The bishop, those in Steyl felt, should not be against this. But when Peil approached the bishop with these new offers, he was no longer interested or willing to enter into a temporary contract, even for three years, or to have the orphan asylum established in a rented house. He did give them permission to stay in his diocese, rent a house in Milton—the community of five could hardly impose much longer on Father Breckel's hospitality—and live there according to their rule.

This they did and, as the founder and Blum had suggested, they began to look around again for another place to settle down. The idea of a mission house to train Americans for the missions came up again, or a combination orphanage and mission house. A house training Americans for foreign missions would be something really new, the likes of which did not exist yet in America.

Father Fischer and the rest of the community agreed with the superior general in his call for caution and delay. In a letter of 16 March 1898, several weeks after the cautionary letter from Steyl, Fischer writes:

> Such caution on your part and, therefore, on our part also, is certainly on target. I have visited several times with the Jesuits who live in the neighborhood of Hanover [Pennsylvania], who are the only religious represented in this diocese, and have discussed with them the caution which Steyl has exercised in these matters and their response has always strengthened my conviction that Steyl handled the situation well and as proper superiors of a religious congregation could not have done otherwise.

Later in the same letter Fischer gives a brief portrait of Peil:

> Personally I get along very well with Father Peil, and I have often thanked God that we have such a superior here at this time. He is one who takes things seriously, and does everything in his power when it comes to following the rules and helping others whenever there is an occasion and in an appropriate way. But as far as his decisions go, I find your description of him very accurate: when he decides something, his nerves go into action and the decision is made with lightning speed as soon as he has thought of something, which he then has to modify when he reflects on it. I pointed this characteristic out to him already as we left for North America, but he has to be reminded once in a while.

In response to a remark on the part of Janssen that candidates to the religious life are rare in the United States, Peil tells Janssen that, contrary to what he might have heard, there is an abundance of vocations to religious life in America. He points out that the Benedictines no longer accept vocations from Europe, and the Franciscans have more vocations than they need.

As the Milton adventure proved, Peil thought big and could act precipitously. Father Janssen thought even bigger, but proceeded cautiously. As he looked at a map of Pennsylvania, at the Milton area particularly, he saw very little hope for any possibility of expansion. There were few people to begin with, and even fewer Catholics. There were Germans there, to be sure, but most of them were Protestant and staunch, conservative Protestants at that. If Janssen was going to introduce his rapidly growing society into America, he did not want to restrict its possibilities right from the beginning. That would not be God's will as he was used to reading it. Was Janssen thinking of a "mission house," for training Americans for missionary life at this point? It would seem so. And Milton was not a good place for this.

Janssen's deliberate way of going about things often blinded those around him to the sweep of the ideas he had and the goals toward which he worked. Enterprises like Steyl and St. Gabriel's, begun by him and built to house hundreds of people, did not happen by accident. And so the small community in America, stuck for the time being in Milton, but only for the time being, began looking again.

What was being fed into their calculations about a foundation in America? First, it must be realized that there was a great deal of ambivalence toward the United States. There were many things about America that the founder and his associates did not understand. Morever, German Catholic thought on the overseas diaspora was in general convinced that German language and German customs had to be kept alive in the United States if the Germans were to remain faithful to the Catholic religion of their forebears. Nor was America much like Argentina and Brazil, where the SVD was already at work with unchurched Germans who lived in their clearly demarcated *colonias*, preserving their language and customs they brought with them. It was commonly thought that it was all the more necessary to keep German customs alive in the United States in view of the American character, which was described as weak and materialistic, looking to make money to the detriment of developing the finer, spiritual side of life. From Father Janssen's perspective, Americans also valued freedom too much. As a consequence, they were excessively prone to question authority, and this, with their stress on egalitarianism, could only lead to social chaos if left unchecked. Finally, there was the general European feeling that the American state was essentially godless. It did not support religion; indeed, by constitution as well as by preference, it kept itself as aloof as it possibly could from religion. In addition, the so-called Americanist controversy that many in Europe thought was threatening to tear the church in America apart fueled these fears. Until he could come to some clarity on all this, or until his confreres in North America could resolve his doubts, Arnold Janssen would hesitate and delay. Finally, no one had invited him to send missionaries to North America, not some bishop, not the Propaganda, not the Holy See. Had this been the case, then the founder would have felt more certain that it was God's will that he enter America with his Society.

In the meantime, the practical activities of the young community went on. While Brother Michael looked after things in Milton, the other two brothers continued their successful journeys selling magazines. In 1897 they sold 20,000 copies of the German *St. Michaelskalendar.* The brothers made many good friends and benefactors as they traveled. All in all, things had not gone badly in the two years since Wendelin had first arrived. He and Homobonus had come for three reasons: to sell magazines; to make the Society known; and to find a place where the SVD might settle down and begin the work for which they had been founded. They had succeeded very well in the first two. And in the third, they had been partially successful. Minimally, it was clear to the small community and the founder that New York and New Jersey were not where the Society should settle. And so the small community continued to live in Milton but began to look around for another place to put down permanent roots, where it would be more clear God wanted them.

2

The Move West

The Foundation in Shermerville Becomes Techny

Because Milton had proven to be a dead end, all began to keep their eyes open for new possibilities. The most traveled person in the community was still Brother Wendelin, who continued to make long journeys selling magazines. On these trips he tried to stay with German pastors whose names and addresses he had taken with him from Steyl. One of his trips took him to Chicago. He spent the night at St. Boniface Church talking with Father Albert Evers. When told of the founder's decision on Milton, Evers informed Wendelin that at Shermerville,[1] not far from the city, a farm belonging to the German orphanage at High Ridge was for sale. Wendelin informed the community at Milton, and Father Peil began inquiries.

THE NEGOTIATIONS FOR THE FARM AT SHERMERVILLE

On 10 July 1898, Father Peil started a two-week trip to inspect places where the SVD could find permanent work. By now he was concentrating on the possibility of a technical school and made sure he checked these out especially. His trip took him to Westchester County, New York, which would become the home of the Maryknoll Missioners in a few years, as well as Clayton, Delaware, where he also visited the Industrial School for Negroes run by the Josephites. He moved on to Pittsburgh; Lafayette and Ft. Wayne, Indiana; Cincinnati; Covington, Kentucky; and finally to Chicago, where he stayed with Father Schäfers, a former student at Steyl, to whom he had written about the orphanage farm. Father Schäfers informed Peil that a committee to which he belonged was in charge of Holy Angels German

---

1. Shermerville's name was later changed to Northbrook, which still calls itself a "Village," but has become a very prosperous north shore Chicago suburb. Shermerville remained the name by which the first SVDs knew the place that would not become known as "Techny" until January 1906. On January 15 that year St. Joseph's Technical School and St. Ann's Home for the Aged got their own post office using Techny as the place name. About this, more will be said below. The Techny post office, still in an SVD-owned building, is in operation with no plans for closure as this book is written.

Orphanage and planned to set up an industrial training school. The children who had to leave the orphanage could be given further training there in a trade they would find useful when they were on their own. This made Father Peil's ears perk up. Father Schäfers put Peil in touch with Father Aloys Thiele, pastor of St. Aloysius German Parish, who was the spokesman for the committee and empowered to negotiate for it.

And so began the process of negotiating at a distance of thousands of miles between Fathers Janssen, Peil, and Thiele. The small SVD community was still based in Milton about 700 miles from Chicago. St. Mary's Catholic Orphanage owned some property on the north side of Chicago. Originally this had been bought for the purpose of building a cemetery, the proceeds of which were to go to support the orphanage. Since cemeteries were quite profitable, the Archbishop of Chicago, Patrick Feehan, was very careful to whom he gave permission to begin one, an issue that almost derailed the purchase from the very beginning. On this property the Society of the Divine Word was to build an industrial school to train young boys in some trade to prepare them morally and physically to find their way in life. This would be, first of all, for boys from the orphanage and primarily for young men of German ancestry, but not exclusively so. The archbishop would officially invite the Society of the Divine Word into his archdiocese for this work, to sell their magazines, to do supply work, and even open a parish on their property to look after the Catholics living in the immediate neighborhood.

So far, so good. Negotiations went forward. Father Blum wrote Peil on 7 October 1898:

> Yesterday evening Father Superior sent the dispatch to buy . . . How sorry you would be now if you were chained to Milton. In Chicago the most extensive activity is waiting for you. Thus you see, waiting was good and according to the plans of Divine Providence. Please send me the purchasing contract, and a copy of the admission into the diocese of Chicago. For your industrial school you need instructors. Who will they be? Shall they be brothers? What is your plan?

When Janssen presented the idea of working in Chicago to his council, he made several points that showed his positive attitude toward making a foundation there:

> Chicago will soon be the biggest city of the Union and lies almost in the middle of the country. Thirty rail lines come together here. If we ever intend to have an impact here in *utilitatem animarum* [for the good of souls], it would be best if we situated ourselves in the middle of this huge country . . . If we conduct an orphanage in Chicago . . . and a farm with a technical school . . . then we can attach other things to this. Things will happen in North America.
>
> Chicago is nothing like Milton. In Chicago one can afford to take some risk; in Milton there was nothing worth risking.

The tone of this circular is enthusiastic, with the result that the council was basically also in favor of the plan. Peil had earlier made a similar point, but a bit more bluntly: "If the Archbishop permits us to take over the administration of such an institution, then we are finally in this city and can then do what we want." And how was he going to pay for all this? Mostly, it seemed from their perspective, by borrowing. Their fears proved to be well founded, for Peil did go into debt. Was this the overly adventurous American spirit with which he was already infected, as the founder often feared?

In this respect, it seems Peil already had a better sense of America and the American character than either the founder or Blum, who seemed to be even more concerned about this aspect of Peil's spending than Janssen. Peil could see how wealthy America actually was. The country also had great potential. By this time he must also have had a sense of the basic generosity that many Americans displayed, certainly, but not only, German-speaking Americans. There was money to be had in North America. Another source of his confidence came, no doubt, from an experience he had when he first visited Father Schäfers, the pastor of St. Martin's in Chicago. He had just built a beautiful church and rectory and ended up $100,000 in debt, a significant sum today, but an enormous debt in those days. "But here," as Peil wrote, "this sort of thing is the fashion." It was the American way, and for most people and institutions it worked.

As negotiations went on, five difficulties threatened to sink the prospects of the SVD getting the Shermerville property. The first has been mentioned, the founder's fear of debt. The second revolved around whether the Society had suitable members and experience to run a technical school. The archbishop of Chicago sought the advice of various bishops on this matter, including the archbishop of Cologne, who responded with a wholehearted endorsement of the new society:

> I gladly recommend the Society of the Divine Word for the industrial school to be erected as a foundation of this society. Its members come to a great extent from the Archdiocese of Cologne. They do not only work very efficiently as missionaries in various parts of the world, but they likewise assist with great readiness and success the diocesan clergy in our Archdiocese. In its Motherhouse in Steyl, which is situated close to the border of the Archdiocese of Cologne, Brothers practice under expert supervision various trades. Thus the Society is well able without any question to conduct such an industrial school with excellent results.
>
> Cologne, January 17, 1899.
Philip Cardinal Krementz

A third problem revolved around the German character of the SVD and the committee's thoughts that perhaps the Salesians (an order founded by Don Bosco in Italy) might be preferable. Early in the negotiations, the founder wrote to Father Thiele:

> Let me say, in connection with the matter of the industrial school, that I, like yourself, am a friend of Don Bosco, whom I visit in Turin. I also think highly of this congregation. If, however, they have to delay taking over this work for 4-5 years, this, too, may be part of God's providential plan, for if you

intend to have the children of German parents keep up the German language, then a congregation whose origins are German might be better for this work than one which is Italian in origin. But you must decide that yourself; we do not want to put undue pressure on you.

At present it is quite well known that Christianity is flourishing in German countries, where the frequent reception of the sacraments is the rule, and vocations to the priesthood and religious life are plentiful. Important consequences follow from this.

I try to avoid and reject excessive nationalism, but it does seem to me, from what I've just said, that the German way of doing things should be cultivated [in such an institution as envisioned], if not exclusively, at least to the extent that it is not completely lost. Whenever possible the German spirit should be fostered, but in a way which does not turn other nationalities away.

If your people in charge over there could agree to something like this, then I would authorize Father Superior Peil to enter into further negotiations to buy the farm from the orphanage so as to have the necessary base for the work. We could then make a small beginning which could expand over time. We have found this procedure to work best with all of the houses we have put up, for, in spite of their small beginnings, they have grown marvelously. In the situation we are now discussing, I have another reason for starting in a modest manner. In this way, as the various departments offering technical skills grow and the students work for the needs of the expanding institution, they avoid competing with other artisans, something to be avoided at all costs.

In this letter of the founder there are also hints that he was already thinking beyond a technical school to a mission house. Just as he had started in a very modest manner with his houses in Germany, so he saw that as the best way in America. But all of his houses in Germany were mission houses.

The fourth difficulty became a veritable crisis in the form of a radical disagreement between Thiele and Peil. Thiele wanted the institute under consideration to be totally charitable. It should not charge tuition and should be there for children of poor families as well as the orphans from Holy Angels, and it should not cater to the children of the well-to-do. Support, he insisted, would come from a group of benefactors, the Don Bosco Society, which he had already assembled and which he would try to turn over to the SVD. Thiele insisted on the charitable nature of the institution because some on his board suspected that once the SVD had control of this technical school they would branch out to build a mission house, which they did not want. Peil, however, did not think it sufficiently safe to rely exclusively on gifts, alms, and the spirit of charity of the lay people and clergy. In a letter of 4 November 1989, Father Peil proposes the following:

I can say that as much as I do not like your plan at all to accept all boys free of charge, I still maintain that the most reasonable thing to do is to fix a minimum charge of $5.00 per month and $1.00 extra for clothes per month. This is to be charged to all that really can pay it. Poorer boys to be charged only half of it; such boys, of whom their pastor attests that they are in no condition to pay, shall be admitted without any charge whatsoever. You will see that this will bring in a fairly good sum, for which nobody else is to be bothered, and which in just measure can be paid by the families of these boys and by nobody else.

In the end, this was accepted.

The fifth difficulty that nearly sank the purchase of the farm at Shermerville resulted from Peil's remembering the founder's fondness for maps. He sent Janssen a map of the area, and on the map Janssen quickly found a section marked "swamp." To fill out the picture, recall that most of these negotiations were conducted by mail exchanged among three parties: the community still living in Milton, Father Thiele and his committee, and the founder in Steyl in the Netherlands. The possibility for confused and crossed messages was unavoidable, particularly when deadlines developed or decisions had to be rushed, especially in areas that Janssen reserved to himself. All the foregoing issues were resolved eventually, but not before the swamp nearly became the straw that broke the camel's back. In Janssen's mind, the swamp meant bad air, insects, malaria, and illness of various kinds. He was eventually persuaded to recognize that what he saw on the map was not the kind of swampland that was quite common in the neighborhood where he grew up, but low ground that stayed wet longer than the surrounding landscape when it rained, otherwise not dangerous or harmful to health in any way. Father Markert says that Peil had to write about a dozen letters over several months to convince the superior general that there were no swamps to worry about.

With all these matters resolved, problems seemed over. There were no malarial swamps. The SVD was able to begin work immediately and the Salesians only after several years. The SVD would scarcely get rich charging the proposed fees, and the charitable institution would not become a cow to be milked for the mission work of the Society.

A final contract was drafted and signed, and was preserved by Father Markert. Nevertheless, in a letter of 18 October 1898, the superior general had many problems with various aspects of the contract, none sufficient to prevent the negotiations from moving forward. He mentioned other difficulties in a long letter of 17 March 1899. One point needed to be changed because it went against canon law, and he wanted the right to be able to dismiss a student immediately, if it was a question of grave danger to other boys, and not to allow them a year to improve. The rest of the points were otherwise acceptable, though he pointed out many things about which they should be wary and careful.

THE CONTROVERSY OVER CHARTERING THE SVD IN ILLINOIS

Connected with the negotiations and lingering on in the founder's mind as an object of suspicion that colored his view of the new foundation was the need for legal incorporation under the laws of the State of Illinois. It was generally agreed by everyone on the scene in Chicago that the Society of the Divine Word as such should be the purchaser of any property to be acquired, not Father Peil nor any other individual. But according to the law of the State of Illinois, if the Society wanted to buy the farm at Shermerville, it would need to be established as a corporation. But to set up a corporation, a charter was required that only American citizens could request or be granted. Consequently, on 11 February 1899, Father Thiele's lawyer, William F. Ryan, and the lawyer's brother, Andrew Ryan—also a lawyer for the Archdiocese of Chicago—drafted the petition. It was granted by James A. Rose, the Secretary of State of Illinois on 11 March 1899. Under the terms of the charter "the Roman Catholic Society of the Divine Word" would be the name of the corporation. The object of the corporation would be

> humanitarian and charitable. To obtain sites and build a college and school buildings for its own use and such other buildings and appurtenances thereto, as may be necessary for its own use. To employ teachers, instructors and such other employees as may be necessary. To provide and establish courses of studies in all branches of learning which may be considered by said corporation necessary to obtain its educational humanitarian and charitable object. To give instructions to pupils in such courses of study and to grant diplomas to graduates therein. To provide a suitable home for homeless and dependent children where they may be cared for and educated under moral influences and taught some useful trade. To provide a home and proper training school for all who may be committed to its charge.

The management of the Society was to be vested in a board of three directors who are to be elected annually, with Father Peil, Father Fischer, and Brother Wendelin serving as the first directors.

When he received a copy of this document, Arnold Janssen almost went into apoplexy. He had all kinds of objections to the identity of the petitioners and clearly he did not understand that the Society of the Divine Word was in fact the corporation being recognized and that it would purchase and own the land. He believed that the owners would be the three petitioners. Janssen feared, in other words, that the ownership rights of the Society were not sufficiently guaranteed, that the three who had incorporated the SVD would be able to cheat the Society out of its property once the SVD had bought it, and if not these three men, who might be honorable, then perhaps their heirs once the three original charter members had died. It seems that he also thought that the way the charter was drawn up could be the first step toward a split of the SVD in America from the SVD in Germany, a worry, as the reader will see, that increased as time went on. Indeed, he was so annoyed with Peil at what he thought was his unseemly haste in handling this entire charter issue that he told Peil he had empowered Father Fischer to investigate and make a report. For this purpose Fischer was no longer under obedience to Peil, who should not interfere with his investigation. He was to go to Chicago and even to the State House in Springfield, Illinois, if that was necessary, to get the information the founder wanted.

The conclusion to all this was permission to purchase the Russell farm. Apparently Father Fischer's efforts and research convinced Janssen and his council that Peil had everything under proper control. With everything straightened out, the founder gave Father John Beckert, the Society's architect, instructions on 12 May to draw up plans for the North American foundation. Father Peil in his memoirs wrote, "The whole process of buying this land took nine long months, something that could have been taken care of in one half hour, all this due to the over-anxious caution of Father Founder." After a post-mortem on the purchase, the air was cleared, and Peil was still "loved and valuable"; the founder hoped Peil would not dwell upon his unkind comment about his hot-blooded insistence.

An important observation can be made here. The decision to buy the Russell farm took nine months to accomplish, almost as long as it took Janssen to decide to found the Society itself, and certainly longer than it took him to decide to build Steyl, new building by new building, or the decision to put up St. Gabriel's, and so forth. Yet Peil was accused of acting hastily. On such a standard, Janssen himself acted much more hastily. The rapidity with which he built up the SVD in Europe was made possible because the founder was on the spot and operating within his own culture. He arrived at "God's will" much more quickly, and once he had a handle on this, there was no holding him back. The obvious conclusion is that he was not yet clear what God wanted the SVD in North America to do. At least now they had something "to which something else can be added later." Obviously a mission house was not out of the question, but neither was the time ripe yet for this. Eventually the founder ended up with grave misgivings about a mission house, as we shall soon see, but these reservations were deeper and even more "philosophically" based, if you will, than the legal questions related to charters and by-laws.

And so the episode came to an end; the official turnover of the 340-acre Russell farm to the SVD for $42,000 on 26 June 1899 was a formality.

THE MOVE TO SHERMERVILLE

During the time this was all going on, the community in Milton continued to go about its business. Both Peil and Fischer were doing supply work in parishes, and Peil made longer trips for supply to Chicago and other parts of the country. He was quickly getting acquainted with America and American ways, as the founder had told him to do. Wendelin and Homobonus were selling almanacs and subscriptions, by all accounts quite successfully. For the year 1899 an English copy of the almanac (*St. Michaelskalendar*) was ready for printing. A printer in Lancaster, with whom Father Kaul had put them in touch, ran off 15,000 copies at $0.08 a copy. According to Wendelin's later memoirs, they were all sold. Brother Michael looked after the home front and kept the magazines and almanacs on their way. All the while they realized they would not be staying in Milton much longer; as soon as the Shermerville property was bought, they would pack everything up once more, this time for the last time. On 4 May 1899, Father Peil rented a house in Shermerville for the five of them. This place was in need of a bit of repair and remodelling, so Homobonus moved in on 9 May 1899, to prepare everything for the rest of the community, who arrived at their new home on 15 May 1899, a few days short of a year since they had settled in Milton.

The first Solemn Mass was celebrated in the house in Shermerville on Pentecost Sunday, 21 May 1899. This event would mark the official opening of the North

American mission for the founder. In his final address to the community at St. Gabriel's in Austria on 19 June 1908, Janssen said: "The North American mission was begun on Pentecost of the year 1899 with the Mass [in honor of the Holy Spirit] which was offered in Shermerville."

The Divine Word Missionaries now had over 300 acres and were living in a rented house in Shermerville while they waited for the farmer who rented the farm to leave and free up the farmhouse. At the same time they were busy making plans to build, a task in which the founder always took a keen and detailed interest. On 29 November 1899, they moved into the farmhouse, celebrating the first Mass there the next day.

Just as leopards find it hard to change their spots, so Janssen and Peil found it impossible to change their characters. Peil continued to move ahead with vigor; the founder kept raising objections, in particular maintaining that Peil did not consult in timely fashion. The dialectic that was such a striking and fascinating characteristic of their relationship continued, with Peil proposing and Janssen opposing—until the founder could be won over. As far as the beginnings of the Society of the Divine Word in North America were concerned, the two founders were good for each other. Had Peil been given his way the efforts of the SVD would have been scattered and dissipated all over North America. Had Janssen had his way, the foundation would have been delayed and perhaps never have taken off, or it may have followed a direction that would have doomed it to insignificance.

PUTTING DOWN ROOTS AND EARLY PROBLEMS

The next stages in the growth of the SVD in the United States—until the decision was made regarding a mission house—revolved around two things: (1) the technical school to which the SVD was committed, and (2) the entry of the SVD and the Missionary Sisters Servants of the Holy Spirit into the apostolate among African Americans. We shall bracket the latter story and develop it in a later chapter. We turn first to the technical school and the question that always lurked in the background: Should the Society open a mission house (seminary) and eventually take North American members?

A topic that came up repeatedly in the letters that were exchanged between North America and Steyl was the question of personnel. Peil would demand help. The founder or Father Blum would respond that he had no right to demand and should adopt the tone of *asking*. And they would usually have to add that they had no one to send. After which, they would usually send someone anyway. Peil would then demand more help again, and the cycle would repeat itself. He needed brothers especially, first, to train the young boys in the technical school, and second, to look after the farm, do the tailoring, and take care of maintenance plus the myriad jobs that needed doing to make the institution self-sufficient. Peil particularly wanted to establish a press quickly. He also requested and got sisters.

Early on, Janssen had promised his support once he could see his way clear to a definite foundation, and he did. In January 1900, he sent two priests and two brothers to Shermerville, one brother to take care of the farm, the other to look after the sacristy and the chickens. In February 1900, he sent Father Beckert, the architect, on a temporary assignment to take charge of the building projects that were just beginning. With him came six more brothers, among them a mechanic-plumber, a postal worker, and a carpenter. By the end of 1900 there were sixteen brothers in the community, and twenty-five by the fall of 1901. By 1905 the founder had appointed thirty-seven brothers and twelve fathers to the technical school.

In the meantime, the ever-energetic Peil writes about all kinds of projects. He suggests establishing a small place in Newark, New Jersey, to assist the many SVDs who were en route to Illinois. The founder says no. Peil wants to build a home for the elderly, since the former chairman of the orphanage board (who was opposed to the SVD and the technical school) had bought the land for an old folks home and would sell it only for that purpose. This was eventually approved. The Society should build branch locations in the New York-Newark area, in the Cleveland Diocese, as well as in San Francisco. The ever-cautious founder replied characteristically on 10 January 1900:

> Please, not everything at once. You'll have so much to do with the industrial school you won't be able to think of anything else, certainly not about new foundations in other dioceses . . . If you want to have a religious congregation make a foundation in Roachton, then pray to God that he send another society there.

The patron of the technical school was St. Joseph, so at first it was called "St. Joseph's Home, Industrial School for Poor Boys." The founder wondered about the phrase, "for poor boys." Wouldn't this turn off boys from the middle and upper class? Whereupon Peil gave him a lesson in American sociology:

> There is nothing particularly offensive about this expression over here . . . In spite of this, the children of better families will come to this school; several have already made application. Here in North America there are no castes. Rich and poor interact peacefully. The one who is clever, who uses his intelligence and makes money is the one who is respected and makes up the "nobility," even though he comes from an ordinary, common, plebeian family. Here there are no earls or counts, princes or barons: everybody is simply "Mister," even if he reaches the highest rung on the social ladder.

At another point Peil wrote to the superior general to say that he did not allow whiskey (in German, *Schnapps*) or beer in the house and he had repeatedly forbidden his people to drink, either at home or on a trip. Two of the brothers, it seems, were overly fond of drinking. He wanted the founder to approve of this rule, because if the prohibition came from the founder, it would be much easier for Peil to enforce his rule. He must have been getting static from some members of the community regarding this rule. In fact, Peil said, Father Fischer recommended that the prohibition be extended to the whole Society. The founder responded by saying that this couldn't be done so easily. He'd have no objections regarding *Schnapps*, although he would need good reasons for this prohibition. But, he continues, "Do you mean you really would not want to allow your people over there to drink beer? And what would you give them as a substitute?" The whole issue may also have been an attempt on his part to imitate the founder in some small way. The superior general, who had himself enjoyed smoking, gave it up as a penance and banned smoking in his religious congregation as well. Beer, however, was something else; it was food as much as anything. The Germans never viewed the temperance movement as their cause. Rather, they considered alcohol and alcoholism an Irish problem. Banning beer could easily become symbolic of something more problematic, as the ban against smoking eventually became.

PUTTING UP BUILDINGS AND FINANCING THE FOUNDATION

In the meantime, an institution had to be built. Janssen did not expect anything much to happen before the fall of 1900, but Peil had already been hauling bricks by September 1899. By the fall of 1900 the first stage of the overall building complex was already well on its way to completion. Father Beckert, with good first-hand experience from having built many of the churches and houses of the SVD in Europe and one whom the founder obviously liked and trusted, had arrived with six skilled brothers on 27 February 1900. Apparently he was mightily impressed with America, with the style and size of the buildings, and with the location and possibilities of Shermerville as well. On 23 April 1900, excavation for the new building began. In a note on 14 June 1900, which he sent to Father Bodems, the founder says: "Father Peil writes from Shermerville that Father Beckert claims the property there is the best we have in the whole society, better even than yours at St. Wendel."

Once Beckert and Peil began working together, the general council had to play catch up, often being forced to give permission for projects and land purchases after the fact. On 11 June 1900, Janssen wrote to Blum:

> Father Peil and Father Beckert are building already and I haven't even given proper permission yet. I didn't receive anything, so I couldn't even make any suggestions. But they think they can defend their way of doing things. I complained about this but it was too late, so we just have to let them go.

Because Beckert was on the spot, there was less need for the founder to go over everything with him in detail. It seems he must also have given Father Beckert a fair bit of leeway in making decisions as to the size of the building and the kinds of materials purchased, so that everything went up rapidly. Already on 15 October 1900, Peil wrote to Father Eickenbrock, a member of the general council:

> Father Beckert has built us a wonderful house, the like of which exists nowhere else in the Society. It has three wings . . . The whole house has over three hundred windows, is four stories high and dominates the whole area. The roof is now being put on, and by December I think we'll be able to move in.

The question of financing the whole enterprise came up repeatedly, and on this score Peil was urged to caution more than once. He, in turn, quoted Father Janssen's own motto back to him: "Don't ask if the money is there, but whether the building is necessary." At this time he estimated the building would cost $15,000, while he also carried a debt of $75,000 for the land he had bought. His credit was still good, and a $100,000 debt did not bother him. It was the American way.

Nevertheless, materials had to be purchased, workers paid. At the height of the building process, that sum could amount to a thousand dollars per week! Some basic foodstuffs were already coming from the farm, to be sure, but some also had to be bought to feed the steadily growing community. Where did the money come from? One important source was the profit that was realized from the sale of almanacs and magazines. The cost of producing these materials and shipping them to America was borne by Steyl. This was carried on Society financial ledgers as debts that Shermerville owed Steyl. There were many letters written and attempts made by Peil to get these amounts reduced. Eventually these debts were paid off, but the superior general did not rush him, nor did Father Blum. On these magazine-selling trips and by direct appeals the new foundation also developed networks of benefactors who donated money to the cause of the SVD. The priests brought in money from their supply work in parishes, and some diocesan priests were beginning to make the SVD the beneficiary of their wills.

All the while, the new community talked up the cause of the Society's overseas missions and the work they were doing at Shermerville. As Brother Homobonus observed in his memoirs, this aid work got organized very early and was a great help during the struggles of the early months and years. Let Homobonus describe this activity as he recalled it some years later:

It was early in the Spring, 1899 when Father Peil and myself went to Shermerville to look over our first property here in the U.S. Reverend Peil did not stay long; he went back the following day . . . So far we did not have a single person in Shermerville who knew about us except Mr. Bellert [their next door neighbor]. Surely I had to get busy to make friends, but how?

The news that priests and brothers had bought the Russell farm spread like wild fire in the town and beyond. It did not take long when people came to see me . . . I had to tell them all about our Mission Work, and what we intended to do here. Of course I did my best to explain everything and asked them to help us, but above all to remain our friends . . .

A fallen away Catholic came to see me, and offered me a bicycle and to be sure, I made good use of it. Now I could go to Deerfield, Highland Park, etc., with very good results. In Deerfield I met an Irish family by name of Duffy, who were so glad to meet a Brother and treated me like one of their own. Of course they also made friends for our work with good success; later on they sent their two boys to our school. From Deerfield I went to the next town, Highland Park, where I met a fine German family. They also became one of our best friends and benefactors. I had the pleasure to meet more friends in Highland Park and Waukegan, and after a few weeks

I could say my, or rather, our friends were not just legions, but many. I enjoyed a bike ride through these towns where almost all the people said "Hello" to me, "come to see us." In Chicago I had a dear friend, who came from the same parish in Westfalia as I did, and of course he and his family did all for me what they could. We paid visits to others, mostly German people in St. Alphonsus parish. From that day on, we had every Sunday visitors from Chicago, and they surely did not come with empty hands, and I was glad to give my Superior a good number of GREENBACKS . . .

For the cornerstone laying—July 8, 1900—a group of men in Chicago busied themselves and brought out about 400 to 500 people on the train from Chicago . . . As a result of this gathering a number of men from various German parishes, consisting of Mr. Anton Braun of St. Theresa's Church, William Rauen of St. Michael's Church, Michael Girten of St. Martin's, Mr. M. Walsdorf from St. Alphonsus, also Paul Spitzer and the family Nahl. Mr. Kobialla, Mr. G. Prescher and Mr. Brabant from St. Aloysius formed a standing committee for the purpose of helping our work. They held regular and frequent meetings in downtown, and planned on a large outing of friends for Sunday, September 9th [1900] to celebrate the silver jubilee of the foundation of our Society.

Two thousand people showed up for this celebration, a number that astounded the founder when Peil wrote him about the event. Homobonus continues:

Someone in Chicago sent a reporter to our picnic, and the next day we could read all about what happened in Shermerville, and how much this immense crowd had enjoyed that picnic. It is understood that publishing our doings in the daily papers brought us friends galore.

Nevertheless, the founder and Father Blum were worried about the debt Peil was accumulating. As he was getting ready to begin building St. Anne's Home for the Elderly, the founder reminds him of his debt in a letter of 4 October 1902:

You already have a debt of $184,000, plus the $40,935 you owe Steyl for a total of $225,168. That is almost 1,000,000 Marks, not assets, mind you, but debts. You tell me that someday you will surely be a millionaire, though right now you are a "debtor-millionaire."

Peil, as superior and procurator, and therefore the one responsible for making sure that payrolls, bills, and interest payments were met, did not seem particularly worried. He wrote to the founder that his debt burden did not cause him to lose sleep. When Father Adolf Burgmer arrived in Shermerville in 1901, he characterized Peil and his spirit as courageous and full of daring, although,

those around him were not so hopeful, but all of us noticed a wonderful response of the Catholic people of Chicago, particularly the German-speaking part. There were a few who called the venture foolhardy, but many more made heroic effort to help. The fact is that Father Peil never failed to pay his interest, though at times he was near despair. Help always came when it was most needed.

By 4 November 1903, the founder himself can cautiously praise Peil for the improved financial condition of the new foundation.

The major reason—never to be underestimated—Father Peil was able to put up such a large building so quickly that the people of Chicago called it the new "world miracle of Chicago" was because the labor of the skilled brothers and priests was free. The brothers' contribution was especially essential to the early success of the SVD in America. And this is not even to mention the contribution they made in the way they called God's blessing upon the young enterprise by the sacrifices they so willingly made, the prayers they said, and the holy rule they followed so religiously. Without the work of the brothers, Shermerville would not have become Techny.

On 26 October 1900, Father Joseph Fischer left to live in Australia as treasurer for SVD missions in New Guinea that had been opened in 1896. His fluency in English got him this transfer, but he did not like this work and was recalled to teach at St. Gabriel's in Austria. This did not suit him either, and he requested permission to leave the Society to enter the diocesan priesthood in the United States. In 1903 he was accepted into the Diocese of Belleville, Illinois, where he worked for many years. The North American SVD owes Fischer a debt of gratitude, if only for convincing Arnold Janssen that everything about the Russell farm, including the by-laws of the charter and the nature of the swamp, were satisfactory.

During the week before Christmas 1900, the brothers moved into the new building. Gradually over the next weeks the transfer was completed. On 24 February 1901, Father Peil and Brothers Wendelin, Placidus, and Blasius took perpetual vows, while Homobonus renewed his vows for three more years. Father Beckert celebrated the Mass. Soon after, Beckert returned to Europe, his major work in America completed. The second wing, the completion of the front wing and the big church would wait till later. The final two wings of his original master plan, the whole of which would form a pentagon, would never be built.

THE SCHOOL BEGINS, THE PLEA FOR MORE BROTHERS

In the spring of 1901 activity at the industrial school began in earnest. On 20 April 1901, the first ten boys arrived from the German orphanage, the first of many. By 28 April, there were 25 boys in the industrial school.

Obviously, brothers were absolutely critical for the success of the technical school, indeed for its very existence. To be sure, everybody recognized this. Lest the founder or anyone else on the general council should forget, Peil kept reminding them how much they needed brothers in North America. Father Janssen tended to be much more generous in this regard than Blum, who was actually in charge of the brothers at Steyl; so Peil wrote both, demanding brothers, cajoling, even threatening that the whole enterprise would collapse if he didn't get more brothers. Peil, the founder, and Blum waged a constant battle over personnel. It was always carried on with a sense of urgency, sometimes acrimoniously, never calmly. Although the first priority was for brothers, the next was for priests and sisters able to teach.

In the context of seeking more brothers, Peil once told the founder not to believe Father Blum when he said he had no brothers to send to North America. The next time Peil wrote Blum to ask for more brothers, Blum snippily complained: "Why should I? You said I lie to the Founder anyway!" By the next letter Blum was his usual helpful self. Sometimes the exchanges were ironic. In one letter, for instance, the founder wrote:

> You've got to rein in your lust for new projects. And this is clear for two reasons: a) you are always complaining about the shortage of priests over there, then you turn right around and do everything you can to take over the Holy Hill project. b) You complain about the way the Sisters are overworked; at the same time you want to introduce them to perpetual adoration, which is totally against their rule. What's this all about? . . . You rush into too many things; for example, you expanded your press activity, added classes, took in very young students. Please, if possible, take your personnel situation into account, otherwise in time they'll all have nervous breakdowns. I don't really like to talk about this, but I feel it's my duty. You have a fiery spirit, but you've got to keep this in check.

After this exchange, Janssen sent him two priests and four more brothers. But it was not easy constantly to come up with more brothers. Even if someone could be identified at Steyl or at St. Gabriel's who was willing to go to the States, he usually had a position already. Then in a veritable game of musical chairs they had the problem of finding a substitute for the one they were sending.

Brothers were worth their weight in gold. Beginning with Wendelin, Homobonus, and Michael, many of those whom the founder himself sent were extremely capable and holy people. Some come readily to mind. Brother Fabian, for example, was a master carpenter, quiet, thorough, and dedicated. It is said that when the founder first went to St. Gabriel's in Austria, one of the crown jewel institutions of the new Society, to lay out the new buildings, he took Brother Fabian along. He has been called *the* builder of Techny. As was said in his obituary: "Every window, door, ceiling, floor and wall at St. Mary's Seminary in Techny felt the hammer, chisel and saw of the good Brother Fabian." In addition, he taught his trade to many a student in the technical school and to later brothers as well. His quiet manner was as much the quiet of prayer as anything else. But Fabian was only one of forty brothers assigned to America by the founder himself. Those who knew them could not forget them, such was the impression they made. Brother Galatius, for instance, was responsible, among other things, for the grillwork in Techny's church; Brother Amabilis was a longtime master typesetter at the press. One could go on naming them in a tour of today's Techny cemetery, where they and so many others finally found rest from their labors.

Father Markert, in his unpublished history of the early years of Techny's community, of which he himself was a member, mentions yet another:

Brother Placidus, in charge of the farm, deserves here special mention. Besides the extensive farm which had been greatly neglected when we took it over, and which Brother improved steadily, he had to do all the hauling of the building materials, take care of the drainage, build the new road, etc. Brother Placidus was a practical man, an indefatigable worker, and excellent religious. Not too much credit can be given him for the great work he did, especially in these first years when everything had to be built from scratch and the building activity made unheard of demands on him and his helpers and equipment. He was a real and typical pioneer, whose name should not be forgotten in the annals of the Society in the U.S. and in the memory of future generations.

Not all the brothers the founder sent to America stayed in the Society. Thirteen of those left over the years, all but two of them still in temporary vows. So desperate were the various missions for brothers that many were still in the initial period of testing, while most of the rest were in temporary vows when they were sent to America and went on to take perpetual vows as members of the Society of the Divine Word. Of the twenty priests the founder sent to America, five left the Society.

WHETHER TO ACCEPT AMERICANS AS BROTHERS

Father Peil repeatedly asked the founder if he could open up the SVD in America to those who wanted to become brothers. Even before they moved to Milton, he had two applicants for the brotherhood. On 15 October 1897, he wrote to the superior general:

Two young men would like to join us as Brothers. Both are German, but speak good English . . . Could I not request you to leave it to me to test them, resp. accept them. I believe you understand me well enough to know that I would not let any useless or harmful person slip into our Society. I would also like to ask you to send some vocational materials for Brothers.

To which the founder answered in a letter of 29 October 1897: "This is not yet the time to accept American applications. You must also first control your zeal as well as that of your confreres over there."

Two and a half years later, Janssen was willing to entertain the idea of accepting Americans into the Society's brotherhood. They would have an additional advantage: they would know English. Around this same time, some in Europe were actually calling for a three- to five-year pause or slowdown in growth, so the Society could catch up with itself and all its commitments. This was seriously discussed in the context of the brothers, so they would have time to train more of them. In April 1901, the founder wrote to say that he would not be disinclined to open a postulancy and novitiate for brothers in America. A month later he asked for some assurance that an adequate novitiate could be set up in Shermerville before he could give permission. Having received such assurance, he wrote on 31

July 1901, "You may begin receiving applicants into the postulancy program." This Peil does on 8 September 1901. Six months later, four postulants put on the cassock and began their novitiate.

One stringent condition put on the permission was that the candidates should all be German. It seems that Arnold Janssen himself was not the principal behind this decision, since he mentions three consultors, namely, Fathers Wegener, Holthausen, and Blum, who wanted this condition placed on the candidates. They singled out the Irish by name as unacceptable. One should direct candidates of other nationalities to other religious orders "in a friendly way and with plausible reasons," but then he goes on to say that if it seems advisable to accept, for example, Polish or Czech applicants, the superior general of the Society should first give permission.

The first candidates were men of German or Dutch birth who had migrated to America. The first American-born brother to enter and persevere would be known in religious life as Brother Andrew (his surname was Schwetner) from Elgin, Illinois. In 1903 the future Brother Andrew enrolled at St. Joseph's Technical School. He was fourteen years old. Two years later he was accepted as a brother candidate and on 24 January 1909, just two weeks before the official blessing of the minor seminary at Techny, he made his first profession of vows. All his life he did maintenance work, cheerfully and competently, in whatever house he was sent to. On 15 February 1969, he died suddenly of a heart attack while he was waiting to catch an airplane to visit his brother in San Francisco. He had celebrated his sixtieth jubilee of profession less than a month before. Brother Andrew was the first of a long line of holy and talented American brothers who devoted their lives of prayer and work to the mission cause in the Society of the Divine Word.

In the meantime, the founder also began sending sisters of the congregation he had founded to Shermerville, the first five arriving on 8 May 1901. Before his death he had assigned fifty-three nuns to North America. They were of tremendous help. Piles of laundry were waiting for their arrival. They also took over the kitchen. Soon, however, they also began to teach, took over the home for the elderly, and were persuaded to work in the southern missions in the African-American apostolate. Later they also went into hospital work and nurses' training. Although they had their own superior in the person of Sister Leonarda, Father Peil was their ultimate superior, because at this early stage Janssen himself was still the superior general of the Congregation of the Missionary Sisters Servants of the Holy Spirit. This soon changed, but the close working relationship between the two, eventually three, congregations continued.

RAISING THE QUESTION OF FOUNDING A MISSION HOUSE

While all this was going on, Peil was busy adding another wing to the building at the institute, all unbeknownst to the superior general. The founder had noticed in Peil's financial report that he had bought $10,000 worth of building materials. On 4 September 1904, before receiving a letter that Father Peil had written on 18 August, he wrote to Peil to ask about his plans. Peil described the building that was nearly complete:

The new addition to the institute—including a chapel, kitchen, dining room, tailor shop, dormitory, etc.—is almost finished. It is 200 feet long and 54 feet wide, 4 stories high with a basement. This building is Father Hoenderop's second piece of work [his first was St. Ann's, the home for the elderly]. This proves he has the makings of a master builder.

Janssen was dumbfounded. He fairly exclaims:

The blessing of the highest God is given to the obedient, to those who submit to their Superior. If you leave this path you start down the slippery slope to perdition . . . I'm telling you this to give you a chance to explain yourself: you wouldn't want to keep this from us, would you?

After seven weeks, Janssen still had not gotten an answer. So he wrote to Francis de Lange on 30 October 1904 to find out what had happened, whether Peil's council had been consulted in the matter, and how they were going to pay for the new wing. Peil answered on 5 December 1904: "As far as building goes, I took it for granted I had your formal permission because you had approved the whole building plan [as submitted earlier by Father Beckert], which included this wing."

Many other letters passed between Father Peil and the founder over this matter, until finally Janssen wrote again to Father de Lange to get his opinion of what was happening. On 25 April 1905, Father de Lange answered that the council had indeed held several meetings and that its members were unanimous in their recommendation to Peil to go ahead with the construction, because there was a definite need.

Although the superior general's council belatedly approved the building, its members also advised Janssen to be more decisive with Peil. The burgeoning debt load was worrying everyone. About this same time, Peil suggested further activities for the Society to take over. Still on his agenda was a school for wayward children, probably in Milwaukee. The archbishop of Chicago was after him to take over a mission for the African Americans in Merigold, Mississippi. And he had received a request to open a place to train American boys for the missionary priesthood. Peil, of course, had no difficulty conceiving work on all these apostolates. In fact, he had earlier challenged those who thought they were not doing mission work in America. He had written the founder on 15 May 1904 in the following words:

It's a pity that so many confreres in Steyl refuse to understand that our technical school and our home for the elderly are acceptable activities according to our rule. Those who say this are probably those who know how to speak so unctuously about the missions, but then build up a high wall of excuses when your Reverence wants to offer them a mission assignment.

Several years before all the events of 1904 and 1905, on 15 July 1900, Peil had presaged his ultimate intentions to build a mission house, or seminary, in a letter written to the founder:

We have definitely dropped the plan to erect a Mission House here. Father Beckert has informed me of your opinion in this matter. I agree with you. Should it later be necessary to erect such a house, undoubtedly the right place can be found elsewhere.

Father Beckert agreed with Peil that someday a seminary would have to be established, but thought it would have to be separated from the technical school. Peil, as a result, put the idea on hold, but did not forget about it. The first letter after this in which he came back to the idea of a seminary was the letter of 15 May 1904, preserved and translated by Father Markert. Because this is really the first letter in which Peil officially requests authorization to begin with a seminary, it is worth quoting at some length:

With this letter I am submitting to your Reverence our plan to train boys from here for the missionary priesthood in our Society. I kindly ask you to consent to it. It is a question of no mean importance. Your Reverence may perhaps remember that some time ago I asked for your permission to accept boys for this purpose. Your answer at that time was: "not for some time yet." Now, however, since the industrial school has been established, and everything here has taken more solid form and stability, it seems that the time has come to return to the original plan.

From the very beginning it was my intention to win from the boys who enter here, vocations for both the priesthood and brotherhood of our Society. I have discussed this frequently with Father Beckert, who agreed with me on the plan as such; only he advised against having both the technical school and Mission House in the same place. In the first building plan which I had submitted, I had provided one wing for the technical school and the other one for students. Your Reverence still has this plan there. The whole was to be arranged along the lines of the institute of Don Bosco. Of course at that time everything was rather uncertain since at that time we did not know whether we would be successful at all.

However, today when we can look back at three years work we can with thanks to God say that we are progressing. With God's help we hope to have, in the not all too far future, 1,000 pupils.

At present we have among our boys several who have repeatedly expressed their desire to become priests in our Society. They are good boys and have given no reason for complaint. No doubt there will be more of their kind who will apply as soon as we can let it be known that we intend to begin to accept boys for this purpose. It is certain that our plan will be hailed with approval by many, if not by priests, certainly by the laity. Likewise the necessary financial assistance will not be lacking.

It is also certain that the applications for our institution will increase in number as soon as we admit prospective candidates for the priesthood. This will be still more the case if the Holy Father is to express himself in our favor.

After having obtained the counsel of my priests here, it seems to me to be the simplest and safest way to proceed in such a way that we first make a small start here in this place. During the next winter the studies may be begun even if it should be only with eight or ten boys. They of course should be completely separated from the others.

We can keep these boys here two years. Meanwhile, we can look for another place. It seems that the diocese of Cleveland, Ohio, may be well suited for it. After two years we will have a sufficiently large number of students that we can begin to carry out a regular study program.

Of course, for all this we need your Reverence's permission and a competent teaching staff. This was always in my mind whenever I wrote for a larger number of teachers. Your Reverence must not overlook the fact that English will have to be the principal element in such a Mission House.

Up to now I have not spoken to our archbishop about such a Mission House, but I can do so when I have your answer. Or shall I not? In case your Reverence will approve our plan—and I can hardly think that you can oppose it—I ask you to give special attention to the next selection of new priests to be sent here. I beg again to be sure to send us only the very best teachers. We need them here more than in any other mission. I have expressed similar thoughts many times before. The best teachers are not too good for us.

I would love to offer this as a special Pentecost gift. May the divine Giver of grace enlighten you in this as in so many others, that we may undertake what God demands of us. I hope that the feast of St. John [Father Peil's patron feast] may bring us your answer, at least as to your preliminary decision in the matter.

The idea of further developing a grade school was not approved and it gradually was dissolved; the home for wayward boys was also rejected out-of-hand. Eventually the Holy Hill project, which had been bandied about for some time, was also abandoned. This left the proposal to set up a seminary. This was delayed for future discussion, while the African-American apostolate was taken up energetically. In the meantime, the founder himself was traveling, staying months at a time in St. Gabriel's; he had many other important things to discuss and decide in other parts of the world. Many different events came together to confuse the effort to open a seminary in America.

To understand the comedy of errors and misunderstandings that follow, it must be stated that Father Janssen had not said no to Peil's plans to start a mission seminary. He had, in fact, stated that nothing new should be started unless the means were available: "We have to move ahead [in North America], but only if the strength [personnel] and means are on hand. I want to stress this . . . He [Peil] is not allowed to start something for which he does not have the necessary resources." Knowing Janssen's mode of operation, Peil could only imagine that the founder would think about it for the future. Knowing Peil, we should suspect that the founder had sufficient grounds to imagine that Peil would be making sure he had the means to do what he proposed. Peil began to teach Latin to five students during the school year of 1904–1905, as he had proposed to do, so no further resources would be required. Janssen had neither forbidden him to do so nor said he should. For Peil it seemed that if he began with a small Latin school, things would be ready to go when the founder revisited the idea "in the future." For the founder, though, opening a small Latin school was the equivalent of starting a preparatory seminary.

On 24 April 1905, Peil wrote to update Janssen on his little "Latin school." When he received that letter, the founder was furious. He said that he wanted the Latin classes stopped, and would not send anyone else to America until this was done. He ordered Peil to dismiss the students, concluding, "I want you to send me a cable as soon as you receive this, telling me that you have complied." Peil responded, in effect, that their disagreements were the result of misunderstandings. In his own words:

> Your letter left me undisturbed. I reflected on how the Savior suffered when he was falsely accused, and why should I also not suffer something similar? May your Reverence permit me to say that I think I have handled the Latin school question correctly and I see no evidence of disobedience here whatsoever. P. de Lange feels the same way, and good Father [Herman] Richarz, that *anima candida*, was speechless with surprise when he read your letter. [The reasons for my decision were:]
> 1. The letter your Reverence sent me on Aug. 1, 1904, was not clear to me. It does not say that we cannot have Latin students. I could read the letter both ways. Had your Reverence simply said you cannot teach Latin to students, then I surely would not have done so.
> 2. The decision of the General Council did not reach me until December, and it was not stated there that I should stop the classes that were already started.
> 3. Rev. P. Wegener and P. Gier expressed themselves positively about the education of missionaries.

This did not pacify Janssen, whose next letter was another lecture on obedience and the dangers of listening to "the evil angel." In his letter to the founder, Richarz explained that they had received his telegram and had given up classes right away, but could only dismiss the students gradually. This they had done, he said. Peil had been on an inspection tour to the South, and on 28 July 1905 he made a report on this trip. He was sorry he had been so sharp in his statements; he just wanted to show his side of things, but not to cause pain. "It would also," he added, "really bother me if such ill-will came of this issue that it would frustrate further work among the Negroes." Thereafter Father Janssen sent the priests, brothers, and sisters that he had promised to send to North America and then threatened to keep in Europe. The matter seemed over and done with. But it was not really, since it took three more years before Father Janssen finally decided to open a mission house in Shermerville. Janssen had decided to reach his hand out to Peil in reconciliation, but he also continues to lecture him on his faults and failings, especially insisting, "You cannot presume my permission just because I don't respond right away or because I delay or put off my decision. You must wait for it."

THE NAME CHANGE FROM SHERMERVILLE TO TECHNY

Before 1906, Shermerville, the small village where the SVDs rented their first home and lived for a while, was the postal address where St. Joseph's Home received its mail. On 27 January 1906, the place officially received the name by which the Society's first foundation has been known ever since, "Techny." This was the day a post office was designated with Techny as its place name. The first piece of mail sent out from Techny was a postcard sent to the founder on 1 March 1906, signed by "Brother Alphonsus, Post Master" and "Homobonus, Assistant Post Master."

How Techny got its name is not completely clear. What seems likely is that the name "St. Joseph's Home" was changed to St. Joseph's Technical School because it was learned that the term "Home" had undesirable connotations in English and would often be understood as referring to a "reform school." Thus someone graduating with a certificate from St. Joseph's Home might not so easily find a job. In addition, there were already too many railroad stations in the Midwest named after St. Joseph by Catholic immigrants. Tradition has it that Father Peil and his councilors put on their collective thinking caps and came up with Techny. The results were not surprising for Germans, who put great stress on locality. The SVDs in Europe had become known and still are known today as the *Steyler Missionare*. In the U. S. a similar thing happened and went on, in fact, until they made a major public relations effort to call themselves "Divine Word Missionaries." Before that, the SVDs in North America were known as the "Techny Fathers and Brothers."

Another version has it that the train conductor found it burdensome to call out "St. Joseph's Technical School" each time his train approached the location, where it had become possible to request a stop even before the official station was opened. He is said to have shortened it to "Techny" on his own, since "St. Joseph's Technical School" was too much of a mouthful. When the stop became an official station, Techny was the name given it, and by extension to the institution as well. This story, however, is probably mythical, since the *Amerikanisches Missionsblatt* ("The American Mission News") stated that in August 1903, St. Joseph's Home got its first telephone connection and said that the telephone central was called "Techny."

THE FOUNDER'S FEARS ABOUT THE AMERICAN FOUNDATION

The period from September 1904, when Peil sprang the word of his new addition on the founder, to the letter of 6 November 1905, was an unsettled period in the early history of the SVD in North America. Janssen knew Peil well from their correspondence. He knew his independent way of doing things, but he also realized that Peil was a good religious who kept the rule, prayed much, and was keenly interested in the salvation of souls. Why, then, did he panic and come down so hard on Peil this time? And why did he continue to wait until 1908 before giving permission to open a seminary in North America?

Probably the major fear the founder had during all the early years the SVDs were in America, and especially during this last crucial time, was the danger he perceived that they would split away from the SVD in Europe to become a separate religious congregation. On 8 April 1905, before he even had clear news that Peil was already teaching Latin to selected students at St. Joseph's, he wrote the following to the general council:

> The conditions in North America have occupied my mind very much recently, and this all the more since I heard that one of the priests, whose opinion I have to respect, said quite openly that our confreres will almost certainly separate themselves from us and look to become independent, which would not be so difficult if the Archbishop of Chicago were of the same mind and were to request permission for this from Rome. I still have enough confidence in our confreres over there that I do not think this will happen, yet real dangers exist, as much as we hope that the good will of those over there will forestall such an event.

The possibility of sending a person known in Catholic religious order terminology as a "visitator" to America was discussed. Father Peil himself had requested that someone from Steyl be sent because he felt the generalate was not well informed about the situation in Shermerville. But the decision was delayed, since the consultor they had in mind to make the visitation, Father John Holthausen, was not well. In fact, he would die in 1906.

The superior general could have had in mind the example of groups such as the Mill Hill Fathers, whose American branch had split from the original Mill Hill Congregation in 1893 to become St. Joseph's Society of the Sacred Heart, or "the Josephites," to do mission work among the African Americans of North America. Another example that was well known in Germany was that of Isaac Hecker, an American-born Redemptorist who left that community in 1858 with four of his confreres to found the Missionary Society of St. Paul the Apostle, popularly called "the Paulists," to work for the conversion of American Protestants. Hecker's was actually the first American foundation of a new religious body for men. He was accused of wishing to "democratize" and "Americanize" the church. And it should not be forgotten that papal condemnations of "Modernism" and "Americanism" were matters of great interest at the turn of the century. Janssen did not want such things happening in his congregation.[2]

This entire movement, as viewed in Germany, may also have been important in leading the founder to caution about establishing a seminary. There is no record that this is the case but it was what German commentators and newspapers of the time were discussing. This helps explain, too, why Janssen hesitated to admit anyone into the SVD except Germans and Dutchmen. But here the founder was caught on the horns of a dilemma. He had apparently gone beyond the point of wanting the Society to be solely German, yet if he were to allow it too swiftly to be implanted in Irish-dominated American Catholicism, he ran the risk of getting

---

2. Pope Leo XIII had condemned "Americanism" in his apostolic letter *Testem benevolentiae* (1899). In that document he found it an error to teach that the church ought to adapt to the times by relaxing its rigor or showing indulgence to modern theories and methods that would result in changes to the "deposit of faith."

sucked into the Americanist controversy and of having the young SVD branch in America break off from the tap root to plant itself anew in American soil.

This was the kind of many-sided predicament that made Janssen put off all decisions. Instead, he sought more information, went slow, and prayed for light to see God's will. As it turned out, the fears that the founder and Pope Leo XIII had of Americanism appear to have been largely misplaced. They did not know the overall context of American Catholicism nor in sufficient detail what was actually happening here. In that regard, Janssen seems not to have known how thoroughly and rapidly the immigrants from Germany were losing their "German-ness" and becoming American. The process of assimilation was practically finished by the First World War. This can be shown graphically by how few German-Americans refused to fight against their former countrymen and how few defected to the German lines once they got to the trenches of France.

THE AMERICAN CATHOLIC CHURCH AND
THE SOCIETY OF THE DIVINE WORD

The American Catholic Church in which the Society of the Divine Word found itself was an immigrant church in its thinking and in its sense of self. Most of its members had come to America as peasants or artisans and were members of the lower classes, generally not well educated, reliant largely on their pastors and bishops for direction and decisions. On the part of ordinary Catholics there was little serious questioning of the authority of the local hierarchy or that of the papal curia and the pope. No great outcry or theological questioning of the basic premises of the pope's condemnation of Americanism was ever raised. At most, educated American Catholics seemed to feel that what the pope condemned was not what was happening in the first place and that Pope Leo XIII was beating a straw man he himself had set up. As Angelyn Dries has shown, while it was to a great extent preoccupied with its internal growth and problems, it was also beginning to look outward and enter into overseas missionary apostolates.[3]

On one thing American Catholics, from the hierarchy on down, would not budge. Here in America they were free of governmental interference, and, given their experience in the homeland, they were not about to give this up, no matter what their European cousins might think of the country as a consequence. The American church, during its long immigrant phase, was also very practical. Churches had to be built, schools had to be constructed and staffed, orphanages and hospitals established, all of which had to be paid for and administered. Seminaries and convents also had to be founded to train staff to look after all these institutions. As a result, there was not much time or inclination to spend resources on extended theological battles related to dogma or liturgy, or to challenge secular sciences like history or philosophy and the relations between these and Catholicism. These issues were vexing European scholars and ended in the condemnation of Modernism by Pius X, an event that did not affect the American church very much.

---

3. See Angelyn Dries, *The Missionary Movement in American Catholic History* (Maryknoll, N.Y.: Orbis Books, 1998), pp. 43–84.

Catholics, in this context, "continued to associate with their non-Catholic neighbors in all the things that were not essentially religious—in labor unions, in chambers of commerce, in business firms, and in sports."[4] In the ordinary activities of society, it was difficult to tell who was a Catholic Christian, or a Baptist Christian, or a Methodist Christian, who was Jewish, or who was an atheist. Something perhaps too little appreciated in Europe, but now very evident, is the genius of both Catholic and Protestant leaders in these circumstances. While industrialization was setting in motion forces that would lead to the secularization of Europe, American religious leaders were finding ways to evangelize people in teeming cities, in wild mining camps, on the Great Plains, and on the furthest frontiers. They managed to enlist the allegiance of this fast-moving people to religious institutions that have proved capable of adapting themselves for over a century now. Protestant evangelists, moreover, were succeeding in evangelizing communities that were totally alienated from Christianity, and in the process creating distinctively American ways of being Christian and missionary.[5]

This is the world in which the seminary at Techny was born and grew. It is hard to know how much the handful of German priests and brothers understood what was happening in the wider context of American religious history in 1906 or its global missionary significance, but they did know they were in a land bursting with growth, one in which the Catholic Church was vital and one in which they felt sure the Society of the Divine Word could thrive. We shall turn to the saga of founding the seminary in the next chapter. In the rest of this one, I would like to draw the story of Father Peil to a close and reflect on the personality and legacy of Arnold Janssen, which is so important for understanding the Divine Word Missionaries of North America.

FATHER PEIL AND THE FOUNDER

To return to our time-line, obscured perhaps by the necessary detour into wider developments in American Catholicism and Protestantism, we are late in the year 1906. Peil asks to be relieved from his office as superior, not because he did not feel up to the work or to carrying all the debts any more, but because in the newly approved constitutions the normal term of a rector was for three years, renewable for a further three years. He had served almost for ten years and he recommended that Father Francis de Lange be his successor. The founder refused his request "for the time being," because he was finally getting ready to send a visitator to America. This finally occurred in December 1906 in the person of Father John Baptist Bodems, who was a member of the general council. Peil again requested release from his office, and Bodems supported the request. On 15 January 1907, the superior general sent a telegram confirming Father de Lange as the new superior. In a letter Janssen sent the next day, he thanked Peil for his stewardship, stating that, despite many difficulties, "everyone who comes after you must recognize your

4. Thomas T. McAvoy, *The Great Crisis in American Catholic History 1895–1900* (Chicago: Henry Regnery Company, 1957), p. 365.

5. See Andrew F. Walls, *The Missionary Movement in Christian History* (Maryknoll, N.Y.: Orbis Books, 1996), chapter 17, "The American Dimension of the Missionary Movement," esp. pp. 227–40.

great service and be grateful to you . . . I too, my beloved and respected confrere, thank you from the bottom of my heart for this. I am also convinced that you have earned great merit before God the Lord for all your great work."

It was now a question of finding another position for Peil, who wanted to remain in the United States to work in the African-American apostolate if possible. As we shall show in a coming chapter, Peil had worked hard almost from the day of his arrival in America to get this apostolate started and to this extent deserves the title of opening that important apostolate for the SVDs in America. His own preference was to work in this full time. It was not to be.

The indefatigable Peil was also willing to be treasurer, take over as director of the Sisters or St. Ann's Home, take charge of the gardens and the farm, help out on supply, or act as proofreader in the press. He had contacted Father Kaul in Harrisburg about possibilities there and was in touch with a bishop in Puerto Rico about the SVD going there, possibly intending to be sent there.

Janssen, in the meantime, moved cautiously. Brothers had complained about the roughshod way he sometimes dealt with them for one thing. The founder did not want Peil in a position where he would have to interact as superior with others again. Peil, he judged, was a good priest and abided by the rule. He was a faithful religious. But he had rough edges. The superior general finally left him in the treasurer's position, but only "provisionally."

Janssen and Peil were similar in many ways. Both worked hard; both were of strong will and tenacious once they had an idea or latched on to a project. Both were very mission-minded. Sometimes they disagreed on what "mission" meant, for example, in the case of the technical school itself. Still, both had a common feeling that the missions deserved the best, even if it pinched the home base. In retrospect, what mission meant for the SVD was clearer in the founder's mind than in Peil's. Janssen stated several times that America was no longer a mission country and should not be compared with other mission countries where his Society worked. One exception, in the founder's mind, was the African-American apostolate, which he considered real mission and which he supported early and vigorously. At times, as we shall see, he and Peil were almost alone in this support.

Each had great respect for the other, yet were able to disagree vociferously with each other, sometimes with an edge of sarcasm. Several times the founder lectured Peil on St. Vincent de Paul's method of getting at God's will by waiting for something to be offered to him rather than take the initiative all the time. To this Peil responded with a touch of irony:

> From my reading of St. Vincent's life, I didn't get the idea that he always waited to be invited and pressured before he started a new foundation . . . In any case, your Reverence certainly did not wait for an invitation to open St. Gabriel's. In fact, you needed six years to overcome the opposition [to this foundation].

Not many persons of great authority brook opposition from those under them as well as Janssen did. Part of the secret of his ability to manage a creative, energetic man like Peil lay, first, in his sense that the work of mission was important and the gifts of all members of the Society must be used wisely. Second, though, Janssen was a man without guile. Even when Peil must have been frustrated at the founder's cautiousness, he sensed that guilelessness and was aware of Janssen's sincerity. A biographer of Janssen, Hermann Fischer, noted that quality dramatically in the following extraordinary testimony:

> I have carefully read some 2000 letters and other pieces which our holy father [Arnold Janssen] wrote . . . I declare before God that I never found any insincerity or intrigue, any holding back or crafty evasion. No matter what the difficulty or however embarrassing the situation, he never allowed himself to deviate one iota from the truth.

As for Peil, there has already been enough said to get a good idea of his personality. There is, however, one item left to mention. It is best stated by the founder himself in referring to Peil in a letter of 21 December 1907. Father Peil had learned of the founder's serious case of diabetes:

> Then you [Peil] wrote [to me]: "May the All-highest deign to add as many years to your precious life as He intended for me. Let him take my life in exchange for yours. I would consider this a great grace, which I will continue to pray for as I have so often done already. Precisely this, dear Father, would I like to give you as a gift on your 70th birthday, together with the promise to cheer your old days as much as I can."
>   That was the best gift I got last November 5 [Janssen's 70th birthday], and I thank you from the bottom of my heart. I pray the Lord to look at the intention behind this offering, and in spite of it give you a truly long life yet to do much good.

The gist of the relationship is best summed up in the special letter the founder wrote to Father Peil on 20 November 1908. Not long before, he had approved the opening of the mission house at Techny. Janssen knew he was dying, but he wanted to write this special letter to Peil himself, the second last letter he wrote to North America. I translate the founder's last letter to Peil in its entirely:

> Steyl. 20 Nov. 1908
>
> Dear Father Peil,
> During the days of my illness I feel compelled to write you this personal letter. It's probably the last time that I will speak to you, because my condition has gotten considerably worse during the past several weeks. I don't believe I have too long to live. My hands and arms have been paralyzed and since November 1, I have not been able to celebrate Mass any more. As you can well imagine, this is a great sacrifice for me, but may the will of God be praised in all things.
>   On the 2nd of November, Father Assistant General anointed me with the last rites, after which I gave my fatherly and priestly blessing to the entire Society and to everyone of its members.

I approach death with confidence. The Lord is my hope and my consolation. When I finish my earthly pilgrimage, I trust that God will not deny me entrance into my heavenly homeland. There we hope to see each other again in great joy and happiness.

I do not want to die, however, without saying this special goodbye to everybody there, but especially you, my beloved Father Peil, whom I treasure so highly. I thank you for all the sincere service you have given me and the Society, over so many years, with such constancy and love. Already in Europe you served the Society well, but have done so all the more in America, where you introduced the Society and were Superior for many years. I have never forgotten this and through my prayer have always tried to show you my gratitude. Now here I clearly want to tell you this again.

Please pray for me. When I stand before the Throne of God, I will not forget you either.

Finally I bestow upon you once more my priestly and fatherly blessing.

May God the Lord repay you richly for everything you have done for me and for the Society.

> With most cordial greetings in the Love of the Holy Spirit.
> Your spiritual father in the Lord.
> signed: Arn. Janssen

A beautiful letter; no recriminations, no last directives; just an expression of deep love and gratitude, the kind of letter anyone would be happy and proud to receive from a saint.

Blessed Arnold Janssen (1837-1909) at the age of 53, five years before he sent the first Divine Word Missionaries to North America.

Father John Baptist Peil (1856-1936), first superior and founder of the Society of the Divine Word in North America.

The pioneers and first members of the Techny community in 1900, from left to right: Father John Baptist Peil, Techny's architect Father John Baptist Beckert (1864-1927), Brother Wendelin (Joseph Meyer, 1857-1927), Brother Michael (Emil Fecken 1860-1925), and Brother Homobonus (Joseph Stiller, 1866-1951).

Machine shop students of St. Joseph's Technical School, Techny, in 1909.

Father Peter Janser (1878-1959) with what is believed to be the first class of high school seminarians at Techny in a picture dated 1909.

Members of the charter convention of the Catholic Students' Mission Crusade held at Techny, 18-20 June 1918. Father Clifford King (1888-1969), CSMC founder, is third from left in second row.

Father Hugo Aubry
(1872-1968).

Father Herman Richarz
(1867-1928).

Father Bruno Hagspiel
(1885-1961).

Father Francis Markert
(1884-1961).

Brother Fabian
(Daniel Quiter,
1877-1961).

From a photo dated 1 May 1921, three of Techny's first ordination class of five, from left to right: Joseph Murphy (1895-1935), Peter Weyland (1895-1969), and Florian Haas (1895-??), who left to become a diocesan priest. Two members of the class, Clifford King and Robert Clark, were ordained in China.

The first three American seminarians sent to Rome for theological studies, from left to right: Emil Lesage (1899-1979), Adolph Noser (1900-1981), Cletus Hodapp (1899-1967).

Fathers Ralph Thyken (1899-1975) and Lester Dooley (1898-1966).

Father Felix Glorius
(1890-1966).

Father Gerard Esser
(1882-1971).

Brother Andrew (August Schwetner, 1889-1969), the first American-born brother to join the Society, was also a student at St. Joseph's Technical School.

Fathers Joseph Finger, left (1901-1989) and Charles Michel (1882-1968).

Three of the four Lesage brothers reunite in Techny in 1971, from left to right: Fathers Maurice from Ghana (1911-1977), Alphonse from the Philippines (1904-1977), and Emil from Techny (1899-1979). Brother Cletus (Joseph Lesage, 1908-1990) was not present for the reunion.

The Techny seminary and Northern Province headquarters in the early 1950s with shops to the left and sport fields to the rear and right.

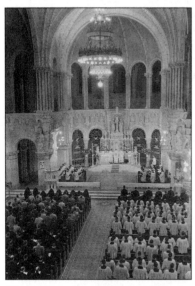

The Techny chapel, filled with brothers, priests, and seminarians during a solemn high Mass in the 1950s.

Bishop William O'Brien, auxiliary bishop of Chicago, assisted by Father Hagspiel, ordains Father Maurice Lesage, in 1938.

3

Opening the Techny Mission Seminary

The Early Years, 1906–1932

MOVING TOWARD APPROVAL, 1906–1908

Even after all that had occurred, Father Janssen was not ready to give final approval to starting a preparatory seminary to accept candidates for the Society in the United States. Still, events and the opinions of men he trusted were moving him inexorably in that direction. We have seen how he sought the advice of priests other than Father Peil, and at each juncture their opinions validated Peil's or moved on parallel tracks. Even those like Father Peter Janser, whom the founder had sent to America with the admonition to keep a close eye on the situation there (meaning, watch Father Peil), were writing to recommend founding a seminary to train young men for the missionary priesthood. No such institution existed to date in the Catholic Church in America. In addition, the issue of founding other technical schools had also been thoroughly discussed, and there was little interest in moving further in that direction.

The founder, as if trying to persuade himself to open up a mission seminary, writes to Father Bodems, the visitator to North America, on 3 June 1907:

> 4. You advise that we begin with an American mission house and that we first use a house about 1300–1400 meters away for this purpose. Isn't this the house close to the [train] station? How many students can it accommodate?
>
> 5. As I remember, St. Joseph's Home is quite large and has several stories. From the beginning already there was always in mind the possibility of opening a mission house and actually in St. Joseph's Home, but naturally with separation between the seminarians and the rest.
>
> 6. If one is to really make something out of a mission house, then it will take a lot of money. I shudder to think of that, because it is so expensive to build in America. Still, every institution used for education needs many rooms, and a private house is rarely useful.
>
> 7. You advise getting in contact with leading people over there, but tell me at the same time that they are Irish, and the Irish will probably never be

satisfied with a German mission house. That being the situation, we would run the danger that they would tell us: No, we Irish will do that ourselves [i.e., set up our own mission house]. So if we announce that we are opening a mission house, the only success it will have is to hurry the Irish into setting up their own mission house. We would come in second then and perhaps would face greater difficulties.

Why was the founder, almost to the end, so concerned about the Irish when he had said repeatedly that he repudiated excessive nationalism? He had also said he would restrict other nationalities only "at first." It really had little to do with the Irish as such, other than the fear of being drawn into the Americanist controversy in the Union, but it had much to do with the unity he expected to reign in his Society. Putting students of Irish and German descent together would be a source of discord, he thought, and would lead to a lack of unity and harmony. Unity and harmony were the marks of a good religious spirit, to the founder, which was one reason he was so concerned that everything be done in the same way it was done in Steyl. If a house had a good religious spirit, it meant that God's will was being carried out there, which also meant that God's blessing rested on the enterprise. A superior, moreover, was obligated to remove anyone who disturbed this spirit of unity, or better still, made sure such an element did not enter in the first place. Why was he willing, then, to let Silesian Poles, Hungarians, Czechs, and Slovaks into his Society almost from the very beginning? Because most such students would know German and would have been educated in German-speaking mission houses. They would have grown up under Prussian political control or would have belonged to the Austro-Hungarian Empire. Thus they would not be a source of discord. Positively, they would be useful in various missions, since they would know several languages. Peil himself had made this point in regard to North America where immigrants speaking the mother tongues of these central European countries had moved. He was not aware, as were those he had sent to America, that unity in the Society would eventually come about on a different level than Germanic monoculturalism. His people in America may not have seen that far ahead, but, as de Lange had predicted, in one generation, it would be difficult to tell the difference between a German and an Irishman. And he was right. This distinction would be a source of discord only if somebody, a priest or a superior, fostered it. With all these responses from America, Janssen finally left the issue alone.

Bodems had written that the idea of a mission house had been repeatedly discussed. Catholics in America, he noted, were getting more and more enthused about the missions and the conversion of the "heathen" (German, *Heiden*). In 1905, for instance, the Catholic Church Extension Society, which was diocesan directed, was founded precisely to foster mission thinking among Catholics in America. This was sufficient reason for establishing a mission house. Father Janssen was nevertheless concerned about staffing such an institution: "Perhaps we are close to this point [of being able to staff a seminary], since the group that was sent there last year was a strong group for this purpose." On 26 February 1908, he tells Father de Lange to begin preparations to start a seminary. On 11 May, getting into reasons why the seminary will be useful, as well as adding practical matters in starting the seminary, de Lange observes:

> An American mission house would be useful because Japan and the Philippines need English-speaking missionaries. We have a house about a quarter of an hour away from the institution, right along the railroad tracks. I doubt that we'll have more than five or six students in the first year. In the beginning one priest would be able to take care of this. One brother, in one or two hours work a day, could keep the place clean while their food would be cooked in St. Joseph's Home and transported there.

In another letter, de Lange requested that Bodems make sure no restrictions were placed on whom they could admit. Better otherwise to drop the whole idea. The idea of opening a mission house in North America was now, it seems, rapidly maturing in the founder's mind. In answer to Father de Lange's letter, he writes (25 June 1908):

> In your letter after Easter you expressed the desire to start a Mission House in the building near the railroad station. You've written about this before. I'm not completely against the idea but I can't answer positively. I do not have the files here to check what I've already written about it. Just some questions at this point: will there be enough interest for pupils and benefactors? You have to think about starting with one class and adding one every year. You need more teachers. Since classes will be in English, you have to start with the teachers you already have there. Who are they? You want to start at Techny and go elsewhere in 2–4 years. What will the cost be? How can this be done with the large debt you already have? Now everything is in the hands of Germans. What will happen when you have Americans, too? Will this yearning for "elbow-room" create problems? Americans will need special mission territories. All these things have to be considered carefully.

Everybody by this time was in favor of starting a mission house/seminary in America, including all the priests and brothers and Father Bodems, who had completed his visitation on 5 July 1907, and was now back in Steyl to add his advice that the Society should go ahead with a seminary in America. Finally, on 28 October 1908, the founder wrote to Father de Lange, the regional superior:

> We spoke of your request in the general council meeting the day before yesterday, and we are not against your making the first trial and opening a mission house. May God the Holy Spirit bless this effort, and in this way, if it pleases him, to show us that this foundation is according to his holy will.

Father Janssen would have liked more information. Other locations—Iowa and Cleveland—had been in the running as the place to begin, but de Lange and Bodems both thought Techny would be best, and later if the seminary was successful, who knows?

Two days after giving his approval to open a mission house in North America, the founder had his first stroke. He lingered, more or less paralyzed, with improvements and setbacks, until his death on Friday, 15 January 1909.

PROFILES OF THE PIONEERS

Before proceeding to the story of the growth of Techny and expansion of the Society in America, I would like to return to the five pioneers who were responsible for putting down SVD roots in America, to whom the Society of the Divine Word in North America owes so much.

Brother Wendelin Meyer. As the first Divine Word Missionary to come to the United States, Brother Wendelin shared in all the excitement and joy, as well as the anxiety and frustrations and even physical hardships, that go with starting anything new in a large and strange country. He continued with his work, which was to travel around the country selling magazines, arousing mission interest and making friends for the Society wherever he went. He succeeded admirably at this. In addition to being a good salesman, he was also quite artistic. He played the organ and violin, wrote poetry, mostly humorous, and designed various mosaics out of stone which dotted the large park at Techny for years. He sang well, and, together with Brother Joachim, also an excellent singer and musician, cut a record which they sold for the sake of the missions. During the last two years of his life, he was ill with tuberculosis, an illness that was not uncommon then. He went to Roswell, New Mexico, where Franciscan nuns ran a sanatorium. By the time he arrived there after an exhausting journey, he was totally drained. His illness had progressed further than anybody realized. Two days after arriving in New Mexico, he died and there was nothing to do but send the traveling brother back on his last journey. Those who were with him when he died on 21 January 1927 were edified. It was five months before his seventieth birthday.

This is not quite the end for Brother Wendelin. In May 1994, the townspeople of Duppach near Gerolstein honored Brother Wendelin by putting a commemorative plaque in their community hall as a way of remembering the first SVD to go to America. It also recalls all those other Duppacher Americans who had migrated to America from the same village, who were so helpful to Brother Wendelin in his first months in America.

Brother Homobonus Stiller. The second brother to come to America, Brother Homobonus saw the Society develop into a large institution. Like Brother Wendelin, he also traveled to sell subscriptions. Later he became office manager, and, for a time, supervised the shipping room of the Mission Press at Techny. He was transferred to the Sacred Heart Mission House in Girard, Pennsylvania, in 1924, where he spent the rest of his life. His sense of humor and cheerfulness not only helped him through many difficulties in the beginning, they also helped him win many friends for the mission cause. He was active almost to the last day of his rich and fruitful life. He died at the age of eighty-five on 27 March 1951.

Brother Michael Fecken. The oldest of the three brothers and second in age only to Father Peil, Brother Michael worked in a textile mill and a creamery before he came to the U.S. as one of the pioneers. He was cook and sacristan, but also worked in the apostolate of the press, soliciting subscriptions. Like Wendelin, he, too, contracted tuberculosis and was ill for about two years before he died on 12 September 1925, at the age of sixty-five. As he had always wished, he was able to celebrate the Golden Jubilee of the Society's founding and the Silver Jubilee of its North American branch.

Father Joseph Fischer. Of the first two priest-pioneers, Father Fischer left America on 26 October 1900, for a new assignment in Australia, where he served as treasurer for the SVD missions in New Guinea, which had been opened in 1896. His fluency in English led to this transfer, but he did not like the work at all. He requested permission to leave the Society to enter the diocesan priesthood in the United States. In 1903 he was accepted into the Diocese of Belleville, Illinois, where he worked until 1932. His relatively short time in the SVD in America, a scant three years, was spent mostly in supply work, helping out in different parishes, giving sermons, meeting many diocesan priests and winning them over to the SVD cause. In this way also he spread the mission message and brought home money, donations, and Mass stipends to help support the early SVD in America. It must have been a satisfying and rewarding experience, for he wanted to go back to it full time. In 1932 he returned to Germany for two years, which he kept extending until he was caught by the war. He remained in Germany until his death there on 8 January 1958. The Society owes him a debt of gratitude, if only for the work he did to convince Arnold Janssen that everything about the purchase of the Russell farm and the by-laws was in good order. He prevailed even in convincing Janssen about the harmlessness of the swamp.

Father John Peil. This brings us to the last years of Father Peil, who did so much in his capacity as superior and founder in North America during the crucial first ten years of its existence here. We left him as treasurer at Techny, a position, according to Father de Lange, his successor, with which he was having some difficulty. At the age of fifty-three, it seemed he was having problems adjusting to the accounting system that the visitator, Father Bodems, had introduced. The other departments did not. Accounts, as a result, couldn't always be reconciled. Peil, thinking he was right in his system and the others wrong, simply ignored their way of doing things. As we have seen before, Peil was a pious, hard-working, honest man—as de Lange would be the first to admit—but, as de Lange also added, "he followed his own way." Apparently he was not happy; so on 3 May 1909, he was transferred back to Austria to take up his old post as treasurer in the huge St. Gabriel's Mission House, where the treasurer had recently died.

Even as treasurer he had occasion to make comparisons to affairs in America. When he arrived at St. Gabriel's, he noted at once that the house had a tremendous debt: "At Techny we carried a substantial debt," he wrote, "but it was child's play compared with that of St. Gabriel's." Peil apparently was correct in not worrying about running up debts in America. The superior in Austria had requested Peil to be treasurer with the observation, "I believe Father Peil would be the man who could best solve our financial situation," and he was right. By 1911, Peil could at least say that the financial situation was good. They had enough wheat, potatoes, and apples on hand for the whole year, as well as a good supply of coal. Also the publication business was satisfactory. Peil, always full of ideas, suggested to Father Blum on 8 July 1909, "Perhaps it would be better and bring in more subscriptions to the *Stadt Gottes* if Austria had its own editor, who could give it an Austrian flavor. We could raise our subscriptions, perhaps to 50,000, as a result of this." This was done, and subscriptions did go up.

In 1924 Peil, who was sixty-eight and was apparently suffering from Alzheimer's, was transferred to Steyl, where he wandered through the shops every day, smiling and quietly laughing to himself. Although his was a "belated vocation"—he was twenty-four when he entered Steyl—he outlived many of his classmates, one of whom was Father John Beckert, who laid out Techny's buildings. His father had wanted Peil to take over his grain milling business, but after his tour of military duty, during which he taught himself Latin, he had entered Steyl. When he spoke with anyone, he tried to use their name and to be a good conversationalist. He was not sentimental and again in this he is compared with the founder: "None of us ever saw the founder raise a handkerchief to moist eyes; the same was true of Peil as well." In later life Peil once stated in a conversation that he had never experienced a sense of what others called "spiritual sweetness." His was an unemotional faith. He died on 8 February 1936, almost eighty years of age.

Father Francis de Lange. The man who succeeded Father Peil in 1907 as superior of the growing SVD community in North America was a Dutchman by the name of Francis de Lange. Born on 16 January 1871, in a village near Haarlem in the Netherlands, Father de Lange came to Shermerville with Father John Hoenderop in the early days of 1900, as the first priests to be sent after Peil and Fischer. De Lange, who later became spiritual director of the brothers and did much else besides, was a good choice to succeed Father Peil, who had described him to the founder on 8 December 1902, in the following words:

> [de Lange] is a good, pious, active, practical and clever priest. Though I have given him the most work, he is always lively and cheerful. Whatever he does, whether as teacher in the school or as spiritual director of the brothers or his pastoral work in the parishes, he does very well . . . Even though his singing and his German leave something to be desired, he will make an excellent superior in due time.

From the beginning, de Lange had urged the establishment of a mission seminary and supported the black parish apostolate. In connection with the latter, his name will come up again in this history. He was transferred to the Dutch East Indies (now part of Indonesia) in 1913. Dutch nationals were much in demand for this new mission. He was one of the pioneers there, to the extent that, on foundations he and his fellow Dutch confreres laid down, Indonesians in the year 2000, numbering about one thousand men, are the largest nationality in the SVD. They supply many new missionaries for the Society's foreign missions and are, as well, active in evangelizing their own people. Worn out by strenuous work in Indonesia and suffering with malaria, Father de Lange returned to the United States to recuperate in 1922. He spent the next years there raising funds to support the Indonesian missions and schools, sixty of which he had built, and a minor seminary that he had been instrumental in establishing.

OPENING THE SEMINARY AND MISSION ANIMATION, 1909–1914

With the permission of Arnold Janssen to open a mission seminary, the situation at Techny changed dramatically. The press, in operation since 1901, for example, had a practical reason to stimulate mission awareness and make appeals for vocations to the missionary priesthood and brotherhood. Also it made more sense to appeal nationally for funds to train missionaries to go to the foreign missions as part of a national and international effort than to seek funds for a local technical school to benefit the graduates of a German orphanage in Chicago.

The original plan was to begin the seminary on 2 February 1909, in the farmhouse situated by the railway station. This house had been rented to a family, but because nobody had given them the required thirty-day notice in writing, they were not able to find another place, so the building could not be prepared properly for the scheduled opening. As a result, classes began in St. Joseph's Technical School with six students. Soon the number rose to seven, and on 9 April 1909, the first seminary in America designated exclusively for the training of priests for the foreign missions moved into the farmhouse, where the chicken coop had to be "remodeled" to serve as a dormitory. During the semester the number of students had increased to twelve and by the beginning of the new school year in September 1909, to sixteen. By any standards this was a small beginning, but it had already made history. Father Peter Janser, whom we have already met and will meet again in other contexts, was appointed rector, and Father August Loechte was the prefect of students. Both, of course, also had to teach many of the courses which had to be offered to the young seminarians.

The seminary, as small as it was, had a magnificent dedication ceremony on 16 April 1909, conducted by Archbishop James Quigley of Chicago. Some forty priests from Chicago and other parts of Illinois and Wisconsin were present for the occasion. In the course of a speech responding to the archbishop, Father de Lange expressed his and the Society's gratitude to those who had come for the dedication and then gave a brief summary of what had led up to the founding of the seminary. In his speech, recorded in somewhat stilted and breathless English in *The Christian Family* of June 1909, he stated:

> The Very Reverend Superior General of the Society had repeatedly been urged by the Propaganda to begin the training of English-speaking missionaries, and that the Missionary Congress recently held in Chicago had greatly emphasized the necessity of such an institution [and] since the Fathers of the Society of the Divine Word, whose special object is missionary work among the pagans, for a long time had ardently wished for the establishment of an American house by their Society, they were induced by these reasons . . . to

found St. Mary's Mission House, which would receive the blessing of the church today; that His Grace had fully approved of the plan . . . that . . . all the members of the Society feel greatly encouraged by the words and actions of His Grace in regard to this matter, and his kindness and zeal toward this movement shall never be forgotten.

Two new items are mentioned in this report, first that the founder had been repeatedly urged by the Roman Curia Congregation *Propaganda Fide* to start such a project. Nowhere in the founder's letters to the United States is this mentioned as a motive for giving permission to open a mission house in America. It would not be surprising if the Propaganda officials, with whom Father Janssen had repeated close contact, had raised this request. Perhaps Father de Lange had heard about this from some source not reflected in the written record. Also mentioned is the impact the call of the Missionary Congress had on the establishment of Techny. Neither is this ever mentioned by Father Janssen. Times, however, had certainly changed since the opening of St. Joseph's Technical School, when clergy and hierarchy were generally opposed to the opening of a seminary for the training of foreign missionaries. Some of this change in atmosphere was due to the hard work and generous help the SVD priests had given the clergy. The traveling brothers also had made an excellent impression on the priests and people with whom they came in contact as they went from place to place and even from door to door selling their mission magazines. Angelyn Dries's study reminds us that there was much interest in overseas missions and support for them at this time, which also roughly coincides with the foundation of Maryknoll in 1911 as the Catholic Foreign Mission Society of America by James Anthony Walsh with the full backing of the American bishops.[1] The SVD was participating in an awakening of the American Catholic Church toward mission that was much larger than the Society's efforts. SVD success, it must be said, came because the times were right, not only because of its members' efforts.

At Techny, the pressing decision to be made was what to do with the rapidly growing enrollments in the high school seminary. The farmhouse was grossly overcrowded with sixteen students, and the first winter had been a fierce one. In a letter the students from America wrote to their counterparts in Steyl, preserved in a 1909 issue of the *Steyler Korrespondenz*, they described their situation as follows:

As a chapel we had a room ten feet in length and six in width. Since the altar took a considerably large space, we were pressed together like sardines in a can. In the dining room we were in an even worse situation [at this time the food was cooked at the Technical Institute and carried the half mile or so to the seminary]. When all were seated there was no space left for anyone to move between the tables. This same room also had to serve as a classroom and conference room. After the basement had been somewhat repaired and calcimined, it had to serve as a dormitory. However, there was room only for eleven beds. Therefore, five of the older boys had to camp in a corn crib next to the chicken coop [all other reports say it was the chicken coop itself]. The

---

1. Angelyn Dries, *The Missionary Movement in American Catholic History* (Maryknoll, N.Y.: Orbis Books, 1998), pp. 67–68.

walls of this "dungeon" consisted of raw boards with cracks that we could stick our hand through without difficulty. Since the first winter we spent here was one of the coldest (the temperature sank as low as 25 degrees below zero), you can imagine that these sleeping quarters were anything but a comfortable dormitory. Fortunately we had plenty of featherbeds . . . There were other inconveniences to which we paid little attention. After all, we knew we had chosen the vocation and life of a missionary, and we knew that this was just a preparation for the future mission life. All in all, the stay in that farmhouse forms one of our most pleasant memories.

There seemed no other choice than to move seminarians to the technical school for the fall semester. But this was intended to be temporary, so where to move the seminary then? And how to staff all the classes that had to be taught? In one of his reports to Father Blum, who was the general administrator of the Society after Father Janssen's death, and who was soon to be elected the second superior general, Father Janser wrote that Father Biskupek and he each taught thirty hours a week, while Father Loechte had thirty-six in addition to twenty minutes each day when he also taught penmanship.

A priest had offered the Society a place in Kingston, New York, on the Hudson River with twenty acres and a house, provided it was used for a mission house. Archbishop John Farley of New York was supposed to be in accord with the idea, but recommended that they wait for two years. Father de Lange also thought they should begin first at Techny and see what had happened after several years, rather than move to Kingston or elsewhere, according to a letter of de Lange to Bodems, dated 2 February 1909. There had always been an interest in setting up a foundation in the East where there were many Catholics, and because Archbishop Farley was favorably inclined toward the missions, the SVDs felt there would be little difficulty establishing a house in his archdiocese in the future. When the SVD turned to Farley some years later, however, he was no longer willing to have the Society in the archdiocese. In the meantime he had given the Maryknoll Fathers permission to begin there. It was not a great blow, since there was no competition between the Maryknoll foundation and the SVD. A round of correspondence between Maryknoll founder James Anthony Walsh, dated 12 April 1912, and Bruno Hagspiel, dated 24 May 1912, shows the cordiality that existed between the two new societies.[2] Techny and Maryknoll agreed to exchange advertisements for the other in their respective magazines, and both men agreed there was plenty of work for everyone, and that each would pray for the success of the other's missionary work. The prevalence of that spirit had been evident earlier in an intra-SVD letter de Lange wrote to Bodems on 6 November 1911, though it is not hard to detect some disappointment that the SVD would not have a house in New York:

We always desired very much to come into the diocese of New York, to erect a mission house. The Archbishop promised last year that within a year he would be able to approve a place for this purpose.

---

2. Maryknoll Archives, W5L2-20 and W5L2-22, courtesy of Maryknoll historian, William McCarthy, MM.

Now I wrote to his Grace that I wished to come to New York, in order to find a place. Some good friends of ours would assist me, and asked his Grace whether he would kindly point out the county or region where about he wishes to have it placed.

To my surprise he writes that since Fathers Price and Walsh [the founders of Maryknoll] are about to establish a mission house for foreign missions in the Archdiocese there is no room for such an institution [as ours]. These fathers [Price and Walsh] also considered that the people in the East are far more prepared for missionary work than elsewhere in the U.S. It seems Divine Providence will direct the Society to some other diocese in the East.

In fact, the Cleveland Diocese and several places in Iowa were other possibilities where they could move the seminary, but gradually the idea that Techny itself would be the best permanent place for the seminary gained currency. It was Father Janser, the rector of the small but growing seminary, who plumped for keeping the seminary where it was, perhaps putting up a new building between Techny station and St. Joseph's Technical School. De Lange even wrote about buying more land to make this possible (20 February 1909, de Lange to Bodems).

Almost from the day he became rector, Father Janser began collecting money for a new seminary building. Certainly the financial situation was not so desperate any more, certainly not as bad as the founder and Blum had thought.

Mission promotion also proceeded apace in other ways. In a very long letter to Bodems on 14 October 1909, Father Janser describes a trip and talk he gave in Indianapolis, Indiana, before two to three hundred delegates of the German Roman Catholic Union convention. "For the very first time in history were the heathen missions so emphatically recommended to the Catholics of the United States in the resolutions of this convention." Techny's press was also busy drumming up interest in the missions and putting out appeals for financial help, not only in the calendars and magazines, but in the many pamphlets and other pieces that were printed and distributed. One early leaflet, not dated but published not too long after the opening of Techny, appealed to benefactors not only for prayers, but also for alms, not just in general, but very specifically for items needed at the new seminary. The appeal concludes: "So far we have no reason to complain. God has been very good to us."

To whom were these informational pamphlets and other pieces of literature sent? Father Janser tells us in a letter he wrote to Superior General Blum on 29 January 1912:

I wrote a small booklet, a sample of which I am enclosing. First we sent this to all of the pastors in the central States: Illinois, Iowa, Wisconsin, Minnesota, Indiana, Michigan, and a few more. Then we inserted a one-page copy of this in every one of our German and English almanacs. Most recently we put a copy in each one of the 17,000 official reports of the Catholic Church Extension Society. Now we also want to send announcements and occasional articles to the newspapers. All this correspondence takes up much time. I myself acknowledge most of the donations received. In general we have no reason to complain about the development of the mission house.

Janser then talks about vocations. He thought there should have been more, though others tell him the SVD is doing well. He adds:

> True, the number of vocations will gradually increase. In the East there are many more vocations to the priesthood, since the mission idea is much better known there. For this reason I have always advocated that we should open a house in the East as soon as possible, be it ever so small. The future of St. Mary's Mission House (Techny) is assured, even if its further growth is slower than I anticipated.

When he wrote these lines there were twenty-five high school students at Techny. By February 1912 this number would increase to thirty. The community at Techny had grown considerably. In addition to the high school students, there were forty-five brothers, one postulant, and one brother novice. Fifteen priests working with St. Joseph's Institute, six with the mission house (seminary), and six in the African-American apostolate.

In spite of the debts it had built up, there is evidence that the SVD in America was already having a positive financial impact on the missions. The press and its publications had much to do with this. Many missions were already looking more and more to America for help. Father Theodore Buecker, SVD, who celebrated the Solemn High Mass on the occasion of the dedication of the seminary, was in America at the time collecting money for his mission in China. America became a common arena for this kind of collecting, and American Catholics responded generously.

CLOSING THE TECHNICAL INSTITUTE,
OPENING A MISSION HOUSE IN GIRARD, PENNSYLVANIA

As 1912 drew on, the seminary still lacked its own home. Over the years different solutions were proposed for putting up a second building close to St. Joseph's so both communities could take advantage of a common kitchen and laundry facilities. Another proposal was to move the seminary into the city of Chicago. Far and away the best solution, everyone eventually agreed, would be to leave the seminary where it was, but this left unresolved St. Joseph's fate. This decision had to await the visitation of the new superior general, Father Nicolaus Blum. He had been elected to succeed Father Arnold Janssen at the fourth general chapter held in November 1909, ten months after the death of the founder.

Blum began his visitation in May 1912. First the decision to close St. Joseph's Technical Institute was made. The institute could not be closed immediately, however, and its last school year was that of 1919–20. In the fall of 1920 the Society began a school for brother candidates as well as a brother postulancy program.

The second major decision of the 1912 visitation was giving permission to open a mission house outside the small town of Girard, Pennsylvania, in the Erie Diocese. De Lange and Janser had already checked out several places and had decided on the Girard property. It consisted of two neighboring farms. An option on both properties was taken in April and a month later the property was shown to

Father Blum on his way to Techny to begin his visitation. Bishop John Fitzmaurice of Erie was glad to have the Divine Word Missionaries in his diocese. The further development of this foundation, which was given the name Sacred Heart Mission House, was left to Father Janser and two brothers, Placidus and Peter, who left on 28 July 1912 to get the farm houses ready for occupancy. That same month the first student arrived in Girard, William Benz, who was soon joined by seven others. Benz had been a student at St. Joseph's Technical Institute for a time before deciding to become a priest. He spent most of his priestly life in parish work in the Society. At its peak as a seminary, Girard, as the Sacred Heart Mission House came to be known, housed as many as 180 students. In the early years Girard was not a paradise. When Father Janser was replaced as rector by Father Arnold Jeurgens, he wrote, "Thank God! I could not endure it any longer."

In 1913, Father de Lange was transferred to the Dutch East Indies. Father Adolph Burgmer, appointed to Techny by the founder in 1901, became his successor. By this time there were thirty priests, fifty-one brothers, two brother novices, one hundred and twenty-eight sisters, and eighty-five students at Techny.

WORLD WAR I AND THE AFTERMATH

August 1914 saw the outbreak of World War I. The United States did not enter that war until 1917, but the entire period from 1914 to 1918 was painful for many of the German priests and brothers who had been assigned to America, some of them very recently. They all had relatives and friends in Europe. In addition, SVD classmates and confreres were drafted into the army and were fighting on the opposite side of their adopted homeland. Numerous Austrian and German priests, brothers, and seminarians drafted into the armed forces were killed. It was, however, extremely useful that the Society was already international, and especially good, as events turned out, that it was already firmly established in the United States. From the beginning, the German SVDs who came to America were urged to become citizens, like most of their German compatriots had done. Because little correspondence passed between the SVD in America and the generalate in Steyl, everything had to be put on hold. Most seriously, perhaps, no new personnel could be sent from Germany.

As soon as the Great War was over in 1918, several dramatic events happened in which Techny played a role that highlighted the value of the growing international character of the Society of the Divine Word. Let us set the scene with a quotation from an article written by Bishop Augustine Henninghaus, SVD, Vicar Apostolic in South Shantung, China, in a 1921 issue of *Our Missions*:

Early in the year 1919 the frightful Repatriation Edict came to the German and Austrian missionaries. If this order had been carried out to the letter, the mission would have been destroyed. Salvation came as a result of the determined and manly efforts of our friends in the United States. From the United States has come in these later years, the monetary aid which has enabled us to weather the trying times. From the United States, too, arrived the first missionaries we had received in seven years—Father Gruhn, King and Clark.

With them the first ray of light broke through the dark clouds. Nine missionaries came from Europe after the signing of the armistice. Some of those who had been expelled in consequence of the Repatriation Edict were also allowed to return.

The first and potentially most disastrous issue to which Bishop Henninghaus called attention was the Repatriation Decree. The Central Alliance, Germany and Austria specifically, had lost the war to the British, French, and Americans. To the victors go the spoils, so Germany and Austria had to pay, first and foremost, by giving up their colonies and protectorates, which included the forcible expulsion of German nationals and their repatriation to Germany. This also meant expropriating anything that belonged to Germans in these areas.

For the Society of the Divine Word, the missions immediately affected were in Mozambique, Togo, China, New Guinea, and the Philippines. German and Austrian missionaries working in Mozambique and Togo returned to these two countries only much later. Some of them, especially those from Togo, were transferred to the United States, where many of them worked in the southern African-American missions. Toward the end of the war, six German priests and one brother who had been working in the Philippines were interned in Camp Logan, an American prison camp in California. One of these, Father Francis Blasczyk, already weakened by maltreatment, became sick with influenza and came to Techny to die. He has the distinction of being the first SVD priest to be buried in the Techny cemetery, but he was not the first Divine Word Missionary to die in America. He had been preceded in death by five brothers. Fathers Henry Bürschen and Hergesheimer eventually returned to the Philippines in a voyage that Brother Benedict, the first American SVD brother to go to the foreign missions, joined them in making.

Much more serious was the distinct possibility that all German missionaries would be deported from China and New Guinea. This, as Bishop Henninghaus stressed, would have meant the ruin of the SVD effort in these areas. In 1918 there had already been articles in the newspapers that German subjects in China were to be deported to Australia, even though the war was still going on. Upon reading this, Father Markert, director of the press at Techny and editor of the *Amerikanisches Familienblatt*, made inquiries of the Chinese ambassador in Washington about the status of the SVD missionaries and whether they would be affected. Having made inquires of his government in Peking, the ambassador said that the German missionaries would not be affected as long as they complied with certain restrictions and did nothing against the Chinese state.

Meanwhile the British kept insisting that Germans be deported and their properties expropriated. On 28 February 1919, we find Father Markert writing to Monsignor Joseph Freri of the Society for the Propagation of the Faith in New York and warning him that German SVDs were to be deported from China and that the consequences would be disastrous. By return mail on 3 March 1919, Monsignor Freri answered:

I cannot but confirm what you read in the last issue of "Catholic Missions" regarding the alarming situation of the mission of your Fathers in South

Shantung. Upon receipt of the cablegram from Bishop Henninghaus I got into communication with His Eminence Cardinal Gibbons and also with His Eminence Cardinal O'Connell. They both promised to use their influence to prevent the expulsion of the missionaries. Cardinal Gibbons wrote to the Acting Secretary of State at Washington, who cabled to our Minister at Pekin. The answer from the Chinese government was not satisfactory. We were requested if possible to make immediate arrangements to send American missionaries to take over the work of your Fathers. I answered that this would be absolutely impossible for the present when all the missions are short of workers, so much the more that it was asked that the new missionaries sent should speak German.

I insisted that the mission of South Shantung be represented as an American mission from the fact that it is in great part supported by American funds.

A few weeks later, on 19 March 1919, Monsignor Freri wrote the following note to Father Burgmer, provincial superior at Techny:

I am pleased to communicate to you the substance of a cablegram received at the Department of State, Washington, from our Minister at Pekin, copy of which has been sent to me: "Exemption is to be granted to missionaries necessary to continuity of work. Missionaries in Shantung undisturbed." Be kind enough to communicate the news to the members of your community and I have no doubt it will be received with great joy . . .

In the face of continued pressure to expel the Germans, Father Blum took concrete measures to protect the China missions. He wrote to Father Janser requesting him to send two or three American seminarians to China. At England's insistence, the Chinese government was to deport German missionaries, who were being detained in camps at the time, whereupon the Chinese government would confiscate the properties which the Society owned and from which they partially supported themselves.

Let Clifford King, one of the two American seminarians to go to China to help turn the tide, tell the story as he recalls it in his 1968 recollections:

After Father Janser finished reading the letter [from the superior general] and explaining its contents, he asked us to reflect on its significance and to pray fervently to the Holy Spirit for guidance. After this any of us who wished to respond affirmatively to Father General's appeal should call on him during the course of the afternoon.

Six students of our class [the entire class] went to see Father Provincial, who announced at table that evening that the two scholastics chosen for the China mission were Robert Clark and Clifford King.

On 1 October 1919, the two scholastics, together with Father Fred Gruhn, a German who had become an American citizen and would accompany them, were given the mission cross in a solemn ceremony of departure at which Archbishop George Mundelein of Chicago gave the farewell talk. The two seminarians were ordained in China on 10 October 1920, by Bishop Augustine Henninghaus as the first native-born Americans to be ordained in the Society of the Divine Word.

Robert Clark would die on 7 July 1923, under circumstances that are not totally clear, as the following two accounts indicate. One version has it that he was ill and was medicating himself with local medicines for an unnamed illness and for constipation. He complained of a loss of appetite and was not able to sleep well. This he is said to have blamed on the humidity and heat. Suddenly he took a turn for the worse and Father George Froewis, the superior, and Father King took him to the Catholic hospital in Hankow, where he was rushed into surgery, his kidneys rapidly failing. The next day he died. A report in *The Independent News* (Hankow, China, Tuesday, 10 July 1923) said the following about the tragic death:

> Father Clark, of the Catholic Mission of Fathers of the Divine Word, died Sunday night at the Catholic Mission Hospital in Hankow.
>
> Father Clark was stationed at the Mission in Sinyangchow, Honan. During the night about a week ago, feeling rather restless, he got up out of bed and took what he believed to be a few headache tablets to quiet his nerves. A few days later, feeling very ill, he came down to Hankow for examination, when it was found out that he had taken bichloride of mercury by mistake. Everything possible was done for him at the Catholic Mission Hospital here, but the poison had taken too firm a hold on his system and it was too late to save him.

Clark was twenty-eight years old. He had been ordained a little over two years and was the first American-born member of the Society of the Divine Word to die.

Father Gruhn returned to Techny on 31 January 1923, before Father Clark had died. He was described as "weak and emaciated" (Janser to Bodems, 10 February 1923). He had been sent to China with the two seminarians as much to chaperone them as to be a missionary in China, it seems, so no one was particularly surprised at his return. He spent the rest of his long life teaching Latin and Greek in SVD high school seminaries and was famous for his rich plain chant singing voice.

FINANCIAL CONTRIBUTIONS TO THE SOCIETY IN EUROPE

During and after the First World War, Germany was going through very difficult times. Because inflation was out of control, German money was worthless. Conditions were better in Holland, but Steyl depended heavily on Germany for sustenance. St. Gabriel's in Austria was no better off. Not only did all of the houses in Germany desperately need help, but it followed that Germany could not help the missions during these years, so the United States Province stepped into the breach. Although it is difficult to come up with an accurate dollar amount, there are indications in correspondence that the contribution was substantial. One can extrapolate relative figures from what we know was the cost of running Techny for the ten months from September 1931 to June 1932 to how far the money would stretch in Holland, Germany, and Austria, where costs were much lower. Food costs for Techny that school year were $37,671; fuel $6,200; clothing and footwear $7,905. The community amounted to 420 persons that school year, and thus it cost about forty cents per day per person to run Techny. After the First World War a dollar in Europe would have stretched even further. Much of the money to support the European SVD was sent in the form of Mass stipends.[3] Father Burgmer sent other funds in 1915 and 1916, requesting that the money be used to write off some of the debt they owed Steyl from the early years, perhaps some of which was the debt incurred for magazines and other items that Father Peil had unilaterally written off. After the war the amounts sent went even higher. Janser, now the provincial superior, sent $15,000 to Steyl on 10 January 1919, stating, "Of this, $10,000 is for as many Mass intentions . . . the rest to reduce our debt." He added another $1,000 as a Christmas present. Father Markert collected well over $100,000 for orphanages in Germany through the *Amerikanisches Familienblatt*. His readers were all of German descent. Many knew the places he wrote about, and knew from relatives how difficult the times were. Money, of course, that was specified for a particular mission was sent to that mission, which is how the China missions, according to Bishop Henninghaus, were able to survive. In the years 1924 to 1928, this amounted to $330,252. In addition, missionaries came to the United States to lecture, preach, and collect money for their bishop and mission as soon after the war as they were allowed into the country to do so. Among others, Father de Lange preached for the Dutch East Indies; Father King, very successfully, for China; Father Drescher for the Philippines.

Partly as a result of Techny's efforts, Americans were developing a strong sense of mission awareness and they responded generously to the call to support overseas missions. Father Burgmer wrote on 22 March 1919: "The gracious Lord has been good to us during the war. The number of our friends and supporters have been steadily growing." It was extremely providential that Arnold Janssen, only ten years earlier, had permitted the opening of Techny as a seminary and, in spite of misgivings to the contrary, gave in to those working in North America who were in the forefront in the internationalization of the Society.

THE NEED FOR MORE SPACE AT TECHNY

As Techny continued to add classes and grow, the need for more space began to become critical again. Classes were now being held at many levels at Techny: four years of high school, two years of junior college, one year of novitiate, two years of philosophy, and four years of theology. The decision was made to continue building at Techny, according to the original plan of Father Beckert. The times

---

3. Mass stipends were the monetary donations that lay people, priests, and bishops sent. The theory behind them was not that the donation paid for the Mass, but that it was to provide sustenance for the celebrant of the Mass. The Masses were then celebrated for the intentions of the donor. In the period from 1918 through the 1930s, stipends rarely exceeded $1.00, and often they were less. In a letter of 22 September 1914, Father Burgmer writes, "We've sent 1,000 stipends to you, and are ready to send more if you can use them. We'll also try to collect other gifts for our needy confreres." Stipends that Steyl could not use were sent to St. Gabriel's and to other monasteries and priests in need.

were as good as they would ever be, and they knew that the cost of building materials was going to go up. Thus they began with the main entrance and two towers of Techny in 1918. This wing faces west along Waukegan Road. They also began planning a new church and were already collecting funds for this purpose. They already had permission from Rome to borrow $100,000 if their investments covered this amount. The debt load at the time, including what was owed to Steyl, came to $400,000, but their investments came to $600,000. Even if one subtracted what was owed at Girard their surplus of investment was $477,000. This did not include the worth of their land, buildings, machinery, and so forth. In the previous year they had taken in close to $200,000 in gifts, not counting donations intended for the missions, which were always separately accounted for and dispatched to the missions when the generalate made its regular apportionments.

In a letter of the period about the building plans preserved in the generalate archives Father Janser stated that they would not leave the SVD in Europe in the lurch, despite the amounts required in the construction projects, because they still received many Mass stipends which they would send. If, by chance, Steyl needed a larger sum, they could manage that, too, if they were allowed to take out a mortgage on their property which was now debt free.

On 22 November 1920, the community moved into their new kitchen and dining rooms in the basement of the new building, just two years and two months, including several stoppages for lack of materials and labor difficulties, after the first shovelful of dirt had been turned. In May 1923 this magnificent structure was dedicated to the Holy Spirit by Superior General Wilhelm Gier.

EXPANSION BEYOND TECHNY AND STRAINS

Another way to overcome the space problems at Techny was to move a group of people or a department from Techny to another house. The first such decision was soon made regarding the "clerical" novices.[4] The search for a proper home for the novitiate went further than the midwest. In February 1921, for instance, Father Herman Richarz, the novice master, and Brother Wendelin went to California to check out a property, called Chittendon, that had been offered to the Society as a possible site for a novitiate or a mission college. Nothing came of this trip, because California was viewed as too far away from Techny for a novitiate. Instead, in May several possible properties were inspected in Wisconsin, with the final choice falling on a piece of land on Lake Beulah near the town of East Troy. The first property bought there, on the western shore of the lake, proved inadequate, and a better piece of property was found on the opposite side of the lake. It was acquired in 1924. East Troy served as the clerical novitiate until 1937, when the high school

---

4. The term "clerical novices" here refers to novices seeking to become missionary-priests and is borrowed from the Canon Law term for priests as members of the "clerical" state (i.e., to become members of the "clergy"). The term distinguished novices studying for the priesthood from novices studying for the brotherhood. Seminarians in vows were also called "clerics," and I will use the term in the pages that follow when necessary. The word "cleric" took on negative connotations in the years after the Second Vatican Council (1962–65) that it did not have during the period we discuss.

seminary still located at Techny changed places with the novices. The latter moved back to Techny where they had started twenty-two years before.

The purchase of property, the building at Techny, and the projected building at East Troy began to put a strain on Techny's finances. Already on 7 March 1922, Father Janser had written to Bruno Hagspiel, who was accompanying Superior General Gier as his English-language secretary on an extended visitation of Asia, that some in the Society think Techny is a "Croesus." He goes on:

> What can we do? We are short in men, we have no funds, we must constantly help others. In January we have sent $12,000 to Steyl, besides many Mass stipends, for December was excellent for stipends; but in order to do so we had to renew a big loan in one of the banks and pay 6% interest. Annuities are still coming in; but they are becoming a nightmare since the amount to be paid for interest becomes embarrassing. During 1921 we received $244,000 in annuities, over $166,000 for free scholarships. China got over $19,000, for pagan babies[5] nearly $15,000.

In an October 1922 letter to Cardinal O'Connell, Janser remarks, "The responsibility for almost our whole Society rests upon our shoulders," a slight exaggeration perhaps, but not by much. Still the North American Province continued to expand and meet its financial obligations.

Janser was next responsible for purchasing a house in Duxbury, Massachusetts, about forty miles south of Boston and just a few miles north of Plymouth Rock, where the first pilgrims had landed. The desire to establish themselves on the East Coast had been present from the first days SVDs landed in America. Because the church had been established here longer than anywhere else, mission interest also seemed to be notably higher here, and vocations were more plentiful. As a mission-sending society, consequently, the Divine Word Missionaries expected much support in the East. Since Archbishop Farley of New York did not want to admit more missionary communities to his archdiocese after he gave Father James Anthony Walsh permission to locate Maryknoll there, the Boston area was especially attractive to the SVD.

The actual invitation for the SVD to locate in Boston came in 1922, when Father Peter Janser traveled to Boston and other dioceses to promote the cause of the seminary for African Americans, which was being planned for Bay St. Louis, Mississippi. He wanted to thank Cardinal William O'Connell, the Archbishop of Boston, for the thousand dollars he had personally given toward the construction of the seminary for African Americans. In the course of their conversation, Janser expressed the desire of his Society to open a mission seminary in the cardinal's archdiocese. He pointed out that the long distances any vocations they got from the East had to travel to get to Techny or even Girard were too much to ask young boys to make. Chuckling to himself, the cardinal said he would think the matter

---

5. The term "pagan babies" refers to the practice of sending in a certain amount of money to "ransom," or save, an abandoned "pagan" baby in China. Five dollars for a girl and ten dollars for a boy were ways of helping the mission support the many abandoned children they rescued. It was also a very effective way of developing mission awareness.

over, and, almost in the same breath, suggested that Father Janser should have a look at the cardinal's own summer house, "Miramar," which he no longer needed. Permission to purchase it was given on 9 June 1922.

Miramar served many purposes for the Society as St. Francis Xavier Seminary. Successively it became a high school seminary with a two-year college, a high school seminary only, a school for belated vocations, and a two-year college with a belated vocation center. While all these changes were going on in the seminary, across the road a magnificent Cape Cod-style house carried on as an SVD-directed lay retreat center, as it does down to the time this book is being written.

Property purchases in the 1920s were rounded out by the 1924 purchase of a vineyard situated on Lake Hemlock in western New York state, thirty-five miles south of Rochester. The purpose of the vineyard was to be the production and sale of wine, especially of sacramental wine. For years the winery lost money and once, during the Prohibition era, became the source of great embarrassment when, according to Father Aubry, the vineyard apparently became entangled with boot-leggers posing as laymen wanting to help the Society turn a profit to benefit its missionary work. Whatever the case was in this colorful period, in 1935 the Society petitioned the Bishop of Rochester, Edward Mooney, for permission to build a sem-inary on the thousand-acre property. Shortly before, Girard had been converted to a central two-year junior college, and the new foundation at Conesus, as the sem-inary came to be known, would take up the task of recruiting and educating high school students in the area Girard had drawn from. Finally, with the trade name O-Neh-Da Vineyard and Winery and under the legitimate direction of a German-born master vintner, Leo Goering, the winery, because of the work of brothers who trav-eled to sell and deliver the wine, made money and helped support the seminary. Known variously as St. Michael's Mission House, or Seminary, the Conesus sem-inary changed its function, and at one time or another over the years was a semi-nary for belated vocations, a novitiate and junior college, a brother candidate school, a clerical novitiate, house of philosophical studies, and a brothers' novi-tiate. German-born Father Hugo Aubry was associated with St. Michael's for many years, as provincial and local superior and later as a resident and retiree. He drew up incredibly ambitious plans for a shrine to St. Michael at Conesus and, though these were never fully realized, in his nineties he kept them alive.

PERSONNEL, A PERENNIAL PROBLEM

With this kind of unremitting expansion, we can well imagine that the major difficulty that the American SVD faced concerned its personnel. This was nothing new; we recall the constant pressure Peil put on the founder to send more priests and brothers to America. The SVD, it is true, was beginning to ordain Americans. And the superiors were gaining permission to keep many of them in the United States to teach and work as formation leaders in new seminaries being opened, to edit magazines, to take over the mission animation and vocational recruitment work that was becoming more and more necessary. American candidates for the priest-hood and brotherhood also wanted personnel of their own culture to whom it would be easier to relate. But English-speaking missionaries were also wanted and needed overseas. New Guinea was now administered by Australia. China was more interested in dealing with Americans than ever before. SVD mission work in the Philippines increasingly became educational work, with English as the medium of instruction in a system patterned on the American model. Many of the letters that passed between Techny and Steyl during the 1920s dealt with the personnel shortage. The correspondents—sometimes bluntly and vigorously—accused each other of holding back or not setting the proper priorities. But the work went on, the expansion continued.

Times were good for most Americans and for the SVD in the period called "the Roaring Twenties." Money was generally plentiful. Women got the vote. But times were not universally good, and SVDs in the African-American apostolate were more aware of the underside of American prosperity and culture than other white Catholics. They knew, for instance, that there had been terrible race riots, generally sparked by labor disputes, in both the North and South, but especially in big cities such as Chicago, Omaha, St. Louis, and Detroit. Before the First World War, the movement of blacks from South to the North had been modest. After 1915, with about a half million blacks migrating North, the trickle became a torrent, and the competition for jobs became intense. But after the painful transition from war time to peace time was accomplished, times again got better and the problems of blacks were again shoved under the carpet. It is hard to judge how deeply awareness of this racial fissure in American culture informed SVD missionary training and awareness, but it is perhaps worthwhile to mention that even in these times of plenty, there were Society members who saw another side of the American reality.

Alongside the invisibility of such social problems to most of white America, overseas mission awareness and a spirit of concern for foreign mission were growing. The hierarchy, no longer so absorbed with the influx of Catholic immigrants that had so occupied their energies for decades, began to take a serious interest in foreign missions. This was so much the case that it led to another problem, one that would have literally brought the SVD in America to ruin had this difficulty not been properly resolved.

CENTRALIZATION OF U. S. CATHOLIC MISSION EFFORTS

The American bishops' 1919 pastoral letter had asked Catholics to engage in missionary works at home and in foreign lands. Their letter was in the spirit of Pope Benedict XV's apostolic letter on the missions *Maximum illud* (1919). The next year, on 1 December 1920, the American Board of Catholic Missions (ABCM) was established, a move that Francis Kelley, prime mover of the Extension Society, had been urging for a number of years. The hope of its proponents was that the ABCM could reorganize and unify missionary efforts in America. The need they felt stemmed from several causes, including experiences resulting from World War I, which left the U. S. carrying the financial burden for many missions. Not to be underestimated as a motivation for the ABCM was the attempt to increase Catholic competition to U. S. Protestant mission efforts, which were much larger than those of Catholics. Up to this time also, money collected in

America for the Society for the Propagation of the Faith was still being sent to France to be distributed from Lyon by the National Council of Laymen. In the November 1922 fund distribution of the Society for the Propagation of the Faith, not one centime went to missions staffed by Germans, although the equivalent of six million francs had come from the United States, much of it from Germans. Politics and national rivalries were rearing their ugly heads, since distribution was clearly according to nationality. The idea now being advanced in the U. S. was to organize the American effort, foster more mission awareness, promote missionary vocations, and to increase mission financial support for foreign missions among American Catholics.

SVD seminarian William Ross, whom we shall later encounter as a missionary in New Guinea, wrote in *Our Missions* that the purpose of the ABCM was "To bring about a nation-wide interest in home and foreign missions, to weld all missionary agencies into close and compact unity, and to make of this unity a mighty force for the spread of Christ's Kingdom. In the first 1921 issue of *Our Missions*, Ross went on to say:

> America is to be made missionary throughout its entire Catholic life. The children will be arrayed under the standard of the Association of the Holy Childhood; all adults will be expected to join the Society for the Propagation of the Faith; the CSMC [Catholic Students' Mission Crusade] will seek to marshal under its banners every Catholic student of the country; members of religious orders will have a special missionary association; the missionary union of the clergy will demand the support of every priest, especially the pastors, whose mission zeal will then react on their flocks; every bishop will appoint a director of missionary activities in his diocese, and a careful diocesan report of missionary contributions will be made by each bishop at the annual conference of the Hierarchy. Every diocese will then know its mission strength; every parish its mission zeal; every school its mission spirit. And guiding, directing, and energizing all will be the ABCM.

Little did he know that soon his own congregation would be leading efforts to dismantle key portions of the ABCM, aspects Ross was praising in his article.

Under the plan, a portion of the money collected in the U. S. would still be sent to Rome for distribution, the rest set aside for home and foreign missions and distributed according to the budget requests that would be submitted by the various [American] groups that were working in the missions. Such ideas were first greeted with enthusiasm. Six bishops and archbishops formed the Board of Governors, one of them Archbishop Mundelein of Chicago, who strongly favored centralization. Not all bishops were enthusiastic. Soon there were second thoughts among many of them, in which they would be joined especially by the SVD and other mission-sending societies. On 17 February 1922, Janser writes to Father Joseph McGlinchey, Director of the Propagation of the Faith for Boston:

> While I surely am in sympathy with the plans in general, I fear that radical proclivities will cause some friction. I am thinking especially of the extir-

pation of ALL missionary magazines except the OFFICIAL papers. Too much centralization is another evil, which is spelling death to private initiative. An autocratic system may work as long as the first fervor prevails and an unusual man directs affairs; it is bound to cause lethargy and stagnation under ordinary leadership. Besides, our magazines are not only a source of revenue, but the spring of many vocations. It is through OUR magazines that we bring our Society and our missions before the public. Rumors have reached me that special efforts are already made with some bishops to win them over to the radical change with regard to magazines. I am sure we all want but the good of the Church and the salvation of souls, but there is also a human side to every human agency.

The issue was especially problematic for an international mission-sending society. It is quite doubtful that the American Society of the Divine Word would have gotten much, if anything, if they submitted a proposal in their budget to send money to Steyl in Holland or to St. Gabriel's in Austria, to save those institutions. And how much would have been allocated for Dutch missionaries in the Dutch East Indies?

The SVD was far from the only group opposing this aspect of the ABCM plan. In addition, the Board began having difficulties with the Roman authorities who wanted a higher percentage of the money collected, as did the Society for the Propagation of the Faith in Lyons. At the SVD provincial chapter of 22–24 April 1924, it was decided that Father Janser would visit the bishops leading the ABCM centralization movement. Soon the religious congregations engaged in mission work began to coordinate their efforts. In a letter to Father Mathis, a member of the Congregation of Holy Cross (CSC), Father Janser suggested that he speak to Archbishop Hurley in Washington. Father Walsh of Maryknoll would speak to Cardinal Patrick Hayes of New York. Janser would meet with Cardinal Mundelein of Chicago. Meanwhile the Apostolic Delegate had told the provincial superior of the Passionists in the East that the bishops could not interfere with mission magazines.

Scarcely to be found in the discussions of the day is recognition of the fact that missionary efforts since 1492 had been carried on by religious communities that, in sociological terminology, were "voluntary, parachurch societies" within the larger church structure. The Congregation *Propaganda Fide* was founded in 1622 to help coordinate these Catholic efforts. De facto, however, founders of communities such as the Jesuits, the SVD, the Salesians, and the Oblates of Mary Immaculate recruited men, raised money from, and animated, local and national churches. Such religious communities and their female counterparts comprised virtually the entire missionary personnel pool of the church. While they enjoyed the support of bishops, the involvement of the official local church in directing such societies was minimal. Nor did *Propaganda* exercise direct authority over them. The strength of the Catholic missionary orders lay in their flexibility, their single-mindedness, and their ability to instill in members a sense of complete commitment. The weakness of this voluntary society structure, from a theological viewpoint, was the duplication of effort and the lack of involvement by the entire local or national church. Mission was in effect an enterprise in the hands of specialists. Nevertheless, one of the greatest compliments paid the structure and methods of these Catholic groups was that Protestant missionary efforts after 1792 utilized similar voluntary society structures.[6]

In that context, what ABCM centralization risked doing was undermining the conditions required by the voluntary societies to create an ethos among their membership and enlist the support of dedicated lay supporters with deep personal ties to the missionary congregation.

In the midst of the ABCM controversy, Father Janser was assigned to China, to open a central mission procure in Shanghai and to coordinate the increasingly large and complex SVD China mission. Father Burgmer became provincial superior to fill out his term. Father Hagspiel had by then returned from his trip with Father Gier to become rector at Techny (and later successor to Father Burgmer as provincial). Hagspiel was a master animator and publicist, a prolific writer and editor, an indefatigable preacher and retreat master. He was a man who had ten ideas on mission promotion and fund raising, it seemed, before he came to breakfast, all of which he tried to carry out by the time he went to bed. Hagspiel immediately took up the banner of decentralization. Quickly he requested and obtained a meeting on 31 January 1925 with Cardinal Mundelein, who favored centralization of animation and fund-raising efforts under the auspices of the ABCM. The results of this meeting were preserved by Father Matthias Braun, SVD, who was one of the participants at the meeting. He reported to Father Gier, the superior general, in a letter dated 1 February 1925, that Hagspiel expressed the concerns of the SVD. Apparently unmoved, the cardinal responded, "You need not fear for the future." But the SVDs objected that, if the plans went through, no mission appeals would be allowed. Missionaries might be allowed to preach in a parish at the request of the diocesan director of the Propagation of the Faith to arouse missionary enthusiasm and get perhaps fifty dollars for his work on a Sunday. Cardinal Mundelein was on his way to Rome to sort out questions and difficulties around the centralization initiative. In a letter attached to his report to the SVD generalate, Braun suggested that the Society should raise the issue in Rome before the cardinal got there, to head off any hasty adoption of Mundelein's views on the part of *Propaganda Fide*.

Janser, Hagspiel, and the members of other congregations needed not to preoccupy themselves with this concern. *Propaganda* had three hundred years experience working with missionary communities and was not about to change the system. The missionary orders, despite all their pluriformity and variety, constituted a dedicated corps of missionaries that Rome was not eager to risk sacrificing for the sake of bureaucratic efficiency that might look good on paper but might not produce the committed personnel and other resources needed. In the end, the ABCM centralization effort failed.[7]

6. The beginning of the Protestant missionary movement is often dated symbolically by the year 1792, in which William Carey published *An Enquiry into the Obligations of Christians, to Use Means for the Conversion of the Heathens*. Carey (1761–1834) was an English Baptist translator, pastor, and founder of the Serampore, India, mission.

7. It should be noted—perhaps with irony—that during Vatican Council II (1962–65), the sixth

CENTRALIZATION IN THE SVD

The idea of centralization of all mission promotion and fund raising in the U.S. was never implemented. In the Society itself, however ironic it may seem, many began to feel a need for internal centralization and control of SVD fund raising. Missionaries came from all around the world to collect in the U. S., the only place where there was much money available for a long time after the First World War. Sometimes the same benefactors received ten and twelve invitations to donate. Many of them were understandably confused. As an example of how one man's idea could have become the Society's black eye, Bishop Henninghaus at one time requested that he be allowed to send one of his Dutch fathers to America more or less permanently to collect funds for the Shantung mission. This priest had been very successful gathering funds in the Netherlands by means of a lottery. Henninghaus thought he would be able to repeat this success in America.

Many ideas for fund raising were brought forward, not all as good as that of a lottery. As a result, Bruno Hagspiel recommended at the provincial chapter of April 1924 that a mission office should be established at Techny to take care of mission funds and mission needs. In 1927 his idea was finally implemented, with Father de Lange as the first mission procurator, the same de Lange who had succeeded Father Peil as the second superior of Techny and who had gone to Indonesia and been so successful there. He had to leave Indonesia (Dutch East Indies at the time) because of illness. When he left the East Indies, he said, they had to carry him out on a stretcher. But as soon as he set foot on United States soil, he immediately felt better and regained his dry sense of humor. In two weeks he was ready to begin lecturing and collecting money for his mission. In this he was very successful. "Where priests would scarcely open the door to us," wrote Father Janser, "he takes up collections."

THE "INTERNATIONAL" CHARACTER
OF THE SOCIETY EMERGES

Before leaving the 1920s, I would like to discuss an incident that again demonstrates the emerging *international* thrust and character of the Society. It was proposed that the mission of Honan in China be assigned to the North American SVD Province. Father Janser wrote to Bishop Allen of Mobile, Alabama, on 13 January 1923, "We are awaiting word that a mission in China will be entrusted to us, so we would not only be responsible in a financial way [for this mission], but also for the

---

superior general of the SVD, Johannes Schütte, the first doctor of missiology to head the Society, was largely instrumental in getting the council to adopt the decree on mission *Ad gentes*. One of the prime goals that he was successful in including in the council's mission document was the principle that local churches and their bishops were to consider the work of mission a primary responsibility. That decree rested on the insight that mission is an activity of the entire church and that something is amiss when it is carried on as if it were the responsibility of certain specialists. To the extent that the vision of *Ad gentes* is implemented, voluntary groups such as the SVD would have to subordinate themselves to ordinary diocesan or national episcopal conference structures. Yet much of their success lies in the ability of religious orders to work outside the sometimes sclerotic channels of local churches.

men." This request was included in the minutes and decisions of the provincial chapter of 22–25 April 1924, which we have already mentioned several times. The vote at the provincial chapter in favor of Americans taking over Honan had been seven in favor and four against. The record and proposals for action were sent to the generalate for approval. The official response from Rome was written on 28 August 1924 by Father Kost on behalf of the generalate:

> All of the decisions of the Provincial Chapter are herewith approved, with the exception of the decision taken at session 7, according to which the mission of Honan would be attached to the North American province. This stands in opposition to the decision of the last General Chapter which rejected such an affiliation. If you wish to use Honan in a special way for propaganda purposes and as the mission for which you will take primary [financial] responsibility, we would have no objection.

The generalate was standing behind a principle that the SVD had begun to understand after World War I. It would not be until after World War II that its utility was fully realized. What we are seeing here is the evolution of the notion that the composition of mission teams in the SVD should be international. Entrusting a mission to the citizens of a single country ran the risk of crippling that mission if political situations made those nationals *personae non gratae* to a host nation. Moreover, internationality gave a much better witness to the universality of the church.

STATE OF THE SOCIETY IN 1932

It may be helpful to close this chapter with a summary of the membership statistics prepared for the society's general chapter held in 1932 to elect the successor of Father Gier. The province reported its personnel statistics as follows:

- one hundred priests, including two who were studying in Europe
- sixty-eight scholastics, among whom eleven were in perpetual vows
- thirty-four clerical novices, sixteen in the first year and eighteen in the second
- ninety-seven professed brothers, among whom sixty-nine were in perpetual vows
- twenty-one brother novices
- seven brother postulants and ten brother candidates
- four hundred sixty students in the first six years of their classical education (four years of high school and two years of junior college); among whom were included five Filipinos, three in the scholasticate and two in the clerical novitiate.

We have not yet arrived at our discussion of the African-American apostolate, but the initial success of this work was revealed in the following statistics from the same year:

- seven scholastics
- five clerical novices
- fifty-five African-American high school seminarians.

Since the first class of scholastics was ordained at Techny in 1920, sixty-four Americans had been ordained to the priesthood, which averages out to five a year for the first eight years, and six a year for the next four. The next ordination class would have eleven and the one following, nineteen. These figures did not include eleven others from Europe, mostly from Germany, who came to America for part of their studies, who were ordained at Techny and then received their assignments.

Comparable statistics for the Society as a whole are interesting, showing that the American SVD was a small percentage of the membership of the Society as a whole. According to official statistics, in 1935 the Society was comprised of: 1,325 priests; 579 scholastics; 575 clerical novices; 1,532 brothers; and 338 brother novices, for a total of 4,359 members. In the ten years from 1925 to 1935, the number of priests had grown from 777 to 1,325; the number of brothers from 914 to 1,532.

Personnel problems did not go away in North America. Requests from bishops to take on new projects, such as colleges or industrial institutes, parishes or missions, kept flowing in from all over the country and world, often with offers of land and money to get the work started. Most had to be refused. The manpower shortage was compounded by so many getting sick in their job. "Weak lungs" was a common diagnosis. This usually meant tuberculosis, which at the time was treated by long rest cures in the West or Southwest. Spanish influenza took many lives. Pneumonia and other infectious diseases caused many to die young. Then too there were the "nervous disorders" that crippled the effectiveness of many. This meant that the one who seemed to be available to take a job was emotionally unable to take over the position. In religious life, the emotionally handicapped are not sent away if their problems emerge after final vows. Rather, less demanding tasks are found for them, and thus simple statistics of numbers of priests and brothers are not always the full measure of an order's apostolic capacities.

Those who filled in at Techny and elsewhere in the early days were often stretched to the point of exhaustion. Many individuals held two or three positions. One priest might teach, be rector, help out in parishes on weekends, and contribute a monthly or weekly column to one of the magazines. This was probably inevitable in the beginning, but it continued to occur well into the 1920s and 1930s. All things considered, however, as the general chapter considered the work the pioneer five had begun in the United States, the judgment was that it had prospered well, and that the present augured well for the future.

4

Maturing as a Missionary Community

World War II through Vatican Council II, 1932–1970

The period of Franklin D. Roosevelt's "New Deal" response to the Great Depression through World War II and its aftermath marked the beginning of many changes in the world that had a tremendous impact on the church and Society of the Divine Word. This was also the period in which the SVD matured into a multiethnic American missionary community.[1] As St. Augustine's Seminary and the African-American parishes developed, so did the ethos that would characterize the Society until the next major sea change occurred in its life as a result of the Second Vatican Council (1962–1965).

The Great Depression and the New Deal saw the beginning of a remarkable transformation of American society. An alphabet soup of agencies from the WPA (Works Progress Administration) to the CCC (Civilian Conservation Corps) insinuated the federal government in dimensions of American life where it had never before been. The passage of the Social Security Act insured the aged. An expanded Department of Agriculture began to affect the way millions of farmers operated. Unions, dominated by Catholics from the urban Northeast through the Midwest, struggled to maintain their gains of the previous decade aided by the unflagging encouragement of Roosevelt and the Democratic Party.

While certainly affected by all these social developments, the greatest impact upon the Techny seminary and its thriving satellites in Pennsylvania, Mississippi, Massachusetts, Iowa, New York, and New Jersey came with the outbreak of hostilities in Europe in 1939. More than most Americans, SVD communities knew men and women whose lives were being uprooted and destroyed. For the many Germans at work in the American Province, their relatives and close friends were

---

1. The most important event that sealed this multiethnic characteristic was the 1920 founding of St. Augustine's Seminary at Bay St. Louis, Mississippi. For practical reasons we have placed that story in part two of this book, on the missionary apostolates of the American SVD, but the reader should realize that the African-American parishes and St. Augustine's were by far the most important and radical emblem of the Society's emerging character. This could easily be obscured by the focus this book is giving to developments surrounding Techny. It should not be.

directly involved. In addition, in a way unimaginable in the U.S., where priests, brothers, and seminarians were given draft deferments, German and Austrian confreres were conscripted into the army. By the end of the war, three hundred German and Austrian SVD—mostly seminarians and brothers—had been killed.[2] Dutch confreres were dominated by the German occupation. Polish confreres were executed in concentration camps. In China and New Guinea, SVDs from the U.S. and Germany were thrown together into Japanese detention centers, and in New Guinea they would be executed together by a power that was supposedly the ally of Germany. Dozens of SVDs would die in New Guinea, too, under air attack by the United States Navy as the Japanese moved them to another location. Life for SVDs, in other words, would become even more complex than it was for most North Americans during the war.

For the rest of the U.S., normal life went on hold when Japan bombed Pearl Harbor on 7 December 1941. For Europeans everything changed on 1 September 1939 with the invasion of Poland. For American SVDs, however, the war had begun eight years earlier than for their countrymen. The life of an international religious community is intimately attached to the cultural ethos and national life of a country. But it transcends that by concrete bonds with persons of different nationalities and concerns for the cultural and political life of other peoples. The fate of China and the Chinese people, for example, under attack by the Japanese since the mid-1930s, were of great concern, and not only because there were American SVDs and members of other missionary communities there. SVDs had heard so many talks about and read so much about China that what happened to the people and the missionaries in China was felt personally.

Let us, though, leave our introductory overview and reconnect our story with the internal life of the Society in the United States.

THE GREAT DEPRESSION AND SVD FINANCES

A major test of the SVD's viability in North America came during the Great Depression. SVD finances were the competence of specially appointed treasurers (who were called "procurators") who served under house and provincial superiors.[3] In fact, because financial competence is so prized in communities such as the SVD, where fund raising and administration are the last things most members want to do, such treasurers tended to have long terms of office and—especially when everything was going well—scant close oversight was exercised by rectors and provincials grateful not to have to raise money. During the early years of the Society in North America, Father Friedrich Reichelt was the treasurer, first at

---

2. Fritz Bornemann et al., *A History of Our Society* (Rome: Collegio del Verbo Divino, 1981), pp. 417–18.

3. At the time, the person in charge of finances and fund raising was called the "procurator" (i.e., "the one who cares for [the material well-being of the members]." At the province level, he was called the provincial procurator, and at the local level he was called the house procurator. In recent years, the word "treasurer" has been substituted for "procurator" and is more intelligible to American ears. Unless the term "procurator" is contained in a quotation, we will also use the term "treasurer." But the reader should realize that procurator was the usual title used by SVDs for their financial and fund-raising officers until the 1960s and early 1970s.

the technical school, and then for the province, until he was replaced in 1925 by Father Bernard Bonk, who handled Society finances from then until the early years of the depression. Bonk was a German who had been ordained at St. Gabriel's in Austria in 1915. One of the many Germans who came to Techny not long after World War I, he taught for several years before his appointment as provincial treasurer. Credit was easy, times were good, everything was booming, and everybody was investing—and investing was akin to speculating. There was no end in sight to the possibilities and few were immune to the fever.

Bonk was trusted universally. Father Hagspiel recalls that when he came into office, his predecessor, Father Burgmer, gave him the advice to leave everything pertaining to finances to Father Bonk, because he not only knew best but would know "more than all the rest of us put together." Nevertheless, as the depression made investments in land and securities less valuable, doubts began to arise concerning whether Bonk had not ventured too far from the conservative financial practices that characterized this group of frugal Germans. Even the ever-cheerful Hagspiel, a great mission promoter, but not one who knew much about or worried a great deal about finances, began to have doubts and difficulties. Father Bonk, whose personal integrity was never in question, finally sought a new appointment from Father Hagspiel's successor as provincial, Hugo Aubry. With the agreement of the generalate, he transferred to the Philippines and took a post as professor and bursar at San Carlos College in Cebu.[4]

Father Aubry was a take-charge sort of person, and he would go on to be a local or provincial superior for the rest of his working years. When he died in his nineties, he was one of the oldest living SVDs. With a mischievous grin, living in active retirement in his beloved St. Michael's Mission House at Conesus, Aubry enjoyed telling young candidates that Father Janssen had once rejected him for membership because he felt his health was too weak. After undergoing a regimen of German homeopathic cures, Aubry walked across the whole of Germany to present his candidacy again, this time with success. In time, he outlived his entire generation in a life of ceaseless activity. His sometime nemesis, Father August Loechte, used to joke, "I want to die before Aubry and tell them in heaven what he was really like. A hard man. The way he keeps being appointed superior, I don't think they understand it." The times called for a decisive provincial superior, however, since the depression made many fear that the American SVD province could go bankrupt. And Hugo Aubry was that man.

A few months after he took office, on 3 December 1934, Father Aubry wrote his appraisal of the situation to Superior General Grendel. He stated flatly that to him and those he had consulted, it appeared nearly inevitable that the Society would suffer bankruptcy. There was some optimism because the Roosevelt admin-

---

4. By all accounts Father Bonk was a good missionary in the Philippines, and his courage was considerable. When the war broke out, the Japanese overran Cebu, took over the college, and began to use it for their own purposes, with which Father Bonk could not agree. Together with some students, he escaped to the mountains, where people escaping the Japanese invasion were plentiful, but food was scarce. Eventually he was captured, tortured, and finally executed on 29 August 1944. He was fifty-four years-old and had been in the Philippines for seven years. (Another source has it that he died on 10 November 1944.)

istration had undertaken measures that could bring stability on the national front. Within the SVD, there had been an upsurge in annuities. The situation was still critical, but there were grounds for hope if they returned to the tried-and-true methods of investing, where security is sought first of all, not the spectacular, the risky, or the speculative. Probably Aubry's most important move was the appointment of a new treasurer.

APPOINTMENT OF ARTHUR MELCHER AS TREASURER

As Father Aubry looked for a new provincial treasurer, the choice fell on Father Arthur Melcher. He had come to the States as a seminarian in 1924 with luggage consisting mostly of rock specimens for Techny's geologist, Father Stephan Richarz (brother of novice master Herman Richarz)—and his figure skates. Before coming to America, Arthur Melcher had experienced a difficult and eventful life. Raised as an orphan, first by his maternal grandmother, then by his father's brother, he "escaped" his uncle's strict care, according to his obituary, by entering the minor seminary in Holy Cross in Silesia (now Poland). Here he contracted tuberculosis, the same disease his mother had died from. He was 17 when he was drafted into the German army and, while fighting on the Western front, was captured by the British and taken to England as a prisoner of war, where he stayed until 1919, getting a head start in speaking English. In 1924 he was sent to Techny to study theology and was ordained in the United States in 1928. Immediately after, he was assigned to Bay St. Louis where he taught botany and was made treasurer of the seminary. A year later he was transferred to Miramar to teach the sciences and to take up the house treasurer's post for the next seven years. In view of Melcher's future, it is quite humorous to read the assessment written by the rector of Bay St. Louis of Melcher's year in the South: He praised Father Melcher's integrity as a priest and religious and acknowledged his ability as a teacher. However, he cautioned the provincial about making use of Father Melcher to manage finances, since he questioned his ability to handle money judiciously. The obituary from which this is taken goes on to say: "Superiors are not known for being infallible."

When Father Provincial Aubry began to look around for a new provincial treasurer, he thought of Miramar's treasurer, Arthur Melcher. He noted that Melcher, alone among all the house treasurers, had kept Miramar in the black during the peak years of the depression. Aubry's council was in favor of appointing him, so Melcher's name was sent to Superior General Grendel as the one to replace Bonk. Grendel appointed Father Melcher as provincial treasurer in 1935.

As Father Melcher took hold of his job and learned the depths of the problems in Society finances caused by the depression, periods of optimism alternated with bouts of anxiety for the future. At the time the province and the mission office were one corporation, with Melcher in charge. The houses, too, were mostly under Melcher's financial management, since most of them were deeply in debt and needed Techny's help. He became famous for squeezing every nickel before he permitted a disbursement of funds. Melcher's objections to proposed expenditures as ill-advised became a ritual at council meetings, and one man who had to deal with him later as mission treasurer succinctly put it, "He yelled a lot in meetings."

But, as Father Aubry had predicted, Arthur Melcher learned fast. Brother James Ryan, his assistant and secretary from the beginning, remembers that Melcher read the stock quotations every day and had a phenomenal memory of trends over time on all stocks in which he was invested. It was this command of detail and personal rectitude that made him the right man in difficult times.

Just as he kept a tight rein on anything in the Society in North America that cost money, he closely monitored the real estate companies, lawyers, and investment firms that handled the Society's property and money. Confident in Father Melcher's administrative abilities, those who loaned the Society money did not call in their loans. Annuities continued to come in from benefactors, and the obligations flowing from those contracts were regularly met. And when Father Melcher had reestablished everything on firm footings, he remembered the lessons he learned. Indeed, years after the struggle for financial stability was over, writing to Father Robert Hunter on 7 May 1949, Melcher said:

> Under no circumstances shall the SVD ever borrow from our Chicago banks! Our first class credit depends upon it and we shall maintain it. The bankers are extremely polite to you as long as you have money. When that runs out, they are ready to hang you. Just remember that! All our worthwhile properties were mortgaged when I came into office and I was fed up with the situation in just no time at all. We shall not start it again.

The secret of Father Melcher's success was the wise use he made of annuity funds sent by benefactors. These he carefully invested and always made prompt payment of interest due on these accounts. The benefactors of the Society in North America, from the beginning, had been generous to the Society. For Melcher, it was always clear that their primary reward was their share in the mission work of the Society. Never once did the SVD miss an annuity payment in his entire tenure, which continued until 1981. Indeed, never once did the Society miss an annuity payment since it wrote its first contract for $7,000 with a priest in the Cleveland Diocese in February 1904. As far as I can ascertain, the SVD was the first religious congregation in North America to write such annuity contracts. When he handed over his office to Father Chester Nowicki, who had been his assistant since 1971, Melcher was eighty-three and had been treasurer for forty years. He retired gracefully and probably gratefully as well, alert in mind and able to move around freely until his death at the age of ninety in 1988. His obituary recalled that his "life and ministry were characterized by integrity, reliability, steadfastness, stability and fidelity . . . More than anyone else, he made possible the growth and expansion of the Society in the States." And although he had the responsibility for millions of dollars during his tenure as treasurer, "He lived a dedicated religious life characterized by simplicity, and he spent very little on himself."

THE SPLIT INTO THREE PROVINCES

It had become evident by the early 1930s that trying to administer all the houses and parishes of the SVD in North America from Techny as a single province was becoming more difficult. Distances between the houses were too great, and the activities of the different areas too varied and diverse. The Society in North America was also growing in manpower, so there were enough people available to fill the new administrative positions. Partly as a result of a visitation he had made in 1937, Father Grendel wrote to the "Revered and Honorable Confreres of the North American Province" that the Holy See had given permission for the general council to divide the one province into three. They would be the Western Province headquartered at Techny, the Eastern Province with Girard as the provincial head-quarters, and the Southern Province with Bay St. Louis as the administrative center. There would still be a common scholasticate and novitiate and, for the time being, a common two-year college at Girard. The treasurer, for the missions and for the Catholic University of Peking, would remain centralized in the Western Province, while the Eastern Province, in close coordination with the central mission office would also continue the collection of mission funds.

Those critical or skeptical about the fairness of the distribution of funds when the province was divided have tended to overlook the fact that, at the time of the separation of provinces, the country as well as the Techny Province were still mired in the depression. What little Techny had, it shared equitably. *Nemo dat quod non habet.* The fact is that it was only subsequent to the separation of provinces (1940) and the end of World War II (1945) that Father Melcher's hard work and perspicacious financial management created a very solid financial basis for the now Chicago Province. This has enabled the province not only to support its own apostolates but, at the same time, to provide significant financial assistance to the other North American Provinces as well as to the Society's overseas missions. When apprized of the criticism and skepticism of the other U. S. Provinces, Father Melcher commented that, if he had been Provincial Treasurer in the Eastern Province, he would have made much more money than he ever made in the Midwest because, in his words, "The money is out East."

ESTABLISHING THE MISSION OFFICE

Before, during, and after the period when Father Melcher was stabilizing the Western Province's financial situation, a second successful agency of the Society in North America concerned with money was also under way. It is known to this day as the "mission office," a name that remains somewhat an anomaly for a society whose entire purpose was missionary. Its origins reach back to the mid-1920s, partly as a response to the American hierarchy's unsuccessful attempts to bring all mission fund-raising efforts directly under its control. But its establishment was owed at least as much to the structure of the SVD community and the need to coordinate the fund-raising efforts of mission bishops from around the world. In terms of inner-SVD operation, a special organ for mission fund raising was needed because, human nature being what it is, each house and province habitually maintained that the money they had raised could be spent best at home. The mission office, by contrast, would raise money *only* for overseas missions, and it would have a special obligation to raise mission consciousness.

Father Hagspiel drafted the first suggestions for such a coordinating office in

1925. Father de Lange, whom Hagspiel had recommended for the office, began setting up the office in the late 1920s, but was soon transferred to the generalate in Rome in 1932. The post remained vacant until 1934 when the mission office was officially established and Hagspiel himself, whose term as provincial had just expired, was put in charge as the first mission treasurer. This was done in spite of his protests that he did not want to be involved in money matters. But he was appointed to the office, and the choice was perfect. From the beginning, when the structure, functions, and purpose of the mission office were being clarified, the mission treasurer was to do more than just collect money. In a set of guidelines issued on 22 July 1927 by Superior General Gier, two objectives other than fund raising were assigned to the office—to foster vocations for the missions, and to develop mission awareness and interest. This last, it was suggested, could be done by writing news releases, and the like. These last two tasks were right up Hagspiel's alley; he was very good at fostering vocations and had a proven record of success in promotion and public relations.

Hagspiel was appointed on 6 June 1934 by Gier's successor, Joseph Grendel. Grendel emphasized that Hagspiel was appointed in the first place for mission promotion. At the beginning, the mission office was under the authority of the provincial and the provincial treasurer, but the exact reporting line was ambiguous. Consequently, relations between various offices and departments in North America were addressed and clarified in a nineteen-page protocol dated 29 July 1937 that spelled out the results of Father Grendel's visitation of North America earlier that year. Much of this document dealt with finances, drafted as it was during the middle of the depression and during Hitler's seizure of power. One senses in it Grendel's attempt to put administrative matters on a solid footing before the impending war broke out. When the province centered on Techny was split first into three, then into four (Northern, Eastern, Southern, and Western) provinces, each province developed its own mission office.

Over the years, various treasurers have filled the post at Techny. Bruno Hagspiel was the first. Father Herman Patzelt, who will return in this history, was another for a brief time, and was followed by the capable Fathers Anthony May and William Hunter. Space restrictions will not permit us to tell their tale. What is possible and necessary is to jump ahead to the generalate administration of Johannes Schütte, which began in March 1958.

Father Schütte, who was the SVD generalate's mission secretary before being elected superior of the entire society, gave the office much greater prominence and put greater demands on it. Schütte decided to centralize the office of the mission treasurers in North America, lest too much effort and money be wasted on reduplication, promotion, public relations, collection. And he wanted it put directly under the generalate. Father Francis Kamp was his choice as director of the centralized mission office, which was to be located at Techny, where it has remained ever since.

FATHER KAMP AND THE MISSION OFFICE

If, as Father Ralph Wiltgen has noted, the public face of much of the first fifty years of the SVD in North America has "Hagspiel" stamped on it, in many ways the same could be said of Francis Kamp and the second fifty years. Ordained in 1947, Kamp was assigned to the high school seminary at East Troy, Wisconsin, to teach English, science, and public speaking. Like so many before him, Kamp had written articles for the various SVD magazines as a seminarian, so it was not long before he was made editor of *The Little Missionary*. In addition, he was appointed the founding director of Divine Word Publications and head of the Public Relations Department at Techny. When he was appointed National Mission Director by Father Schütte, he owed it to the superior general's recognition of the quality of his many ideas and suggestions in correspondence between them. Kamp himself would characterize the appointment and his life as national mission director as follows in 1997:

> This position became the turning point of my life as an SVD. The welfare of our overseas missionaries became the driving force of all my activities for the next quarter of a century and more. My work was accomplished by establishing a personal interest in missionaries around the world and attempting to meet their many needs by telling our missionaries' stories to as many people as possible and encouraging them to pray for and support them.

The ways of gathering funds for the missions and of increasing mission awareness have changed over the years. At one time "ransoming pagan babies" was an attractive target of appeals in a day when missions in China were overwhelmed by the number of abandoned babies that they felt an obligation to care for. Today this approach would be viewed both as the result of bad theology and paternalistic as well. It is no small part of the fund raiser's art to be tasteful in what he highlights while casting appeals in ways that generate the help needed. That art was no small part of Kamp's success, but even more was owed to the self-evident concern he had both for the people among whom the missionaries worked and for the missionaries themselves. Ask any SVD who has worked overseas during the years of Kamp's tenure as national missions director and you will find a long list of acts Kamp and the mission office performed that go beyond mere efficiency and physical resources to a spirit of kindness and concern with which the office has been imbued.

In addition to collecting money for the missions, the mission office was given the responsibility for looking after missionaries on home leave. They were always given a complete medical and dental check-up, and frequently serious conditions needed to be treated. In the early days of the Society many missionaries died young, which was a tremendous loss in terms of the time and money spent in getting them educated to the brotherhood or priesthood. It is much better and surely more economical, not to mention humane, to keep them alive and well.

THE SVD CATHOLIC UNIVERSITIES OFFICE AND FATHER RALPH THYKEN

Another fund-raising effort of the Society in North America, now part of the mission office, deserves at least brief mention in this chapter, as we discuss the maturing of the Society in the U.S. It is the group that came to be known as the

"SVD Catholic Universities Office." Its inception occurred when the Society was asked to take over Fu Jen University in Peking in the early 1930s. Because it was the first university entrusted to the Society, it would be a learning experience, and one of the first things learned was that running it would take a great deal of money. Post-World War I Germany, the Society's core and long its center of support, had little surplus money. And, as the Nazis consolidated their control of the government, it appeared likely it would be able to do even less. Holland, though wealthy, generous, and rich in vocations to the SVD, was a small country. Other relatively well-developed countries where the SVD missionaries worked, for example, Chile and Argentina, were barely able to support themselves, and could not be expected to do much for Fu Jen. Yet neither could Father Grendel, the superior general, put the main financial burden of Fu Jen on the province in America. As we have seen above, it had enough to do to keep its own head above water. The central mission office was just getting itself organized at Techny and would have *all* of the SVD missions as its responsibility. They could not be made to suffer to keep one university afloat. Yet it would have to be the U.S. that would have to bear the brunt of the cost of running Fu Jen.

To solve the problem, Grendel stepped totally outside of the Society's traditions to create a special office to collect money exclusively for Fu Jen University, not for the SVD as such. In establishing it, he took care to keep this office separate from the SVD's other efforts. The next question was who to put in charge of this office. Bruno Hagspiel and Clifford King were mentioned, but Hagspiel declined and King did not seem the right man. Father Ralph Thyken was finally appointed. The initial plan for the "Peking Procure" was to set up offices in New York, Chicago, and San Francisco. Scaling back the plans, Thyken opened an office in Chicago alone.

By background and temperament Thyken was ideal for the position, even though his tenure was not without problems. After ordination he was first assigned to Girard as house treasurer. He had always been interested in writing and, like so many of the other early SVDs, quickly saw the value of this kind of activity. In 1929 he was recalled to Techny to be Father Bonk's assistant as provincial treasurer. As assistant procurator, he also took over as editor of *Our Missions*. So when the Society began looking for someone to take over the financial care of Fu Jen, it was no disadvantage that "Father Ralph," as he became known to millions of benefactors, quickly came to mind as the right person to take over the task of collecting and promoting for Fu Jen. Following tried and true methods, he established clubs, sold Christmas cards, and promoted vigil lights. He invested wherever he thought he could make money, even to the extent of purchasing a boat to transport goods along the Chinese coast. Above all, he canvassed for Mass stipends and annuities with a zeal that caused him and his office a good deal of embarrassment with church authorities outside the Society. Moreover, the independence from normal American SVD structures that his office claimed to have from Father Grendel would become the source of further conflict.

In fairness it must be said that Ralph's problems were not all of his own making. Greater demands were placed on him as the years passed. When Fu Jen in Beijing was closed, his office was not closed, but expanded. Father Ralph was given the responsibility of financing Nanzan University in Japan, the University of San Carlos in the Philippines, the new Fu Jen on Taiwan, seminaries at Fatima in Portugal, in India, Japan, Philippines, Mexico, even in Maynooth, Ireland. Often, it seems that money was sent to the generalate for such institutions without due consideration whether the SVD Universities Office could afford it and continue with sufficient reserves to meet obligations.

By 1970 Father Ralph was seventy-one and in poor health, less and less able to stay on top of his busy office. Ominously, no one had been groomed to take over his office when he resigned in 1970. The mission office, directed by Father Kamp, was assigned to assume Father Ralph's position that year and brought the office into order, while maintaining SVD Catholic Universities as a distinct corporation. Father Ralph, who, it is estimated, raised over twenty-five million dollars for the SVD higher education effort worldwide, died in Queen of Angels Hospital in Los Angeles on 11 January 1975 of the heart problems with which he had been afflicted for several years. His body was brought back to Techny for burial.

DEVELOPMENTS IN THE 1950S AND 1960S

Taking the Name "Divine Word Missionaries"

Before moving to more important matters, an item that, although not earth-shaking, was nevertheless important at the time and exercised the creative talents of many people almost from the beginning of the SVD in North America. In many ways, it marks symbolically the emergence of a distinct North American SVD identity. How should the members of the Society be known in North America? The terms "Techny Fathers and Brothers" and "Techny Missionaries" were popular in the beginning and for many years afterward. But this name became more problematic as the Society expanded to other parts of North America, especially as it expanded in the African-American apostolate. It was important, too, because English was spreading as the standard international language for commerce and cultural exchange. Furthermore, as English, Irish, Filipino, Australian, and Indian Provinces became established, it seemed more and more important to have an international English-language title. The most common appellation was "SVD" used as shorthand for the Society and "SVDs" for its members, but many felt the Society needed a name that said in a few words what the community was about.

Some suggested using a variation on the terms common in Italian and Spanish, namely, *Verbiti* or "Verbists." This, according to Father Joseph Shendill, writing in the Society's journal *Verbum* in 1961, was quickly rejected. The problem was not a new one. As early as 5 April 1934, in a letter written in English and preserved in the Techny archives, Father Hagspiel, then provincial at Techny, wrote to Father Superior General Grendel, inquiring whether they had problems with the name in Europe. In that letter, he averts to the fact that members of the province were trying to substitute "Divine Word Fathers" for "Techny Fathers" and "Society of the Divine Word," arguing that the one is too local and the other too cumbersome. Then he noted:

Especially our houses outside of Techny would probably prefer the name "Divine Word Fathers" over "The Techny Fathers," although I doubt whether these efforts will achieve anything at all. Another difficulty in this regard has been presented by just a few Brothers, who think they are slighted, if only the Divine Word Fathers are mentioned and not the Brothers also. In German you have, as far as the name goes, the same difficulty, but I wonder if the Brothers over there have made the same difficulty as just a few of them did here. May I hear from you concerning this matter as soon as possible?

One detects a note of condescension to the brothers in Hagspiel's letter, perhaps a foreshadowing of complaints yet to come on the part of the brothers that the priests too easily assumed that they were the key members of the Society.

The issue was not resolved until 1953, when Father Ralph Wiltgen was director of publicity. He suggested to Father Lawrence Mack, the provincial who had appointed him to this post, that "Divine Word Missionaries" might work very nicely, and it did. Father Mack initiated the change in a circular of 24 November 1954, and the name was quickly adopted. In all news releases and other publications, the term "Divine Word Missionaries" was to take the place of "SVD" and the "SVDs." In the late 1950s, it was decided that all SVD mission houses would change their names to "Divine Word Seminary." It was not easy for houses that had been known as "Holy Ghost Mission Seminary" or "St Michael's Mission Seminary" to change overnight, and some members were still using the old stationery many years later. Whether they did so out of preference for the old names or out of the legendary spirit of poverty that characterized an older generation of Divine Word Missionaries, it is hard to say. Nonetheless, it is also true that the new name remains a mouthful. Although attempts to get members to stop using the abbreviation SVD resembled nothing so much as attempts of the language police to enforce political correctness in the 1980s, SVD still tumbles so easily from the tongue that one doubts it will ever completely be supplanted by the new term.

Several more important concerns dominated the Society in the 1950s and 1960s. The first had to do with accreditation and internal changes in the educational program. The second with a rush of building and remodeling. The third with vocations. The three were interrelated. Let us begin with accreditation.

Accreditation and Educational System Changes

By the middle 1950s, the day had passed when ordination automatically gave a priest the ability to teach or the graduates of and departees from a diocesan or religious order seminary entrée into union training programs, colleges, or professions. "Professionalization" was underway in all fields, and the Divine Word Missionary education program could not avoid getting involved. Soon the move to accreditation would embrace all education units, but it would start in the high school seminaries, where great effort and expense were put into upgrading libraries, sending teachers to universities to work on higher degrees, upgrading facilities to meet both state standards and those of various accrediting associations. Self-studies became routine; house, provincial, and interprovincial committees were set up to monitor and facilitate all this.

Connected with this effort were long discussions on the question *where* the various units were to be established. Should the central junior college be at Miramar, Conesus, or Epworth? Where should the seminary for "belated vocations"[5] be placed? How could one tailor the requirements of SVD training to the demands of accrediting agencies? Various combinations were tried, new facilities were built. The desirability of seeking accreditation, once accepted, seems never to have been seriously questioned, despite the great sacrifices that had to be made to accomplish this.

At meetings held in October 1959, Superior General Johannes Schütte was at Techny for a crucial meeting on accreditation, at which the necessity of accreditation was established without difficulty. The minutes record him enunciating a crucial principle: "Our principle objective is the religious missionary priesthood. Competency in a secondary profession should also be sought, but only to the extent that training for the secondary profession does not interfere with training for the religious missionary priesthood." Father Schütte then went on to say, "Our goal should be that ALL MEN WHO GO TO THE MISSIONS SHOULD HAVE A MASTER DEGREE BEFORE THEY GO" (capitals in original).

He said this was necessary in Japan for prestige for the priests in parish work. A master's degree was obviously useful for anyone directly involved in school work, as was mostly the case in the Philippines and Africa, but also in Indonesia and India. Even for the bush missionary in New Guinea, who would likely become a supervisor of schools, a higher degree would be a great advantage. A fortiori, it was necessary for those teaching in the high school seminaries to have a higher degree if schools were to be accredited. Accreditation of SVD educational institutions would, in its turn, facilitate the process of the newly ordained getting a master's degree before leaving for overseas assignments.

Another reason for hurrying the accreditation process that was often mentioned was related to the huge percentage of students who dropped out of the seminary at all stages—to "return to the world," as the phrase then current had it—where they would finish their education. Not to offer them the benefits of an accredited educational program, it came to be felt, was to do them an injustice.

With the principle of pursuing accreditation quickly accepted, much discussion in the October 1959 meeting took up the problem of where the various units would be placed, with participants from the existing units plumping for their own place as the ideal spot for this or that enterprise: novitiate, junior college, school for belated vocations, and the college and philosophy programs for professed seminarians. Again the question of the timing and length of the novitiate came up. All this had a profound effect on future formation. The discussion of the length of novitiate resulted in returning the novitiate to its former place, after the first two years

---

5. The term "belated vocations" referred to candidates who presented themselves after the "normal" time for entry, that is, in the first year of or during high school. In the days when priesthood candidates had to be able to follow philosophy and theology lectures in Latin, it was important to provide training that would bring belated candidates up to the standards of candidates who had gone through the full minor seminary and junior college classical education program with their heavy emphasis on languages.

of college, and making the second year of novitiate coincide with the first year of philosophy. Miramar figured prominently as the place to put some or all of the units involved in such a change. With the first two years of college coming before the "canonical" or strict year of novitiate and philosophy (the major subject taught in the second two years of college), everybody agreed that novitiate and philosophy should be in the same place.

As he had previously, Father Edward Norton pointed out that the trend in American seminary education was toward four-year colleges. He urged that a binding decision should be delayed "because it would be premature at this time." His advocacy of a four-year college program fell on deaf ears.

The years between 1960 and 1965 were full of decisions to do one thing and another. During that time, the first two years of college and the belated vocations department were located at Miramar. The novitiate and philosophical studies went to Conesus. A new junior college building was put up at Epworth, Iowa, a house that had been closed for some years. Once Epworth was built and standing handsomely in the cornfields of eastern Iowa, the pattern of education that Norton had urged seemed less a stretch to those in the educational hierarchy. It was quickly decided to delay novitiate till after college and reduce it to one year, while all four years of college would be combined at Epworth. At the start of the 1965–66 school year, the new pattern was instituted.

During these same years, which coincided with the sessions of Vatican Council II, enrollments to the high school seminaries diminished for a variety of reasons. We shall discuss this and the consequences below. Briefly said, however, the minor seminaries fell out of favor. Although it would be argued for years whether closing the minor seminaries was the result of changes in American Catholic culture or the cause of a decline in the number of young men who would enter religious life and the priesthood, the 1970s brought the need to cope with a steep drop in the number of candidates presenting themselves to enter the Society of the Divine Word and all other religious communities. But this is getting ahead of our story, for in the 1950s and through the 1960s, the problem the SVD and many other communities faced was an abundance of candidates overwhelming their physical capacity to house them. Virtually every society built facilities to cope with that problem in the early 1960s, only to find at the end of the 1970s that they had white elephants on their hands.

The Society Begins a Building Boom

Despite the impression that the preceding section may have given of a recruitment and educational system in trouble, the reality is that the North American SVD was full of optimism in these years. Partially, this can be traced to a cultural optimism that makes Americans take it for granted that every problem has a solution. For non-Americans, however, that same trait is experienced as ambiguous—irritating to many as an expression of a naivete that overlooks many tragic problems they judge cannot be fixed. It is, though, attractive to others who dislike the fatalism and pessimism of other cultures represented in the Society. In any case, for some time after World War II, vocations seemed plentiful. And in the mid-1950s, the creative force of new formation directors in the high schools gave SVDs a feeling that their minor seminaries were improving as places for general social maturation and, because of accreditation, becoming much more up-to-date as academic training centers.

In the formation area, Father Edward Dudink, for example, initiated forms of student government at East Troy that saw the students themselves, by means of a student council, taking charge of student activities and even the ordinary discipline of student life in the house. When he became prefect (dean) of the junior college at Miramar in 1958, he introduced these methods there too, attempting to expand the area in which the older students could enjoy autonomy in their lives and grow in a spirit of responsibility and initiative. Dudink's innovations were not universally approved, since many felt the growth of student councils and such "democratic" methods of student governance were undermining the spirit of "obedience" that characterized the religious life students were preparing for. But for most SVDs and students, Dudink's methods and the growing number of priests with masters' degrees teaching in accredited education programs were part of an optimism about the future that warmed every American's heart in the the years after John F. Kennedy was elected president. Catholicism appeared to have found its place in the U.S., and the American SVD felt confident about its place in the world.

At the same time, some of the best newly ordained priests were put into recruiting for the newly accredited minor seminaries, the belated program, and the junior college. Ordination classes that would routinely reach thirty and forty were confidently predicted just as Vatican Council II was beginning in October 1962. To make that happen new buildings had to be put up. And no matter where a building went up, it seemed, Brother William Krick was to be found. He more than any single individual insured that everything in the plans was translated into solid craftsmanship on the ground from the way the excavation went to how the roofs were constructed. His eagle eye was the bane of many a contractor over the years, but the proof of his expertise was the quality of many of the buildings we shall describe. Let us, then, look briefly at some the most important developments.

Bordentown, New Jersey. Shortly after the split into three provinces in 1940, the Eastern Province bought an estate that had once belonged to Joseph Bonaparte, the elder brother of Napoleon I. After passing through several owners when Joseph returned to Europe in 1832, the estate, located in Bordentown, New Jersey, was purchased by the Society in 1941. After remodeling, it opened in 1947 as St. Joseph's Seminary for belated vocations to the priesthood. By tapping into a new pool of potential candidates, namely, those who were older but who felt they might have a vocation to the religious and missionary life, vocations would increase. No doubt there were older aspirants, but to bring these to the priesthood was a challenge and a struggle from the beginning, not least of all because of the overriding necessity at the time for everybody to learn Latin. Bordentown remained the belated vocation department until 1958 when it was changed to a high school seminary and the seminary for belated vocations was transferred to Miramar. At the same time the high school seminarians still at Miramar were transferred to Bordentown, where a wonderful set of buildings had been constructed near the old

Bonaparte mansion, which served as the faculty house. (The mansion would burn to the ground in a spectacular fire on 2 February 1983, which SVDs living there at the time recall with a mixture of exhilaration and sadness. The fire also forced the decision to close the minor seminary at Bordentown. It was a decision that seemed both inevitable and necessary to its proponents, because of dwindling enrollments, but considered by its opponents as tantamount to giving up on the only means of vocation recruitment that worked.)

Expansion into Canada. Not long after purchasing Bordentown, the Eastern Province began to ask whether plans to expand into French-speaking Quebec should be reconsidered or carried out. Canada was not exactly new for the SVD as a place of work. Father Albert Florian had been working in the wide open spaces of Canada's western provinces since the mid-1930s, ministering primarily to Czech and Slovak immigrants. In so doing he brought Canada as a new field of mission work to the attention of the superiors in the U.S. Finally the Society accepted the offer of a small polyglot parish in Chipman, a small town about 35 miles east of Edmonton in Alberta. Father Anthony Humel was to pioneer at Chipman and Father Joseph Faikus was appointed to assist him. Faikus spoke Slovak, Hungarian, and Croatian and understood Czech, Polish, and Russian, all useful languages in Chipman. The *Techny Chimes* of July 1939 says the following about this first Canadian foundation:

> In time other mission stations within a radius of five or ten miles may be developed and attempted from Chipman at Bruderheim, Lamont, and Ross Creek. For the present no mission house is contemplated but perhaps after some years of study and reconnoitering such a foundation may be found feasible. By its entrance into Canada the Society enjoys a great opportunity for missionary work in an up-and-growing country and for further expansion of its activities.

In the period we are dealing with, Father Joseph Eckert was asked to do a preliminary investigation of a likely place to start a minor seminary. Monsignor (i.e., Bishop) Ildebrando Antoniutti, a long-time friend and supporter of the Society, happened to be the Apostolic Delegate of Canada at the time and put the Society in contact with Arthur Douville, Bishop of St. Hyacinthe, who approved of the foundation of a mission house near Granby, some 50 miles from Montreal. On 13 April 1948, SVD Superior General Aloisius Grosse-Kappenberg had written Antoniutti about the matter in a way that puts the entire matter in context:

> It is just at this time when our missionary Bishops and Superiors are everywhere calling for more help and when new horizons of missionary opportunities are rising everywhere, we feel extremely shorthanded due to our heavy losses in Europe during the war and in the general dearth of vocations which are the hope of the future.

Given the number of missions in Africa and Asia where French was the common language, getting a ready supply of French-speaking missionaries was an attractive proposition. The new foundation in Canada would start with Bruno Hagspiel as the builder, first rector, and publicist. It was placed in the Eastern Province. By 1951, three years after its opening, St. John the Baptist Mission House had eighty students in three classes. On 21 September 1951, the new rector, Father Albert St. Pierre, a French Canadian from New York State, wrote the superior general: "I wish we could have this great number of vocations in the United States . . . our houses down there are far from full." Over time, some talented missionaries came from Granby, but the numbers never became as high as the beginnings at Granby foreshadowed.

Perrysburg, Ohio. Still another new high school seminary was begun at Perrysburg, Ohio, along the banks of the Maumee River near Toledo, in the mid-1950s. Intended to tap a new market and implement a principle established earlier (that the distance minor seminarians should travel to a Divine Word high school should be reduced greatly), it opened its doors to the first class of seventeen students in 1956. Initially it grew quite dramatically, so much so that a much larger complex of buildings was constructed and ready for occupancy by the fall of 1960. Perrysburg would eventually become one of the SVD's most beautiful houses, the center of which was a magnificent church with a dramatic roof design that spoke volumes about the high hopes of the Society not just for Perrysburg, but for the other seminaries as well.

Riverside, California. By 1946 it was clear to all that dust-bowl era migrations to California and the immense growth of defense industries on the West Coast had made California the "Golden State." Huge numbers of Catholic ethnics, newly discharged from service in World War II, were deciding to remain in California. Migrations of Hispanics to work in the burgeoning agricultural industries or with hopes of achieving the so-called American dream by finding high-paying jobs in factories meant that California would bend and then break the rule that the West was Protestant. The West was also short of priests and its bishops welcomed religious orders to settle there. Any religious order that was serious about its future had to think about locating there and recruiting there. Thus, in 1956, the SVD opened a new minor seminary in Riverside, sixty miles east of Los Angeles. For the first years of work in the West, operations there were part of the Southern Province, governed out of Bay St. Louis. In 1964, the West split off from the South as a separate province dedicated to St. Therese of the Child Jesus. The location in Riverside had been an orange grove estate, but as with the vineyard in Conesus, expectations that the orange grove would produce great income for the province were never fulfilled.

Epworth, Iowa. We have already discussed the momentous October 1959 meetings that decided on pursuing accreditation. On an interim basis, though it was not clearly a temporary location when the first two years of college and the belated school were shifted to Miramar in 1958, the college would be in the East. It would not remain there for long. As the result of continuing discussions, it seemed logical to locate the junior college nearer the center of the country, thus making the distance students would have to travel from the South and the West more manageable. The decision was to erect a new college at Epworth. It was the biggest construction project of all those that occurred in this time of almost frantic building. In September 1964, Epworth opened its doors again as a completely new and impressive facility, this time as a multimillion dollar college with accommodations for 160 seminarians and 25 faculty and staff. In the fall of 1965, the newly professed class of novices that had begun their novitiate at Conesus in 1963, the class that had begun novitiate in 1964, and the class that would have begun novitiate at Conesus in 1965, all converged on Epworth, in one fell swoop overwhelming the brand new edifice's living facility and making real Edward Norton's longtime vision of a single, unified four-year college in one place. Critics, however, would answer: "But why in the cornfields of Iowa?" To which the classic response was, "The majority of Divine Word Missionaries will work in rural environs. Much of their education should take place in similar circumstances."

Washington, D.C. One last major construction project was Divine Word College in Washington, D.C. It began as a place where newly ordained priests would spend a year being introduced into the pastoral life of a priest in a program that was called the "Pastoral Year." Since the decision that every priest who could do so was to get a master's degree had also been made, and since Washington was the site of several good universities, the pastoral year program was placed there. During this year, the newly ordained missionaries, all of whom had been given their mission assignments before they were ordained, also pursued a graduate program that the priest and his future bishop and provincial superior had agreed upon. Although the program began its existence in several rented houses near Catholic University in Northeast Washington, pressure soon mounted to have something more permanent, so an impressive building was erected on Michigan Avenue and dedicated in 1962. Helping in the decision to build it was the existence of insurance money from the Techny press fire that could be spent only on the press or in building an educational institution.

Elsewhere: Upgrading, Remodeling, Expanding. In addition to all the building we have described, other houses were upgrading their facilities. East Troy first put up a Quonset hut gymnasium and stage to provide recreation facilities for the students. That was followed by a new classroom and dormitory building, a permanent gymnasium, a beautiful new chapel, and a convent for the sisters who did the cooking and laundry for the growing community of high school students. Later a new faculty house would be built, unfortunately just as high school vocations began to plummet.

At Conesus, an entire new wing went up as the clerical novitiate, and later the philosophy program was located there too. Conesus also housed the brothers' novitiate and a brother candidate school. Its design was ambitious, and the location on a hill in the Finger Lakes region was beautiful. The scale reflected the desire of the Eastern Province to have facilities the equal of Techny's and of Father Aubry's plans for a major pilgrimage site and basilica dedicated to St. Michael the Archangel. The designs, though, were pared back eventually for lack of money, much to the disappointment of Father Aubry who continued to run St. Michael's

League and raise money for the basilica well into his nineties. The new building that was actually constructed was occupied by juniorate[6] students in vows in the fall of 1956.

Girard upgraded its facilities also during the 1950s, with a new building, including a new boiler room, laundry, and kitchen. Miramar, too, was busy adding a new wing to the north side of the building that dozens of Divine Word Missionaries remember with great fondness and not a little pride in the hardiness they developed living there. The top floor of the old building was a dormitory with large, factory-style, crank out windows. Legend has it that the windows bowed so far inward that when a strong wind blew off the ocean not only did copious amounts of water get in through the cracks but also an occasional seagull.

In spite of the fact that the whole vocation issue was still very unsettled, construction went on. Bordentown, also, began a building expansion in 1961. At Bay St. Louis new buildings were going up. Not one of the major educational units of the Society in North America was left out of this tremendous building boom of the 1950s and 1960s. The bulk of this extensive construction and renovation—according to Brother James Ryan, who worked closely with Father Melcher during these years—was financed by the Northern Province and its provincial finance office under the direction of Father Melcher. And with Father Melcher in charge of the financing, when a building was finished, it was also paid for.

THE LINGERING PROBLEM:
VOCATIONAL RECRUITMENT, RETENTION, AND DROPOUTS

If the purposes of the SVD in establishing its impressive minor seminary and college system was to provide huge numbers of missionary priests and brothers for the missionary work of the church, all this effort produced ambiguous results. Viewed from another perspective, if the SVD was also imbuing the laity with a sense of vocational identity and deep spirituality, there is very little in its results that were ambiguous, for SVD alumni generally departed the Society with rich memories that translated into devotion to the church wherever they went.

The Society's leaders always accepted the fact that a great number of those who came would leave. They made it clear to candidates that, while they could remain in its seminaries while they were resolving doubts about joining, once they had decided that life as a missionary religious brother or priest was not for them, they were to depart. Whether the number of departures was acceptable and whether all the effort put into recruitment and education could be justified were problematic. An unsigned communication sent in 1951 to Superior General Aloisius Grosse-Kappenberg in Rome surveyed the fate of entrants to Miramar from 1941 to 1951. According to this report, from 1942 to 1946 vocations were plentiful and the two vocation directors, Fathers Daniel Driscoll and William Hunter, were to be given the credit. After these

---

6. "Juniorate" was the term used to describe the program of seminarians who had finished high school and novitiate, and had taken their first vows. They followed a curriculum roughly like that of a classical first and second year college. It emphasized Latin, Greek, English, and the natural sciences, and it was designed to prepare the seminarian for the two years of philosophical and four years of theological studies that would precede final vows and ordination.

two vocation directors were reassigned after only two years in the position, others replaced them and the numbers went down, The blame was put on ineffective vocational directors. The solution? Put the best men on the road to recruit and put more men to work on recruitment. Another solution was to make the Society better known: "we need more publicity," and "the publicity we need is good publicity."

The report goes on to say that competition for vocations was increasing and that sometimes it was almost cutthroat, with the vocational director from one society running down the work and value of another society to boys who might be interested in the priesthood or brotherhood. The reader of this report today will, no doubt, marvel that there is no questioning whether modern advertising methods were the proper method to attract men to the religious and missionary life, a life that offers few of the ego-enhancing rewards advertising and publicity are able to draw on to motivate. Were the heavy dropouts that would occur later among men recruited to the SVD, the diocesan priesthood, and to other orders during this period, the critical contemporary reader begs to ask, to some extent, the result of recruiting boys with implicit promises of a kind of fulfillment without the cross that religious and missionary life could never fulfill?

To return to the 1951 report, in that period the most disturbing trend, according to an anonymous author, related to the high rate of dropouts from the seminary:

> We are getting too much unfavorable publicity. I refer to departures. We must expect losses in High School. We are sorry when Miramarians leave the novitiate, but we can explain these losses quite easily when we are asked. But we run into difficulties when we are questioned about departures after the novitiate . . . And there are so many losses after novitiate. There are only ten Miramarians in the Seminary at Techny on June 21st [1951] . . . I do not say that any superior is at fault, but there are so many losses every year. Often the boys apply for entrance into the Diocesan Seminary and the authorities wonder. The way things have been going of late years, about half of the students from Miramar who go through our novitiate and take their first vows quit before they get through the Seminary. And surprising is the number of students who develop nervous tension after their novitiate.

The hope of the Eastern Province was to have their own novitiate, college, and philosophy program. It was thought that for a province to be complete, it should have all of these divisions under its own control. In fact, for a time this happened. In 1949 the novitiate was divided. High school graduates from the Eastern Province stayed in the East and had their novitiate at Conesus, New York. Although St. Paul's Mission House at Epworth, Iowa, became the central juniorate from 1952 until 1955, the juniorate was relocated to Conesus in 1955. Epworth then became a school for belated vocations for two years. In 1958 the clerical novitiate at Techny was closed and also moved to Conesus where it remained until 1965.

There were some asking deeper questions even then, as is shown in a round of correspondence between Lawrence Mack, the provincial of the Western (Techny) Province, and Bishop Adolf Noser, at this time the Vicar Apostolic of Alexishafen in New Guinea. The highlights are well worth quoting at length because Mack and

Noser were among the canniest and most intelligent in their generation. They were also men who looked below the surface to discern the deeper causes of what was occurring. On 29 September 1955, Noser wrote to Mack.

> It is quite depressing for us in the missions to hear of the annual exodus of so many men after the Novitiate, for it causes our hopes of help to drop almost to freezing point. I just do not understand why so many should drop out after the thorough Novitiate and have been wondering whether other Congregations have the same high rate. Must one say that all these men who leave really have no vocation or only found it out just now? or does a fair proportion of them become priests elsewhere? The fact that it is an annual recurrence does make it very serious and deserving of a very earnest and objective investigation. In our seminary days comparatively few, as a rule, left after the passing through of the Novitiate. Perhaps it is the spirit of the times; perhaps it is something else for which there is a remedy, and it is a heavy responsibility, for the salvation of some thousands of souls in the missions may depend on men persevering or not persevering in their calling.

In this letter, Noser hints at the possibility that times may have changed, but does not dwell on this. He also wonders whether other congregations are having the same problems. From Mack's response, we are given to understand that they were. Mack's letter of 15 October 1955 is interesting in spelling out some of the thinking of the time.

> Your Excellency's letter of September 29 touches upon a sore spot which has been bothering us for some time. Out of 134 Seminarians [in vows studying philosophy and theology] 11 left us during the past year. Out of 73 Juniors 10 did not renew vows in September last. This is the average mortality for the past four or five years. Of the Seminarians who left us this year, one was rejected by the General Council, two were advised by the Provincial Council [to leave], one had to go because he failed for the second time in Philosophy. The rest left of their own accord. Of the ten Juniors one was rejected by the General Council, one had to leave because he failed in four branches. The remainder went of their own accord . . . Of the eleven Seminarians who left the past year, only three want to go on for the priesthood . . .

Mack continues:

> In trying to explain the heavy losses each year, I can give only my own opinion. However, I would wish to add that other Fathers agree.
>   First of all, in addition to all the dioceses nearly all religious institutes of the Church are competing for vocations. High pressure is exerted in recruiting boys who later defect. Furthermore, some of our Vocational Directors have not made it clear that we are religious, missionaries. Some of the students reach the Novitiate before they really learn the nature of the institute. They make an heroic effort during the Novitiate but later prefer not to

follow our life. Add to this the fact that our lack of personnel prevents us from making the Society better known in the States with the consequence that we do not receive enough applicants to be selective in admitting candidates. Without doubt, the young man has changed. He no longer has the stamina, the maturity of former generations.

A good percentage are told by their confessors to leave because of impurity. Other forms of selfishness play a leading role with many others who leave. All this is traceable to a lack of the spirit of sacrifice. The proximate cause of this deficiency is lack of spirituality.

For years I have been of the conviction that the appointment of a Spiritual Director in our Seminaries, whose only duty would be to give conferences for the Seminarians and hold ratios [the Latin word *ratio* was used for one-on-one conferences of members with superiors] who would be no official in any other capacity, would do away with much of our trouble. I proposed this matter to the last General Chapter. I suppose one reason for failure to appoint a Spiritual Director is the lack of proper personnel to care for our candidates at the home base.

The fact that other institutes have similar troubles is no remedy but does offer some consolation in as far as it shows that our Society is not completely responsible for our losses. Recently I spoke with the superior of a seminary in a highly rated religious society in the States. He had charge of the Seminarians in College and Philosophy. He told me that the last man of a class of 75 who had begun first year minor seminary had just left. By the end of college there was not one left of 75 who had entered the first year High School.

A few comments are in order. Father Mack's last figure confirms that many men were delaying their final decision as long as possible. Were the reasons Mack speculated to be the causes the real ones? It is hard to know how the case could be proved. In any case, the major blame was laid by Mack at the feet of the seminarian. But the question raised above must also be considered as possibly relevant. Vocation ads made their appeal to "the all-American boy," and the all-American boy loved sports. Vocational literature and the films emphasized the sports one would enjoy in a high school seminary: skating and basketball in winter, baseball and handball in the spring, football in the fall. The object was to get boys interested in the minor seminary. Once there, their suitability for the missionary and religious life could be sorted out.

There was, though, no cynicism in Noser's or Mack's letters. What clearly concerned Noser was the "salvation of souls" in an age that took the possibility of the damnation of the unbaptized very seriously. Compared to the numbers of unbaptized in the non-Christian world, the number of missionaries seemed small. Noser and Mack were among the many for whom SVD institutional success was not the key goal. That success was necessary to achieve the greater goal, winning the world not just to Christ but to the Catholic Church.

To give the reader a sense of where American SVDs were laboring, here is a list of the countries and numbers of American SVDs as of Christmas 1946, a decade before the Noser-Mack correspondence. This is taken from the roll of those to whom the *Techny Chimes* was sent that year. The list is probably the most accurate reflection of the results of the Society's efforts in North America to prepare and send missionaries in the forty years since accepting the first candidates.

China	32
Philippines	27
New Guinea	21
Africa	14
Australia	4
Dutch East Indies	2
Italy (Rome)	2
Ireland	1
Canada	1
England	1
Total	**105**

These numbers do not, it should be stressed, include the considerable number of men working as missionaries in the African-American apostolate or in other direct parish ministries. It should be remembered, too, that the SVD was a semi-monastic organization. Many members, especially brothers, were involved in support roles. It was part of the ethos that the members should do everything possible to run the houses and that the money saved should be sent to the overseas missions. Brothers did the skilled work. Seminarians and brother candidates took care of domestic chores such as cleaning, washing dishes, folding laundry, and gardening. Everyone, often including the priests, pitched in when special help was required at harvest times and on special projects. Indeed, some of the fondest memories of SVDs and their alumni are of summer days at Techny bringing in hay and helping with the threshing of wheat and oats. To those memories others will add brilliant fall days at Conesus picking grapes. Many of the other houses had farms to cultivate. Every seminarian and priest was imbued with the philosophy that *all* work was holy, that they would have to supervise or carry out major portions of the construction of buildings, such as their own houses, clinics, and schools in the missions. Thus a fuller picture of the results of their work is shown in the following statistics of those living and working in the American provinces in 1946:

Fathers	201
Scholastics	67
Juniors	33
Clerical Novices	52
Brothers	122
Brother Novices	3
Brother Candidates	11
Minor Seminarians	377
Total	**866**

MAJOR CHANGES IN THE LATE 1960S

As late as the mid-1960s, the kind of SVD community spirit that had been lived since the 1880s seemed to be thriving. The numbers of recruits entering the minor seminaries and brother candidate programs were high. They were so high, indeed, that it was possible to ignore the fact that retention rates continued to go down. We shall be discussing in greater detail the kind of ferment that began to occur during and after the Second Vatican Council, and for reasons of space we will not give the figures that show how retention was becoming a greater problem. Suffice it to say that by 1968 a major shift had occurred. Many SVDs, both in educational and vocation recruitment work, began to question whether minor seminaries were the right way to train future religious missionaries. Without passing judgment on any of the sides in these vigorous arguments, we turn to the study that was devised to analyze what was happening, sort out the options, and help the Society plan a way forward.

The CARA Study

In the early 1970s, the Society commissioned the Center for Applied Research in the Apostolate (CARA) to study their high school seminaries. The SVD study was not the first look at minor seminaries undertaken by CARA. In 1975, in his preface to the protocol on the SVD seminaries, Father John V. O'Connor, SJ, CARA's executive director, stated:

> In the six high school seminaries which it maintains, the Society of the Divine Word found itself with problems similar to those besetting other high school seminary administrators. It courageously undertook to seek realistic solutions to the problems through an intensive evaluation of its seminary programs and costs.

The study calls attention to the fact that problems in the high school seminaries were not peculiar to the SVD. Indeed, according to the report, there was solid evidence that the SVD high schools were better than most in their various formation programs. The report has this to say in its first conclusion and observation:

> Today [1975] all six seminaries [Bay St. Louis, Bordentown, East Troy, Perrysburg, Riverside, Girard] . . . have adequate, even promising programs. (In fact, in terms of their formation programs, the SVD seminaries in general were well above the average of all the seminaries represented at the CARA minor seminary workshops this summer, which included over half of all minor seminaries in the country.) From the standpoint of adequacy and promise of current programs, there is no indication that any seminary should be closed.

It was suggested that the promise the seminaries still gave should be tested for four more years before any drastic decisions were made. Several responses, however, had been decided already: Girard had closed as an independent free-standing high school seminary and had amalgamated with St. Mark's, the diocesan high school seminary. Bordentown had begun to accept high school seminarians from other congregations into their high school seminary. In both cases this was done to ensure sufficient enrollment to enable an adequate and genuine high school experience. CARA pegged this number at about one hundred.

But CARA also pointed out that in 1975, it took, on average, ten entering high school freshmen to get one graduating senior to enter the central college at Epworth. One in four of those entering college went on to novitiate, while three out of four starting the novitiate took vows and went on to the seminary or advanced brother-training programs. About fifty percent of those who took first vows lasted through the four years of theology to reach ordination. Analogous figures could have been given for the brotherhood. The conclusion was that "to produce a single ordination, on the average 107 freshmen have to start out in the high schools."

But nothing seemed to improve either the recruitment or retention numbers. Looking back from the late 1990s, we can see that the general collapse of the minor seminary begins in the late 1960s; experimentation and improvements continue through the 1970s; closures begin during the 1980s. The last Divine Word Seminary high school to hold out was East Troy in Wisconsin, which closed in 1991. A method of recruiting boys and keeping them in special programs until they were ordained as young men had lasted since the Reformation in the sixteenth century. In hardly more than the twenty years from the close of Vatican Council II to 1985, it was demolished.

In a final letter to Mack on the subject of vocations, Noser had remarked, "If the cause [of so many leaving and the difficulty of recruiting] is an outside one—the spirit of the times—you can do little about it, and even vocation directors would have a hard problem to discern the true from the false . . ." Since the recruitment issue has been so important for the SVD and other religious congregations, and for the church as a whole, a few words outlining some of the factors that have gone into it in North America are in order.

Family demographics surely has something to do with the "vocation" crisis (as the recruitment and retention crisis is called in the church). Among other things, it is easier for parents to give one or two children out of seven or eight to religious life and the priesthood than to offer one of one or two. Another feature has to do with the length of commitment expected in our culture. As recently as seventy-five years ago, many who entered religious life or marriage at the age of twenty would be dead by forty or fifty years of age. Today the twenty year old can expect to live well into his seventies, many into their eighties. If one adds to this the immense changes experienced from the middle of the twentieth century, and which are likely to continue as far as we can see into the twenty-first, the young person is looking at a long commitment, indeed. Little in our culture makes him or her think that such a long commitment is a positive value. On the other side, we are seeing in the entrance of second-career candidates for priesthood and religious life another side of that coin, as persons who have had success in business or teaching, for instance, decide to enter religious life.

For the son or daughter of immigrants in the last century and even through the middle of the twentieth, one of the most obvious choices for educational advancement and high social status lay in the church. Since at least the 1960s, perhaps even earlier, other opportunities abounded, and the sons and daughters of European Catholics began choosing them. It is often said that young people are no longer willing to make the sacrifices necessary to become a priest or religious. Difficulties in "giving up the world" and accepting celibacy are often mentioned in this context. There may, however, be something more basic at work, namely, that there is a growing conviction that sex and married life are themselves good and that there is no virtue in giving them up. Second, it has become axiomatic that secular vocations are also capable of Christian meaning and that the ordinary way to serve God and one's neighbor is in such vocations. Even more basic perhaps, as the notion of a fixed human nature and therefore of a "natural law" became more problematic toward the mid- and late-twentieth century, there was a weakening sense that there are true absolutes in a world that appeared plastic, fluid, and ever-changing. It is not clear in the year 2000 that such factors will necessarily continue. It is clear from reading the Mack-Noser correspondence that two intelligent men of an earlier generation were concerned about a tectonic culture change long before the current vocation crisis assumed its present proportions.

In SVD history, the discussions from the mid-1960s onward on how best to train men in changing times resulted in centering the emphasis in vocational recruitment for both the brotherhood and priesthood on the four-year Divine Word College in Epworth. It is important to note the addition of "brotherhood" recruitment and training to the college's tasks. In changes brought about by the Second Vatican Council and discussed at greater length in the chapter on education and training, the goal was set to train all brothers at least to the level of a bachelor of arts degree at Epworth, or in an advanced postsecondary technical program in approved fields in some other place.

Closing the School of Theology at Techny

While all was churning in the feeder system, other changes were also underway. They would end in closing the school of theology at Techny and sending Divine Word seminarians for their theological and ministerial studies to the new seminary consortium operated by several religious orders, Catholic Theological Union in the Hyde Park neighborhood in Chicago. The change was major, perhaps the most momentous in the seventy-five years since Brother Wendelin landed in Hoboken. Since the beginning of the century Techny had been the center of the Society in North America. From the time the first brotherhood and priesthood aspirants reached final vows and ordination, these rites and the mission cross ceremony had been central to life at Techny. These ceremonies were the occasion to take stock of the young men who represented the result of the labors of dozens of SVD brothers and priests in seminaries, mission procures, and parishes throughout the country.

When mission assignments were given at about the time perpetual vows were pronounced, brothers and priests would begin packing their trunks. They began to correspond with their new mission provincial superiors and bishops about what to bring, what courses to take, how to make the trip. The mission office loading docks swelled with trunks, and Techny enjoyed a sense of fulfillment and pride. They left in ones and twos over a period of weeks. Wherever the brother or priest went, to an assignment in the U.S. or overseas, those last weeks at Techny took on a special flavor. Decades later it would be common for a misty-eyed missionary to recall it to a newly arrived confrere in a faraway mission. Across the years and the miles, generations would connect. It is small wonder, then, that this history has been so occupied with this house and province and everything that went on there. The location of this educational unit had remained constant through all its history. For four years every American priest and brother, with the exception of some men trained at Bay St. Louis, spent time at Techny.

The decision to close the theology school was not made lightly, nor was it a response to any single factor. It is also clear that much discussion over many years went into it, since it was a decision that had the potential to tear the Society apart and whose outcome could scarcely be anticipated. It was truly a decision demanding faith, for in many ways it was a leap in the dark. And when it occurred, it almost did tear the Society apart. One still senses the hurt feelings. Some suspend judgment, hoping for the best; others, who are quickly becoming the majority, speak positively of the open, person-oriented style of formation that occurred as a result of the change.

The background of the decision lay in the ferment that accompanied Vatican Council II. As the documents of Vatican II appeared, they were passed around in mimeographed form, eagerly read, discussed, and implemented in the theology department at Techny. The faculty at the time was young, enthusiastic. "Unfortunately," some would say, with some justification; the "old guard" had retired and younger men had joined the faculty, but there was no significant in-between group to mediate between old and new. Others maintain that it was good that this gap existed, believing it made it easier to make the changes in one fell swoop as the times demanded. Some of the changes made at Techny under the leadership of the seminary department, in retrospect, appear insensitive. For instance, many older members were horrified to see the old altar rail and several statues torn out. Seminarians increasingly appeared in lay clothes, and the cassock rapidly disappeared. A major cultural change was underway, yet the ideological stakes were so high that it was not seen in such terms.

In a four-year span, the SVD decided that Techny as a free-standing, self-contained seminary should not be maintained. In part, the decline in numbers forecast to enter the theologate would make the expense inordinately high. That in itself necessitated that the Society and other communities cooperate, for without this, many small institutions could not maintain accreditation. More important, given the evolving thinking on what was involved in theological and ministerial education, it was argued that a small, stand-alone seminary at Techny could not provide adequate professional training that met the new standards.

At first it was suggested that the Society should invite other groups, especially other missionary orders, to join forces at Techny. Nothing ever came of this proposal, partly because such communities thought it would be equally fitting for the

SVD to come to their campuses. Other proposals were made, such as opening the classes at Techny to adult education and lay ministry training, but none of these proved viable either. The consensus was emerging that the Divine Word Missionary training program would have to join some cluster of like units. When the decision was made, it came more quickly than anyone expected. John Boberg recalls: "When I left for Rome in January of 1969 to defend my thesis, there was no talk of moving seminarians out of Techny. In the summer I received an appointment as Dean of those students going to CTU [Catholic Theological Union in Chicago]."

According to the criteria developed, the new theology program for training Divine Word Missionaries should: (1) be located in the city, since isolation in the countryside emphasized an other worldly approach to formation, while the city with all its poverty and racism would acquaint the future missionary with the kind of environment he would likely work in; (2) be within easy reach of a university, since the university ethos would have a stimulating effect on and force the seminary to professionalize its educational program as a true graduate school; (3) given Vatican II's emphasis on ecumenism, be located in a place where ecumenism might be promoted and different Christian traditions might work together to help break down the barriers that had been erected over the centuries.

Among other criteria developed was the need to develop a mission orientation in the teaching of theology. Other societies participating in conversations about forming a coalition of orders made it known that other mission-sending societies looked to the Society of the Divine Word for leadership in this enterprise. By participating in a coalition of orders, the SVD would be doing its part to accentuate the teaching of the council that baptism had an essential missionary character that obligated all the faithful to consider themselves missionary. All the more reason for the SVD to make every effort to provide this emphasis and orientation.

Given the criteria, seven possibilities were identified for investigation in a 1969 report compiled by Fathers Robert Flinn and Eugene Ahner:

1. Catholic Theological Union (CTU) at Chicago, which had opened its doors to its first classes in October of 1968
2. Dubuque, Iowa, where the Dominican-led St. Rose Priory had become a center of innovation
3. Notre Dame University, South Bend, Indiana
4. St. Louis University, St. Louis, Missouri
5. St. Mary of the Lake, Mundelein, Illinois, the site of the seminary of the Archdiocese of Chicago
6. Washington Theological Coalition (WTC), which was similar to Catholic Theological Union
7. Scattering seminarians among the above six schools.

CTU and WTC quickly became the two primary possibilities. A CARA study commissioned to look into the matter of where to move was known to be pointing to WTC as the cluster of choice, but the program there offered the student fewer electives and choices. In trying to cover all of the branches of theology as more traditionally understood, it appeared more static. From the beginning the faculty majority at Techny favored CTU. But some who were familiar with Washington, D.C., and Catholic University, including some in positions of authority, wanted the theologate to move to WTC. From the perspective of cost, not an insignificant consideration, WTC was the best choice, for the Society already had a residence there that had been built for the pastoral year program not many years previously.

A stalemate resulted and a compromise was called for. This took the form of dividing the four classes of theology on an experimental basis. The first and second year students would go to WTC, the third and fourth year to CTU. The opinion of the students could also be evaluated when the final "decision" was made. In a meeting held on 2 June 1969, the four provincials approved several items, among them the dispersal of the theologate community to the two locations for the 1969–1970 school year. Curiously, a final report had already been drafted by February 1970 comparing the two clusters after roughly four months' experience. Although many doubted that both places had been given an equal chance and although, according to the criteria used and the method of weighting applied, WTC actually came out slightly ahead,[7] the faculty was still strongly in favor of CTU, and they carried the day. If one were to ask why the four members of the faculty who were to carry out the decision insisted on Chicago and CTU as the location of the theologate, the chief reason to tilt the balance seems to have been a perception that CTU would be more flexible and innovative, that it had more potential for development and seemed less tied into traditional ways of viewing and doing theology, though this is nowhere explicitly stated in the record.

The decision to relocate to CTU in Chicago was made at a meeting of the four provincials in a three to one vote in favor of Chicago. In short order this decision was ratified by the superior general and his council. Techny, which had opened its doors as a seminary in 1909, was effectively closed as a seminary in 1969 and officially so in 1970.

As it turned out, the SVD did make a significant contribution in placing mission studies at the center of the CTU program, one of the considerations in making their decision to move to Chicago. Paul Bechtold, CP, one of the founders of CTU, had the following to say in his history of the early years of the Union:

> The Program in World Mission is largely the history of the Divine Word Missionaries at the school. While all of the communities who were at CTU at its beginnings had a missionary-sending apostolate, no group had world mission as its primary work. A vibrant program in mission studies awaited a missionary society to sponsor and staff it.[8]

Father Lawrence Nemer, church historian and missiologist, and one of the four SVD faculty who favored the decision to move to CTU, makes the following statement in his 1989 paper, "A Recommendation Revisited":

---

7. The criteria used were: 1) Theological program, 2) Faculty, 3) Student body, 4) Administration, 5) Academic setting, 6) Ecumenical possibilities, 7) Urban setting, 8) Possibility for mission dimension, 9) SVD presence, 10) Library, 11) Finances.

8. Paul Bechtold, *Catholic Theological Union at Chicago: The Founding Years 1965–1975: History and Memoir* (Chicago: Catholic Theological Union, 1993), p. 194.

History has proved that the insight [to move to CTU rather than WTC] was indeed sound. Not only has CTU developed the strongest theological program in the U.S., but, thanks especially to the SVD, it has also become the outstanding Roman Catholic Center for Mission Studies in the U.S. It was a decision carefully studied and wisely made.

Much more could be said about the dramatic and traumatic period when the Techny theologate closed. I would like to close this very brief account of the close of Techny's theologate with a quotation from Father Joseph Connors, provincial superior at Techny during the years of decision. In the concluding paragraph of a letter to all the members of the province informing them of the decision to close Techny's theologate, he wrote:

Even in a brief account such as this, there must be place for one more thought. It is the thought of the sixty years of dedication and devotion that have gone into the theologate at Techny, and its graduates all over the world who are even now doing the work of the Lord for which the Techny theologate prepared them. Over the decades, the Techny faculty and the whole Techny community have served them well, and it is hard to feel that what we have known and loved for so long is about to become part of our history. And yet, as times and circumstances change, as they have indeed changed for theologates everywhere, and as the Church itself makes newer and greater demands on the theological education of priests, the Techny community and theological faculty can only be worthy of their own admirable tradition by now providing for our present and future seminarians the location and facilities which are necessary to equip them as well for the future missionary era as their predecessors were equipped for their own.

5

Animating the Mission Cause, 1901–1970

Utilizing the Media and Popular Movements

When the first members of the Society of the Divine Word arrived in America, the first thing they had to do was make themselves known and self-supporting. Because their goal was primarily to aid in the church's missionary life, there was also compelling need to put effort into developing mission awareness and educating the church in America of its obligation to be mission-oriented. At the same time, this German society needed to win the good will of the American church. This was attempted and accomplished in a variety of ways, beginning with the apostolate of the press, developing the Catholic Students' Mission Crusade, involvement with the lay retreat movement, plus a host of other, more individual efforts as they tried to spread the Word and make the Society known.

THE APOSTOLATE OF THE PRESS

Arnold Janssen's interest in and use of the burgeoning popular medium of the press was continued by his followers wherever they went. In the first issue of *Stadt Gottes* ("City of God") in 1878, the founder of the Divine Word Missionaries is the presumed author of an unsigned article introducing his family magazine. In that first article, Janssen observed the following about the power of the printed word:

> If anyone wants to accomplish some good and have a good effect on his fellows in these times [i.e., Bismarck's *Kulturkampf*], he must make use of those methods which seem to be most appropriate for the times. And right now the best means would be the press. The spoken word quickly fades away; the printed word remains, to be read again and again. With the press I can speak to people who are far from me, whom I have never seen nor will ever see. And still my thought has an effect on those people. Indeed, they become my spiritual children the more they accept my words and my beliefs. My thought is embodied in my writing, and this is multiplied many times

and can be spread around easily today. Just as a bad press can cause much harm, in the same way much good can be accomplished by means of a good press.

Stadt Gottes became successful beyond all expectations. Its contents were mainly educational and entertaining and only partly religious. It was truly a family magazine for the masses, with many illustrations and a great variety of reading matter. It soon became the most popular Catholic magazine in German-speaking Europe; it supported much of the Society's early work in both Europe and in North America. *Stadt Gottes* became the editorial exemplar for much of what the SVD published in the U.S. as well as wherever the SVD went.

Brother Wendelin, you will recall, came to America in the first place to sell Steyl's magazines and almanacs to German Catholics. In his letter to the founder after his first foray to look for a place where the SVD might settle, he made explicit mention of the possibility of setting up a press "like the one at Steyl." Already in 1900 as Father Beckert planned and laid out the shops for the future technical school in Shermerville, he included a press building. The press was to be an integral and major part of the industrial school. At the same time it would serve the same mission animation and fund-raising goals as Steyl's press. Father Janssen overcame his initial reluctance to approve the plans and soon permitted the establishment of a press at Techny with Father Herman Richarz in charge, on 30 June 1901, with the printing of the English translation of the 1902 edition of *St. Michaelskalendar* as *St. Michael's Almanac*. Sending brothers from the Steyl press to direct the Techny press was seen as the only solution to the problem of operating the machinery until Americans could be trained.

In 1902, under the editorship of Father Richarz, the press began to print a mission magazine in German called the *Amerikanisches Missionsblatt* ("American Mission Magazine"), the title and focus of which was soon changed (in 1911) to *Amerikanisches Familienblatt* ("American Family Magazine"). At first a small English-language supplement was included, but it soon became obvious that an English magazine was needed to keep in contact with their English readers and benefactors, so *The Christian Family* formally began publication as a monthly in January 1906. Father Richarz was editor of both the German magazine and of *The Christian Family* when it first appeared. He was also teaching some 100 students in the technical school and needed help desperately. Father Janssen came to the aid of these fledgling magazines by sending Fathers Frederick Lynk, Bruno Hagspiel, and Francis Markert.

Originally, Father Lynk, who was ordained in 1906, was assigned to Japan, and was to come to the U.S. to learn English. This he did quickly and exceptionally well. As a result, shortly after he arrived in America he replaced Father Richarz as editor of *The Christian Family*. Under his long tenure, this magazine became very popular and successful. Even though he suffered from diabetes, he was a prolific writer and poet, both in English and in German. As chaplain of St. Francis Hospital in Evanston, Illinois, he was able to receive medical attention when he needed it. It was also at the hospital that he did his writing and editing, the major activities of his whole priestly life. Without the constant writing and publishing done by people like Father Lynk, Techny and the SVD in North America would have developed in quite a different direction, or would have failed to develop at all.

Father Hagspiel, about whom we have heard much in other contexts, was in the first group of SVDs sent to the U. S. who did not get their appointment from the founder himself, since he died early in 1909. In 1914, very soon after he arrived in America, Hagspiel, perhaps the greatest promoter and prolific writer of the early SVD, started a phenomenally successful magazine intended to develop mission awareness and stimulate vocations among the youth in America. He called it *The Little Missionary*, and at its peak it reached 150,000 school children a month. Three popes, Benedict XV, Pius XI, and Pius XII, gave their blessings to the magazine and its work. Then in 1921, realizing that the SVD really had no magazine for adult readers devoted exclusively to the missions, he founded *Our Missions*. In the first issue of this magazine in 1921, he reported on the Techny press's output. *The Christian Family* and *Amerikanisches Familienblatt*, each appearing monthly, had a combined circulation of 100,000. *St. Michael's Almanac* came out once a year with a run of 90,000. *The Little Missionary* was sent to 100,000 students every month in 1921, while over half a million free leaflets and mission pamphlets were distributed each year.

The SVD became well known and was widely associated with the apostolate of the press. One of the traveling brothers, Paulinus, once brought home a story. He was staying with a community of Jesuits and at the dinner table one of the older Jesuits asked Brother Paulinus if he thought Mars was inhabited. "I'm sure I do not know," was the brother's answer. "Well, I'm sure it's not inhabited," was the quick rejoinder, "and the convincing proof that bears me out has been overlooked by scientists who are studying the question. Mars is the only place the Society of the Divine Word has not sent its mission pamphlets."

Father Hagspiel was largely responsible for this work. He was also at the origin of many other movements in the U.S. or was very quick to support them. Like Peil, Hagspiel was a man of ideas. Father Hagspiel had an optimistic, exuberant personality that spilled over into the many books and pamphlets he wrote. From the beginning of his priestly life he was also engaged in the retreat movement, so much so that Pius XI personally gave him his encyclical on the retreat movement (*Mens nostra*, issued in 1929), urging him to spread this practice throughout the United States—and spread it he did, especially in his later years, sometimes preaching as many as forty scheduled retreats of six or ten days in English, German, or Polish annually. He gloried, it was said, in concluding one retreat at his morning Mass and opening another retreat somewhere else the same evening, and was especially proud of the retreats he gave to Trappists (the popular name for Cistercians).

The third great media man of the U. S. SVD was Father Francis Markert, a classmate of Hagspiel. The two came to America together. He took over the editorship of *Amerikanisches Familienblatt* and made it the most popular German-language monthly in the United States. It continued in existence until December 1950. Soon after his arrival in America, Markert also became the director of the press, which allowed Father Richarz to become the novice master for the candidates for the priesthood, a position he held from 1914 until his final illness and death on 12 February 1928, a position in which he was respected and loved by all who came into contact with him.

Father Markert held the position of press director until 1950, when he was replaced by Father Lawrence Wagner, and under his long direction it grew into an impressive, modern operation responsible for much of the SVD's success in North America.

Father Markert's influence extended beyond Techny. In 1920, for example, Markert was attending the annual meeting of the Catholic Press Association in Washington, D.C. According to Markert's recollections, he was talking over lunch one day with Bishop William Russell of Charleston, South Carolina, who had been appointed the first episcopal chairman of the newly organized Press Department of the National Catholic Welfare Council. Markert recalls talking to Bishop Russell about the small number of subscribers to the Catholic press and suggesting how to remedy this problem. If the Catholic press were to have an impact, he suggested, it needed to be publicized and supported by the hierarchy. An annual drive lasting for a week or more, with appropriate sermons in every parish pushing the value of a strong Catholic press might work. "I told the Bishop," Markert recalled, "that this system had been employed very successfully in Spain." The idea was picked up and presented to all of the U.S. bishops at their annual meeting in September 1920 where it was approved unanimously. February became Catholic Press Month. In Markert's words in an undated letter in the Techny archives:

> The results have far surpassed my fondest dreams. Not only has the circula-
> tion multiplied to 26,000,000 in 1960 [from an estimated 1,000,000 in
> 1920], but with the greater interest on the part of the Catholic population
> and the larger financial income for the Catholic Press on the whole, it has
> been able to extend and improve itself in such a way that today there are
> available innumerable publications dealing with every phase and problem
> of Catholic life . . . thus making Catholic thought and the Catholic way of
> life more readily accessible and more highly esteemed than it ever was in
> our country's history.

THE GROWTH OF THE PRESS AT TECHNY AND ITS PROBLEMS

Through the 1920s, the Techny press continued to grow to the point that a new, larger building became necessary. By the fall of 1929 operations began in the new building. Subscriptions to the magazines went down somewhat during the depression, but the presses were kept busy with many other jobs: books, pamphlets, leaflets, inserts, and other mission literature, much of which was given away free. Yearly calendars were sent to benefactors. Printing for other American SVD houses was also done at Techny's press. Some magazines, such as *Our Missions*, folded or were merged with existing magazines; others were started up for specific purposes, like *Fu Jen* magazine, to support the Catholic university which had been assigned to the SVD by Pius XI in 1933.

When the press began operating in the new building, it was a complete complex comprising the press itself, the typesetting department, the bindery, the shipping department, plate making, electroplating and engraving, and eventually a photography department as well. There were some thirty to thirty-five brothers working in the press, several full-time lay people, with occasional help coming from the brother novices and postulants.

Throughout the operation of the press, several issues kept surfacing. To understand them, the reader must know that Catholic religious communities are commonly organized at three levels—internationally under a superior general; regionally or nationally as "provinces" under a provincial superior; and locally under a "rector" or local superior. Each level has its own area of autonomy in making decisions on matters such as personnel assignments and for raising and spending money, and thus the question of boundaries and competence to decide controversial matters frequently arises. In the case of the Techny press, a recurring problem was that of the relationship between the press, owned by the provincial administration, and the other operations going on at Techny that belonged to the local community. The press operation clearly belonged to the province, yet the brothers and priests who worked in the press lived and ate in the same house at Techny as people working for the house, and in questions of daily order and life, they were subject to Techny's rector. In principle, the province had to pay the house for its personnel's room and board. But many men held down several jobs, for example, one job as sacristan in the house chapel, a second as a typesetter for the province press. Who was to pay for printing done for other houses or pay the printing bills for Father Wendel's magazine *The Colored Messenger*, which promoted the African-American apostolate?

All this was connected with a broader and more complex question: What was the primary purpose of the magazines and books that were published and printed at Techny? Were they meant to be a way of advertising the Society in North America? A means of stimulating vocations? Or a way of raising funds? If the question is answered one way, they should be given freely or be sold at the minimum amount possible, and the provincial administration should then pay the bill. If they were meant to break even or to make money, then the real cost of producing the magazines had to be dealt with; there should be no giveaways; and each house should be required to pay the full amount for what they ordered to be printed and sent out. Such questions bedeviled the press operation from the beginning. The ambiguity was present already in the word "press." Taken literally, it means the machinery that prints. Taken more widely, it stands for the entire gamut of activities that go under the name "publishing," where nothing is complete until a reader buys and reads a publication. Looking back over the years, it is clear that the North American SVD was seminally a great publisher in the context of American Catholicism, but also that it did not put the resources necessary into its publication efforts to meet the changes in the publishing world that occurred in the first two decades after the Second World War.

In 1923, in a report on the press to the provincial council and the superior general, Father Markert wrote: "We had the first press of this kind in North America and had, as a result, a great advantage over all the other congregations . . . but now we are constantly losing ground, for the most part because we do not have enough personnel in all departments [of the press]. There is competition from all sides."

The problem did not go away. In 1947 Markert thought the situation was getting desperate. In the typesetting department, he complained, Brother Amabilis was sixty-five, while the other two, Brothers Cyril and Clement, were not robust in health. If any one of them were forced to take some time off, as the doctor had already suggested in the case of Brother Clement, it would not be possible to set the magazines. "Instead of three, we should have seven typesetters." The same situation, he wrote in this letter to the provincial chapter, held true for the press proper and for the bindery. This shortage meant that the equipment was not fully utilized while, at the same time, only the most necessary work could be done. Also, Markert did not feel that they could do the work by hiring outside workers. The press had to have more brothers, he felt.

Stepping aside from the situation at Techny, one realizes that the problems experienced there were but a small part of a larger national Catholic press apostolate dilemma. Individual communities of men and women had taken advantage of the relatively inexpensive means of spreading their message and supporting themselves by means of the printing press. Each community did its best to provide reputable publications, but the bottom line is that the missionary groups were in a real, if genteel, competition with one another. A score of mission magazines were being propagated by as many orders. The question must be asked whether the advantages of these relatively small scale operations outweighed their disadvantages. Would a national magazine, designed to inform Catholics of what was happening as missions founded in the early years of the nineteenth and twentieth centuries became local churches, have nurtured a more global Catholic consciousness?

In the case of the North American SVD, the Techny press continued with the infusion of some new blood for another thirteen years after Father Markert spoke of its dire personnel situation. Then, on a cold January day in 1960, the entire press went up in flames. The exact cause was never established. Electricians had been doing repair work in the press building and some think that they might have forgotten to turn their equipment off properly. Others blamed the fire on baled paper that had gotten wet and suffered spontaneous combustion.

The fire was a shock to everybody, and soon a decision had to be made: to rebuild the press or not? Insurance covered only a fraction of what would be needed to replace the equipment that had been destroyed. Also, the times had changed. There was no longer any need for the SVD to have its own press. Within days, two big presses in Chicago offered to do whatever printing commitments the Society had outstanding, and whatever else they needed to have printed in the future as inexpensively as they could do the job in their own press. Father Markert, possibly remembering his letter of 1947, was the first to speak against rebuilding the press, to which he had devoted his entire life. The superior general of the Society, John Schütte, who had flown from Rome to participate in the meetings, concurred in the decision that the press should not be rebuilt. The decision's effects were manifold, especially on the lives of the brothers who worked in the press. Their identities were bound up with the press and their lives had to be redirected. Some went to the missions to continue their work as printers. Others retrained and took other assignments. All accepted the changes gracefully.

There was at least one other consequence of the fire that deserves mention. When the press went up in flames, Father Markert was working on the history of the early years of the Society in America. He kept all of the archival materials, such as letters, diaries, memoirs, copies of contracts, and so forth, from the early years of the SVD in North America in his office in the press building. All this material, much of it existing nowhere else, also went up in flames. Only his manuscript copy of the events recorded in these archives survived. It has been an important source of material for the present history.

DIVINE WORD PUBLICATIONS

With the appointment in 1950 of Father Lawrence Wagner as director of the press to replace Father Markert, the press operation was divided into a publications department and a press department. The publications part continued, after the press was destroyed, as Divine Word Publications. Although the publications division had operated as "The Mission Press" before the press burned and had published such classics as Father Matthias Braun's translations of two seminal missiological works by Joseph Schmidlin—*Catholic Mission Theory* (1931) and *Catholic Mission History* (1933) and five of Bruno Hagspiel's popular *Along the Mission Trail* (1925–28)—it became more important after this event.

The SVD book and pamphlet publishing operations should be considered alongside the establishment of The Liturgical Press by the Benedictines of St. John's Abbey in Collegeville, Minnesota, and Paulist Press by the Paulist Fathers in New York and New Jersey. Similarly, Maryknollers such as John Considine and Robert Sheridan were publishing highly successful pamphlets and books, as well as films such as "Maryknoll on the Hudson" and "Maryknoll in China" in the 1930s. Each of these communities published materials that suited its apostolic goals. The Benedictines had an interest in renewing liturgical life; the Paulists in materials that would put forward an attractive face of Catholicism to promote conversions; the Maryknollers and the SVDs in animating mission consciousness and making their societies better known. The Benedictines, like the SVDs, would operate their own presses, but in all cases the principle of distinguishing between a *printing* and a *publishing* operation was crucial. And then the critical question: Was the community to subsidize the press in order to achieve apostolic goals or was the press supposed to make a profit to subsidize the community's apostolates? In the case of the SVD, oscillation between these two ideals reflected the ambivalence of the community's leadership. Historically, as we have seen, the press in Steyl produced popular materials that paid for themselves and helped support the community. Some had little to do with the missionary ideal but were quite successful in inculcating Christian and Catholic ideals. That model was followed in the U.S, but the subsidization of publishing by the contributed services of the brothers made exact accounting easy to avoid. Furthermore, the relatively modest cost of the first several generations of equipment used in composition, printing, and binding made it easy to stay in business as long as that equipment functioned reasonably well. The Techny fire forced a decision concerning how to proceed in the publishing apostolate in the American SVD province. The capital expenditures necessary to rebuild and furnish the press with modern equipment would be huge. Normal printing firms need to operate such equipment for two or three shifts a day in order to pay for the equipment and produce a profit. The SVD press, by contrast, was a semi-monastic operation carried on by a majority of religious brothers who could normally work only one shift a day. Furthermore, the fire came at a time when it had become necessary to buy new and expensive equipment to operate efficiently in the conditions obtaining in the late 1950s and early 1960s, as offset printing and "cold-type" technologies began to replace the "hot-type" presses of an earlier day.

The early 1950s decision to separate the printing from the publishing operation was a logical one. It became evident in the aftermath of the fire that the Society could purchase printing from outside firms as economically as it could print books, magazines, and pamphlets itself, once the capital costs of building a new facility and replacing the aging brothers with laymen were factored in. The dynamic Father Francis Kamp, who was at this same time developing the new mission office to promote knowledge and support of the SVD's overseas missions, was involved in the decision to separate the press operation from the publication activity and was given the responsibility for developing Divine Word Publications (DWP). DWP received its first full-time director in 1959, worked valiantly, and at times enjoyed success. It even built its own building. In spite of the best efforts of such talented priests as Vincent McMahon, Edward McGuinn, and John McHenry, however, DWP could neither pay its own way consistently nor show a profit. In addition, there were other, very basic difficulties connected with the enterprise. On the one hand, a statement of the provincial council on 16 December 1968 showed that the province administration appreciated the work of DWP. "The Publication Apostolate is a worthwhile, justifiable and commendable apostolate in itself. If it has a definite missionary thrust it is all the more worthwhile, justifiable and commendable; and if it also broke even it is even more worthwhile and commendable." On the other hand, the bottom line of the province administration's analysis was contained in the recognition that the press apostolate had been subsidized for years, and that the losses had long been overlooked for reasons discussed above. It had been impossible to put a dollar figure on such benefits as making the SVD better known, and promoting the missions, vocations, and public relations.

By 1968, however, the issue of cost had come to the fore. In the heady days of post-Vatican Council II, DWP began to operate rather independently of the Society's self-interest and to produce books and other materials for persons interested in the general renewal of the church. DWP had begun to look as if it were independent of the Society, and from there it was a short step to saying that it should at least break even. In the meantime, publishing houses like those run by Maryknoll, the Paulists, the Benedictines, and the Franciscans of Cincinnati were facing similar issues. Each responded differently, but it is noteworthy that all but the Maryknoll operation managed to produce books and other materials for ordinary people and scholars while breaking even. Maryknoll made the decision in 1968 to increase its commitment to book publishing and to give it a new third-world, missionary focus when it charged Father Miguel D'Escoto and the lay editor Philip Scharper to start Orbis Books, a publisher that has relied on Maryknoll subsidies since its foundation. The SVD never resolved the conflict in favor of granting a continuing subsidy to DWP. Each year the subsidy question was hotly debated as budgets for the departments were set. By August 1972 the staff of twenty-three, the great majority of whom were lay, were let go, and a significant work of the Society in North America came to an end.

CHANGE AND CONTINUITY

The previous section has narrated the developments that led to the SVD withdrawing from printing its own materials and publishing books and magazines. All during the period from 1950 through the early 1970s, however, publishing went on. In 1953, *The Little Missionary* became *Missionary Youth*, and with the change of name came a change in content as well. While *The Little Missionary* was geared to grade school children, *Missionary Youth* was edited to appeal to high school students. The implication was clear: the target audience in vocation recruitment was changing from grade school to high school students. *Missionary Youth*, in its turn, came to an end with the June 1967 issue. Vatican Council II had intervened and subscriptions to *Missionary Youth* collapsed. Recruitment to the priesthood and brotherhood, which until the late 1960s had been directed to filling its high school seminaries and brother candidate programs, began to dry up. An attempt was made to achieve the vocation-recruitment goals of *Missionary Youth* by two other publications, *The Shepherd* for vocations to the missionary priesthood and *The Brother* for the brotherhood. All this was to little avail. The large numbers of high school-age recruits characteristic of the late 1940s and 1950s were no more.

Shortly after *Missionary Youth* ceased publication, *Divine Word Missionaries*, the creation of Francis Kamp, appeared. It was styled as "A Magazine for Friends of The Society of the Divine Word, Chicago Province" and it still appears quarterly in an attractive, colorful format. Its main purpose is to stay in touch with benefactors and friends of the Society and it is sent free in a mailing of 250,000. Produced by the mission office, it also mounts appeals for money to help support the overseas missions of the Society. It has been successful ever since its commencement and remains so today.

Although the media apostolate of the Society has changed over the years, interest in and the attempt to utilize these tools have not disappeared. In the decree approving the revised *Constitutions of the Society of the Divine Word*, on 19 October 1983, Cardinal Pironio, head of the Vatican Congregation for Religious, called special attention to the use of contemporary means of communication to spread God's word:

The Society's members share personally through their missionary service in the purpose and mission of Christ's life; in this way they glorify God's name, and work for the salvation of the world's peoples. The founder saw in the printed word a powerful means for evangelization, and his sons wish to follow him in this by utilizing the various communications media in the service of spreading and deepening the faith and of making the whole church aware of its missionary task.

CATHOLIC STUDENTS' MISSION CRUSADE

One of the most successful mechanisms of mission animation in the first half of the twentieth century, not just for the Society of the Divine Word but for the entire Catholic Church in North America, was the Catholic Students' Mission Crusade (CSMC), which had its origin at Techny in the minds of Clifford King and Bruno Hagspiel. Catholics in America were obviously waiting for something like this to happen, so rapidly did the Crusade grow and such an impact did it have. Protestant example and enthusiasm for mission, which were at an all-time high in the first years of the century, were an added incentive for the establishment of the CSMC. In 1900, for example, some 200,000 people attended the Ecumenical Missionary Conference held in New York City, out of which came the slogan "the evangelization of the world in this generation." One group that had done much to increase Protestant mission interest was the Student Volunteer Movement, and it appears also to have captured the imagination of SVD seminarian King.

It was King, a member of the first class to enter the new mission seminary, who got and, with his fellow seminarians, carried the idea of the CSMC through its beginnings. Seminarian King, like later Father King, was not only a man of ideas; he was even more a man of action. Brooking as little delay as possible, he began to carry out his ideas. As one of his classmates, Father Joseph Murphy whom we will meet in another context remembers it, an article from the Maryknoll magazine *Field Afar* was read at table one day in 1914, describing the Kansas City convention of the Student Volunteer Movement, where five hundred students had gathered. It started a heated discussion among the seminarians. In the meantime the war intervened and it soon became clear that, with European help closed down, American Catholics had a serious responsibility to the foreign missions. King took the initiative and drafted a circular that he called the "Coming Crusade." In it he solicited answers to nine questions he had formulated in conversations with other seminarians. He was outlining the way the CSMC would function.

The purpose of the Techny seminarians' work was intentionally limited. First of all, they called their effort the "Students' Mission Crusade Bureau," by which to indicate that it was "merely provisional in character," according to their second bulletin. The sole purpose was to organize the Catholic students of America to involve themselves with a concern for the missions, to become active for the missions, according to the slogan the bureau was trying to promote: "The Sacred Heart for the world and the world for the Sacred Heart." At the time of the first convention in 1918, the SVD and Maryknoll were the two major groups in America devoted exclusively to mission work. In spite of this, during one of the sessions of the convention, Father Hagspiel suggested that neither Techny nor Maryknoll should be the place where the central headquarters of the Catholic Students' Mission Crusade be established, lest the crusade be identified too closely with one mission society and be perceived as advocating the interests of one to the prejudice of others. The crusade was to be a *students'* crusade and should cast its net for membership as widely as possible. As it turned out, this proved to be excellent advice, for the crusade under this nonpartisan management expanded rapidly.

In the beginning it was not clear that the crusade would be successful at all. King and his seminary confreres sent out 900 copies of his first circular to institutions of higher learning, colleges, academies, universities, seminaries, and the like. He received only nine answers to his questions. Discouragement, however, was not a word to be found in King's vocabulary. One important person who supported the idea was Joseph Husslein, S.J., the editor of the Jesuit magazine *America*, an influential Catholic weekly. In the 2 June 1917 issue, Husslein wrote:

It is dangerous to speak in superlatives. Yet it is no exaggeration to say that one of the most important events in our Catholic educational life is the appeal recently sent out by the new Mission Crusade Bureau to the students of our academies, colleges, seminaries and universities . . . the publication of this invitation can become epoch-making for the Church.

During his summer vacation, King read through the meager responses he had received, working out the answers to his own questions. In October 1917 he had 2000 copies of his summer's work printed and sent again to educational institutions, to every bishop in the country, to every Catholic paper and magazine. This time he and his coworkers at Techny received a good response, especially encouragement from the hierarchy, in particular from Cardinal Farley. The thirty-one seminaries and colleges that pledged their cooperation with the Students' Mission Crusade decided to hold their first convention at Techny, 27–30 July 1918, the day that is marked as the founding day of the CSMC. Bulletin III, the last to be published by the bureau, described the results of this first convention, at which the national leadership was entrusted to the students and rector of Mt. St. Mary's Seminary of the Archdiocese of Cincinnati. Their delegates had been very active at this first convention, supported in this by their rector, Monsignor Francis Beckman.

The CSMC grew rapidly over the next years and made an enormous contribution in fostering mission awareness, with all that means for prayers and vocations and for financial support of the missions. In 1921, Hagspiel had the following to report:

The CSMC is doing very much to increase vocations among the young men and women who come in touch with its beneficent influence. An example of this is seen in the fact that every member of the Executive Board (of the CSMC) last year has entered the seminary or convent. The great increase of vocations at Techny, by over 70 this year, can be traced partly to the Crusade. Maryknoll, Omaha (Chinese Mission Society of Omaha),[1] and other missionary colleges say the same thing. The students of America need only be instructed in the mission idea and then the wonderful ideal of the missionary

---

1. In its early years in the U.S., St. Columban's Foreign Mission Society (SSC) went by different names, the most common being Columbans. In the literature of the SVDs of the period, the Columbans were normally called "Omaha" where they had their headquarters. Originally founded in Ireland, the SSC initially worked only in China and are, like the Maryknollers, a group of secular priests banded together in a "society of apostolic life" dedicated to the missions.

vocation is brought home to the idealists. As long as the Crusade prospers and spreads to the still-untouched student ranks, more and more vocations will arise in these quarters.

The Crusade Castle in Cincinnati became the headquarters of the CSMC; here were published the different magazines, bulletins, and study guides that were sent out to the units of the CSMC; selected students spent time at the castle learning leadership skills, and how to establish and run a mission club. Over the years, as many as a million students would be enrolled in more than 3000 units. Every two years the CSMC held a convention, many of them at the University of Notre Dame. At the 23rd National Golden Jubilee Convention, held at Notre Dame, August 22–25 1968, the delegates honored Father King, who was ill and unable to attend the convention. The telegram sent by the CSMC read:

Delegates to the Golden Jubilee Convention of the Mission Crusade at the University of Notre Dame, by standing vote in the final general meeting, voiced their great esteem for you as the Founder of the Crusade and the source of continuing inspiration in your half-century of service in the missions.

Father King died in 1969. The CSMC survived him by one year, and was disbanded in the convention of 1970, a casualty of the winds of change brought by the Second Vatican Council. For this history of the SVD, the important thing to note, perhaps, is how quickly its earliest American recruits inserted the Society on the national Catholic stage in creative ways. They were helping enlist popular support for Catholic missions that was not surpassed in the twentieth century. Indeed, the demise of the CSMC may even be symptomatic of the decrease in popular Catholic enthusiasm for world mission, as American Catholics began to share their neighbors' suspicions and judgments that missions had been the fellow traveler of colonialism.

RETREATS

Another important activity that made the Society known in North America and that helped form the outlook of every American SVD were the retreats for laity that were conducted at Techny, just as they were at Steyl. A "retreat," in the sense we are using the term, refers to a specified period of time when one "retreats" to a place of silence, usually a weekend, from Thursday or Friday evening until Sunday noon, to pray and reflect in the context of a series of meditations and conferences given by a retreat master. A retreat has always meant a withdrawing somehow from the world of the quotidian, according to the example and recommendation of Christ himself to his apostles: "Come away by yourselves to a deserted place and rest awhile" (Mark 6:31).

No sooner had the SVD settled in at Techny when they began to think of introducing retreats, but they could not begin right away. They needed space, and they also needed time to promote the whole idea of retreats, something largely unknown in the Midwest. A brochure by an anonymous layman that was printed at Techny in 1954, *The Origin of the American Retreat Movement: A History of the First Decade: 1903–1912*, includes a picture of one of the pioneer retreatants, John Reiner, Sr., with his son and grandson, taken with Cardinal Tien and Father Charles Kelty, the retreat master. "John Sr.," read the caption, "had made the very first retreat at Techny in 1906."

A young man who had made a retreat in 1903 in Cleveland where he was visiting a relative in a Jesuit novitiate, according to the brochure, "made it the ambition of his life" to develop the Diocesan Union of Young Men's Societies of the Archdiocese of Chicago into an organization that would rival the Young Men's Christian Association (YMCA). It occurred to him, facing difficulties in getting the organization going, that if the members of the union made a retreat they might not be so apathetic about their work. Because he was of German ethnic background, he knew about the Society of the Divine Word at Shermerville (Techny) and their retreat work in Europe. He decided to address the union delegates on the subject of retreats at their upcoming annual convention. Stymied in his first attempt, the young man went to Shermerville, where he found open minds. If he could drum up enough men, the Society would furnish space in their technical school and find someone to preach the retreat. It would have to be in German. So on the date for the first retreat, 19–22 July 1906, from Thursday evening to Sunday afternoon, seventeen men showed up. By all accounts the affair was a spiritual success; to commemorate the occasion the retreatants commissioned the erection of a crucifix.

When the crucifix was finished some two months later, the retreatants returned for its installation. They also resolved to keep the idea and fervor of the first retreat alive by meeting together during the course of the year. In preparation for the next year's retreat, they decided to have some printed materials prepared to interest others. On 13 June 1907, twenty-six men, one from 250 miles away, arrived. At the conclusion of this second retreat the men enthusiastically approved of the establishment of the Sacred Heart Retreatants' League, which had a twofold purpose, to secure the personal fruits of the retreat and to extend the good work of retreats among the laity. They were enrolled in the Apostleship of Prayer and received monthly leaflets as a reminder of their retreat. Quarterly meetings, which they promised to attend, would do the same. According to the tenets of the gospel, they were to leaven their families, parishes, and workplaces by their good example and by fulfilling the obligations of their state of life.

In 1908, thirty-six men came for a June retreat and fifteen for another one on September 1, a total that summer of fifty-one retreatants. There were occasional setbacks, but the cause of laymen's retreats was becoming more acceptable to priests, who began to promote them. Articles began to appear praising this work. Retreats in English soon followed at Techny, as well as retreats for women, which were first conducted in 1909 at St. Ann's Home for the Elderly across the highway from the seminary.

As times changed, needs changed, and retreats changed to adapt to new situations. Increasing vocations to the SVD has always been of concern to the Society. One means of developing such vocations, it was thought, could be to bring altar boys to Techny or to East Troy for retreats. This rewarded the altar boys for their dedication in their parishes; they were able to leave home for a break. It was also a chance to acquaint these young men with the SVD and its work, while fostering any vocation God might be offering them. Popular from the 1950s on, altar boy retreats were attempted to uplift the spiritual life of the young retreatants so they could return to their daily activities strengthened in the Spirit. In 1958–1959 alone, over a thousand altar boys made a retreat. As long as this effort lasted, it, too, was very successful.

Over the years, the SVDs in North America expanded their retreat work by giving longer retreats to groups. We have already mentioned the great success Hagspiel had in this regard. Others also developed a reputation for this, for example, Father Lawrence Lovasik, who spent much of his priestly life in retreat and other related work. Father Lovasik also wrote books and pamphlets, founded two congregations of nuns, and was able to preach and conduct retreats equally well in Slovak and English. Born in Tarentum, Pennsylvania, on 22 June 1913, he worked in the Eastern Province of the SVD most of his life, preaching the Word of God in season and out of season. He wrote more than 80 books and pamphlets, gave as many as 36 retreats a year, each a week long, as well as parish missions. He was active until his death in 1986, a few days shy of his seventy-third birthday.

THE PARISH MISSION BAND AND PREACHING IN PARISHES

The parish mission, known as the *Volksmission*, was very popular in Germany during Arnold Janssen's lifetime and was brought to this country also. Jesuits and Redemptorists, in particular, had great success with these both in Germany and in America. The parish mission was not a closed retreat, but took place over several days for a week or two, sometimes even longer, in parish churches. The preachers would hold services every evening, make themselves available for counseling and giving talks to women's groups during the day, all with a view to deepening the laity's understanding of and commitment to their faith. They became the highlight of a parish's year and provided an occasion for parishoners to confess their sins and for the parish to reach out to people who had drifted away from strict observance of their Sunday obligations. To the orders that conducted such missions, it was a prime opportunity to spread word of their societies' works and enlist lay spiritual and financial support. The SVD was engaged in this apostolate for a few years. It deserves mention as another way of spreading the Word and of being of service to local churches, which would often offer support to the Society and its members in tangible ways.

In 1935 the provincial council at Techny approved a proposal by Father Joseph Ford to form a mission band that would give these parish missions. The members of this band were centered at Miramar on the East Coast. According to the proposal, the members of the mission band might also teach in SVD seminaries at Miramar or Girard. Some could labor full time in their parish mission and retreat work. The SVD became very well known throughout the East as a result of this work. Besides Ford and Lovasik, Fathers Lester Dooley, Robert Hunter, Joseph Eckert, Anthony May, Edward Luis, Theodore Bauman, and Lawrence Poetz were engaged in this work.

Perhaps Father Lester Dooley's story can stand for them all. Dooley was born in a small Illinois town called Odell in 1898. He entered high school at Techny in 1913, was ordained in 1926, and not long after was asked to replace Father William Ross as editor of *The Little Missionary*, a position he held until 1934 when he handed it over to Father Charles Erb. Dooley joined the newly organized mission band that year. By all accounts he had a great sense of humor, but was also a hard worker. Father Hunter, who knew Dooley well, comments extensively on his sense of humor, calling it "a singular charism of joy for others":

> He was the wittiest man I ever knew. It was a native noble wit, unstudied and spontaneous, which now after reflection was a singular charism of joy for others. It was enhanced by his sparkling blue eyes, a bit mischievous in their glint, an irresistible smile, an almost imperceptible dimple and thinning hair.
>
> His humor was always in the situation, never a personal reflection. The sarcastic remark, the put-down, the rapier-thrust was not part of him . . . When he would remark, "My German is poor and my Scotch low," there was added piquancy. He might ask you if you had heard about two men on the Chicago El. One said, "Was sagst du?" and the other replied, "They split a double-header with the Yankees."
>
> His coming into a silent dining room brightened up the atmosphere. He could dispel grumpiness wherever found. To live with him in a rectory or small community was a joy. When he said, "Good morning, Miss O'Malley" to the dourest German housekeeper, there was instant cheer.
>
> Community living needs a generous seasoning of his type and style of humor . . . If St. Teresa of Avila counseled her Sisters not to suppress the precious spark of humor within them, she knew the importance, maybe necessity of that commodity in religious life.

Father Dooley continued his interest in writing and produced several books, one of them a book of sermons for children which he titled *Hello Halo*. This was very well received. In 1965 he had his first heart attack and died suddenly of a second one in 1966, just as he was walking into the sanctuary to give a conference to the Missionary Sisters of the Holy Spirit, on what was probably his favorite topic, devotion to the Holy Spirit.

An activity in which virtually every SVD priest engaged in over the years was preaching and helping out in parishes near the seminaries they were assigned to. Typically the priests went out, "on supply" as it was called, on Saturdays and Sundays to help out in parishes. On Saturdays they heard confessions, often from 3:30 to 6:00 in the afternoon and from 7:30 to 9:00 in the evening. On Sundays most celebrated two Masses, preaching at both. When missionaries came home on leave, they did the same. In addition, they might be assigned to give talks and take up collections in parishes assigned to the Society by the bishops for this purpose. These talks and sermons were taken seriously and diligently prepared.

The results of this work were important in forming the attitudes of candidates for the Society. While the ethos of some religious orders was such that helping out in parishes was infrequent, SVDs learned from their early days in the Society that they should make themselves available to help out the diocesan clergy. This they did selflessly, often after a full week in the classroom teaching Latin or mathematics or running an office. At other times an SVD might take over a parish for an extended time so the pastor could take a vacation or sabbatical, as we saw shortly after Fathers Peil and Fischer arrived in America. In this way the Society became known. It built up good will among priests and bishops. They made it clear that they belonged to a missionary society and brought the topic of missions into their sermons. Often they left printed materials behind for the parishioners to take home. In this way they also won many benefactors for SVD missions. But most important of all, the way in which SVD priests kept active in parish life insured that the ethos of the society would be pastoral and practical, even though many of its members would go on to higher studies.

Boxes of supplies leaving the Techny loading dock for missions in the Philippines, China, and the Dutch East Indies (today, Indonesia) in March 1926.

The Mission Press at Techny. Brother Disibodius (Franz Hageni, 1882-1967), one of the press's stalwart, long-serving brothers, stands in the left background.

In 1947, forty-two Divine Word Missionaries, the largest group ever to receive mission crosses at the same time, left from Techny for India, China, New Guinea, Japan, Africa, Indonesia and the Philippines.

The annual staging of a major play or musical by the seminarians was a key event in the Techny year. Here is the cast of The Pirates of Penzance, in which the pirate king is Ernest Brandewie, the author of this volume.

Brother Archangel (Jan Przybylski, 1881-1973), baker, beloved by all who knew him, renowned for his spirit of prayer, gives guidance to brother novice Larry Winkler.

Brother Tiberius (Wilhelm Beckers, 1887-1978), who worked in the press and then as head sacristan, was also Techny's candle maker, using wax from Brother Frederick's (Heinz Huelsewische, 1879-1956) bees.

Brother Regis (Ernest Leuthner, 1895-1969) made his watch-repair hobby a valuable asset for the Techny community.

Brother Roman (Norbert Hertel, 1907-1996) at the organ console he helped build, keep in repair, and play masterfully to accompany Techny's liturgies.

Brother Charles (Victor Reckamp, 1905-1996) managed the Techny Gardens, which he made nationally famous.

The seminary at Girard, Pennsylvania, opened in 1912, the first mission house established after Techny.

In the foreground of this picture of Miramar, near Duxbury, Massachusetts, is Cardinal William O'Connell's summer home, which he offered to the SVD in 1922. The addition to the right was added later as a school and dormitory.

This building at Epworth, Iowa, became the central, four-year college of the Divine Word missionaries in 1965, replacing a Civil War era Methodist Church building used for various purposes by the SVD (inset).

This building was erected as the home of the SVD's first Canadian seminary and mission house, founded at Granby, Quebec, in 1949.

The chapel and south wing of St. Michael's Seminary, Conesus, New York, used variously from the 1930s through the post-Vatican Council II era as a brother candidate school, brother and clerical novitiate, juniorate and school of philosophy. A sacramental wine vineyard was also located at Conesus.

An aerial view of the SVD seminary in East Troy, Wisconsin, which served as a clerical novitiate and minor seminary and today as a residence for retired brothers and priests.

The Divine Word Residence in Bordentown, New Jersey, that replaced the original, stately nineteenth-century mansion once owned by Joseph Bonaparte, King of Naples and Spain and brother of the French emperor Napoleon, that served as the first Divine Word Seminary at Bordentown.

In 1956, the SVD opened its first seminary on the west coast in Riverside, California, east of Los Angeles.

When this building was opened in 1960, the Perrysburg minor seminary was the most striking of the Divine Word seminaries in North America.

Divine Word College in Washington, DC, was opened in 1962. It was built with insurance funds from the Techny Mission Press fire to house a post-ordination "pastoral-year" graduate program. The Brother Wendelin house for brother formation is out of view to the right.

6

Formation of SVD Missionary Priests

Continuity in Change, 1909–1960

INTRODUCTION

The work of formation is the most important activity of a religious congregation, whatever its particular purpose or charism might be. It is lifelong, but especially important in the early years of initiation into the society that aspirants have chosen as the group they would like to join. As Joseph Becker in his book *The Re-Formed Jesuits* states: "Formation is the key to the character of any group. 'Formation' imparts the 'form' to the body; that is, it determines what the soul, the animating principle, will be. To emphasize the prominence of formation he claims that "no change is so important as a change in formation."[1] Though Becker writes about the Jesuits, the same could be said of the Society of the Divine Word and all other religious societies as well.

Formation for brothers and seminarians was quite different in the pre-Vatican II SVD. And for this reason they are given separate chapters in this book. The first chapter of this part of the history deals with the formation of seminarians, who were usually called "clerics" in the SVD. That formation was threefold: intellectual, spiritual, and missionary. All are important, and all three were present in every educational unit of the Society, from high school through junior college, philosophy, and the years of theology. Neither did formation stop with ordination or perpetual vows. It was lifelong. This book, however, intends to give only the highlights of SVD formation and point out some of the changes that occurred after the Second World War and Vatican Council II.

Briefly, we shall show that at the high school level, the emphasis was put on *intellectual* formation, stressing Latin and other languages. During the novitiate the concern was *spiritual* formation, but it returned to the intellectual again in junior college, philosophy, and theology. Missionary formation received its own section. The following chapter is on the formation of the brothers and the changes

---

1. Joseph Becker, *The Re-Formed Jesuits: A History of Changes in Jesuit Formation during the Decade 1965–1975* (San Francisco: Ignatius Press, 1992), p. 13.

that occurred when the two types of formation, clerical and brother, came together. The different styles of formation for brothers and seminarians derived from the times in which they developed. It must also be emphasized that the pre-Vatican II formation was successful in its day. Anyone who doubts that SVD formation produced self-giving missionary-religious priests and brothers who vowed their lives to carry out the great commission of Christ to make disciples of all nations will have a hard time proving the point.

BACKGROUND

To appreciate the history of formation goals and practices before Vatican II— and this is true for all religious communities—one has first to understand the impact of monastic and mendicant orders on the church. Second, one must keep in mind the legislation imposed to establish seminaries at the Council of Trent (1545–1563). Equally important in the case of most congregations founded since Trent is the *Rule* of the Society of Jesus and *The Spiritual Exercises* of St. Ignatius of Loyola. These two documents have had an impact that is hard to overestimate. The pattern of apostolic religious life established by Jesuits must be included as one of the most important influences on formation in the Society of the Divine Word, along with seventeenth-century seminary education developments shaped by the Vincentians founded by St. Vincent de Paul in 1625 and Sulpicians founded in 1641 by Father Jean Jacques Olier. This background, plus general directives regulating formation that were periodically issued by the Vatican, produced a great uniformity both in the intellectual and spiritual formation of priests. While there were many cultural differences found among priests and religious in various countries, it is also true that there was an international "clerical" culture of amazing homogeneity.

In addition to these elements that the Society had in common with other orders and societies of apostolic life, the original element in the formation of Divine Word Missionaries came from the spirituality and personality of the founder, Arnold Janssen. His style of spirituality and intellectual life, as well as the missionary purpose for which he founded his congregation, affected the formation of his members. This is useful to address in more detail, because, as in so many other instances, it directly affected the kind of formation that characterized the SVD in North America.

THE FOUNDER AND FORMATION

Before founding the Society of the Divine Word, Father Janssen was a diocesan priest, dedicated from the beginning to a teacher's life.[2] His education in Germany, not unique for the times, was quite different from what it would have been either in France or in America at the time. Although the SVD would institute a pattern where attendance at a minor seminary was the ordinary entrée to novi-

---

2. The source for what follows is Fritz Bornemann, *Arnold Janssen der Gründer des Steyler Missionswerkes, 1837–1909: Ein Lebensbild nach zeitgenössischen Quellen* (Steyl: Sekretariat Arnold Janssen, 1969).

tiate and membership, only after graduating from the *Gymnasium* in Bocholt did Janssen leave home to go to Münster to begin his higher studies. On 2 August 1856, Janssen wrote to one of his former teachers:

> I came to Münster with the clear intention to stay here for a time and study mathematics. I did this very diligently for the first year. But now that the time has come to make the decision whether I should begin my theology now or later, I firmly decided to spend two or three years more studying mathematics and the natural sciences in order to get a [teaching] certificate in these subjects and then to do my theology . . . The reasons for my decision are first my interest in these sciences and secondly my desire to get a teaching certificate.[3]

In Münster he stayed for three semesters in the Borromeum, a seminary for those who were interested in the priesthood. Janssen then transferred to the University of Bonn where he studied for the next five semesters, living not in a seminary but in a private home. Here he continued his studies in mathematics and the sciences and he received his teacher's certificate. At Bonn he competed successfully for a prize in mathematics. His twenty-six-page paper was written in Latin, had more than seventy diagrams, and won first prize. After this he returned to Münster. His bishop was satisfied with Janssen's overall progress, also in theology, for he had attended some theology lectures also while attending the University of Bonn, so the bishop dispensed him from all but four more semesters of theology. These two years of theology he took in Münster where he lived in the Borromeum for the first year. By this time it was organized as a real seminary. During his last year of theology before his ordination he lived in the regular seminary near the Ueberwasser church. During these last two semesters he also took more examinations in the sciences and other secular subjects, for which he had to give demonstration lectures. One of his worst marks was in religion, and his best were in chemistry and mathematics.

Janssen had to be bright to achieve what he did in so short a time. He also had very little experience living the life of a seminarian, which meant he had little first-hand experience to fall back on when he was setting up his own training center for religious priests and brothers. In another sense, one could say he had been in an excellent formation program ever since he was a young boy at home.

Later, when developing the SVD formation program, Janssen had problems, but he was flexible and learned fast. His first appeal for people who might be interested in working for the foreign missions, especially in China, resulted in three applications, one a priest, Peter Bill, and two major seminarians, Franz Xavier Reichart and John Baptist Anzer, certainly a meager enough beginning. Bill and Reichart left six months later. Anzer stayed. The disagreements were significant in light of issues that would become important in Divine Word Missionary spirituality and formation. Father Bill, who had already been a pastor and was older than Janssen himself, wanted an association of diocesan priests who would go to the China missions. The new house also needed statutes and the question of who

---

3. Fritz Bornemann, *Arnold Janssen der Gründer*, p. 13.

would be superior had to be solved. Janssen was elected and ratified by the Bishop of Roermond as superior. By this time, Janssen was thinking in terms of some kind of religious vows.

First Janssen insisted that everyone who joined should be a member of the Third Order of St. Dominic. For diocesan priests and laity in those times, joining a third order was quite popular. For Janssen this was an interim solution that could have become permanent. His cofounders, however, objected. They were convinced that the restrictions of the Third Order's rules would not make sense in the missions. The rule most frequently objected to was the dietary regulation that specified four days of abstinence from meat per week and one day of fast. In the first draft of the statutes of 1876, Janssen already began to modify the Third Order rules. For those in a mission house he kept three days of abstinence and recommended a fast day. These should be observed in the missions "if possible." In the first statutes of the Society he also spent much time describing the devotions and patrons that were to become such a large part of the Society's formation program later, also in America. In one part of this long section, a third of the length of the statutes, he described what he considers should be the "spirit of our congregation":

> It should be a spirit of devotion, a spirit of faith and hope, a spirit of humility and self-denial . . . for our congregation can only do something worthwhile, if we seek to do his will alone . . . For this reason the Society follows exactly the teachings of spiritual writers that God the Lord shows us his will most surely in the directives of our superiors, as well as in the signs of the times. Although the superior should certainly not presume to think that every command he gives is actually God's will, the subjects who obey are following God's will and a loving God will never hold it against them for following and obeying the commands [of this superior].

When the congregation finally got around to holding its first general chapter and began drafting its first constitutions, the entire rule of the Third Order of St. Dominic was dropped in 1885. The reasons were the same that had been given in 1875–76 by his cofounders.

As Bornemann tells the tale, the whole issue of formation, whether into the spiritual, pastoral, missionary, or intellectual life, proceeded in ad hoc fashion. Also, once the idea of the kind of Latin school which the founder started caught on, the rapidity of growth required experimentation. In the beginning, the founder had to make do with a minimum of resources. But it must also have been exciting to be part of such success, whether in terms of the many retreats conducted, the students accepted, the constant building going on, the rapid expansion into new mission fields, and the recognition of the Society's significance on the part of the Holy See.

THE INFLUENCE OF FERDINAND MEDITS, CM

One person who became a close friend of the founder and had a great impact on formation in the SVD was a Vincentian priest born in Hungary, Ferdinand Medits. Younger than Janssen by four years, Medits first got acquainted with

Janssen through correspondence. As a preacher of parish missions, he was well acquainted with the ins and outs of the Austrian bureaucracy and was very helpful to the founder as he tried to develop St. Gabriel's, the Society's major seminary in Mödling, near Vienna. The two met personally in Vienna in 1883, and Medits became one of the founder's important advisers and the only priest, other than his own brother John, with whom he used the familiar form *du* ("you"), rather than the formal second person German pronoun *Sie*. As a member of the Vincentian congregation, which was dedicated to the education of priests and the direction of seminaries, Medits was in a position to help the founder in many ways.

In 1886, the founder invited Medits to come to Steyl for several months to conduct the novitiate for the brothers and clerics and to train the new novice master, Bernard Eickenbrock. Before he left he had several recommendations for Father Janssen to consider. First, the novitiate should last for two years; second, the novices should be separated from all other students and should have their own separate dining room, chapel, recreation area, and classes; third, there would be strict maintenance of the separation of the novices from lay people. He also recommended that the amount and quality of the food be improved. Anything saved in expense in this area would just go to the doctor. By this time the buildings were all completed and more money was available, so the founder took Medits's advice on all counts and conditions, and moods began to improve.

An additional point must be made about Janssen's ideas about intellectual formation in his Society. He envisioned a cadre of well-educated priests within the Society dedicated to the study of science, especially but not exclusively, theological science. These were to be the teachers of those going to the missions. This was vigorously opposed by his cofounders, who insisted that everyone joining the Society should go to the missions. Janssen remained firm on this and always supported higher studies for those who had the ability and interest. Many of his seminary professors went to Rome for higher studies, and in 1888 he rented a residence for his priests studying there. He also supported advanced studies in other universities. Among the early members who followed such a course were Wilhelm Schmidt at the University of Berlin and Stephan Richarz who came to the U. S. after studying geology in Munich.

THE STAGES AND PLACES OF SVD FORMATION IN NORTH AMERICA

When the first German SVDs came to the U. S., they brought with them what they were familiar with from their own training and formation as they went about setting up the seminary at Techny. Again, in the beginning it was haphazard. Students were accepted at different ages and stages of education. Those few available teachers ended up teaching all kinds of courses, two of which, Latin and religion, it was understood, any priest could teach. Germans teaching English to American students was problematic. For the first twenty-five years, the program followed the European model, which featured a six-year classical course called the minor seminary, plus six years of philosophy and theology called the major. Many other seminaries in America followed this same 6+6 sequence rather than the customary American model of four years of high school, plus four of college, plus four of graduate school. As we have seen, it was not until the 1960s that the SVD adopted the American format totally. After the first six years, the original pattern called for a two-year novitiate, the second year of which included some courses in philosophy.

As each of the early seminaries was opened—Techny (1909), Girard, Pennsylvania (1912), Bay St. Louis, Mississippi (1923), Miramar in Duxbury, Massachusetts (1922)—they were envisioned as six-year seminaries, a close facsimile of the German *Gymnasium*. The two-year novitiate that followed the minor seminary was located at East Troy, Wisconsin, which opened in 1921. Very soon it was clear that such a system would be very costly, especially in manpower. Also there was a push to Americanize the system. Thus a central two-year college was established at Girard in 1935. Techny, Miramar, and the newly opened seminary in Epworth, Iowa, were or included four-year high school seminaries. Seminaries that were built later followed this four-year pattern. Novitiate at East Troy followed the two-year college at Girard. Through all these years, with the exception of Bay St. Louis, which was a full major seminary, the two years of philosophy and the four years of theology were at Techny.

A major change took place in 1941, when the two-year novitiate was placed immediately after high school. There were several reasons for this decision, the primary one being to save vocations. In practical terms, the change was introduced by Father Felix Glorius, who had gone to Florissant, Missouri, to investigate how the Jesuits handled the juniorate system. Getting future SVDs into novitiate at the age of eighteen instead of twenty, it was thought, would increase the chances that more would persevere. At this younger age, they would be more malleable. Such future stalwarts as James Artzer, John Fincutter, Paul McVinney, and Robert Myers were among the first to go through the new program.

HIGH SCHOOL SEMINARY FORMATION

Most American boys entering the seminary were about fourteen years old. Two prominent reasons were given for taking them so early. The first was to help them grow up uncorrupted by "the world." The second was the need to know Latin. In regard to the first, the Council of Trent (1545–1563) had legislated that every bishop should establish a seminary in his diocese where boys would begin to live, be given the tonsure, and be required to wear the cassock. Thus, they could be protected from submitting to the attractions of the world and be trained in piety. Realizing that adolescence was a tumultuous time in a boy's life, it was thought best to isolate boys from "the world" as early as possible. The radical matter of the step to enter the SVD minor seminary was underscored best by one symbolic event. High school seminarians were forbidden to go home for the Christmas holidays, the quintessential American family holiday. Thus the Divine Word Missionaries signaled to the candidate that if he persevered, the SVD would be his home. This rule against letting minor seminarians go home for Christmas was changed only in the 1950s.

The second key rationale for the minor seminary was the need to learn Latin, the official language of the Western, Roman church and the common language of international clerical culture, and of the liturgy. The breviary, the official prayer of the priest, which he was obliged to recite daily, also was to be prayed only in Latin. In addition, lectures in philosophy and dogmatic theology, the core curriculum for the priest-to-be, were conducted in Latin. Texts in these disciplines and others, such as moral theology and canon law, were also in Latin. Like mathematics for physics, Latin was the gatekeeper for higher studies in philosophy and theology. Without passing grades in Latin no one could hope to be admitted to vows and the major seminary. And the emphasis on learning Latin, too, signaled to the student that he was entering an international fraternity that would take precedence over his family by birth. Father Herman Richarz said of the American boys with whom he worked, "Arithmetic is generally easy for them, and even though Latin case endings are foreign to them and cause difficulty in the beginning, they make up for this by the speed with which they learn their vocabulary."

Greek was also important in the curriculum. This, too, was part of a classical program, but another reason for studying Greek was to be able to read the New Testament in its original language. It was also considered critical to learn German, which students began in the second year of high school. The reader will recall how important it seemed at the beginning of the Society in North America to maintain the good German spirit. As non-Germans entered, the theory was that learning German would aid in the adaptation of attitudes that were felt to be prominent in German culture: a sense of discipline, hard work, perseverance, and so forth. American students were required to take five years of German language courses, three years in high school and two years in college. The daily routine of prenovitiate students from 1909 through the 1960s underwent only minor changes. Students rose and retired early. Between those two pillars of the day, they were kept very busy. The daily order was arranged as follows:

School Days

5:30	Rising
5:55	Morning Prayers
6:05	Holy Mass
7:30	Breakfast. Recess
8:15	First Recitation [class period]
9:05	Second Recitation
10:15	Third Recitation
11:05	Fourth Recitation
11:50	Examination of Conscience
12:00	Dinner. Visit to Blessed Sacrament. Recreation
1:30	Study Period
2:00	Fifth Recitation
2:50	Sixth Recitation
3:30	Recess
4:25	Visit to Blessed Sacrament. Study
6:00	Supper. Recess
7:00	Study Period
8:00	Night Prayers or Devotions
9:00	Retire

Wednesday

3:30	Visit to Blessed Sacrament. Recreation
7:30	Conference or Silence

Thursday

7:10	(a.m.) Manual Work
4:20	(p.m.) Stations of the Cross. Study

Friday (p.m.)

4:25	Confessions. Study

Saturday (p.m.)

3:30	Bathing

5:00	Study	6:20	Morning Prayers
6:00	Supper. Silence during and after supper	6:30	Holy Mass
		7:15	Breakfast
7:00	Conference or sermon	8:15	High Mass
7:30	Devotions/Compline (sung)	4:00	Vespers (sung)
		5:15	Study
	Sunday	7:15	Silence
5:50	Rising		

Some comments are in order. The brief recess after breakfast, for example, might be spent cleaning up the washrooms or clearing the dining room, perhaps dust mopping the dormitory. Students would be assigned to these tasks. Although Wednesday was a class day, beginning at 3:30 in the afternoon, students were free. For generations of SVD students, the announcement, "This afternoon we will have 'Wednesday order'" (before the Thursday free day or a special holiday) was the best news of the week. It meant a chance to organize a basketball, baseball, or softball game, depending on the season, or hockey if the ice was good. Handball games on outdoor courts were popular for many. Everyone was encouraged to take part in these and other games, as vigorously as possible. This activity, too, was part of the daily routine and, therefore, important. Often the Latin adage *mens sana in corpore sano* ("a healthy mind in a healthy body") was quoted.

Because Thursday was not a class day, Saturday morning classes made up the difference. Manual work occupied the morning on Thursdays. The afternoon was free for extracurricular activities, writing letters, practicing for an upcoming play. But it came to an end at 4:20, at which time the regular school day schedule started again with an afternoon study period. On Saturday evening, time was set aside for music practice, when the community would prepare the Gregorian chants for the next day's liturgy. It was a busy schedule, and it was to be followed rigorously. A quote from the brief introduction to the *Book of Rules for the Mission Students of the American Province of the Society of the Divine Word* (1935), from which this daily order is taken, shows how the daily order was regarded:

This booklet will tell you how you can become a good mission student. It shows you what God demands of you during your classical course in the Mission House, which is a preparation for your future religious, priestly, and missionary life. It points out to you which virtues you should practice and which duties you should fulfill.

Perform everything well and faithfully, and you will experience that to serve God means to reign over the evil passions of your heart and to rule in the realm of virtue. For the conscientious observance of these rules trains you in the spirit of self-sacrifice, in obedience and humility, in the love of God and your neighbor. It strengthens you to fight the temptations of the enemies of your soul and your holy vocation.

Often ask yourself the same question which St. Bernard put to himself: *Ad quid venisti?* "Why did you come here?" With a self-sacrificing heart answer it in the words of your Divine Master: *Ecce venio facere voluntatem tuam.* "Behold, I come to do thy will." God's will is expressed to you by your rules. If you perform them well, the Mission House will be a place of peace, joy, and blessings for you. The exact observance of the rules will also be the greatest help to develop your character and to persevere in your sublime vocation. *Qui regulae vivit, Deo vivit* ("who lives for the rule, lives for God") St. Gregory Nazianzen.

As the minor seminary and the brother candidates' schools developed in the Society of the Divine Word, they became more and more like a private boarding school for boys with the special purpose of testing their vocation to the religious and missionary life either as a priest or brother. Mixed in throughout the weeks and months were extracurricular activities, plays, mission club meetings, sports and games, a sensible prayer life and liturgical celebrations, which concentrated on the devotions handed down from the founder. The liturgies, Mass every morning, special solemn liturgies on Sundays and high feast days were always well prepared at Arnold Janssen's insistence. Holy Week, Easter, Pentecost, and the feast of the Holy Trinity were always solemn occasions, as were Christmas and all of the feast days of the Blessed Mother, to whom every minor seminarian and brother candidate consecrated himself repeatedly. Every night, prayer concluded with the *Salve Regina* ("Hail Holy Queen") or other seasonal hymn to the Blessed Mother and was followed by the prayer: *Nos cum prole pia benedicat Virgo Maria* ("Mary with your loving Son, bless us each and every one").

The busy days passed quickly, and a sense of community and camaraderie developed. Many, of course, left even during the year, more during the summer holidays. The question of a vocation was one in which both the Society and the individual had a great stake and both had the obligation to discern whether there were signs of a true vocation to the Society. All who had any knowledge of the candidate for promotion were consulted, including faculty and superiors. Confessors were limited to exerting their influence on what was called "the internal forum," that is, in the privacy of the confessional. If a confessor had serious doubts that a boy had a vocation, he was expected to advise the aspirant to leave the seminary, but he could not take any other steps to get a student to leave. The officials whose opinions were especially sought and decisive were called "prefects." In contemporary terminology, prefects would be called "deans of students."

The Prefects

At all levels of formation, the prefects were important. Although the faculty as a whole exerted an influence on the students by their example and teaching and in the way they attended community exercises, it was the prefects, often aided in their duties by one or more assistant prefects, who had the most influence and impact on development. They were carefully chosen and many were remembered with fondness and appreciation for the good they accomplished. Among those who served long and with great distinction are men such as Charles Malin, Ray Sanders, Andrew Rentko, Edward Dudink, Casmir Murawski, Wilbert Wagner, William Adams, Charles Leisring, William Shea, John McHenry, and Paul Jacobi.

One seminarian compared the prefect to the father of a family, the one person immediately responsible for the physical, intellectual, and spiritual life of every seminarian. In the high school seminary he perhaps had to keep a sharper eye on his charges, making sure, for example, that they were actually studying during study periods, instead of reading a Western paperback between the covers of a large Latin grammar. A seminarian describes a prefect as follows:

> By means of a weekly conference, occasional private chats with individuals and little reminders when needed, he keeps a check on our total welfare and constantly spurs us on to become the kind of missionaries we ought to be. Of course, his main concern is for our spiritual life and our studies. But that doesn't mean he has no interest in our health . . .
>
> Our prefect, realizing that he can do more for his seminarians by example than by preaching, tries to spend as much time with us as he possibly can. When the seminarians come to the dining room or chapel, Father is right there with them. And it is by no means a rare sight to see him out on the campus, working up an appetite with the rest of the seminarians . . .
>
> Father has been prefect of the major seminarians for ten years. But if you knew him you would realize why. For whether he is on the campus, in his office or in chapel, our prefect is always the perfect example of what we seminarians should strive to become.

Emil Lesage epitomized the ideal prefect. He held that office in different houses over many years, alternating between being prefect and local superior (or rector). Emil was born in Belgium in 1899, the oldest of ten children. When he was still a child, his parents migrated to America and settled in Moline, Illinois, where Emil grew up as a typical American, interested in sports and the active life. He never got to go to the foreign missions, but found his mission in instilling the missionary spirit in the minds and hearts of many.[4]

Lesage was a gentle man, not in the least pretentious. He always seemed awed by little things that happened, reacting with a sense of surprise and satisfaction at small successes, for example, when his seminarians won a baseball game against another seminary, or when he, with one of the seminarians as his partner, became handball champions at Epworth. He enjoyed drama and encouraged seminarians to write and produce their own scripts. Lesage had a great spiritual influence on those under his care and was remembered for the "conferences" he gave wherever he worked. These conferences were a regular part of the seminarians' week, and were often on spiritual topics, for example, on how to keep recollected during the day and make one's studies an offering to God for the success of the missions. Other conferences would be on practical matters or the condition of the house. Lesage was long remembered for his conferences. The present writer found him-

---

4. Father Lesage (1899–1979) was joined in the SVD by three brothers. Alphonse (1904–1977) worked as a missionary priest in Indonesia and the Philippines; Joseph (1908–1990) became a brother and took the name Cletus; he also worked as a missionary running a press in Ghana, West Africa. Maurice (1911–1977) went as a missionary priest to Ghana in West Africa, where he worked mainly in education; he became famous as an expert on West African snakes.

self talking with two priests who had celebrated their golden jubilees as Divine Word Missionaries. They still remembered conferences Emil Lesage gave when he was prefect at Girard when it was the central college, especially those that dealt with sexual matters. While not remembering many specific details, they recalled the impact these conferences had on them, explaining many things and confirming them in their vocations at the same time.

If a student gave promise that he had good health, requisite intellectual, spiritual, and moral character, and the desire to continue in his vocation, he proceeded to the next stage of formation. Before 1941 this meant advancing to the first two years of college. After 1941 it meant going directly into novitiate.

The Brothers and Teachers

Prefects were not the only influence on the minor seminarians. The entire SVD community was meant to give an example of what the student's later life would be like, and an effort was made to station at these houses only brothers and priests who were "regular" in their observance of the vows and exemplary in their attendance at community liturgies. While it is true that brothers in later years, when the pressure was on to increase their educational level and make them equal members, accused superiors of using them as cheap labor and denying them requisite professional training, it is also true that few seminarians left the SVD without feeling intense admiration for the brothers. Brothers such as Otto at Miramar, Henry and Leonard at Epworth, Joseph at Conesus, and Conrad, Felix, and Nicholas at East Troy were the spiritual and physical core of their communities. It is unfortunate that the very nature of their work makes it hard to single out their accomplishments, for their impact came from year after year of faithfully caring for the buildings, working the farm, insuring that there was food in the kitchen. Not spectacular accomplishments, but the work they did in a spirit of prayer taught generations of boys, both those who went on in the SVD and the far greater numbers who left, what religious life was about.

The corps of teachers was similarly dedicated, even if their daily interactions with the students in the classroom and the need to grade the students' result exposed them to greater scrutiny. It is hard to pick a single teacher to exemplify those who taught the core courses of Latin, Greek, biology, history, and English in high school and college. Names such as Joseph Shendill, John Beemster, Terrence McGurk, Arnold Lang (Langenkamp), Lawrence Bohnen, James Artzer, Anthony Deppe, and Joseph Busch come to mind. For our purposes, though, Father Joseph Finger may represent all these and others.

Immediately after his ordination in 1927, Father Finger was assigned to teach at Miramar in Massachusetts. Two months later he came down with tuberculosis, almost an occupational hazard for the early generation of SVDs. Twice he had these health problems and twice he spent months in sanitaria in the West and Southwest. It cost him one of his lungs. He came back to teach at Miramar, then in the high school and college at Techny, at Bay St. Louis, at Girard when it was the central college, and finally, in 1941, back to Techny to the novitiate where he remained until he retired from teaching in 1958 after 31 years in this apostolate.

After his retirement from teaching he began to give retreats and conferences to various communities of religious and was very successful at this too. With a master's degree in English, he was virtually without a trace of the accent of his native German language, an accomplishment in which he took great pride. In addition to Latin and Greek, Finger also taught English literature, as well as homiletics (preaching) at times. He could display a keen sense of irony and sarcasm, though he often made himself the butt of his humor. As John Donaghey remembers Father Finger, when he was teaching Greek to his novice class at Techny, he was a lifesaver:

> [His] evenhandedness and kindness . . . humor and good sense, enabled us to survive the pressure cooker that was novitiate. I recall one episode. We had a test in Biblical Greek. The following class Fr. Finger walked in, ran through the test and then called out dramatically to one of the novices: "Frater, you translated the Greek sentence 'Our Lord healed them from evil spirits' with the words 'Our Lord cured them from bad breath.' Did he use a mouthwash or a toothpaste?"

In a more serious vein, Donaghey, who had been Finger's student, and later lived with him as a confrere, and still later was his provincial superior, described Father Finger's personality in a brief sketch of formation in the early years of this century:

> As a person, our confrere and friend, Father Joseph was very emotional and highly sensitive. He was naturally affectionate and needed personal affirmation and emotional support constantly. As with us all, he appreciated attention and treasured and welcomed love. Unfortunately he had come through a system of training that was not only not responsive to emotion or affection but was highly repressive. He was never able to shake that training that had taught him only too well to distrust his emotions and had drilled into him that emotions, however good, were usually at fault in all human situations and that, if not actually evil, they were borderline sinful. And so he was frequently torn between what he innately felt to be right and what he had been taught to see as wrong.

Joseph Finger died in 1989, at the age of eighty-eight.

THE NOVITIATE

More important than intellectual formation, according to authorities on religious life, was the training one received in the ways of the spiritual life. The minor seminary and college were certainly replete with such formation, as the major seminary would be after novitiate. Novices began wearing the habit when they entered the novitiate on investiture day. The newly invested were told that they would wear the habit the rest of their lives, if they persevered—a gift for which they should pray daily. Their habit was basically the same garb as that worn by Divine Word priests (and with slight differences, by the brothers): a plain black cassock, a long dress-like garment that reached to the ankles, with a white collar around the neck, and a broad cincture around the waist. On investiture day, they were given the title *Frater* ("Brother") by which they would be known until ordination. (*Frater* was also convenient as a way to differentiate "clerics," seminarians in vows, from the brothers in the large Techny community.)

During novitiate, the novice was to dedicate himself to understanding and advancing in the spiritual life and to the study of the constitutions of the Society. In regard to the rule, or constitutions, the core idea imparted in novitiate was that the rule was a means to the salvation of one's soul. If one followed the rule, he would also have success in his work for the salvation of the souls of others. And one's personal holiness, it was stressed, would become the means God would use to bring more souls to salvation. Following the rule, furthermore, was the practical way to achieve "perfection" as a religious. In language that after Vatican Council II many would find offensive, the novice was told that theirs was a higher state than that of the laity and that the three vows of poverty, celibacy, and obedience, if followed sincerely, would be an occasion for great grace. They were to strive to be worthy of the favor God showed them by calling them to this state, and they were to be aware that this call imposed a greater obligation to become perfect in the Christian life than that of the laity.

The actual daily order of the novitiate did not differ greatly from that of major seminarians in vows or for the priests and brothers. It was thought that this life of days spent mainly in silence, work, study, and prayer in the mission house was the ideal for missionaries in the field and for those working in parishes in the home countries. Every SVD, he was taught, whatever his work, whether he lived alone or in community, was to have a daily order to follow. This he was to submit to the provincial for approval. That daily order included time for meditation and for Mass in the early morning, for spiritual reading, for an examination of conscience at noontime, and a general examination of conscience at night and night prayers. A clearly specified time of retiring at night and rising in the morning was also required. Exceptions were, of course, possible, but they should remain just that, exceptions. To be faithful to such a daily order meant you were a good Divine Word missionary religious.

The best way to consider the daily order is in the context of "striving." This may also give the reader a sense of the atmosphere of these two years, which were more active than quiet, contrary to what one might otherwise think. This emphasis on striving, moreover, reflects the long years when Father Felix Glorius was novice master. Many times, Father Glorius told novices that they had to strive. For what? For perfection. After all, Christ in the sacred scriptures had said: "You must be made perfect, as your heavenly Father is perfect" (Matthew 5:48). What did it mean "to strive" in the setting of the novitiate and the daily order?

The wake-up bell, the loud clanging of a large hand-held bell, jolted everybody awake at 4:45. Novices slept in a large open dormitory, each bed surrounded by curtains that were drawn only at night. The novice needed little space for clothes, because he had few. A narrow locker and a small dresser sufficed. As soon as the bell had rung, the dormitory "senior" (as the one responsible for the room was called) flung open all the windows, whether it was spring, summer, fall, or winter. He was quick at this, because he was striving. Everyone sprang out of bed as quickly as possible, fell on their knees for a brief prayer, when they were to recollect the points they had prepared the night before for the meditation that would follow morning prayers. To lie in bed definitely meant one was not striving. As quickly as possible the novice washed his face, brushed his teeth, and shaved — in cold water if he was really striving—so he could get to chapel as soon as possible. To strive meant one got there by 5:00, 5:10 at the absolute latest. Morning prayers in common started at 5:15 promptly and were taken from the official Society book of prayer, the *Vademecum* ("Come with me") that Society members carried with them wherever they traveled. After morning prayer came meditation. If he was really striving, the novice knelt upright for the whole forty-five minute meditation.

The novice was trained to follow the methods and spirit of prayer taught by St. Ignatius of Loyola. He recalled the topic of his meditation and read a passage from the sacred scriptures related to this topic. He was to imagine the scene and mentally reconstruct it. Then he reflected on three key points, prayed over them, and applied the lessons learned to the betterment of his life. All this was intended to lead to insights called *lumina* or "lights." The *lumina* he wrote down in a small notebook kept for this purpose. Periodically the novice master would ask to see the *lumina*. Of course, if one had fallen asleep during meditation—and with practice it was possible to fall asleep even while kneeling—then one was not striving and appropriate admonitions and penances would be given.

After meditation came Mass, to which an hour was devoted. If Mass took a half-hour, then the novices had a half-hour more for meditation and thanksgiving for the benefits received during Mass before they went to breakfast at 7:15. Everybody was enjoined to eat a hearty breakfast meal comprised of cereal, coffee, eggs, and bread. There was always plenty of butter and honey from Techny's own cows and bees, though if the novice was really striving he would never put butter and honey together on Brother Archangel's whole wheat bread, because this could slip into *gula*, or gluttony. There might be cold cuts to put on the bread. On Sundays and feast days there would be strudel and liver sausage on the table, a custom that went all the way back to the founder's practice in Steyl and was recommended for every house in the Society. Since the early days of the Society, when the first missionaries convinced the founder that the many fast days he recommended were impossible for missionaries, there was never great stress placed on denying oneself food. To give up sugar in coffee was recommended. To give up a dessert now and then was acceptable, but it should not always be done, for such penances could lead to ostentation and pride. What was primary was to keep up one's health in order to endure the unavoidable rigors of missionary life. There was always enough to eat.

All meals were eaten without conversation. Instead, novices took turns reading to the rest from a spiritual book, the life of a saint perhaps, or a letter from a missionary, perhaps—though rarely—from an article describing an activity of the pope. On Sundays and certain specified feast days conversation at meals was allowed, and this was much appreciated. On ordinary days, however, silence was first broken at 1:45 p.m. when the novices had a recreation period. They then kept silence again until after supper when there was a recreation period from 6:30 until it was time for meditation preparation beginning at 7:15. If one had to say something, for example, to give directions during work or during other periods of silence, this was supposed to be done in Latin. While this helped develop facility with spoken Latin, it also helped maintain the silence, since many found it more difficult to speak in Latin than to keep quiet. Indeed, as late as 1964 when Father John Musinsky explained the rules of the Society to the last incoming novice class at Conesus, the standard explanation for the rhythms of silence and conversation was that the normal pattern of life in Divine Word communities was to remain silent—and this included those in final vows and those who had been ordained—except during stipulated recreation periods. Otherwise, one was to practice silence and recollection.

In all the activities of the daily order, one was expected to be punctual and to do one's best. As one moved from place to place, one was expected to hold doors open for those coming behind, even if they were as much as thirty yards behind, since this was a way to show charity and respect. It could also be annoying for the one following, who rushed to get to the door being held open, lest he inconvenience his fellow *frater*. One strove to be recollected and to concentrate, for example, on the virtue one had resolved to practice that day or on the fault to be eradicated. This resolution would then become the object of the midday examination of conscience, as well as the examination of conscience at night prayers. On a weekly basis, the novice was encouraged to bring his failures to follow the resolution to confession. And at the annual retreat, novices were taught, time should be spent examining how one was progressing in combating the major faults that were identified during novitiate, as well as in practicing the virtue that would be the surest antidote to the fault.

Practically every day the novice master gave a conference to the novices. Every day they read from one of the three volumes of the spiritual writings of the Jesuit Alphonsus Rodriguez (1526–1556). When the three hefty volumes, called *Practice of Christian and Religious Perfection,* were finished, the novice started over again. Reading Rodriguez was one of the contributions to Society spirituality suggested by Father Janssen's Vincentian friend, Ferdinand Medits. Many novices came to think it a dubious gift. A second classic that novices were acquainted with and expected to read daily both during novitiate and the rest of their lives was the *Imitation of Christ,* written by Thomas à Kempis. This little book became the anchor of what became known as *devotio moderna* or "modern devotion" that held sway in the spirituality of religious congregations until the 1960s.

After the noonday dinner, the main meal of the day, came a period of manual labor performed in silence. Novices kept the mission house clean, even sparkling clean if they were striving. The mop crew scrubbed down the long corridors with buckets of soapy water, every drop of which had to be mopped up. Those who scrubbed the terrazzo floors with hard bristled brushes did so vigorously. Steps had to be cleaned, the church damp mopped. When finished, the mops, wagons, and the like, all had to be cleaned. After swishing the mop around in what were meant to be foot baths, the mop would be rinsed out in a clean bucket. If the water was still cloudy, the work senior would say the dreaded Latin words, *iterum, Frater*

("Do it again, Brother"). The water wrung out of a clean mop was supposed to be clean enough to drink. There are few reports, though, of novices actually drinking it! Mops were worn out at a rapid rate, sacrificed to the novices' need to strive for perfection.

Only from 1:45 till 2:45 did novices have a chance to talk during first recreation period of the day. Games were organized. In the proper season, handball, basketball, and softball were played. Everybody had to participate. When the bell for the end of recreation rang, the novices raced to the locker room and donned their cassocks (without taking a shower, unless special permission were given, no matter how much they had sweated during the exercise period). Novices then rushed up four long flights of stairs to get to chapel for a visit, then to a class or study hall. Every minute of every day was taken up with some activity or other.

After the evening meal, novices queued up in "the bread line," where they were periodically to tell the novice master of some fault or faults they had committed during the day. After all, if the just man sinned seven times a day, what must it be like for a lowly novice? If one could not come up with anything, he was obviously not looking hard enough, or was too proud of himself for thinking he had not sinned that day, which was an even greater sin.

A critical extension of this self-examination was the *votatio* ("voting"). This entailed everyone voting on the suitability of everyone else in his class before taking their first and subsequent vows. This went forward even after first vows in the major seminary where, not only one's classmates but anyone who had contact with the candidate for vows or orders voted on their suitability. Although the confessor did not take part in the annual *votatio*, if he knew that the candidate had difficulties with the vow of chastity, as evidenced by a habit of masturbation or the inability to control sexual fantasies, the confessor was to urge him not to continue. Specific instructions from the Holy See and the Society detailing the guidelines a confessor should follow in this matter were issued, and in the years immediately before and during World War II became the cause of bitter disagreements among the priests, though little or no word of this ever leaked out among the seminarians.

How did the novitiate "work"? For many, the experience was satisfying and achieved what it was intended to do. There was stability, consistency, a sense of tradition that bound people together and bonded them in mutual support one for the other for a lifetime. "In the novitiate I laid the foundation for my later spiritual life," was a common way approval was expressed. Others would say, "I developed a sense of discipline in my spiritual life that has stood me in good stead," and still others, "I found myself." As times changed, especially around the time of Vatican Council II, deficiencies were identified. Criticisms were directed especially to the way little was left to individual initiative and to the lack of insight into human growth being a process of developing emotional and psychosexual maturity. Looking back on that era, the juridical way things were spelled out came in for special criticism. Controls, it was later judged, were not so much matters of inner conviction but externally imposed.

It is important, though, to balance such criticisms with insight into the fact that a major part of the formation program was derived from the rich liturgical and devotional life of the entire community. While many of these devotions deserved the criticism that they were overly sentimental, subjective, and pietistic, the liturgy of SVD houses was well and seriously celebrated. On Sundays the whole community gathered in the main church for Solemn High Mass sung in Gregorian chant by all or, on special occasions, by the polyphonic choir. The most impressive and moving liturgies, which all looked forward to, were those of Holy Week and Easter, a time of intense prayer and recollection of the passion, death, and resurrection of Christ. It also meant the end of somber Lent. In addition, the sung prayers of the novena before Christmas and the solemn midnight liturgy of Christmas brought tears to the eyes of young and old alike. All these experiences were an essential part of the spiritual formation of the brothers, novices, seminarians, and fathers, all in common. For the founder, nothing was too good for the chapel, and this legacy was passed on in forming the American branch of his Society.

The Novice Master

Crucial to the way spiritual formation took place in the novitiate was the "novice master," who was often referred to as the *magister*, Latin for "teacher" with the connotation of a master teacher. In 1914 the first novitiate for SVD priests in North America was opened under the charge of Father Herman Richarz. By the early 1920s, Techny was crowded with six classes of minor seminarians, novices, and the major seminarians, in addition to the brother novices, junior brothers, and all the priests and brothers who served as teachers and workers both in the seminary and the expanding press, not to speak of the farms, the orchards, and the various shops that provided everything from meat to shoes. One solution to the overcrowding was moving the novices in the summer of 1921 to East Troy, Wisconsin. Father Richarz had been a belated vocation, having entered Steyl at the age of 23. Ordained at the age of 33, he was sent to the United States by the founder in 1900. Soon after he took over the fledgling printing press. In addition to his heavy involvement with St. Joseph's Technical School, he soon began editing the *Amerikanisches Familienblatt* in 1902 and the English magazine *The Christian Family* in 1906. He oversaw them until Fathers Markert and Lynk took them over. From 1914 until he died in February 1928 he was Techny's only novice master. For an interim period of less than a year Father Bruno Drescher served as novice master, making a good impression on the novices in the few months he was their *magister*. In the meantime, Father Felix Glorius, who had come to Techny in 1920, was appointed novice master. He held that position from the fall of 1928 until 1958.

Whatever faults or personality quirks Glorius had, that he lived the life of a novice for thirty long years has to be to his everlasting credit. He got up with his charges every morning and meditated with them in chapel. Simply listening to hundreds of lantern slide presentations prepared by succeeding classes of novices on the lives of the saints, the visions at Fatima or Lourdes, the life of Christ, the Blessed Mother, and St. Joseph would have tried anyone. Yet he sat patiently through all these, and every year for thirty years he met a new class without ever seeming bored by his life's work.

Father Glorius evoked strong reactions from those who had him as novice master as well as from those who lived and worked with him. He took his job very seriously and permitted no intervention in the affairs of the novitiate. Although the *magister* was theoretically subject to the provincial, this did not impress Father Glorius. He had many critics. Early in his appointment, for example, Provincial Hagspiel wrote to Superior General Gier that something had to be done about Father Glorius, since he was not cooperative with the provincial council, took no suggestions about running the novitiate, and was very nervous, to the extent that he started shaking when a topic came up he did not agree with. Hagspiel also felt he was too hard on the novices, offering as evidence the fact that many of them were developing knee problems brought about by too much kneeling. In response, Gier acknowledged the nervous weakness of Father Glorius, yet maintained that he seemed to be the best man for the job. In this climate of criticism, Adolf Noser, Glorius's assistant, also wrote the generalate ("on his own initiative") saying that Glorius was the best man for the position. "In judging his weaknesses we should be willing to close one, or even both, eyes." In 1937, Hugo Aubry, now provincial superior, was hearing complaints from those living with Father Glorius, and he commented, "even Fr. Noser has his problems." In the bill of particulars, it was alleged that Glorius did not give enough opportunity for the novices to develop "in a more natural way," but was too forceful and demanding. Aubry said Glorius was temperamental and unable to let well enough alone, but he then goes on to say that Glorius nevertheless seems to have found his right niche in the Society.

Glorius began as *magister* at East Troy, when novitiate was placed chronologically after two years of college. He continued when it was moved physically back to Techny and chronologically back to immediately after high school. The reasons for these changes were many and involved, and will not detain us here. Suffice it to say that Techny was getting crowded again and debates on how to staunch the flow of departures from the major seminary were ongoing. The move was made smoothly and Father Aubry comments on the pleasant quiet in the house at Techny after the minor seminarians left.

A more significant change came in 1949 when a new novitiate was established in Conesus for those who finished high school studies in the Eastern Province. Father Wilbert Wagner was appointed novice master. We have already noted that in the Eastern Province feelings of suspicion had developed that far too many of their graduates who went to Techny for novitiate under Father Glorius were dropping out. Some felt, too, that training at Techny was too German and that the faculty there just did not understand the American boy, and their boys were predominantly of Irish extraction. There was no hard evidence presented that this was true, but it played a role in the decision to open the novitiate. Nor did the decision lead to a total split between the provinces in terms of education. After novitiate, novices from the Eastern and Western novitiates came together for juniorate at Epworth, Iowa, and Techny remained the major seminary for both provinces. In 1958 the two novitiates were merged in Conesus and returned to the chronological place in the candidates' formation it held before 1941, after the first two years of college.

When Father Glorius gave up his position as novice master in 1958, relieved of the responsibilities he had shouldered for so many years, he became much more relaxed. He applied for and was assigned to the post of chaplain to St. Ann's Home for the Aged, a task he carried out faithfully and cheerfully for the next eight years. He was struck and killed by a car as he was crossing the dark and busy Waukegan Road on 19 December 1966, on his way back to Techny after Vespers and Benediction at St. Ann's. He had become an admirable community man, and in spite of his years of training and teaching in the pre-Vatican II style, he readily adjusted to the new ideas that were struggling to emerge at the time of his death. In the special bulletin published on the occasion of his death he and the formation he offered were characterized vividly:

> As Novice Master for thirty years, Father Glorius was in a position to do more, perhaps, in the spiritual formation of hundreds of Divine Word Missionary priests, than any other single individual. During the two years of novitiate for each future priest, it was Father Glorius's task to help him lay a solid foundation of religious missionary conviction and commitment. For this purpose, Father Glorius lectured at least an hour a day to the novices, interviewed them individually each month, led them annually through the month-long Spiritual Exercises of St. Ignatius, lived with them, prayed with them, recreated with them—for thirty long years.

MAJOR SEMINARY FORMATION AND EDUCATION AT TECHNY

Philosophy

Having finished novitiate and having taken first vows, during most periods of SVD history, the educational pattern saw students enter the major seminary for the study of philosophy and theology.[5] With the exception of those who studied at Bay St. Louis, the major seminary was always at Techny during most of the years covered in this history. Philosophy was also taught at Conesus from the late 1950s through 1965 and then at Epworth, when the curriculum was revised to place the four years of college and the bachelor of arts degree before novitiate.

Now all the years of preparation in Latin were to bear their fruit. Studies were still the primary task of the major seminarian, but now they were more directly related to the priesthood and their future work. Until the year 1966, the core philosophical curriculum was taught in Latin: logic, metaphysics, epistemology, psychology, and cosmology. Only the history of philosophy was taught in English. During the first two years of major seminary, which were also actually the last two years of college, philosophy was the core subject.

Both philosophy and theology were taught in the manualist tradition of scholasticism that Pope Leo XIII, updating the decrees of the Council of Trent, had mandated in all seminaries of the Catholic Church. By "manualist" I mean that the philosophy taught was one that was handed down in manuals that had been approved by higher authorities. In these manuals certain key questions and their answers were carefully laid out, for example, concerning the principle of *causality*,

---

5. As previously noted, at various times novitiate came immediately after high school. During these periods, the newly professed would begin junior college studies dominated by Latin, Greek, and the physical sciences, after which they went to Techny or Bay St. Louis for philosophy and theology.

which would be used to demonstrate the necessity of God's existence, and on the nature of a "thing" as necessarily composed by matter and form, which would be used to demonstrate the necessity of a spiritual soul as the form of the human person. By "scholasticism" I mean the tradition of philosophy begun in the great European universities of Cambridge, Paris, Bologna, and Oxford in the high Middle Ages. In that period, roughly from the twelfth through the fourteenth century, Aristotle, Plato, and the other great Greek philosophers were retrieved in Arabic translations in Spain and translated into Latin. Theology moved from being practical "wisdom" taught in monasteries to a "science" taught in the schools, whence the name "scholasticism." Chief among the characteristics of scholasticism was the use of logic and dialectic to clarify terms, to identify sure principles upon which arguments could be reliably constructed, and to point out fallacies in opposing arguments.

Although scholastic argumentation has been often attacked by moderns with scant understanding of its brilliant achievements, it is important to realize that the central purpose of the manuals used in seminaries like Techny and Bay St. Louis was to keep "critical realism" in play in an age that was in constant danger of falling victim to skepticism, materialism, and subjectivism. The tenor of the times, at least from the age of David Hume (1711–1776) and Immanuel Kant (1724–1804), was to utilize "enlightenment" to release humanity from its "self-incurred tutelage" to authority. Instead, Kant urged, "*Sapere aude!* Have courage to use your own reason!"[6] Against such figures as Hume and Kant, Catholic thought was concerned to maintain the authority of tradition and confidence in human reason, guided by the light of faith as clarified by the church's teaching authority, truly to know the world as directed to God and show the reasonableness of what was revealed in revelation.

In scholastic manual philosophy taught in the seminaries, proficiency in understanding and using certain basic terms, concepts, and distinctions handed down since the Reformation was demanded. Imparted by the manual and the teacher was a style of argumentation that the seminarian would employ in theological studies. Philosophy was viewed as the "handmaid of theology" and, therefore, extremely important. Many hours were spent learning the basics of this system. Philosophical distinctions between nature and person, substance and accident, act and potency, necessary and contingent, and essence and existence would later be important in the language theology used to discuss the doctrines of Trinity, human and divine natures in the one person of Jesus Christ, and Eucharist, where the emphasis was placed on how the substance of bread and wine is "transubstantiated" to become Christ's Body and Blood, while the accidents of bread and wine remained.

Catholic theology since the Council of Trent was preoccupied with defending what it considered the entire deposit of faith against the "partial truth" and "mis-

---

6. The quote is from Immanuel Kant, *On History*, trans. Lewis White Beck et al. (Indianapolis: Bobbs-Merrill, 1963, original German, 1784), p. 3. The easiest works of Hume and Kant to grasp the importance that Catholic philosophy and theology placed on rebutting them are the following: David Hume, *Dialogues Concerning Natural Religion* (Indianapolis: Bobbs-Merrill, 1947, original dated from the period 1751–1755); Immanuel Kant, *Religion within the Limits of Reason Alone*, trans. Theodore M. Greene and Hoyt H. Hudson (New York: Harper & Row, 1960, original German published in 1792).

understandings" of Reformers such as Luther and Calvin. Their break from Rome, it was alleged, created conditions that weakened confidence that reason, aided by faith, could discern natural law and confidently guide the faithful in all areas of life. As a consequence of the Reformation, furthermore, the Catholic world attempted to oppose empiricist and skeptical thought in the British tradition; critical and romantic thought in the German tradition; and rationalist thought in the French tradition. In addition to thinkers such as Hume and Kant, Catholicism also opposed the thought of D. F. S. Schleiermacher, Jean-Jacques Rousseau, and the entire tenor of post-Enlightenment thought their names represent. How many SVD seminarians studying philosophy knew the stakes when they memorized formulae and distinctions? It is hard to say. What was clear, though, was that the Society of the Divine Word had come of age during the period of Catholic anti-Modernism and it would obey Roman legislation to ground its members in the scholastic tradition of St. Thomas. Through the entire period we are discussing, Divine Word seminarians were trained in the scholastic manuals' attempts to expose the errors of the non-Catholic world. As late as 1950, Pope Pius XII issued his encyclical *Aeterni patris* to reiterate the fact that no other approach to philosophy was licit. In the pope's words:

> If one considers all this well, one will easily see why the Church demands that future priests be instructed in philosophy "according to the method, doctrine, and principles of the Angelic Doctor" [Code of Canon Law 1366] since, as we well know from the experience of centuries, the method of Aquinas is singularly preeminent both for teaching students and for bringing truth to light; his doctrine is in harmony with divine revelation, and is most effective both for safeguarding the foundation of the faith, and for reaping, safely and usefully, the fruits of sound progress.

And lest the reader think that only benighted conservatives considered this important, one of the first acts of Pope John XXIII (pope from 1958 to 1963) was to issue *Veterum sapientiae*, an encyclical on the importance of Latin and the need to retain it in the study of philosophy and theology.

The professor most responsible for teaching philosophy was Father Gerard Esser. Esser was born near Bonn in 1882. Ordained in 1906, he was assigned to do graduate studies in philosophy, then assigned by Father Janssen to the Bishop of Sutri-Nepi in Italy to teach in the diocesan seminary. He did this for three years, after which he returned to St. Gabriel's. He was active at St. Gabriel's and was quite highly thought of by Janssen and Father Wilhelm Gier, at whose recommendation Esser became clerical novice master. He was drafted into the military during World War I and served as a military nurse in Munich and Cologne. The war over and Techny needing both a novice master for the brothers and a philosophy teacher, Father Esser was transferred to Techny in 1920. In 1934, when Hugo Aubry, his classmate, was provincial superior, Father Esser was appointed rector of Bay St. Louis and philosophy professor in the major seminary there. As superior, Esser, it seems, left something to be desired, and after one three-year term as rector, he returned to Techny to devote himself full time to teaching philosophy and to writing. He also became confessor and spiritual director to many. It was his niche in life. Bright and complex, Esser's was not an attractive personality. He tried to live by *all* the principles he had learned from the *Imitation of Christ* and the writings of Alphonsus Rodriguez, SJ. The result was a somewhat cramped style. He was nervous and displayed a variety of tics that got in the way of a comfortable relationship with his confreres. John Donaghey, himself a teacher of philosophy and the SVD of the next generation who perhaps knew Esser's work best—and who also knew Esser when he was Esser's provincial superior in the last years of his life—described him in the following words:

> Fr. Esser was a man of hard work, dedication and duty. Intense self-discipline enabled him to do an immense amount of reading, writing and revising. This same quality drove him to economize on time and energy and, while it hardly helped him to relax nor others to relax in his presence, it provided the incentive never to waste a moment and to use his time in teaching, researching, writing, hearing confessions, and spiritual directing.

His career forming Divine Word seminarians in America spanned 40 years, which means that, with few exceptions, he had every Divine Word missionary in his class for the entire first half of the Society's time in North America. Most would recall his classic *avis in fenestra* ("bird on the window sill") example, though few remember what the bird on the window sill was supposed to exemplify. When asked a question by a confused seminarian, Esser often ended up repeating the same point in the same words as the first time, only louder and more emphatically. This made his students read again and more carefully what he had written in one of the six volumes of philosophy he wrote and published over the years. The books, like the classroom lectures they expanded on and provided background for those who wished to go further, were in Latin. He also lectured in Latin, a language he was more familiar with than English. My own reading suggests that his volumes on metaphysics and rational psychology were well done. They were, of course, very scholastic; questions were put and answered, objections were given to the answers, and *adversarii* such as Kant were refuted in the answers to the objections.

Whether his work and that of so many of the manualists is fully "Thomistic" is a difficult question to answer. While the manualists endeavored to be faithful practitioners of the methods pioneered by the great medieval theologian St. Thomas Aquinas (d. 1274), if one follows the work of the great reforming Thomists—Yves Congar, OP, Karl Rahner, SJ, and Bernard Lonergan, SJ—manual scholasticism had lost sight of St. Thomas's dynamism. By the 1800s, in large measure, it had become a sterile enterprise dominated by ahistorical logic-chopping. Most importantly, it had not engaged the central insight of both Catholic and non-Catholic philosophy, the reality of historical change and consciousness.[7] This did not mean that intelligent men did not study and teach it, nor that the critical realism that the manuals tried to inculcate was not important. But it had ceased to be a system fully engaged with contemporary intellectual currents. And even talented philosophers

---

7. See Bernard J. F. Lonergan, *A Second Collection* (Philadelphia: Westminster Press, 1974), pp. 1–11, "The Transition from a Classicist World-view to Historical Mindedness."

like Gerard Esser, who clearly knew the issues in contemporary thought, found themselves trying to teach difficult concepts in Latin that many students could follow only partially and with great difficulty. In spite of everything militating against success in his branch of learning, Gerard Esser was one of the towering intellects in North American Divine Word history, and made a great contribution both to the intellectual formation and spiritual formation of its personnel. After retiring from teaching he became a chaplain at St. Ann's Home and worked in this position until two weeks before his death in 1971 at the age of 89.

Esser was followed by other SVD philosophy teachers, such as John Donaghey, Luis Manuel Rodriguez, and Bernard Wrockladge. In some ways their courses were the antithesis of Esser's, yet in a deeper sense they carried on his legacy of meticulous preparation and consummate professionalism at Techny, Conesus, Bay St. Louis, and Epworth in the decades that followed Esser's retirement.

During the years of philosophical studies, other subjects also occupied the students, philosophy serving as the major subject, the others as a constellation of courses—often one-year or one-semester courses that were deemed useful for the future priest and missionary: Hebrew, education, anthropology, geology, missiology, art, astronomy, and music. Not all were taught every year, and some courses might be added on a temporary basis. During the Korean War summer classes were given at Techny, and in later years seminarians with special interests in areas like science, history, psychology, education, and literature took summer courses at Loyola and DePaul Universities in Chicago.

Theology

The core course for the last four years in the seminary was theology, and of the various sub-divisions of theology, the most important was dogmatic theology. As Roger Arnold, then a seminarian writing in a 1959 issue of the *Seminary Bulletin*, put it: "All the other branches of Theology are to an extent like planets, spinning around one big sun—Dogma. They are separated, but never completely out of range of its influence."

The theology courses must be considered the core of intellectual formation for those preparing for the priesthood. Over the years they had been carefully monitored by Roman authorities to ensure a high degree of uniformity, so whether one were a Divine Word religious preparing for the missionary priesthood or a student at nearby Mundelein seminary preparing for the diocesan priesthood, the course of studies was by and large the same. The theology course as a whole was divided into various subspecialties with dogmatic theology, the study of the central truths of the Christian and Catholic faith, the heart of it all. Such doctrines as Trinity, Christology, sin, grace and redemption, ecclesiology, and sacraments were taught in the dogma classroom.

The second major area of study was moral theology, the goal of which was to prepare effective pastors and confessors. In the moral theology curriculum types of sin, their seriousness, mitigating circumstances, with emphasis on acts and the number of acts of sin, were taught. In addition, the virtues and vices were enumerated and explained. Much of this was done in the context of making fine distinctions. In the two pages introducing the topic of virtue in the first volume of the *Summa theologiae moralis* authored by Hieronymus Noldin (1838–1922), a commonly used textbook on moral theology, the author makes some fifty distinctions to clarify what he meant by "virtue." Similar sections could be found with distinctions based on the notion of law, in the writings of medieval philosophers, on habits, and so forth. In addition to moral theology there was fundamental theology, often called apologetics, as well as pastoral, ascetical, and mystical theology.

There were great benefits to be derived from the type of formation just described. The student was exposed to an integral philosophical and theological system on the basis of which he could preach and teach. The whole course of studies ensured a high overall level of learning on everyone's part. The student learned to think of himself as part of a tradition he was to help pass on and not as a freelancer to make it up as he went along. Those who could not grasp Latin were not allowed to go on. Since everyone followed the same curriculum and had the same teachers, a community that led to a deep and sincere concern for others developed. It bound men together and again produced a sense of togetherness and camaraderie, of unity and, therefore, of community. As an older priest I interviewed put it when he was trying to explain this sense of easy connectedness on the part of those who went through the pre-Vatican II course of formation, "We suffered together."

What is to be said about scripture in the years before the Second Vatican Council? The way to answer the question most directly is to observe that the study of scripture was subordinate to dogmatics. Indeed, the Old Testament was taught not as the dynamic record of God's dealings with the Israelite people, but as a preparation for the New Testament, which surpassed and did away with the old covenant. The New Testament was studied in much more detail than the Old, and the emphasis was to use it as a mine for apt quotations for sermons, conferences, retreats, and spiritual reading. As the distinguished University of Chicago historical theologian B. A. Gerrish, a member of the Reformed Church, once aptly put it, "Scripture, in the era when dogmatic theology reigned supreme, was considered a marvelous source for texts to prove that the Church's dogmas were correct. The role of the theologian was to systematize truths scattered haphazardly in the Bible." Although SVD scripture professors such as Bernard LeFrois were meticulously educated and aware of European developments in scripture, it would not be till the 1960s that scripture would begin to challenge dogmatics, despite earlier protestations that biblical studies were of equal importance.

It is easy for a note of sarcasm to creep into a paragraph such as the previous one. It should not be forgotten, though, that a benefit of the kind of training that Techny and Bay St. Louis provided for an international missionary society was to provide a common basis of understanding for their labors. After World War II, the Society was self-consciously assigning its men in multinational teams, rather than assigning missions to one province to staff and support, which was the most common practice at the time in other orders. There was a core intellectual culture imparted that helped men of quite different national cultures collaborate fruitfully in mission work. A German, an Argentine, an American, a Filipino, and a Dutchman working together in a school in Taiwan, for example, could fall back on a common experience of novitiate followed by philosophical and theological studies when their native cultures made them presuppose quite different things in administering an educational institution.

Although the formal education was straightforward, and the daily order did not allow much deviation, there was still space for creativity, initiative, competition, and fun throughout the major seminary. Playoffs after a season of intramural sports like basketball stirred up interest not unlike the National Basketball Association playoffs. There were two to three major stage plays a year—during Christmas vacation, for example—to bring together the entire community and to stimulate the major seminarians' creative juices. *H.M.S. Pinafore*, with female parts either written out or the sex changed to that of male cousins, with the stage transformed as the foredeck of a ship, was produced. And if the play customarily presented on Christmas day itself called for pagan idols, in a flash large papier-mâché statues were conjured up. During recreation after supper, especially on Wednesday nights, a group might form to sing Bach chorales or put together a Dixieland band. And elections for president of the Mission Club, if not taken as seriously, were surely as much fun and as elaborate and vicious, in a spoofing way, as elections of any kind anywhere. This is only partly why the seminary years before Vatican II are remembered by so many in retrospect as being a happy, satisfying and fulfilling time.

As we did above with the story of Father Esser, I would like to single out a man who epitomizes the teaching of theology, in this case Father Charles Michel. His impact as professor of dogma for many years was enormous. After ordination at St. Gabriel's in 1908, Michel was sent for further studies to Rome, where he earned doctorates in both philosophy and theology. He returned to St. Gabriel's to teach and, like Father Esser, was drafted into the army to serve as a medical orderly in Munich. He continued his studies during these years, this time in theology, philosophy, mathematics, and physics. He was a brilliant and superbly educated man. In 1922, Michel was assigned to teach dogma at St. Mary's Seminary at Techny. With the exception of the eight years he was provincial superior during the Second World War, he served as professor of dogma from 1922 to 1962.

The dogmatic theology courses were taught in Latin and all the texts were in Latin. When Charles Michel lectured, they were explained and expounded in what amounted to classical Latin. Other professors made concessions to English and the sometimes meager Latin talents of their students. Not Charles Michel. And his method of presentation followed the scholastic *sic et non* style throughout. Nevertheless, he expanded on that question-answer-objection-rejoinder method by quoting at length from the early Fathers of the Church, more than was customary at the time. He explained that scripture and what was called tradition were the sources of dogma, the deposit of faith. He delighted in explaining the great theological controversies of church history, which he could drag out for class after class if he had the time to spend.

The question was sometimes asked why Michel never published, as Father Esser, his colleague in philosophy, had done. The legendary explanation, which quoted Michel himself, was that a teacher should have his work published only after his death, lest he puff up with pride. This is almost certainly a fictitious explanation. It was another, mostly hidden, side of this troubled man that was really responsible: Charles Michel was scrupulous. He feared damnation and despaired of his own salvation right to the moment of his death. As an example of how seriously he took everything, it might be recalled that in 1936, when he was a member of the provincial council, he had to make a report on the state of the Society in the North American Province. He went on for thirteen single-spaced, typewritten pages. Most of the reports of his fellow councilors were brief and to the point. Michel wrote in painful detail, usually negatively, in answer to almost every one of the eleven points for which information was requested. (Correspondence I found in the generalate archives from Father Grendel, superior general at the time, did not help matters. He thanked Father Michel profusely for the insights he had given, which he said were helpful to him in making his decisions!)

Though fundamentally kind, Charles Michel was dour. He had a stern visage, with long bushy eyebrows. A hint of a smile might crease his lips when, after a long discussion of some topic had led some students to the portals of slumberland, he would whip off his glasses and ask: "Cursh?" his way of pronouncing the Latin *cur* (why?). He would then look out over the class and call on someone whom he had seen struggling to keep from dozing. As the poor man floundered about looking for an answer to a question he hadn't heard, Michel would sit up straight in his chair, look about as if surprised, a half smile nearly breaking through. He was not an easy man to approach, much less get close to, but he possessed a towering intellect, knew his material thoroughly, and did his job well, according to the style, method, and purpose of the times.

In a 1989 eulogy to Father Joseph Finger, who admired Father Michel greatly, Provincial Superior John Donaghey had the following to say about Michel and his last days:

> Fr. Michel was a brilliant man with an incisive mind who suffered his own anxieties. He rarely, if ever, preached for fear that he might commit heresy. He was tormented because of the scholastic teaching on predestination. On our way to the 1967 General Chapter, Fr. Provincial Connors, Fr. Bukovsky and I visited Fr. Michel and his sisters in Tetringshausen near Bingen. Fr. Michel, himself an affectionate person though his affectivity was hidden by a stern facade, had retired with his family. He was unable to sleep at night because of his fear of eternal damnation. He himself had taught that not even a good life merited the grace of perseverance since salvation itself was a free gift of God. Fr. Michel's sisters took turns sitting up with him each night because of this oppressive fear.

Fr. Michel died in January 1968 and, by special permission, was buried in a chapel of the church in Tetringshausen.

SVD FORMATION TO *MISSIONARY* LIFE

When a young man decided to join the Society of the Divine Word, at about fourteen, the most important attraction was to life as a missionary. Moreover, according to the Arnold Janssen's traditions, anyone, whether wealthy or poor, who thought he might have a vocation to be a missionary was welcome to test this inclination to try life in the Society. Whatever else motivated the applicant for entrance into the Society, the goal of becoming a missionary was almost certainly present, however inchoate or vague in detail. This was nourished, developed, and encouraged by missionary formation. This said, a paradox appears. Although spiritual and intellectual formation procedures were clearly laid out, the plan for *missionary formation was not concretely or formally specified*. Moreover, little formal educational time was spent on missionary formation. Until late in the major seminary, for example, there were no missiology courses (the study of mission theory and history) in the curriculum. Sometimes a newly ordained priest might be sent to a university for a summer course in missiology or to study the people, culture, and history of the place he was being sent to. Still, this is not placing missionary formation at the heart of the curriculum, as one would expect it to be in one of the church's premier missionary communities, a society, moreover, that was leading the way in the application of linguistics and anthropology to missionary theory and practice, a society with members like Wilhelm Schmidt and Paul Schebesta, who were famous worldwide for their pioneering work. And in the 1950s and 1960s, an American SVD missionary anthropologist, Louis Luzbetak, was becoming famous for insights into how anthropology should be used in mission work. Yet, even though it received little academic time, the mission ideal remained foremost in the thinking of the seminarian. It is this that we must explain in our final section on formation and education.

Always in the background was a robust belief in the adage of the great third century bishop, St. Cyprian of Carthage: *extra ecclesiam nulla salus* ("outside the church no salvation"). Despite the fact that Catholic theology mitigated that stern adage with what a great Jesuit theologian of the late twentieth century calls "substitutes for the Gospel,"[8] Arnold Janssen and his Society presumed that faith in Christ, baptism, and incorporation in the life of the church were the ordinary way of salvation. The first words of Jesus' "great commission" (Matthew 28:19) were embedded prominently in virtually every SVD house: *Euntes ergo, docete omnes gentes . . .* ("Go therefore and teach all nations, baptizing them in the name of the Father, and of the Son, and of the Holy Spirit"). Those words emblazoned in the form of a mosaic on the floor of the Techny chapel are found also on the cover of this book. One became a missionary, in other words, because the greatest act of love possible was to lead the people to God through Jesus Christ. No one argued against this, though there was great interest in religion class when the teacher would expound on such tried and tested Catholic escape clauses as the invincibly ignorant being saved.

In that context, vocation directors, with the assistance of every parish priest and teaching brother, priest, and sister in the world, recruited boys for the high school seminary. And when they were successful, students arrived in communities where everything was focused to remind the candidate that this was a mission house. That the term "mission house" sounded odd to American ears did not matter. That's what it was called from 1900 until the late 1950s.

---

8. See Jacques Dupuis, *Toward a Christian Theology of Religious Pluralism* (Maryknoll, N.Y.: Orbis Books, 1997), pp. 110–29.

In that context, prefects talked constantly of "mission spirit." It became the atmosphere that surrounded the seminarian, something in which he moved and breathed. Mission spirit and the missionary ideal and spirituality were developed in various ways. Prefects and novice masters, for instance, urged all students, including those with scant talent for athletics, to participate in sports and other physical activities because they had to be healthy to be missionaries. Hobbies and extracurricular activities were encouraged not necessarily because they were useful in their own right, but because they were directed to the missions. A seminarian might get the brothers to teach him basic carpentry and auto mechanics because they would be useful "in the missions." The German teacher would urge students to master that formidable language because it would be helpful to ease social life "in the missions." The biology teacher urged students to learn to identify the essential qualities of plants and animals because they could use such observations to help local people develop better agricultural methods "in the missions." And so it went. The "Mission Book Brigade" collected and packed books to ship to the libraries of schools and universities that SVDs conducted in Ghana and the Philippines. Another group made rosaries in their spare time to be sent to the missions. Such efforts focused the minds of the seminarians on the needs of the missions and reminded them that they themselves would someday go to the missions.

The main source for developing mission awareness and interest, both for the brothers and for the seminarians, were their respective "mission clubs." Each unit in a large house like Techny had their own mission club. Each mission club became a chapter of the Catholic Students' Mission Crusade and held meetings once a month throughout the year. Every year new officers were elected, the preparation for which went on for weeks and rivaled in importance, to the seminarians and brothers, campaigns for the presidency of the United States. These elections were extravagant, complete with primaries, slogans, humorous mud-slinging propaganda and platforms, but they also kept the idea of the missions in the forefront of everyone's thinking. The brothers' mission club at Techny took on the task of keeping missionaries in the field informed of events at home in the *Techny Chimes*. This came out once a month and was sent to all SVD missionaries around the world and to anyone who desired a copy. Not only was it full of news about the SVD in North America, it also published letters that missionaries sent in from around the world. Although it appeared in mimeographed format, it was eagerly awaited and read.

The years of the *Techny Chimes* were filled with news. One could almost compile a chronology of events at Techny from this source alone. Just working on this publication, recounting all of the happenings at Techny, listing all the jubilees celebrated and the people of all states of life who graced Techny's corridors with their visits, requesting the prayers of readers for those who were sick or had died, publishing letters that had been received from missionaries from all around the world for the edification of other readers, was a wonderful missionary formation for everyone. The following letter from Clifford King published in the August 1935 edition of *Techny Chimes* gives the flavor of many more:

Dog-days are on in China. Every day about two or three o'clock p.m. the mercury in the thermometer creeps up to the neighborhood of 105 (in the shade). It's hard to remain peppy in such an atmosphere. A fellow's cloth-ing gets all limp and sticky with perspiration and the psychological effect is that the wearer also feels like a superannuated dish-rag. Nevertheless there are certain tasks which call imperatively for attention. It is then that one must draw upon the reserve-fund of vocational grace which he still has to dispose of, if he is the right kind of a missionary . . . For instance yesterday I was invited out to a dinner by a group of men who have just decided to embrace the Catholic religion, in the large village of Lianbaosih eight miles from Tangkiataokow. A Chinese dinner in a country village is not much to attract one, even under the most favorable circumstances, and it was only the love of God, and souls, which could have induced me to attend this particular repast, as I had to travel those eight miles under a broiling sun, over roads covered by several inches of dust. Arrived at my destination I had to sit in a small stuffy room with a crowd of some twenty perspiring peasants sur-rounding me. This I had to put up with for four hours and keep smiling throughout. First the crops were discussed, then the political situation, and then I gave them a long earnest talk on [the] purpose and benefits of being a Christian. Those good, unspoiled men were impressed. I could see that and felt recompensed. They then served a tolerably good meal and also partook in common of a kind of agape. It reminded me of early Christian times.

Thus the foundation of a new Christian community had been laid and I felt well repaid for the slight hardship incurred on that trip.

Please excuse me for making this letter short . . . Best love to all at Techny!

Such letters portrayed a life of adventure for the sake of souls and the cause of Christ, and it was this that the prefects and teachers understood by "mission spirit" when they urged their charges not to give up. Another major source of knowledge about life in the missions were the lantern and later Kodak slide lectures given by missionaries on home leave. Each missionary made it a point to get to all the houses where they would be invited to talk to the priests, brothers, and seminarians. Sometimes, too, they would be asked by the local superior to give the Saturday night sermon or be the celebrant at the Sunday High Mass. Spellbound, everybody lis-tened with attention. Some of these talks were especially memorable. Students at East Troy still talk at alumni gatherings of Father Maurice Lesage tossing a fake python out into the audience. Students in the juniorate at Epworth in the early 1950s recall the visit of Father Henry Hoff, then one of the New Guinea mission pilots who flew the bishop, missionaries, and supplies from mission station to station in the vast Central Highlands. He also took reel after reel of film of the ceremonies of the Highlands people, who lived in a region that had only recently been declared "controlled" by the Australian government. The students were enthralled and many wanted nothing more than to hurry through their studies and go to the missions.

How was mission understood *theologically*? Undergirding these informal means of maintaining a high interest in the missions was the missiology of the papal mis-sion encyclicals and that of Joseph Schmidlin, widely acknowledged as the founder of Catholic missiology. An early attempt to start scientific Catholic mission stud-ies by Divine Word Father Friedrich Schwager had come to naught, but Arnold

Janssen clearly saw the importance of a scientific study of mission. The founder assigned the newly ordained Anton Freitag to work on this project. When a department of missiology was established at the University of Münster in 1914, with Joseph Schmidlin as its founding professor, Freitag went there to become Schmidlin's first doctoral candidate. In the SVD in North America, Schmidlin's influence was enhanced by the arrival of Father Matthias Braun, who came to Techny in 1920. For some years he taught in the minor seminary at Techny where he was also librarian. When he was put in charge of mission history in the major seminary, he began to develop an extensive section on missiology. This led him to translate and publish Schmidlin's two massive works, the first as *Catholic Mission Theory* and the second as *Catholic Mission History*, into English. He also offered courses in missiology from 1931 till 1940 when he was assigned to other tasks, among them to a ten-year assignment to the southern missions. Braun was not a professionally trained missiologist, nor was missiology a core course in the seminary at Techny or Bay St Louis. Indeed, after he left teaching, offerings in missiology were haphazard for lack of faculty. Only with the 1958 election of Johannes Schütte (a trained missiologist) as superior general was missiology given prominence in the Society and many priests were assigned to study this subject. Under Schütte, Fathers Ralph Wiltgen, Lawrence Nemer, and John Boberg from North America went into higher missiological studies. In Europe by this time missiology was well established as an academic discipline. In the United States it never achieved that recognition in Catholic seminaries and universities, though its importance was accepted much better in Protestant seminaries and in divinity schools on university campuses.

Schmidlin's understanding of mission, I have already said, became important in the American SVD. There is no space here to summarize his two huge volumes, but it may be useful to point out a few key points at which he affected mission thinking in the Catholic Church as a whole and in the SVD in particular. First, the object of mission for Schmidlin, "is the still unconverted world—that is, the unconverted, non-Christian world, or the pagan world in the wider sense" (*Catholic Mission Theory*, p. 38). The people populating such regions were termed "pagans" or "heathen," and they coincided conveniently with the colonized people of Africa, Asia, and Oceania. Schmidlin further divided the order of groups that were the object of missions as: (1) Pagans, (2) Muslims, (3) Jews, (4) non-Catholic Christians, whom he further divided into (a) heretics (Protestants) and (b) schismatics (the Oriental Orthodox Churches), and finally (5) fallen away Catholics.

The SVD had taken pagans as the primary object of the Society's mission interest and made it clear that those who entered the Society had, first, to have a call for this work and, second, be willing to go wherever his superior assigned him to further the mission cause. In the second place, pastoral work in Catholic countries to strengthen the faith and help the diocesan clergy, including the unchurched, was taken as another legitimate activity for the Society, as was work that helped the Society attain its missionary objectives: work in seminaries, vocation work, fund raising, mission animation, and the like.

For Schmidlin, the work of mission properly so-called was over as soon as it had established the mission church on a hierarchical basis with relative autonomy, financial independence, and a native clergy (*Catholic Mission Theory*, p. 47). Also, according to Schmidlin, all were to be given the opportunity to become Catholic. The universality of the church meant just that. It was not a question of converting a "small flock" to represent the whole people in the economy of salvation. And the process was to begin with individuals, not with an entire community. Eventually as more and more individuals were converted they would form a Christian community and become part of the Body of Christ. Only at this point might one talk of social conversion.[9] It should come as no surprise that this universal effort to convert individual pagans should lead to judging success by numbers. Conversions and baptisms, as well as the administration of other sacraments, were meticulously counted. Missionaries dutifully sent a numerical accounting regularly to their superiors, who, in turn, sent them to the Congregation for the Propagation of the Faith. Competition between Catholic and Protestant missionaries was intense, and they read each other's statistics and used progress by their adversaries as reason to urge their supporters to provide more material and human resources to convert the heathen.

How could the church, amid all the diversity of culture and language to be found in mission, maintain its unity? Schmidlin gave the answer that all Catholics then accepted, SVDs among them, when he answered: "Individuals are everywhere bound to the common Supreme Head by the same dogmas, the same cult, and the same hierarchy" (*Catholic Mission Theory*, p. 272). In practice this meant unity in truth and in liturgical observance. The entire Divine Word training program emphasized exactly these principles, which were taught to be absolute and for all time and for all peoples. Another implication was also clear: only the church had all the truth; other religions did not.

What were the results of SVD mission formation? Without considering here two essential dimensions of formation, namely, God's grace and what each individual brought to the formation process, it can be said that SVD formation produced a hard-working individual, one who was dedicated to the work assigned, to which he always gave his best. He was task-oriented and disciplined. Generally the American SVD tended to be more practical than theoretical, not easily impressed by theory nor deterred by obstacles. This is not to say he was always comfortable or felt equipped to do the work he was given. He might often have felt ill-prepared for many things, but others, he had been taught, had faced greater obstacles and succeeded. The bottom line for each missionary was his experience to date that convinced him that the Society was interested in him and would support him.

There was, however, a shadow side to missionary formation, especially in the context of what has been termed "colonialism." Missionaries felt themselves invested with the responsibility to fulfill the great commission of Christ to bring the truth to all people and nations. Their scholastic training taught them that it was well founded and irrefutable. Moreover, they came from the developed West and

---

9. These issues were hotly debated and each attitude cited has been modified or rejected. For up-to-date studies on these and other missiological principles, see David Bosch's magisterial *Transforming Mission: Paradigm Shifts in the Theology of Mission* (Maryknoll, N.Y.: Orbis Books, 1991); and Timothy Yates, *Christian Mission in the Twentieth Century* (New York: Cambridge University Press, 1994).

were able, therefore, to bring the benefits of development and technology to "benighted heathen" who could not help but be grateful for all this advantage. For citizens of the U.S., in addition, there was the added danger that came from being part of a people whose technological prowess, they believed, was unequaled. In the eyes of persons from other cultures, American missionaries too often brought with them the cockiness they saw exemplified in the motion pictures from which they learned how the U.S. had single-handedly won World War II. If a confrere were Dutch, Polish, or Slovak, he had a different view. And if he were German or Austrian, it was quite something else again. World War II and its lessons were tragic and sobering, and should not have been a cause for nationalistic self-confidence. The formation program tried to equip young Americans with sensitivity, but it was hard to teach the importance of modesty. If all Western missionaries run the risk of feeling superior to those among whom they worked, Americans after World War II carried a special burden.

"Mission spirit" could lead readily to paternalism, which was clearly both supported by and supported colonial thinking. Indeed, in many cases, missionary paternalism outlasted colonialism. It had any number of consequences from not properly preparing the local church expeditiously enough to run its own affairs in its own way. It kept many churches dependent on the West and Western styles of organization and cultural systems, impeding local churches from reliance on their own financial resources, often maintaining expatriate missionaries as superiors long past the appropriate time to elect locals.

Still, these failings were not the whole story. As Lamin Sanneh, himself an African convert to Christianity from Islam, reminds us, missionaries were also liberators of local cultures and defenders of local languages that would have disappeared if colonialism had arrived without missionaries.[10] With the demise of colonialism in the years after World War II and Vatican II, seeds sown in the mission era were freed from their connection with colonialism. The most important thing about the history of mission, then, is that it is an integral part of the history of peoples who, in Sanneh's terms, translate the gospel into their own languages and cultures. For those with eyes to see and ears to hear, missionaries trained in the North American SVD were agents of this process, one that we are only now able to see in historical perspective.

---

10. See Lamin Sanneh, *Translating the Message: The Missionary Impact on Culture* (Maryknoll, N.Y.: Orbis Books, 1989).

7

The Brothers' Life and Formation

Faithful Servants and Master Craftsmen, 1895–1960

The brothers have been a key component in the Divine Word Missionary community since the beginning. For a number of years, in fact, brothers outnumbered the priests. Most important, their spirit of prayer has inspired the entire corps of students and future missionaries. Then at a practical level, traveling brothers (*Reisebrüder*) sold huge numbers of subscriptions to the Society's publications. Moreover, the expertise of other brothers in running the press at a high degree of efficiency insured that maximum profits could be poured into the expansion of Arnold Janssen's dreams. They performed yeoman service in all the details of building and maintaining the SVD's expanding system of satellite seminaries, again saving huge sums of money that could be freed up for the missions and further expansion. And when the SVD began new missions in places as distant as China, New Guinea, and Togo, brothers erected the buildings in which the missionaries lived. For missions where there were no construction companies or support services, they devised ways of prefabricating basic buildings, shipping them to the mission, and putting them together where they were needed.

Despite their integral nature as a key component in the Society, two factors impeded them from equality with the priests. While it interrupts our story, those two factors must be adverted to at the beginning. Their official or canonical stature was a step down from that of the priests because of the church's universal Code of Canon Law. According to that law, a "non-cleric" cannot have jurisdiction, the power to regulate a priest in the performance of his office. The brothers were not clerics, despite taking the same vows according to the same SVD constitutions. Because the SVD had priests, it was, according to canon law, a "clerical" institute. If brothers were not priests, then, they had to be laity, hence the odd name they were given, *lay* brothers, or *lay* religious. The issue ultimately becomes one of enfranchisement and having an official voice in Society "chapters" where policy matters are decided. According to canon law, only the clerics (priests) could be elected to positions of authority and had decision-making power. They, and only they, could vote and have a voice in the running of the congregation, none of which was allowed to the "lay" brothers. This enfranchisement issue never came up with women religious, for as females they could not become clerics in the first place. Sisters, "nuns" as they were often called then, were simply "religious." In their congregations sisters governed themselves and elected their own superiors.

The second issue coloring the brothers' membership stemmed from the long history of brothers in monastic and mendicant congregations and the European class system. Because of that history, the work of those who entered religious communities and took vows, but were not ordained, was manual labor, even if it was in the skilled trades. The nobility, university-educated people, and professionals had higher social status. Priests, even if they came from lower social orders, were granted de facto membership in society's higher ranks. This carried over into the Society of the Divine Word, not because the founder wanted to have a servant class in the Society, but because it seemed completely natural, indeed, the only way to organize the membership. Indeed, it appears that the lot and the social status of the SVD brothers were higher than in other comparable religious societies. In the main, then, it was the provisions of canon law, much more than European social status attitudes, that will underlay certain problems we shall discuss in what follows. With this as background, we turn to the main story.

THE BROTHERS AND THE FOUNDER

Although he had a clear idea about founding a German mission-sending society, Arnold Janssen had few fixed ideas on how to work out his vision in detail. He improvised as he went along. This was all the more necessary because of the rapidity with which his congregation grew in the first years. Very early on he thought of making his Society a religious congregation living under the three vows of poverty, chastity, and obedience, but was persuaded to start it as an institute of priests who did not take vows but made a promise to work in the missions. As Father Johann Kraus put it: "Arnold Janssen . . . was not thinking of a religious order before he started the work in Steyl. The idea of having brothers was far from his mind. His cherished image was that of a society of secular priests for the service of the pagan missions."[1] The issue of authority and obedience in the new society, however, became the first major crisis. Two of the four original founders, Father Bill and Seminarian Reichart, rejected Janssen's point of view and departed, leaving seminarians Anzer and Janssen to go it alone.

As the community grew, Janssen was faced with a dilemma. He needed people to help him, especially with the press he had decided to build. To solve his labor problems, he first thought of recruiting for his new enterprise students who would have the skill both to work and to study Latin in preparation for the priesthood at the same time. According to Fritz Bornemann, Janssen was quickly disabused of this idea even before he started his congregation. In the summer of 1875, a Professor Hengesch, whom he had consulted, suggested he include brothers. They could do the manual work that would have to be done.[2] The founder did not do this

---

1. Johann Kraus, "Die Steyler Brüdergemeinschaft und ihr Wirken," *Nova et Vetera* (September/December 1975): 235.

2. Fritz Bornemann, *Arnold Janssen der Gründer, des Steyler Misionswerkes 1837–1909: Ein Lebensbild nach zeitgenössischen Quellen* (Steyl: Secretariat Arnold Janssen,1969), p. 115.

right away. First he recruited men who would be willing to work for room, board, pocket money, and for God. Some of these lay helpers themselves, however, put pressure on Father Janssen to take them as postulants for the brotherhood. In 1878, Janssen was definitely thinking of incorporating brothers as vowed religious into his new society. Finally, in the spring of 1879 he began to accept lay helpers as postulants. In 1882 the first brothers took their vows, while the first clerics took their vows in 1884, after the first general chapter. Thus brothers were the pioneers in changing the Society from an association of diocesan priests into a religious congregation.

From the beginning the founder expected the best from his brothers and gave them the best opportunities and machinery available to attain their goals, a practice which was stimulated by the need of the press to operate at a high degree of efficiency and quality. Moreover, the founder respected and trusted the brothers. As a consequence, the SVD way of incorporating the brothers, as Superior General Henry Heekeren said in his 1979 circular letter to the Society, *Witnessing to the Word*, "was, without doubt, one of the most modern in Europe at the turn of the century." That Janssen should expect his brothers to be the best in their fields should not surprise us, for skilled workers and craftsmen were highly respected and rewarded in Germany then as well as today. Nor were the brothers during the founder's lifetime regarded as second-class members in his Society. They were as fully religious, as fully missionary as any of the priests. The constraints put on them came not so much from Arnold Janssen as from the *Code of Canon Law*.

When the Society was translated to democratic, meritocratic America, paradoxically something of this was lost. The brothers became more isolated than they ever were in Europe. Their education and training here were generally limited to what they were able to receive from other brothers, which, of necessity, consisted primarily of the skills they brought with them from Europe. As the brothers at Techny got older, however, so did their knowledge and skills. This was not true of all the brothers; many did much to improve their skills, some of them even turning hobbies or special skills into full-time occupations and useful contributions. Brother Regis did this with his watch-repairing, Brother Amabilis played the organ for St. Norbert's parish, Brother Richard developed a duplicating machine business on his own, Technygraph. Some brothers developed significant reputations in their respective fields of work, such as Brother Frederick in the apiary and Brother Charles in the nursery. The same situation held true in all the houses of the Society in North America. The pattern was for trades to be learned at Techny. A brother assigned to Girard as cook, for example, spent time learning to bake under the tutelage of Brother Archangel at Techny before taking up his assignment.

Because of the brothers, Techny was as self-sufficient as possible, like the monasteries of old. Brothers grew and produced whatever was needed to feed the community: wheat, potatoes and other vegetables, and fruit. They kept cows for milk, butter, and meat, and kept chickens for meat and eggs. They kept bees for honey and made Techny's candles from the beeswax. Brothers tailored the clothes, and both made and repaired shoes. Anything that could be grown, made, repaired, or produced by the members themselves in isolation from the surrounding world was done. It bred a sense of self-reliance and frugality, and thus Techny was considered an ideal place to prepare young men for the missionary brotherhood and priesthood in a religious congregation.

Over time, we have said, the sense of equality that characterized the founder's dealing with the brothers diminished. At the very least, many brothers *thought so,* and in matters of this kind, perception and reality are identical. One old brother, who has died since I spoke with him, held up the report card he had brought with him to Techny when he entered in 1921 as a candidate fourteen years old. He had preserved it in mint condition and it was a very good report card. His only comment was: "And they [the priests] thought we [the brothers] were not talented enough to become priests!"

Not all priests and seminarians thought this way, but some surely did, and this brother's perception definitely had a basis in reality. He had suffered because of the distinction between clerics and brothers. At Techny, in fact, clerics and brothers had little sustained social interaction. What occurred was on major feasts such as Christmas and in the common liturgies in the main church. Each unit at Techny—priests, brothers, major seminarians, minor seminarians, and brother novices—had its own dining room and recreation room. Younger members played sports with their own department and each unit had its own part of the building. Since silence was the rule and not the exception, most of the time when members of one department encountered another, a nod served as the sole greeting. Very little passing-time occurred. Indeed, it was frowned on, and the junior brother who spent time talking with the seminarians could expect the director of the brothers to tell him to refrain from doing so. Genuine friendships between members of different groups were discouraged.

There are indications that already in the first quarter-century of North American SVD history this kind of dissatisfaction was felt. In the provincial chapter at Techny in 1924, the brothers, through their representative and director (a priest!), Gerard Heffels, voiced the following grievances, which I found in the generalate archives:

[There are] various complaints which may be summed up in the following points:
1. The Brothers are not considered as full members of the Society, they are only its workmen.
2. The Brothers have too much work. Fathers and students have free time on certain days, while the Brothers have to work (Washington's Birthday, observed only by the Fathers and students). Every American laborer is entitled to a few weeks' vacation.
3. The personal liberty of the Brothers is restricted, they are held down by their superiors, etc. They desire advance [*sic*]; ascetical, intellectual, social.

As one brother put it in a personal interview with me, reflecting on the life of the clerical novices and seminarians compared to that of the brothers, there really was not that much dissimilarity in the way they lived, with one big exception. The lives of the clerics changed after ordination. The brothers, in a sense, lived a perpetual novitiate; they continued their life of abnegation and denial. They continued to need permission for everything; they never even reached a time when they could seal their letters,[3] which were always subject to being read by their superiors, as if they remained on probation perpetually.

Unless a man had a useful skill when he applied to the Society to become a brother, he was assigned to do whatever was needed at the time. The system of training for long years in the Society in North America followed the apprentice system. There was little formal schooling for the work assigned to a brother. He learned on the job, the older brothers teaching the younger ones, following the German method of craftsmanship, but without the German habit of being part of a large national guild that kept updating and improving skills. While the brother candidates brought superb raw material to the SVD in terms of motivation and character, until the 1960s the clerical outlook that dominated the Society did not see fit to send brothers out for professional training. The needs of the kitchen, the farm, and the press took precedence, and because the world was largely a closed world, it was not immediately apparent that the American SVD was not developing the human potential of its brothers.

At the risk of making this section sound overly negative, still another fact must be brought to the fore. The needs of Techny and the rest of the North American houses were so pressing that it was rare for a brother to be sent to the missions. The generalate or a mission provincial might ask for brothers, but U.S. provincials and rectors were loath to release them. Thus a far smaller percentage of brothers than priests went overseas.

Brother Norbert Hertel (known for many years as Brother Roman, the name given him when he took first vows) may serve as an example. He came to Techny carrying a small chest of woodworking tools his father had given him to build bird houses. He was, of course, assigned to the carpenter shop under the tutelage of Brother Fabian, from whom he learned the trade. Most SVDs remember Brother Norbert as the community organist. But the opportunity to learn the organ came to him by accident. In addition to being musically gifted, his father had bought a piano two years before Norbert had left for Techny. On it Norbert learned to play. One day the regular organist in the brothers' chapel was sick and Father Burgmer, who was in charge of music at the time, asked if anyone could play simple hymns. They thus found that Brother Norbert could. And how he would play! He was allowed to practice for one and a half hours a day, on his own, for five years. Father Paunder, who succeeded Burgmer in charge of music, gave Norbert permission to study for two semesters at the Chicago School of Music. After this he studied privately with a church organist who lived near Techny. And Brother Norbert even got to use the skills he had learned as a carpenter when it came time to build and repair the two organs in the Techny church. Brother Norbert thrilled the Techny community with his virtuoso abilities. Until his death in 1996, people came from all around the northern suburbs to hear him play. The quality of the organ he helped build and maintain was recognized by Northwestern University's music department and was used for the university's recitals in the Techny chapel for a number

---

3. It was the rule that everyone but priests were to leave all their letters unsealed in a box near their superior's office. He had the right to read both outgoing and incoming mail. Though relatively few superiors availed themselves of the right, it remained a symbol of dependence.

of years. In this context, a quote from Father Robert Flinn's unpublished manuscript description of Techny's church is instructive:

> The magnificent grand organ and the special antiphonal organ were constructed on site by Vienna-born Bartholomew Wiener, his son Carl, and Brother Norbert Hertel, SVD. The old organ moved over from the east wing chapel was clearly inadequate for the new edifice and an instrument worthy of the chapel was planned from the beginning. From 1924 to 1927 the Wieners and Brother Norbert built the large organ with its four manual consoles and 3500 pipes and ornate setting . . . All metal pipes were new except fifteen ranks which came from an organ at the Busch Temple Conservatory of Music. This building was destroyed by fire, but the organ was virtually unharmed and purchased for the unlikely sum of $500 . . . The reverberant acoustics of the chapel and the wide range of the organ's capabilities lent splendor to the sacred liturgies and concert performances. Brother Norbert played the organ for sixty-six years until his recent retirement.

Brothers did not often change their work assignments. Those assigned to work in one of the offices usually spent their lives doing office work. Their first job upon entry into the Society frequently established their life's course. This was especially the case when a particular job demanded a lengthy apprenticeship for its mastery, as was the case for many tasks in the print shop. Only a catastrophic event such as the fire in the press was able to free a number of brothers to pursue other occupations in the U.S. and in the missions.

In the first half of the Society's history in America, formal education was not in demand for the kind of work brothers traditionally did. This changed after World War II, but before then, it was common for many working-class men and women not even to finish grade school, let alone high school. Thus when a boy fourteen years of age applied to join the brotherhood, he became an aspirant and was put to work immediately to learn a trade. If the applicant was older, he entered and remained as a postulant for a minimum of six months. After a two-year novitiate the candidate took first vows, which could not be taken until he had reached the minimum canonical age of eighteen. For boys entering in the early years, then, their training for their work was their education, in much the same way as if they had followed their father into the mill or plumbing business. As things developed, then, brothers played a supporting role in a clerical society. Anthony Thottan, in a 1988 article in *Verbum SVD*, stated that what we have been describing characterized the situation and the relationship between clerics and brothers up to Vatican Council II. A series of general chapters of renewal that occurred at five-year intervals after Vatican Council II (in the years 1967, 1972, 1977, and 1982) developed new Constitutions which "do not portray Brothers only as support personnel in an overall mission strategy but rather imply their full participation in the missionary-religious life to which they are consecrated by vows."

Even though there was occasional friction between clerics and brothers, given the acceptance of church law and teaching, the *system* was perceived to be legitimate. The system, however, began to crumble when society at large and the church in the conciliar decree on religious life (*Perfectae caritatis*) recognized that the brothers must be given equal rights in clerical congregations.

In spite of it all, or perhaps because of it all, many brothers acquired a deep dedication to the Society and its work, along with a prayer life that was palpable, even to young seminarians very full of themselves. If St. Therese of Lisieux, who never left her cloistered Carmelite convent, could be proclaimed the Patroness of the Missions for what she did for the conversion of souls by her prayers and sacrifices, one may also conclude that much of the Society's success is owed to the prayers of the many brothers who did their work so prayerfully for so many years.

THE FORMATION OF THE BROTHERS

Where did this deep prayer life of the brothers come from? This is not an easy question to answer, but an attempt can be made. Their lives, from their entry into the Society, revolved around work, at which they became masters, which meant also it often became routine. The mind could wander off to explicit considerations of God. Most work, moreover, was done in silence, and this fostered an atmosphere conducive to prayer. In addition, the work done by the brothers had intrinsic worth that could lead to what another generation would term "Zen-like satisfaction" when it was done well. Like everyone else in the house, they began the day with morning prayers and meditation, followed by Mass, which amounted to an hour and a half of prayer before breakfast, prayer that started when it was quiet and dark outside. Work started and stopped with a prayer. Then, every fifteen minutes throughout the day, they stopped work for a few moments to raise their thoughts to God in the Quarter Hour Prayer. At noon there was the particular examen, followed by dinner and one hour's recreation with their first chance for friendly conversation with their confreres. After that recreation, it was back to work until it was time to clean up and get ready for supper.

Several brothers I interviewed made the point that there was little difference between being in novitiate, being junior brothers in formation while in temporary vows, and being senior brothers with forty years in the Society already behind them. It seems to be an accurate assessment. Unless a brother was given an assignment, for example, as a purchasing agent for the house or dealing with contracts for the provincial administration, he had little contact with the outside world. His life did resemble that of a novice. And in time he became much more like a contemplative monk than a missionary, even if he directed all his prayers and intentions to the missions.

Brothers experienced the life they would lead all their lives long, if they persevered, while they were in novitiate. The relationship between training and future life for the brothers was a far closer fit than that of the clerical novices. As novices, brothers had two classes daily. They included careful instruction in the constitutions of the Society and lessons in Catholic doctrine. In addition, they were instructed on how to pray and prepare a meditation and on other practical matters, as well as on what the Society expected from a brother and what it means to be a missionary. For the rest, silence reigned during most of the day, and there was both a lot of hard work and prayer in common.

All the brothers' virtues were summed up in obedience. This was supposedly true of the clerics as well, but the brothers lived obedience in a much more direct way than the priests. It was a rare brother whose work was not directed by a priest. Even though the brother was master of his craft, what he did, when he did it, in what order, was up to the priest in charge. Sometimes the results could be hilarious when a priest did not respect the brother's expertise. Brother Albert delighted in telling a story from the days when an addition was constructed at East Troy. He tried to tell the rector, Father Robert Studeny, a man with advanced degrees and a well-deserved reputation for brilliance, that a larger return tank was needed in the boiler room when several hundred new feet of radiators were added. Father Studeny told him that an engineer had drawn up the plans and that he (Studeny) would trust the engineer. Albert remonstrated to no effect and, in religious obedience, accepted the rector's decision. When the return tank overflowed and deposited a couple feet of water in the boiler room one winter day, Albert admitted to feeling more than a little satisfaction in telling Father Studeny that major repairs were now needed in the boiler room. Studeny, he said, accepted the news with a sheepish smile, but never admitted he should have listened to Brother Albert and questioned the engineer. It seems that the engineer had never even thought about the potential problem.

There were certainly brothers who were not only listened to but whose advice was sought by their superiors. Indeed, a smart rector or provincial knew that only a fool would try to make these wise men do things against their better judgment. But it was not until the currents that flowed into the upheavals of the Second Vatican Council began to challenge the notion that the SVD was a clerical community with lay brother helpers that the brothers' vocation began to be appreciated for what it really was in and of itself. We turn in the next chapter to that era and in so doing we merge the story of the formation of priests and brothers in a single storyline. Perhaps the greatest impact of the council on the SVD was to help the Society grapple with the fundamental equality and dignity of the two main components of its membership.

Changes begun at Vatican II worked their way into the Society's constitutions. The Society's basic documents now stress the fact that brothers and priests are religious missionaries and that before some are ordained as priests, *all* are brothers, and that this fraternity is the fundamental relationship that should obtain between the two groups. Although clericalism, like racism, does not always die easily in all its manifestations, Society legislation and constitutions have removed every excuse for retaining a two-tiered kind of association. In addition, since the general chapter of 1988, brothers can be elected or appointed rectors, provincials, and members of local, provincial, and general councils. Brothers have served as rectors and vice provincials in the Chicago Province, and the same is true in other regions.

A REVOLUTION ON THE HORIZON

Did Vatican II and its revolutions sneak up unbidden? How is one to assess the kind of training we have been talking about in this and the previous chapter on the formation of the priests and the formation and life of the brothers? As a transition to our next chapter, it may be useful to borrow a long quote from a former SVD, who by most people's accounts was one of the most beloved priests at Techny. Father Charles Kelty, who was a seminarian at Techny during the first half of the 1940s, left the Society in 1961, after the fire we spoke of in chapter five burned down the press he managed. He became a Cistercian monk and was renamed Father Matthew in Gethsemani, Kentucky. With humor and affection, but also incisively, Kelty sums up these years brilliantly. And though he speaks explicitly from the position of having been a seminarian and priest, anybody who was part of the SVD from the 1930s through the 1960s will recognize himself in it:

There was much about life in minor and major seminary in a totally active order [the Divine Word Missionaries] that was contrary to my taste, yet necessary and good for me. I had to adapt and to adjust in order to survive, and so cultivated out-going qualities with zest. I was no good at all in sports; I think because I did not have the basic aggression necessary, or, if I did, could not express it in that way. But there were many other activities and I was involved in most of them: publications, drama, music, debate, clubs, and committees. We had endless discussions, arguments, exchanges, and I developed a flair for quick retort and effective ridicule and sarcasm. Since manual labor in that particular era at the seminary was perhaps in higher repute than the intellectual life (World War II was on, labor was short, and we had an open invitation to help on the big farm—a new world to many of us), I managed to acquire some prowess in that, too, and enjoyed working with horses and pigs, in garden and flour mill. In my studies I was about average and had to work hard, not really knowing how to study.

Today, the seminary training that we underwent is looked back on as something depraved and bizarre. True, there was a good deal wrong with it, but at the time, few of us felt so and took it all in with enthusiasm. There were only a few rumblings of the revolution to come and we did not understand them. We thought of ourselves as competent, alive, and aware—did we not speak forthrightly on such progressive issues as liturgy in English, cooperatives, back-to-the-land and organic farming, indigenous art forms in mission lands? And we looked forward with joy and confidence to the mission work we would be assigned.

There was a great sense of close fraternity in that enclosure which was fostered by almost every factor of the life: a heavy routine of public prayer and liturgy, an almost constant being together, a great sense of sharing in a common ideal. We found it stimulating and we stimulated one another. It occurs to me now that we had innumerable celebrations of one kind or another: programs or plays or speakers, musicals, banquets, picnics, get-togethers, hikes, outings, investitures, professions, ordinations, the cycle of liturgical feasts. Our time was tightly controlled and day followed day in Spartan discipline. I frankly loved it and I sensed most of us did. We complained endlessly about the administration, the faculty, the prefects of discipline, but that was as much a part of the life as ritual. And through it all ran a spiritual current that only added to it and bounded it together.

It was a "good seminary" and we were proud of it. We were further proud to be members of a worldwide missionary group and felt ourselves superbly blessed in that. We looked on students in diocesan seminaries and even in other orders and societies with a kind of sympathy, quite assured that what they had could not possibly come up to ours.

It was a fabulous creation, really, and over it hung some aura of God's and the Church's blessing; it was divinely right. The tight control that Rome kept on us was only further proof that evidently we were important. Eventually, the whole thing fell apart, though many years later.[4]

One can argue whether SVD formation and training fell apart or has begun a process of evolution into a new way of bringing the light of the Word into the darkness of the night of unbelief. It is less ambitious and more pertinent to tell the tale of what happened in the late 1950s and through the 1960s. To do so, we turn to the next chapter.

---

4. Matthew Kelty, *My Song Is of Mercy: Writings of Mathew Kelty, Monk of Gethsemani*, ed. Michael Downey (Kansas City, Mo.: Sheed & Ward, 1994), pp. 5–6.

8

The Second Vatican Council and Its Impact

Changes in Religious Life and Missionary Formation, 1958–1970

INTRODUCTION

From the beginning of Techny as a seminary, there was a strong undertow that threatened to weaken the legitimacy of mission house life. While everyone in authority spoke of the relevance of the semimonastic life that brothers, seminarians, and priests lived "for the missions," it was also clear that actual life in the missions diverged sharply from the ideals spoken of in novitiate. For those preparing for the missionary priesthood especially, it was common knowledge that they would soon live in ones and twos and threes and would spend long hours on jungle trails moving from village to village. When they came back to the main station, where theoretically several other confreres lived and where it was possible to observe community prayer hours and the like, they often returned to find that their fellow priests were themselves off on trek and the brother who managed the attached sawmill had been called away by the bishop to help another brother rebuild a church knocked down by a hurricane. In other words, there was a certain split between the religious-community ideal and the religious-missionary ideal.

Second, a strength of Arnold Janssen's heritage of singling out some of his members for advanced studies to spend their lives preparing younger members to become missionaries and of making each of his mission houses self-supporting was the dedication his priest-educators and brothers brought to the task. One of the disadvantages was that over the course of years, two cultures had grown up in the Society, that of the mission house and that of the missionaries. Johannes Schütte, who became superior general in 1958, set out to remove the bifurcation. He wanted to help the Divine Word Missionaries become a group where the form of religious life was determined by being missionary, while the form of missionary life would be informed by religious vows that enabled the individual and the community to dedicate themselves totally to mission.

JOHANNES SCHÜTTE AND THE SVD AT MID-CENTURY

Times change. The nineteenth century became the twentieth and soon the SVD was in the midst of the postwar 1950s. Did what worked well in years past need alteration to answer the needs of another age as circumstances changed? Would structures established when the colonial era thrived function when that era was condemned by the peoples Divine Word Missionaries worked among? We get a sense of the direction of the change already in the first years after the Second World War. Missionaries were expelled from India first, and then China. The socialist and even the communist ideal was at war with the notion that Christianity would become the organizing principle of the world. At another level, theologians were retrieving insights from scripture studies and history. These insights challenged the notion that the Roman Catholic Church's organization and certain of its practices were the only possible way to be a catholic church. Though these "new theologians" were condemned and forbidden to publish in the 1940s and 1950s, by 1962 they were the *periti* ("experts") called by the bishops of the Second Vatican Council to draft the council's decrees.

In the 1950s things begin to change. In the Society of the Divine Word, the man who saw most clearly the necessity of changes was Johannes Schütte. Ordained in 1939, Schütte was conscripted as a medical orderly in the German army but, according to SVD historian Fritz Bornemann, was able to talk himself out of this and went to China where he joined a group of American SVDs in Honan. Expelled from China by the communists in 1952, he returned to Germany and earned a doctorate in missiology at the University of Münster. Father Aloysius Grosse-Kappenberg, the superior general at the time of his return, had been Schütte's prefect in St. Gabriel's as well as a good friend and supporter. It was he who appointed Schütte to be the mission secretary of the Society in 1955, a completely new position in the generalate, which forced Schütte to reflect on the missions and missionaries, their needs and formation. Shortly after his appointment, Schütte went to North America, among other things to implement and adapt, if need be, the "Statute on Mission Propaganda" that he had written as the first fruit of his new position. He stayed for eight months, traveled all over the U.S., and became well acquainted with the American SVD. On 27 August 1957, Grosse-Kappenberg died, which meant a general chapter had to be called to elect a superior general. As mission secretary, Schütte was automatically a member of this chapter.

Johannes Schütte was elected superior general on 28 March 1958, the first superior general who had not known the founder personally. More important, he was the first superior general who had been an overseas missionary. Up to his election, the mission houses had become primary in the thinking of many and the ideal for what constituted proper SVD community life. In 1954, Grosse-Kappenberg had this to say in reference to Schütte, who was just finishing his studies in Münster:

> We must remember that for almost fifteen years now he had not lived in a regular religious community. The last time was more than a decade ago at St. Gabriel. Even then the regular life of the community had been very seri-

ously disturbed by the conditions before and after the outbreak of World War II. It is, therefore, necessary that he should become accustomed once more to regular community life. Then he will all the more certainly have the proper religious spirit which a leading position in any of our houses of formation clearly requires.[1]

One imagines Father Schütte looking down from heaven and smiling at his mentor's opinion of his irregular life to that point. Schütte, in fact, would set out to change this kind of thinking, because in his opinion, the Society was not founded to produce mission house priests and brothers. In an article published in *Verbum*, rich in quotes of the founder and earlier superior generals, Schütte argues that mission, not the needs of established houses, must determine how the Society is organized and forms its members.[2] An established mission house Schütte calls a *domus formata*, and he insists such a house is a means to an end, and the end, he insisted, was to prepare men for the "conversion of the faith," a clumsy expression perhaps, but one that indicates that the purpose of the mission house is to lead to the conversion or deepening of the personal and vocational life of the candidate. To bolster this argument he quotes the founder, and then goes on to quote former Superior General Joseph Grendel, "mission work . . . is the main task of the Society." And again, "Our apostolic vocation according to the will of our Father and Founder is the specific characteristic of our family" (quoting his predecessor Grosse-Kappenberg). The article notes that only a quarter of those ordained or in vows live in mission houses and another quarter live in a *domus formata* in the missions, but these houses in the missions are quite different from those in the sending countries. The rest of the membership goes to assignments in missions where community life is simply impossible. Yet mission house living, Schütte continues, has been held up as the ideal. He points out the dangers of seminary formation that stress dependence on superiors or emphasize external observance of matters like the daily order, silence, and so forth. In contrast, for Schütte, love of God and neighbor must always motivate the SVD wherever he works.

Father Schütte enumerates three other traits a successful missionary must have. The first is the ability to adjust and accommodate. Here empathy becomes important as does the capability to share in the life of the people one is sent to. Not just the will and the head, but the heart also, must be formed. The second trait a good missionary must exhibit is independence (*Selbstständigkeit*), which, in turn, must also be linked with a sense of personal responsibility. Third, what is finally required is guidance and instruction, but also inner, personal direction, not just external control and supervision.

Another major point Schütte makes in the article has to do with the mission house itself, insisting that its atmosphere should also be missionary, to the point

1. Quoted in Fritz Bornemann, *In Memoriam: Father John Schütte, 6th Superior General SVD* (Rome: Collegio de Verbo Divino, 1972), p. 56.

2. Johannes Schütte, "Der bestimmende Faktor in Erziehung und Ausbildung unser Scholastiker," *Verbum* 1 (1959): 32–45. By the term *domus formata*, Schütte meant a fully developed house engaged in formation, having a sufficiently large community to have a common life and daily order.

that people should recognize immediately that the mission spirit holds sway in an SVD house of studies.

Several important steps were taken to implement this program of turning formation to one suitable for a mission-sending society, the majority of whose members were assigned to overseas missions, where many might live alone for weeks at a time, dealing with people with strange customs and difficult languages. To help direct the tone and style of formation in a mission direction, he urged as many of those engaged in formation as possible be given the chance to spend time in the missions. One of the resolutions of the eighth general chapter, which had elected Schütte, was to revise the *ratio studiorum SVD* (the Society's "order of studies") to provide a year's pastoral apprenticeship after ordination. For the North American provinces, one of the practical results of this was to establish a pastoral year in Washington, D.C.

VATICAN COUNCIL II AND DIVINE WORD FORMATION

The year Johannes Schütte was elected superior general, Angelo Roncalli became pope. Roncalli, as Pope John XXIII, convened the Second Vatican Council, perhaps the most significant religious event of the twentieth century. If one considers the twenty-one councils called "ecumenical" by the Roman Catholic Church, Vatican Council II stands out as singular in several important ways. It was more truly international in membership than any previous council; it had more participants than any previous council; it was more ethnically mixed than any other; the participants from Oceania, Latin America, Asia, and Africa showed the face of a church that by the end of the twentieth century would no longer be a Western church. It included non-Catholics as observers, and the sessions of the council were conducted under the view of the world's communication media.

The opening session of the council occurred on 11 October 1962, and in the words of John XXIII, it was to be a council of *aggiornamento* ("updating"). We could spend a good deal of time discussing the movements and countermovements at the council, but they are familiar to many readers and readily available in other sources to those who did not live through that era. Suffice it to say that the presence of more than twenty bishop-members of the Society, most of whom lived in the Collegio del Verbo Divino, spoke to the SVD about the impact of its eighty-year-history. It reminded the entire Society of the internationality of the church. And in practical terms, since Superior General Schütte became one of the most important people behind the council's Decree on Mission (*Ad gentes*), his stature within the Society was immensely enhanced. This meant that the direction in which he was pointing would gain ascendancy over the older, semimonastic philosophy that ruled in the "home countries."

What Schütte had suggested in regard to the renewal of the Society, now had added authority in the spirit of the council. In particular, to take the question of the position of brothers in the Society, the council's emphasis on the metaphor of church as a pilgrim people of God, in which the integral mission of the Church is the responsibility of all the people of God, and not primarily of priests and bishops, one recognizes the ingredients for dramatic change. In its Decree on the

Appropriate Renewal of the Religious Life, change was mandated and all congregations were to update and renew themselves. If formerly change was reluctantly accepted as a means to maintain stability, now change was simply an empirical fact, and virtue was found in how one directed it. There was a revolution implied in this alteration. If an institution becomes stable, one suspects that it is ossified and self-serving.

The emphasis on the pastoral approach changed the emphasis of studies in the brother training centers and seminaries. Concretely, it placed future SVD priests in pastoral ministry much earlier and more intensely than ever before. Perhaps even more significantly, brothers were welcomed to enter pastoral ministries, and many began to see a future for the brotherhood in areas other than supporting the work of priests. In an amazingly short period of time, the consensus arose that in all matters priests and brothers were equal in the inner life of the Society. Indeed, it is probably not an exaggeration to say that this consensus formed within the Society far faster than in the church at large, certainly faster than the Code of Canon Law would allow.

Father Schütte, who had been intensively involved in Vatican II in various capacities, called for a general chapter to be convened in 1967 to formally legislate how the updating and renewal process would be carried on. Since the renewal chapter would almost coincide with the regular general chapter at which a new superior general was to be elected, Schütte decided to have the renewal chapter serve also as a chapter for choosing new international SVD leadership. There are indications that Schütte felt he would be reelected, but it appears his style of leadership and the energy with which he pushed change caused a backlash. The capitulars chose Father John Musinsky, an American, for the Society's highest office.

FORMATION AFTER VATICAN II

After Vatican II, the formation program for priesthood- and brotherhood-bound students drew closer until finally they merged. In 1967 the brother candidate school at Techny and the minor seminary program at East Troy were merged. At the same time, brother candidate programs in Conesus and Girard merged. In 1969, junior brothers began attending Divine Word College at Epworth, and the expectation grew that brothers would receive full postsecondary education, either in technical areas or in bachelor's and graduate degree programs. For brothers, as for priests, educational programs would be approved according to the talent of the individual and the needs of the Society, not on the artificial basis of cleric versus lay brother status. Finally the brothers' novitiate was combined with the clerical novitiate, and both were put in Bay St. Louis, which in the meantime had been closed as a theologate. In reaching these decisions, the will of the brothers themselves prevailed. These views had coalesced in the course of intense discussions held during the years immediately following Vatican II and in preparation for the first renewal chapter (1967). Despite the recognition of two groups within their ranks—an older and a younger group—the majority clearly favored the new direction, and this is the way SVD went.

One of the major tasks in Musinsky's generalate administration was to carry out the renewal and reforms mandated by the Second Vatican Council. This was done in many ways, but one of the chief were four "renewal" chapters preceded by a lengthy self-study of the Society. Musinsky himself was elected at the first of these in 1967. He presided over two more, one in 1972 and the second in 1977, when Heinrich Heekeren was elected to replace him. Father Heekeren served for eleven years.

As the American provinces looked forward to these general chapters of the Society, Father Joseph Connors, then provincial superior at Techny, wrote a letter that gives a very profound sense of the direction all this would take. In it he contrasts religious life before and after Vatican Council II.

> A generation ago characteristics such as consistency of routine, punctuality, deference toward age and experience, authority, gravity, strictness of interpretation of rules, cherishing the unique religious spirit of one's own congregation, and predominance of decision-making by those in authority, were quite highly esteemed by most religious. In a cultural shift, however, in the rising generation, energetic activity, flexibility of routine, respect for youth and initiative, democracy, affability, freedom of spirit in the interpretation of rules, desire to communicate and collaborate with other congregations, desire for team-work and general discussion and a measure of collective decision-making, all form a new set of values which most younger religious esteem where ever they find them.

The renewal chapters had much to do. One of the most important tasks was discussing the nature of community life, and this became a major theme for all the subsequent chapters. One capitular reflected, "Our community life [in years past] was more an isolated living in community. We performed duties and exercises in physical togetherness but had little opportunity to form personal relationships. It was possible to be in community and still live in total isolation." The solution he proposed was to break larger communities into smaller ones. In small groups, it was thought, a person could develop the ability to grow and work with others. Most SVDs would live in small communities later in life anyway, it was known. In the attempt to implement such insights, there was much experimentation both among the brothers and the priests. The alterations in SVD lifestyle were immense and speedy. Many were left gasping for breath.

From an inspection of the new SVD constitutions, one might conclude that the community was now the primary formation unit. "Community" also became the most frequently referenced word in the constitutions. Rather than the hierarchical model prevalent for many years, a communion of faith and love was to become the model. This called for fraternal relations, a community that was Christ-centered with Christ present in the community as a brother, not above it. The model is baptismal.

But this posed another problem for the capitulars, the question of authority and obedience. The dialectic between authority and obedience and the necessity of dialogue before authority could act flowed through chapter discussions no matter what topic was on the table. It was presciently observed by one capitular, "Perhaps our greatest future task will be a serious search for a proper balance of freedom within commands, and dignity within submission." According to another capitular, the key would be found in the meaning of authority as service, which is a biblical understanding of that term. What was patently clear, however, was that the key to renewal in the Society was community.

BROTHERS AND PRIESTS

The brothers had the task of building up among themselves a community that epitomized their hopes for a revitalized religious missionary life, on the one hand, and simultaneously create a more healthy relationship between themselves and the priests, on the other hand. Even after the council, the Society remained a de facto clerical institute with a large cadre of non-clerical members. So, twist and turn the issue whichever way you will, there were two very distinct and different groups in the one Society, if one takes the canonical distinction seriously. While section 15 of the council's Decree on the Appropriate Renewal of the Religious Life called for brothers "to be brought into the heart of its life and activities . . . on the same basis and with equal rights and duties," it also added the words "excepting those which result from ordination." The canonical conundrum remained.

Let it be said clearly that for many members the issue of cleric-lay distinction is of no consequence, causes no difficulty, and canon law on the subject is simply not taken seriously. For priests and brothers in this group, the canonical distinction is painful. Still, in ways that remind a social scientist of the differences blacks and whites give on the extent to which racial prejudice exists in the U.S., brothers often see things differently, differently even from priests who think of themselves as pro-brother and against the canonical division.

Other issues are equally important. Among them are those that result from the changes mentioned in the intellectual formation of brothers and priests. These have led to dramatic changes in the style and shape of spiritual formation, though not in the final goals of this formation. By 1970, formation was taking place "in the world" rather than isolated from it. Pastoral engagement began early and occupied a significant proportion of time. This serves both as a preparation for the future apostolic work of the student as well as a vehicle for his formation, for much of spiritual formation regards helping the candidate understand himself and his reactions to the people he works with. He learns to understand his strong and weak points and also how to develop approaches that will make God's love more tangible for those he works among, both while he is in training and later. Formation by 1970 was much less structured by attendance at a multitude of community prayer exercises—though such exercises were still an integral part of formation at houses like the theologate in Chicago—than around events that must be tailored to an individual's own schedule. In the traditional program, the student had a private *ratio* (interview) with the prefect once or twice a year; in the program that emerged by 1970, he would share what was happening in his *inner* life and its struggles *in community discussions* with six to ten community members and a priest- or brother-director. One can wonder whether Johannes Schütte could have imagined the direction that formation would take in North America even before his death in 1971 and eleven years after his pioneering article in the 1959 *Verbum*, but it is clear that his American confreres took him at his word. They indeed tried to fashion a formation program in which the inner religious conversion of the candidate is the primary object, so that he, whether as brother or priest, can be an ambassador of Christ and one who carries on his entire life as a *socius Verbi Divini* ("a companion of the Divine Word"), to use a phrase that was dear to Schütte and that his successor John Musinsky thought should epitomize Divine Word spirituality and missionary life.

In contrast to the overriding concern before Vatican II to teach the truth, sometimes a truth that could rightly be called a tad narrow, the contemporary formation of brothers and priests together presupposes that the missionary has had a faith experience of Christ that he attempts first to embody and then to share. Constitution 521 states that members "must be attuned to the Holy Spirit and so be able to share their faith experience for the benefit of others. The more their words are borne out by their deeds, the greater will be their influence."

When the formal renewal process begun in 1967 had run its course through four chapters of renewal, the revised constitutions, now tested for fifteen years, were presented to the Congregation for Religious and Secular Institutes. They were approved on 19 October 1983 by the congregation, and the following words were placed at the beginning of the constitutions. The congregation, it says:

> recommends all members of the Society to accept the renewed constitutions willingly and to observe them faithfully. Through them they are helped to put in practice perfect Christian love in the following of Christ.

PART TWO

APOSTOLATES OF DIVINE WORD MISSIONARIES AT HOME AND ABROAD

Father John Musinsky, born in 1918 in Farrell, Pennsylvania, and ordained in 1944 at Techny, was prefect of the major seminary and novice master from 1949 through the mid-1960s. Father Musinsky served as the first and (to date) only American superior general of the SVD from 1967 through 1977, the years of tumultuous change after the Second Vatican Council.

9

Staffing African-American Parishes

The SVD's Most Radical Venture in America

When the final period is put at the end of the last sentence in the eternal book recording the work of the Society of the Divine Word, looming large in that book will be the contribution SVD missionaries have made to the African-American apostolate.[1] To tell this story in its entirety requires more space than this history can devote to it. Here only the highlights and their importance for the church in the United States can be touched upon. Together with their sister congregation, the Missionary Sisters, Servants of the Holy Spirit, the Divine Word Missionaries began their work by establishing a series of parishes and schools in the South. The Society's founder was still living when this apostolate began, so the story begins with him and, of course, with Father Peil who was superior in North America when the question of moving in this direction came up. As a matter of fact, at one point Father Peil and Father Janssen alone favored entering upon this work.

---

1. Various terms have been applied to African Americans at different times over the course of history, which makes it difficult to settle on one expression. One such is "African American," which parallels the term "European American" for those whose ancestral roots are found in Europe and "Asian American" for those whose origins lie in Asia. The term "African American" is quite recent, however, and was unknown to the founder or to the early SVDs who worked in the South. The terms they used were "black" or "Negro," especially as it is used in the German word *Negermission*. Negro was also the term used in official church circles, as in "The Catholic Board for Mission Work among the Negroes," which was established by the bishops of the country on 12 May 1907. Earlier at the Third Plenary Council of Baltimore (9 November to 7 December 1889) the bishops established the "Commission for the Catholic Missions Among the Colored People and the Indians" which was to oversee the collection and dispersal of the money that was collected annually for these missions in every diocese—at Rome's insistence. Even then, they could not decide on any one consistent term for African Americans, which is my own preference. In translating I will be literal: if the German uses *schwarz*, I will use "black," if *Neger*, I will use Negro. I will also use these same terms when "African American" would be a historical anachronism. Whatever term is eventually decided upon, the decision, as Father Edward Braxton said in the bulletin insert *In a Word* of June 1989, will have to come from the black community itself.

BACKGROUND OF THE SVD
AFRICAN-AMERICAN APOSTOLATE

The founder was first made aware of the Negro home missions in 1896. A Franciscan priest by the name of Otto Jansen, who had applied to enter Steyl one year after its opening but was not accepted, wrote to the founder on 1 March 1896 about this apostolate. In a letter of 5 June 1896, Father Lambert Welbers, who had studied in Steyl from 1877 to 1882, but who left to join the Josephites, urged Janssen to establish a mission among the Negroes. Over the early years of the SVD's work among the blacks, Welbers was often consulted. He was one of the many so-called ex-Steylers who had gone on to become priests and worked in North America.[2]

Because the Josephites were the main group working for the conversion of the Negroes, it will be fitting here to give a brief sketch of this group of missionaries. They trace their roots to Father Herbert Vaughan, an English priest who later became Archbishop and Cardinal of Westminster. Vaughan founded St. Joseph's Society of the Sacred Heart for Foreign Missions in 1866 in the London suburb of Mill Hill, hence the name "Mill Hill Fathers." They were not a religious congregation but a society of apostolic life, that is to say, they are a group of diocesan priests like the Maryknollers and the Paris Foreign Mission Society. They bound themselves by a promise to the work of their foundation. Wherever they labored, they put themselves more under the jurisdiction of the bishops.

One of the concerns of the Second Plenary Council of Baltimore, which opened on 7 October 1866, the year following the end of the Civil War, was the religious plight of the Negro. Not much was actually done during this council, but it did highlight many of the objections later raised regarding the evangelization of blacks. Bishops from the North felt that the problem was not theirs, but was for the southern bishops to work out. The southern bishops recited their enormous poverty of resources as an excuse for their reluctance to devote themselves to the cause of the Negro. Although Vaughan's main interest was Africa, he was persuaded to send missionaries to work among blacks in the U.S. His commitment was the first of its kind by Catholics. Vaughan intended that his missionaries not only "labor among the Negroes of the South, but to found in America a Missionary College . . . in which the African population may there be trained to carry the faith into their own land."[3]

In 1871, Vaughan came to America with the first contingent of four Josephites and toured the South. He wrote, "The dislike of the Americans . . . to the Negroes . . . far exceeds in intensity anything I had expected." In his diary he wrote that

---

2. See Fritz Bornemann, "Ehemalige Steyler als Priester in USA," *Verbum* 5 (1963), 188–98. *Steyler* referred to anyone who had studied at Steyl and was also the standard way of referring to SVDs in German-speaking regions.

3. Stephen J. Ochs, *Desegregating the Altar: The Josephites and the Struggle for Black Priests 1871–1960* (Baton Rouge: Louisiana State University Press, 1990), pp. 29f. Much of this material on the Josephites and on conditions in the South relies heavily on Ochs's Ph.D. dissertation, *Deferred Mission: The Struggle for Black Catholic Priests, 1871–1970*, University of Maryland, 1985. I have cited the dissertation in the U.M.I. Dissertation Services edition (1985) rather than the later book because the documentation is fuller and the number of quotations of contemporaneous opinions richer.

even priests regarded blacks as no more than dogs. He saw a priest refuse communion to a black soldier in a cathedral, which probably enables one to make some judgment about the bishop's policies toward blacks also. He also commented on the low, backless benches marked "for Negroes."[4]

On 30 May 1893, the Mill Hill missionaries in America separated themselves from the rest of the community and renamed themselves "St. Joseph's Society of the Sacred Heart," but they are much better known as Josephites. Ochs's book gives a good account of the reasons for the split and should be consulted for more on the subject. Father Janssen knew of this split and corresponded with Father Vaughan concerning it.

SVD BEGINNINGS

As he was in so much else in the early years of the SVD in North America, Brother Wendelin is involved with the development of the African-American mission. In a letter to the founder dated 21 January 1897, he called the founder's attention to the proposal of Father Welbers that the SVD take up work among the Negroes. On 29 March 1897, Wendelin again writes the founder after he had returned from Philadelphia, where a Father Thomas Hammeke, a cousin of a SVD brother, had suggested that the SVD take over an orphanage. He continues:

Perhaps we could consider another kind of work also, namely, a mission for Indians and Negroes. I enclose the annual report [of the bishops] regarding these missions to give you an overview. A great field of work lies open to us in the South and in the West [at this time the Society was still trying to focus on a place where they could concentrate their operation]. Yesterday I visited a nun—her name is Kath. Drexel—who gives about $250,000 a year to the Indian missions, and that's just the interest on her capital! She had already heard of our Brothers and would like to have some for her mission stations in the West. Of course, she would also like to have priests.[5]

The Drexel of whom Wendelin speaks, of course, is Saint Mother Katharine Drexel, founder of the Sisters of the Blessed Sacrament, an order founded to work among Indians and African Americans, and only the second native-born American to be canonized by the church. She helped SVD missions among African Americans and later supported the seminary. She is an amazing figure in American Catholic history. It is an indication of how ubiquitous Brother Wendelin was that

---

4. Ochs, *Deferred Mission*, p. 30.

5. Josef Alt, ed., *Arnold Janssen: Briefe in die Vereinigten Staaten von Amerika* (Nettetal: Steyler Verlag, 1994), p. 14, n. 3. Unless otherwise stated, quotations from contemporaneous correspondence are from the original German edition of this book, not the English translation (see bibliography), which was not available when I did my research. Because it is relatively easy to identify by date the letters being cited and the notes in which Alt explains the letters, I have generally given only the date of correspondence. The reader may find the relevant passage in either the German or English edition. Translations of these letters are my own.

he had met her and enrolled her among the Society's supporters. Some months later, on 5 April 1897, Brother Wendelin again writes the founder:

> The way I see it, we will have to work among the Indians and Negroes, which will enable us to do much good [for the church] over here. If we take on this work, we will have to establish a base in the South.

After Father Peil had arrived in the States, the possibility of working in the South again came up. Markert mentions a letter of Peil to the founder written on 12 April 1898, in which he tries to sell Janssen on the idea of combining an orphan asylum and a mission house somewhere in the Harrisburg Diocese in Pennsylvania. Father Peil stressed the possibility of getting a considerable number of candidates for the missionary vocation. In addition, starting a mission house would be something new in America; nothing like this existed. In the meantime he had discussed this idea with others, including Father Welbers.

Nothing more appears in the literature about a mission to the blacks until the fall of 1903, after the SVD already had settled on the north side of Chicago at Techny. Father Peil met with Archbishop James Quigley of Chicago to present two new confreres who had recently arrived from Europe. In the course of the conversation the archbishop mentioned the sad situation of the blacks in the South and in ways that seemed to invite the SVD to work for their conversion.

The next indication that Father Peil was involving himself with the idea of opening a mission for the Negroes came in the form of a response of Father Hermann auf der Heide to something Peil must have written to him. Auf der Heide, under the founder, was in charge of the sisters and it was possibly in this connection that the issue was brought up. Peil knew he would need sisters for the schools that would have to be opened eventually in the South. Auf der Heide writes to Father Peil on 26 February 1904:

> The information you sent that Father Heick could have started a mission for Negroes in Vicksburg on the 2nd of this month, was good news. I hope this mission among the Negroes in the United States will be successful and richly blessed, all the more, indeed, because the beginnings, I'm sure, will be difficult.

It is not so clear what auf der Heide was referring to, because Vicksburg in Mississippi was not the first place the SVD tried to establish a mission. The first attempt, which was made further north in Merigold in Bolivar County, also came close to being the last. If the South in general was a difficult mission, the toughest place to work would probably have been Mississippi, and in Mississippi, the most difficult area would have to be the central and northern counties of the state. There were practically no black Catholics, and not much of any other Catholic presence either. The blacks were mostly Protestant and had their own black ministers and churches. Those who were not Protestant were, in the terminology of the day, "pagans." In those churches, though, blacks felt at home and were wanted, and were, indeed, the only institutions they could control. It was primarily the unchurched "pagans" that the Catholic missionaries set out to convert. They were about to try it in Bolivar County, Mississippi, one of the counties most antagonistic to Catholicism in the nation.

Merigold was to be an example of a German colony in which German language and culture would be maintained along with Catholic identity, somewhat after the fashion of the colonies founded in Argentina and other parts of South America. Early in the history of the Society, the founder had sent his missionaries to help the Germans living in these colonies to preserve their Catholic heritage. Merigold was the site of one such colony and had been founded in 1895, the year the first SVD came to America. The Marquette Colonization Company purchased 5000 acres in Bolivar County, and forty Catholic families were persuaded to settle on the land. In 1896, Bishop Thomas Heslin assigned a German priest, Father Andrew Gmelch, who will appear in this history again, to offer Mass there twice a month. The colony, though, was a disaster. The land was low and swampy, and when it rained, everything turned to mud. Malaria and dysentery were common, nor was it uncommon for the Mississippi River to flood, ruining whatever cotton was planted. The weather, the terrain, and the way of life were nothing like what these Germans had known at home, and soon all left.

One of the investors in this colony, David Bremner, a Chicago businessman, purchased 640 acres of land near Merigold when it failed. He persuaded one hundred forty black families to move there to work the cotton plantations he sought to establish. Among these was one Catholic, the only person who had any education at all, something Bremner proposed to remedy. In the summer of 1904, having consulted Father Gmelch and Bishop Heslin, he approached Archbishop Quigley to help him find a religious community who would be interested in this work. Archbishop Quigley thought of the Society of the Divine Word and put the two in touch with each other.[6]

Several other events conspired to make this new enterprise of the SVD look attractive. The Society in North America was looking for a field of labor that would be in line with the purpose for which it was founded in the first place, and work among the pagan Negroes in America would satisfy that requirement, even if it was not strictly "foreign" mission work. Secondly, the work was being offered to the Society; the Society was not requesting it. For the founder this automatically gave it the earmark of God's will. He must also have known that Rome wanted more priests and missionaries working among the Negroes and Indians. In addition, not every priest or brother sent to America was cut out for the teaching work which was the only outlet for their talents up to this time. Some, both in Europe and in America, would definitely be interested in working among the Negroes. Promotion work for foreign missions would also make more sense if the Society was engaged in such work in the States itself. Around this same time also, according to a memorandum of Father Janssen to the general council, dated 2 November 1904, the founder and his council were beginning to question whether running

---

6. My account of these events relies on the doctoral dissertation of Michael Meier, SVD. See Michael Meier, SVD, "Das Negerpriester Seminar in Bay St. Louis," *Verbum* 3 (1961): 329–408; and "Die Negermission SVD im Süden der USA" (Steyl, Holland: Pontificia Universitas Gregoriana, 1961). As of this writing, Meier is Archbishop of Mt. Hagen in the central highlands of Papua New Guinea.

technical schools or orphanages was really what the SVD should be doing. This was also the time Father Peil was recommending that the Society take responsibility for Holy Hill in Wisconsin, an offer that was finally rejected as unsuitable. One final point Peil made in his letter of 8 July 1904, in which he describes his meeting of 4 July with Bremner and Archbishop Quigley, was that the initial establishment would cost the Society nothing, since Bremner would donate 320 acres of land, erect the buildings, and contribute to the maintenance of the missionaries.

The founder's reactions to the proposed projects was one of immediate interest. He was responding to several letters of Father Peil in 1904 that are no longer extant. Janssen has the following to say on 4 January 1905:

> You suspected that your letter would stir up our interest. That it did, but we still have to study the details. Much more surely has to be done for the Negroes of America, and we want to help to the degree we can and as the will of God is made known to us.

As their correspondence develops, the main problem Janssen foresees is the problem of personnel. He goes on to say that he knew that the Negro was perfectly capable of being educated, alluding to reports he got from Togo. But, he asked, are they ready to accept what they perceive as the white man's religion? What sort of family life do they have?

In short, the founder was interested in this project. He would repeatedly return to the question of the black apostolate, and from the tone of the very first letter one gathers that he was already convinced of its value. It is a stance from which he does not deviate. In a letter of 2 February 1905, shortly, therefore, after he had received Peil's response of 16 January to all his questions, he writes that he had sent a second circular, together with Peil's letter, to his council. The council gave consent, with the condition that the beginning would be made with a minimum of personnel and that favorable arrangements could be made with Mr. Bremner and the bishop. On 11 March 1905, however, Janssen writes that opinion on the council remains divided and that the time was not yet ripe. There were still questions to be answered. In the letter of 11 March, there was no question whether the SVD would begin work in the South among the Negroes, but rather where and how. Was Merigold the best place? There were recommendations that they check out other places; that Father Heick make an exploratory trip; that either Father Peil or Heick should visit Father Welbers again, who might be able to give some advice on how to go about setting up a mission among the Negroes and how to handle whites who may pose objections.

From the context of the founder's response, Peil had asked for one priest, two brothers, and four sisters to be assigned to this work. He had suggested that Father Aloysius Heick be the one to begin the mission at Merigold, to which the founder had no objections and was ready to make the appointment. Once again the founder was accurate in his reading of personality and put the right man in the right place. Father Heick had come to Steyl in 1888 to be a brother, but transferred one year later to the seminary at the age of twenty-five. Ordained in 1900, he was sent directly to the U.S. A Bavarian by birth, he was forty-one years old when he began his work in the South. He was wiry and energetic. He had spent five years in the United States. Among problems facing the founder in attempting to assign more priests and brothers to the Unites States was that none of the new priests and brothers wanted to volunteer for North America, and certainly not for the Negro missions. Peil wrote about this in a letter of 23 April 1905, addressed to the founder: "These 'rabbit-hearted' characters! These confreres should ask themselves sometime whether they think Christ also died for blacks or not, and what they actually promised the Savior on their ordination day. I am ashamed to even have to talk about such things."

Nonetheless, Peil was already talking about expansion into the whole diocese of Natchez, which meant to the whole state of Mississippi. For this the Society would have to get permission from the Propaganda (which they later did on 19 July 1907). Peil traveled to Merigold and all through the South, then to the Benedictine priory in Allegheny, Pennsylvania, to talk to the prior there, who had much experience in the black apostolate. He went to consult with the superior of the Josephites in Baltimore as well as with Father Welbers. Later he and Heick together made a study trip through the South from which both came away convinced of the need to work among the Negroes. On this journey they both got some idea of the way whites treated blacks. The numbers of blacks to be missionized was almost overwhelming. Meier quotes one mother superior in New Orleans who told Peil:

> Even in the cities where there were relatively large numbers of blacks . . . who gladly came to church . . . were joining Protestant sects because of the shocking treatment they had received. Not only the laity, but Catholic priests treat the poor blacks with contempt. Many who came from old Catholic families leave the Church.

Mother Drexel, whom Peil had also visited, felt that the possibilities for conversions among blacks was promising, and Meier says Peil thought that "Mother Drexel had a better opinion concerning blacks than any one in the country."

By 23 April 1905, in the context of deciding on the list of new assignments, the founder informed his council about the mission in the American South:

> As soon as agreement has been reached between the Bishop of the Diocese of Natchez [Mississippi] and us, Father Heick will take up a 2-3 month residency in the Negro town of Merigold. After this time we will decide definitely whether we will take over this station . . . At the same time the situation of the mission on [Bremner's] property, as well as and especially the situation in the rest of the diocese where there are some 900,000 Negroes [needed more study]. Only after this will we decide whether to take over any missions, and if the Propaganda gives permission we can take over this mission.

ARRIVAL IN MERIGOLD

On 15 July 1905, Father Heick arrived in Merigold, Mississippi, for the month trial period. On 24 July, Peil came to help him settle in. Father Meier reports that

Peil wrote the founder, "Early today [24 July] at about four thirty I arrived here where Father Heick was staying. We offered Holy Mass and I helped him buy the first things for his own housekeeping."

Everybody had done their homework; the foundation at Merigold had been prepared as well as humanly possible. True, nobody, it seems, had discussed the venture with the white planters around Merigold. Bremner was optimistic that the missionaries would succeed. Peil foresaw few difficulties and really would have liked to start the mission himself. Father Heick, never as enthusiastic as Peil about anything, feared he might have difficulties because of the heat and his English.

In the actual playing out of the drama, however, things went from bad to worse. In July it rained hard and everything turned to mud. This brought on a huge crop of mosquitos, including the anopheles mosquito bearing malaria, which Father Heick caught. Word got out that the new missionary intended to open a school and bring in white nuns to teach the blacks. Heick quickly learned that there was only one fully Catholic family, and that most of the the blacks were not pagans but Protestants, and, therefore, much more difficult to convert. Heick wrote to the founder:

> If I had my choice, I would not stay here for any amount of money. There are no Catholics here, so there's not much to do . . . I've said Mass three times, and the number who showed up were never more than three. Not once did I have a server. Just yesterday, on Sunday, nobody showed up until the Gospel. It's good I had the foresight to get permission to celebrate mass *nullo praesente et sine ullo ministro* [with nobody present and no server].

The founder attempted to cheer him up in a letter of 5 September 1905. He, too, was somewhat surprised that most of the blacks, as it turned out, were Protestant. This concerned Janssen greatly; Heick was to try to find out from others more experienced in this field whether black Protestants would eventually convert to the Catholic faith. The founder realized that schools might be a way of converting Protestants, but for this sisters would be necessary. Working with the children would be a way to reach the parents, while the priest would also be trying to win over the people, all the while showing great love and friendliness. There were possibilities of achieving something. Because too much pointed to God's will being at work, he was definitely not yet ready to give up on Merigold or on the black mission apostolate. He still had some questions about Bremner's offers of land and money, then tried to console Heick in his misery, but told him to stick it out some more.

Actually sisters were scheduled to come to Merigold, but an outbreak of yellow fever had put much of the northern part of Mississippi under quarantine. The pupils, however, came anyway, eventually thirty of them, with more promised when the cotton crop was in. Then something happened, but exactly what is not totally clear. Heick, with his life suddenly put at risk, had to leave Merigold with unseemly haste. Here myth and history become mixed. Some people said the danger was so great that Father Heick had to be hidden in a piano box and rolled out of town on a wagon; other stories turned the piano box into a coffin. Why did he have to leave so suddenly? The usual reason given had to do with the fact that he was trying to educate blacks. To be sure, the area of Mississippi where he was working was deeply committed to keeping the races separate and the blacks in their place, by keeping them uneducated, but this was true of the rest of Mississippi as well. Blacks, on the other hand, were keenly interested in having their children educated. This was proven time and again in the schools that the SVD began in all of the first missions they started. The whites were equally intent on keeping the Negro uneducated, according to Neil McMillan, because they feared "the revolutionary social and economic implications of educating a subservient work force."[7] For some during these years, keeping blacks from becoming educated was justified by claiming that blacks were incapable of formal learning. But from other instances it is clear that whites feared they would learn too much in schools, not too little. In this context McMillan notes:

> Broader educational opportunity for Blacks, many Whites recognized, could profoundly unsettle the patterns of southern life. It could breed black discontent; it could technically qualify Blacks for suffrage. Educated Blacks were thought to be less dependent and deferential than their ignorant cousins, less comfortable with caste sanctions, more likely to challenge the acceptable limits of white supremacy. Not least, they were less likely to work for Whites on white terms.[8]

Although they had to face great odds and much prejudice, the Divine Word Missionaries and the Missionary Sisters of the Holy Spirit were trying to do exactly what the whites feared most, educate blacks. So one can imagine that the white planters in Merigold in Bolivar County were not too happy when this German priest began to turn an old cotton warehouse into a school. To make it worse, he was bringing white nuns to town to teach black children. In her book on the history of the Missionary Sisters of the Holy Spirit in the South, Mary Best mentions that Father Heick had told his friends about escaping from Merigold in a piano box but that he is "strangely silent about his exodus in his writings."[9] And this is true; not much is found in his letters regarding the incident. The letter of 20 September 1905, in which he tells the founder about his escape, is no longer extant, but one gets a sense that something dramatic must have happened from the letter of 7 October 1905 Janssen wrote to Father Heick after he had received his report.

> Present prospects surely do not look good and my councilors do not want to have anything more to do with the Negro mission. In spite of that I do not want to make that decision until I have heard more from you. It often happens that something succeeds, even though the majority think the whole effort is hopeless. We experienced that ourselves in Steyl. People thought I

---

7. Neil R. McMillan, *Dark Journey: Black Mississippians in the Age of Jim Crow* (Urbana, Ill.: University of Illinois Press, 1989), p. 90. McMillan gives an excellent account of the Jim Crow years in Mississippi from 1890 to 1940, the exact years during which the SVD was beginning its work in Mississippi. Much of the information on social background that I include here comes from this book.

8. McMillan, *Dark Journey*.

9. Mary E. Best, *Seventy Septembers* (Techny, Ill. : Holy Spirit Missionary Sisters, 1988), p. 13.

was reaching way beyond my means, that I was even crazy. But in spite of it all, I kept my hope and eventually, with God's help, I was able to succeed.

That can happen here, too. We have to check, though, whether Protestant Negroes are able to be converted. Perhaps those who have already worked a long time with Negroes can give you information about this if you ask them.

Beyond that you must have recourse to prayer and beseech God the Lord earnestly: O Lord, show us your holy will. If it is your will that we stay here and take over a Negro mission, then show us somehow that this is your holy will, so we persevere here, even though there was so little hope for success in the beginning.

Nor is it enough to pray this way one, two, or even three times. If you want to be an apostle to the Negroes, you have to wrestle with God, the way our ancestor Jacob once did, so that God gives you the victory in the battle.

What happened? Albert Foley gives us an account that is credible, one that he perhaps learned from Father John Bowman, SVD, who in 1949 was assigned to open a mission in Mound Bayou, Mississippi, not far from Merigold in Bolivar County. Bowman, who died in 1992, was black. Foley writes,

Bolivar County had a long reputation of hostility to Catholics, especially Catholic priests. In the beginning of the century, Father Aloysius Heick, S.V.D., had endeavored to inaugurate some missionary work for the neglected Negroes of the cotton plantations in the county. He built a frame chapel in Merigold, Mississippi, two miles from Mound Bayou. He won a few converts and started plans for the opening of a Catholic mission school for colored children. He mentioned this to the planters of the area, naively hoping for their support. Instead, he was warned that if he ventured on any educational project, he would be run out of the county. A short time later, he was actually chased out. Riding down the road one day, he saw a planter horse-whipping a colored lad. Father Heick rode up and snatched the whip from his hand, scolding him for his cruelty. The man immediately rounded up his fellow Ku Klux Klanners and threatened to tar and feather Father Heick if he stayed overnight. He was forced to leave.[10]

The question now was whether to abandon the Negro mission or try again somewhere else. Father Peil, it will be recalled, had traveled through the South gathering information for the founder and his council. Just as he was primarily responsible for the Society settling down at Techny and also for founding the first seminary in the U. S. to train priests and brothers for the foreign missions, so he must also be given the credit for convincing the founder to involve the Society in the Negro missions. In a letter sent to the founder in early November 1907, Peil indicates that he considered himself better informed regarding the situation in the South than Heick, who could only base his report on his limited experience in Merigold. In Peil's judgment, depending on the area one was talking about, from

---

10. Albert S. Foley, S.J., *God's Men of Color* (New York: Farrar, Straus and Company, 1955), p. 191.

about twenty-five to fifty percent of the Negroes in the South could be considered heathen and Protestant Negroes would not be too hard to convert. Taking all things into consideration, he suggested Vicksburg as the place to try again. Janssen answered him in a letter dated 21 October that trying to convert Protestants would rightly bring the SVD into bad repute. He counsels Peil to be patient and humble, and on 2 December 1905 responds to the question of opening missions in Vicksburg and Memphis, Tennessee. He notes a number of matters that favor Memphis but does not foreclose on the Vicksburg plans. Vicksburg was chosen and on 7 January 1906 Father Heick went to Vicksburg to found St. Mary's Church. The whole matter was cleared up quickly—indeed, in nearly record time for Janssen, who wanted the SVD to remain in the African-American apostolate. Janssen was resolute, the record shows, in the face of opposition from confreres who felt he was putting too many men in the Americas and was now starting off in a whole new direction.

VICKSBURG, THE FIRST SVD PARISH IN THE SOUTH

On 2 February 1906, the Vicksburg mission was officially opened with the dedication of a provisional chapel. About thirty people were present. From the founder's perspective the whole operation was still provisional, his favorite term for situations in which he was still trying to make up his mind "definitely." In addition, he wanted a report in hand when he approached the Congregation for the Propagation of the Faith for permission to take up in a permanent way a new mission among African Americans. Peil sent optimistic reports. Heick, who tended to view things more pessimistically and probably more realistically, sent in more sober reports.

Father Heick was disappointed that so few of the adult black Catholics came to Mass on Sundays. He offered several reasons for this and for the difficulties of converting them. As for fulfilling their Sunday obligation, Heick saw this as a general fault in America, not peculiar to the blacks. Also he recognized that many "blacks have to work in the kitchen and make breakfast for Whites at Mass time. This keeps many from their obligation, especially if they work for people of another faith." He was beginning to learn some of the customs of the South and the substance of the relations between blacks and whites. Nor could he at that time change the time of Mass to the afternoon or evening to accommodate his parishioners.

Before taking over this mission, a contract had to be drawn up and agreed upon between Bishop Heslin of Natchez and the Society of the Divine Word, always a touchy issue for the founder. The contract proposed to entrust the central and northern part of Mississippi to the Society of the Divine Word. This was the most prejudiced and least Catholic part of Mississippi. Since the SVD was a mission society, this was eventually accepted. Another clause that said much about race relations in the South at the time had to be modified. After saying that the Society had to build their mission stations (churches, schools, social centers) a "reasonable distance" from the churches of whites, the contract went on to say, "In their ministrations and social intercourse they shall confine themselves strictly to the Negroes." Whether the bishop put this in every contract he drew up with religious groups working in his diocese or to avoid a repetition of Merigold, or to educate these Germans to the proper way of carrying on with white-black relationships in the South is not clear. But the conditions were viewed as excessive, even for Vicksburg, and the generalate was unhappy with this language. To limit social contacts, even in private life, to the black population was too strict and excessive, so it was changed to read: "The social contacts with the White population should be so arranged that they give no reason for founded complaints." It must have been difficult for these foreigners to understand the system. Blacks could work in white homes, cook meals for whites, and clean their clothes, yet when Heick tried to rent a house in Vicksburg, he was told by the whites with houses to rent that it was impossible for them to rent their place to him. Why? Because "Whites would never use the house again once blacks had used it."[11]

Such matters as the contract taken care of, there was need to define goals. In his report to the generalate on 18 January 1907, Heick shows that he is gaining insight into the situation in Mississippi. Among other things, he gave some reasons why adult blacks would be hard to convert. He felt blacks themselves have a great prejudice against the Catholic Church. They saw it, he said, as a white church in which they are merely tolerated, drastically limited in their active participation, forced to sit in places restricted to them, and so forth. It does not take a long leap of imagination to conclude that a black clergy would have more understanding of other blacks and their ways and would be able to minister to them more effectively. This would at least begin to solve the problem blacks had of identifying with the Catholic Church. Nor, as it soon developed, did it take long for Divine Word Missionaries to begin thinking along these lines. For African Americans, the Catholic Church was another sect, little different than the Baptist or Methodist church. The strict, austere Latin liturgy of the Catholic Church did not much grip blacks either. Heick realized fully that the black church was not only a vehicle for teaching religion, but a place where they could sing and dance, get up and preach, where they met neighbors and socialized. In other words, it was also a place of entertainment. Heick, according to Meier, said that African Americans

> take religion as a question of feelings. They arrange their divine service as they feel, or as they say, as the Holy Spirit moves them. For this reason the Baptist Church is considered the church of Blacks, since they can play and sing every possible song and make noise to their hearts' content. Anyone of either sex is allowed to preach and they make rich use of this until later in the night.

Heick mentioned other problem areas, like the strict moral and marriage codes of the Catholic Church, bans on freemasonry, and the opposition of Protestant ministers to Catholic proselytizing, and concluded by saying that few adult conversions could be expected. Prospects looked much brighter, however, if schools were established. Both Peil and Heick agreed on this, so they requested permission to begin one, even though the mission in Vicksburg was still "provisional." On 31

---

11. Michael Meier's dissertation is the source of this and the other incidents recounted.

July 1906, Father Janssen wrote to Peil, "The Fathers here, Father auf der Heide and I as well, and the Sister Superior, have nothing against your assigning the three Sisters you suggested, Bertranda, Maria, and Sebastiana, to Vicksburg with Sister Bertranda as the Sister Superior."

So began involvement with schools in the SVD's Negro missions. At about the same time, Janssen requested official permission from Propaganda to undertake this work on a permanent basis on 19 June 1907. In his letter he outlined the difficulties the Society faced and would continue to struggle with, but in only a month, on 19 July 1907, he received the answer. Not only was the Propaganda "pleased" to give permission, it was "very pleased." For decades, they said, Rome had been concerned about the pastoral care of the blacks in America and had repeatedly tried to stir the hierarchy to more action, working especially through the Plenary Councils of Baltimore. Immediately many offers to undertake new projects came to the Society, and as manpower became available missions were opened. The first were: St. Mary's in Vicksburg (1906), Holy Ghost Parish in Jackson (1908), St. Joseph's Church in Meridian (1910), Sacred Heart Church in Greenville (1913)— all in Mississippi—and St. Bartholomew's Church in Little Rock, Arkansas (1910).

Father Heick founded St. Mary's in Vicksburg. Father John Hoenderop, who was in the second group of priests the founder sent to America, had arrived in January 1900. He became the builder of the southern missions, a skill he learned at Techny before he was transferred to the South. When Heick went to Jackson to begin the Holy Ghost mission there, Father Hoenderop became pastor at Vicksburg. As new people were assigned to the South, new parishes were opened or taken over. Soon they were joined by Father James Wendel in 1910, in time to open St. Joseph's in Meridian, Mississippi. Although Wendel's first assignment after ordination in 1906 was to New Guinea, after four years there he became very ill and was transferred to the United States to the southern missions. He did magnificent pioneering work in the South. Among other things, he increased school enrollments dramatically, collected money in the North for his church and mission, and by means of *The Colored Messenger*, a yearbook he founded, agitated for the priesthood of African Americans. In 1913 he invited Josephite Father John Dorsey, a colored priest, to give a two-week mission in his parish. It was a smashing success. Father Dorsey also gave missions in other SVD churches in Jackson. A common prejudice at the time had it that black Catholics preferred white priests to priests of their own color. It was a bias that Father Wendel and the other early Divine Word Missionaries in the South did not share. Father Dorsey's success confirmed their convictions.

Father Wendel will appear again in this history in the context of the origin of St. Augustine's Seminary. At Meridian he did another thing that deserves remembering. In 1914 he built an auditorium at his school. No one had thought of doing this before. Father Matthew Christman said, "Father Wendel built an auditorium, which proved such a help in the education and social uplift of the children, and so important a factor in the progress of the mission, that during the next year such auditoriums were built in every one of our missions."[12] What the Catholic Church

---

12. Matthew Christman, "Our Negro Missions," *Our Missions* 1 (1921): 27. In German, Christman's surname was spelled with two n's. He dropped the one letter early in deference to English spelling con-

could not supply in its liturgy and ritual by way of satisfying spiritual experience it supplied by making the auditorium available to the community.

Early in this same article Father Matthew Christman pays grateful tribute to Mother Katharine Drexel "for the financial help she has continually and generously given to the cause of our missions among the Negroes." Michael Meier details the amounts she gave:

Vicksburg	1907	$12,500
Jackson	1909	$16,000
Meridian	1910	$10,000
Little Rock	1910	$3,000
Greenville	1913	$10,000

These were significant sums for the early 1900s, and Peil writes (on 9 March 1906, also according to Meier), that she did not hand out her money without conditions to make sure "that her money really was used for blacks and did not somehow flow into the pockets of the Society." Because the mission at Little Rock was already built up when the Society of the Divine Word took it over, there was no need for her to give so much money to get it started.

Not long after the elementary grades began, classes on the high school level were also offered in 1916. At this time, there were no Catholic or any public high schools for blacks in Mississippi. Because there were only five denominational high schools in the state that blacks could attend, almost from the beginning the sisters and fathers offered high school classes to students properly prepared to handle them. Sacred Heart in Greenville pioneered in this work, graduating their first student, Mamie Upshaw, on 2 June 1916. She went on to college and eventually held the position of Dean of Women at Howard University in Washington, D.C.[13]

The high quality of the elementary and secondary schools was primarily the work of the Missionary Sisters of the Holy Spirit, who, as Bishop Gunn wrote in 1919, "are doing magnificent work everywhere."[14] As much as the civil authorities were interested in vocational and industrial schools for the blacks, the priests and nuns were concerned to give them much more. But it was always a delicate matter. In 1920, for example, a Mississippi law stated that anyone found "guilty of printing, publishing or circulating printed, typewritten or written matter urging or presenting for public acceptation or general information, arguments or suggestions in favor of social equality or of intermarriage" could be fined up to $500.00, sentenced to prison for up to six months, or both.[15] The kind of education the Missionary Sisters of the Holy Ghost were giving their students was not geared to teach them to accept the status quo.

---

ventions, but it was often retained, especially in intra-Society references, which can make identifying him with precision confusing.

13. Best, *Seventy Summers*, pp. 129ff.

14. Best, *Seventy Summers*, p. 133.

15. McMillan, *Dark Journey*, pp. 8–9.

EXPANSION AND CHANGES AFTER 1918

After World War I, with the help of SVD missionaries from Europe, the Southern missions began to expand, opening new mission stations in Louisiana, Texas, and California. The missions suffered through the great migrations of the African Americans from the South to the North, which began in earnest in 1915 and reached a peak, after the Second World War, in the 1950s and 1960s and which still continues. As many converts to Catholicism as the Southern missions made, they lost at least as many to the North.

Nothing brought as many changes in the African-American apostolate as the Civil Rights Movement that began in 1954. Painful and deadly as the hand of racism was in Mississippi, the movement brought changes in attitudes even there. One of the casualties was the Catholic school dedicated to African Americans. Given the revolution in thinking, it was now accepted that the state was responsible for operating a single school system to the benefit of both races. Thus sisters' communities, which were being hit by large numbers of departures from their ranks and few recruits, no longer had the same motivation to staff schools. On top of this, facilities that by now were fifty and more years old had to be replaced or updated at tremendous cost. Racism, of course, had not disappeared because of the Civil Rights Movement, even in the church. And it often surfaced in discussions about Catholic schools originally built for blacks and those built for whites. How were they to be integrated? Bishops and their school boards knew it had to happen if they were to have credibility. Strong letters went from group to group when the white Catholic schools, because they were private, threatened to remain all white to circumvent the new law of the land. The very existence of all-black schools, such as those the Divine Word Missionaries and the Missionary Sisters of the Holy Spirit conducted, was even used as reason not to integrate.

Beginning with the high schools in the early 1960s, then moving on to the elementary grades, the schools were gradually closed. St. Bartholomew's was to be the last of the five original pre-World War I missions to close its school. All the turmoil of social change notwithstanding, the five original parishes are still pastored by Divine Word Missionaries. In addition, many others that were entrusted to the Society remain, in all twenty-seven parishes in 1996. In the meantime others that the Society took over were closed or given to the care of the diocese. Much more deserves to be said about these events. Within the scope of this volume, however, it seems best to outline the early history and then turn to issues such as the methods the SVD used in the South. To do justice to the scope of the SVD's activity in both North and South would take another book.

THE METHOD OF THE SOCIETY OF THE DIVINE WORD

While doing his original research for the founder during the process of deciding whether or not to begin work among the African Americans in the South, Peil identified two basic feasible approaches to what was called the "colored" or "Negro" apostolate. To gain these insights, Father Peil contacted the two religious congregations that up to 1905 had the most experience in this field, the Benedictines and the Josephites. They had quite different styles and modes of operation. The Josephites, as a society of apostolic life, were dependent on the good will of the bishops under whom they worked. The Benedictines were monastic and thus tied to monastery conventions that emphasized "stability of place." They were also what was called "exempt religious," which meant that the internal life of their communities was exempt from episcopal direction. Theirs was a life of *ora et labora*, prayer in community and "work" in ways suited to the times and situation. Going out from their established centers, monks-in-mission tried to evangelize their surroundings. That method was best suited for rural areas. The Josephites exemplified another approach, which Peil described in the following way to the founder:

> The superior gives a priest the task to start a community somewhere. In the beginning the priest has to make it on his own. He has to see where the money is going to come from. He gets twenty dollars a month from the superior, but for this he has to apply [Mass] stipends every day. Generally a black woman keeps house for him, or he lives with other priests or Sisters.

If the parish develops, Peil notes, a second or third priest is sent to help the first. Given this method and the fact that they were the first group to work exclusively with blacks, they chose to work initially in places where the density of Catholic Negroes was the greatest.

Peil did not recommend either of these approaches, but wanted to see the circumstances to which divine providence would bring the SVD. That turned out to be one of the most difficult parts of the southern missions as far as prospects for accomplishing much among blacks were concerned. Schools, as we have seen, were considered the best approach, because these would give respect to the Catholic missions and would build up good will among the black Protestants by whom they were surrounded and who were quite antagonistic to Catholics, but might be impressed by well-run schools. The education provided would raise the status of blacks and thus contribute to their betterment. This very goal, of course, was why so many whites were opposed. Eventually the SVD hoped to make conversions also. It was certainly a long-range and expensive project, but the Society had several advantages in this work which other groups did not. First, they had a companion group of nuns, the Missionary Sisters Servants of the Holy Spirit, who could staff the schools they opened. Over the years the sisters did a marvelous job. Their example of dedication and the contribution they made to liturgy and to the cultural and social betterment of the communities they lived in, as well as the advice and the counseling they gave to so many young women over the years, made a significant difference.

The second advantage the SVD had was its international scope. It could draw on support from many other countries. When the German Divine Word Missionaries were forced to leave Togo in West Africa after the First World War, several were transferred to the southern missions. This is how Fathers Patzelt, Baltes, Wolf, Klaffl, and Heffels came to work in the African-American apostolate. And this international help still continues today. While it may not appear on the surface, one of the advantages that the SVD had in bringing in Europeans, such as most of their early missionaries were, is that they were outsiders. As outsiders to American culture, these priests and sisters saw things differently and were less likely to fall into ingrained American cultural patterns of anti-black prejudice. But they came with their own biases. Mention has already been made how this affected their views of the Irish as well as to much that was thought to be typically American. In that regard, they had a negative regard for what they regarded as excessive freedom, materialism, the desire for comfort, an overriding interest in sports, and the inability to work very hard. Yet as far as the South and the structure of relations between whites and blacks were concerned, they came with a far different mindset. Southerners had been taught from the cradle that blacks were inferior to whites, and that they were capable of work solely as field hands and servants. They were judged incapable of being educated and had to be "kept in their place" at all costs, by which was meant, in a subservient position.[16] The early Divine Word Missionaries and Sisters of the Holy Spirit became catalysts for change. They learned quickly to proceed as the founder had urged them after Merigold, *suaviter, prudenter, fortiter*, "gently, prudently, courageously."

Ironically, in spite of the emphasis on schools, many of the first Divine Word Missionaries who were sent to the southern missions were sent there because they did not have a knack for teaching at Techny. It was a different case for the sisters. As time went on, especially after the First World War and during the time the St. Augustine's Seminary was getting approval and later being built, criticism regarding the heavy reliance on schools as a mode of conversion was common. In retrospect, was their approach a failure or a success? The answer requires other questions: What does success mean in the context of Jim Crow Mississippi with its legalized segregation and edifice of laws to insure that whites remained in power in every important area? What does it mean for Catholic missionaries in areas where there were few black Catholics to begin with, and where at least half of blacks were Protestant, and Protestants generally well content with their church affiliations? And all this before contemporary religious studies by African Americans would reveal that even the word "Protestant" is misleading when applied to black Christianity. Conversion success in these days was measured in numbers, numbers of catechumens, of baptisms, of confessions, of communions. According to this measure, the emphasis on schools as a vehicle of conversion was a failure. But what would be considered dismal failure in one mission could perhaps count as glowing success in Mississippi where conditions were so different. Of course missionaries in Mississippi got discouraged, so much so that there was discussion of pulling up stakes and moving elsewhere. These musings eventually reached Father Wilhelm Gier, the superior general, who said in a letter dated 17 December 1924, "On the Mission to Blacks in North America":

> Precisely because she is Catholic, the Catholic Church can neglect no people in the world. If she is not in a position to offer the gift of grace as she

---

16. McMillan, *Dark Journey*, gives a multitude of examples of Mississippi's race relations and attitudes in this period.

might desire, she can and must be concerned that the *testes veritatis* ["the witnesses of truth"] remain at their posts . . . In this witness to faith rests the most profound presence of missionary work, as far as it can be carried out by human beings. The spiritual conversion remains forever the result of God's grace which we must merit for those who stray, and we do this through much prayer and an innocent life and fidelity to pastoral work and teaching.

In spite of this encouragement to persevere at what they were doing, as they gained more priests, the Divine Word Missionaries in the South began to decrease their reliance on schools and looked for parishes in black areas with more Catholics, especially in Louisiana. When possible, superiors assigned two men to each parish, so they could have some kind of community life. The lack of community life had not been a major problem for the sisters. Being in school work from the beginning, they always had the possibility of community life. Pictures of the teaching staff of sisters in the five African-American missions, taken in 1925, showed that two missions (Jackson and Vicksburg) had ten nuns each, two (Little Rock and Meridian) eight nuns each, and one (Greenville) had nine nuns. Though it was a policy of the SVD to station at least two or more priests and brothers in every station around the world, it was not always followed. In the American context, the need to open a parish was sometimes so great or a window of opportunity so unique that those involved felt it could not be ignored. Thus somehow someone was set free to take up the post. This did not make them bad religious and missionaries. On the contrary, many of them, by any standard of measurement, were very successful missionaries and faithful. Another Society policy was for new missionaries to have a chance to work with veterans. The pioneer Germans had little chance to learn, even from each other. Janssen himself recognized this problem, and suggested that new men assigned to the South should spend time with a veteran missionary to get accustomed to the life and situation in this unique mission field.

The chance to open a church for blacks often came at the request of the black Catholics themselves, not bishops. Such Catholics would have been going to Mass in the local Catholic church operated for the whites, where they had to sit discreetly in the pews off to one side or in the rear. At communion they went up last. They had no say in church affairs, took no part in church socials, and were generally treated as second-class citizens, as they were everywhere else. This was an era when signs "For Blacks Only" and "For Whites Only" were everywhere, and the facilities so marked were far from equal. When black Catholics became numerous enough, their white pastor, the bishop, or they themselves would look for someone to open a parish for them. Many more requests of this kind to open parishes came to the Society than it could accept. The Society did the best it could to respond.

THE CALL TO PARISH WORK IN NORTHERN CITIES

For long years, Catholic dioceses in the northern states did very little for African Americans, despite the increasing numbers who were moving north because of rural southern poverty and the lure of good jobs in factories, especially during the two world wars. For a long time, even after the Civil War, there were relatively few African Americans in the North, and most of those followed Protestant and indigenous forms of African-American Christian traditions. Catholic bishops in the North were preoccupied during the years of migration from Europe with looking after immigrant Catholics. In their thinking, moreover, the black problem was a southern problem, and priests and bishops in the North were more than happy to wash their hands of the difficulty. The few blacks in the North who were Catholic went to white churches. There was racism in the North, never legalized, as there was for years in the South. That the view that it was somebody else's problem and had to change was already felt after the emancipation of slaves during and after the Civil War.

The story of St. Elizabeth's, the flagship parish of the Divine Word Missionaries in Chicago, is inseparable from the life of a black priest, Augustus Tolton. To tell the story of St. Elizabeth's and the black Catholic communities that the SVD came to pastor in Chicago we must at least briefly tell the story of Father Tolton. He was the first black priest in America who was clearly recognized as black, and he worked for blacks for the eleven years of his life as a priest. Born a slave in Missouri in 1854, Tolton escaped with his mother during the Civil War to Quincy, Illinois. His father had escaped earlier but disappeared in the confusion of the Civil War. Tolton wanted to be a priest, and after many difficulties and shifting from one priest-tutor to another, he was finally taken under the tutelage of the Franciscans. After spending some years in Quincy College, which was founded and run by the Franciscans, Tolton was admitted, with the support of the friars, to the Urbaniana College in Rome where he was ordained in 1886. He was thirty-two years old.[17]

The same problem that later faced the Divine Word Missionaries as they prepared to ordain the first graduates of St. Augustine's Seminary in 1934 faced Father Augustus Tolton in 1886. What was he to do, a black priest in a white church? The original plan was to have him go to Africa as a missionary, but this was changed, as he himself describes it:

> I heard the words of St. John "prepare the ways of the Lord" and God gave me strength to persevere, for Rome had heard that no one of us could be found here to preach the Gospel. I rejoyced when I heard that I was [to] be sent to America. God is over us all, and he has many blessings for men of every race. When on the eve of going to St. John Lateran to be ordained, the word came expressing doubt whether I would be sent here. It was said that I would be the only priest of my race in America and would not be likely to succeed. All at once Cardinal Simoni said, "America has been called the most enlightened nation; we will see if it deserves that honor. If America has never seen a black priest, it has to see one now."[18]

Tolton had problems with loneliness, and, although his primary support as a priest should have come from his fellow priests, they were all white. He never felt

---

17. See Cyprian Davis, *The History of Black Catholics in the United States* (New York: Crossroad, 1990) for the story of Tolton, the source of most of my material on Tolton's life.

18. Davis, *Black Catholics*, p. 155.

their sympathy or good will. In addition, he was not a member of a religious congregation, so he did not have the support he might otherwise expect from his confreres in religion. This might account for the longing, Davis says, that he expressed to join the Josephites. He was accepted by black Catholics with enthusiasm, but there just weren't many of them.

As a priest of the Diocese of Alton (now the Diocese of Springfield), Illinois, Tolton became the pastor of a black church in Quincy, where he worked for three years. Eventually he asked to be transferred to Chicago because he was lonesome where he was and felt unsupported by his neighboring priests, primarily because many of their white parishioners attended Father Tolton's church. Nineteen of the black converts he had made in Quincy moved to Chicago with him. Tolton felt he had failed in Quincy, but how many priests can boast of nineteen converts in such a brief time and against such great odds, let alone gain nineteen who would leave their homes and move with them to a new place? He was made to feel a failure by those who should have been the first to give him support, his fellow priests.

Tolton arrived in Chicago, in December 1889, where he was asked to form a parish for blacks at 35th and Dearborn, which he did. It was dedicated to St. Monica, the mother of St. Augustine, the famous Bishop of Hippo in North Africa. Tolton died as the result of a heat stroke on 10 July 1897, at the age of forty-three. Father Davis sums up his contribution to the African-American apostolate:

> Today we can look back at the priestly career of Augustus Tolton and recognize the courage and the faith of a man who persevered in his vocation despite insuperable obstacles and opposition. Neither brilliant nor clever, America's first black priest whom all could recognize as black was a man with whom all African Americans could identify. He was a pastor, first and last, and justly merits the title of father of all the African American priests who would come after him. More than he realized, he was the inspiration for the remarkable movement of faith and evangelization among the African American Catholic laity in the last decade of the nineteenth century.[19]

For a time after Tolton's death, St. Monica's, which was at the time the basement of a church that was never built, became a mission station of St. Elizabeth's until Father John Morris, a priest of the Chicago Archdiocese, was assigned to St. Monica's as permanent pastor in 1909. When he was transferred to another parish in 1917, Archbishop Mundelein asked the Society of the Divine Word to take over the parish. One might fairly wonder why St. Monica's was offered to the SVD. The most "correct" answer would be that the diocesan clergy were not trained for missionary work among blacks, whereas the SVD already had achieved national recognition for this work. And it was true that when American bishops had entrusted the local clergy with Negro missions or parishes, they had failed. "Or," as Father Joseph Eckert, a SVD priest who later became a pastor in Chicago, said. "Cardinal Mundelein told me himself, they have used such works as stepping stones to something better."[20] Thus the American bishops appealed to religious communities of

---

19. Davis, *Black Catholics*, p. 162.
20. Report of Father Eckert to the SVD Provincial Chapter in 1927.

men and women, such as the Josephites, the Holy Spirit Fathers, the SVD, and other congregations, to take up this work.

Mundelein wanted St. Monica's to be reserved exclusively for the "colored" Catholics of Chicago on the South Side. The letter he wrote on 16 October 1927 to Father Burgmer, then provincial superior, officially entrusting St. Monica's to the Society, was also read to the parishioners of St. Monica's on the day the SVD began work. In the letter, which is still preserved in the Techny archives, the archbishop said, "all other Catholics of whatsoever race or color are requested not to intrude." The reasons for this appear to be that there were two large parishes close to St. Monica's and blacks were not wanted in them. St. Monica's, moreover, was small, and the buildings were not even completed, and if anybody else were allowed to go there, the church would be too crowded. In the final analysis, however, the need to attend to blacks stemmed from the arrival of African Americans in unprecedented numbers, seeking jobs, and the number of Catholic blacks who need to be cared for had grown proportionately. It should be recalled, too, that this was the age of ethnic parishes throughout the American Catholic Church. The archbishop's letter continues:

> In a word, because of circumstances that do exist here in this city I am convinced that our colored Catholics will find themselves much more comfortable, far less inconvenienced, and never at all embarrassed if, in a church that is credited to them, they have their own sodalities and societies, their own school and choir in which they alone will constitute the membership and for even stronger reasons the first places in the church should be theirs just as much as the seats in the rear benches are.

Mundelein was doubtlessly referring both to the nature of ethnic Catholicism and to the tense relations that existed between the races, which would soon be demonstrated by the riots of 1919 in Chicago.

Because of his letter, Mundelein came in for sharp criticism in the Negro press. Some Catholic Negroes, members of the parish, also accused Mundelein of being an advocate of segregation and an enemy of the Negro race. In another part of the letter, however, he had made it clear that he had "no intention of excluding colored Catholics from any of the other churches in the diocese, and particularly if they live in another part of the city, but simply of excluding from St. Monica's all but the colored Catholics." There is, though, little question that many Catholic priests and bishops were prejudiced against blacks. As Thomas Wyatt Turner, chairman for the Committee for the Advancement of Colored People, had put it in a letter he wrote to Archbishop Bonzano, apostolic delegate at the time, racism has "passed up the aisles and found its way through the railing to the Sacristy."[21]

Not to be forgotten, too, is the question that this nation has never definitively answered one way or the other: Is the way to deal with the "problem" of white-black relations one of integration or separate development? Blacks to this day are not united in answer to this question. As for Mundelein, he shows himself to be a

---

21. Quoted in Davis, *Black Catholics*, p. 220.

pragmatist, not a visionary, when it comes to the crucial question of race relations in America, as the following words show:

> It would be puerile for us to ignore the fact that a distinction as to color enters very often into the daily happenings of our city. I am not going to argue as to the reasons for or against this line of distinction which causes so much bitterness, nor will I say anything as to the justice or injustice of it. It is sufficient to say that it does exist and that I am convinced that I am quite powerless to change it.

It is also clear that Mundelein thought of himself as a man with benevolent intentions and as a friend of blacks, as his letter to Father Burgmer indicates:

> But when I consider their many good qualities, their peaceful family life, their love for their children, their strong religious spirit, I fail to see how they can fail [to build up the parish of St. Monica]. I have never yet met a colored man who was professedly atheistic or blasphemous. The Creator seems to have given them a spirit of reverence and religion that is often lacking in other races.

For better or worse, in the midst of all this ambiguity, the white priests of the Society of the Divine Word took over St. Monica's. The first SVD pastor there was Father August Reissman. He had been assigned to America by the founder himself in 1905. He put St. Monica's solidly on its feet financially. When Reissman was transferred back to Techny to teach in 1921, Father Joseph Eckert became pastor of St. Monica's. From this time on, the names of Joseph Eckert and the African-American apostolate become synonymous.

In the meantime, the tide of black immigration northward, a trickle since the Civil War, became a river before and during the First World War, and a virtual torrent thereafter. As they moved into the South Side neighborhoods of Chicago near St. Monica's, white Irish and German immigrants, who had come in earlier torrents, by now prosperous and rich, moved out, leaving their big houses and beautiful churches behind. The process was painful both to blacks and whites. The one group wanted only to find work and live in peace and dignity. The other would not stay and resented the drop in property values that occurred because they left in droves. In the seething ebb and flow that is every major American city during this period, the process, never really complete, is marked by animosity and resentment, by fear and suspicion, sometimes erupting in riots.

St. Monica's Becomes St. Elizabeth's Church and Other Developments

By the time Father Reissman left St. Monica's in 1922, the buildings were too small for the growing congregation, so Father Eckert approached Mundelein for a solution. A few blocks away stood St. Elizabeth's church, almost empty. It had been the (white) parish whose pastor had at one time been responsible for St. Monica's as a mission. Founded by Father Daniel O'Riordan on 10 November

1881, the feast day of St. Elizabeth of Hungary (1207–31), it got its name from a valiant woman, whose life had been dominated by men. By 1922 most of its white parishioners had fled the neighborhood, leaving it to the African Americans who continued to pour in from the South. Two years of reflection and negotiation followed, filled with much bitterness and recrimination, but on 6 December 1924, St. Elizabeth's became a black church and was turned over to the Society of the Divine Word. Father Eckert was appointed pastor. Two years later St. Monica's was closed and merged with St. Elizabeth's. With new facilities the school could be expanded, and the first Catholic high school in Chicago for African Americans could be opened. St. Elizabeth's church burned one cold morning in January 1930 and it was never rebuilt. Instead, the parish hall was remodeled to serve as a church. The parish and its neighborhood changed over the years. During the late 1950s and 1960s, the two- and three-story apartment buildings and stores that dominated this old residential neighborhood were razed to make room for the Dan Ryan Expressway. A second and equally important purpose of the expressway construction was to provide a wall to impede the progress of black migration. Over time, in the place of solid working-class black families, huge apartment complexes owned by the Chicago Housing Authority became the homes of the urban poor. Few living in these apartments were Catholic, and almost all were poor and poorly educated. Nevertheless, the SVDs who have labored there over the years did their best to keep the school running. Countless young men and women received an education there that enabled them to escape the fate of so many of their age and social cohort. Though many others served, the names of Joseph Eckert, George Stephan, Aloysius Zimmerman, Dominic Carmon, Donald Ehr, and Gary Burr will be remembered by many. Theirs was and is a mission field like no other in history, however one defines mission.

In 1926, this time in St. Louis, the same process of black migration and white flight left St. Nicholas Church almost empty. It too became a mission of the Divine Word Missionaries, who still minister there to African Americans.

The next inner-city black church to be turned over to the Society of the Divine Word was St. Anselm's, which also had been Irish at one time. In 1932 when Father Eckert was appointed pastor, the neighborhood was rapidly becoming African American. Father Eckert remained pastor at St. Anselm's until 1940, when the one American SVD province divided into a Western Province (Techny), an Eastern Province (Girard), and a Southern Province (Bay St. Louis). Eckert was appointed as the first provincial superior of the Southern Province, where he continued to work in the African-American apostolate.

Joseph Eckert was, in many ways, the most prominent and well-known SVD engaged in the African-American apostolate. Born to a German family in Silesia, which was a part of Poland governed by Germany when he was born (17 January 1884), he was a vigorous missionary and pastor, and he was also a child of his times in quantifying success by the number of converts made. Judged by this standard, Eckert was enormously successful. He had convert classes that once numbered as many as three hundred people. During the thirty-four years when he was in the direct parish apostolate, he baptized almost four thousand people. In my research, I heard accounts that Eckert was overbearing and paternalistic toward his black parishioners, even biased and prejudiced in regard to the abilities of African Americans. In his defense, several African American SVDs who had lived with him and had him as their superior simply responded, "He was German." By that they meant he was culturally and generationally a pastor or superior who thought it was his role to act decisively and as if he were a notch above those he led. Another African American, too, denied that Eckert was prejudiced. He was happy to add that he was "dictatorial and undiplomatic. Yes. But prejudiced? No!"

Eckert was certainly a man who heartily enjoyed meeting people. In a book edited by Father John A. O'Brien, Eckert writes the following concerning his methods:

> Whenever I meet Colored people on the street, or in stores or in their homes, I seize the opportunity to have a little conversation with them; and often I ask them to what Church they go on Sundays. Whatever the answer may be, I heartily invite them to come, at least once, to our services . . . It may interest many, at this point, to learn that more than once I have been told: "Father, you are the first person who has ever invited me to the Catholic Church. I have heard about your church, but no one has ever asked me to come to it."[22]

Following the example of Protestant ministers, Eckert and his assistants also began greeting parishioners outside of church on Sunday, something that was not the practice in those days, when the Catholic priest generally held himself aloof from his congregation. The people came to him, not the other way around. Eckert also used home visits on the occasion of doing the parish census as an occasion to make personal contact and break down anti-Catholic prejudices. But, along with his confreres in the South, Eckert judged that the best way to get in touch with non-Catholics was through the school. A good school would attract many students of all faith traditions. Through the children the priest could invite the parents to special liturgies or to programs in which the children participated. It was clear, then, that for Eckert, there was no question whether making conversions to Catholicism was a goal of his parish. Indeed, he insisted that every Catholic had an obligation to be a missionary to their friends and neighbors, which he comments on in the same chapter:

> According to custom, parishioners introduce their non-Catholic friends to me after the services, and thus the way for a better acquaintance is opened up. We have one man in our parish who has brought at least forty converts into the Church through his personal efforts. Here it must be mentioned that I impress upon converts, during instruction, the beauty of the lay apostolate; and I have found that converts make most zealous and most successful convert-makers.

Father Eckert became a successful apostle to the African Americans, a legend in his own lifetime. In spite of what seemed to some to be his "dictatorial and

---

22. O'Brien's book is (somewhat ironically) entitled *The White Harvest: A Symposium on Methods of Convert Making* (New York: Longmans, Green & Co., 1927). Father Eckert's chapter (pp. 93–109) was entitled "Methods of Convert-Making Among the Negroes of Chicago"; the citation is from p. 99.

undiplomatic" manner, those he served in the parishes knew his heart was in the right place. He died in Meridian, Mississippi, on 17 March 1965. He had asked that his funeral be held at St. Anselm's, where he had served as pastor from 1932 to 1940. It was a sad but triumphal return.

OTHER SVD MISSIONS AND SVD MISSIONARIES IN THE UNITED STATES

In researching this book, I continually found men and apostolates that did not fit into neat chapter divisions. I hope I may be forgiven, as I conclude this chapter, for writing at least briefly about several notable apostolates and apostles.

One is St. Francis Xavier Mission in San Francisco, California. It was founded by a Paris Foreign Mission priest, Albert Breton, who had spent thirteen years in Japan. Breton came to the United States in response to concern by California bishops that the Japanese were not being cared for. He established missions in Los Angeles in 1912 and in San Francisco (St. Francis Xavier Mission) in 1913. Breton returned to Japan and became Bishop of Fukuoka. Jesuits took over the San Francisco mission until it was turned over to the SVD in 1925.

The first SVD pastor, William Stoecke, qualifies as one of the many "forgotten" members of the Society who did so much work that will never be properly recognized. His first assignment after ordination in 1908 was to the SVD's newly opened mission in Akita, Japan. In 1918 he was a pastor and in charge of an orphanage in Nagoka. Like so many others, he was sent to the United States after World War I to collect money in 1920 for the orphanage and for the entire SVD mission in Japan. He did this very successfully for five years, when he was assigned to take over the St. Francis Xavier Mission for Japanese in San Francisco, a post he held until his retirement in 1951 at the age of seventy-four.

Never great in number of Catholics, the mission had significant impact on Japanese life in San Francisco. "Through the children to the parents" was Stoecke's motto and mission method. He started a kindergarten, then a Japanese language school for children whose parents wanted them to maintain the Japanese language, which they would attend after their regular public school classes. In 1929 an elementary school was opened. In the early 1930s, Stoecke bought over a hundred acres of barren land in Napa County near a running brook. This eventually was improved and became a vacation place for Japanese children, a country experience most of them would otherwise never have had. Eventually even a swimming pool was constructed by damming the brook.

During the Second World War, during one of the darker episodes of American history, when the Japanese, including those who were American citizens, were rounded up and interned, Father Stoecke followed his beloved flock into voluntary imprisonment in the desert near Topaz, Utah. He returned with them when the government allowed them back in 1945. He lived in retirement in a house adjacent to the mission from 1945 to 1963 so he could keep in touch with his people. He was assigned to Bay St. Louis, Mississippi, where he died a few months later that same year.

The next pastor, another SVD missionary from Japan who spoke Japanese fluently, was Father Joseph Guetzloe. Guetzloe stayed for over forty years until he went into semiretirement in the same house adjacent to the church that Father Stoecke had occupied. He died on 31 May 1994, not long after St. Francis Xavier Mission was closed by the archdiocese as part of its retrenchment program in 1994.

St. Francis Xavier was a specialized mission. It had never been a large parish in terms of numbers, but it was an active parish, not just for Japanese Catholics but for the Japanese community as a whole. It was known in Japan as a place of connection bridging the Pacific, especially but not only for Catholics. The Japanese community in San Francisco continued to support the parish until its sudden and unexpected closing, the end of an apostolate that had been successful and seemed to have the potential to continue its good work.

A LIFE TO STAND FOR MANY

One man among the many who have already been mentioned may, I hope, represent all those who worked in the parishes but who have not been mentioned, Father Bruno Drescher. Born in Bavaria in 1881, he was ordained in 1910 and sent shortly after to the Philippines as a missionary to Abra, the first mission of the Society in the Philippines. Toward the end of World War I, Drescher and several other Germans were rounded up by the Americans who then ruled the Philippine Islands. They were shipped off to an internment camp in San Francisco. Released soon after their arrival, Drescher was asked to take over Father Wendel's mission parish in Meridian, Mississippi. Wendel had died suddenly in 1920. This was Drescher's first contact with African Americans. At Father Wendel's parish, where he stayed almost a year, Drescher learned to appreciate the value of a social center in the African-American apostolate. It was a lesson he would apply to great advantage in his future missionary life.

In 1921, Drescher returned to Abra to continue his interrupted career. Like so many other SVD missionaries in that era, Drescher was sent back to the United States to collect money for the Philippines, something he had done during his first stay in the United States. After about eighteen months collecting funds, he returned to the Philippines, but a year later he returned to the States, this time for good. At about this time, Father Herman Richarz, the novice master, died and Drescher was asked to replace him until Father Glorius could take over as the permanent novice master. Among the thirty-one novices placed under his care, there were five black students from Bay St. Louis in Mississippi, four of whom went on to become the first black SVDs to be ordained. It was Drescher's second contact with the African-American apostolate.

As soon as Father Glorius arrived, Drescher was sent to the South, this time as pastor of St. Peter's Parish in Pine Bluff, Arkansas. In 1934 he was appointed as pastor to St. Elizabeth's in Chicago, at the time practically bankrupt. When he left eight years later, the parish was solvent with $13,000 in the bank. Like Eckert, he was also effective in contacting and making converts.

In 1941, at the age of 61, when many begin to look forward to retirement, Drescher was assigned to St. Benedict the Moor Parish in San Francisco. Here this Bavarian-become-American's ministry began to flourish in many directions. Blacks came to his church from all over the city. In Father Drescher's parish, they were always welcome. In Drescher they had a forceful advocate. These were the years of the Second World War, and many blacks were moving to San Francisco looking for better jobs in the war industries. This influx made for racially tense cities throughout the North and led to several race riots. To forestall this in San Francisco, an emergency meeting of civic leaders was convened in the winter of 1942–1943. Drescher attended and told the participants, many of whom were tiptoeing around the issue of prejudice, that San Francisco was also prejudiced. He related that he had himself seen a black man pulled off a streetcar and beaten. Then and in later years, when integration and social change were moving ahead, if Drescher heard that a Catholic school would not allow black children into the school, he approached the pastor at the first opportunity and asked, "Why not?" Often the black students would be admitted as a result. He became known in the city of San Francisco as the advocate for full rights for blacks, for which, suspected of being a communist, he had the honor of being investigated by the Federal Bureau of Investigation.

Reflecting his experience in Meridian, as soon as Drescher became pastor of St. Benedict the Moor Mission, he began to collect money for a youth center. In this he involved the whole parish and blacks from all over the city. After twelve years it was finished and dedicated "to serve all young people of the neighborhood, regardless of race, creed or color." In its day it was extremely successful. When Father Drescher "retired" at the age of seventy-six in 1957, he went to live in the SVD parish in Oakland. The mayor of San Francisco and the governor of California gave official testimony to the work he had done for the African Americans of San Francisco and for the betterment of race relations. Two vice presidents, Richard Nixon (1957) and Lyndon Johnson (1963), invited Drescher to participate in government seminars on discrimination and equal opportunity. In retirement at St. Patrick's he continued work with adults interested in becoming Catholics and his advocacy work for African Americans. He died at a convalescent home in Riverside, California, on 14 June 1970 at eighty-nine years of age.

Drescher represents many other Divine Word Missionaries, both of his own time and today. His first appointment was not his last. He stayed open and kept growing. He filled in wherever he could help. He represented the best of the internationalism of the Society. He identified as totally as he could with those he worked among. Professor Andrew Walls has often said, "To be a missionary means to live on terms set by others." This is exactly what Bruno Drescher did throughout a long life.

CONCLUSION

As the years have rolled on, at the request of bishops, the Society of the Divine Word has taken over numerous other rural and urban parishes: four in New Jersey; five in West Virginia in the Appalachians; seven in the West Indies; seven in California; and one in Indianapolis. In the meantime also, parishes have been returned to dioceses or to other religious orders. As they did from their arrival in North America, Divine Word Missionaries involved in administration and teaching helped out in parishes, proclaiming the Word as Arnold Janssen intended when he founded his society.

Father Aloysius Heick (1864-1929), the first Divine Word Missionary in the black apostolate, with parishioners and students in Jackson, Mississippi, about 1920.

Sacred Heart College, Greenville, Mississippi, in 1920, the first seminary dedicated to the education of African Americans to the priesthood, precursor to St. Augustine's Seminary. Father Christman is standing on the veranda.

Father Matthew Christman (1887-1929), the moving force behind SVD efforts to establish an African-American Catholic priesthood.

The major seminary building at Divine Word Seminary, Bay St. Louis, Mississippi (1925-1967).

Ordination day of the first black SVD priests (23 May 1934), from left: Fathers Anthony Bourges (1904-1991), Maurice Rousseve (1906-1985), Francis Wade (1892-1976), and Vincent Smith (1894-1952).

Brother Vincent (Louis Webb, b. 1908), the first African-American SVD brother to persevere to final vows (middle), shown here as a novice in 1935.

Father Anthony Bourges (1904-1991), a beloved pastor at Our Lady of Perpetual Help parish in St. Martinsville, Louisiana, laid to rest prejudices against black Catholic priests. Shown here in 1956 after twenty-two years as a priest.

Father Joseph Eckert (1884-1965), with a confirmation class and parishioners. They stand in front of St. Elizabeth's Church, which was destroyed by fire in 1930.

Bishop Harold Perry (1916-1991), first African American to be ordained a bishop in the twentieth century, and the first black SVD to be ordained a bishop in the United States, served as provincial of the Southern Province and as auxiliary bishop of New Orleans, Louisiana.

Bishop Joseph Francis (1923-1997), the second African-American SVD to become a bishop, was a national spokesman for black Catholics, provincial superior in the South, and battler for civil rights as auxiliary bishop of Newark, New Jersey.

10

Saint Augustine's Seminary

The First Seminary for African Americans

The crown jewel of the work of the Divine Word Missionaries among African Americans was the seminary they established for the education of black priests. It did not sprout up overnight, nor did it grow and expand without many incidents of opposition and prejudice. Many groups were watching the experiment carefully, some expecting and hoping it would fail, while others doubted it would succeed, but prayed that it might. In the end, it prospered beyond most proponents' fondest hopes and predictions.

PREVIOUS EFFORTS TO ESTABLISH
AN AFRICAN-AMERICAN PRIESTHOOD

Before going further, I must note that the Society of the Divine Word was not the first to train and ordain African Americans to the priesthood. A brief history of previous work in this area is in order, to show how the SVD attempt differed, why it succeeded, and in its own way was a first.[1] The three Healy brothers were sons of Michael Healy, a wealthy Irish immigrant-become-planter and his light-skinned slave Mary Eliza. They had ten children together, three of whom became nuns and three priests. James Augustine, the oldest of the brothers, was ordained in France in 1854. When he returned from there, he became the personal secretary of John Fitzpatrick, Bishop of Boston. In 1875 he was ordained Bishop of Portland, Maine, the first African-American bishop in the United States. The next brother to be ordained was Alexander Sherwood Healy. He studied canon law in Rome, where he was ordained for Boston. He became personal theologian to Bishop John

---

1. This section relies heavily on the following sources: Cyprian Davis, *The History of Black Catholics in the United States* (New York: Crossroad, 1990); Stephen J. Ochs, "Deferred Mission: The Josephites and the Struggle for Black Catholic Priests, 1871–1960," 3 vols. Ph.D. diss. (Ann Arbor, Mich.: UMI Dissertation Services, 1985), and *Desegregating the Altar: The Josephites and the Struggle for Black Priests 1871–1960* (Baton Rouge: Louisiana State University Press, 1990); Caroline Hemesath, O.S.F., "They Spread the Good News" (Unpublished Manuscript, 1967); and Albert Foley, S.J., *God's Men of Color* (New York: Farrar, Straus and Company, 1955).

Williams, who had succeeded Bishop Fitzpatrick. The third brother became a Jesuit and in 1873 became president of Georgetown University in Washington, D.C., a position he occupied until 1882. After working hard and successfully, though not without opposition because of prejudice and whisperings about his "tainted blood," he went into semi-retirement because of poor health brought on by overwork. Cyprian Davis observes:

> It is, again, one of the ironies of history that this university—which owed so much to a former slave who became known as its second founder—did not admit African American students until the middle of the twentieth century, and then only as a result of the civil rights movement.

The Healys' success did little for the cause of an African-American Catholic priesthood. They did not exactly conceal their African-American roots or try to deliberately pass as whites, but neither were they obviously black, in the way Tolton clearly was. Nor did they did use their background and position to try to upgrade and improve the condition of blacks. Few outside of the areas where the three brothers worked were even aware that there were any black priests in America. None of the three ever identified with their race or spoke or wrote publicly against conditions in the South. Until they were recognized as African Americans by historians, they left no significant trace of their heritage in terms of the African-American apostolate.

The same must be said of Augustus Tolton, whose career we have already introduced. In *God's Men of Color*, Albert Foley mentions a handful of other black priests who were ordained during the 1920s and early 1930s, but once again they were individual cases, and the de facto color bar was not breached.

The first systematic effort to develop a black Catholic priesthood was led by the Josephites, according to Stephen Ochs, upon whose account I rely in what follows. Father John Slattery, who was to be the first superior general of the Josephites after their split from Mill Hill in 1893, had been agitating for black priests long before the foundation of the Josephite community and had already succeeded in having Charles Randolph Uncles ordained as a Josephite on 19 December 1891. Convinced that blacks could be priests and that their own would accept them, Slattery nevertheless labored under the burden of some of the same prejudices that his contemporaries displayed, according to Stephen Ochs. Bishop Patrick Lynch of Charleston wrote in 1864 that blacks "[were] a race very prone to excess; and who, unless restrained, plunge madly into the lowest depths of licentiousness."[2] Ochs reports also the answers of several bishops to a questionnaire sent out by Archbishop Martin Spalding in preparation for discussing the "Negro" issue in 1866 at the Baltimore Council. Bishop William Elder of Natchez, Mississippi, felt that "immorality loomed as a great problem for the Church in its work with the Afro-American."[3]

---

2. Ochs, "Deferred Mission," p. 20, quoting Edward J. Misch, "The American Bishops and the Negro from the Civil War to the Third Plenary Council of Baltimore, 1865–1884" (Unpublished Ph.D. diss., Georgetown University, 1968).

3. Ochs, "Deferred Mission," p. 26.

To Father Slattery's later credit, he refused to accept that the African Americans' "deficiencies" were in any way racial. He recognized the true basis of the difficulties they faced in their systematic abuse by the slave system. Three priests were ordained as the result of Slattery's early efforts, the first being Charles Randolph Uncles. Ordained by Cardinal James Gibbons of Baltimore on 19 December 1891, Uncles was the first African American to be ordained in the United States. Slattery wanted him visible among his own people; Uncles found it distasteful to be trotted out like an exotic specimen. Uncles also felt obligated to his family and wanted to help them; Slattery found this difficult to appreciate. Uncles served out his priestly life as an effective teacher at Epiphany Apostolic College, the Josephite minor seminary and junior college, until he died in 1933.

The second Josephite in Slattery's push for a colored priesthood was ordained in 1902, John Henry Dorsey. Slattery delivered the sermon on the occasion of Dorsey's first Mass. Filled with anger at the way the Negro missions were being treated by the white church, angry and exasperated by the prejudice and bias he saw directed toward black priests, Slattery let out all his frustrations in this sermon. It proved to be his farewell to the Josephite congregation, to his work for the Negro missions, and to the church as well. Dorsey himself, in the relatively short time he lived, was hugely successful and gave the lie to the slur that blacks would never accept a black priest as their pastor, though many still repeated it. Blacks, according to Ochs, welcomed him with open arms wherever he went and demanded more like him.

It was largely the reception of Dorsey that convinced SVDs in the South that African Americans would accept African Americans as their pastors and representatives of Christ and his church among them. In 1914, Father Heick invited Father Dorsey to give a mission in his parish in Jackson. It would be a "daring undertaking," for if there was to be an audience it would have to be drawn from non-Catholics, because the number of Catholics was so small. The Protestant preachers tried to undercut the mission by having special talks and services in their own churches every night of the mission. "But they had no success," wrote Father Heick in an article in the first 1916 issue of *The Colored Messenger*; "the people came in ever greater numbers to hear Father Dorsey, because they considered him one of their own." Father Heick, the superior of the SVD southern mission, was one of the more pessimistic of the group on the question of a black priesthood, but he was convinced by Dorsey: "Men like Father Dorsey could do much for the conversion of their race, especially among the people in the country, where it is most difficult for a white man to reach those people and get their confidence."

Still, opposition to the step of recruiting and training African Americans persisted. Dorsey felt keenly the snubs and opposition of his fellow priests. He died in 1926, the result of a blow on the head he had received two years earlier from the irate father of a child he had disciplined. He was fifty-three years old.

The most tragic of the three early black Josephites to become a priest was John Plantevigne, who was ordained on 21 September 1907. No doubt because of the terrible sufferings he and his family had experienced—one brother was killed by white terrorists while he was in the seminary—John Plantevigne felt a special antipathy for racism and adopted a confrontational style. For example, in an article he wrote in 1909 for the *Afro-American Ledger*, he had this to say:

> The blood of the Negro boils in resentment of a "Jim Crow" system in the Catholic Church. The doors of the Church must be opened full wide, not a side entrance, if the Negro is to be saved by the Catholic Church. Negroes have followed their masters into the Catholic Church, but have fallen away in great numbers because they have not been given an active part in the organic life of the Church. Social circumstances compel us to compromise. This is unfortunate, because it loses the Negro and fails to develop true religion among the Whites, for true religion is charity.
>
> The Negro wants [black] Catholic priests, non-Catholic people are accustomed to colored ministers and refuse to enter the Catholic Church under white priests.[4]

Pantevigne wanted to build a school for blacks in his home parish in the Archdiocese of New Orleans but was refused permission by Archbishop James Blenk. Nor was he allowed to preach a mission in New Orleans. Plantevigne contracted tuberculosis, suffered a nervous breakdown, and died on 7 January 1913 at the age of forty-two. The last of the three black Josephites, he was the first to die. His ordination was the end of any further systematic effort on the part of the Josephites to develop a black clergy until the 1940s.

THE SOCIETY OF THE DIVINE WORD ENTERS THE SCENE

Such was the situation when the Society of the Divine Word began its work among African Americans. As they considered the vastness of the work of "converting the Negro" and the meagerness of the resources they could muster, they realized there was no proportion between the two realities. Coming with the enthusiasm and optimism of a young Society founded barely twenty-five years earlier and aware of the string of successes the Society had experienced thus far, they were also confident that the situation could be improved. Very early they began to think of establishing a "native" clergy, just as they, from their German perspective, had done at Techny, only this time the clergy would be African American. All the SVD missionaries in the South were German. They had not grown up in the United States, and so the manner of handling race relations that permeated every aspect of black-white relations had not lost the capacity to shock them, as it apparently had most other white Catholics. Concretely, these German missioners did not share the common prejudices concerning the "racial" inability of African Americans to be educated, nor did they accept that they had "innate" lack of high moral sensibility, nor believe they were incapable of rising to and maintaining the standards of the priesthood as did so many others.

Still, it was not patently obvious to the SVD that work among African Americans ought to be undertaken. The founder, Arnold Janssen, wondered aloud

---

4. Cited in Foley, *God's Men of Color*, pp. 89–90.

in a letter of 1 May 1907 to Father Bodems, visitator general in the United States, why there were so few religious congregations working among Negroes:

> There are many religious congregations in North America. Everybody can see how many Blacks there are and easily recognize that the Josephites are too few in number to handle this great work. A person has to ask why none of these other congregations, with many German members, like the Jesuits, Franciscans and Benedictines, have not gone into this work. This is one of the reasons I hesitate [to commit more to the Negro mission]; I won't mention the other reasons.

The Divine Word Missionary initially most responsible for promoting the idea of a seminary for the training of black priests was Father James Wendel, who was also the first pastor in Meridian, Mississippi. Apparently the topic came up frequently in the annual meetings of the SVD missionaries in the South. Probably because it was more obvious in Mississippi that blacks were held in low repute in the church and that they enter this white church only with great difficulty, the men working in Mississippi were forced to contemplate more drastic solutions than elsewhere. At any rate, the conviction quickly grew among them that only an African-American clergy could approach their own people as credible representatives of the church and Christ.

There was, however, an even earlier stimulus to the whole thinking of the SVD regarding a seminary for African Americans. Credit must be given where credit is due, and in this case it must be given again to Father Peil. From his post as procurator in St. Gabriel's Seminary near Vienna, Peil was still interested in the SVD work in North America, and especially in their work among African Americans, the apostolate to which he had asked to be assigned. Janssen had refused that wish because he thought Peil's personality would create too many problems. In spite of this refusal Peil did not lose his interest in and concern for the African-American apostolate. It happened this way. Father Karl Friedrich, the SVD's procurator general,[5] who normally lived in Rome, was taking his vacation at St. Gabriel's during the summer of 1911. Alt says in his centenary history of St. Gabriel's that the procurator general and Peil exchanged ideas about the African-American apostolate and that these conversations included the need for a black priesthood if the race problem was ever to be resolved. Peil urged Friedrich to get curia officials involved with the work for Negroes in America. They continued corresponding about these issues after Friedrich's return to Rome. Peil also sent tips to Rome how best to present the issue to the curia. In the meantime Peil also wrote letters requesting ideas from the priests in the United States.[6]

Friedrich needed to have answers to two questions. First, he asks, is a seminary for blacks possible? Will there be enough vocations and will social conditions allow it? In a letter of 7 September 1911, Friedrich says:

---

5. A procurator general handles the relations of a religious community with the Holy See.

6. Joseph Alt, *Die Geschichte des Missionshauses St. Gabriel der Gesellschaft des Göttlichen Wortes: Das erstes Jahrhundert, 1889–1989* (Rome: Collegio del Verbo Divino, 1990), p. 181.

If such an institution is possible, then there will be open a source of grace for the black apostolate, which, with God's grace, will never run dry. If, indeed, many priests do not want to have anything to do with the conversion of Blacks and put no effort into this apostolate, not much will be accomplished in the long run. Many would be saved, however, if not all, as soon as the Blacks have their own priests. Everything else would automatically follow. In a word, this issue is worth serious study, so that we can go forward quietly and confidently, without danger of having to call off the project halfway through.[7]

The second question was whether the SVD was in a position to begin such a seminary. Not only would it require money and personnel, but also courage. Nevertheless, by educating African Americans as priests, he judged that the Society would be doing much more for the African-American apostolate than they ever could by staffing parishes. He quickly got answers from Peil on 25 August 1911; from de Lange, at this time superior in the United States, on 17 September 1911; and from Heick, superior of the Southern missions, on 25 September 1911. Their responses can be summed up in the following points:

1. For the time being it is not possible to start the seminary, but we should continue to work toward that goal.
2. Black priests are necessary if we want to push forward the conversion of blacks.
3. The first thing we have to promote is the higher education of blacks.
4. If they prove qualified in the course of their studies, we can direct them into philosophy and theology.
5. The Society must be allowed to open missions in areas where there have long been Catholics. To try to fill a seminary with recently converted Catholics would be foolish.

With these answers Friedrich did not have enough to go to the curia, yet he wanted desperately to do something. If he had no concrete proposal to present, Rome would tell him what to do, and the project might not succeed.

Peil again came up with the solution. It was too early to bring up the seminary idea, but the way had to be prepared. First, they should offer Rome some occasion to praise the African-American apostolate and thereby also urge bishops, clergy, and laity to do more for this neglected and despised people, "for the matter becomes different for the public if the Holy See has spoken about it."[8] This would be the first petition.

The second petition would consist of a request to allow the Society to set up missions anywhere in the United States, or in lieu of that, in the areas where black Catholics are concentrated. From these Catholics they could expect candidates for the priesthood. Of course, this latter rationale need not be mentioned yet. The first

---

7. Michael Meier, "Die Negermission SVD im Süden der USA" Ph.D. diss. (Steyl, Netherlands: Pontificia Universitas Gregoriana, 1961), p. 83.

8. Peil to Friedrich, 11 December 1911, cited in Meier, "Die Negermission SVD," p. 85.

petition received a positive response in the form of a letter from the Holy See's secretary of state to Archbishop Quigley of Chicago, dated 22 January 1912. In it, Meier reports, the Holy Father expressed his wish that the American Catholics, clerics and laity, should not neglect the people of the black race, but rather help these poor people in a true Christian sense, and that they should support the mission work for the conversion of blacks.

FIRST STEPS

The first small step toward developing a seminary was made in 1913 in Greenville, Mississippi, with the opening of a boarding school for boys. It consisted of a dormitory set up in the attic, and permission to proceed came from Father Heick. The priests and sisters hoped that vocations would develop from this small attempt. But because the First World War broke out in 1914, a halt was put to everything, including expanding the Greenville seminary. Nobody could be sent from Europe to help the priests or nuns, and the seminary at Techny was only four years old, so no American-born SVDs were yet available. All new projects were put on hold.

Discussions on a seminary for African Americans continued, including suggestions from the German missioners in the South that Heick petition the provincial, Father Burgmer, and Bishop John Gunn, the bishop of the diocese in which Greenville was located, to allow a beginning. In the meantime, Father Matthew Christman was assigned to Sacred Heart in Greenville to replace the pastor who had to leave because of poor health. From this time on, Father Christman was associated with plans for the first seminary for African Americans and became one of the key men responsible for success. Father Burgmer, never as enthusiastic for the southern missions as his successor was to be, answered that he was not himself adverse to the idea of a colored priesthood, but wished to have more time to study the question thoroughly. On 2 January 1915, Bishop Gunn wrote to say that the idea of a colored priesthood is interesting, but also that he does not think it is necessary or even advisable for the work of converting African Americans. "I would not, however, be opposed to the formation of a colored priesthood in general, but I do not think that the principle could be reduced to practice, at least here in the South. Under certain conditions the attempt could be made."[9]

He reminds the SVDs that the attempt had been made before and failed and he suggested that Africa was the place to begin such an enterprise, which could perhaps be extended here later. Bishop Gunn did not want a seminary in his diocese, yet he left the door open for the possibility of granting permission later. Finally, he hit upon what he thought would be a good solution. He concludes his letter denying permission for the time being to begin a seminary in his diocese with the counterproposal that married "colored deacons . . . could preach and administer most of the sacraments." In the bishop's mind, this would "avoid the difficulties and dangers most to be feared," by which he meant difficulties related to remaining celibate. Although he was ahead of his time in the matter of a married and permanent diaconate, he favored it for all of the wrong reasons.

---

9. Gunn to Heick, 2 January 1915, from SVD Archives, Bay St. Louis, Mississippi.

As we have indicated, little could be done for the seminary during the war years, but they were not wasted years. In the summer of 1915, Father Provincial Burgmer and Father Heick attended a conference of prominent missionaries working in the African-American apostolate. During it they brought up the idea of a seminary for blacks. Opposition to the idea, they found, was vigorous, and the SVDs, especially Father Wendel, began the subtle and painstakingly long process of preparing the ground for a seminary, first of all by promoting the idea of a black seminary. Wendel toured northern parishes to get a sense of what priests there thought, while collecting money for his mission in Meridian. He started *The Colored Messenger*, in which he explained the need and value of ordaining African Americans, promoting the cause in season and out of season. The last issue of *The Colored Messenger*, almost entirely devoted to the question of black priests, appeared in 1918.

ADVANCING THE IDEA

When the war ended, Father Peter Janser replaced Burgmer as provincial. The missionaries in the South, who often felt overlooked and neglected by Techny, wanted the new provincial to take an interest in the southern missions and the seminary idea. They were happy when he began to push the seminary project along. The southern missionaries had a sense of pleasant surprise, according to documents I found in the archives at Bay St. Louis.

Had the men in the South been privy to the founder's thinking when he appointed Janser to the States in the first place, they would not have been surprised. In a lengthy circular letter to his council members at Steyl, the founder tried to convince his councilors to let Janser leave Steyl and go to Shermerville (Techny). On 28 April 1905, the founder wrote:

> I gather that you think I should leave Father Janser there [in Steyl] . . . From the letter of Father Janser, however, I notice that he has always been keenly interested in the Negro missions. I must confess that I had this assignment in mind [as superior of the Negro missions] when I thought of appointing him to America.

Soon after the First World War, German missionaries were forced to leave the Togo mission in West Africa and were transferred to the Negro mission in America. Rome was still interested in an African-American clergy and began again to remind the American church of the obligations they carried for the African Americans. Benedict XV had issued the apostolic letter *Maximum illud* on 30 November 1919, in which he put great stress on the development of a native clergy taken from among every people. In the United States, including in the North where blacks began to pour in during the war, bishops were slowly beginning to change. They could no longer conveniently limit responsibility for blacks to southern bishops any more. Thus they, too, became more sympathetic to the idea of a black priesthood.

MAKING THE CASE FOR THE NEED
FOR A BLACK PRIESTHOOD

Father Wendel became the most active supporter of a colored priesthood and had some interesting things to say in a letter sent to Superior General Blum on 29 September 1919:

The prejudice of the Whites against the Blacks reaches deep into the Church. People consider us second class priests, because we work for the despised Blacks. But let me tell you what we have been able to do to convert the bishops and priests. Six years ago we could not get permission to open a high school for Blacks, even though the Protestants had eighteen in Mississippi alone. Catholics did not have a single one. The reason the Bishop gave: Why, what would my priests say if you have a high school for Blacks? We insisted on the need for high schools, and now we have five, one on each station . . . About six months ago [the bishop] was converted to the most important matter of all, one we scarcely dared to bring up directly but about which we kept writing and discussing whenever possible, namely the education of black priests. We brought it up and prayed about this and the Bishop went so far that he and other bishops publicly stated that it was not advisable to ordain black priests, but that they would petition Rome to allow them to ordain deacons, who then could marry, because the Blacks are unable to live a celibate life. The matter never went to Rome; it was all so ridiculous and terribly insulting to Blacks. We ignored this proposal and thought it laughable. Even the Lord Bishops realized what nonsense they were talking. So far has the conversion of the bishops progressed that at their meeting in Baltimore at this very time they are discussing, officially, the question of Negro priests. They finally realize that black priests are absolutely necessary if their people are ever going to be converted. They have also come around to the proposal of the SVD that these Negro priests must live in some sort of community and be kept together, for the prejudice against black priests among white priests born in America and Irish priests is just too much otherwise to deal with. German, Dutch, and French priests are quite different in this respect. This insight also marks a conversion on the part of the Bishops. All this talk about conversion might seem to be a joke, but it is a bitter reality that took much struggle and prayer, and will take even more before they are fully converted. But at least everything is on the right track.

It is also the wish of all of us working here in the missions that the SVD work for this. We have good schools which is a good basis for such work, nor is there any lack of good vocations, though we still have to go out and encourage them. As I see it, the education of black priests would be one of the most important contributions we could make here in America . . .

Please allow us to begin this work by sending us personnel from over there; this is the only thing we need. Money will not be that much of a problem . . . Two months ago I went north on a four week begging tour and I turned up many benefactors for just such a project. They all kept talking about black priests. When I got to Baltimore, I met Cardinal Gibbons and he also urged me how much black priests were needed, and only German priests could do this. American and Irish priests would never go into this work, because it was too demeaning. "A nigger is a nigger, and anybody who works with them will also be considered a nigger!"

This reminds me of St. Paul, who became all things to all men for the sake of Christ.

Wendel concludes his long letter:

Fr. General, for the Lord's sake help us educate Blacks to the priesthood. The bishops, with all their good will, realize that they are powerless but the SVD can do it if we put our hand to the wheel. At least let us make a small beginning with a boarding school. The details can be worked out later as the project develops. What we need is your permission and your blessing.[10]

In his letter of 21 October 1919, one of the very last he wrote to America before he died on 29 October, Blum grants them tentative permission, but wants to see a more complete plan sent through the provincial before he can give permanent permission. Father Janser, in the meantime, officially asked Bishop Gunn for his permission, which he granted in view of the fact that these priests were to be religious rather than diocesan priests.

As superior of the mission, Father Heick also sent a report to the generalate. In this report on how things had gone in the South during the war years, he points out—almost in awe, as if finding it difficult to believe—that the mission had advanced. They could hardly have expected this in normal times, but in war time? As Germans? Teaching American children? They were not molested during the war, though people treated them with caution. What a chance this would have been for their enemies to have them thrown out of the missions, he exclaims. He then points to the main reason for this success:

Gladly and with gratitude we recognize that we owe this success to the Sisters [Missionary Servants of the Holy Spirit]. They were tireless in their work, which demanded of them much sacrifice, time and real hardship. Six years ago, they were almost all novices in the subjects they had to teach, with little experience in education. Today they are all tested and proven teachers. Six years ago there were few who could take over the upper classes; now they are prepared to teach high school, even the more difficult subjects like Latin, mathematics, physics and chemistry. And on every one of our stations we now have a high school . . . It is now generally recognized in church circles and acknowledged that we were the first to seriously address the school problem [of going beyond the elementary grades] and have real success.[11]

---

10. This long report is preserved in Father Bonner's *Chronologium*, 29 September 1919.
11. *Chronologium*, 1 November 1919.

BEGINNING TO REALIZE THE DREAM

It was left to Father Matthew Christman to implement this idea and bring it to fruition. To this work, beginning in 1919 at Greenville, Mississippi, he devoted the rest of his life.

Immediately after his ordination in St. Gabriel's in 1912, Christman was assigned to the southern missions, to Sacred Heart Mission in Greenville, Mississippi. By 1914 he was hard at work developing a regular classical high school. Bishop Gunn had wanted the Society to begin an industrial school which he thought would better prepare blacks for a job and would not be much of a threat to the status quo. Finally and reluctantly, he gave permission to establish a classical high school and Christman, together with the Missionary Sisters of the Holy Spirit who were teaching in the school, set about to develop what came to be a successful, well-equipped, and professionally staffed high school. This gave the SVDs experience administering an educational institution in the South, knowledge that was to be useful when the time came to set up a seminary. It seems Christman always had the seminary in mind, because from the start intensive Latin was part of the curriculum, and it was to be later joined by Greek.

By 1919 the stage was set and the curtain was ready to go up on the drama that began a new phase of the Society's work in the United States. Bishop Gunn also finally approved but set two conditions. First, any future African-American priests would form or belong to a religious community. Second, the spiritual direction and education of African-American candidates to the priesthood was to be taken over completely and for all time by the Society of the Divine Word. When the SVD accepted them, it neatly relieved the bishop of the responsibility of doing something himself and of accepting the black priests as secular priests in his own diocese.

Others also needed convincing. In 1920, Janser met with Archbishop Mundelein of Chicago not long after he had come from a meeting with Apostolic Delegate, Archbishop John Bonzano. The delegate had told him that a delegation of black Catholics had given him three petitions: (1) to allow blacks to join the Knights of Columbus; (2) to allow blacks to study at Catholic University; and (3) to ordain black priests for their own race. "Naturally," Mundelein said, "I explained to the Apostolic Delegate, that the American bishops did not feel the time was ripe for the education of black priests."

Father Janser continues his report, admitting that he could hardly keep from laughing: "And I told the Cardinal [Janser wrote these recollections after Mundelein had become a cardinal] that really was interesting news, and it would become more interesting because I had come to inform him of our plan for the foundation of a new community for black priests and Brothers." He approved of a community for brothers, but could not be convinced that black priests would be possible in spite of Janser's arguments. Two days later, having had time to think on the matter, Janser reports that Mundelein was full of enthusiasm for the idea. "The plan," he said, "is terrific, and now I'm convinced that it is the only way."[12]

---

12. Meier, "Die Negermission SVD," p. 93.

Unexpectedly, 24 February 1920, on the same day permission to open the first seminary exclusively devoted to the education of an African-American priesthood and brotherhood was granted, Father James Wendel died of the Spanish influenza. He was an indefatigable advocate of blacks, a champion and defender of their rights who repeatedly argued that they were capable of doing anything they wanted, if only they were given the opportunity. Although he had spent only ten years in the South, they were ten crucial years in the history of the church there. On 8 March 1920, he would have been thirty-nine years old.

Messages of condolence came from many quarters. Father Dorsey, the black Josephite priest who had preached such a successful mission in Father Wendel's parish, wrote to Provincial Superior Janser on 25 March 1920:

The sad news of Father Wendel's death reached me yesterday. I cannot tell you how I feel his loss. He was a friend most dear, tried and true. There was no sham in his love for the colored people. I always admired the stand he took even amongst prejudiced priests and bishops. He was fearless for he knew he was right. When shall another Father Wendel be raised up? We need such men, especially at this time when there is so much cowardice. Father Pastorelli [the superior general of the Josephites] is reporting that he never said he would not take any more colored priests. When I heard this I thought of your words to me. Namely, that Father Pastorelli told you that he would not take any more colored students. Well, those who are fearless, and who are working for the honor and glory of God and the salvation of souls must help the Colored Race in its hour of untold trials. Your community has my sympathy in the loss of such a worthy priest of God. At God's altar I shall remember his soul. Yours in Xto, J. H. Dorsey. P.S. I would to God that another Archbishop Jansens be raised up to fight the battles of neglected, despised Colored Catholics. J.H.D.[13]

BEGINNING AT GREENVILLE

Once all formal permissions for starting the seminary were in hand, Father Janser sent a letter to every priest who worked among the African Americans, announcing the opening of the new seminary in Greenville, Mississippi, in the fall of 1920. In this letter he solicited the help and advice of priests and nuns:

If you know boys and young men showing signs of such a vocation [to the religious priesthood or brotherhood], either as a member of the Society of the Divine Word or a new religious community still to be established [this, he had said, need not be decided today], will you be good enough to direct them to us? Only the sympathetic help of the Reverend Pastors and Venerable Teachers will assure success. Boys who wish to become priests should be graduates from grammar school, possessed of good talents and health, above

13. *Chronologium.* By "Archbishop Jansens" Dorsey must have meant Arnold Janssen, who really must be given much of the credit for what the Society of the Divine Word accomplished in the South for the African-American cause.

all pious and docile. Ordinarily only children of Catholic parents can be considered. Candidates for the Brotherhood need no special training, but should be morally good and healthy, and not over thirty years old.[14]

The letter brought a good response, especially from the Josephites, many of whom went out of their way to send vocations to the SVD. Father Christman, in the meantime, in spite of all his other work of teaching and serving as pastor of Sacred Heart Church in Greenville, went out giving talks on vocations and begging for money to support the seminarians and to build a seminary. Finally, the first high school seminary for African Americans opened its doors in the fall of 1920. As this first year went on, students dribbled in at different times and at many different stages of development and preparation. By the end of the year the students numbered twelve. Christman was satisfied. On 20 July 1921 he writes to one of his firm supporters, Monsignor Burke, the editor of *Our Colored Missions*:

> The first year of the seminary is now coming to a close. The first year of the College was certainly a success. We have good students and I believe, with the exception of one, all will come back next year. Three new students will come within the next two weeks. Several applications from New Orleans are also on hand, and then some Northern boys have already sent their required papers. So we shall be able to start the next school year with a goodly number of boys.
>
> Among the most enthusiastic friends of the College are some Josephite and Jesuit Fathers, also several secular priests; Mr. Markoe, S.J. sent an excellent boy here and writes me regularly. It is mainly through them that I receive the students of the College. There is a good religious spirit among the boys, a great love for their studies, and discipline is good.
>
> The greatest difficulty in the beginning was to grade the students; almost every student belonged to a different grade. Now I have two well-organized classes.

He continues:

> Then knowing well that Greenville is not a suitable place for a seminary, we already bought a very desirable property at Bay St. Louis, Mississippi. So it was decided not to enlarge the original building here to accommodate new students or add any improvement, but save all the money we can get in order to be able to soon move to the Bay.[15]

That a new place would be necessary soon became obvious. The number of students in the second year jumped to twenty-five. They had to live in a house that Christman had described as only big enough for twenty. These twenty-five students, which had actually risen to twenty-seven by the opening of school, represented ten states of the Union and Central America.

---

14. Letter dated 1 July 1920, taken from the "House Chronicle," Archives, Bay St. Louis, p. 11.
15. "House Chronicle," Archives, Bay St. Louis, pp. 25–26.

As soon as Father Heick returned from the general chapter, where William Gier had been elected as the third superior general, he rushed to Greenville to see how the seminary was doing. From him we might have expected a somewhat jaundiced description of the first semester's results, but to have a dozen students as a beginning was even beyond Heick's wildest dreams, and the zeal of the students was more than satisfactory. The seminary was off to a good start.

BEGINNING AT BAY ST. LOUIS

Almost from the beginning Christman realized that Greenville was not the place for a seminary, so Father Heick had begun to look around for a more suitable place. His old friend from his Merigold days, Father Gmelch, was now pastor of a mixed black and white parish in Bay St. Louis. He was German and had always been well disposed to the Society. It seems very likely that he was the one who called Father Heick's attention to this location. As thoughts advanced, it began to seem that if the SVD built their seminary in Bay St. Louis, it might be advisable to open a parish for blacks in town also. Thus Father Janser proposed that Father Heick be Gmelch's assistant, build a school for blacks, and eventually, as the project developed, invite the blacks in Gmelch's parish into a separate parish under the care of the Divine Word Missionaries. This is what happened when St. Rose de Lima parish was established in 1928.

Bay St. Louis proved to be an excellent place for the seminary, for there were more Catholics, also black Catholics, in this part of Mississippi, and relations between the races were not as tense as they were in central and northern Mississippi. New Orleans, the center of Catholicism in the South, was also nearby and easily accessible. All in all, it was a good choice. There were the usual difficulties of scraping together the money to build the seminary, which was named after and dedicated to the great doctor of the church and Bishop of Hippo, St. Augustine. The deed to the property was transferred to the SVD by the Voorhies family on 13 June 1921, for the sum of $5,650.

Bishop Gunn had given permission for the move, once he had again been assured that the African-American priests would not be diocesan priests. He offered to help financially with the purchase of the land and to pressure his fellow bishops, through the Indian and Negro Commission, for financial assistance for the seminary. The members of this commission were glad to oblige. Southern bishops could do the same and be content at the same time that they would be religious and would not have to intermingle with white priests. At the same time the southern bishops would "not be tormented any longer," as Bishop Gunn put it, "about our unChristian color line."[16] His priests, though, "are hopeful that the thing will die for want of support." He admired the Society for its bravery in the matter, but attributed it to their "invincible ignorance" of southern ways, which might just "bring these good SVD men to save themselves and . . . their brunettes."[17] In addition, as members of a religious missionary society, they could

16. Ochs, "Deferred Mission," p. 286.
17. Ochs, "Deferred Mission," p. 286.

always be sent abroad to Africa and might not ever be assigned to work in the southern United States.

Father Janser in the meantime sent a letter to every bishop in the United States in November 1921 that is worth quoting in full:

I feel that you will be interested in an account of the work for the education of colored boys to the Catholic priesthood, which the Society of the Divine Word undertook about a year ago.

For the past sixteen years our Fathers have been successfully laboring among the colored people of our country. But since our work was generally among the Protestants, unusual difficulties stood in the way. On account of the many restrictions imposed upon the missionaries by the existing social conditions, our activity was almost entirely limited to the school room with the natural result that progress has been very slow. Thus the conviction grew upon us that the conversion of the colored RACE could not be looked for, unless there would be a COLORED CLERGY, as non-Catholic denominations had provided them ever since the Civil War.

We realized the difficulties of having a colored SECULAR clergy; but after many conferences with competent men, including several members of our American hierarchy, we could find no valid or serious objection to a colored RELIGIOUS priesthood. It is to the Right Rev. John E. Gunn, Bishop of Natchez, that most credit is due for carrying out this plan. He had always been a zealous shepherd of his colored children, and so very generously consented to have the beginning made in his diocese, at Greenville, Washington Co., Miss.

While the "Sacred Heart College" found a temporary home at Greenville, a more suitable property has been acquired at Bay Saint Louis, Miss., where the institution will be permanently established to be known then as ST. AUGUSTINE'S MISSION HOUSE.

As you will note above, the candidates will be trained for the religious life of Priests and Brothers. At the suggestion of the Roman authorities the plan of an AUTONOMOUS province has been decided upon. Hence, while all are candidates of the Society of the Divine Word, they will receive their education in separate institutions. Remaining under the same Superior General, and, for many years to come, under white local and provincial superiors, they will ultimately form a province of their own. It is our ambition to train them according to the purpose of our Society, for missionary work among their own people, both here in the United States and eventually also in foreign countries.

We are pleased to tell your Lordship that twenty-eight candidates for the colored priesthood are studying today at Sacred Heart College, Greenville, Miss. As a rule, only the best boys of Catholic parents are accepted. It has been very gratifying that the priests and sisters laboring among the colored people have enthusiastically welcomed our foundation, and we are particularly grateful for the promise of their faithful cooperation.

While the Society of the Divine Word is entirely responsible for the enterprise, we must rely, as in all our missionary efforts, on the generous support of the Catholic public. So far the funds have been meager, and nothing as yet could be done for the erection of new buildings at Bay Saint Louis, Miss.

You are, no doubt, aware, my dear Bishop, that we have assumed a very difficult task. It is well known that the work of educating colored boys for a religious priesthood does not make the strong appeal to many people that it should make. More than ordinary patience and prudence will be required, and only God's special blessing can make this work a success. Since we believe it to be His work, we trust in Him, the more so, since we have no other end in view than to win souls for Christ, to prepare for the ultimate conversion of the whole colored race, and to do this by the most efficient means. You have often heard the missionary axiom, universally recognized as such, that no people has ever been converted except by men of their own blood.

The Holy Father himself has but recently given strong expression to this truth, and he surely did not wish to exclude the Negroes of the United States. Brazil has shown the way. A colored Catholic Archbishop is admired there for his scholarship and sanctity; our own Fathers are working under his jurisdiction. Besides, over 200 Negro priests are giving an excellent account of themselves.

The race problem has become a troublesome one and may lead to a crisis. While we do not consider it within the scope of our activity to seek directly for a solution of the social, economic, or even political aspect of that problem, we think the best solution would be to make the NEGRO CATHOLIC. It is his birthright as much as ours, of which he has been too long deprived.

In submitting this statement to your Lordship, it is not only to obviate misunderstandings, but to ask for advice and guidance. Though principally an organization for foreign mission work, we are nevertheless desirous of being helpful at home and do some missionary work, where we can lighten the burden of some of our bishops. We hope to do our work quietly, without hurting the susceptibilities [*sic*] of opponents; but you will agree with us that God's holy will and the wish of the Holy Father should not be frustrated by prejudice and lack of charity.

In conclusion, may I humbly ask for your episcopal blessing and the alms of prayer for our Community, our whole mission work, and especially for the young seminary? With the assurance of profoundest respect, I beg to remain, Your Lordship's most obedient servant.[18]

The response from the bishops was encouraging and many of them put their money where their mouth was by sending in donations for the proposed seminary at Bay St. Louis. Cardinal O'Connell, who knew the Society of the Divine Word well already, was one of the first to give a personal gift of one thousand dollars,

---

18. Bonner's *Chronologium*.

with the remark, "You Germans are the only ones who can do it." At that very time the Society was negotiating to enter his archdiocese, and the Cardinal offered to sell his summer home, "Miramar," to the Society for its work. This became St. Francis Xavier Mission House.

THE FORMAL OPENING

The Bay, as the seminary came to be called, had its share of difficulties. On the part of many inside the SVD and outside among bishops, clergy, and laity there was ambivalence and prejudice, as well as enthusiasm and relief that finally something was being done. The seminary at Bay St. Louis was finally opened formally with much fanfare and a solemn blessing on 16 September 1923. The House Chronicle describes the day thus:

> Today is marked as a "RED LETTER" day in the annals of St. Augustine's Mission House at Bay St. Louis, Mississippi. It was the day of the dedication of this new Mission House; and in the history of the Catholic Church among the Colored people of America, the day of the opening of the portals of the first seminary for young men of their race with a vocation for the priesthood, a day that will be long remembered particularly by the hundreds of visiting Knights of Peter Claver, and thousands of Colored Catholics from New Orleans and other points along the Coast, as an epoch-making forward step, and as a pledge of their most hearty endorsement of the great enterprise . . . A grand parade was formed . . . Thus they marched through the business section of the town, then to the Seminary grounds.
>
> As soon as the visitors arrived on the Seminary grounds, another procession was staged. At the head of the procession was the bearer of the standard of our faith, the Cross with which the new Seminary will soon be crowned; beside him two altar boys; then "Old Glory" and the banner of Peter Claver, followed by the Knights themselves, dressed in immaculate white uniforms with swords held aloft. After these came the faithful at large; then a great number of Sisters and Brothers, the Seminarians, the Clergy and His Lordship, the Bishop. This beautiful procession wended its way from the Rectory to the new Mission House where Rt. Rev. John E. Gunn, Bishop of Natchez, before the main entrance of the building, implored the blessings of God upon the new Seminary and sprinkled the exterior of the building with Holy Water.
>
> After this Father Janser celebrated a solemn Mass, at which Father Kane, a Josephite priest, gave the sermon.
>
> At five-thirty a parade was once more formed, and the visitors in step with the music, marched back to the station to board the trains that would take them to their various homes in Louisiana, Mississippi, Alabama, and Texas. Just before they boarded the train, the air was filled with the strains of "Home Sweet Home."

THE LETTER OF PIUS XI

In preparation for the move from Greenville to Bay St. Louis, Pope Pius XI had sent a letter to Father Gier, the superior general of the Society of the Divine Word. In this letter, dated 5 April 1923, the pope approved and praised the effort to begin the work of educating blacks to the priesthood. This letter reads in part:

It is to Us a source of deep joy to learn that the college for the education of Negroes which you have established temporarily at Greenville, in the Diocese of Natchez, will shortly be transferred to Bay St. Louis in the same diocese, and converted into a mission seminary for the training of Negro youth according to the rule of your Order . . .

In your new undertaking you are following the very principle which, in so far as circumstances allowed, has always guided the Catholic Church. To this mother has arisen, especially in recent times, a numerous progeny among the colored race—a host of children who have frequently displayed virtues so splendid that they sealed their faith with their blood as in the most glorious epochs of Christian history. The Negroes occupy enormous areas of the earth, and it is undoubted that these races, which the Church takes so loving and maternal an interest in gladdening with the knowledge of her joyful message, will in the course of time be trained in all branches of human civilization, and will thus arise from their present lowly stages of culture, and attain a high level in their mode of life and moral training. If therefore We wish to accomplish useful and solid work in this field, it is indispensable that priests of the same race shall make it their life's task to lead these peoples to the Christian faith and to a higher cultural level . . .

Does it not follow from the very nature of the Church as a Divine institution that every tribe or people should have priests who are one with it in race and character, in habit of thought and temperament? Aside from the fact that such priests will find a friendly welcome will they not also prove far more effective in leading their brethren into, and confirming them in the faith than any priest of any different race and from another country? May Saint Augustine's Mission House prosper greatly under the care of the American Episcopate, and may it attract a large attendance of Negro pupils inspired with pure intentions![19]

STATUS OF THE AFRICAN-AMERICAN
PRIESTS AND BROTHERS

From the day it decided to open a seminary for African Americans, the Society of the Divine Word was faced with a dilemma that troubled it until the first class of four was ordained in 1934. It even lingered on for a time after the ordination. The dilemma had to do with the status of the African-American priests once they

---

19. *Acta Apostolicae Sedis* 15 (1923): 216.

were ordained and the work they were to do. Since it takes twelve or more years to bring a minor seminarian to ordination, the problem could be ignored for a long time and eventually the whole concern would become moot. At the time, however, the issue of the status of the African-American priests in a white-dominated American church was a critical problem.

When permissions were first sought to open a seminary for African Americans, there were several possibilities regarding what kind of priests they would become and the kinds of work they would do. They could have been trained by the Society of the Divine Word but ordained for the diocesan priesthood. Given the fact that whites would do almost nothing in any way that even hinted at the equality of blacks and whites, this possibility was scarcely feasible. That they would not be ordained for a diocese was indeed the condition on which Bishop Gunn gave permission to open a black seminary in the first place. Initially, therefore, they would be ordained as SVDs. But this solution created another problem. Father Bodems, the general administrator of the Society at the time and the one who wrote Father Janser giving official permission to open the seminary at Greenville, posed the possibility, the likelihood even, that not every black who had a vocation to the priesthood would also have a vocation to the religious life. Some would surely want to become diocesan priests. What would be done for these?

It had also been suggested that Rome appoint a prefect apostolic or create a *praelatura nullius*, the head of which would have exclusive jurisdiction over blacks, including black priests. That prelate would be responsible for assigning these priests to work among their own people. The American bishops, however, had repeatedly and roundly rejected this idea and any others like it that threatened their authority or split their jurisdiction.[20]

Another proposal was to found a congregation for African-American men who would work among their own people. The Society of the Divine Word would keep them under their own control until such time in the future when they had developed enough of them to become independent. This would solve the problem of having white SVDs and black SVDs breaching the law of the land by living together in one community. This idea had been raised by some Josephites, who were interested in a black priesthood but were unable to get their congregation to move energetically in the matter. Initially many Divine Word Missionaries were inclined to this solution. But then Father Karl Friedrich, still the procurator general, approached Roman authorities to get papal approval for what would become St. Augustine's. If this permission were forthcoming, the opposition from within the Society would be muted. Father Friedrich first approached Monsignor Camillus Laurenti, secretary of the Congregation for the Propagation of the Faith, who had always been interested in a seminary for African Americans. But since the United States was no longer under *Propaganda Fidei*, as of 1908, Laurenti was no longer officially engaged with America, though he arranged an audience with the Holy Father, during which Father Friedrich could bring up the matter himself. As Father Friedrich remembered it in a report he made years later to the 1932 Society general chapter, he mentioned the opposition the Society could expect from American

---

20. Ochs, "Deferred Mission," p. 26.

bishops. The pope (Benedict XV) replied that the seminary would not fail because of the bishops, especially if he, the Pope, wanted the work done. If the provincial in the United States should have any problems with the bishops, said Benedict XV, he should contact the pope directly.[21]

Because the Society's operations in America were now under the supervision of the Congregation for Religious, the pope directed Father Friedrich to discuss the matter of an African-American seminary with the prefect of this congregation, Cardinal Valfre. Before Friedrich went to Cardinal Valfre's office to get papal approval for the seminary, he asked Janser for information on what they intended to do in America. The answer was that the Society in America was not yet clear on what would happen when the time came to ordain black priests. The primary decision was to begin with the minor seminary immediately. The decision on assignments of ordinands, he said, had at least twelve years to mature. When the matter was brought up to the prefect of the Congregation for Religious, however, Cardinal Valfre recommended that the Society take the black priests into the Society of the Divine Word, but create a separate, autonomous province for them. They would then be directly under the generalate, and separate from the white priests, which would then give no reason to fear for the unity of the Society in America.

Having considered all these possibilities, the path the Society eventually followed was to admit African-American priests and brothers as full-fledged members of the Society of the Divine Word, with no distinction.

The question came to the fore again shortly before the first black SVD seminarians were to take their perpetual vows. The occasion was a request from Superior General Gier regarding the future status of the African Americans. Father Gerard Heffels, an ex-Togo missionary who succeeded Father Christman as rector of the Bay when he died in 1929, responded to Gier's request for information with a thirty-six page memorandum. That report was very negative toward African Americans. Heffels had come to the United States in 1921, but he was new to the South when he came to the Bay in 1929 to be rector.

When Father Heffels sent his yearly report for 1930 to the generalate, he mentioned that he had also prepared a report related to the important question of the future of the black students at the Bay. When Father Gier read this, he had Father Grendel request a copy of this report. "This matter," Grendel wrote to Heffels on 17 April 1931, "should have been thought out and regulated much earlier." To move this matter along as quickly as possible, Heffels was asked to send a copy of his memo to others, including the provincial, for their comments on this issue. Father Hagspiel asked for comments from Peter Janser, now working to establish the Society in England. Janser, of course, had been deeply involved in the founding of the seminary at Bay St. Louis. All were dismayed that the status issue, which they thought had long ago been settled, was being raised. That is to say, were they to be SVDs or secular priests? Were they to found their own congregation? The generalate, before reading Heffels' report, was concerned about the future work assignments of the African-American priests. Heffels' memorandum, however, had raised once again the more basic questions discussed above. He had nothing to say about their future work.

---

21. Meier, "Die Negermission SVD," p. 87.

Heffels indicated, first, that it was morally impossible to combine the two races into one religious community in the United States and, second, that it was practically impossible to segregate the African Americans into a separate province which would be totally coequal. He then rehearsed the accusations that whites, especially in the South, have made against blacks since they were first brought from Africa, namely, that they were intellectually and morally inferior, that they cannot control their emotions and are more sensual than whites, and that they have never been taught to regard marriage vows as sacred.

Not everyone agreed with Heffels's sour assessment, and, as Meier says, paraphrasing Father Patzelt, another of the former Togo missionaries, if the pioneers of the black apostolate and original champions of the black priests were still alive, the solution to the whole issue would not have been so difficult.[22] Father Wendel had died in 1920; Fathers Christman and Heick had died in 1929. It was now 1931.

Father Heffels's report had certainly confused Father Provincial Bruno Hagspiel, who wrote the following to Father Gier on 19 May 1931. The letter is extant in the generalate archives. Hagspiel writes in English because people in the generalate wanted to practice their English, and though the style is awkward, the meaning is clear. In regard to the matter Father Heffels has raised,

> there is absolutely nothing to be discussed . . . because everything as to the education of these candidates of the colored for the priesthood has been settled from the beginning carefully and conscientiously, not only by Father Janser, who at that time was Provincial . . . furthermore by Fathers Christman and Wendel, who sponsored this cause with all the enthusiasm that was theirs, but also Bishop Gunn, at the time in charge of the Diocese of Natchez, and the whole hierarchy, and even by yourself and your council—but no doubt you forgot. You surely must remember that as early as 1922 when St. Augustine's came into existence, it was emphatically stated and approved that in that institution only such colored boys should be trained for the priesthood who at the same time would express a desire for the religious life as members of the S.V.D. The new enterprise at that time was advertised in the whole of the United States and all over the world as something unique and so different from all previous attempts in this regard for the reasons just mentioned, and in papers and magazines it was hailed as the safest solution of the racial problem in the United States as far as the training of a Catholic priesthood was concerned. It was pointed out emphatically that the Negro could never stay by himself as a secular [diocesan] priest, but that if he could be a success, he would be so only as a member of a religious community, and the Society was congratulated upon because it showed itself generous and truly Catholic in offering its services not only to train a colored priesthood but also to admit such promising candidates into our society as full-fledged members who were to work upon their ordinations for the conversion of their own race and eventually also, if there should be a superabundance, go forth to Africa or other places wherever there are pagan Negroes to work

---

22. Meier, "Die Negermission SVD," p. 101.

for their conversion. On top of all that, don't you remember, Father General, that you yourself asked the Holy Father for his blessing which the Holy Father most cheerfully granted by handing you that beautiful brief in behalf of the new seminary, opened in 1923 in Bay St. Louis? When you read those rather awkward remarks of Father Heffels, you surely must have forgotten the details of the Holy Father's letter, and therefore I take the liberty of inclosing a translation of that letter which was published soon after the original reached us in 1923, and a copy of which was forwarded at that time to every member of the American hierarchy. I take the liberty to mark with blue pencil those sentences which are of greater importance. To make the points a little clearer yet: you must remember that the Catholic hierarchy—as far as I remember not one of its members wishes to have in his diocese a colored secular priest. A colored secular priesthood is as yet unwelcome in the United States. It is a pity that such is the view not only of the layman, but even of the Catholic clergy and hierarchy. But shall we, that means you or I, or Father Heffels and all our councils taken together be able to change this sad condition, the apparently un-Catholic attitude?

One of Heffels's suggestions had been to turn St. Augustine's into an apostolic seminary and educate only those black candidates for the priesthood sent there by their bishops for their own dioceses, not for the Society of the Divine Word. Hagspiel continues:

This racial difficulty must simply be taken as a matter of fact, and it will require much time and patience yet till gradually perhaps it will disappear, gradually perhaps one, or two, or three bishops of the United States will be ready to accept secular priests into their dioceses to work among their own, and then we shall be able to approach this question with great interest. For the present and for the next ten or twenty years to come, it was thought to be the only advisable solution of training a colored priesthood to train such candidates as members of a religious community because only thus they would have a firm hold, a certain moral protection whereas otherwise no Bishop would be willing to assume the responsibility for a colored priesthood.

Father Gier did not appreciate being lectured to in this manner, and in his response said that the question he had posed had to do with the work the black priests would be doing within the Society. Yet the superior general may also have been waffling on the question of the status of the African Americans, perhaps without wanting to admit it. On the 28 March 1932, the provincial council confirmed and reiterated what the province had obligated itself to years earlier: (1) African Americans should be educated to be religious and should work primarily for the conversion of their own people, though also in other countries eventually; (2) they should be members of the Society of the Divine Word as full members of the Society; and (3) until such time as they had sufficient numbers to form an autonomous province, of necessity they would be subject to superiors not of their own race.

To all of this, Father Gier and his council agreed, but went on to add special requirements the African Americans must meet to ensure that they would measure up to the full status of being SVDs. Given the implied tone of wariness about African-American members, the requirements do not make pleasant reading today. The essence of these conditions were the following: (1) There was to be strict screening of applicants, no converts were allowed, and only children born in wedlock of recognized good Catholic families could be admitted. (2) There were to be restrictions on home vacations as a way of overcoming the supposed weakness of the African American. (3) The period of trial in temporary vows must be longer. (4) After the third year of theology, which would still be before perpetual vows, a trial year of pastoral work under direction of a priest should be introduced as another test of their vocation. (5) Superiors should not be seduced by the "magic of numbers."

These extra precautions exclusively for black SVDs made little sense. There was no basis for applying them, since up to this point the black seminarians had successfully passed through all the training and spiritual exercises that their white confreres had to follow. They had made a common novitiate with whites, their course of studies, though separate, was essentially equal, regulated not by the faculty of their respective seminaries, but by Rome itself. They lived the same common religious life and followed the same practices as all other members. These extra requirements could only proceed from a lack of understanding or prejudice, or a large bit of both. In the end, the policy was never implemented and was rejected by Father Grendel, Gier's successor. So came to an end the dispute over the status of the African-American priests that were trained and ordained at Bay St. Louis.

In the first years, most of the candidates who came to St. Augustine's and finished their education there became members of the Society of the Divine Word. Even in the first classes, however, there were some who studied at Bay St. Louis for dioceses in places such as Central America and the West Indies. These numbers declined over time as blacks were able to enter other seminaries. But it is clear that Bay St. Louis had an immense impact on breaking the barrier to the ordination of blacks in the United States, as these statistics show: By the middle of the 1960s, the total number of African-American priests in the United States was 146. Of these, 103 were religious priests and 43 were diocesan. The Society of the Divine Word claimed 54 of the religious, while 22 of the rest had received at least part of their training at Bay St. Louis.

ASSIGNING THE NEW BLACK PRIESTS

All this did not end the difficulties, since there was still the concrete question of where to assign the new black priests, and a host of questions on how they would be received. As time passed, the first four seminarians took their perpetual vows in the Society of the Divine Word. From the beginning they were educated to work among their own people, which was one of the major reasons constantly put forth to justify the effort and expense of establishing a seminary in the first place. Because no people will ever be converted except by their own race, priests of their own race must be provided for them. As Father Burgmer had said, they are not being trained for China. And here the Society ran into the same wall that the Josephites, before them, had. Bishops refused to accept black priests into their dioceses, however enthusiastic they had been that the SVD had opened a seminary to educate black priests, but always, in their thinking, as members of the Society of the Divine Word. They could always be sent to Africa or some other place where the SVD had missions.

ORDINATIONS

The ordination day of the first African Americans as members of the Society of the Divine Word was set for 23 May 1934. About that event, Stephen Ochs wrote: "The ordinations of the first four black priests from St. Augustine's seminary in 1934 represented a watershed event in the history of black priests in the United States."[23] Just as Father Provincial Peter Janser wrote to the bishops to announce the opening of the seminary at Bay St. Louis, so now Father Provincial Bruno Hagspiel wrote the 130 bishops again to tell them about the forthcoming ordination on 23 May 1934:

Fourteen years ago Father Peter T. Janser, S.V.D., then Provincial Superior of the Society of the Divine Word, submitted his plan for founding a seminary for colored candidates of the priesthood to the Hierarchy of the United States. With the approval of the Most Reverend Bishops of America, and the hearty endorsement and encouragement of the Holy Father in Rome, the plan materialized. A humble institution for the education of colored priests came into existence, and has been functioning as St. Augustine's Seminary ever since.

To-day, after fourteen years of waiting and watching, of praying and laboring, we again approach the Hierarchy of the Church, communicating to its members the joyful news that their good advice, the people's sacrifices and our own efforts have not been in vain. Four of our first seminarians have completed their long course of preparation, of studies and training. They have passed a six-year classical course, a year of religious training in the Novitiate, a year of teaching, two years of philosophy, four years of theology. Now, after having consecrated their lives to the service of God in the missionary career of the Society of the Divine Word by the profession of perpetual vows, they stand before the altar asking the Most Reverend Ordinary of the diocese to make them priests of God.

On May 23, at 9. a.m., the Most Reverend R. O. Gerow, D.D., Bishop of Natchez, will confer the holy Order of the Priesthood on Maurice Rousseve of New Orleans, Louisiana, Vincent Smith of Lebanon, Kentucky, Anthony Bourges of Lafayette, Louisiana, Francis Wade of Washington, D.C. Besides these, Philip Marin, of British Honduras, who also made his studies at St. Augustine's Seminary will receive sub-Diaconate on the same day. He will

---

23. Ochs, "Deferred Mission," p. 367.

be ordained priest at a later date for the Vicariate of Belize, British Honduras, C.A.

The great "watershed event" marked the end of a long, difficult road, which zigged and zagged as often as it ran straight. Many obstacles had to be overcome. Many also gave support, advice, and encouragement to those walking the rough road. Now came the great day, which marked the end and the beginning, for as the Society of the Divine Word continued to educate and ordain blacks, other bishops and seminaries were forced to reflect and change their policy of not accepting African Americans. St. Augustine's Seminary and the first four black ordinands broke down the barriers and paved the way for those who followed.

The crowd that came to witness this ordination exceeded all expectation. Although a tent to accommodate eight hundred people had been set up on the seminary grounds, two thousand showed up from all over the South and beyond, and this during the depths of the depression. Most of these were African Americans, who, as the *Techny Chimes* of June 1934, put it, "had come from far and near to see 'how they make a priest'." In addition, some one hundred priests and three bishops attended. *The Catholic Standard*, newspaper of the Archdiocese of New Orleans, commented in May 1934:

> The ordination of four colored priests, members of the Society of the Divine Word . . . may well mark an epoch in the missionary history of the Church in this country. The young men to be ordained will be the first colored priests of the Society of the Divine Word in this country. The Fathers of this Society have seriously undertaken to apply to the Negro missionary problem in this country the ideal of the Church in every age and country, that is, that the work of the Church be carried on by a native priesthood.
>
> It is true that there has been missionary activity among the Negroes both by diocesan and regular clergy and there have been Negro priests at work among their own people. But the foundation of St. Augustine's Seminary at Bay St. Louis a dozen years ago marked the first organized effort to secure for the Negroes of the United States the services of their own race. The seminary is devoted exclusively to this work and with the advancement of its first class to the ranks of the priesthood its success may be regarded as certain.

The course of ordinations after 1934 was not one of regular annual additions to the number of priests, since students were taken in at different ages and stages of educational development. In 1935 and 1936, for example, there were no ordinations; in 1937 two were ordained, and in 1938 there were none. Six were ordained in 1939, one of whom was white, John Kist, who finished his studies at Bay St. Louis for reasons of health. In 1940 again there was no ordination class, but in 1941 there were four. In 1940 as well, the Southern Province was created, with headquarters at Bay St. Louis, but the new province was not, as once anticipated, for African Americans only. It was and has remained a province of blacks *and* whites. Whites would remain as superiors until 1957 when Father Harold Perry became the first African American to be appointed as rector of a major seminary in America, and six years later the first to be a provincial superior.

Harry Sylvester, writing in *The Commonweal* issue of 11 April 1941, reflects on the work of the Society and the contribution made by St. Augustine's Seminary to the African-American apostolate:

> In its implications the work is so terrifying that it is only by an effort that the ordinary mind can bring itself to contemplate it . . . Other orders of priests in this country are beginning to be actively interested in work among the Negroes. The Jesuits and Redemptorists have made definite moves, and the Congregation of the Holy Cross, despite the fact that it still bars Negroes from its University of Notre Dame, has priests with Negro parishes. But none have done the truly awesome thing that this small and comparatively newly-founded order of priests has done: given to this continent native Negro priests . . . any work that the Church may ever do on this continent with the Negro can only follow where this small and poor order of priests has gone before.

STARTING THE AFRICAN-AMERICAN BROTHERHOOD

Not long after their decision to accept African Americans as seminarians, SVDs in the South decided also to recruit African Americans for the brotherhood. The first of these, still living as of the writing of this book, is now in retirement at Techny. That brother, Louis Webb, took the name of Vincent in religion. He was born in Fordyce, Arkansas, on 7 April 1908 to Wesley and Ella Webb, the seventh of ten children. At the age of seventeen he went north to Toledo, Ohio, where he found a job in a creosote plant. One Sunday his white supervisor at work, who was a Catholic, invited Louis to go to the Catholic church, St. Patrick's, for Mass. As soon as he entered, he said, he felt that this was the place for him. The next Sunday he returned on his own. It was January and to be on time he got there before 6:00 a.m. Mass, however, did not start until 7:00, so he walked around and around the block trying to keep warm, until the doors of the church were opened. Since then, he said, he has never missed Sunday Mass. Soon he realized that Catholics were also the targets of Ku Klux Klan aggression and hatred, which, of course, made him even more sympathetic to the Catholic religion, and he decided to become one himself, the only one of his family who did. Louis began to think about becoming a priest. He heard about St. Augustine's and applied there. The long course of studies for the priesthood was thought impossible for a young man who had not even finished elementary school. After a year, he left Bay St. Louis and returned to Toledo. But the idea of doing more for God stayed with him and in 1934 he returned to Bay St. Louis, this time as a candidate for the brotherhood. In 1937 he took first vows and in 1943 took perpetual vows. Though he was never assigned to missions, he did more than his share in supporting the missions in various houses of the Society throughout North America, doing what was needed, whether in the laundry, on the farm, or as cook—his usual occupation. Brother Vincent was the first of a long line of black SVD brothers who came to be respected throughout the Society.

FATHER MATTHEW CHRISTMAN AND
THE SOUTHERN MISSION

The joy of that May 1934 ordination was bittersweet for the newly ordained, because Matthew Christman, the man they most wanted to be with them was not there. He had died on 14 February 1929, two months shy of his forty-second birthday. More than anyone else, Matthew Christman was responsible for the successful development of St. Augustine's.

Father (later Bishop) Joseph Francis was ordained in 1950, and assigned after ordination as teacher and prefect to the minor seminary at the Bay. There he told the students, as he had been told by one of the first ordained graduates of the seminary: "Son, when you hear the name of Christman, bow your head!" Maurice Rousseve, a member of the first class to be ordained, had this to say about Father Christman:

> Of all the priests of the Society, I never found any to come even close to the late Father Christman our beloved Founder . . . He learned to identify himself with his black flock, working rather with them than for them. His was empathy, not sympathy . . . Wherever we went, whether in the store or on the street or in the country, he was always with us. He ate at the same table and served himself from the same dish as we ourselves . . . Everywhere we went the whites called us Father Christman's boys and gave us all respect. He wished us to KNOW our people, and so he kept the first students well supplied with papers from the Black Press . . . He'd burn with indignation whenever he learned of any injustice anywhere . . . He was a true Man of God, a devoted son of the Church, and an exemplary priest and religious.

Overworked, worn out, clearly in need of a long rest after years of worry over finances and all the other concerns that went with running the seminary, including the wanton prejudice, antagonism, and threats he and his students had to endure, Christman had been unwell for some time. On the day he died he went to New Orleans with Father Gmelch to consult a heart specialist. The doctor advised him to commit himself to the hospital for treatment. This was not possible, Father Christman insisted. He had so much to do at Bay St. Louis. That night he died of a heart attack. Dying as young as he did in the new community, however, he was the first to be buried in the cemetery on the grounds of the seminary to which he had devoted his life.

WHERE TO ASSIGN THE NEW PRIESTS

As joyous as the day of ordination was, behind the scenes people were scurrying around trying desperately to find work that the newly ordained would be allowed to do. The American Catholic world, both its blacks and whites, was watching to see if the experiment would succeed and where it would lead to. Sending them to the foreign mission was apparently not even considered. For a time it was suggested that one be assigned as assistant in St. Rose of Lima parish in Bay St. Louis, that one be sent to Rome for higher studies, and that two be assigned as teacher and prefect at the seminary. But it was generally felt that they had become priests to work as pastors among their own people.

Cardinal Pietro Fumasoni-Biondi had told SVD Superior General Joseph Grendel that when he had been apostolic delegate to the United States from 1922 to 1933 he had asked all the southern bishops if they were prepared to assign parishes to black priests. All had answered that they would. Nevertheless, now they all refused, citing the difficulties they foresaw if they took a black priest into their diocese. A way of getting around the Southern bishops would be to make a Divine Word Missionary the bishop of a diocese that contained many African Americans. Such a bishop would have jurisdiction over both whites and blacks, but would be able to withstand the opposition that was sure to erupt. It was also suggested that an auxiliary bishop could be assigned to a diocese to take charge of African Americans. Unable to find a satisfactory solution, SVD Provincial Superior Bruno Hagspiel went to consult with Cardinal George Mundelein on 22 March 1933. Hagspiel sent his summary of the meeting to Grendel two days later. In it he related that Mundelein judged it impossible to assign black priests to Chicago and advised that they be assigned to "some parish work among Catholic Negroes of the State of Louisiana, either in the archdiocese of New Orleans or in the diocese of Lafayette, or the one of Alexandria."

Mundelein's reasons for not wanting the black priests in the North are a repetition of long discarded reasoning, but he at least gave Hagspiel a positive direction. At this point the rector of St. Augustine's, Father Heffels, was asked to consult with Bishops Richard Gerow of the Jackson, Mississippi, Diocese; Jules Jeanmard of the Lafayette, Louisiana, Diocese; and Daniel Desmond of the Alexandria, Louisiana, Diocese. Bishop Desmond, a northerner, was new to the South. None were interested in having the young SVD black priests work in their dioceses.

On 31 May 1933, Hagspiel made a second visit to Cardinal Mundelein. Hagspiel reported to Grendel in a letter of 3 June 1933 that the idea of a special prelature for blacks (*praelatura nullius* in Latin terminology) had come up, and that Hagspiel was advised by Cardinal Mundelein to contact the new apostolic delegate, Archbishop Amleto Cicognani, and invite him to exert his influence. Mundelein promised that he would ask Cicognani to do just this. The apostolic delegate arranged to meet with Cardinal Mundelein and Bishops Gerow, Jeanmard, and Desmond at a meeting of the American bishops in November 1933 to decide the assignment of the SVD's African-American priests who had not yet been ordained. No SVD representative was present to argue for the Society's position. Afterward, Cardinal Mundelein reported to Hagspiel that Jeanmard had backed away from his willingness to take them in the Lafayette Diocese, and that Gerow expressed a willingness to accept them in his diocese, but only in Bay St. Louis at the seminary and St. Rose of Lima parish. At this point, Bishop Desmond of Alexandria offered to accept all of the new priests into his diocese.

As soon as the details of the meeting became available on 3 December 1933, Patzelt wrote to Father Provincial Hagspiel, his very good friend and classmate, that Alexandria would be a disaster for the black priests. Introducing them into the diocese as Desmond suggested would almost surely result in failure. On 13 December 1933, Bishop Desmond published the details of his plans to build a house for the small community of black priests in Mansura, Louisiana, in Avoyelles Parish, where they would care for the eight hundred black parishioners of St. Paul's and direct a school for boys the bishop intended to develop. They would also look after black Catholics in the outlying districts of Bunkie and Moreauville. There had been no consultation on or approval of these plans by the SVD provincial and superior general. In fact, Bishop Desmond had not even consulted his own priests or advisers about any of this. Thus nearly everyone involved mounted opposition to the plans. To all opposition Desmond insinuated, and sometimes stated very clearly, that he was being asked to do this by the apostolic delegate, that this was something in which the Holy Father himself was very interested. Nevertheless, because of the opposition he had stirred up, Desmond had to change his original plans. The next time, however, he consulted his priests and advisers, all of whom signed on to the changes, many of them reluctantly. Partly because of this reluctance on the part of some of his own clergy, Desmond practically insisted that Father William Brambrink, a Divine Word Missionary who later joined the ranks of the diocesan clergy, be assigned to the South to introduce and supervise the black priests into their ministry. Desmond had gotten to know Brambrink when they were both in the Boston area and wanted him as director of the African-American priests to smooth the way with his own white priests. As far as the SVD was concerned, the insistence on the Brambrink assignment was yet another mistake.

Father Patzelt, in a letter of 16 December 1933, quotes Bishop Jeanmard of Lafayette as saying about the entire decision:

> At the *conciliabulum* in Washington he was sitting on hot coals and practically was convinced [to take the African-American priests into his diocese], but Bishop Desmond reacted too quickly since he had been in the South only a year, and did not sufficiently know the situation and the true feeling of the people: above all, the publication of the plan could be disastrous.[24]

In the meantime, by 15 February 1934, Bishop Jeanmard had stated his willingness to Patzelt to accept the African-American priests into the Lafayette Diocese. He too had the plan all worked out. Under it, he would establish a parish out of which the priests could work in the black apostolate as assistants under a white priest as nominal pastor. He would do this under several conditions, and required utmost secrecy on everyone's part. He also wanted the change of venue for the introduction of the priests to come from the apostolic delegate so as to avoid any possible difficulties with Bishop Desmond.

A letter written by the apostolic delegate to Hagspiel on 16 May 1934, however, repeated all the details of Desmond's altered plans, even to the detail of his wanting Brambrink to introduce the black priests.[25] Hagspiel replied, expressing chagrin that Desmond's plans were still under consideration, because the superior general, in the meantime, had suggested the compromise solution of sending two

---

24. Meier, "Die Negermission SVD," p. 114.
25. The letter is preserved in the SVD Generalate Archives in Rome.

of the four black priests to Alexandria and two to Lafayette. This was not an ideal solution, but one that would be the best possible for Desmond, who had made everything so public that he could back down now only with great difficulty. By this time, too, the apostolic delegate wanted to get out of the dispute and left the entire matter to be solved by Father Hagspiel, delegating to him the task of explaining any further changes in plans to Bishop Desmond. It was now 13 June 1934; and the four new African-American priests had been ordained and had spent their time traveling through the South giving talks, saying Mass in different colored parishes, conducting missions, waiting to take up their first assignments in September. They were doing all this with great success.

Five days after the apostolic delegate had turned the whole problem over to him, on 18 June 1934, Father Hagspiel wrote a long letter (preserved in SVD generalate archives, Rome) to Bishop Desmond. It constitutes an excellent summary of everything that had occurred in the discussions on placing the SVD's first four African-American priests. Diplomatically but firmly, Hagspiel says that Lafayette is the choice.

1. The diocese of Lafayette (contrary to Your Excellency's view, as expressed to me during my visit in Alexandria) with its 50,000 or more Negro Catholics, is evidently a far better field for a pastoral start, and for a definite religious community house of our colored priests than Alexandria with its approximately 4,000 Catholic Negroes.

2. The more congenial attitude of the population (colored and white) in Lafayette territory towards the Colored priests will mean a great deal, nay everything, in the further development of the newly ordained priests. While in Avoyelles of the diocese of Alexandria, the type of the population, their character and temperament, is in itself by no means the right pastoral material for the new priests, and while the opposition to the latter is still sufficiently evident, there need be no fear and apprehension whatever in this regard in the diocese of Lafayette. Let it be remembered that it always has been Lafayette where we for years had planned to place our colored priests, but because of the rather reserved attitude of Bishop Jeanmard, could not come to any terms until of late. We are grateful to the Lord for His Excellency's change of mind in this regard. We appreciate it more than we can say. I wish to state here once more emphatically, that it was only because of our own frequent, and rather insistent and pleading requests, especially since we ourselves got aware of the far less favorable conditions in Avoyelles, that he became a "convert" to the cause, realizing that actually there would be hardly any opposition in his territory, and the prospect for the further development for the Colored clergy in his diocese much more promising than anywhere else. It stands to reason that only the best and most congenial district should be definitely chosen for the new priests, for their first pastoral activities.

Bishop Desmond sent a telegram on 21 June 1934 to Father Hagspiel.

Your letter of eighteenth in which you exposed the plan of beginning colored project is on hand. My sincere good wishes for you all in the work. Maybe at some future date the Diocese of Alexandria may have its community.

THEIR ASSIGNMENT BEGINS

The new African-American priests were assigned to the new parish of the Immaculate Heart of Mary, which Bishop Jeanmard had established for them in Lafayette, with Father H. J. Patzelt, who lived not far away at Holy Rosary Institute, appointed as pastor. Thus the four black priests were assigned to be his assistants, and he was responsible for introducing them into the work of the ministry. Among other things he was to make sure they abided by all the southern rules of etiquette between whites and blacks, rules that did not change just because they were now priests, at least not according to Patzelt's thinking. Over the years of his work in the South, Patzelt had picked up much of the paternalism so characteristic of white priests working in the South. Among other things, the black priests had to be kept in their proper place in society, as a symbol of which they were not to shake a white man's hand, including that of a white priest. They were not allowed to accept dinner invitations from white priests, nor were they allowed to substitute at neighboring black parishes if the white pastor was ill or wanted to go on vacation.

The arrangements for administering the parish were sometimes strange. Although Patzelt never went to Immaculate Heart of Mary to celebrate Mass in the five years he was pastor, he hired all parish help, handled all the parish funds, and even picked up the parish mail. According to the author's personal correspondence with Father Anthony Hemphill, SVD, when Patzelt delivered it, he would honk the horn, and one of the black priests would come out to get the mail. When complaints were later lodged against him, Patzelt laid all the blame for complaints against him on his "special assistant," Father Smith, or on people in the seminary who, he claimed, were stirring up race consciousness, not only among the seminarians but also among the colored priests.

After five years of this arrangement, in perhaps the most acrimonious chapter in black-white SVD relations, Father Patzelt was removed as pastor of Immaculate Heart of Mary by Father Hugo Aubry who had succeeded Father Hagspiel as provincial. By this time, two new black priests had been ordained, Clarence Howard and Francis Wells. With Patzelt removed, Anthony Bourges was made pastor at Immaculate Heart of Mary, and Francis Wade, pastor of the parish in Duson, Louisiana. The newly ordained Father Howard was assigned as assistant to Bourges, and the newly ordained Father Wells as assistant to Wade. Maurice Rousseve was assigned as assistant to Cosmas Schneider, the white SVD priest at St. Martinville, Louisiana. Vincent Smith was assigned to inner-Society promotion work and to give missions in various parishes. Father Aubry was certainly right to note in a letter of 13 January 1939 to Father John Gasper, which I found in the Techny archives, that this "really meant a new phase in the development of our colored confreres in the South."

Watched by priests and laity, by both blacks and whites, by bishops and cardinals, and even by the pope himself, the four priests were definitely put on the spot.

In the judgment of any fair-minded person, they marked the way for those who were to follow and set a high standard of service. None of them were Uncle Toms, as they were sometimes accused of being by some blacks who favored confrontation as the high road to equality. Nevertheless, they made their own statements of independence, as a story that occurred after the death of Pope Pius XI shows. Every parish church celebrated a Solemn Mass for the deceased pope, including the cathedral parish. According to Stephen Ochs, though Father Bourges knew that black priests were expected not to attend functions at the cathedral, he had received an invitation from Bishop Jeanmard, so he went to the Mass for the dead pope. Monsignor Anthony Isenberg received him coolly as Bourges passed through the receiving line. That evening, the monsignor dined with Father Patzelt, according to their usual custom, and the next morning Patzelt told Bourges that Isenberg wished to see him. When Bourges arrived, Isenberg accused him of taking advantage of his light skin and his priesthood by attending the service. Ochs preserves the rest of this incident using Bourges's recollections: Bourges calmly told Isenberg that he intended to take up the matter with the bishop. The next morning Bourges called on Bishop Jeanmard and recounted his conversation with Isenberg. Jeanmard claimed that he had heard no complaints about the black priests and dismissed Isenberg's comments, "Some old crank must have said that." Isenberg gave Bourges no further trouble.[26]

We have said the first four black priests set a high standard for those who followed. At least a few details about their lives and later careers are in order.

Father Vincent Smith, born near the Trappist monastery in Gethsemani, Kentucky, in 1894, had always wanted to be a Trappist contemplative. At the time, this was impossible, because, as the twelfth of thirteen children, he had to go to work when he was seventeen. At the age of twenty-seven, he joined the SVD. When new priests from later classes were added to the parishes in Louisiana, Smith was set free to give missions and talks around the country, both North and South. He was much in demand and did an excellent job for twelve years, until he was eventually assigned to black parishes that the Society of the Divine Word had taken over in New Jersey. The desire to join the Trappists remained with him, however, gently calling him to his first love, the monastery. Because he was doing such a good job as pastor of Our Lady of the Divine Shepherd in Trenton, New Jersey, his provincial superior, Father Robert Hunter, urged him to postpone his application to the Trappists. Finally, Hunter gave in, and in 1948 Smith was admitted to Gethsemani. As soon as he finished his novitiate in Kentucky, he was sent to the new Trappist monastery of Christ the King in the Genesee Valley in upper western New York, now as Father Mary Simon. At Christ the King he became novice master, a clear recognition both of his ability and of his deep spirituality, an office he held, however, only a few months before he died of a heart attack on 11 March 1952, the first of the four to die.

Father Francis Wade was born in Maryland, and from early on he wanted to be a priest, but there was no place to go. His family moved to Washington, D.C., where

---

26. Ochs, "Deferred Mission," p. 385.

he went to school and grew up. While working in an office in New York as a young man, he learned about the Graymoor Friars, a group of former Episcopalian Franciscans who had joined the Catholic Church as a group. He thought perhaps they might accept him. This they did, but as a brother, not a priest. He stayed with the Graymoor Friars as Brother Benedict for seven years. When St. Augustine's was opened, knowing of his great desire to be a priest, Graymoor released him from his vows and with a strong letter of recommendation sent him to Bay St. Louis, which he entered on 13 September 1924, at the age of 30. Having had Latin and high school already, he advanced rapidly to ordination with his class in 1934. Wade spent all his priestly life in parish work in and around the area where he had started. He was pastor for seventeen years in Lafayette at Immaculate Heart of Mary parish, where he had begun his priestly work. Wherever he went, he was well liked and very successful, because he was always totally dedicated to those who were committed to his care. Not flashy nor an activist, he lived the life of his parishioners, sharing in their poverty and humility. He concluded the little talk he gave on the fortieth anniversary of Immaculate Heart of Mary parish, which coincided with the fortieth anniversary of his ordination, with the words:

It's forty years that I've been working. I am not able to work anymore. Sometimes I fall. I have to go up and down steps slowly. It's hard for me to get in and out of a car. There are a lot of things, but I'm not complaining. I've been so happy these forty years. I am happy here now. Thank you for all you did to help me to work for you. God love you.

Father Wade died two years later, on 28 February 1976, of a massive stroke, at the age of eighty-two, rich in the grace of the God he served so long and so faithfully.

Father Maurice Rousseve came to the Society of the Divine Word by way of the Josephites, Since they were no longer accepting young boys as candidates for the priesthood, many Josephite priests urged boys from their parishes who might have a vocation to apply to St. Augustine's. On a trip to New Orleans to check out possible recruits for the seminary he planned to open in Greenville, Mississippi, Father Christman also interviewed young Maurice, who had already contacted him about becoming a priest. Maurice came to Greenville in the fall of 1920 at the age of fourteen. As one of the first entrants to the seminary, he shared in the difficulties, the privations and hostility of the early years. Maurice was very bright and was duly ordained with his classmates in 1934. After his period of introduction under Patzelt, during which time he also went about giving missions, talks, sermons, and later also substituting in other parishes, he was assigned as an assistant to Father Schneider in 1939. This was in St. Martinville in the Lafayette diocese. Two years later he became pastor, soon after which he was able to put up a new convent for the nuns, Sisters of the Blessed Sacrament, who taught in his school, the first time ever that white nuns worked under the supervision of a black pastor. There was talk, but Father Rousseve handled it smoothly and diplomatically, while Mother Katharine Drexel, the foundress of the Sisters of the Blessed Sacrament, must have been proud of her nuns. The SVD provincial appointed a white priest to be Rousseve's assistant—another first. One Sunday, indeed, the pastor of the white parish in town invited Rousseve to say Mass for the white men's quarterly communion. According to Albert Foley's account,[27] one of the Knights of Columbus, a completely white organization at this time, served Father Rousseve's Mass, thanked him for coming and shook hands with him, this in a parish that Patzelt insisted would never accept a colored priest. After ten years of successful parish and mission preaching, Rousseve was transferred back to Bay St. Louis, where he was made prefect (dean) of the theology students. After this he returned to parish work until he "retired" back to Immaculate Heart of Mary parish where he and his three classmates had begun their fruitful work as SVD missionaries. The last years of his life were spent at St. John Berchman's Manor in New Orleans. He died there and was buried at Bay St. Louis on December 30, 1985.

Father Anthony Bourges, born on 7 January 1904, grew up in Lafayette, Louisiana. He applied to Sacred Heart College, the seminary for blacks in Greenville, and entered in August 1921. Part of his assignment at Immaculate Heart of Mary was to work among the blacks in outlying areas, many of whom had been baptized as infants but had never really had much chance to learn about or practice their faith. Soon he had developed the nucleus of a parish in Scott, where he was actually born, and in Duson, where he soon took up his residence. When Patzelt relinquished his position as pastor, Bourges was appointed first as administrator and later as pastor of Immaculate Heart of Mary, a position he held for eleven successful and fruitful years. The whites in Lafayette became accustomed to having black priests in their city and began accepting them as full-fledged Catholic clergymen, even coming to them for confession. When Rousseve was appointed to the seminary, Bourges took over the parish in St. Martinville. His entire priestly life was spent as pastor of various parishes: Immaculate Heart of Mary in Lafayette, Louisiana, where he was the first black pastor, from 1939 to 1950; Notre Dame in St. Martinville, Louisiana, from 1950 to 1962; Holy Ghost Parish, Jackson, Mississippi, from 1962 to 1972; St. Gabriel's, Mound Bayou, Mississippi, the all-black town near Merigold, from 1972 to 1978; Waco, Texas, from 1978 to 1983. He moved for the final time when he left Waco and went to Bay St. Louis to retire. For the last few months of his life, Father Bourges was confined to the Lafon Nursing Home in New Orleans, his warm, cheerful personality intact till the end came on 6 November 1991, the last of the four pioneers to die.

THE QUESTION OF AN AUTONOMOUS PROVINCE

Recall that to avoid the problems that some feared would eventuate if black and white SVDs lived and worked together, it was originally thought that black SVDs would eventually form a province that would be directly under the superior general. The Southern Province was erected in 1940, but not as a province made up exclusively of African Americans. When the province was split off from Techny,

---

27. Foley, *God's Men of Color*, p. 138.

the numbers of African Americans, to be sure, did not warrant it, but more importantly the relations between white and black SVDs in the South were such that
there was no need for separation. There never really was. Black SVDs would be
as SVD as anybody else. In fact, at least as far back as 1920, many had pushed for
an independent Southern Province. This was long before there were any black
priests to integrate into the Society. By the time African-American priests started
to be ordained in greater numbers, there was no longer the same pressing need for
separation into an autonomous all-black province, as had been suggested by
Cardinal Valfre much earlier, much less that they should form a separate religious
congregation. Black and white priests and brothers were effectively integrated long
before the Civil Rights Movement forced the South to acknowledge the injustice
of its system. The brothers had been integrated and were living together, recreat-
ing together, eating together, since the 1930s when Brother Theophane was
assigned to the Bay. Shortly after this, three more white brothers were sent to the
South from Europe. The major seminary was also integrated when seminarian John
Kist became ill and requested a transfer to Bay St. Louis to finish his studies. Quiet
and unostentatious as he was, he passed his seminary time without incident, as did
the brothers. As uneventful as it was, they made history as the first to study and
work at an all-Negro school with Negroes in Mississippi.

The seminary at the Bay was openly and obviously integrated in 1950 when
four white seminarians came to the Bay to finish their theology. As small as their
numbers were, they posed a challenge to the Jim Crow system and the seminary
almost lost its exemption from taxes of the state of Mississippi. In the meantime,
American society as a whole was also beginning to change. Was the process always
smooth? Father Elmer Powell, a black SVD priest, remarked in 1965, when racial
tensions were running high in America:

> One must say that the SVD was instrumental in making the American
> Church see and remedy to some extent her awful sin of refusing qualified
> black men admission to the ranks of the priesthood. The pioneer members
> of the Society in the southern U.S.A. underwent verbal and bodily assaults
> from prejudiced whites for living with blacks and promoting the education
> of blacks.[28]

THE RIPPLING EFFECTS OF STARTING
ST. AUGUSTINE'S SEMINARY

The apostolate of the Society of the Divine Word among the African Americans
and its efforts to educate and introduce African Americans to the Catholic priesthood had an impact on the church in America far greater than the modest numbers
would seem to warrant. Their success changed such stereotypes as those that held
that blacks could not master Latin and Greek, let alone philosophy and theology.
Another prejudice that fell in the face of their dedicated work and the upright and
spiritual life of which they were models was the position that African Americans

---

28. *Word in the World* (1994–1995): 192.

did not have the moral fiber to live a priest's life. The early African-American members of the Society of the Divine Word, brothers and priests alike, lived exemplary lives of poverty, chastity, and obedience. The final argument dragged on the longest, the idea that blacks would never accept or respect priests of their own color and preferred white priests, but it too died in the face of the reception of the black priests who came out of Bay St. Louis. The seminary, small as it was, became an inspiration to black youths to study for the priesthood in other orders and for the dioceses that now began to open their doors to blacks as a result of the example of the Bay. St. Augustine's graduates were educating white priests and bishops and members of other religious orders, whether they realized this or not. Father Pastorelli, who had closed down the Josephite effort to ordain black priests, as he watched the work of the early black Divine Word Missionaries, wrote a memo to himself to bring up again the issue of a black priesthood and brotherhood to his Josephite confreres:

> We might as well face the cold fact that we will be compelled to staff our southern parishes little by little with colored priests of our own Society— else the people will clamor for Colored priests not of our own Society. Even bishops will eventually reach this conclusion. We have allowed feeling, yes even I will say prejudice to blind us to our best interests. Time to arise and to wake up to the needs and present and coming conditions.[29]

At about this time, according to Stephen Ochs, the Benedictine monks of St. Vincent's Archabbey in Latrobe, Pennsylvania, met in chapter to discuss the question of admitting black men as candidates. The conclusion was a declaration that race would no longer be a consideration when it came to admitting applicants to St. Vincent's. The ripples were spreading out across the land. According to Ochs's research, by 1950, twenty-three male religious orders and seventeen diocesan seminaries admitted blacks, including New Orleans. Nevertheless, there were still seminaries that did not accept blacks, but the barrier had been broken through.

Influenced by post-World War II events such as Harry Truman's integration of United States armed forces, and the Civil Rights Movement that began in 1954 with the Supreme Court's Brown versus Board of Education decree, St. Augustine's Seminary at Bay St. Louis continued to educate African Americans for the priesthood and brotherhood. It was not untouched by the events of these decades. In fact, St. Augustine's was accused by blacks who were struggling against the Jim Crow system as being a Jim Crow school and just another expression of a Jim Crow Catholic Church. The seminary at Bay St. Louis, however, was not to keep blacks oppressed, but to educate, liberate, and give opportunity to African Americans when most efforts on the part of whites, using Jim Crow measures, were intending exactly the opposite. St. Augustine's was not a direct attack on Jim Crow, but it was one of the death-dealing blows that would destroy the system. Moved by a sense of justice, its founders believed that the Catholic priesthood must be open to

---

29. Quoted in Ochs, "Deferred Mission," p. 397.

African Americans.[30] In forcing other seminaries and religious congregations to rethink their policies of refusing blacks entry to their schools, the Society of the Divine Word and St. Augustine's Seminary were part of the onslaught by conscientious Christians that over time had a major impact not only on American Catholic society, but on American society as such.

The South was the first battlefield in the struggle to create a more just and integrated United States. Within a few years, the struggle moved North, to the cities where millions of blacks found themselves in conditions as bad as the ones they had left in the South. Many northern blacks began to question the value of integration, which they perceived as paying too little attention to themselves as a people with the need to retain identity and pride for who and what they were. Integration, it was said, ran the risk of fostering assimilation and loss of the strengths blacks must bring into the relationship between blacks and whites. These highly charged currents of social consciousness still pulse through relations between blacks and whites and are even reflected in the lives and goals of two of the first SVD African-American bishops, graduates of St. Augustine's. Telling a little of their story will be a fitting conclusion of this long chapter.

St. Augustine's was founded to educate and ordain African-American priests. But from its ranks of some seventy priests it has also produced nine bishops.[31] The first graduate to become a bishop, Joseph Bowers, was born in the West Indies and was sent as a missionary to the Gold Coast, now Ghana. The next appointment of an SVD African-American bishop, this time for the United States itself, has its origin in Ghana with a 1964 letter from Father Charles Erb, a white SVD missionary there. He wrote on his own initiative to the apostolic delegate in the United States and to every bishop in America, urging the appointment of a black bishop in the United States. In the letter, Erb refers to race riots that were occurring around the United States, but most concretely in his home town, Rochester, New York. African newspapers, Erb reported, were alleging that churches were giving mere lip service to the plight of American "Negroes." He went on to say that the American church is "limping with prudence."

He inquires whether there is not one of the 147 black priests in the United States capable of becoming a bishop.

> Perhaps there are some reasons why my suggestions are out of order, but I am unaware of them. I'm a bush missionary with plenty of problems of my own. But be convinced, Your Excellency, we here in Africa are very much concerned with what goes on in the United States. It affects our missionary work. Be assured also, our Catholics here are praying earnestly for God's blessings on what you are doing for the Church at the [Second Vatican] Council.

Erb received a variety of responses. Most were, frankly speaking, patronizing. They either said that a black bishop would be appointed when an "adequately qualified

---

30. See Edwin Cabey, "Liberation and the SVD," *Word in the World* (Techny, Ill.: Society of the Divine Word, 1976): 142–47.

31. Archives of the Southern Province, provided by Provincial Clifton Labbé.

man" was found or downplayed the importance of the riots as "outbreaks of irresponsible mobs" that "actually set back the cause of our Negro people." One, for example, told Erb that "it is quite evident that you are badly informed with regard to conditions existing generally in the United States, even as compared to Africa . . . I would recommend that you read another side of the picture in the literature on the subject."

Harold R. Perry. Whether Erb's letter had anything to do with the matter, it was a year and a week later, on 9 September 1965, that Pope Paul VI appointed Harold R. Perry, SVD, auxiliary to the Archbishop of New Orleans. Bishop Perry, born on 9 October 1916 in Lake Charles, Louisiana, was the first African American in the twentieth century to be named a Catholic bishop and the first ever in the South. He was forty-eight and wonderfully qualified by a variety of works performed with great competence, including serving as provincial superior of the SVD Southern Province. Perry came from an exemplary home and was one of several siblings who rose high. Although Bishop Perry's parents had not even finished primary school, they made sure each one of their children went on to college and beyond. Two brothers became dentists, a third the first black cancer surgeon in the United States. One sister was a teacher and the second a homemaker for her doctor-husband. All of them were staunch in their Catholic identity as well.

Many expectations were piled on Perry's shoulders. The Civil Rights Movement was sweeping the whole country. Some in the movement were turning to violence. Black nationalism was on the rise. Just as this cauldron of hatred and anger was starting to boil over, Perry was ordained bishop. Many were hoping he would be the Catholic Martin Luther King, Jr., but Perry rejected the comparison. He displayed less a political and activist orientation and was more dedicated to an inner-church, pastoral life, which would, he judged, also be an important part of the solution of the problems of his people. In his response to the pope's appointment he said:

> I am also aware that this signal appointment will have a meaningful impact and a special significance for many sections of the United States. It is my resolve to lift their hopes for a life of Christian dignity and to stimulate their desire for virtuous living here on earth and eternal life hereafter. With God's help I sincerely pledge myself to accomplish these religious objectives.[32]

Yet in many ways he was like King as a reconciler, and he had a passion for justice and peace. Like King, he was concerned with tearing down the walls of segregation, but always with true equality as the goal. As the movement took a turn toward violence and a reemphasis on segregation and even separation, this time demanded by many blacks, Perry suffered frustration and rejection, even from his fellow African Americans. Still, Harold Perry was the first and served as model for African Americans who followed him into the episcopate. When he died on 17 July

---

32. *Divine Word Messenger* (January–February, 1966): 30.

1991, he had just celebrated the silver anniversary of his ordination as bishop, and in his last years had suffered from Alzheimer's.

Joseph Francis. Present and speaking at Perry's funeral was Bishop Joseph Francis, the second African-American member of the Society of the Divine Word to become a bishop.[33] In 1976 he had been appointed auxiliary bishop to Archbishop Peter Gerety in Newark, New Jersey. Francis, like Perry, was well prepared in his family as a Christian. His parents' educational attainments were meager, but they were hard-working and insisted that their four children be educated. His two sisters became teachers and his brother became an attorney and later president of Xavier University in New Orleans. After ordination on 7 October 1950, Francis earned a master's degree from Catholic University and became dean of students in the seminary at Bay St. Louis. Later he directed the largest coeducational high school in the South in his hometown, Lafayette, Louisiana. For several years he worked in parishes until he was transferred to California to become the founding director of Verbum Dei High School in 1962, three years before the devastating riots there, riots that left Verbum Dei untouched because its reputation in Watts was sterling and its principal, Joseph Francis, was respected as a community leader.

After serving at Verbum Dei, Francis became the second provincial of the new SVD Western Province centered in California and then provincial of the Southern Province. During that time as a major superior, he was elected president of the Conference of Major Superiors of Men and of the Black Clergy Caucus. In the ten years that had passed since Perry's appointment, things had changed in the Civil Rights Movement, and the approach of Francis to such questions as segregation versus integration, black identity and culture, confrontation, and separation mirrored these changes. In a newspaper article written when he was ordained bishop, Francis said: "My early teachers in the Society of the Divine Word taught me that black is beautiful long before I was able to say 'Black is beautiful.' But they also made me realize that it is not sufficient to be beautiful . . . one must also do beautiful things for those to whom God has sent one."[34]

Bishop Joseph Francis could be frank and forthright, even confrontational, especially in matters having to do with racism, oppression, or injustice. The motto on his coat of arms was, "Justice, Peace, Liberty," and to these he dedicated his life. One way he and his fellow black bishops—ten of them by now—pursued these goals was by writing a pastoral letter, "What We Have Seen and Heard: A Pastoral Letter on Evangelization From the Black Bishops of the United States." Bishop Francis was the chairman of this committee, which issued the letter on 9 September 1984. It is divided into two parts, the first on the contribution that blacks and black spirituality can make to the church as a whole: the gifts of contemplation, holism as contrasted with dualism, joy, and emphasis on community. By "contemplative spirituality" the letter meant the spontaneity and all-pervasiveness of prayer that

---

33. In the ten years between Perry's and Francis's ordinations, a Josephite and a diocesan priest had been made bishops as well.

34. From a special issue of *Divine Word Messenger* (Summer 1976): 48, celebrating Bishop Francis's ordination.

characterized black spirituality, with its sense that God is to be found and recognized everywhere. Black spirituality is also holistic, with a sense that emotions, the feelings, the body, as well as mind and spirit are good. Black spirituality, they said, is joyous and should bring that sense of joy in religion to others. Finally, community, beginning with the family, is very important in black spirituality. This is so even to the point, as the letter states, that "even children conceived outside of marriage were cherished and given a place in the extended family."

> Part two indicts the racism that still exists in the Catholic Church and is a call to denounce racism as a sin and to work for justice and inner renewal . . . This racism, at once subtle and masked, still festers within our Church as within our society . . . Our demand for recognition, our demand for leadership roles in the task of evangelization, is not a call of separatism but a pledge of our commitment to the Church.

Earlier the letter had defined evangelization to mean:

> Not only preaching but witnessing; not only conversion but renewal; not only entry into the community but the building up of the community; not only hearing the Word but sharing it . . . Unless *all* are free, *none* are free.

Almost certainly Bishop Francis would have been named a bishop of a diocese had his health been better. He had had heart surgery before his appointment as bishop. He spoke of this experience as "no big thing," but he had to be careful of his diet and exercise regularly for the rest of his life. He died on 1 September 1997, just after he had finished his daily exercise. He was seventy-four.

Differences between the styles and emphases of Bishops Perry and Francis can be explained by the change in the tenor of the times in the decade between their appointments. These differences are clear in their coats of arms, a heraldic device chosen by a bishop to be a symbol of his sense of vocation. It has this role today rather than what it once had as an emblem of his position of honor and power in

the church and society as a member of the ruling class.

The issue of *Divine Word Messenger* celebrating Bishop Perry's appointment, explains his coat of arms, noting that his shield is vermeil (red), above—the liturgical color of love and the Holy Spirit—and contains a dove, a symbol of the Holy Spirit. It is azure (blue) beneath—the color of the limitless sky—and indicates that love should be boundless, transcending creed or culture, caste or color. The flaming torch is pointed out as the symbol of faith in Christ and of his love for us as the Light of the World is upheld by two clasped hands symbolizing the love for one another which is the sign whereby, "all men will know that your are my disciples" (John 14:35), a gesture of good will and cooperation.

The fleur-de-lis on Perry's coat of arms alludes to his Louisiana origins and the founding of the Louisiana Territory by the French. His motto is a verse taken from the Pentecostal hymn *Veni Creator Spiritus* ("Come, Holy Spirit") and reads, *Infunde amorem cordibus* ("Pour love into our hearts"). Choosing this verse from a hymn to the Holy Spirit was meant to recall the devotion to the Holy Spirit that the Society of the Divine Word received as a legacy from Arnold Janssen.

All things considered, his was a traditional, noncontroversial coat of arms.

Bishop Joseph Francis' was quite different.

This shield is divided in half horizontally. In the center of the upper red field is a gold cross flanked on each side by a broken black chain. This cross is a symbol of Christ who frees us by his death on that cross and is, therefore, the sign of our ultimate liberation. The chain is the symbol of the bishop's slave ancestry and symbolized the violence that separated his people from their African ancestry and home and kept them in bondage in a foreign land. The cross in the center of the broken chain indicates how it was broken and symbolized the faith that sustained the bishop's ancestors in their bondage. On one side of the lower half, against a black background, is a cluster of green sugar cane stalks. They symbolize the main agricultural product in the area where the bishop was born and the hard, dirty work done by African Americans before and after slavery. They mark both oppression and survival. On the other side are the Watts towers, located in Watts, California. It was in Watts that Bishop Francis felt he had spent the most productive years of his life. The spires of the towers, two black and one silver, bespeak hope, facing ever upward. The white and black towers show the beauty of blackness as enhancing whiteness and vice versa, each contributing to the goal, each reflecting uniqueness and dignity. And his motto? "Justice, Peace, Liberty."

The day of his appointment was in the time of "Black is beautiful." The previous effort at integration was now looked upon with suspicion and skepticism by many. Black Power, not necessarily merely limited to political power, had become the battle cry of blacks, and some were pushing for total separation. Though not embracing this agenda in its totality, Bishop Francis did stand for black rights and rejected an integration that threatened black self-determination. Liberation of a sort there has been, he knew, but too many were not free to make realistic choices. True equality, he maintained, deserves real integration and must be built on a solid base that will never be reached until the burden of racism is removed from the back of both white and black. As Bishop Francis repeated often, true integration is not the kind that can be legislated. Instead, "It must first be a 'coming together of peers,' then a 'mutuality of love and service.'"[35]

CONCLUSION

In the years following Vatican II, the seminary in Bay St. Louis found itself buffeted by the same pressures and forced to undergo the same changes that affected all other educational units in the Society, and in 1967 the major seminary in Mississippi was closed. Its students went to Techny, which was in its final two years. A few months after the closure of the major seminary there, St. Augustine's became the Society's novitiate, as well as remaining the location of the high school seminary that had begun it all. In 1980, the decision was made to close the high school seminary, and this occurred in 1982, a sad decision made necessary by changing patterns in vocational recruitment. In order to provide an educational center into which African-American candidates might have an initial experience in continuity with the Southern Province's traditions, in 1983 Tolton House was opened in New Orleans, with Father Curtis Guillory as director,[36] Tolton House, a formation center where black seminarians could stay while taking college courses at Xavier University, was modeled on a house of formation opened by the Western Province in 1976 as Casa Guadalupe under the inspiration of Father Gary Riebe.[37] Both houses were a part of the trend to bring prospective candidates for the SVD into contact with the Society during their college years and to bring seminary training into the highways and byways of the world. The goal was to help the student experience pastoral and missionary life in the Society, while also staying close to their black and Hispanic/Latino roots.

By the time of its closure as a major seminary in 1967, St. Augustine's Seminary had become an anachronism. For years it was practically the only place in the

---

35. *Divine Word Messenger* (Special Issue, Summer 1976): 48. For more of Bishop Francis's ideas, see his "New Directions in the Black Apostolate," *Word in the World* (Techny, Ill.: Divine Word Missionaries, 1975). The latter article was written when he was provincial of the SVD Southern Province.

36. Guillory was ordained bishop in 1988 and at the time of writing this book is auxiliary bishop of Houston and Galveston, Texas, and chair of the United States Bishops' Committee on Mission.

37. Riebe has become a major figure among United States Hispanic and Latino theologians and at the time of writing this book is Dean of Catholic Theological Union, Chicago Province.

United States where a young black man who felt he had a vocation to the priesthood could go to test his vocation. Because of the pioneering work of this effort, other seminaries and religious orders began to accept and even actively recruit candidates from the African-American community. By its existence and because of the success of its ordinands, St. Augustine's had accomplished the historic work God willed of it. Serene in this knowledge, the SVD could move on to other forms of ministry and formation. The German pioneers, Christman, Wendel, and Janser, and the first four to be ordained, the pioneer black brothers, and many others marked a way for those following them. Their names are written large and clear in the Book of Life and will not be forgotten.

On 2 June 2000 Curtis Guillory was named Bishop of Beaumont, Texas, by Pope John Paul II, another symbol of the success of the SVD's work among African Americans. He took up his post there on 28 July 2000

11

China

Rural Missions and an Urban University

OVERVIEW

China was the first mission of the Society, and the experiences the SVD had there were to have a major impact on missions undertaken subsequently. This was all the more true since Arnold Janssen had the habit of taking successful missionaries from one mission and putting them in charge of new missions. Since China was the first, many missionaries were taken from there to begin the mission in New Guinea, Indonesia, and the Philippines. China is also important because it was here that the Society began its first foray into university work. China is important in the history of the Society of the Divine Word in North America for analogous reasons.

In the first part of this chapter on missions in China, we shall concentrate on the men who worked in rural areas, usually among the poorest of the poor, in the tumultuous years from the end of World War I through the communist revolution. Much more could and should be said about these missions, and one can only hope that the story will be told in the detail it deserves in the future. In the second half of the chapter, we will take up the story of Fu Jen University, which becomes especially important as a particularly dramatic chapter in the lives of SVD missionaries caught up in a maelstrom of bloodshed, violence, and radical social change.

The first Americans to go to the foreign missions, Clifford King and Robert Clark, were sent to China. We have already discussed them in an earlier chapter. The bulk of SVD missionaries in China, however, were German by nationality, although some of these had studied in the United States. Others worked in China and were later sent to the United States. Peter Janser, whom we have also already met, began his work in the United States and then went to China. Over the years some sixty or more missionaries from the United States were assigned to China. Because of the strategic position of the United States in Chinese affairs, however, and through their connections with the Catholic Church in the United States, American members of the Society had an influence on the work of the SVD in China that went beyond their relatively small numbers.

THE FOUNDATION OF THE CHINA MISSION

As in so many other areas in this history, so also the story of the American SVD in China begins with Arnold Janssen. The Society was founded in 1875, and in 1879 the decision was made to send John Baptist Anzer, one of Janssen's cofounders, and a diocesan priest who had only entered the Society in August 1878, Joseph Freinademetz. On Sunday, 20 April 1879, the two landed in Hong Kong. They would work in China the rest of their lives.

Father Freinademetz had a great impact on how subsequent SVD missions were conducted, not just in China but around the world, and thus on the ideals and concrete practices of the way many Americans worked in the missions. For this reason he and his methods need to be described. Freinademetz had been a priest for three years before entering the new society. He entered because he felt he was called to go to China as a missionary. Janssen, for his part, was anxious to get members into mission work to give his rapidly growing student body and the brothers something concrete for which to strive. No sooner had they arrived than Janssen began urging them to send descriptions of their work, of the people they lived among, their customs, anything that might be useful for promotion purposes.

Father Anzer was appointed the superior of the fledgling China mission. Later, when a mission in South Shantung province was entrusted to the SVD, he also became vicar apostolic of the mission and was ordained a bishop.[1] Freinademetz was acknowledged as the better grass-roots missionary of the two, and it was he who set the tone for those who came after.

The first thing Freinademetz did when he arrived in Hong Kong was begin to learn the language, in this case Hakka, one of the major dialects of South China. He took on a Chinese name, by which he was always thereafter known. He became "Fu," meaning "happiness," which stood for the "F" in his last name and "Jo Shei" ("Joseph"). More commonly, however, he became "Fu Shen-fu" or "Priest Fu." Freinademetz went first to a small fishing village where there was a poor, small Christian community. Here he stayed for six months, mostly by himself, learning Chinese and getting adjusted to Chinese culture. It took some time and the loss of weight he could ill-afford to lose before he accustomed himself to a Chinese diet, mostly of fish and rice. "The Chinese," he wrote, "eat rice and always more rice, even on their deathbed."[2] Every one or two months he would make the four- to five-

---

1. It may be important to explain that in Catholic mission work, members of religious orders usually have two superiors. An order's superior has responsibilities for the well-being of the members of the community in the mission. A bishop, however, is the *ecclesiastical* superior in charge of all facets of a given mission's life. Until the post-World War II era, the ecclesiastical superior appointed by Rome was called a "prefect apostolic" or "vicar apostolic," the latter being a higher responsibility. Prefects apostolic were seldom bishops, vicars apostolic usually were. The mission over which the prefect or vicar apostolic had jurisdiction was generally entrusted to a single order of priests. After World War II, however, this system was changed. Prefectures and vicariates apostolic generally became dioceses with diocesan bishops, though some were combined with other prefectures to become dioceses. Under the new legislation, missions were no longer "entrusted" to a single order, though in practice the order to which a prefecture had been appointed under the old rules often predominated in the new diocese.

2. Fritz Bornemann, *As Wine Poured Out: Blessed Joseph Freinademetz SVD Missionary in China*

hour trip to Hong Kong to confer with Father Anzer, who was assigned by Bishop Raimondi to teach in the seminary there. In the meantime, negotiations were underway to split South Shantung from the large area for which the Franciscans had been responsible. Anzer moved there when this was completed.

In May 1880, Raimondi decided Freinademetz should have another kind of experience, more like the one he would meet when he moved to South Shantung. As his biographer puts it, he should now learn something about the more difficult work of traveling from station to station, even to villages where there were no Christians in order to make the first contact with the people. He already discarded his European-style clothing and dressed completely in the Chinese fashion. He wrote: "The Chinese clothes are light and loose and very comfortable; they make the heat much more bearable." Except for some strands at the back of his head to which he attached a queue, or pigtail, he shaved his head completely. As he penetrated more deeply into Chinese life and culture, gradually learning Mandarin, he began to appreciate the magnificence of the civilization they had developed over the years. As a result of traveling from village to village scattered far and wide, he also realized quickly how absolutely crucial good catechists were to the whole enterprise of founding and then building up the church in China. It was also brought home again that there was no substitute for learning Chinese, and time had to be set aside for this. On 23 May 1881, he joined Anzer in South Shantung, where they began work in a mission founded by others and thus exemplifying the lessons learned in the past fifty or so years of mission work in China. While the SVDs would do some things differently from other communities, on the whole, their first task was to staff an ongoing mission founded by Franciscans and to broaden its outreach. They insisted that Chinese who were interested in becoming Christians should remain in their own village among their own families and neighbors. Every new Christian was to be another missionary. Freinademetz once said, "Our Christian men and women must become apostles. We must awaken prudent zeal and holy enthusiasm in the hearts of our catechumens and newly-baptized so they will win others for the faith."

As soon as one or two families had expressed an interest, the missionary would send a catechist to the area and would himself visit these places. In short order he would often have twenty and more such places to visit. They were to be themselves missionaries to their own. As a result, the missionary was often away from his own center, if he can even be said to have a central place at all. For weeks at a time he would be traveling from place to place, encouraging the catechists. Eventually a catechumenate would be established. In the meantime a house would be leased or purchased that could be used as a gathering place, an oratory or a chapel perhaps and even a place for the missionary to stay on one of his visits. The catechist would have attended a special catechist school for a period of three years and had to pass an examination in Christian doctrine at the end of this time.

To be underscored in all this is the fact that the primary task of the mission was to teach the catechism and the basic prayers to prospective Christians. All essential teaching and every essential prayer had to be memorized. In contradistinction

---

(Rome: Divine Word Missionaries, 1984), p. 51. Bornemann is the source for much of what follows on Father Freinademetz.

to Protestant missions that were being carried on at the same time and with much success as well, little was said about the scriptures, nor was the Bible systematically taught. Catholic missionaries were children of the post-Reformation reform movement seminary where the emphasis was on imparting the core dogmatics of the church, particularly where they diverged from Protestant teaching and practice. This was carried over to China. Protestants in the meantime were singling out those teachings in which they differed from the Catholics, and one of the principal ones had to do with the primacy of the Bible. The truths of the Catholic faith were typically catalogued in catechisms. Certainly Catholic catechists and foreign missionaries used stories from the Bible, but primarily to exemplify what Christians were to believe and how they were to act, but leading the catechumen to the Bible, where he or she would find personal teaching coming directly from God, was a Protestant, not a Catholic, practice.

One consequence of this, according to Maryknoller John Considine, was that the primary purpose of teaching the catechism was to inculcate individual religious practices rather than emphasize the communal dimension of religious conversion. That, however, is to look at things from a perspective developed a century later and ratified in the Second Vatican Council. What is being emphasized here is that for Catholic missionaries, including SVDs, the approved catechisms contained the truths of Christianity and these truths were regarded as unchanging and unchangeable, whether one was teaching people in Germany, the United States, New Guinea, or China. It was, in fact, an extension of the way the missioner had been taught in the seminary.

One problem was recognized with the system, the lack of women catechists. Freinademetz complained of this lack. Whether it was original with the SVDs or not, under Freinademetz's leadership they did try to train female catechists. This innovative style of carrying on mission work, it seems, is what SVD Father Schu reported when he writes to the generalate that the apostolic delegate had praised their mission methods and marveled at how hard SVD missionaries worked. In a letter to Joseph Grendel in 1933, then the newly elected superior general, Schu also says, "The new Vicar Apostolic DeJonghe requested me to send him a copy of the *Fructus Spirituales* ["spiritual fruits"] of our Shantung mission: he is so enthusiastic about our mission method that he wants to introduce everything that we do into his vicariate."[3]

It is clear that the SVD in China worked primarily among the poor peasantry. The reasons for this option were rooted in theology of mission that emphasized the absolute necessity of baptism for salvation. In reports detailing mission progress, therefore, the number of infant and adult baptisms was always listed as well as numbers of catechumens in preparation for baptism. In addition, the number of baptisms of infants in danger of death was also included. It was also acceptable to baptize babies secretly, even if their parents disapproved, provided the infant was in danger of death, a condition capable of broad definition.

The missionaries often had a difficult life, as an example from Freinademetz's life will show. The year was 1889, the place Tsaohsien. The success of the Catholic

---

3. SVD Generalate Archives, Rome, letter of 3 June 1933.

mission began to concern the local gentry, who tried to put an end to what they characterized as a secret and false sect. They first went after the village chief, himself a catechumen. Father Freinademetz came to his aid and both, together with some teachers connected with the mission, were beaten. In Freinademetz's own words:

> They yanked out my hair, twisted my arms, and from the place where the whole world goes to ease nature, someone scooped up a handful of excrement and "lathered" my face. Then I was dragged through the main street of the city. How long this lasted I do not know. I must have been too heavy for them since time and again I was jerked to my feet and forced to march under my own power. All the while someone was twisting my arm, pulling me by the hair and yanking it out. I could only look upwards at the sky; I had to force myself to move forward . . .
>
> I really thought our last hour had come . . . At the same time, however, I was afraid of the martyrdom I thought was imminent and so I prayed continuously for strength.
>
> [When the leader called a halt for rest] I used the momentary lull to speak a few words to the mob. "This is the first time in our lives that we see one another. I have never done you any harm and yet this is the welcome you give me! Though you are maltreating me in a most inhuman manner and are at a loss how to vent your anger against me, I do not bear you the slightest resentment. And as far as the religion I preach is concerned, you know nothing about it. If you did, you would be even more enthusiastic for it than you are opposed to it now."
>
> Lying on the ground, I preached for about a quarter of an hour about the glories of the Christian religion. The fury of the mob abated, my bonds were loosened and gradually the rabble melted away . . .
>
> The first thing we did when we were alone and looked at one another was to have a good, hearty laugh at our tattered clothing, our swollen and bloody bodies, our faces smeared with dirt and filth, hatless and shoeless, complete strangers in a strange place, eleven hours from our Christians.[4]

This story is an excellent example of why Joseph Freinademetz's memory loomed so large among his successors in China, why he was eventually beatified, and why many feel he will eventually be canonized. Much more should be said about both Freinademetz and the mission he was so instrumental in inspiring, but it is time to join the story of the North American SVD and the China mission.

AMERICAN SVDS ASSIGNED TO CHINA

As already mentioned, although the concentration in this book is on SVDs from the United States, theirs was a small part of a much larger international effort. Their numbers were dwarfed by the number of European Divine Word Missionaries, especially by the Germans. Father Clifford King was the first American to make his

---

4. Bornemann, *As Wine Poured Out*, pp. 133–34.

mark in China. King was a short and stocky man. In terms of his character and personality, King is best described as "peppery," "determined," "full of ideas," "persevering." By all accounts, he learned Chinese well. He also fell in love with the Chinese and their way of going about living their lives. This seems to have happened to all of the American missionaries who lived and worked in China for any length of time. In old age, after working in a variety of apostolates around the world, King always returned to China for his examples and memories of his good times. His talks and sermons invariably began with the words, "In China . . ." or "When I was in China . . ."

His decisive nature is revealed in an episode that took place several years after he arrived. Wilhelm Gier, who was elected the third superior general of the Society in 1920, began a visitation tour of the entire Society, accompanied by Bruno Hagspiel as his English-speaking secretary. By 1922 he was in China. Father King had a chance to converse with him about the idea that when the Society took over another mission area, it might eventually become a mission staffed by priests and brothers from the United States. His idea apparently received a positive reaction, for shortly thereafter, part of Honan Province was ceded to the Society with the idea that it would eventually be turned over to American SVDs. The idea, of course, was premature. At the time there were only two Americans in China, King and Clark, and Clark died in the near future. Apparently King's idea was received critically when Father Gier discussed it with the general council in Rome and with the SVDs in America. They, of course, were predominantly Germans. Gier clarified his decision to say that a mission in China might be "assigned" to the American SVD for promotion and collection purposes, but that all money so collected would be disbursed centrally, that is, to the advantage of the entire mission.

As we have already discussed, there was little money to be raised in Germany at that time and even through the Second World War and its aftermath. First, the economy was poor and then, after the ascent of Hitler to power in 1933, it became difficult and later forbidden to send money out of the country. Austria, dealing with the end of its empire after the First World War, was going through its own hard times. That left the Netherlands and North America as islands of relative wealth and an SVD contingent to seek donations. The United States, because of the relative size of its economy, would be expected pick up the slack in SVD fund raising. Thus began a new chapter in the now fairly seasoned missionary life of Clifford King. King's ecclesiastical superior, Prefect Apostolic of Honan, was an SVD father named Froewis, and he was in charge of the mission as a whole. Monsignor Froewis decided to send Father King to the United States on a collection tour. He was not alone. Father de Lange was back raising money for the SVD mission in the Little Sunda Islands (today part of Indonesia). Father Bruno Drescher was doing the same for the Philippines. Father George Stenz was also raising money for China. He had been through hard times in China, including having almost been tortured to death at one point. In Germany recuperating from his injuries, he tried to raise money there and then in America, about which he says:

> This beautiful country, which is choking with wealth (as the saying goes), must be an Eldorado for a beggar: such was my impression, and it was shared

by not a few others. On one occasion I sat at one table with nine colleagues of our venerable calling [fund raising]: they had come from all the lands of the world, and were begging for Germany, Austria, China, India, Asia Minor, Africa, etc. And not one of them went away empty-handed. The Americans give much and give willingly. The hospitality of the American clergy is truly magnificent, and I am under a deep debt of gratitude to them.[5]

King began his tour in February 1924 and carried it on into November. He purchased a projector to give "stereopticon" slide lectures, for each of which he received an average of ten dollars. The slides, all on China, were made of glass and were heavy. He recalls:

For over a year I must have lugged that clumsy projector and those heavy slides through the length and breadth of a dozen northern states. I must have given about three hundred lectures, receiving an average of ten dollars as an honorarium for each talk. It took all that time for me to discover that attaining my exalted goal might thus keep me engaged for a decade or two.[6]

Three hundred lectures spread over eighteen months meant he averaged a little more than a lecture every two days. He changed his tactics and launched an advertising campaign for aid toward the building of chapels for his Honan mission "in memory of departed loved ones." By using these and other techniques he collected $75,000 for Froewis and the Honan mission.

When King's bishop asked him to go to the United States again in 1930 to collect money, the provincial superior in Techny, Father Hagspiel, said that he did not want him in America. He claimed that King was hypernationalistic, which probably meant, among other things, that he did things his own way and was too independent of superiors in America. To these Germans, Clifford King seemed like a loose cannon. Add to this his impetuosity and success, often at the expense of other SVD fund-raising operations, the conflict is understandable. Because of just this kind of conflict, the province and mission office were just beginning to operate under statutes designed to clean up this kind of messiness. But it also seems likely that King represented the nascent feeling of the now-maturing American SVDs that it was time to Americanize the Society. In any case, the superiors and fund raisers in the United States did not want King running around, subject to no one but his bishop in China, siphoning benefactors away or turning them off. The final reason Hagspiel said King should not come to the United States to beg was that there was very little money to be had from any one during the Depression, which was in full force and beginning to cause all kind of problems for everybody at this time. Since King was in Rome on his way to the States, Hagspiel suggested that he be sent to work in England where the first SVD house had just opened. This suggestion was acted on and by 8 January 1931, King was in England recruiting vocations for the coming school year. But he was not happy. He had taken personally the refusal to grant him permission to collect money in the States. Five

---

5. George M. Stenz, "Recollections of a Beggar," *Our Missions* 5 (1925): 28.
6. King, *I Remember* (Techny, Ill.: Divine Word Publications, 1968), p. 28.

months later, on 8 May 1931, he requested permission to be dispensed from vows and leave the Society. He wanted to go back to the missions, even if that meant joining another order or becoming a diocesan priest.

Gier came to the conclusion that King's vocation could not be saved. Hagspiel thought otherwise and wrote the following to Gier, to give the substance of what he had written to King:

> I briefly requested him [King] to reconsider his petition for dispensation from the vows and to have patience. Why should he be in such a hurry, going back to China this very year? Was he not satisfied before that he would go back to China perhaps after two years? I believe that if he would know for sure that it is more than probable that after the two years would elapse he would return to China or go at least to India, he would be satisfied. I personally worried a little about this radical step which he wished to take because he is the founder of the Catholic Students' Mission Crusade, and if it would become known that Father King left the Society, it would not make the best of impressions.[7]

In a letter of 22 July 1931, Gier told Hagspiel that King had withdrawn his request for dispensation and that he was being assigned to a position as professor in the university in Peking. Gier, too, had been concerned about King's leaving. He was the first American missionary of the Society, and his departure would not have been easy to explain, especially in an era when resignations were considered a great shame. Despite King's change of heart, Gier remained doubtful whether King would persevere in the SVD over the long haul, even though he admitted that King had done a wonderful job recruiting vocations for the new house in Hadzor. Fifteen English boys were there to begin the first school year, largely as a result of this remarkable man's effort. Gier was completely wrong about King. Much was still in store for him.

THE DARKENING POLITICAL SITUATION AND ITS IMPACT

We must turn to a short discussion of the China missions and international politics as background to the rest of our story, for it is the ever-darkening political situation that alone makes our story understandable. The China to which Clark and King went had been forcibly opened to the work of Christian missionaries by the gunboats of European nations. The British efforts to use the rationale that missionaries should be admitted so that Britain might spread the benefits of "Christian civilization" are well known. This claim of a higher mission was responsible for the early and vigorous start that English-speaking Protestants got in the mission rush that began early in the nineteenth century. Cynics have questioned whether the push by the British to admit missioners was a sincere goal of the British government or a sugar-coated pill to make it more palatable to the British public. It is hard to discern motives in such cases, but it is clear that France wanted to be sure there were Catholic missionaries in China to counteract the influence of the British,

---

7. SVD Generalate Archives, Rome, Hagspiel to Gier, 6 June 1931.

and French missionaries began to come in large numbers before the SVD entered the scene. The French, as "elder daughter" of the Catholic Church, claimed and got the right to be protectors of non-French missionaries as well. Thus all Catholics, including the early SVDs, entered China with France as their protectors. To the Chinese, of course, being forced to take missioners was a bitter pill to swallow. It also caused them to view the religious work of missionaries as Trojan horses whose loins would inevitably sprout Christians with divided loyalties.

Modern Germany began the race to accumulate colonies only during the era of Bismarck's unification of the German principalities. The Germans felt that they too needed the prestige and favored trading relationships that Britain and France had been garnering. It is clear that the SVD's entry into missions in West Africa, and New Guinea, which occurred *after* the start of its China missions, were the direct result of Germany's sense that it needed missionaries sympathetic to German colonial policies. If it did not succeed in its colonial ambitions, it feared its global, great power ambitions would be strangled by its neighbors and rivals. And were it to lose the race for colonies, it was felt that its European ambitions would suffer as well. While there is no evidence of SVD collusion with the government to gain protected status, the murder of two German SVD priests, Richard Henle and Francis Xavier Nies, as they slept during the night of 1 November 1897, gave the German government the occasion to demand special treatment for its nationals, both commercial and missionary, much to the chagrin of Father Freinademetz. The murder of Henle and Nies was the work of the Society of Long Knives, whose members had taken a vow to drive all foreigners out of China. Their death gave the German government the excuse to send the German Far East fleet to secure a suitable harbor for themselves and carve out a protectorate. The protection of German missioners was one way of extending sway further into China. It carried with it the risk that German missioners would be considered agents of the German state, and whether they approved of German protection or not, SVDs definitely found themselves viewed by many Chinese as agents of a foreign power.

The year 1908 saw the demise of the last imperial dynasty. Three years later Sun Yat-sen founded the Chinese Republic. One result was the rise of warlords who carved out fiefdoms for themselves and entered in and out of alliances with one other. Banditry and lawlessness spread through the country, and all this affected missions. In 1921 the communist party was founded in Shanghai but it really began to achieve importance when a librarian named Mao Tse-tung became the head of the party in 1924. In 1928, Chiang Kai-shek took over the presidency of the Chinese Republic and later also became commander-in-chief of the Nationalist army. He took steps to oppose the communists and quickly a bloody conflict began, which would not end until the communists completely expelled the Nationalists in 1949. From the time of the 1931 Japanese invasion of Manchuria, of course, the Chinese were also at war with the Japanese, and by 1937 it had become widespread. The three-sided war that resulted had a great impact on all Christian missions. The Catholic Church, always suspicious of socialism and in direct conflict with communism because of its atheism and materialism, condemned communism officially in 1939. Thus, for the last ten years of the conflict, Catholic missionaries found themselves identified with the Nationalists, whether they wanted to be or not.

As if this situation was not confusing enough, when the Second World War broke out in 1939, but especially after the United States entered the war in 1941, everything became even more mixed up. German missionaries were usually able to continue their mission work in areas controlled by the Japanese. Americans were usually allowed to go about their mission business in territories under the control of the Chinese, unless the Chinese government in a region happened to be communist. The exceptions to these rules and the continuing shift of control in the various areas rendered the situation bewildering, and dangerous, even impossible to sort out. It became sticky for American missionaries after Pearl Harbor, because not only were the Americans at war with Japan, they also had uneasy relations with the communists, because they, the Americans, poured in thousands of advisers, pilots, airplanes, and soldiers, but gave assistance only to the Nationalists. One can get a sense of the situation from a few lines that the American SVD Father Joseph Henkels wrote to the Brothers' Mission Club paper, *Techny Chimes*, in 1932:

> After the "commies" got all my stuff over in Loshan I was transferred to Chengyang, where I spent the winter of 1930–31 . . . During the summer the floods here in China were very bad . . . This would not have been so bad after all had everything remained peaceful . . . But it so happened that just then the campaign against Sh Yu-san (a warlord) was being carried on in an effort to subdue him. That campaign being at an end, all of a sudden all of the [Nationalist] soldiers, returning from the North, got off the train right here in Mingkiang. You can imagine the result when 30,000 soldiers tried to crowd into a village with a normal population of 15,000. They do not carry any tents with them either so that wherever they go they crowd themselves into empty pagan temples or into the houses of the people. And the mission was not spared either . . . During their three weeks stay we had no peace. No matter where we would meet a soldier we would always be greeted by the salutation "yang-kwei-tse" (foreign devil). Father Megan says if he would be given a choice he would choose to deal with the bandits and communists just as soon as with the soldiers, for the latter are just as bad if not worse than the former.

Many had variations of this tune to play. King, for instance, was kidnapped by one bandit brigade and held for ransom. He was rescued by another freelance army, but had to give this commander one thousand Chinese silver dollars with which the commander was to buy socks and shoes for his soldiers. After his 1931 disagreements with superiors, Father King went to the university in Peking for one year. He then returned to the South Shantung mission where he had gotten his start in 1920. When the Japanese took over this area in 1937, he found it difficult to deal with them and finally decided, with his bishop's and the Society's permission, to leave Shantung temporarily. He was transferred to the Philippines where the Society was looking for people who spoke English to move into school and university work.

During these very years, King's 1922 idea about assigning a mission specifically to American SVDs was partially realized. In 1933, SVDs were sent to assist

Italian missionaries in North Honan, a place the Chinese called "Paradise." The area was soon turned over to the SVD. In many ways the area was a paradise. It had coal mines, no small gift in a land strapped for fuel. The climate was good, transportation was good. The area was not spared the periodic flooding of the Yellow River, nor the locusts that sometimes darkened the skies, eating everything that was green, but generally it was a good place. Five American SVD priests were sent. Thomas Megan went from the catechetical training center that he still directed for Vicar Apostolic Froewis in South Shantung. After that retreat in Paradise in 1934, Father Edward Wojniak, another American SVD who served in China, quoted him.

The intention of the Society of the Divine Word is to make Paradise an American mission field — not in the exclusive sense that missionaries of other nationalities will not be sent there, but in the inclusive sense that the majority of the missionaries will be Americans. Our Society is an international organization dedicated to the promotion of mission work. Because of its cosmopolitan character, it boasts no exclusive mission field for members of any one nation. Rather, the Society endeavors to display the universal character of the Church by the harmonious efforts of many nations for the purpose of saving souls.[8]

Not long after writing this, Megan, a farm boy of Irish extraction, born in Eldora, Iowa, in 1899, became the prefect apostolic of the new Catholic prefecture of North Honan. His family was one of the largest landowners in Harden County, and Thomas was one of ten children. He made his way to Techny in 1913 to begin studies for the missionary priesthood. Twenty-three years later, in 1936, he became the first American SVD to be made a prefect apostolic and thus assumed a kind of exemplary role for all the American SVD bishops—black and white—who followed him.

THOMAS MEGAN AND THE AMERICAN SVD EXPERIENCE OF WAR AND REVOLUTION IN CHINA

The experiment of assigning a mission to Americans had little chance to prove itself. In 1936, Megan was appointed; in 1937 full-scale war between China and Japan was officially declared. The United States entered the war against Japan in 1941. Even though the communists and Nationalists worked out a truce in order to fight the Japanese, it was a shaky truce, repeatedly broken by both sides, and destined to be totally discarded as soon as the Japanese were defeated in 1945. If the Japanese in their advances and retreats did not wreak enough havoc, the communists, Nationalists, warlords or bandits, who were still around also, more than made up the deficit. There are constant reports from missionaries in this period describing how their stations were wiped out, themselves escaping with their lives

8. Edward Wojniak, *Atomic Apostle: The Life Story of Thomas Megan* (Techny, Ill.: Divine Word Publications, 1957), p. 70.

and little else, sometimes by lowering themselves over the walls of a besieged city by rope or escaping by mingling with Chinese peasants, dressed as coolies going out to work. To make it worse for Megan and his confreres, Honan was a battleground for all factions. And what armies were unable to destroy was periodically accomplished by floods and famine or drought and famine during these years. One such famine, the result of a prolonged drought in the summer of 1942, reached its peak effect in the winter of 1942–1943. Thirty million people were affected. Theodore White, a correspondent for *Time* magazine, spent two weeks on a tour of starving Honan, with Megan as his companion, and wrote the following:

> In Loyang we went to call on Bishop Thomas Megan of Eldora, Iowa, a great hearted Irish padre, who is reported to know more about the famine than anyone else in the north. When we came out of his relief dispensary, which is supported by American funds, the refugees tried to mob us. Men fell on their knees, surrounded us, folding hands in supplication.
>
> When we rode forth two days later, the bishop accompanied us. Our objective was the town of Chengchow, a three-days' journey—one by truck, then two by horse. The quick and the dead confused us. There were corpses on the road. When they die they just lie down in the slush or gutters and give up. One man moaned as he lay, and we shook him to try to make him get up. Then we turned to a woman in rags who was clutching a baby; we begged her to help us move the man to the refugee camp. As she bent, the baby fell from her arms into the snow and cried pitifully. We saw them off, all three, toward the compound, and Bishop Megan, who was escorting us, said, "At least let them die like human beings."[9]

Megan and his confreres did what they could, but the famine was so immense and the government's ability to alleviate the suffering so weak that countless innocent civilians perished. It also says something about the state of China's transportation system that instead of collecting excess grain in the west and transporting it east to Honan, the starving people had to try to go by whatever means they could to where the food stocks were.

Megan began to organize relief efforts as soon as the dimensions of the tragedy became known, as did the Protestants also. Megan's work came to the attention of Chiang Kai-shek, who appointed him the head of the Honan Relief Commission. This was no favor, as events turned out, for then Megan, and all Catholic missionaries by extension, were viewed as direct and active supporters of the Nationalists when civil war broke out again.

During the Japanese war with China and into the final civil war, there were Americans stationed in Xian in western China. Father Henkels, who had escaped west with Megan, became chaplain at an American air base, while Megan became a translator and liaison between the United States military and Nationalist Chinese authorities. He traveled on military airplanes and quickly got used to the military way of giving orders with the expectation that they be followed. When the Second

---

9. Wojniak, *Atomic Apostle*, p. 134.

World War was over, Megan and Henkels, along with other missioners, thought a new era for the church in China had begun. They were destined to be disillusioned as the final phase of the civil war between communists and Nationalists began again and each side scrambled madly to occupy as much of China as possible after the defeat of the Japanese. Initially, Megan hoped the communists might be persuaded to allow the missionaries to continue their work, at least the humanitarian labors, keeping the hospitals and dispensaries open, for example, and the schools operating. It did not take too long to realize it was not to be.

After twenty-two stressful years in China, during ten of which he was subject to threats from one or another of the three sides, Megan desperately needed a break and a rest. The year was 1947 and the civil war had ground to a temporary halt, allowing the two sides a chance to recuperate and rebuild their strength for the last push to victory. On paper the odds were in favor of the Nationalists because of their enormous superiority in resources, but people in the know—including Megan, who had seen the Red Army in action and witnessed their dedication and efficiency— should have had more doubts. In addition, the mission was bankrupt and needed money desperately to rebuild and expand for the future. So everyone agreed that Megan should return to the States for a rest and to collect money. In October 1947, Megan felt he could be back in time to look after his mission during the war that was sure to come in the spring. There was also talk of raising the prefecture apostolic of Sinsiang to a full-fledged diocese. Father John Schütte, the future superior general of the Society, was left in charge by Megan. Schütte describes the departure at length and writes for us the last words recorded of Megan in China:

> While on the train, the bishop confided to me: "Johnny, I have a feeling—in fact, I'm almost sure—I shall never become the consecrated bishop of Sinsiang. But don't worry. You can be sure of this—I'll be back! I'll ask to be made pastor of Chi-Li-Ying, and then I'll spend the evening of my life there. I have given my very best to China, and in China I want to die and be buried."[10]

On the first point he was correct; he was never made a diocesan bishop, or "ordinary" in the technical language of the day. On the second point he was wrong. He never returned to China, but was reassigned to Hattiesburg, Mississippi, in the Southern Province. His new "method" was emphasized, approaching adults directly rather than through a school. In the few short years he worked in the South, he was very successful. In his heart, though, he seems to have doubted that his return to China would ever happen, as Father Edward Wojniak cites his words in an account of his return:

> The future of the Catholic Church in China is intimately connected with Communism. Based on our experience of the past decade, the Communists will destroy our churches and installations; they will exile our priests and Brothers and Sisters; they will discriminate against our Christians. Whether

10. Wojniak, *Atomic Apostle*, p. 169.

they can effect the eradication of Catholicism is another question. Stronger
forces than Communism have tried and failed.[11]

He was correct on all accounts. After World War II was over, Megan returned
briefly to Paradise before returning to the United States. Over the next few years
the rest of the missionaries were exiled and given other assignments. And as events
since 1972 have shown, the seeds that missionaries sowed in these troubled years
bore fruit. But countless missionaries, like Megan, men and women who had fallen
in love with China and would have returned gladly, were destined to spend many
years in exile from their adopted homelands.

Megan himself was refused permission to return by his religious and ecclesiastical superiors at the highest levels in Rome. Over the years in China, it was felt,
he had done great work, but he also was believed to have fatally compromised himself by identification with the Nationalist and American sides. And he had undoubtedly been pro-Nationalist and pro-American to the extent of helping American
forces. Before that he had accepted the honorary rank of colonel in the Nationalist
army so he could more easily command ordinary soldiers in his position as chaplain to the Chinese army when he wanted them to help the wounded and dying.

In 1949 Megan had what was probably a minor stroke and there is evidence that
he may have had a similar cerebral event earlier in China. As a result of the stroke
in the United States, however, he collapsed. Over the next year and a half he had
several more of these episodes, each time recovering sufficiently to take up his
work again in his parish in Hattiesburg, Mississippi. Finally, on 4 October 1951,
he died in his rectory, at the age of fifty-two. With him died a major chapter in
North American SVD history, since he cut such a quintessential "American figure." Whether or not the image corresponds to the reality, Megan came to represent an ideal for the generation of American SVD seminarians and brother
candidates who were swelling the ranks of members-in-vows in the years from
1935 through the early 1960s. They were the years also when Americans were taking over from the Germans as superiors, and there was an unquestionable swelling
of American nationalism when the United States began to take virtual single-
handed credit for defeating the Axis powers. It was also a picture that the story of
Clifford King in the war and postwar years only amplified.

For this generation of SVD candidates, the story of King going from China to
the Philippines, where he taught in several places over the next few years, capped
the image that a missioner's life was filled with heroic deeds. When the Japanese
bombed Manila, shortly after Pearl Harbor, and then invaded and quickly con-
quered the Islands, King went into hiding from the Japanese in the mountains of
Mindanao. There he looked after a small parish and its outstations, from January
1942 until March 1944, when he and thirty-nine others were secretly transported
by submarine to Australia. Later he returned to America where he joined Cardinal
Tien as his English secretary and translator, returning to China with him on his
way back to Peking. For the next ten years, King devoted his time and energies to
Cardinal Tien. During much of that time, Tien would reside at Techny, where, as

---

11. Wojniak, *Atomic Apostle*, p. 172.

the only SVD ever to be named a cardinal, he became an instant hero to American seminarians. The story of Tien and his influence on that generation of Americans deserves to be told at greater length than this history can go into. Suffice it to say here that the legacy of the China mission ethos was, along with that of the New Guinea experience that we shall turn to in the following chapter, one of the greatest shapers of future American Divine Word Missioners.

We turn now to the SVD's assumption of Fu Jen University in Peking, a momentous addition to the kind of apostolates that the Society engages in, entry into tertiary-level education.

INTERNAL SVD MATTERS RELATING
TO THE FU JEN TAKEOVER

The most significant addition to the Society of the Divine Word's missionary activity—after the difficult years of the initial founding and obtaining full recognition by the Holy See of its constitutions and status as a group that could work without oversight of local bishops in its internal life—is almost certainly the decision to enter into higher education by taking over Fu Jen University in Peking. True, Arnold Janssen had always envisioned his Society as an order that would be involved in the promotion of science. But from the foundation in 1875 until the year 1933, when the question of taking over Fu Jen University arose, members of Janssen's community had mainly been involved in higher education in relation to training SVD candidates in the philosophical and theological "sciences." (In German, it should be recalled, the word *Wissenschaft*, which is usually translated as "science" in English, includes empirical sciences such as chemistry and medicine, on the one hand, and what are called the "humanities" in English.)

The request from the Holy See to take over the direction of Fu Jen University in Peking, because of the founder's commitment of the society to advance both kinds of "sciences," did not, then, present a matter of great principle that would alter the character of the Society. Members had been accustomed to hearing advancement of science as a goal of the Society in the daily reading of sections of the constitutions in the dining room for more than fifty years before the decision to undertake the direction of Fu Jen University was made. Moreover, SVDs knew about and were proud of the efforts of their confrere, Father Wilhelm Schmidt, and other confreres he had gathered to advance ethnography as a science and to help missionaries understand better the cultures of the peoples they worked among. Schmidt insisted that the work of his Anthropos Institute must first of all pass the highest academic standards as *wissenschaftlich* ("scientific") or run the risk of being considered inferior by the then-burgeoning science of anthropology. Success in achieving this had been a matter of pride for SVDs for a generation. Selection of the Society's members to plan an ethnographic exposition in the Vatican in 1925, moreover, had been a matter of great pride to the Society's members. They reveled in signs that Pope Pius XI considered the SVD as an especially astute and capable group, in no small measure because of his friendship and respect for Schmidt and his band of scientific anthropologists. Moreover, this emphasis on anthropology and providing "scientific" accounts of what they found in their missions had become one of the distinguishing characteristics of the Society already in the first decade of the twentieth century.

What was new and frightening in the request to take over the direction of a Catholic University in Peking was the scope of practical issues involved for a group that was constantly short of qualified personnel to staff its seminaries and mostly rural, parish-based missions. And when one thinks of how young the Society was in North America, how few men had been ordained, and how much specialized talent and academic preparation was required to staff a university with its host of departments, the idea that the province in the United States would have a special responsibility for Fu Jen was a decision that gave the most enthusiastic and energetic people reason to pause and consider whether they ran the risk of being unwise men who began to build without calculating the resources necessary to finish the task. From previous chapters, we realize that Fathers Ralph Thyken and Arthur Melcher would succeed in shoring up the financial base of the Society, which would make the task of rescuing the floundering university feasible. But in 1933, in a country undergoing the ravages of the Great Depression, no one knew that the requirements for success had been met. Taking on a university in Peking—one of the most important cities in China, in the midst of great political unrest and the likelihood of war and revolution engulfing the nation—meant that what was undertaken would be carried on in full view of every Catholic and Protestant missionary organization, as well in the face of a Chinese political class that was highly ambivalent about the progress of Christianity.

THE BENEDICTINES FOUND FU JEN

The idea of a Catholic University in China begins in 1912, with a Chinese Catholic journalist and scholar, Dr. Vincent Ying (Ying Lien Cheh), who wrote to Pope Pius X about the possibility of establishing a Catholic University in Peking. Although the Jesuits had opened Aurora University in 1903 in Shanghai, and although the man who was probably the most prominent Catholic in China, Vincentian Father Vincent Lebbe, had been directing his educational efforts to the educated elites of China by means of his public lecture halls the first of which he opened in Tientsin, there was no formal Catholic higher education for ordinary Chinese in Peking itself. In 1913, Ying opened the Fu Jen She in Peking. *Fu Jen* translates as "fostering true humanity."[12] Ying's school was an academy of Chinese letters for Catholic young men.

The next step in the foundation of a university occurred in October 1920. George Barry O'Toole, a Catholic priest, an Oblate of St. Benedict, and a professor at St. Vincent's Archabbey in Latrobe, Pennsylvania, was traveling in China. O'Toole met Vincent Ying and was shown the letter Dr. Ying wrote to the pope seven years earlier. From this point on, O'Toole became one of the forces behind the establishment of a Catholic university in China. Returning to the States by way of Europe and Rome, he consulted with Pope Benedict XV and the abbot primate of the Benedictine Order. Once he was back in America, with the blessing and

---

12. Richard Arens, "The Pursuit of True Humanity," *Word in the World* (1967): 58.

encouragement of the abbot primate and the pope, he took the matter of a Catholic University in China up with the Benedictines of the Cassinese congregation. In 1923 the Prefect of the Propaganda in Rome made a formal proposal that the Order of St. Benedict start a university in Peking and at their general chapter the American branch voted to undertake this project. At the same chapter the order also decided to establish a monastery in China.

It must be recalled that Benedictine monasteries are independent of each other. When it was agreed that the American Benedictine Congregation would start and support a university in China, the constitutions of the congregation of Cassinese, a conglomerate of monasteries and priories, did not permit any enterprise to be conducted by the entire body as such. It became necessary to entrust the project to a particular abbey, in this case St. Vincent's in Pennsylvania, which was under the direction at the time of Archabbot Aurelius Stehle. He was enthusiastic about the idea of a Benedictine university in China, took charge of the project in the name of his abbey, and eventually became chancellor of the university and promptly appointed O'Toole as the rector on 15 January 1925. Dr. Ying was named dean of the School of Chinese Studies at Fu Jen. Ying, his health failing rapidly, died 10 January 1926.

On 29 July 1927, the university achieved the rank of University of Peking. Only two years later, however, the Nationalist Ministry of Education, now located in Nanking, issued new regulations. Under them, Fu Jen lost university status and was demoted to the rank of college. To repair this loss of face, there was nothing to do but purchase the necessary equipment and add the faculty that could justify the return of the lost university status, which required a faculty of science. The science faculty and a new faculty of education, along with the original faculty of arts qualified Fu Jen for getting back its university title, and it was so recognized again on 2 August 1929. On 13 November 1929 a cornerstone was laid for a new building.

In the meantime the Great Depression had taken hold in America and around the world. There were building expenses to be paid but the monks and abbots found themselves short of resources and, at least according to Father Bruno Hagspiel, reporting on a conversation he had with the prior of one of the congregation's houses in St. Leo, Florida, Father Lewis Peser, "there was a great lack of interest all the time, especially since the death of Aurelius Stehle, and consequently, lack of unity of action on the part of the fourteen or sixteen abbeys in the American Cassinese Benedictine Congregation."[13] This situation occasioned the invitation to the Society of the Divine Word to assume responsibility for Fu Jen. To that story we now turn.

THE SOCIETY DECISION TO ACCEPT FU JEN

The SVD became involved in February 1933, according to Superior General Joseph Grendel. He states that on 9 February 1933, Society representatives met in the home of the prefect of Propaganda Fide because he was ill. They were told that

---

13. Rome, SVD Generalate Archives.

Fu Jen was on the verge of collapse and "that it was the wish and will of the Holy Father that the Society take over the Catholic University in Peking."[14]

The next day, the general council was presented with the Holy Father's request made at the previous day's meeting. It was clear to all that, even if couched in polite terms, they had been presented with a virtual order. Still, each member was to reflect on this matter, both in favor and against, and put it in writing. Each consultor was asked to offer Mass the next day for the light and guidance of the Holy Spirit. Everybody realized how important and far-reaching the decision would be.

At the meeting on 11 February, Grendel received the consultors' opinions. In thorough and logical fashion he drew up a summary of the reasons for and against accepting the university. On the plus side, the chief one was the will of the pope. There were numerous intrinsic reasons why such a university was an important apostolate. Among them, it would be a means of putting into practice the founder's concern that the Society advance science and knowledge in addition to being missionary. Given all this, it was urged, the practical problems could be overcome and obeying the pope would bring with it God's blessings.

Among the reasons against accepting the request were the lack of personnel, the "American" character of the university and the lack of sufficient qualified Americans to assign to it, possible resentment from the Benedictines and other orders, and the difficulty of financing the operation.

On 12 February, the council discussed these issues again, and each of the points militating against accepting were addressed and answered. Specifically, it was felt that the SVD had the resources and that in regard to the American character of the university, that could be retained by having Americans in the administration. Persons of other nationalities could be found for teaching posts. It was felt that the university itself could be made responsible for fund raising and that thus it would not become a permanent burden on general Society funds.

The council voted to accept Fu Jen and on 13 February 1933 a letter to this effect was sent to Monsignor Salotti at Propaganda, who handed it to the pope on the same day. The apostolic delegate to China, Celso Constantini, was summoned to Rome so the transfer could be made. Constantini arrived in April and on 29 April, Propaganda announced the transfer of Fu Jen to the Society of the Divine Word. That all this could happen between 2 February and 29 April 1933 is an indication how concerned Pius XI was to get the issue of Fu Jen resolved.

WHY WAS THE SVD CHOSEN?

One might well ask why Pope Pius XI chose the SVD for this task. It was easy to understand why another *American* order or the American province of a community like the Jesuits or Dominicans would be tapped. Insofar as the Chinese were enthusiastic about foreign influences in education, for instance, it was American models they were following, for a variety of reasons. American incursions into and demands on China had not been as imperialistic as those of the Europeans and their gunboat diplomacy. In the Pacific, the United States was per-

---

14. Rome, SVD Generalate Archives.

ceived as the power most likely to defeat the Japanese with whom the Chinese knew, a deepening of war was inevitable. English was the language of preference for Chinese students. Germans were respected in China, but the United States and its institutions provided the model most generally adapted in China. This does not mean that Chinese ambivalence about *all* foreign influence had abated.

Nevertheless, the American province of the SVD was weak, and if it were a matter of high priority to retain an American character at Fu Jen, any number of male Catholic communities would have been in a better position to take over the university. But the pope bypassed all of these and ordered the Society of the Divine Word to get into what was, for it, an entirely new area of the apostolate. The most plausible explanation is Pius XI's relationship with Wilhelm Schmidt. To prove this friendship stood behind the choice is impossible, but it is clear that Pius XI had a high opinion of Schmidt. In 1922 the pope invited Schmidt to Rome because he wanted to meet Schmidt personally and discuss his work in ethnology and linguistics. On 23 April 1923, Schmidt had the first of many meetings with the pope. In his account of this first meeting, Schmidt says the pope talked about a new era in mission work and of the necessary connections between science and religion. He repeated these concerns when he asked the SVD to take over Fu Jen. Schmidt was selected to direct the ethnological exhibits prepared for the Holy Year observances in 1925, and as a result of the many conversations the pope had with Schmidt, he had become familiar with the Society, its interests, its capabilities and strengths. It seems likely, therefore, that the pope felt confident that the SVD had the resources to take over the university, and also that it would become an occasion for the Society to firm up its efforts to bring science into the missionary enterprise as a whole.

On 6 May 1933, Grendel sent a circular letter to all members of the Society outlining what had happened and why the Society was taking this dramatic step and asking that they accept this challenge decisively and with joy. Following ecclesiastical traditions, Father Grendel was appointed chancellor of the university. In that position, while he would not be responsible for day-to-day operations, he would be responsible for staffing the university with faculty and could act to resolve disputes when necessary. Curriculum matters, so intimately linked with staffing questions, also required the chancellor's ultimate approval. Through Chancellor Grendel, then, the Holy See would be able to settle important matters.

FATHER MURPHY'S APPOINTMENT AS RECTOR

Grendel's first task as chancellor was to appoint a rector for the university. In a letter to Provincial Hagspiel, written on 11 May 1933, the superior general and his council suggested that Father Joseph Murphy would be the right person to fill the positions as rector both of the SVD community and of the university. Combining the roles of superior of the house and the rector of the university had been a strong recommendation of the apostolic delegate. The separation of the two offices by the Benedictines, it was said, had caused conflicts of interest and a divided authority. The next issue Grendel raised concerned the appointment of promoter and treasurer of Fu Jen. Father King had been mentioned and recommended by the apostolic delegate, but in the generalate people had reservations about King. He asked whether Hagspiel himself would take on the job. Everyone in Rome was said to think that Hagspiel would be good in the position as well.

In the end, Father Joseph Murphy was selected. He was a native-born American of Irish ancestry and a member of the first class to be ordained at Techny. Born in 1895 in Chicago, he came to Techny for high school studies in 1909, the year the seminary was opened. He was, therefore, a classmate of King and Clark, both of whom had gone to China. Bright and talented, he was put to work after ordination teaching at Girard and later at Miramar. In 1928 he was sent to Rome for post-graduate studies in theology and he received his S.T.D. in two years. Generalate members, including Father Grendel, got to know him there and were impressed with his work and the type of person he was. In the fall of 1930 the new professor was teaching theology, church history, and scripture to the African-American seminarians at St. Augustine's in Bay St. Louis, Mississippi. The American province did not want to let him go. They lost the tug-of-war, and on 18 June 1933, Murphy wrote to the superior general to accept the assignment offered him to be the rector of the Catholic University of Peking.

In that letter, Murphy suggests the names of Fathers King or Dooley to work full time on finances, and says he will get ready to leave directly for China as soon as possible. He went by way of Europe to get a chance to talk the matter of Fu Jen over with Father Grendel. He arrived in Peking on 9 September 1933, to get ready for the first school year at the Society's first university. Money became the main concern of the new rector. The world was suffering through the Great Depression. In addition, in the background, like a somber basso continuo, there were the many wars large and small that were ravaging China—wars between the Chinese and Japan, wars between the Chinese Nationalists and communists, wars of opportunity when theater commanders and warlords found an opportunity to enrich themselves too good to pass up. Add to this the ferocious floods and famines that continued to sweep over parts of China and the ambience was anything but tranquil for Murphy as he tried to sort out finances, pay bills and teachers, recruit new staff, and cope with the conflicting demands of the government educational bureaucracy, elements of which were not sure China needed a Catholic university and were prepared to make that university's life difficult.

In spite of everything, the Catholic University of Peking continued to grow, both in numbers and in quality. An interesting feature of Murphy's letters from the beginning and through his tenure as well is his positive tone. He does not bemoan the lack of money but makes positive suggestions of what could be done, what might perhaps be attempted, possible suggestions on how to assure a steady income. In time Father Ralph's operation, about which we have spoken above, began to click in.

An improvement in finance came but it proved to be too late for Joseph Murphy, who had a weak heart. In January 1935 he contracted the flu. It weakened him but he was able to continue working until the school year finished. According to a report to Father Grendel on Murphy's last days written by his confrere Father Joseph Goertz, one of the Fu Jen faculty, Murphy never gave himself a chance to fully recuperate. Even while he was supposed to be resting, he continued writing, answering letters, making decisions regarding the upcoming school year, and assigning faculty. On 30 August 1935, he took a turn for the worse and listened to the advice of his doctor and confreres to go to the hospital. He died on 5 September 1935 and was buried on 9 September—the second anniversary of his arrival in Peking. Fr. Goertz was the last to see Murphy and sums up the contribution Murphy made there:

> What the deceased was able to accomplish in the two short years he was Rector, through his quiet, untiring labor, cannot be expressed in words. The difficulties facing the university when it was first handed over to the Society were not minor. There was no end of worry and concern during the whole two years. Even though he came to China as a novice to Chinese ways, still he knew how to make smooth the way for the successful development of the university. In this he was helped greatly by his basically kind nature and his tireless, humble work. He felt uncomfortable with flashy show, and empty ceremonial also turned him off. But he could work, he could produce; in this· he was a real man. Even with all of these administrative duties, he maintained a teaching schedule equivalent to that of a full-time professor.[15]

MOVING AHEAD AFTER MURPHY'S DEATH

After Murphy's death, an American SVD priest from Dyersville, Iowa, Joseph Henkels, was called from North Honan to serve as acting rector of Fu Jen. By the third year of the SVD's administration, the financial difficulties began to lessen somewhat, as Father Ralph's work began to bear fruit. The bulk of the faculty were German, but Americans were studying to take up positions. Father Henkel departed when Father Rudolf Rahmann, his German-born replacement, arrived. Rahmann grew into his position quickly and thoroughly, and was able to interact with others quietly and diplomatically and persistently. He was thus able both to hold the university together and move it forward through the difficult period of the Second World War. He served as rector from 1936 to 1946. During the years from 1943 to 1946, the main accomplishment was the physical one of keeping the university open. Fortunately for the university, Rahmann was German. Even so, the war years were hard, but with the help of his confrere, Father Eugene Feifel, he kept the university open through the entire war. Feifel had worked in Japan after his ordination in 1927 until he was reassigned to China. Speaking fluent Japanese, he assisted Rahmann in constant negotiations with the Japanese occupation forces necessary to keep the university open. By all kinds of machinations, Rahmann was also able to find money to pay the bills and salaries of the professors, some of whom were imprisoned. A later generation of SVD students who studied in Miramar and Epworth were sometimes treated to the tales of Fathers John McDonough, Edgar Oehler, and William Fitzgibbon, American missionaries who were assigned to Fu Jen to teach English, biology, chemistry, and physics. They were rounded up and spent the war in Japanese detention centers in quite grim circumstances. Their tale

---

15. Goertz to Grendel, Rome, Generalate Archives, 12 September 1935.

is told best by Langdon Gilkey, a young American Protestant from Chicago.[16] Gilkey came to China to teach shortly before the outbreak of hostilities between the Americans and the Japanese. After the war, his book *Shantung Compound* became a best-seller, and in it some of the most vivid characters were the Catholic missionaries. In Gilkey's judgment, they did better than any other identifiable group in the compounds, bearing heat and cold, food shortages, and other deprivations with an equanimity that others found hard to imitate. Those who recall earlier chapters in this volume about the Spartan but intense communal life at Techny during the years when men like Fitzgibbon and Oehler were in the seminary will not be surprised by Gilkey's judgment.

The student body of Fu Jen university actually grew during the war. A report drawn up for the SVD general chapter of 1947 by Father Rahmann gave enrollment figures from the time the Society took over the university from the Benedictines. Not including middle school students, enrollments grew as follows: From 570 students in 1933 to 810 in 1936; from 1,265 in 1938 to 2,245 in 1941; from 2,354 in 1942 to 2,611 in 1946. Between the years 1942 and 1943, enrollments dropped to 2,061; they went back up to 2,303 in 1944 and dropped to 2,271 in 1945.

An event that added to the luster of Fu Jen in the eyes of the Chinese, according to Rahmann's report, stemmed from its refusal to join a public parade the Japanese put on in Peking in early summer of 1938 to celebrate their victory over the Chinese at Hsuchowfu. Chinese were being ordered to celebrate a Japanese victory over Chinese disguised as a victory of the Japanese over communism. Fu Jen's middle school was summarily closed because of this refusal, and the university's closure was to follow. Rahmann and Feifel's diplomatic skills were put to the test and six weeks later the middle school was permitted to reopen and freedom for the university guaranteed through an official decree. Because other universities had closed, students began to transfer to Fu Jen to the point that the university could not accept them all.

THE REVOLUTION, HAROLD RIGNEY, AND FU JEN'S VICISSITUDES

The next dramatic event in Fu Jen's history concerns its fate during and after the Communist Revolution. The events of that revolution are well known and have been written on extensively. Our focus will be on what they meant for Fu Jen and SVD missions in China.

As soon as World War II came to an end, the Society started sending missionaries to Peking. Among them were several from the United States, which was now producing larger numbers of priests and brothers. At the same time, Father Ralph and the mission procures in the three provinces had continued to collect money during the war years. As soon as communications were established, money raised by Ralph Thyken was sent to pay off the loans that Fu Jen had contracted to keep

---

16. See Langdon B. Gilkey, *Shantung Compound: The Story of Men and Women under Pressure* (New York: Harper & Row, 1966).

itself open during the war years. Most concretely, in regard to the American connection, Father Harold Rigney was also assigned to succeed Father Rahmann as rector. He did so on 4 August 1946.

Rigney was born in Chicago on 18 December 1900 and decided early on that he wanted to be a priest. With this in mind he entered the Chicago diocesan seminary. After two years he decided he really wanted to be a missionary, so in 1916 he entered Techny and was ordained with nine others in 1930. His first assignment led him to Girard to teach biology, mathematics, geography, and Bible history. As the Society was seeking to improve its teachers and schools, and since Rigney was very bright, he was asked to pursue further studies. On the recommendation of the superior general that "if he is to be respected in his field, he should attend the best school in the country," he became the first of a number of SVDs who over the years earned doctorates at the University of Chicago. Rigney received his degree in vertebrate paleontology in 1937, after which he was assigned to Ghana on the west coast of Africa. Ghana, long known as the Gold Coast, had only recently been assigned to the Society. Rigney taught at Achimota College until World War II broke out.

An American air base was built not far from the college, and Father Rigney began to celebrate Mass and help out. He joined the American army as chaplain, a position he held until the end of the war in 1945. Pictures of a natty-looking Rigney in his U.S. army uniform were quite widely published and disseminated. In 1946 he was appointed to Fu Jen as rector. Like Megan in Honan, Rigney in Peking was very friendly with the American military and embassy officials during the years immediately after the war. By the beginning of the 1948 school year there were thirty-four Divine Word priests and three brothers attached to Fu Jen, a number of them American, many not long there when the communists entered Peking. These were quickly reassigned to the Philippines and other missions or back to the United States.

One of those assigned to Fu Jen was Father Joseph Bates. He tells the story of the communist takeover of Peking in a letter written to Father Ralph on 30 March 1949.

At the request of Very Rev. Harold Rigney, S.V.D., I am writing a brief statement of conditions at the University as of March 22, 1949 . . . On January 22 the city was surrendered by agreement to the Communists. On January 31st the Communists marched in without any advance announcement or fanfare . . .

The most impressive aspect of the parade was not the material but the men. Although recruited from the same peasant stock and—with the exception of those wearing fur caps—clad in the same faded yellow uniforms as the Nationalists, the Communists looked very different. The average Nationalist soldier looks dazed; the Communist recruit looks purposeful. This is, of course, a product of their indoctrination which teaches them that they are what their name implies: The People's Liberation Army. The seriousness with which they take themselves was discovered by two students who asked some Communist soldiers, "Any of you [Communist General] Lin Piao's troops?" "No," was the reply, "We are the people's troops."

The wave of anti-foreignism that was brought into the city with them is the result of a suspicious attitude of a people who have lived too long in inland isolation, feeling the anti-communist world was actually against them. While foreigners are not molested in any way, they have to have road passes to move any place outside the city walls and these are secured with great difficulty and always with a great deal of questioning. When Fr. Rigney attempted to contact the head of the Educational Ministry of the Communists to find out what policy they had towards private schools, the man in charge refused not only to talk to him but to look at him and demanded that he be taken out of his presence. The Consulates have not been recognized because as the Communists put it, "you do not recognize us."

RIGNEY'S MEMORANDUM AND THE
BEGINNING OF THE END OF FU JEN IN CHINA

The years from the victory of the Communist Revolution to the closing of Fu Jen University were incredibly dramatic. They left an indelible impression on all who stayed in China through the entire period. The general course of events that followed the communists' consolidation of power is well known and will not be repeated here. Much of what I shall report is based on an almost day-by-day account of the events that revolved around Fu Jen from 22 January 1949 until the last entry on 24 October 1950. It is contained in a twenty-nine-page, single-spaced account that Fu Jen's rector, Harold Rigney, sent to Cardinal Pietro Fumasoni-Biondi, Prefect of the Congregation for the Propagation of the Faith, more commonly known then and now as Propaganda.

Only days after the communists took over the city of Peking, the road to the end of the institution as a Catholic university became inevitable. Rigney's memorandum tells how that demise occurred. The first steps involved ad hoc attempts to accommodate to the situation as it was developing. Under the ideology of the revolution, the Chinese faculty and the students were part of the newly recognized "people" of China. Because China was now a "democracy," the students felt they had a right to a significant say in running "their" university. Accordingly, demands were made on the German and American foreigners in administration. Over time, a form of agitation developed, and the SVDs attempted to react to the demands being made. Consultations with Archbishop Riberi, the pope's representative to China, and the SVD superior general on whether to keep Fu Jen open were answered in the affirmative. When it became apparent that all schools would have to teach Marxism and atheistic materialism, the authorities would be asked if this could be done, and the answer came that it would be acceptable if the person teaching the course was not paid by the university, since it would simply constitute material cooperation. Problems would arise in dealing with the government as well. A change in regulations might be proposed, but the Ministry of Education would be unsure just what it should do. Confusion reigned when a Chinese president of the university was named and the foreign rector or chancellor did not agree. This had been a problem in earlier years, but now the pressure to give authority over all university matters to the Chinese president became inexorable.

As time went on, the university's fate became entangled in Chinese-American government enmity as the Americans began their search for an answer to the question, "Who lost China?" and the communists realized that their revolution was not going to be recognized by Washington. On 25 July 1949, Chou En-lai, the most important man in the hierarchy of Communist leaders after Mao Tse-tung, gave a speech at the All China Labor Congress on furthering the revolution. In this speech he pointed to the United States as the worst imperialist enemy and called Fu Jen an imperialistic university.

On 1 October 1949, the new People's Government of All China was inaugurated with great pomp. Two days later the university, still under the SVD, opened with 1,291 students, down substantially from the previous year's enrollment of 2,324. The matter of foreign SVD and church subsidies and control of the university became critical issues, both of which reached the highest levels of the government. The second great problem that runs through Rigney's account of the last days before Fu Jen was occupied by the communists was the question of foreign money and control. Without a certain minimum of control over curriculum and the staff, the SVD and Propaganda would not support the university. For a cash-strapped government, the amounts were not small, since Father Ralph sent $355,000 between July 1949 and June 1950.

In retrospect, it seems odd that anyone then could imagine that the new communist government would give ground, but in 1949 and 1950 matters were not so clear. Would the communists finally consolidate their hold on China or would the Americans find a way to support Chiang-Kai-shek's military to an extent that he might manage to return and begin a reconquest? Viewed from a vantage point of fifty years, that too seems fanciful, but Chinese communist fear of the United States in 1950 was not paranoid but realistic.

In the meantime, German and American SVDs were joining religious from many nations in leaving an increasingly inhospitable country. The majority were expelled by the communists. Still others were not permitted to return from trips abroad. Father Edgar Oehler, for example, had been on a geological research trip in the interior of China. When he tried to reenter mainland China from Hong Kong, he was unable to get a reentry permit and was reassigned to the University of San Carlos in the Philippines, where he worked for thirteen years. When Father William Hogan left in late September, the only American SVD left in China was Rigney.

All through the school year previous to the university takeover, there were escalating demonstrations and acts of agitation by the students and denunciations on the part of the Chinese faculty. Demands were made that could not be satisfied. Accusations included charges of aiding and abetting imperialism, followed by accusations of dictatorial behavior toward "the people," in this case, the students, and of infringing on the sovereignty of the country. In that environment, then, the foreign priests began departing.

The drama was moving to its denouement as more agitation and circulation of petitions to the government to take over Fu Jen were spread. Father Rigney's account becomes a list of provocations that he tries to deal with, but he is merely sticking his finger in a failing dike. The government by now has certainly decided to carry out their plans. Since Rigney was unable to get an exit permit, he could only stay behind at Fu Jen, where he continued to live in what had been his private quarters in the garden. For all practical purposes he was a non-person. "As time went on," as he wrote in his account of this period and his imprisonment after being released, "I was more and more avoided by those I knew, until finally I was practically deserted by all. I was abandoned."[17] He lived in Limbo until 15 July 1951, when he was finally arrested on charges of being an American spy. Although it is an oversimplification to put it this way, Harold Rigney had given the communists all the plausibility they needed to level those charges: his years of service in the United States army as a chaplain and later his socializing with American diplomats and military personnel in Peking.

Rigney's stay in prison was characterized by brutal and dehumanizing treatment. The story of that stay, written not long after he was released, is chilling even today. For about two months he was subjected to an intense interrogation phase. Every night, often all night, he was accused by a judge of being a spy for America, for subversion of the will of the people, for a host of violations of the law—whatever, it seems, that came into the judge's mind. Rigney was expected to confess, though no proofs were offered, no counsel allowed on the principle that you were punished not for what you confessed, but for what you did not confess. During this phase he was fettered and handcuffed, once for seven days and nights, because he refused to admit the accusation of the court that two German colleagues on the Fu Jen staff, Father Joseph Meiners, SVD, and Dr. Wilhelm Bruell, were Gestapo agents. He could not sleep lying down, so he had to do so sitting up; he had to eat his food as best he could, like a dog. Nor was it simple to go to the latrine trussed up this way. The rusty fetters breaking through the skin finally caused blood poisoning and were removed. Apparently the government could not afford to let Rigney die. Under such torment he confessed his crimes, but later would retract the confession. The process would continue.

Finally, on 21 September 1954, Father Rigney was sentenced to ten years in prison and was sent to a match box factory in Peking. The time already spent in prison would count toward the sentence, so he could expect to be released on 25 July 1961. Nevertheless, on 15 July 1955, his treatment improved. Packages came through more regularly. Then he was returned to the place of his initial imprisonment, where he was put in solitary confinement. He was being prepared for his release, which was confirmed not long after. On 11 September 1955, he was once again brought to a court away from the prison. The judge read a statement saying that he had worked well in prison, had kept the rules, recognized his crimes, and reformed himself by work.

Without knowing it, Rigney had become an international *cause celebre* and China could no longer afford the price they were paying, losing face in the world community. Great efforts had been made on his behalf, about which he only learned when he arrived in Hong Kong on 16 September 1955. While Rigney languished in prison, the Techny community, under the leadership of Father Ralph Wiltgen, had started a "Freedom Crusade," whose purpose was to free their con-

---

17. Harold Rigney, *Four Years in a Red Hell* (Chicago: Henry Regnery Company, 1956), p. 29.

frere and other American civilians held prisoners in China. The crusade consisted in sending petitions for their release to anybody and everybody who might have some influence in accomplishing this. A petition was also addressed to Mao Tse-tung, Chairman of the People's Republic of China, requesting that he free Rigney and the other half-dozen civilian Americans whose names were on the petition. The crusade sent out copies of the petition to anyone requesting them, and soon thousands of the two-color petitions were being printed by the brothers in the Techny press. Requests for additional copies of the petition, announced in the press, began to arrive from midwestern cities and states and soon from all over the country.

After his release Rigney returned to the United States, well known and a hero to many. After one year of giving speeches, partly as a way of repaying all those who helped him out of prison, Rigney was ready for reassignment. The first was a term as provincial superior of the English-Irish Province, followed by a stint as president of the University of San Carlos in the Philippines. In 1965 Rigney came to Epworth to head up the science department and to do research. Then in 1970 he was called to be president of the new four-year Divine Word College in Epworth, Iowa. It was during his tenure here that he was able to continue his own research again in vertebrate paleontology and identify the unique quality of the fossil his good friend, Fr. Oehler, had found in China.

By 1973, Rigney suffered a kidney disease and was forced to undergo dialysis. He suffered through seven years of this, gradually getting worse with many complications. At the end he was down to 87 pounds, much less than he was during his imprisonment. He was witty, obviously intelligent. Born in the Back of the Yards area in Chicago, an area so-called because it bordered on Chicago's famous stockyards, he was Irish-American to the core. He met people easily and would have made a wonderful politician if he had not gone into the priesthood. He loved life and people, a good drink and a good meal now and then, ready at all times with a joke. Yet, as the fruits of his life prove, he was also steel-willed and serious about his vocation to the missionary priesthood and religious life.

But this was not the end for Fu Jen. After the school was taken over, the staff and part of the campus were joined to Beijing Normal University. Father Frank Budenholzer, an American Divine Word priest who works in the chemistry department of the new Fu Jen in Taipei, Taiwan, made a trip to Beijing and visited the old campus. In personal correspondence with me, Budenholzer reports that the main building of the old university was, for a while, the chemistry department for the normal university. A new chemistry building has since been built, and the old structure is now used for the humanities. The main building has been declared a cultural landmark, which means that at least its exterior must be kept in its present state. Other sections of the campus have been used for a high school, since the academy of social sciences and one part that had been the palace of a prince is now a sort of museum park. Budenholzer reports that there is an alumni association that is allowed to offer extension courses using the name, "Fu Jen Evening School." The number of persons enrolled is relatively small and no recognized diplomas are granted. Still, he says, "it is their hope that from this beginning a new Fu Jen might emerge."

THE NEW FU JEN

Fu Jen, in a drastically changed format, still exists on the island of Taiwan, to which Chiang Kai-shek and the remnants of his government and Nationalist army fled. There they set up a government that claimed to represent all China. The People's Republic of China, however, claims sovereignty over Taiwan, and over this political fault line a new Fu Jen University has risen.

Already in 1948 the Society of the Divine Word was looking into the possibility of beginning a mission on Taiwan, or Formosa as it was then known. This included plans for transferring Fu Jen to Taiwan as well. In 1949 a piece of property was bought near the railway station in the capital city, Taipei, for a future Fu Jen. That land was sold in 1953, a decision the Society in Taiwan would later regret.[18] The SVDs who were forced to leave China, so went the thinking, could be reassigned to Taiwan. The discussion went so far as assigning possible superiors for the project. Eventually, however, the idea was abandoned and the China missionaries received new assignments. Taiwan was kept in mind as a possible site of a new mission, a possibility that was acted on in 1958. By this time the Nationalists on Taiwan had consolidated their position, and with the two Chinas facing each other belligerently across the Straits of Taiwan, it seemed unlikely that much would come of this posturing in the near future. Moreover, the Society held a general chapter in 1958 and had elected Johannes Schütte, a former China missioner, as their new superior general. To Schütte it was inconceivable that the SVD would not have a presence in Taiwan, in part to prepare missionaries to return to the mainland.

The Society had actually begun work on Taiwan provisionally in 1954. In 1959 all was ready to make this tentative entry a permanent one and included plans to reopen Fu Jen University in some form. Many of Fu Jen's Chinese staff and alumni had gone to Taiwan with the Nationalists and had begun to request that Fu Jen be opened again on Taiwan. In 1959, Pope John XXIII asked the head of Propaganda, Cardinal Agagianian, to look into the possibility of a new Chinese Catholic university. Archbishop Paul Yu Pin, formerly a member of the board of trustees of the old Fu Jen, was instructed to promote the project. Plans moved rapidly, as such things go. By 1963 the university was officially recognized and students were accepted into the new Fu Jen, located in Hsin Chuang, a suburb of Taipei. Not only were the location and buildings new, but the administrative structure of the new Fu Jen was different. No longer could the SVD alone take on the heavy financial and personnel burden of a modern university by itself. The task had to be shared. The colleges of liberal and fine arts, as well as the central administration of the university, were assigned to the Chinese diocesan clergy. The colleges of science, engineering, and foreign languages were entrusted to the Society of the Divine Word. The Jesuits assumed the responsibility to manage the colleges of law and management. This division of labor has worked well, and the university has pros-

---

18. Anton Weber, "Across the Strait to Taiwan," *Word in the World 1990/91* (Steyl: Steyler Verlag, 1991), p. 61.

pered and grown, both in terms of the quality of its programs and by adding new facilities. One of the key people in making that happen was Father Bernard Doyle.

Doyle, who would die at the age of thirty-five of lung cancer, may serve as a representative of another group of Americans who strove to serve the mission of Christ in China. Told by his father that he could not enter the SVD minor seminary, he finished high school in three rather than four years and went off to novitiate at Techny. During his novitiate, the joke was told that Father Glorius was so convinced that Bernie would not persevere that he wrote his name on the roster with a pencil rather than an ink pen. Perhaps Bernie made up the joke himself, for many were the practical jokes he played on his confreres.

His China interest was keenly stimulated during the years that Cardinal Thomas Tien lived in exile at Techny. Tien, the SVD's only cardinal, was in exile from his post as Archbishop of Peking and a much beloved member of the Techny community. Doyle offered to teach the cardinal English. In return, Cardinal Tien introduced Bernie to the Chinese language. When Clifford King was not available, Doyle served as Tien's secretary, and the two became close friends. The cardinal attended Bernie's first Mass celebration and later, when he returned to Taiwan to become apostolic administrator of Taipei, Doyle was his first choice to be his secretary there, according to Father Bartley Schmitz who did become his secretary. By this time, however, Bernie was already assigned to the new Fu Jen in Taiwan.

After his ordination on 15 August 1955, Doyle was assigned to the Philippines where he worked in St. Jude's, the Society's Chinese parish in Manila. Soon he was national chaplain for the Chinese Catholic Youth Organization in the Philippines. In the Philippines, Doyle's capacity as an astute money manager surfaced. Thus in 1959 as plans were being developed to reopen Fu Jen on Taiwan, Doyle was sent to the United States to get a master's degree in business administration. His studies completed, he returned in 1962 to Taiwan as treasurer of the College of Science and Engineering and the College of Foreign Languages, both existing only in plans. Bartley Schmitz, who was in Taiwan when Doyle arrived, marveled at what he was able to accomplish so quickly. According to Schmitz, Bernie Doyle distinguished himself within months of his arrival by negotiating virtually overnight the legendary complexity of purchasing and obtaining deeds to numberless small land parcels that went to make up the thirteen hectares, about thirty-two acres, of the original campus area. In two and a half years Doyle directed and completed a five-building complex for the two colleges to be conducted by the SVD.

He was diagnosed with cancer and returned home for treatment. Instead, he died within three months, much to the shock of his confreres and countless Chinese friends in both Taiwan and the Philippines. Fu Jen University in Taipei, however, went on to become an integral part of the development of modern Taiwan. By the 1960s, of course, it was no longer possible or desirable for an order such as the SVD to dominate an institution of higher learning with its members, so the ratio of SVDs to Chinese and foreign lay staff has always been modest. Citizens of the United States and persons from other lands who received degrees in American universities have, nevertheless, been a major influence on the development of colleges entrusted to the SVD. Francis Budenholzer has already been named. We cannot complete this chapter without adding to his name those of Edward Vargo, James Liebner, Daniel Bauer, and Patrick Hogan.

And while mentioning men of a new generation who served and serve Fu Jen, it is worthwhile to call to mind a man remembered principally for service in Ghana who came to Fu Jen in 1979 after retiring from the University of Ghana. The priest is John Koster, about whom more will be said later. At the age of sixty-one, when most are beginning to think about retirement, Father Koster took up the invitation to teach physics on Taiwan in 1979. Brother Patrick Hogan, who served with him during many of the years Koster worked there, recalls a man of supreme discipline, who believed firmly that the role of an SVD professor was to model respect for his academic branch and who carried on research both for its own sake and to infect his students with love for learning. Koster worked at Fu Jen from 1979 until 1994 when he returned to the United States to go finally into retirement. Hogan recalls how much his years and students in Ghana meant to Koster. When he heard any word of disparagement for Africa and the capacities of its people, which sometimes occurred among the Chinese, Koster always stated firmly, in a tone that indicated he wanted to hear no more ethnic prejudice, "My students in Africa were the equal of any I have had here or anywhere else." Despite his great learning and heavy research and teaching commitments, Koster is also recalled as a man observant of all the community's religious and social exercises, and a man who exuded a sense of spirituality. We shall meet Koster again in the chapter on Ghana, where he began his career.

Will Fu Jen ever be reopened in the People's Republic? If recent history has taught us anything, it is that anything is possible. Today's enemies become tomorrow's friends. Will SVD missionaries ever return to the People's Republic? As soon as it is permitted, we may be sure they will go.

12

New Guinea

The Land That History Found

The mission work of the Divine Word Missionaries in New Guinea is a fascinating story. It is the area in which SVDs have had the longest sustained work with major responsibilities for a large segment of a church. The island of New Guinea itself is often referred to as "the land that time forgot." It was discovered during the early European voyages of exploration, but it was only in the nineteenth century that it became the object of much sustained interest from the outside world. In reality, it became the "land that history found" in the age of colonial empire-building. The SVD and missionaries from other Catholic and Protestant groups were a good part of the intercultural interchange that would bring the island into the modern world. We can only touch the surface of that story here. It is a land whose whole history is being written as Melanesians increasingly move from being "exotic" peoples anthropologists study to citizens of a global civilization. As the twenty-first century begins, over ninety percent of the Melanesians identify themselves as Christians. It is hard to believe that as the twentieth began, one percent would have chosen that designation.

In discussing the foundation of the China mission, I have already adverted to the fact that SVD missions in China, West Africa, and New Guinea were in areas controlled by the Germans or where the German government wanted to broaden its influence. There were differences in nuance in each of these missions, and this is true of the mission in New Guinea. Here the German claim was preceded by commercial and scientific expeditions that had been sent out by the emperor's (*Kaiser* in German) government. The only available areas in New Guinea were the northeastern third of the island and the group of islands further to the northeast that were named the Bismarck Archipelago. Political and judicial controls were delegated to the New Guinea Company in an arrangement similar to that employed by the British in India. Their rule was backed up by Germany's naval might, much like the way the British allowed the East India Company to form their India army. The New Guinea Company was to exploit the colony for the profit of its stockholders. In terms of profits, the system never worked well in New Guinea, but while it lasted, from its charter in May 1885 until 1899 when it requested to be released from its obligations, the arrangement would cause much grief.

A few geographical facts should be given. "New Guinea" is the name for the entire large island that lies to the north of the Australian landmass. It is the second largest island in the world, larger even than Great Britain, but smaller than Greenland. It is one-and-a-half times the size of Spain, twice the size of Japan, and larger than the states of Texas and Louisiana combined. The coastal areas are sparsely inhabited compared to the Highlands, which were still *terra incognita* during the first thirty years the Society worked in New Guinea. Swamp, jungle, and mountains made up most of what the missionaries encountered, or so it seemed to them. In 1896 the Dutch held sway in western New Guinea; now known as Irian Jaya, that part of the island that is now a province of Indonesia. The British administered the southeastern part of the island as British New Guinea or Papua. The German colony was comprised of the northeast portion and it was called both Kaiser Wilhelmsland and *Nordost Neu Guinea* in German. The northeast and southeast were united into one country known as Papua New Guinea in 1975. Throughout this chapter we shall use the term New Guinea, referring mainly to the northeast portion of the island and the many islands off the north shore, on many of which the Society also established missions.

ARRIVAL OF THE SOCIETY OF THE DIVINE WORD

In the mid-1890s, the German Colonial Office and Colonial Council was negotiating with the Holy See to obtain German nationals as missionaries in German colonies as a means of avoiding the difficulties that had developed between the New Guinea Company and French Missionaries of the Sacred Heart who were then working in New Guinea. The foreign office reported itself

> pleased to learn that the mission work in New Guinea was entrusted to the missionaries of the Divine Word. Under the direction of their very respected superior, Arnold Janssen, they have already performed great service in China and in German Togoland.[1]

On 13 August 1896, the first SVD missionaries landed at Friedrich Wilhelmshafen, later and still called Madang (the name we shall use throughout) to begin the SVD New Guinea mission. At the time the New Guinea Company was still in control and pursued a policy of assigning various areas to different Christian denominations to try to avoid competition among them. The area around Madang was already assigned to the Lutherans, and the SVDs were not allowed to open a station by the government in Madang, although the founder believed he had been promised the opportunity to purchase land there. The administration would not

---

1. Fritz Bornemann, *Arnold Janssen der Gründer des Steyler Missionswerkes 1837–1909. Ein Lebensbild nach zeitgenössischen Quellen* (Steyl: Sekretariat Arnold Janssen, 1969), p. 398. Bornemann is the source for most anecdotes and facts reported in this section. For a clear, concise description of what preceded the entrance of the SVD into New Guinea, see Ralph Wiltgen, *The Founding of the Roman Catholic Church in Oceania*, vol. 1 (Canberra: Australian National University Press, 1979).

change its policy, however, and the mission had to find another place to begin. Upon the invitation of a German planter—who, it seems, wanted German company to ease the burdens of a lonely settlement on the island—and his assurance that Tumleo Island, about 272 nautical miles from Madang, was free from fever, yet close to the mainland, the Society moved its headquarters there. Headquarters for the SVD were finally established in Alexishafen, known also by its indigenous name, Sek. Here was a protected deepwater harbor. Over the years, sawmills, butcher shops, mechanical shops, schools, aid posts, and catechetical centers would go up around Alexishafen. It became the headquarters both of the mission and the site where the regional, and later provincial, superior lived. A large regional house was erected and in it would stay traveling missionaries, missionaries in for retreats, and so forth. As missions up the coast in Wewak, in the Simbu, and Mount Hagen grew, each developed similar facilities, but Alexishafen always retained a special place in the memories of most SVDs assigned to Papua New Guinea if only because most new missionaries spent several days there before they went off by boat and plane, and later by pickup truck and jeep, to stations scattered across the island.

Father Eberhard Limbrock was the first SVD religious superior and prefect apostolic in New Guinea. Limbrock came to Steyl in 1877, at the age of eighteen, and had trained as a mechanic and blacksmith, or iron worker, before he arrived there. He was sent to China in 1883 and was thirty-six when Janssen asked him to go to New Guinea. His appointment is an example of Janssen's habit of sending men who proved successful in one mission to start new ones, rather than entrust such pioneering work to men without missionary experience.

Since Janssen wanted each mission to be self-supporting as soon as possible, Limbrock's first concern was to establish plantations, a task made difficult by the fact that the New Guinea Company did not want competition. Limbrock was a man of vision, determination, and hard work. Following mission methods learned in China, he established main stations up and down the coast and outstations in the villages in the hinterland at about the distance the missionary could walk or ride a horse in a day or two. As soon as possible, schools were established, both for catechist training and general schools. To support all this he bought land, developed sawmills in strategic places, planted coconut palms and rubber trees, and raised cattle at the recommendation of the founder, who even agreed to donate the first pair. In a report to Father Janssen in 1906, Limbrock wrote that 600 acres were planted with 28,650 coconut palms and 120 acres with 28,550 rubber trees. He reported 100 head of cattle and 20 horses. By 1925 the animal population had increased to 1,374 cattle, 170 carabaos, 80 pigs, 116 horses, 19 donkeys or mules, 817 sheep, 365 goats, and 1,117 chickens.

Some might find it strange that so much time, energy, and money was spent on plantations and other activities seemingly quite far removed from missionary work. The reason is that both Janssen and Limbrock realized how undeveloped New Guinea was and how necessary it was to have means of self-support for two reasons: first, if contact with Europe should be cut off because of an event like war, and second, lest the mission drain the coffers of the young Society and make other work impossible. At this time there was no other source of money than Germany and Holland. Another SVD missionary, Father Andreas Puff, writing in 1921, gave more pastoral reasons for plantations:

> The natural development of the mission suggested plantations . . . as the best means of making contact with the distant and diverse linguistic groups of natives, acquainting them with our intentions and purposes, and facilitating the mission's task of instruction and education.[2]

Puff's rationale notwithstanding, there was much disagreement among the missionaries as years went on. Especially after World War II, as independence drew near and the government tried to make the nation more self-sufficient, plantations owned by churches and mission groups, including the SVD, were highly controversial.

Not to be forgotten as we tell the story of the early fathers and brothers is the magnificent work and dedication of the Holy Spirit Missionary Sisters in education and health, particularly. The first five sisters arrived on Tumleo Island on 16 March 1899, only three years after the fathers and brothers. By 1907, sisters were working at stations in Ali, Bogia, and Alexishafen. From the beginning they were intensely engaged in teaching and nursing, Their clinics were spotless and many sisters developed talents equal to those of the best-trained physicians. A young American who arrived sick in Alexishafen in 1972 learned that first hand when the brother in charge of the SVD regional house whisked him off to the clinic. Sister Christophilda, a veteran of untold years of missionary service, quickly diagnosed the problem, gave him a shot, and prescribed a medicine. The sisters cared for countless priests and brothers over the years. They oversaw the domestic arrangements of several of the larger stations as well, and the missioner from an outstation could always look forward to a well-cooked meal when he visited such a station.

These missionaries lived and died subject to unfamiliar diseases, heat, and the ravages of war. Their history calls out to be told, and our brief tribute here does not do them justice.

During the early years, a multitude of problems were faced. Many were solved, and many simply became the difficulties that the missioners took as integral to working in New Guinea. The question of how the mission was to be governed and whether the distinct offices of religious and ecclesiastical superior should continue to be linked in New Guinea, as it had been from the beginning, was resolved after the founder died. As the size and complexity of the missions grew, this combination of authority became more and more problematic. Conflicts of interest were almost inevitable, on the financial as well as on the spiritual level. As the constitutions were revised, the separation was effected. Nicholas Blum, the second superior general, implemented the new policy and in 1914 replaced Father Limbrock as religious superior with Father Vormann, as "regional" (i.e., "religious" superior). Limbrock then resigned as prefect apostolic, a resignation he had earlier submitted to the founder, who refused to accept it. This time it was accepted by the

---

2. Fritz Bornemann et al., *A History of the Divine Word Missionaries* (Rome: Collegio del Verbo Divino, 1981), p. 388.

Holy See after consulting the Society. The relationship was a stormy one at times, but very fruitful for the New Guinea mission. Part of Limbrock's reason for resigning was the outbreak of war in Europe and the Australian takeover of Kaiser Wilhelmsland on 14 September 1914. On 7 December 1914, the Australians, belligerents in World War I on the side of Britain, arrived in Madang. Foreseeing the Australian ascendancy over all of eastern New Guinea, Limbrock argued that by resigning he made it more likely that the Australians would be willing to let the German missionaries continue their pastoral work in New Guinea.

In fact, however, no successor to Limbrock was named until 1922 when Bishop Francis Wolf, SVD, who had been ordained for Togo on 28 June 1914, was appointed the day that Archduke Franz Ferdinand was assassinated in Sarajevo. Wolf was not permitted to return to Togo, since all German missionaries there were interned during the war and forbidden to return after it, when the colony had been stripped from Germany's control. New Guinea was elevated to the status of vicariate apostolic and placed under Bishop Wolf. On 14 August 1923, he finally made it to his new vicariate. When he settled into the job and began to interact with the Australian civil administration, Wolf felt a need to have a native English speaker and writer on his staff to make his relations with the government easier. From that need came the appointment of the first citizen of the United States to New Guinea.

Father Peter Weyland, a member of Techny's first ordination class, was to be that man. Fate or providence intervened, however, and his appointment was changed to the Philippines. Bishop Wolf had to wait until 1926, when Father William Ross, known to everyone as "Willie," arrived in New Guinea to serve as the bishop's English-speaking secretary. Ross, born in Kingston, New York, on 23 September 1895, one of three to be ordained in the second class at Techny in 1922, would become both a pioneer and a legend in New Guinea. As a seminarian, he wrote for *Our Missions* and *The Little Missionary*. A good public speaker and writer, he was assigned to teach at the new seminary in Miramar, though not long after getting that appointment, he was drafted to edit *The Little Missionary*. It was difficult to be the sole American among a virtually all-German team in these early years, but Ross impressed Bishop Wolf and was well liked. In a letter to the superior general, Bishop Wolf wrote:

> You remember that when we discussed opening a seminary in Australia, I voted with you all that Australian Catholics, who seem to be mostly of Irish descent, will never be tough enough to be our kind of missionary. Now, however, I am changing my mind. I have an Irish-American priest here, Father Ross, who is excellent in every way. If the Irish-Australian priests can be as good, they will be very good missionaries. I would now vote to open the seminary.[3]

Ross worked in coastal stations and as Wolf's secretary for some years. Wolf's praise of him for toughness was strong praise indeed. But the fact that Wolf felt the need to make it at all speaks volumes about the German confreres' attitudes

---

3. Bernard Fisher, "Techny Highlander," *Word in the World 1994–1995* (Steyl: Steyler Verlag, 1994): 96.

toward Americans. During the years between the time Ross arrived in New Guinea and took up work in the Highlands, the work that would make him famous, a variety of policy issues had to be worked out. Many of them revolved around the question of what language or languages should become the medium of missionary work. The choices on an island with eight hundred languages were basically three-fold: (1) the missioner could learn and use the local vernacular; (2) he could speak English and use interpreters to translate his words into this vernacular; (3) he could avail himself of the rapidly spreading trading language called *Tok Pisin* (pronounced "talk pidgin," whence the common but misleading term "pidgin English"). This matter was hotly debated on the coast during the time Willie Ross was there. The first generation of missioners tended to favor learning and using the local vernacular. In the end, though, that proved impractical for two reasons. First, there were so many languages that any given missionary might have to learn three or four just to work in a single area. How could he be replaced in case of sickness or when he needed a vacation? Second, how could catechetical materials, hymnals, and bibles be prepared quickly enough in all the languages? But the second, speaking English and having it interpreted, held little attraction to the Germans. Moreover, this opinion would rob missionaries of the only proven way to enter into a local culture, by learning a local language. In time, the decision was taken out of the missionaries' hands. Tok Pisin began spreading like wildfire and became the *lingua franca* of Melanesian peoples as they traveled and traded in the wider environs that the peace enforced by colonial administrations opened up to them. We shall discuss Tok Pisin more below. In the meantime, it may suffice to close this section by saying that from 1896, when German SVDs first arrived, through the mid-1930s, a network of mission stations was established up and down the coast with main centers as far from Madang as Aitape and Wewak. Large stations were built inland as well, especially along the Sepik River. This work was almost entirely done by German and Austrian confreres. The Dutch were concentrated in the islands today called Indonesia, then the East Indies, a Dutch colony. It is in the next chapter of New Guinea church history that Americans make a distinctive contribution, and to that we turn.

THE OPENING OF THE HIGHLANDS

When the SVD came to the New Guinea, everyone on the coast thought that the mountains that loomed on the inland horizon continued unbroken to the southern shores of the island in Papua. Thus Europeans believed that the interior was uninhabitable. Correcting that error would become one of the most important chapters in the modern history of exploration.

There had been some early indications that the inland area was more than just steep mountain ranges. In 1930, on one of his exploratory trips up the Sepik River and its tributaries, for instance, Father Franz Kirschbaum had viewed a vast inland plain stretching from the southeast to the west. In light of later knowledge, he could have viewed the Wahgi River valley but more likely he saw the Baiyer River valley. Kirschbaum urged Bishop Wolf to send an expedition into the area. Wolf applied for permission but was refused by the Australian administration in Rabaul.

The Australian system of pacification and exploration decreed that government patrols had to enter unexplored areas first, partly to protect local peoples, partly to protect foolhardy explorers from their zeal and curiosity. When the administration knew what kind of people were there and a modicum of protection could be guaranteed, patrols would move further into new areas. Permission could then be given to missionaries or commercial persons to move into the area if the administration judged it safe. Fathers Willie Ross and Richard Nowak had even been assigned by Bishop Wolf to accompany Kirschbaum on the expedition for which permission had been denied.

As Kirschbaum was associated with the Sepik River, Nowak knew the Ramu River and the area behind Alexishafen. Villagers along the Ramu had told Nowak that the mountains that loomed beyond the Ramu were filled with people, "as numerous as the leaves on a tree."[4] Because Father Nowak needed a rest and home leave, his successor, Alphonse Schäfer, was entrusted the task of mounting the first SVD expedition into the Highlands. He did so from the north, leaving from Alexishafen and proceeded via the Ramu river. Unbeknownst to Schäfer or Bishop Wolf, another attempt to enter the Highlands was already underway from the east under the aegis of a group of gold miners who wanted to investigate new areas where gold might be found. Entry into the Highlands from the east had been unsuccessfully tested by the Lutheran missionary Leonhardt Flierl in 1922 and again in 1926.

At this point the airplane entered the picture. On 8 March 1933, Ken Spinks, a surveyor, and James Taylor, a government patrol officer, flew from Bena Bena over the Wahgi valley all the way to Mount Hagen. It was the first time any white men had seen these valleys. Their trip demolished the belief that the center of New Guinea was a mass of uninhabitable mountains.[5] It was obvious, even from the air, that the area they had flown over was quite densely populated. Shortly thereafter they walked all the way to Mount Hagen.

Before that airplane landed, in early 1932, Father Schäfer, Father Anthony Cranssen, and Brother Anton Baas began moving from Alexishafen up the Ramu, then into the Bismarck mountain range, preparing a base camp for the journey by foot that the first SVDs would take into the Highlands. They built a house at Bundi and finally in October 1933 began the trek into the Simbu valley. They were guided by a man named Kawagl. By 9 November they reached the 9,200-foot Bundi pass, and on the next day celebrated the first Catholic Eucharist in the history of the Simbu valley. Five years later, in 1938, the first ten young boys from this area were baptized at what is now the mission station of Denglagu. Schäfer will return in our story, but since our focus is on the American presence, it is important to stress that Alphonse Schäfer is one of the great pioneers of Catholic missionary work in New Guinea, a man as important as Willie Ross, whose story will serve to focus our story.

---

4. Bornemann, *A History*, p. 392.

5. Michael Leahy and Maurice Crain, *The Land That Time Forgot: Adventures and Discoveries in New Guinea* (New York: Funk & Wagnalls Company, 1937), p. 150. See also Michael Leahy, *Explorations into Highland New Guinea 1930–1935*, ed. Douglas E. Jones (Tuscaloosa, Ala: University of Alabama Press, 1991).

FATHER ROSS AND BROTHER EUGENE
IN THE WESTERN HIGHLANDS

After Schäfer's return with his description of the Highlands and his report detailing all of the opportunities awaiting the missions, Bishop Wolf made immediate plans to send more missionaries into the mountains. Father Ross was a natural choice. Among other things, he knew Mick Leahy, who was already laying the foundations of the business interests that he and his three brothers would establish there. In July 1933, Mick Leahy wrote to Ross from Mount Hagen: "This is a fabulous country, a vast population, beautiful climate."[6] At the same time he invited him to come to Mount Hagen and open up a mission. Mick and Dan Leahy left Mount Hagen in October to spend the Christmas holidays in Australia. On the way they passed through Alexishafen to report to Bishop Wolf and further encourage him to open a mission in the Hagen area.[7] Wolf quickly made the judgment that the Highlands were in the SVD's future and he pursued it with all the vigor he had. He did not live to see the flowering of the church in the Highlands that took place after the Second World War, since he was killed during the war.

Father Ross was put in charge of the expedition to Mount Hagen. He, Father William Tropper, and Brother Eugene Frank were to go by boat to Bogajim, ten miles south of Madang, then proceed up the Gogol River into the Ramu River valley and on to Bundi. Here they would meet up with Schäfer, who would take over and lead the expedition the rest of the way to Hagen. Ross estimated the whole trip would take thirty-eight days. In addition to food supplies for six months, the group also took along essential building materials like nails, locks, hinges, bolts, as well as household items, and church goods like mass wine, hosts, candles, and missals. A line of seventy carriers boarded the mission ship *Michael* to make this trip. They began their six-week journey on 15 February 1934.

Let us take a moment to introduce Brother Eugene, the second American assigned to the New Guinea SVD missions. Brother Eugene was born at Mount Carmel, Illinois, the fifth of eight children, on 21 December 1900 and was named Francis Anthony Frank. He first wanted to be a priest and went to a minor seminary of the Congregation of the Sacred Heart at the age of fifteen. He left in less than a year and returned home, where he became a skilled carpenter. At the age of eighteen, he went to the Trappist monastery in Gethsemani, Kentucky, where he stayed for three months. When he read that the Society of the Divine Word was accepting young men as brothers, he applied there and was accepted. He entered as a postulant on 31 August 1921, and was trained as a baker. In the summer of 1929 he was appointed for New Guinea, where his skills as a carpenter were put to use as a builder of houses, churches, and schools; after a period he was in charge

---

6. Quoted in an unpublished, undated manuscript by Bernard Fisher, SVD, *Father Alphonse Schaefer, S.V.D., One of the Great Men and Women Who Built Up the Catholic Church in Papua New Guinea* (Kundiawa, Simbu, PNG: Divine Word Missionaries), p. 3.

7. John Nilles, SVD, *They Went Out to Sow. The Beginning of the Work of the Catholic Mission in the Highlands of Papua New Guinea 1933–1934* (Rome: Collegio del Verbo Divino, 1987), p. 19.

of drying coconuts to produce copra. In 1933 he was sent with Ross on the expedition to the Western Highlands. Here he stayed, putting up buildings for the fledgling Highlands mission. That he was happy with this appointment is clear from a letter he wrote home:

> Hip, hip, hurray . . . our destination is Mount Hagen. It's about 13,000 feet high. We shall be working in the valley. That the good Bishop [Wolf] has appointed me to work in the interior of our vicariate, among the wilds and the cannibals makes me feel very happy. Thousands of natives are there, some fifty or sixty thousand . . . We will take over a hundred young men as carriers, and enough food for one year . . . Am happy and well as ever.[8]

According to Father Bernard Fisher, himself a missionary in New Guinea for many years, this was to be a reconnaissance trip. The bishop had drafted plans for the Highlands based on what he had learned from Schäfer and the Leahys. Mick Leahy recalls their arrival in Mount Hagen:

> Much shouting and excitement from the countryside announced the arrival of the first white missionaries in the area. Dan and I walked from our camp and met Frs. Ross, Schäfer, Augenunger [*sic*], and Tropper and Brother Eugene, a tall lay brother from Mt. Carmel, Illinois. It was Wednesday, March 28, 1934, when they arrived on Mogei airstrip. They brought back Rebir, a small boy from Palinger whom we had taken out the previous year and had lent to Father Ross so he could learn the language. They were very enthusiastic about the great highland valleys through which they had traveled after crossing the Bismarck Range from their Gueabi [*sic*] station on the lower Ramu River side. As Dan and I were by now ready to move on to the small plateau above to start work on the alluvial gold in the small creeks, we handed over our partially built grass and pitpit camp to them so that they could start their missionary activities.
>
> The first Mass was celebrated in a tentfly rigged on the still untried airstrip on Sunday, April 1, 1934. Perhaps it was not a very appropriate or propitious day, but given the energy and enthusiasm of Fathers Ross and Schäfer, the mission seemed certain to succeed. They later made their headquarters at Rabiemul near the present Mt. Hagen strip. Father Schäfer was about seventy to eighty miles down the valley at Mingenda [*sic*]. Fathers Augenunger and Tropper were later assigned to other stations away from the Highlands, and Brother Eugene busied himself with constructing new grass, pitpit, and vine-tied buildings for the temporary camp on the airstrip.[9]

On 1 April 1934, the first airplane ever to land in Hagen, on a strip built by Mick and Dan Leahy, touched down. Bob Gurney, a pilot from the Morobe Gold Mining

---

8. Doris Burton, *Heroic Brothers: Ten Great Religious* (Fresno, Cal.: Academy Guild Press, n.d.), p. 99. Though Brother Eugene did not know it then, there were no cannibals in this part of the island.

9. Leahy, *Explorations*, pp. 168–69.

Company, stepped down from his Tiger Moth airplane to the welcome of the two Leahy brothers and the five SVDs.

Since their trip was exploratory, the missionaries declined Mick Leahy's offer to use his house and returned east in early April 1934 to build facilities in this area first, as the bishop had instructed them to do. Willie stayed at Dembi with Father Tropper, but his heart remained in Mount Hagen. Then Lutherans made their appearance, passing through Dembi around 22 May 1934 on their way to Mount Hagen. Ross, with Tropper and Brother Eugene, immediately rushed to Mount Hagen, fearing that the Lutherans would occupy the area and the houses the Leahys had given to them. When Ross, Tropper, and Eugene appeared at Hagen, they were welcomed by Danny Leahy, who was surprised but pleased to see them again so soon. The Catholic land was safe in a pre-ecumenical age.

Schäfer, the Highlands superior, was not around when Ross and the rest hastened off to Hagen. Without consulting Schäfer, Ross wrote to Bishop Wolf, seeking permission to remain in Mount Hagen. Wolf responded positively on 15 June 1934. Father Schäfer was not pleased and called Ross back to the Simbu. Ross protested with a detailed explanation why he should not return.

Schäfer complained bitterly to Bishop Wolf about Ross's behavior as undermining the plans that had been so meticulously made a few months before. By this time the bishop was probably getting tired of the bickering. He knew Ross's capabilities better than Schäfer and wrote: "In God's name, let Fr. Ross remain and work in Mt. Hagen."[10] Forever after, Alphonse Schäfer and Willie Ross could not see eye to eye, yet together the two were the great pioneers in the Highlands.

Although it is running ahead of our story, this may be the best place to say a few words about Father Schäfer's career. He went on to build a central mission station in Mingende. He introduced a generation of missionaries to work in Simbu, perhaps the most challenging SVD mission in New Guinea. He was legendary as a stern but fair taskmaster at making the new priests learn the difficult Simbu language, and learn it they did. He even became a legendary figure to the Simbu people for other-than-missionary reasons. His success in raising pigs larger than anyone had ever seen was astounding in a region where pigs were the possession that guaranteed prestige and power. In 1958, after twenty-eight years in active work in New Guinea (as well as in Australia during the war years), he was sent to Europe as a delegate of the New Guinea region to the eighth general Chapter of the Society. This itself is a sign of how much he was respected by his fellow missioners, for the post was elective. He was to get medical attention for a heart condition, but it came too late. While in the hospital in Arnsberg, Germany, he had a severe heart attack and died on 19 August 1958 at the age of fifty-four, much beloved by his people and coworkers. When the news of his death reached the people of the Simbu and Wahgi valleys, Christians and non-Christians gathered at Mingende where Father Schäfer had baptized more than ten thousand of them. There they held an immense funeral celebration, with prolonged wailing because they had lost their father.

---

10. Nilles, *They Went Out to Sow*, p. 30.

THE DEATHS OF BROTHER EUGENE
AND FATHER MORSCHEUSER

Ten months after Ross, Schäfer, and their confreres reached Mount Hagen, an enormous tragedy engulfed the entire Highlands mission. It was a tragedy made worse by an impetuous threat that today sets one's teeth on edge, revealing, as it does, a note of arrogance in missioners sent to announce the gospel of God's love. It began in the Eastern Highlands where a house at a station at Womkama, built as an overnight stopping place for missionaries in the upper Simbu, had accidentally burned down. Father Cornelius van Baar, recently appointed to the Highlands,[11] erected a frame for a new house and insisted that the people weave the matting for the walls and put on the thatched roof. He threatened that if they did not have this done by the time he returned, he would shoot some of their pigs. The more experienced Father Schäfer urged him not to shoot pigs if the house wasn't completed. What made the situation potentially more dangerous was the ongoing clan fighting in the area. Nevertheless, when van Baar, Father Karl Morscheuser, and some carriers returned to Womkama to find the house still unfinished, van Baar felt he had to carry out his threat. He killed two pigs and ordered everyone in his party out of the area. He walked at the head of the column of carriers, with Morscheuser at the rear. Soon they were under attack. One arrow struck Morscheuser in the neck and another in his chest. Shortly after, he died on the spot. It was 16 December 1934.

This essentially ended the actual hostilities, but the violence-poisoned atmosphere continued. In the meantime, Brother Eugene felt he needed a rest from the construction at Mount Hagen and decided to go to Bundi to make his annual retreat. To get to Bundi meant passing through and up the Simbu valley, now agitated by the events we have described, which were still not known in Mount Hagen. On 2 January 1935, Eugene set off with fourteen carriers. By 5 January the small party reached Dembi where they were told of the death of Morscheuser and warned not to proceed up the Simbu. But Schäfer had left for Alexishafen to report to the bishop, and Eugene thought he could make it to Bundi. As he proceeded, a few arrows were shot at them, and men attempted to snatch some of their cargo. Finally, the group was surrounded and Brother Eugene realized the danger. He told the carriers to leave their cargo and they began to descend into the valley. Soon a full-scale attack ensued, and the carriers emptied their guns into the air to frighten the attackers off. But the attackers took this ineffectual shooting as evidence that they were invincible. The attack was pressed, and Brother Eugene was struck by seven arrows. According to one of the carriers who survived the attack, Eugene collapsed to his hands and knees, which enabled one of the attackers to drive a lance twice into his back, piercing his lungs and causing his death. Except for two carriers who were also wounded, the rest were able to run away unscathed.

---

11. There were three van Baar brothers assigned by the SVD to New Guinea. The other two were Engelmundus and William. The latter was appointed apostolic administrator of the mission after World War II and before new bishops were ordained.

The attacking party had accomplished what they set out to do, and when another group from across the river rushed down the mountain to help those under attack, they scattered. This new group from Barengigl took Brother Eugene and his carriers into a men's house and treated their wounds according to their own traditions. The carriers recovered. Brother Eugene did not. He lingered in the native hut from 8 January until 15 January, when he was finally found by a government patrol sent out to look for him. Robert Melrose, the patrol officer who found Eugene, kept watch over him with the Reverend Wilhelm Bergmann, the Lutheran missionary at Kundiawa, while they waited for an airplane to evacuate him to Salamaua. He died in Salamaua without a priest to give him the last rites. He was buried there, but a few years later his body was exhumed and brought back to Alexishafen to be placed in the SVD community cemetery. He was thirty-five years old.

In the aftermath of Morscheuser's death, Cornelius van Baar, depressed because he was responsible for Morscheuser's death, had left for the coast where he worked thirty more years. The government forces arrested forty men from the tribe responsible for Morscheuser's death and forty from the group that had killed Eugene. They marched them to Salamaua, and later to prison on the coast, a long and difficult trek. Not many returned. Some died of illnesses in prison. Some were killed by the Japanese bombing runs during the Second World War. It is hard to find any silver lining in the dark cloud that settled over the area. Missionaries, including native Lutheran evangelists from the coast who were working in the area, were restricted to their stations, and both Protestant and Catholic missions were forced to restrict their efforts. In 1960 Father Cornelius van Baar returned to Womkama to participate in a final peace ceremony.

DEVELOPING THE WESTERN HIGHLANDS MISSION

After Eugene was killed, Ross was essentially alone in the Western Highlands from 1935 to 1937. Until a young American SVD priest named George Bernarding[12] came to help Ross in 1941, he was sometimes without contact with the outside world for months at a time. He continued to make contact with as many people and areas as he could, identified future mission stations, supervised his schools, usually staffed by locals from the coast, and preached the Word in whatever way he could, all the while trying to learn the language as fast as he could. In retrospect, it might have helped if he had been forced to curtail his travels like missionaries in Simbu had been, for according to Father Bernard Fisher, the two years of restrictions were used profitably there to learn languages, prepare materials in local languages, and secure a solid material base for future work.[13]

Ross's was an ever-active life. His dedication and his concern for the people's welfare, his willingness to live with and like them and to help them however he could, all out of the love of Christ and his gospel, made an indelible impression on

---

12. George Bernarding, from Pittsburgh, Pennsylvania, went on to hold a number of high offices. Within the Society he became regional superior. Still later, he became the first vicar apostolic when the Alexishafen vicariate was split into three in 1959, then first bishop in 1966 when the vicariate became a diocese, and finally first archbishop when the church in the highlands developed to this stage in 1982.

13. Fisher, *Father Alphonse Schaefer*, p. 11.

the locals. After three years of schooling, the first of Ross's school boys requested baptism. In 1939 the first sixty-six Hagen people received the sacrament of baptism. By the time Ross had to leave the Highlands in 1943 because of the war, 470 persons had been baptized.[14]

Willie Ross strove to meet as many people as he could, and always walked wherever he went. He was short, slimly built, wiry and athletic, and able, it was said, to outwalk any of the locals. I got to know Ross well while doing anthropological field work among the Kumdi Engamoi from 1963 to 1965. They lived twenty miles north of Mount Hagen on the eastern slope of the Hagen range. The older people still talked about the time when Ross first walked through their area. From the evidence I have put together, this would have been around 1937. One of Ross's bearers from the coast had married a local woman and was living with her and his family exactly where I was doing field work. Even after the war, Ross never drove a car or jeep when they became available. Other American SVDs who began to pour into the Highlands were willing to drive Ross when he needed to go a distance; otherwise he preferred to walk.

When the missionaries entered the Highlands, there were huge numbers of people, some of them living in quasi villages, many of them scattered across the landscape in houses near gardens. The area was so densely populated that a group of three thousand or more could gather in a half hour in most places, even more in others. Groups were often at war with each other, but there were also extensive periods of peace, especially when a large exchange of pigs or shells was underway. Such exchange ceremonies were the peak moments in social life and took years to arrange and weeks to carry out.

The highland languages were unlike any others that the missionaries were familiar with and there were no Tok Pisin speakers in the beginning, though this developed quite rapidly as young highlander men were recruited to work in the gold fields or on the coastal plantations. The culture and social customs were far different from those of the coastal people among whom the missioners had been working. A good deal of learning had to occur before the missionary could hope to make major inroads. Nevertheless, from the day of their first steps into the Highlands, they began to preach Christ. According to Father Nilles, Alphonse Schäfer's first speech to the Simbu people was given the day after the missionaries' arrival, first in the Bundi language which he had learned, and then, through the guide Kawagl, in Simbu. John Nilles adds wryly, "I suspect they did not understand much of what Father was saying."[15]

The general procedure was to make the mission known and to make it clear also that the mission intended to stay. Part of the first work was to identify and contact the "big man," the leader in the area, and then wait for an invitation from him for the missionary to stay in their area. Such leaders in the New Guinea Highlands were in constant competition with one another and were generally quite interested in having a missionary in their area of influence. The mission was a source of trade

---

14. These figures are taken from the papers prepared for the visit of Pope John Paul II to Papua New Guinea, 7–10 May 1984.

15. Nilles, *They Went Out to Sow*, p. 15.

goods such as axes, sea shells, cloth, beads, and the kinds of things that meant prestige in New Guinea. It was clear to a people who, when they first saw an airplane, went looking for the genitalia of the big bird that the Europeans had a level of material well-being and technological prowess that they did not. It is unquestionably the case that first contacts were often greased by the desire of the locals to gain the secret to obtaining such goods. And it was also true that when such goods did not flow, a mission went into crisis and the time had come to teach and learn more deeply what the new faith was really about.

It was just this task that Ross excelled in over the next thirty-five years. Even as stations multiplied and scores of new and sometimes less talented missioners arrived, Willie Ross remained a man to whom the peoples of the Western Highlands could go, knowing they would be treated with respect and get straight answers. This said, it is important to remember that here as everywhere else in the missions, *native catechists were the indispensable link between the missionary and the people*. Without them very little important work would have occurred. Initially catechists were brought into the mountains from the coast, but as soon as possible local men were recruited as catechists. And until a catechist training school could be started in the Highlands, locals with promise were sent to the coast for training and education.

First and foremost, Willie Ross made friends with local people. And by his example, Highlands missioners learned the importance of relationships in this face-to-face, oral society. Paradoxically, Ross appears not to have fully mastered the local language. It was known to be a difficult language for a native English speaker, but there is also the fact that language learning was not the greatest gift of the Americans in the Western Highlands in comparison with missionaries trained by the redoubtable Alphonse Schäfer. Nevertheless, the people understood Willie Ross's dialect version of their language, and he understood them. By the time I knew him, he had been with the highlanders for thirty years, and it was obvious that they loved and respected him mightily. A diminutive man with a distinctive, long white beard, he kidded them and they gave it back to him in good measure as well. To see Willie and his old, long-time cook, Dubai, interact was to watch two people interact and love each other in a deeply Christian way.

Even though he worked in a man's world, Ross was always considerate of women and they flocked into the church. But he had special sensitivity for the sick and elderly, and that endeared him to everyone.

> When he was told that an old man or woman was dying, he would take a lantern, if he needed it, and walk for hours over the mountains by day or by night, in good weather or in rain, to come to the distant hut. There he would go inside to instruct and anoint the sick person . . . When he got home, Father Ross might be too exhausted to sleep, but the dying man was ready to greet God with joy and go to heaven. Father did this many hundreds of times even when he himself became old.[16]

---

16. Bernard Fisher, *The Catholic Church Comes to the Central Mountains of Papua New Guinea* (Kundiawa, Simbu, PNG: Mission Procure S.V.D., n.d.), p. 12.

Ross never built a comfortable central station with a large house for himself. He lived very simply, in a house made of pit-sawn timber with a small detached building of the same rough material, which he used for a parish office. The food Dubai prepared for him was not sumptuous. In his early years, isolated for months at a time from his confreres, Ross took up smoking the rough, locally grown tobacco wrapped in a special leaf, lit and shared with others. Smoking, however, was forbidden to the members of the Society at the time. Years later Willie recalled how he had not had mail one time for several months from anyone, including his bishop or any of his religious confreres or superiors. He was feeling low, abandoned, anxious for news. Finally an airplane came with a letter all the way from Rome. He opened it eagerly. One of the first sentences he read stated that a rumor had reached Rome that he was smoking. If this were true, he was admonished to stop this practice if he ever hoped to become a superior in the Society. Ross, untroubled by the admonition, told Brother Stephen Pardy that he rolled the letter around tobacco and smoked it. The idea of being a superior was of no consequence to Ross. Twice, it is true, his name floated to the top to be bishop, but each time he made it clear that he would not accept. He was content where he was and thought that this was where God wanted him. But he had expected more from his superiors and recalled this incident with pain.

By the time of his death on 20 May 1973, Father Willie Ross was living history. He had received the Order of the British Empire on 14 June 1971 for helping refugees from the Japanese during World War II, but that honor was always lower in his estimation than being a friend of the Hagen people. He did not live to see his beloved people gain their independence on 15 September 1975. He celebrated his golden jubilee of ordination a few months before he died. As he was preparing his celebration for 8 September 1972, delayed a few months because of a broken hip which never healed right, he had the following to say in a note he added to the invitations he sent out:

> May I invite you to join me in thanksgiving to God for the great grace of a golden jubilee in His priesthood. On the Feast of Our Lady I shall offer a concelebrated Mass at Mt. Hagen to say thank you to Almighty God. On this occasion I would like to thank you all, my good friends and fellow members of the Society of the Divine Word who over the years have helped me.
>
> Many of those who were with me in the seminary have passed on, some ever so close to the Golden Jubilee.
>
> I am the only one of my class left to celebrate, the first American New Guinea S.V.D. priest to reach this goal.
>
> In looking over the past years, I can see the finger of God everywhere and His protection, love and care have never failed. Everything has come from God—nothing from myself, good health, strong physique, confidence of the natives, love of the work.
>
> Forty-six of my fifty priestly years have been spent in the New Guinea Mission, and in thanking God for His wonderful goodness to me, I ask Him to continue His blessing on all of us.[17]

---

17. Quoted in Mary R Mennis, *Hagen Saga: The Story of Fr. William Ross, Pioneer American*

Father Willie Ross was a pioneer and his picture hangs in the gallery of pioneers in the Mt. Hagen Town Hall. He was also honored by the country with a commemorative stamp in 1976.

WORLD WAR II AND ITS AFTERMATH

"Devastating" is the best word to describe World Wart II and its effect on the missions in New Guinea. The American SVDs were only seven in number. In addition to Willie Ross in the mountains, there were Fathers Michael Clerkin and William Hagan, and Brother Berchmans Bloner, all of whom survived the American strafing of the Japanese ship the *Dorish Maru*. Father Joseph Kotrba was beheaded by the Japanese. Father Arthur Manion and Brother Victor Salois were murdered by the Japanese off the coast of Kavieng and thrown into the Solomon Sea. An American Missionary Sister of the Holy Spirit, Sr. Adelaide Koetter, suffered the same fate, while Sr. Martitia Haag, another Missionary Sister of the Holy Spirit, died in the strafing of the *Dorish Maru*. Many more European SVDs and Holy Spirit Missionary Sisters were killed, including both SVD bishops, Francis Wolf and Joseph Lörks. Missionaries from other churches were also killed, as were other expatriates, even children. In spite of Japanese insistence that they were executing spies, these last at least were innocent.

Most of Japan's military objectives were accomplished swiftly and with less loss of Japanese life than they had anticipated. Singapore and the Malay peninsula fell, as did the East Indies and the Philippines. As a base for operations to take Australia, the Japanese occupied the Bismarck Archipelago and began the conquest of the New Guinea mainland. After extending their control around Rabaul and New Britain in January 1942, they landed on the New Guinea mainland, first at Lae and Salamaua in March and then moved onto Papua at Buna and Gona, which they reached in July 1942. In the bitter fighting over the Kokoda trail the Japanese exhausted themselves and could go no further. At one point, they had patrols pushed so far south that they could see Allied shipping coming in and out of Port Moresby harbor on the south coast.

Their advance to the southeast and Australia effectively blocked, the Japanese began to move up the northwest coast of New Guinea, where they moved into areas of large SVD missions. By this time they were losing the war, but their army, navy, and air force still had a lot of fight left. Many would die on both sides, including members of both Protestant and Catholic mission communities. The Catholic Missionaries of the Sacred Heart (MSC), whose center and strength was in Rabaul on New Britain and then down the island chain from New Ireland through Bougainville and Guadalcanal (where Marist missionaries predominated) suffered greatly.

On 18 and 23 December 1942, the Japanese occupied Wewak and Alexishafen. Troops swarmed over the two missions, taking whatever they wanted, often destroying what they could not use. This pillage began a destruction that was completed by Allied bombing later in the war. Together the Japanese and Allied war effort practically destroyed the physical base of the SVD missions on the coast and

---

Missionary to Papua New Guinea, with notes and articles by Father Ross (Boroka, PNG: Institute of PNG Studies, 1982), p. 147.

its hinterlands. At first the German missionaries thought they, at least, would be allowed to continue working, since Germany was an ally of the Japanese. But almost from the beginning all of the missionaries were confined to their mission stations under a form of house arrest, and all missionaries were suspected of being spies, including German missionaries. John Tschauder, one of the Germans thus affected, says that their fate was sealed, ironically, because the German SVDs had good relations with the Australian government. From 1939 through the occupation by the Japanese in late 1942, the Australians let them continue their missionary work under a fairly loose regimen of supervision. The Japanese, Tschauder felt, believed that if he and his fellow Germans were friends of the Australians they must at least have helped shelter the coast-watchers whose monitoring of Japanese naval and air forces was so helpful to the Australians during those years.[18]

By the time the Japanese landed at Wewak and Madang, they were already in retreat from General Douglas MacArthur's force. Their losses were mounting. Their sense of superiority had been successfully challenged; their losses both in manpower and in shipping were steadily increasing; their frustration and concern to root out any spies also grew in proportion. The American SVD missionary, Father Joseph Kotrba, was interrogated and imprisoned within a few months of the Japanese occupation of his station and quickly beheaded as a spy because he had been auxiliary chaplain for the American troops stationed in the Wewak area before the Japanese invasion. In 1950 his body was exhumed, returned to Techny, and reburied in the community cemetery with military honors. Father Arthur Manion was stationed outside Wewak and was secretary to Bishop Lörks when he received a message that a group of American aviators who had been shot down by the Japanese had been washed up on Vokeo, a small island off the coast from Wewak, near Kairiru Island where Bishop Lörks and Manion had their residence. Manion decided to help the downed Americans, which soon became known to the Japanese. His fate was sealed. Crueler things were to come.

SLAUGHTER ABOARD THE *AKIKAZE*

As the war turned against the Japanese, most of the missionaries from the Wewak vicariate were interned on Kairiru Island "for their protection" in January 1943, although some were permitted to stay in their missions some time longer. The worse things became for the Japanese, the more restrictions were placed on the movements of the missionaries and the more dangerous it became for them. Father William Jakob and Brother Emmanuel Wagner, both German SVDs, were killed, for example, at the Catholic mission station at But.

In the Battle of the Bismarck Sea, 3–14 March 1943, the Japanese lost what MacArthur called "the decisive aerial engagement" in his theater of the war, and

---

18. Father Ralph Wiltgen's work corroborates Father Tschauder's firsthand experience. I base much of what follows on Wiltgen's fascinating articles in *Verbum*. In these articles he goes into interesting details, especially regarding the Japanese occupation of the central vicariate of Wewak. We have already had occasion to refer to another of these articles in conjunction with the return of German SVDs to New Guinea after the war. All of these articles are highly recommended to the reader.

"one of the most complete and annihilating combats of all time."[19] On 10 March 1943, the Japanese destroyer *Akikaze* arrived at Kairiru, loaded down with materials for the construction of a seaplane base on this island. It was Ash Wednesday. This base, of course, gave military importance to Kairiru Island and the missionaries were ordered to be loaded aboard *Akikaze* on 15 March 1943. They were forty-two in all: one bishop, six priests, fourteen brothers and eighteen sisters. Three were Americans: Father Manion, Brother Victor Salois, and Sister Adelaide Koetter.

On its way to Rabaul, *Akikaze* was ordered to Manus Island, where the Japanese officer in charge was ordered to round up all foreign nationals for transport to Rabaul. Here twenty were added to the forty-two already aboard. Among these there were three Catholic Sacred Heart (MSC) priests and three Sacred Heart sisters (OLSH), two Lutheran missionaries and their wives, one child, and a Lutheran nurse. In addition there were an Australian planter and a German plantation manager, two Chinese, and four other men, thought to be Indian or Burmese. They were put aboard at Manus Island on 16 March 1943.

Somewhere between Kavieng on New Ireland and Rabaul on New Britain, all sixty-two were killed by a secret order that had been given to the ship's captain while *Akikaze* was idling in Kavieng harbor. One by one, they were brought up from below, their clothes removed, their hands tied in front of them, and each hoisted into the air by a hook fastened to the bonds around their hands. They were then shot, the ropes around their hands cut, and their bodies thrown off the stern of the destroyer where the execution platform had been placed.[20] The speed of the destroyer practically blew the bodies off the boat. The whine of the engines running at full speed also muted the sounds of the shooting for those prisoners who still waited their unknown fate.

THE *DORISH MARU* TRAGEDY

The story of the second tragedy to befall the New Guinea mission occurred at the hands of the United States Navy. The episode begins at about the same time as the previous one. Alexishafen, Bishop Wolf's central station, was occupied, and the missionaries who remained behind were kept on a short leash. As MacArthur's joint American-Australian force worked its way west, the missionaries, beginning with the bishop, were rounded up, transported, and interned on Manam Island, off the north coast, midway between Madang and Wewak. The Japanese said it was for their protection. From Manam, the Japanese decided to move the missionaries to Hollandia in Dutch New Guinea, which they intended to build up and defend vigorously. On 5 February 1944, after repeated delays, the missionaries were all finally loaded aboard the merchant vessel *Dorish Maru* that also carried Japanese troops. As the ship began the first leg of its trip to Hollandia, it was planned to sail first to Wewak during the night to avoid enemy aircraft. She was then to remain in Wewak during the day where she would be protected by the air defenses of Wewak.

---

19. Quoted in Ralph Wiltgen, "The Death of Bishop Loerks and his Companions," Part 1, *Verbum* 6 (1964): 372.

20. Wiltgen includes a sketch of this gallows-like platform, drawn by a Japanese gunnery officer who witnessed the executions.

Unfortunately, the ship was unable to reach Wewak, though missionaries on the deck could see a pall of dark smoke hovering over the area in the distance. A squadron of Navy A-20 Havoc planes had bombed the barges that were tied up in camouflage around Muschu Island not far from Wewak. On the way back to their home base the squadron turned its attention to *Dorish Maru*. The Japanese soldiers aboard began to fire at the Navy fighter-bombers when they began their strafing run. The prisoners, about 150 of them, including Catholic and Lutheran missionaries, half-castes, and planters, were kept on the deck. They were ordered to lie down as the squadron approached. In the few seconds it took the planes, flying at 280 miles an hour, to make their strafing run and fly off, seven SVD priests, twelve SVD brothers, and twenty-seven Missionary Sisters of the Holy Spirit (SSpS) were dead, as were many of the Lutherans and others. One of the dead sisters was the American Sister Martitia Haag, who had worked hard to introduce Tok Pisin into the mission's liturgy and school. A great many more were wounded, many seriously, including Bishop Wolf. The wound in his left shoulder was so severe that his lung was exposed. He died on 23 February 1944 after indescribable suffering in the prison camp in Hollandia where those who survived were finally brought. Two more SVDs and seven Sisters of the Holy Spirit also died of their wounds in the prison camp at Hollandia. A total of twenty-two SVDs and thirty-four SSpS sisters died as a result of the strafing.[21] Fortunately, one of the Lutheran missionaries, who was also a medical doctor, escaped uninjured with his wife, a nurse. They were able to help care for the injured, though greatly handicapped by a lack of instruments and medicines.

On 22 April 1944, American troops landed at Hollandia against minimal opposition, since the Japanese were expecting the main attack at Wewak and had deployed their main defenses there. Three days later the survivors of the attack on *Dorish Maru* were liberated from a makeshift prison camp in the interior and were evacuated to Australia to recuperate.

A few of the missionaries escaped the tragedy that befell so many others. A group of five Holy Spirit Sisters stationed at Marienberg on the Sepik River was brought up the river as far as possible and then guided by Danny Leahy and his carriers to Wabag. From there they went to Mount Hagen and eventually to Bena Bena further east, from where they were evacuated by air to Australia. The trip took from 6 June 1943 to 30 August 1943. In spots the nuns were pulled, pushed, even carried by the local carriers, all of the time garbed in their habits. Their trip also proved what Father Kirschbaum had argued so many years before, about the possibility of making a trip into the Highlands from the Sepik side of the island.[22]

The toll taken by the war in lives lost and shattered among the SVD Catholic missionaries in New Guinea was high. Father Bornemann gives the following figures.

---

21. A complete list of all of the church personnel killed in this tragic incident and in others during the Pacific war can be found in Theo Aerts, ed., *The Martyrs of Papua New Guinea: 333 Missionary Lives Lost During World War II* (Port Moresby: University of Papua New Guinea Press, 1994), pp. 37–47.

22. This story is told in a small, privately published book written in 1945 by Sister Vinciana Engberink, SSpS. Her account also appears in shortened form in Aerts, *Martyrs of Papua New Guinea*, pp. 76–81.

Of the 230 priests, brothers and sisters active in our New Guinea mission before the outbreak of World War II, 122, or 53 percent, lost their lives during the war. And 90 percent of our churches, schools and other buildings were destroyed.[23]

REBUILDING THE MISSION

While war was still raging little could be done, even in areas liberated by the Allies. A number of SVDs had been evacuated from the island to Australia, including Fathers Willie Ross and George Bernarding. To their numbers were added the sisters and others who escaped by similar routes overland to places from which they could be extracted by American and Australian airplanes. Father Ross wrote a letter from Australia published in the March 1944 issue of *Techny Chimes* that nothing was then known about the large number left behind. By this time also, with some fluctuation to be sure, the number of those being ordained was on the increase.

In the same March 1944 issue of *Techny Chimes*, Bernarding gives an idea how the missionaries from New Guinea (including the Germans) occupied themselves in Australia:

I am doing parish work. Have been at St. Joseph's (Enfield) for the past 6 weeks. It's one of Sydney's larger parishes with over 4000 souls. Plenty of work to do: two hospitals, an orphanage, two outside churches, etc. Two of our brothers are doing farm work at Springwood, the minor seminary. Have met many of the boys [servicemen?], some from my hometown, Pittsburgh. Have given twenty lectures since I am in Australia. Our Society was hardly known down this way until the missionaries were evacuated from New Guinea. The Australian Catholic public wants to know about New Guinea.

While the war was on, few American missionaries were able to go overseas. Ordinations mounted in several missionary groups, and during this period Maryknoll made the decision to open missions in Latin America. The men they sent there were the vanguard of an enormous commitment of priests, sisters, brothers, and lay persons who would eventually travel south. At Techny, too, the results of years of work began to bear fruit, and there were sixty-five ordinations during the war years. Knowing of the devastation of the missions in New Guinea, General Douglas MacArthur was sympathetic to having missionaries return to New Guinea as soon as possible, seeing them as a force for development, especially in the field of education. When he was asked by the apostolic delegate in Sydney to allow American SVDs back into New Guinea as soon as possible, he was glad to oblige. He appointed twenty of the young priests at Techny to the rank of auxiliary chaplains. That made it possible for them to be sent to Australia by military transportation even before the war was over. In addition, Ross and Bernarding were permitted to return to the Highlands before the end of the war. On 8 September 1944, they returned to Mount Hagen. In the April 1945 issue of *Techny Chimes*,

---

23. Bornemann, *A History of the Divine Word Missionaries*, p. 396.

five months before the end of the war in the Pacific, the editor paraphrases from a letter of Ross:

> It is interesting to read how Father Ross spent his Christmas [25 December 1944]. He said Midnight Mass in a station 8,000 feet above sea level with 2,000 natives present. All the light that was used came from small kerosene lamps, and from torches held by the native men. How they did sing! And 300 went to receive Our Lord in Holy Communion. During the day, Father baptized twenty infants, and validated three marriages.
>
> During the course of two tours through the Bismarck [mountains] region, Father Ross heard 2,062 confessions, distributed 3,949 Communions, baptized 225 babies and performed 90 marriages. What a wonderful consolation both for the Kanakas and for Father himself after an absence of two years!

And so the repair of the mission began in the Highlands.

On the coast, on 30 September 1945, Monsignor William van Baar, the apostolic administrator, and his two brothers, Engelmundus and Cornelius, returned to Alexishafen with his English-speaking secretary, the newly arrived American Father John Hannaher. Twenty-one priests and five brothers followed. These were mostly Americans, and a few Dutchmen arrived 9 October 1945. In 1947, German SVDs were allowed to return to work again in New Guinea. In 1948 two Americans, Stephen Appelhans and Leo Arkfeld, were ordained bishops to succeed Bishops Wolf and Lörks. In the years following, more and more Americans were assigned to New Guinea. As they were, more and more stations were opened, new areas were explored, and the Word spread more and more widely and successfully.

The basic model was still followed. Catechists who lived in the outstations the missionary visited regularly were still the backbone of the method. In addition to catechists, who were paid, the missionary also "appointed" mission leaders or "mission friends" who were responsible to call people together when the missionary was scheduled to make an appearance; these need not be, and usually were not, Catholic. After the war, which had forced the different Christian churches to cooperate if only for survival, many other barriers also came down; certainly after Vatican II, the attitude became much more one of cooperation, beginning with the bishops and extending to the various Christian churches, especially but not only between the Lutherans and Catholics. There was more than enough work for everybody, whether in education, in social or economic development, or in a variety of other important areas.

The growth of the Catholic Church in New Guinea is reflected in the growth of ecclesiastical jurisdictions. But the growth of Catholics, it should be remembered, was paralleled by growth among Anglican, Wesleyan, and Lutheran Churches. While Catholics were and remain the largest single denomination in New Guinea, other churches were active and very successful. After about 1950, in fact, so-called independent or Bible-church Protestants and groups such as the Seventh Day Adventists began entering the country in large numbers, and from that time on, the percentage growth of these churches exceeded the historical churches, such as the Catholic and the Lutheran.

Within the Catholic Church, including SVD areas, new vicariates were created as numbers of Catholics increased and as missionaries from other communities of missionaries (such as Franciscans and Passionists) were introduced when the three orders that had been there from the beginning (SVD, Missionaries of the Sacred Heart [MSC], and the Marists [SM]) needed assistance. Let us survey this growth in ecclesiastical jurisdictions briefly. In 1955 the vicariates apostolic of Madang (the name that replaced Alexishafen) and Wewak were divided into three vicariates: Mount Hagen, Goroka, and Lae. Lae was assigned to the Marianhill Fathers, the rest were entrusted to the SVDs, who were already staffing them. George Bernarding was named the first vicar apostolic of Mount Hagen, which then included the Wabag district (now known by the political province named for the area, "Enga"), and a German SVD, Bernard Schilling, became the first vicar apostolic of Goroka (the Eastern Highlands). Still later the Simbu area would become the diocese of Kundiawa. On 15 November 1966, the vicariates apostolic of New Guinea were officially established as dioceses and archdioceses, with Madang the archdiocesan center for all the dioceses created out of the old German Northeast New Guinea area. Then in 1982, Mount Hagen became an archdiocese, and under it were all the mountain dioceses, including Mendi (which had been entrusted to the Pittsburgh Capuchins in 1955, had become a prefecture in 1959, a vicariate in 1965, and a diocese in 1966, all under the leadership of Bishop Firmin Schmidt, OFM, Cap). When Mount Hagen became an archdiocese, Madang retained its symbolic leadership of the dioceses of Wewak, Aitape (split off from Wewak in 1952 and entrusted to Australian Franciscans), Vanimo (split off from Wewak in 1963 and entrusted to Australian Passionists), and Lae. Still later, Papua New Guinean priests would be named bishops, including a Tolai named Benedict ToVarpin who became archbishop of Madang in 1988.[24] In that same year, three of the other eighteen dioceses of PNG were directed by local bishops and archbishops. Church policy, of course, is to place local men as bishops at the earliest possible moment, though the process is proceeding slowly because of the relatively small numbers of Melanesian men being ordained to the priesthood. Because of this, the church in Papua New Guinea still relies more heavily on foreign missionary priests for ordinary pastors than would be considered ideal.

THE PLANE AS EMBLEM OF THE POST-WAR MISSION

As men arrived from America and Europe, they were sent out in ones and twos to take over prewar stations along the coast and in the mountain ranges and river basins behind the coast. At the same time entirely new missions were being erected both on the coast and in the mountains. The mission was hard put to bring in the

---

24. Benedict ToVarpin was a Tolai, the major tribal group around Rabaul in New Britain, an area evangelized by German Sacred Heart Missionaries. Another Tolai, Herman ToPaivu, was named archbishop of the national capital, Port Moresby, already in the mid-1970s both because he was a wonderful priest and because the Holy See wanted a national priest as bishop in the nation's capital. The MSCs in New Britain and New Ireland (the latter, an island on which American MSCs were numerous), and the Marists in the islands to the south of New Ireland had been at work in their missions longer than the SVDs and consequently were able to recruit men for the diocesan priesthood and for membership in their own societies earlier than the SVD.

material necessary to construct these missions. Out of that problem came reliance on the airplane, and its increased use became a sign of the mission's "progress," according to Mary Taylor Huber, an American anthropologist who has written one of the most interesting and perceptive books on the SVD missions in Papua New Guinea.[25] To put the mission on a sound basis, Limbrock and his confreres started plantations, and these model projects became an emblem of their progress. Later, Bishops Wolf and Lörks began missions up and down the coast and on the offshore islands. The ship became an emblem of their work and of their mission's progress. In the prewar era the mission had begun to use planes, but in the postwar period they became the most identifiable symbol. Although Protestant and other Catholic missions used airplanes, Bishop Leo Arkfeld, SVD, came to personify missionary aviation and the New Guinea mission around the world. But first some background.

Mining companies had pioneered the technique of walking into the mountains, preparing a landing site for planes, and then flying in supplies for the next push into the Highlands. This began in the fall of 1929 in the Wau-Bulolo areas, and the missionaries were watching. Father Schäfer, always the man to think of efficiency, recommended very strongly to Bishop Wolf that the mission purchase an airplane. Indeed, the first stations were chosen with the possibility in mind of building airstrips. Already in 1934 the bishop wrote to the MIVA ("Missionary International Vehicular Association").[26] By the end of the year, MIVA supplied two planes and a pilot named Willy Schaffhausen. The two planes were named *Petrus* and *Paulus*, and in July 1935 *Paulus* landed in the Eastern Highlands. Early in October 1935, *Petrus* made its first run, landing at Hagen.

The runways were grass covered, short and narrow, and in the early years, there were several minor accidents, the damage from which was always reparable. But in 1939, *Petrus* landed in the sea at Bogajim. The pilot swam ashore, but the plane was a total loss. It was replaced with *Theresia*, a larger plane. *Theresia* flew only a few months before it crashed on 6 August 1939. Among the Fathers to die in that accident was Father Kirschbaum, the great pioneer of the Sepik.

Air operations were begun again immediately after World War II by the SVDs who came to New Guinea from America. Some of the early equipment was army surplus. Henry Hoff, SVD, was assigned to New Guinea and instructed to learn how to fly first. He did so at Parks College in East St. Louis, Missouri. When Hoff arrived in New Guinea in 1948, he joined Father John Glover, a diocesan priest and former air force pilot. They began with two twin-engine Dragon DH84 biplanes and a Tiger Moth DH82 with open cockpit. Glover died in an accident at Mingende on 31 December 1948 when his plane was hit by a sudden crosswind while landing.

Over the years many people flew for the missions, lay missionaries as well as SVD brothers and priests. In the early years, the emphasis was on priest-pilots, because most of the mission stations to which the pilots flew were isolated for long periods of time, so a priest-pilot would give the missionary a chance for spir-

---

25. See Mary Taylor Huber, *The Bishops' Progress: A Historical Ethnography of Catholic Missionary Experience on the Sepik Frontier* (Washington, D.C.: Smithsonian Institution Press, 1988).

26. MIVA was founded by an Oblate of Mary Immaculate (OMI) priest to provide transportation for their missionaries in Canada.

itual direction, to go to confession, or to have some help when a special liturgical event was in the offing. In addition to bringing in supplies and transporting
the missionary from place to place, the priest-pilot could help in all of these situations. As isolation became less of a problem because of road-building, lay missionaries and brothers were gradually added to the ranks of the mission pilots in
New Guinea.

Leo Arkfeld came to epitomize the flying missionaries of New Guinea. From
Panama, Iowa, Arkfeld was one of the first group of American SVDs assigned to
the coastal missions after the war. He went to Lae, which meant he was also
responsible for the Catholics working in the gold fields of Wau and Bulolo. As a
youngster in Iowa, he had become enamored with planes and wanted to be a pilot,
fascinated by pilots who barnstormed around the countryside in the 1920s, offering rides as they landed and took off from a level cow pasture. In Lae he quickly
realized how useful, even critical for certain purposes, it would be to have a plane,
so he bought a small plane, took flying lessons, and got a license.

Arkfeld was not just a pilot. On 8 July 1948, three years after he arrived in New
Guinea, he and another young American, Stephen Appelhans, were ordained bish-
ops to replace Bishops Lörks and Wolf (killed during the war) and put in charge,
respectively, of the vicariates apostolic of Central New Guinea (Wewak) and East
New Guinea (Madang). In a personal communication with me, Father Frank
Mihalic describes Arkfeld's first flight after being named vicar apostolic:

> Bishop-elect Leo Arkfeld, who had earned his wings just a few months
> before, climbed into an old fashioned, open cockpit Tiger Moth, pulled his
> goggles over his eyes, and flew from his parish in Lae to get a first-hand
> bird's eye view of his new vicariate. The very first time he touched Wewak
> soil as its bishop, he stepped out of a plane. That was perhaps an omen of
> things to come.
>
> By the time the "Flying Bishop" made his last flight on 18 January 1990,
> he had held a pilot's license for 42 years and logged 8,653 hours in the air
> which, he says, amounts to about 30,000 flights.

Over the years two different SVD air services were formed, Divine Word
Airways in Madang and Wirui Air Services in Wewak. Flying out of Madang to
the Highlands was particularly dangerous. Clouds or fog or rain could roll in while
the plane was negotiating the few passes that allowed air passage into the
Highlands. And even if the pass was clear, the airstrip where one was to land might
be overcast or fogged in. Tragically, more pilots were killed flying into the mountains than was the case in Wewak. The list of those priest-pilots killed in the mountains are John Glover, the Australian diocesan priest, and SVD Fathers Joseph
Walachy and Harry McGee. Henry Hoff, who by the time of his death had left the
Society and retired from the priesthood, was also killed while flying for a commercial airline. In Wewak there was one fatal crash, the pilot a diocesan priest from
New Zealand named Zampese.

Planes and their maintenance were expensive. The question is sometimes asked
whether the results were worth the cost. No simple answer can be given. We have

already talked about the loss of life. But it is certainly the case that more lives were saved by medical evacuations using planes than were lost in crashes. And it is also true that many of the inland missions, particularly in the Highlands, would have been developed much more slowly if they had to wait until roads were pushed through to them in the 1960s and 1970s. Whatever the evaluation one makes of their usefulness, they were a peculiarly American enterprise after the Second World War when Bishop Arkfeld, Father Ivo Ruiter, and Brother Lawrence Camilleri were running the Madang and Wewak air services.

GENERAL AND SEMINARY EDUCATION

Undoubtedly the greatest effort expended by missionaries in Papua New Guinea went into education. Beginning in the early years with catechist training, it expanded to the point that elementary schools were built at every station. Later a string of secondary schools, teacher training colleges, minor and major seminaries, and finally even a university-level program at Divine Word Institute (now Divine Word University) were founded. SVDs taught in some of them, but the bulk of the teaching was done in early years by foreign brothers, sisters, and lay people. In terms of significant contributions to the development of both the church and the nation, schools and healthcare institutions are at the top of the list. While non-SVDs staffed virtually all these institutions, the Society's members were often the agents who found the sites, spearheaded the planning, and pushed them through to opening day. In the case of Massachusetts-born Father Paul McVinney, for a number of years the national education secretary for the Catholic Bishops' Conference, the contribution to education was to broker improvements in the method of planning and funding educational services throughout the country. The integrated school system that McVinney helped bring about facilitated cooperation between public and private educational authorities. As a result of the integration and introduction of the independent Teaching Service, a significant financial burden was lifted from the shoulders of all missions. McVinney's work was one of the first major and tangible results of the spirit of ecumenism that virtually all missions embraced in the 1960s. Although many in Papua New Guinea do not know his name, his work made it possible for both religious and secular education at the primary and secondary level in Papua New Guinea to make progress together without the acrimony of church-state conflict and competition. By 1969, half the children in New Guinea were estimated to be in schools. Of these, one-third were in Catholic schools, one-third in Protestant schools, and one-third in public.[27]

Another American SVD who had a great impact on education in the area of language and communication over the half century after World War II was Father Frank Mihalic. Born in 1916, ordained in 1944, and sent to New Guinea in 1947, Mihalic spent most of his fifty-one years in the mission involved with Tok Pisin, the main language of the country.

Mihalic's first accomplishment was to standardize the spelling of this widespread trade language in 1957, when he published the first edition of his *Dictionary*

---

27. Adolph Noser, "Yesterday, Today and Tomorrow," *Word in the World* (Techny, Ill.: Divine Word Publications, 1969), p. 59.

and Grammar of Melanesian Pidgin.[28] That book gave status to Tok Pisin, a language that had developed almost spontaneously in the first half of the twentieth century among the thousands of indentured laborers from all parts of the country who worked on coconut plantations on the coast and in the outlying islands. They took it home with them to their villages in the Highlands and other inland regions. Mihalic's first job was to explain to linguistically illiterate and therefore prejudiced expatriates that Pidgin English was not "baby talk" but the natural evolution of a language that develops between two groups, neither of which speaks the other's mother tongue. A pidgin language, he showed, is no one's first language. Rather, it is a "compromise language" that develops with use. Today there are some 179 pidgin languages in the world, according to Stanford University linguists. Tok Pisin is one of them, and its basic vocabulary comes from English.

Because of its widespread usefulness, Tok Pisin gradually became a *lingua franca* that overcame the Babel of (at last count) 857 local languages in New Guinea, virtually none of which had yet been written down. It became the first unifying factor in this polyglot country's history when it became the medium of short wave broadcasts by government radio, which penetrated the most inaccessible outback before roads even existed.

When Tok Pisin schools had developed a literate public, Father Mihalic, himself a teacher, started *Wantok*, the first Tok Pisin newspaper in the country in 1970. He did not have a single high school graduate on his original staff. He reports that "I muddled along from very primitive beginnings in Wewak, far from the centers of trade and industry. I had to coax people to read the first issues before they used it as 'smoke paper' to wrap tobacco, the main use of newspapers in those days."

In its first years in existence, *Wantok* weathered distribution problems and the government's decision that Tok Pisin should be banned from schools. Equally important, it won over the advertisers necessary to pay for the paper. In the only language that the man on the street and in the rural areas understood, the newspaper explained how one voted, how the government operated, how one ran for public office, and it coined the names of the dozens of government departments. It ran the first pictures of the new money that would soon be introduced and published competing versions of the proposed national anthem to be adopted after independence. On independence day itself, *Wantok* ran pages full of scenes of events and people that were making history. Most of all, politicians learned quickly that they had to speak to people in the language they used, and that is what *Wantok* had been doing all along.

In the late 1970s, *Wantok* moved to the capital city of Port Moresby. There it developed into an ecumenical Christian publishing house known as "Word Publishing," which was spearheaded by Fathers Jim Franks and Kevin Walcot (an American and a British SVD respectively). Word Publishing soon began to publish *The Times of PNG* and the largest monthly magazine in the South Pacific, *New Nation*, which went to every school in Papua New Guinea.

According to the authoritative *World Press Encyclopedia, Wantok* has 400,000 readers nationwide in the 1990s, with each copy being read by twenty-two per-

---

28. This seminal book was published again as the *Jacaranda Dictionary and Grammar of Melanesian Pidgin* in 1971 by the Jacaranda Press.

sons, although few of them had ever been formally taught the language. Tok Pisin is today spoken by fifty percent of Papua New Guinea's 4.5 million inhabitants. In recognition of that fact, Tok Pisin has come back into the classroom at the preschool level, where it is used as a literacy tool in the classroom. Mihalic's original shoestring operation was staffed by some forty computer-literate Papua New Guineans who serve at every level from editors and reporters to distributors and printers. Since its humble beginnings, *Wantok* had published over 1,500 issues as the twentieth century ended. Receiving hundreds of letters to the editor on every conceivable topic, it is today the place where issues in the developing nation's life are discussed, showing a more pervasively Christian spirit than one finds in the homelands of the missioners who brought the faith from Europe, the Americas, and Australia. As the twenty-first century began, the Pennsylvania-born Father Mihalic has shrugged off his notoriety, awards, and acclaim to retire at the SVD house in Riverside, California. There he keeps occupied translating from German into English the letters that Blessed Arnold Janssen sent to New Guinea between 1896 and 1906.

If the work of the missioner is ever to be brought to a close and the local church is to replace the mission, the ordained ministry must be handed over to local bishops, priests, and deacons. Theirs is not the most important vocation in the church, but if they, plus religious sisters and brothers, are not present in sufficient numbers and educated in ways that will make them respected leaders, a local Catholic Church does not develop. The decision to open the first seminary in Rabaul was made in 1936 by the bishops of Rabaul, the North Solomons, and Papua. In Rabaul and the Solomons, German Missionaries of the Sacred Heart (MSC) and Marists from several lands predominated. In Papua, French and Belgian MSCs predominated. The seminary began, but the war intervened. The MSCs continued the education of the seminarians while under Japanese detention, and after the war six men were ordained from this effort. Among them, Herman ToPaivu, whom we have already mentioned, would become the first Melanesian archbishop of Port Moresby. The SVD was not involved in this cooperative effort in the northern islands and Papua. The Alexishafen SVD vicariate opened its own minor seminary in 1938.[29] The war intervened, however, and the seminary died leaving hardly a trace.

After the war, the Holy See and the bishops realized that getting a seminary in operation was a matter of the highest priority and in order to do so cooperation among all the bishops was demanded. Given the insistence of the church that priests in mission lands must receive an education comparable to that in Europe and America, it was obvious that the church would have to provide a higher level secondary education for its priesthood candidates as a foundation for philosophical and theological studies. Accordingly, following the Australian system, the bishops decided that a full, six-year minor seminary had to be established. Thus, with the approval and assistance of Propaganda, a minor seminary for all vicariates of

29. Reiner Jaspers, "An Historical Investigation into the Foundation of the Catholic Church in Papua New Guinea and the Solomon Islands" (in "Papers prepared for the Visit of Pope John Paul II to Papua New Guinea 7–10 May 1984"), p. 67.

Papua and New Guinea was to be established as St. Peter Chanel College at Ulapia on New Britain in 1955 and entrusted to the MSC.[30] When the full six forms were running, Ulapia would have the highest educational level institution in the entire nation, according to SVD Father Patrick Murphy.[31] In addition, on Kairiru Island, off the coast near Wewak, a minor seminary named after St. John the Apostle was opened. A number of American SVDs worked there over the years, including Frank Mihalic, Francis Swift, and Raymond Kalisz. Kalisz went on to become Bishop of Wewak in 1980 after Bishop Arkfeld was transferred to Madang and made archbishop there.

In 1960 it became clear that there would soon be graduates of Chanel College ready to enter the major seminary for studies in philosophy and theology. Propaganda asked the Society of the Divine Word, through its superior general, John Schütte, to administer this regional seminary, which was built at Kap near Alexishafen and put under the aegis of Bishop Noser. The SVD committed nine priests to the seminary staff. Named Holy Spirit Regional Seminary, it opened its doors on 1 March 1963, to a class of 22 students. Father Patrick Murphy, an Australian-born SVD who had studied in Techny and later in Rome, and whose first missionary post was an assignment in India, was named the first rector. An American black priest named Raymond Caesar was assigned to teaching philosophy. The first class was ordained in 1966, all of whom came from the outlying islands where the MSCs had first begun minor seminary training. In 1968 the first mainland priest from a diocese staffed by SVDs was ordained, Ignatius Kilage of a Simbu village named Denglagu in the Diocese of Goroka. A New Jersey-born SVD, John Cohill, was by then Bishop of Goroka. Denglagu, it should be noted, is in the area in which Father Morscheuser and Brother Eugene were killed.

The Kap major seminary quickly discovered it was laboring under immense disadvantages. First, it was far from any other tertiary-level educational institution and was isolated on a section of the coast that was not accessible from the rest of the country. Students and staff were dissatisfied. The MSCs decided independently that a location near Port Moresby, the national capital, was preferable for seminarians for their own order. Since the decision to put their students in the Port Moresby area was their own to make without need to consult the bishops, it was quickly made. Facilitating their move, the Archdiocese of Port Moresby was led by an Australian MSC, Virgil Copas, so the ecclesiastical approval was also a quasi-internal matter. The MSCs, it should be noted, had a large number of impressive students, since they had concentrated on seminary education for men from New Britain, New Ireland, and adjacent islands in a major way much earlier than any other order. The fact that Kap would not have MSC students had two effects. The MSCs, the largest group of seminarians, would be missing. Second, the largest group of diocesan priesthood candidates were *wantoks*[32] of the missing MSCs.

---

30. Reiner Jaspers, "The Unity of the Catholic Church in Papua New Guinea and the Role of Holy Spirit Seminary: A Historical Analysis of Facts, Events and Development" (in "Papers Prepared for the Visit of John Paul II to Papua New Guinea, 1–10 May 1984"), p. 67.

31. Patrick Murphy, "Holy Spirit Regional Seminary: The Evolution of a Training School for an Indigenous Clergy," *Word in the World* (1969): 86.

32. *Wantok*, a Tok Pisin word meaning literally "one talk," connotes a person who speaks the same language as another. It takes more than language, however, to denote a tribal, clan, and cultural unity.

These students didn't want to be isolated in a strange area, away from their *wantoks*. Bishops in the MSC and Marist missions, accordingly, chafed under the requirement that their students be sent to Kap, since they knew instinctively that they would not be happy there.

Father Murphy, one of the truly pivotal figures in Melanesian church history, was at one moment resentful of the MSC reluctance to send their students to Kap, yet he was also convinced that Port Moresby was the right place for Holy Spirit Seminary to be located. His ambivalence (and that of the rest of the SVD staff, a mixture of Germans, Dutchmen, and one American) would be a fateful ingredient in the next chapter in the history of seminary education in Papua New Guinea. By contrast, Highlands missionaries (SVDs and the American Capuchins from Pittsburgh in the Mendi Diocese) never felt Moresby was the right location, while the people at Madang felt resentful of losing the major seminary. The western coastal dioceses (Wewak, under the SVDs, Aitape under Franciscans, and Vanimo under Passionists) had a wait-and-see attitude, but were not convinced that the right step was being taken, even though Bishop Arkfeld, for several years president of the bishops' oversight committee, made an effort to stifle his misgivings.

Urged to do so by Murphy, the bishops' conference of Papua New Guinea decided to transfer the seminary to Port Moresby and acquired land at Bomana, owned by the Archdiocese of Port Moresby, adjacent to the fledgling MSC major seminary. Bomana was about twenty minutes by a good road from Port Moresby, now the so-called territorial capital of eastern New Guinea, soon to become the national capital of the independent nation of Papua New Guinea. One of the attractions of locating in Port Moresby was that it would be the site of the University of Papua New Guinea, which actually opened in 1966. The actual transfer of the seminary from Madang to Bomana took place in February 1968.

The move gave the faculty and students the opportunity for joint enrollment in seminary and university programs while creating the occasion for a good deal of ill feeling, which quickly developed. The MSCs had become used to running their own show at Bomana. Now a much more impressive physical plant than theirs—complete with up-to-date classrooms, a library building, better student rooms, a beautiful chapel, playing fields, and dining room—was going up next door to their more frugal buildings. When the MSC joined forces with Holy Spirit Seminary, the institution gained many of the finest and best-prepared students and several well-trained MSC faculty members. But relations between the two formerly independent faculties were destined not to become cordial for quite some time, in part because one of Father Murphy's most important strengths—a keen, decisive mind that cut to the quick and became impatient when others would not quickly concede the merits of his case—was a liability in exerting the diplomacy that the situation required. A frustrated Murphy left to become secretary of ecumenical affairs of the Catholic bishops and to work full time with the Pacific Council of Churches. His contributions to peace and justice and to ecumenical cooperation among the churches were immense. Ironically, he found it easier to be diplomatic with Lutherans, Anglicans, and Methodists than with his fellow Catholic missionary

---

In Melanesia a person away from his or her home immediately seeks to be with *wantoks*, with whom they can feel *wanbel* (literally, "of one belly"), a way of easing the pain of leaving one's clan.

priests, Dutch SVDs, and members of other orders. Murphy was replaced by a gentle Dutch SVD and canon lawyer, Klaus Beutener. Father Caesar was made bishop of Goroka in the Highlands, and the only American presence at the seminary was a Marist missionary, Gerald Frey, until Nick de Groot, an Australian SVD who had studied in the United States and Rome, and Bill Burrows, an American who had studied in Rome also, arrived in 1971 and 1972. Two years later, another American, Arnold Steffen, a veteran Highlands missioner, was named president of the seminary. "Arnie," as he was known to everyone, was popular among the bishops because of his years of field experience. They feared that the Bomana seminary was staffed by too many teachers, SVDs and from other orders, with too little pastoral experience. From the relocation of the seminary in 1968, Marists, Capuchins, Franciscans, and SVDs began sending members of their orders to Bomana.

The question whether the celibate, Western form of the Catholic priesthood will produce sufficient priests to provide pastoral care for the hundreds of thousands of Melanesian Catholics is one on which the hierarchy, Rome, missionaries and local peoples still differ among themselves. There is no question, however, about how hard formation personnel and teachers at Bomana have worked with generous, intelligent Melanesian young men, and how richly God has blessed the men who have been ordained after training in Bomana. In addition, for the new Melanesian priests, time spent near the national capital is an important moment where the world beyond their mountain valley or coastal village begins to open up. And the number of Bomana students who have been snapped up by government departments and commercial firms when they left the seminary or the priesthood (as frequently occurs) is a tribute to the qualities of the minor seminaries in Ulapia and Kap,[33] as well as to the education received at Bomana.

CORE CULTURAL ISSUES FACING MELANESIAN CATHOLICS

Beyond the institutional history of the Bomana seminary, the struggle to find a form of training for future priests adequate to the Melanesian reality has been faced as well in every other area of church life. It is important to remember that theological education is not confined to the seminary. Catechetical training centers have been a second area of concern and antedate the seminaries by many years. As congregations of religious have opened their doors to Melanesian men and women, their training centers, too, have become places where questions of "inculturation" arise (the term used denote a variety of processes whereby Christian and Catholic doctrine and practices are translated into terms Melanesians understand and accept).

One of the most fruitful means of discussing inculturation issues in Papua New Guinea had significant American input from both a Lutheran and a Catholic viewpoint. As the Second Vatican Council was drawing to a close, Catholic-Lutheran relationships became quite friendly. Members of both missions felt strongly the need for a center that would combine the efforts of both Catholics and Protestants

---

33. When the major seminary left Kap, the Capuchins took over the facilities and began directing a minor seminary there for students from the northern part of Papua New Guinea.

to better understand the cultures of Melanesia and to help missionaries and local peoples make decisions on how Christianity and Melanesian cultures should be related. The final result of these conversations was the establishment of the Melanesian Social Pastoral Institute, which was later named the Melanesian Institute for Pastoral and Socio-Economic Service.[34]

The institute was quickly nicknamed the "MI" and began giving courses to new missionaries in the late 1960s. It was an instant success, filling an obvious need felt by all churches and religious orders for a program to help introduce new missioners to Melanesia. As success was recognized, so too was the need for a permanent home. At first it was felt that it would be better not to build facilities for the MI, since using the facilities of the various churches meant that the MI would interact more vitally with them. The need to locate a library that could house materials that were beginning to accumulate and to have a center where the staff could dialogue about what they were learning in research and from interactions with missioners and local people led the MI to build a modest center in Goroka, where the institute is still located. The MI has continued for thirty years now to be a vital source of insights and locus for dialogue on various issues concerning inculturation. MI members, expanded to include women as core staff in the 1970s, traveled widely, lectured, and taught in seminaries and catechetical centers. Respected in their churches, they were invited to observe and give presentations in synods and bishops' conferences. Among the critical insights they provided are several that follow. In this section, I will attempt to outline several of them that have been important in the deepening of Christianity in Melanesia.

The first of these are "Cargo Cult Movements" that revealed to the missionaries that the message they had preached had been received in ways very surprising to Westerners. Also called "adjustment" movements and "millenarian" movements, most cargo cults occurred along the coast and on neighboring islands, not in the Highlands, and the most famous of them occurred in areas staffed by SVDs. Their root lies in the fundamental Melanesian worldview. In it, religion and practical life are intimately bound up, and the spirits of ancestors are believed to be close to life and a source of blessing. In addition, ancient "culture heroes" and semidivine figures were believed to be the source of all their technologies, such as axes, bows and arrows, methods of hunting, and so forth. Without question, the locals became Christian out of genuine motives, but in many areas one of those beliefs included belief that in time—when the Melanesians had passed a probationary period and had proved their sincerity as Christians—the missionaries would reveal the secrets that accounted for their impressive technology. Steamships, two-way radios, planes, and medicine, missioners came to realize later, were, for the Melanesian, not the products of centuries of gradual technical advance, but the result of the white man's ancestors' revelations and gifts. The cargo cults, accordingly, were a combination of rituals and other practices that, it was hoped, would open the *rot blong kago* (Tok Pisin for "the road to obtain cargo" [i.e., modern material goods]). In traditional religion, what was conferred by the ancestors was sometimes understood

---

34. For more on the origin of the Melanesian Institute, see Ennio Mantovani, "Silver Jubilee of the Melanesian Institute," *Point* 19, (1994). *Point* is a publication of the MI.

as (mystical) power to make things happen and enjoy the blessings of the spirits that made material well-being possible. The cults, accordingly, were means to obtain this "power." When a cult began, thousands of Melanesians could leave everything behind to follow a leader who promised he had found a way to unlock the cargo road. In many places, missionaries were believed to be perfidious and selfish because they would not give their faithful new Christians the secret to the "power" needed to obtain these material goods. When it took this turn, the foreign priests, brothers, sisters, and lay missioners at a station could be in danger of physical attack.

The greater isolation and smaller size of groups along the coast encouraged a greater number and variety of cult movements there. Many reasons help explain the difference between the coastal and island peoples, as opposed to the highland peoples, as far as cult movements are concerned. They include the fact that coastal, island, and river societies had been exposed longer to foreigners, including missionaries and the church. Christianity on the coast had more time to influence traditional thinking and in its new form be applied to make sense of the new world in which the people found themselves. Few Catholic missionaries were prepared for the outbreak of the cults that seemed to undo much that they had worked so hard to achieve over so many years. Missionaries were dismayed, interpreting the movements as a revelation that they had simply not understood their people and had labored in vain. On more reflection, they learned that they need not be so troubled. The Melanesian Institute was one of the key sources of better information for Catholic and Protestant missionaries, helping them understand the kinds of fundamental interpretations of the cults that I gave in the first paragraphs of this section. This was the case, at least, for missionaries in cargo cult areas in the 1960s and later. Prewar cargo cults and those occurring immediately after the war were a difficult trial. For years the missionary had worked tirelessly to extend the influence of Christianity by reaching as many people as quickly as possible. Given the theology of mission at the time, this made sense. Most missionaries believed that only those who had heard of Christ, however superficially, and were baptized would be saved. Thus knowledge of Christ had to be spread as rapidly and as best one could do it. In the light of the cargo cults, it was clear that an in-depth dialogue with local culture was required so evangelization could go deeper.

Among the areas that the mission began stressing in dialogue was the difference between power as understood in Christianity and in Melanesian religion. Power was *pawa* in Tok Pisin. *Pawa*, as the control of secret knowledge to get access to influence and especially to an abundance of material goods, had to be differentiated from the ends of Christianity in a slow and laborious process of dialogue. Few expatriate missionaries realized the extent and deep roots of cargo thinking. Missionaries usually knew something was happening, but often only in a very general way. When a full-scale cargo cult, which could no longer be ignored, swept through an area, the missionary was tempted to blame it on the materialistic outlook of the Melanesians who wanted to have everything immediately but not have to work for all they craved. The task of the Melanesian Institute in relation to the adjustment movements we have been discussing, as well as in regard to a host of major and minor other issues, was to help the missionaries understand the worldview out of which their people were working. In the final analysis, what is also revealed is the need for a local clergy, working with the people they are much more capable of understanding, and much better able to translate the message of the gospel properly into the idiom and mentality of the people. In that process, the importance of contextualizing the biblical message can hardly be overemphasized. The same holds true for stressing the Bible as the ordinary way of catechizing the Melanesian people. Expatriate missionaries, such as American SVDs, staffing parishes and catechetical centers, working through programs like the Better World Movement and Renew, are still making specialized contributions to the further growth and development of the church in Papua New Guinea.

Father Clifford King (1888-1969) stands at the entry to a mission in China. The addresses on the boxes from Techny evoke the worldwide scope of Techny's first missionaries' concerns.

Fathers Peter ("Happ") Heier (1895-1982) and Thomas Megan (1899-1951) in China. As a prefect apostolic in China, Megan was the first American SVD to hold a mission ecclesiastical office.

The North American SVD's first overseas missionaries, Clifford King, at right of Vicar Apostolic Augustine Henninghaus, SVD, and Robert Clark (1895-1929), with three Chinese diocesan seminarians in 1920.

Father Harold Rigney (1900-1980), appointed rector of Fu Jen after World War II, was sentenced to four years in a communist prison as a spy.

Father Joseph Murphy (1895-1935), first SVD rector of Fu Jen University.

The main building of Fu Jen University in Peking (Beijing), taken over by the SVD in 1933, the Society's first venture in higher education.

This group of twenty SVD priests who went to New Guinea in 1944 included three future bishops, Stephen Appelhans (1905-1951), John Cohill (1907-1994), third and fourth from left in first row, and Leo Arkfeld (1912-1999), third from left in back row.

Brother Eugene (Francis Frank, 1900-1935), the first American SVD brother in New Guinea, a highlands pioneer, standing with workers in front of the mission's pre-war headquarters in Alexishafen, was killed by arrows in January 1935.

On 1 April 1934, the first SVDs in Mount Hagen greet the first airplane to land there. From left to right, Fathers William Ross, Henry Aufenanger, Alphons Schäfer, Brother Eugene, and Father William Topper.

Archbishop Adolph Noser (1900-1981), Bishop of Accra, Ghana, Archbishop of Madang, Papua New Guinea.

Archbishop Leo Arkfeld (1912-1999), Bishop of Wewak, Archbishop of Madang, Papua New Guinea.

Archbishop George Bernarding (1912-1987), Archbishop of Mount Hagen, Papua New Guinea.

Bishop John Cohill (1907-1994), Bishop of Goroka, Papua New Guinea.

Father William Ross (1895-1973), founder of the Mount Hagen mission as he looked late in life.

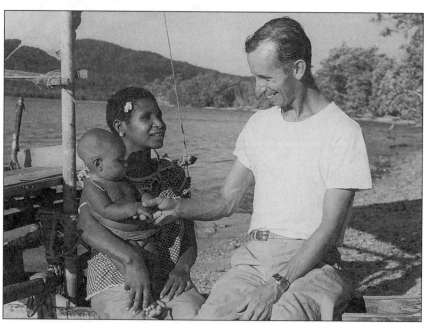

Father Francis Mihalic (b. 1916), persistent advocate of Melanesian Pidgin and founding editor of *Wantok* newspaper, on Kairiru Island off the coast of Wewak, Papua New Guinea.

Christ the King Seminary, Quezon City, Philippines, nurtured Filipino vocations to the Society and was the predecessor of today's Divine Word Seminary in Tagaytay City.

Brother Raphael (Ralph Felix, 1912-1978) with a troop of the Boy Scouts he energetically fostered during his years in the Philippines.

Father Bernard LeFrois (1908-1997), long a popular scripture teacher at Techny, went to the Philippines in 1956 to continue teaching Sacred Scripture to Filipino candidates to the Society.

Bishop Joseph Bowers (b. 1910), the first alumnus of Bay Saint Louis to become a bishop, was bishop of Accra in 1953 and later obtained SVD missionaries for the Caribbean Islands apostolates when he became bishop there.

In 1939, Father Alphonse Elsbernd (1899-1997) was the first American assigned to Ghana.

Father Richard Winters (b. 1911), an alumnus of Bay Saint Louis, was the first American SVD to go to the Congo in 1952.

Brother Damian (Jerome Bockman, 1919-1994) began his missionary life as a builder and later became a highly successful prison chaplain, an example of the way many brothers entered pastoral ministries after Vatican Council II.

Brother Cletus (Joseph Lesage 1908-1990) set up a Catholic press in Ghana and trained Ghanaians to take it over.

Brother Lucian (on right, Urban Orians, 1904-79), master builder in the Ghana mission, with Father Thomas Halleran (b. 1906).

13

The Philippines

Strengthening a Church through Education

The situation facing the Society of the Divine Word in the Philippines was quite different from what it had confronted in missions elsewhere. A different approach had to be adopted, thus causing a significant shift in the understanding of the mission of the SVD. To understand this shift, we must look briefly at the history of Christianity in the Philippines.

BACKGROUND

That history begins near the beginning of the colonial era when the Portuguese explorer Ferdinand Magellan discovered a group of islands, later to be called the Philippines, in March 1521. He died there the following month after trying to impose Christianity and Spanish sovereignty. In 1542 the Spaniards took possession of the archipelago, naming the country after the Infanto and later king of Spain, Philip II. As the Spaniards planted the flag, they planted the cross. They took it as a sacred duty to win the newly discovered lands for the Christian faith. Supported by the Spanish crown, the missionaries built magnificent churches and monasteries, near which they grouped schools and colleges, going about their work with zeal and success. As early as 1611 the Dominicans established the University of Santo Tomas in Manila. Eventually, due to the munificence of the government, many of these monasteries became wealthy, but the dependence of the religious orders on the Spanish government proved to be a problem, for in 1896 the Filipinos mounted a successful revolt against Spanish domination.

Backed by the church, Spain had imposed unity on the Philippines, not an easy task when one recalls that the archipelago consists of some seven thousand islands and many different languages. The country was also split into various kingdoms, villages, clans, tribes, and the like. A revolution led by José Rizal began in 1892. Rizal was executed by Spain in 1896. In June 1898, revolutionaries led by Andres Bonifacio declared their independence from Spain, the first country in Asia to do so. The republic that was proclaimed did not last long, since it was not recognized by other nations. Then the Spanish-American war, which had started over Cuba, spread to the Philippines. Just as the Philippine government was consolidating its control of the country, Spain was forced to cede the Philippines to the United States. With overwhelming force and a hankering for a colony, the United States crushed the Filipinos in a war they called the "Philippine Insurrection," though Filipinos refer to it as the "Philippine-American War."

When Spain was forced to leave the Philippines, so were more than five hundred of the Spanish friars on which many of the church's institutions depended. Among the Americans there was much opposition to the church. Part of it was because the church was so closely identified with the oppressive Spanish regime as to be considered itself oppressive and exploitative. Undeniably a major part of that opposition from the Americans came from their reflexive Protesant identity. On top of it all, the Catholic Church was weak because the Spanish friars had been slow to develop a local clergy.

In addition to the lack of priests, another issue soon worried the church in the Philippines. With the American takeover, Protestant churches rushed to the islands to fill the spiritual vacuum they perceived to be there, and tried to convert Filipinos away from the Catholic Church. This was not discouraged by the American colonial regime. One thing the new masters positively encouraged was the introduction of the American public school system and the use of English. It too would be used to weaken the church. Over a thousand American teachers flocked to the Philippines, now willingly accepted as America's burden and responsibility. These teachers became widely known as "Thomasites" after the name of the ship on which five hundred of them came to the Philippines in August 1901. They were to introduce English and an American style of public school education to the Philippines. In those schools, no religion was to be taught. Eventually, as devout Filipinos demanded religious instruction, priests and nuns were permitted to teach religion after school hours.[1]

Freemasonry was a third area of concern for the church. Many Filipino revolutionaries were already masonic in their thinking, and that translated into anticlerical, liberal, anti-Catholic actions. Many of the Americans coming over to spread English and the American school system were also masons, so there was danger, from the standpoint of church leaders in the Philippines, that the next generation of Filipinos would be lost to the Catholic Church.

THE SOCIETY OF THE DIVINE WORD COMES

SVD involvement in the Philippines goes back to the period a few years after the Philippine-American War, and was decided upon by Arnold Janssen. The correspondence goes back to 1904, when the archbishop of Manila, through the Vatican secretary of state, wrote Father Janssen requesting help for the Philippines. Even though Janssen was willing to send it, his councilors were divided. The dissenters argued that the Philippines was already largely Catholic, while the Society had been founded to work among the "heathen." The reader will recall that the same objection had been made when the Society was preparing to work among the

---

1. For more on this era, see Stanley Karnow, *In Our Image: America's Empire in the Philippines* (New York: Ballantine Books, 1989), p. 201.

African Americans in the United States. How often had the founder inquired of Peil: How many pagans, or heathens, are there among the blacks in the South? Although Peil did not know, he gave an exaggerated percentage, knowing it would help his cause. The founder always prepared himself thoroughly before coming to any decision, and the Philippines were no exception. He also enlisted the help of Father Limbrock, the Limbrock who had been a missionary in China and was later transferred to New Guinea. Limbrock, whose opinion Janssen valued highly, sent a long report back to the founder in 1907 after he had stopped for a time in the Philippines to investigate the situation. In this report he pointed out how many "heathen" there still were in Abra, which was then part of the Diocese of Vigan, and concluded his letter of 27 March 1907, "Good Father, don't leave unheard this heartfelt appeal. I feel that God wants you here. Your mission in the Philippines will be a success, and will draw upon your Society the choicest blessings of God."[2]

In 1909, Janssen sent two priests to Abra to work among non-Christians. According to the custom of the founder, the first superior and missionary in the Philippines, Father John Beckert, was an experienced missionary who had gotten his training in China. They landed in Manila on 15 August 1909, seven months after the founder's death. The conditions they found were different from what was expected, and the China experience of working to establish the faith among "heathen" would not be relevant. Of the two, Father John Schleiermann died of a fever after less than six months in the mission. The superior, Father Beckert, died in Manila in 1913. The Missionary Sisters of the Holy Spirit arrived in 1912 and were able to keep the school work going all during World War I. By the time the war broke out in 1914, there were ten priests, two brothers, eleven sisters, fifty-one catechists, and forty schools serving about 1,700 students in the then very difficult Abra mission.

By 1916 the mission had already lost five missionaries to death. The war, as elsewhere, put a stop to any further progress. Abra was poor, practically priestless, taken over by the Aglipayans,[3] isolated during the rainy season by flooding rivers. All in all, it was a pristine mission field in the strictest sense. Yet it was soon plain that the task was as much one of reclaiming people who had once been Catholic as it was to convert people in the first place. As more experience was gained, it became clear that in virtually every other place in the Philippines as well, it was predominantly a task of bringing people back to the observance of their Catholic duties, a work that required education.

AMERICAN SVDS IN THE PHILIPPINES

From the beginning of his decision to enter the Philippines, the founder had the American SVD in mind, expecting them eventually to be able to help the Philippines. He was also on the verge of permitting the Society in America to open its own seminary. The first time the American SVD had direct contact with the Philippines was at the end of World War I when six German SVD priests and one German SVD brother were sent to an internment camp in San Francisco. This was

2. Rome, SVD Generalate Archives.
3. The Aglipayans were a native sect seeking an independent church.

part of an incipient policy initiated by Great Britain to deport enemy nationals, especially Germans, after the war and to confiscate their property as part of war reparations. The Australians were attempting the same thing in New Guinea and the same process was being attempted also in China. The effort, largely due to American influence and pressure, was not ultimately successful, except for the SVD missions in Africa. Shortly after the war, these German SVDs were released from internment and came to Techny. Immediately they began to get ready to return to the Philippines. One, Father F. X. Blasczyk, run-down and ill as a result of his captivity, contracted the flu which developed into pneumonia. Instead of going to Techny, he was taken directly from the train in Chicago to the hospital, where he died.

When the interned missionaries returned to the Philippines in November 1920, the first American missionary, Brother Benedict, went along. Not long after he left the Society, simply disappearing. In 1922 two more Americans, Father Peter Weyland, a member of Techny's first ordination class in 1921, and Brother Jerome Wagner, set sail for the Philippines. Originally assigned to New Guinea, Weyland's appointment was changed to the Philippines as a result of Superior General Gier's visitation of the Philippines. Protestant groups had been busy setting up dormitories for students in Manila, for those who were attending universities in the big city, and it was decided to build such a place under Catholic auspices as well. Father Weyland was to be the prefect. After two years he returned to the States. Weyland, many felt, was temperamentally unsuited for a foreign missionary's life. According to his own account, as prefect of discipline he had once turned an unruly boy upside down. According to the personal recollections of Father Stanley Plutz, once a student of Father Weyland and himself a long-time missionary in the Philippines, when free masons heard about this incident, it was magnified and used to have him deported. Father Weyland eventually found his niche as a sculptor. He did much fine work. Perhaps the most famous one involved sculpting the figure, supposedly of Christ himself, traced on the Shroud of Turin. To do this, Weyland did experiments that included suspending himself from a cross with leather cuffs long enough to have plaster casts made of his own chest, so that the torments that Christ's body must have been subjected to might the better be shown. He died on 20 May 1969 at the age of seventy-four.

As the first American to stay in the Philippines, Brother Jerome Wagner deserves a few words. Born in Decatur, Illinois, on 16 December 1889, he was called into the army during the First World War. During this time, he decided to become a missionary. He was twenty-nine when he came to Techny to be a brother. Two years later he took his first vows. Under the tutelage of Brother Fabian he learned the art of carpentry. He also worked for a time in the circulation department of the press. He must have impressed people at Techny, as well as the superior general, whom he had written that he would like to go to the missions, for he received an appointment to New Guinea while still a novice. Like that of Father Weyland, this appointment was changed to the Philippines, and the two of them left for their new mission in May 1922. He stayed first at St. Rita's Hall for girls studying at the universities in Manila, then at the Catholic Trade School when it was opened in 1924. Eventually he became assistant procurator, the one who ordered and received supplies for missionaries all over the Philippines. This meant clearing customs, not always an easy task in the Philippines, and buying materials locally for churches and schools. He was also the purchasing agent for the Catholic Trade School and for Christ the King Seminary for many years. He was a conscientious, hard worker and prayerful, qualities that made him an example to scores of Filipino candidates for religious life over the years.

When the Second World War broke out, Brother Jerome, like all the other Americans, was interned during the entire war. He was liberated in 1945 and offered a free trip back to the United States, courtesy of the United States navy. He had been in the Philippines for 23 years, but he turned down the offer and went back to his work as purchasing agent as soon as he was able.

For many years, Brother Jerome was the only American SVD brother in the Philippines. Like all successful missionaries, he crossed over to a different world and culture and quickly adapted, making many friends. Finally in 1950, after twenty-eight years away from home, he returned for a brief visit to the United States. After three months he was on his way back to Manila, which by now had become his real home. By this time he was sixty-two. As more years went by and he became much older, Jerome had to give up his usual work, but did not stop contributing. He became the eyes of another long-time missionary in the Philippines, Father Michael Hergesheimer, who was blind. Almost to the day of his death of a heart attack, he was faithful to his charge to take care of Father Michael. The last entry in his diary was: "I shall take care of Fr. Michael until I die," and he did. Brother Jerome died on 27 June 1968, at the age of seventy-eight. Father Michael followed a year later, almost to the day, both of them after years of service to the cause of Christ in the missions of the Philippines. In his eulogy at Brother Jerome's funeral Mass, Father Walter Joyce (another American missioner in the Philippines, who died in 1997) said, "Although Brother Jerome never preached from this pulpit, his entire religious life was one great sermon more forceful than words can be. His deep humility and thoroughly religious spirit have been an inspiration for us."

EXPANSION INTO EDUCATION

In Abra, the place where the Society began its work in the Philippines, it still preaches God's Word today. But as the SVD grew and developed, it spread out. In 1922, the Society moved into its next mission, this one on the small island of Lubang, off the northeastern coast of Mindoro. While continuing and expanding parochial work in such areas as Abra and Lubang, the two other major contributions that the Society of the Divine Word has made in the Philippines have both been in the educational field. In these, the Americans had a great deal to contribute, first, in schools established for general education and, second, in seminary education both of candidates for membership in the Society itself but also and equally important, for the dioceses of the archipelago.

In addition to elementary and secondary education, emphasis came to be placed on higher, or tertiary, education. The American colonial government had stressed public education, which meant that no religion could be taught in these schools.

But government support for the most part extended only to elementary and secondary education. Higher education was left to private initiative, and the church moved into this area with vigor, quickly developing a reputation as having the better schools in the country.[4] The SVD, with its commitment to work among the unbaptized and the poor, did not move into higher education until 1935, when it assumed the direction of San Carlos College in Cebu City on the island of Cebu, in the central part of the archipelago. It was the Society's second foray into tertiary education, Fu Jen University in China being the first.

San Carlos had been in continuous existence as a school of various sorts since 1595, when the Jesuits opened it as a simple parochial school. After the Jesuits, the Dominicans had it for a time, then the Vincentians, who used it for a seminary and college, until the SVD took it over as a college. Cebu City was growing into the second largest city outside of Manila, and the college grew also, from forty-eight students when the Society took it over in 1935 to eleven hundred by the time the Japanese invaded the Philippines in late 1941. They commandeered the university buildings for military purposes and turned the college into an ammunition depot. This depot blew up in a 1944 air raid, completely destroying it. Prewar experience, however, had unequivocally demonstrated the need for a school of high education, so the Society set to work immediately to rebuild San Carlos.

Father Ralph's SVD Catholic Universities operation was expanded to include San Carlos University, which, in 1948, had been granted university status. In the postwar years, it expanded rapidly. By 1952, after the flush of post-war reconstruction was over, the May-June 1952 *Mission Secretariat Washington Service Bulletin* had this comment to make about the Society's educational work in the Philippines:

A group of Divine Word Fathers met in Manila on May 9, 1952, for their first national Educational Convention. The aim of the meeting was to exchange views and experiences in the educational field, acquaint school directors with current trends in education, particularly in vocational guidance and to standardize the community's own special code of school administration. The Divine Word Fathers have one of the best organized chains of schools in the Islands, which are noted for both their high enrollment and high standards. The Fathers operate the largest and best equipped school outside of Manila, San Carlos University in Cebu. In addition they operate eight colleges, twenty-seven high schools and nineteen elementary schools in various sections of the Philippines. The total enrollment of these schools is over 28,000. The Society also has charge of five diocesan seminaries in addition to their own Christ the King Seminary in New Manila. There are 185 Fathers of the Society in the Philippines, among them a substantial number of Filipino priests.

Two of these high schools, one in Manila and the other in Dagupan City, north of Manila, were primarily intended to educate the large Chinese population in the

---

4. The University of the Philippines is an obvious exception to this statement. For a long time it was the only national university and was lavishly supported by the government as well as by outside funding sources, such as the Ford and Rockefeller Foundations. It was and remains a top-rate university.

Philippines. With the communist takeover in China in 1949, many priests and seminarians, including eight Chinese SVD seminarians, went into exile, many to the Philippines, to work among the overseas Chinese. Before 1949, there were two Catholic schools for Chinese; by 1970 there were sixteen. Before 1949 there was only one Chinese parish, which had been established in 1587 by the Dominicans in the Binondo district of Manila, where most of the Chinese immigrants had settled from as far back as the year 982 C.E. By 1970 there were twenty-six Chinese parishes and missions. The number of Chinese Catholics had also increased. It should be noted that this growth was not all the SVD's work, since many religious congregations took part in it.

The tremendous and rapid growth of the SVD in the Philippines, especially in its educational work, was made possible partly because of the closure of the China mission and the subsequent exodus of scores of talented missioners. Of one hundred sixty ex-China SVDs, forty-nine were reassigned to the Philippines. Among them, for example, were Father Harold Rigney, named president of San Carlos, while his good friend Father Edgar Oehler was assigned to teach chemistry in San Carlos. Later Father Rahmann, the rector of Fu Jen before Rigney, also came to San Carlos to be its president. Father Goertz, whom we met in our history of Fu Jen, also was assigned to San Carlos and spent many fruitful years there. Even the dedicated lay teacher of chemistry in Fu Jen, Dr. William Bruell, moved to San Carlos, where he worked for many years.

Some of the missionaries sent to China barely got there before they were reassigned because of Mao Tse-tung's takeover of China. Consider, for example, the last six Americans to go to China, Edward Norton, Thomas Cassidy, Joseph Bates, Bartley Schmitz, Hilbert Wiesen, and Paul Auer, all of them ordained toward the end of the war. They had barely begun their Chinese language studies when they were reassigned, three of them to the Philippines.[5] Norton was sent to San Carlos where he helped start the Girls' High School. He returned to the United States after a few years to get a doctorate in education from the University of Chicago, with the intention of returning to San Carlos. He was, however, reassigned to the States and appointed secretary for education with the special assignment to guide the SVD's accreditation work in America. Cassidy remained in the Philippines to teach in a variety of schools, but mostly in seminary education. He is still active, now in the SVD Chinese parish in Manila. Father Bates remained many years in the Philippines, mostly in education.

A description of Bates's work in the Philippines, as an example of activity similar to that carried on by others in the Philippines, is in order. I base much of what follows on a report written by the Filipino SVD Father Flor Camacho, who worked with Father Bates as a scholastic while they struggled to build a college in Albay province in the Bicol-speaking area of the Philippines, located at the southern tip of Luzon, the largest island in the Philippines.[6]

---

5. Bartley Schmitz at the time this book was written was working on Taiwan, while Fathers Wiesen and Auer were both reassigned to Japan, where Wiesen, who died in 1998, had a long and fruitful career. Father Auer left the Society to become a diocesan priest.

6. See Flor Camacho, "At the Foot of Mount Mayon," *Word in the World* (Techny, Ill.: Divine Word Publications, 1965), pp. 102–105.

Camacho recalls that there had been a high school and college in Legaspi City, the capital town of Albay. It was called the Liceo de Albay, administered by diocesan clergy as soon as World War II had ended. It had prospered until the whole complex was almost totally destroyed by a typhoon in 1952. The Liceo was a shell, which the bishop tried to restart as a high school, but even this proved too costly; the institution continued to deteriorate, only attracting students who, for one reason or another, could not get into any other school. By now it was in private hands and going deeper and deeper into debt.

In 1960, the provincial superior of the Philippines, Father Alphonse Lesage, another of the brothers Lesage, had a study of vocations done; it became clear that (1) most vocations came from schools run by the SVD, and (2) there were few vocations from the Bicol area, where the SVD had no school. Father Bates, who had already been in school work in the Philippines for twelve years, mostly in Bohol, an island south of Cebu, was asked to make the start. In 1961 the Society bought the almost defunct Liceo de Albay and, with two male student workers and two women teachers, whom he brought from Bohol, and with Flor Camacho, an SVD scholastic also from Bohol, Bates began to get the school ready for classes. The pioneers had from the end of May to the middle of June, when the school year started, to get ready. Camacho writes:

> His greatest cross was the problem of raising money to prepare for the school year. Books alone would require 5,000 pesos (about $1500). Repairs would take another 2,000 pesos. While I was busy with the manual workers, poor Father Joe was busy writing letters to his benefactors in the United States, not to mention numerous letters to the Provincial. He himself went downtown to buy the needed materials, such as plywood, nails, paints, etc. Hardly any store would give him credit. The reason was that the Liceo had formerly been notorious for not paying its bills.[7]

The beginnings were difficult, but within three years the Liceo had become Divine Word College, Bates completed a new three-story addition to the school and developed plans for a much larger building program. At the time of this book's publication in 2000, the college is still going strong. Note that Father Bates was expected to find as much financing for his school as he could on his own. This custom went all the way back to the founder, who expected each mission to be as self-supporting as possible. His members were to live the vow of poverty, but they also were expected to do as much as they could financially to support their mission work. This was a way in which SVD mission work was different from that of many other communities, whose fund raising and disbursement were centralized. The advantages of the SVD system were that the SVD had a broader base of support and could undertake projects that other groups would shy away from. The disadvantage was that missioners with generous benefactors could become more influential than those without them.

When the time came, by government decree and Filipino agitation, to Filipinize (i.e., turn schools over to the Filipino SVDs) the administration of all

___

7. Camacho, "At the Foot of Mount Mayon," pp. 103–4.

foreign enterprises, which included schools, colleges, and universities, Father Bates volunteered to go as chaplain to a penal colony on Palawan, an island in the South China Sea in the west central part of the archipelago. He was a builder of schools, had good benefactors to back him up, but he was foremost a priest interested in people's well-being. Bates's fund raising was typical of what Americans of many communities were doing. As one of the two great powers left standing after the Second World War, the United States was the wealthiest nation on earth, especially in the first ten years after the war. For some time its funds were virtually the only source that could be counted on for financing Christian mission. Russia carried on its own brand of mission in its export and support of national liberation movements. The struggle to improve the lot of the poor in the Philippines was a work that the SVD had engaged in mightily. This was accompanied by another struggle, namely, to liberate the Philippines from all domination, including that of the United States. Filipinos intended to take decision making over their affairs into their own hands, in short, to nationalize, or Filipinize, everything, including church institutions. This movement also swept the Society of the Divine Word. This, however, belongs more to a history of the Filipino SVD provinces, and will be told elsewhere. For our history, the important thing to recount is that Joseph Bates got caught up in the Filipinization of the institution he had done so much to found and that he found it very difficult to adapt to these changed circumstances. He went to the prison at Palawan, and after several years of effort trying to develop a profitable project for prisoners who were kept on this isolated island, he requested to be transferred back to the United States. He was reassigned to the Society's mission in the West Indies, where he died on 28 January 1995, one of the postwar generation of Americans who labored so intensively in the Philippines.

To get still another picture of the kind of work in which American missionaries were engaged in the Philippines, it might be useful, in the form of a chronology, to list the assignments of two missionaries, Fathers Eugene Stoll and Alphonse Lesage. Stoll was born in Canton, Ohio, in 1904 and entered Techny to begin his studies for the missionary priesthood in 1917. Ordained in 1930, he was sent the same year to the Philippines and arrived in November 1930. From early 1931 till May 1932, Stoll worked in Abra at Tayum as an associate pastor. He was then assigned to seven years of work as an instructor at the diocesan seminary in Vigan, along with work in the grade and high school at the College of the Immaculate Conception. Reassigned in 1939 to San Carlos University, and several months to the Tacloban Catholic Institute, his life was put on hold when the war broke out. From 1942 to 1945 he was interned by the Japanese in various locations, after which he spent two years recuperating on home leave in the United States. He dropped from his normal one hundred fifty pounds to ninety-eight pounds during that ordeal.

Stoll returned to the Philippines to be rector of Aklan College from 1949 to 1953, and then spent the period till May 1958 as the liaison officer between SVD schools and the government's Bureau of Private Schools, following which he served at San Carlos as a teacher in 1958 and 1959, when he returned to the grade and high school of the College of the Immaculate Conception for four years between June 1960 and June 1964. With time off for home leave, he spent most of the years from 1964 till his transfer back to the United States in May 1973 at Divine Word College (later University) in Tacloban. True to the spirit of the Society, he did not retire while he had strength to work. He lived and worked in various SVD communities and parishes until in 1994 it was finally time to return to the Techny community where his principal activity is praying for the Philippines, a land and people he still loves deeply, and keeping up an extensive correspondence with his beloved Filipinos.

Fr. Stoll's career in school administration, during which he also kept himself pastorally engaged with counseling students, giving retreats, hearing confessions, teaching religion, and the like, might not have been typical or the same for every SVD in the Philippines, but his experiences would have been shared by many during most of the first sixty years of the Society's work there.

A second member of the ten-member Techny ordination class of 1930 who went to the Philippines and who merits special mention is Alphonse Lesage, known endearingly as "Fons" by all who knew him. Father Lesage was sent first to Indonesia, but in short order it was decided that his qualifications in education would be of greater use in the Philippines. He soon found himself in Cebu, in the southern Philippines at the school that eventually became San Carlos University. Progress toward becoming a university came to a screeching halt when Pearl Harbor was bombed and the Philippine Islands were invaded in late 1941 and early 1942. Lesage was captured by the Japanese and treated ruthlessly by them. He eventually ended up in the Los Baños concentration camp with Eugene Stoll. The classmates showed unselfish, courageous spirit by encouraging their fellow internees both to work and to engage in activities. They found a way to make jelly out of young coconuts, for example, and spread it around. Lesage somehow got cards, organized a poker-playing club, and even ran competitions among his fellow impoverished internees. He kept track of who owed how much and to whom. The debts were to be repaid after the war. To the embarrassment of the Sisters who wondered whether a priest should be running a gambling enterprise, Lesage's name was generally at the top of the list with nearly everyone owing him money. It is not recorded whether he was ever paid. All reservations about gambling aside, such boyish pranks kept spirits up and kept many prisoners alive in spite of the horrors of camp life.

After the war, the indefatigable Fons went right back to work and got his plans for quality education pushed through SVD councils. His passion was for affordable education, especially for programs that would benefit women and the poor. Soon there were SVD schools in many of the capital cities and on the outer islands. Lesage not only pushed the *idea* of education, he took up his own share of the hard work. In 1946 he began Holy Name College in Tagbilaran on Bohol, starting from the ground up by obtaining the land and then buildings from the local bishop. He searched for and found quality teachers for all levels, and scrounged everywhere for suitable textbooks at a time when everything needed to start a school was in short supply because of the ravages caused by World War II. Ever living a life of frugality and simplicity, Lesage got the reputation of being very thrifty, to the extent that he was rumored to have cut up automobile inner tubes for rubber bands or that he patched old basketballs in order to get another game out of them—accusations he steadfastly denied with a grin on his face till the end of his life. Whatever the truth, whatever his secret, both as an ordinary confrere, head of a school or college, or during his time as provincial superior, Fons Lesage coaxed results out of scanty resources. Ever putting into practice the adage he learned at Techny, *mens sana in corpore sano* ("a healthy mind in a healthy body"), Father Lesage loved to swim from the beach at Tagbilaran to a distant lighthouse and back. His confreres felt it was fitting that on the day of his death on 30 December 1977, at the age of 73, Alphonse Lesage died of a heart attack as he admired the reefs of Bohol.

RATIONALE FOR SCHOOL WORK

Wherever the SVDs worked among the unbaptized or the unchurched and fallen away, they have also engaged from the beginning in school work as well. At first these may have been little more than a gathering of people who expressed an interest in becoming Catholic Christians, a school where they learned their prayers and catechism from a catechist. This was certainly and most obviously the situation in China and New Guinea. Even here, though, these catechetical schools developed and were quickly expanded into primary and, often later, secondary schools. Mission schools had a twin goal, imparting the essentials of the faith, to be sure, but also to contribute to the development and freedom of those educated. Education makes choice possible, because it gives a person insight into oneself and the surrounding world and thereby offers options. This is both positive and negative. Positive, in offering freedom; negative, in that traditional cultural bonds are often weakened when students begin to realize that their culture is only one among many. Such Christian education, when it goes well, both makes choice possible and imposes upon the educated person the necessity and responsibility of making one choice rather than another. To the extent, however, that an education makes a variety of choices possible, to that degree the person is more free, less constrained by ignorance to one or two possibilities. An education, therefore, also makes one more human; it is a humanizing process. Learning more about oneself, about one's world, and, in Catholic schools at least, about God and divine revelation to humankind, also makes our religious and moral choices more adult. Small wonder that the Society built schools right from the beginning.

If it is true as well that an educated citizenry is a country's most valuable resource, then educating such a citizenry is a distinct contribution to a country's development, not a small matter when working in a country or area where the level of human development is low. There is, to be sure, a shadow side to the enterprise of education in the missions. With it often came European and American values and culture as well. In themselves this is fine, but in the typical mission situation of the late nineteenth century and down to the present, there is also the problem of furthering a Euro-American cultural hegemony over the non-Western world. That process can alienate Melanesians or Filipinos or Africans from finding appropriate solutions to their problems in their own cultures. One cannot avoid the judgment that those going into missions during this period thought of themselves as bringing the "benefits of Western civilization" along with Christianity. The two were considered to be so closely linked as to be practically inseparable. Looking back with the benefits of hindsight, some suggest that this educational enterprise smacks of colonialism, the monster that brooded over everything, coloring and, in many cases, vitiating the missionary's benignly intended effort. Deliberately mixing nationalism and religion can be dangerous and destructive. Whatever the drawbacks of an educational philosophy introduced from outside, however, the benefits seem to far outweigh them.[8]

CONTRIBUTIONS TO SEMINARY EDUCATION

The second major contribution of the SVD, with representation from American SVDs, is involvement in the education and training of priests. Despite the importance of this task in a country that had been largely Catholic for at least two hundred years, the Society was unable to move into seminary formation at first. Too few missionaries were sent in the beginning, and many of those sent died of fever, of accidents, of overwork. After the First World War, little help was available for years.

When that war was over, the Society began to expand, and some American SVDs also began to arrive. In 1923 the Missionary Sisters of the Holy Spirit of Perpetual Adoration also came to carry out their work, to pray for the grace of God upon the missions. In this same year, Father Bürschen, then the superior, suggested that a seminary be built to educate Filipinos to become priests and brothers for the Society of the Divine Word, but this recommendation was judged to be premature.[9] In 1925, however, three SVDs joined the staff of the diocesan major seminary in Vigan. A year later it was totally entrusted to the Society. The Society took over the seminary in Binmaley, Pangasinan (1930). Members of the Society pioneered seminary formation in Leyte (1944); in Tagbilaran, Bohol (1950); in Pidigan, Abra (1960); in Cabanatuan City (1964); in San Jose, Western Mindoro (1964); in Calapan, Western Mindoro (1969). The Bishop of Mindanao asked the Society to begin and administer the Regional Major Seminary in Davao (1976). But as a diocese or region grew and became capable of directing its own seminary, some were turned over to the bishops again to be administered by their own priests.

An example of how this assistance to Filipino dioceses was given occurred during World War II. With the permission of the bishop, Father Alois Paulsen, a German who took his theology studies at Techny, went to Manila and obtained permission to start a diocesan seminary. He received permission and started in Holy Infant Academy of Sisters near the parish church in Tacloban, Leyte. Since all regular academic schools had been closed, the building was unoccupied. With about ten young men, he operated the seminary under the title of a technical school. After the war, the seminary went to Tanauan, where next to the church stood a former

---

8. In *The Missionary Movement in Christian History* (Maryknoll, N.Y.: Orbis Books, 1996), Andrew Walls makes many interesting observations on the style of American evangelical mission work, many of which hold true also for American Catholic missions. The entire collection is relevant, but here I call special attention again to Chapter 17, "The American Dimension of the Missionary Movement," pp. 221–240.

9. Fritz Bornemann et al., *A History of the Divine Word Missionaries* (Rome: Collegio del Verbo Divino, 1981), p. 339.

Franciscan rectory. Makeshift dormitories were added and Quonset huts served as classrooms. In 1956 the seminarians transferred again, this time to a new buidling that the bishop had been constructing in Palo. In 1969 the administration of the seminary was turned over to the bishop and his priests by the Society. Today Sacred Heart Seminary, in Palo, Leyte, is a complete seminary with a high school, college, and theologate with some two hundred seminarians. This was the kind of contribution that the Society made to the proclamation of the Word.

FILIPINO VOCATIONS TO THE SOCIETY

As the 1930s began, the question of accepting Filipinos into the Society began to be discussed in earnest. It was eventually decided to take the step to open Christ the King Seminary. The American province had a great deal to do with getting it going. Superior General Grendel wrote to Techny that they were to find the money somehow, despite the depression, to buy the property and start the building. Land was mortgaged at Techny and benefactors came through.

On 8 June 1934, the feast of the Sacred Heart of Jesus, the first sixteen seminarians were consecrated to the Sacred Heart. The academic year began on 11 June with seminarians in the first year of high school and the first year of college. A year later, in 1935, a novitiate was opened. In another two years the first six novices took their first vows. By 1940, thirty years after the Society had started its mission effort in the Philippines, there were seven Filipino priests and twenty-two seminarians in vows preparing for the priesthood. In another thirty years, by 1970, the early years of work began to pay off. There were ninety-seven Filipino SVD priests, twenty Filipino brothers, one hundred thirty scholastics, seventy clerical novices, eleven brother novices, and three hundred and five minor seminarians. Among the contributions of American SVDs to the development of the Filipino component of the Society, the work of Father Walter Joyce and Brother Gary (Gerald) Burr stands out. Joyce came to the Philippines after years in which he was a much beloved novice master of the brothers. Burr, a superb athlete and one of the leaders in the brothers' success at upgrading brother training in the United States, brought all these gifts with him.

As devastated as the church in the Philippines was when the Spaniards were forced out of the country, it was true, nevertheless, that the Philippines was the only Christian nation in the whole of Asia. And just as the church as a whole, so every local church, including the Filipino church, had an obligation to preach and bear witness to Christ before their non-Christian neighbors and beyond. To help the Filipino church carry out this task may have been the primary reason in God's design why the SVD was led to the Philippines in the first place. Who knows the mind of God? All we can hope to do is read the signs of the times as best we can. It is, however, a fact, according to Constante Floresca, that *"the SVD was the first religious order to open its ranks to Filipinos to full membership for the specific purpose of preparing them to become missionaries."*[10]

In 1951 two Filipino SVD priests were sent as missionaries to Timor and Flores

---

10. Constante Floresca, "A Missionary Church," *Word in the World* (Techny, Ill.: Society of the Divine Word, 1979), p. 93. The italics are his.

in Indonesia. Since then Filipino SVDs have been sent to practically every mission field in which the Society works. Many more Filipinos have stayed to work in their still priest-poor country, where they now administer most of the schools, universities, and parishes entrusted to the Society. Because so many Filipinos are still poor and exploited, Filipino SVDs have also long been engaged in efforts at human development, in the struggle to better the lot of the poor and dispossessed, and to build a better life for Filipinos of all classes.

Among those most heavily committed to this effort was Edicio de la Torre, SVD. Many other SVDs disagreed with his tactics, preferring to use nonviolent means to bring about social change, but there is no denying that de la Torre became the best-known SVD in the Philippines.

These efforts to change Filipino society in the years of President Ferdinand Marcos's dictatorship involved many diocesan priests and religious from many communities, but especially the laity. Many of those lay persons and priests were the graduates of Catholic schools, some of which American SVDs had worked in. They had planted seeds of the ideals of human dignity as taught in the Bible and as concretized in Catholic social teaching.

With only a few exceptions, most American SVDs and other expatriate missionaries could go home or be reassigned. Filipino SVDs, in the meantime, have been going to the missions, both in their own country as well as to places like New Guinea, to Africa, to every mission where the Society is active, as they should. According to the listing of members in the *Catalogus* of 1995/96, there was a total of 477 Filipinos in the Society of the Divine Word, which counts all those who are in vows and are considered members of the Society, including scholastics in the major seminary and brothers. Of these, 367 are in the Philippines, which means 110 are working as missionaries outside of the Philippines. The Society continues to stress its international character; may it never lose this characteristic.

No event is more symbolic of the way in which the SVD's decision to open itself to membership on the part of non-EurAmericans has transformed the Society than the election of Antonio M. Pernia as superior general on 26 June 2000. Born the eighth of nine children to a Filipino physician and his wife in Tagbilaran on 2 January 1949, Pernia earned a doctorate in theology in 1987 at the Gregorian University with a dissertation on the Kingdom of God in the work of liberation theologians Gustavo Gutiérrez, Leonardo Boff, and Juan Luis Segundo. Pernia served as a seminary teacher, provincial superior, and member of the general council before his election as superior general.

14

Ghana

Return to Africa

The modern history of the Catholic Church in Ghana goes back to 1880, when two members of the recently founded Society for African Missions sent two priests there. Within months one of them was dead. The second survived him by five years. In the meantime four others had been sent. In the twenty years between 1880 and 1900, thirty-four priests and sisters died, and many others were forced home, broken in health. The average span of missionary work was three years, and their average age at death was under thirty. Truly the Gold Coast lived up to its reputation as the "white man's graveyard." Conservatively, Father Albert Kretschmer estimates, over three hundred missionaries lost their lives in the early days in the Gold Coast. The majority were killed by the unseen parasites causing malaria, yellow fever, and black-water fever, all caused by an infected mosquito. By the time the Divine Word Missionaries got there, much of this could be controlled by quinine and other medical discoveries.

The Society's second mission after China was Togo in West Africa. The first missionaries went there in 1892. In 1887, Pope Leo XIII had suggested to Father Janssen that the SVD send missionaries there. When it was agreed to and plans set in motion, the mission was opened as part of a *quid pro quo* arrangement. The Society would send missionaries to Togo in West Africa, in return the state of Prussia would allow the Society to open a mission house in Silesia, then part of Prussia. A second African mission, this time in Mozambique in southeast Africa, was undertaken by the SVD in 1913 during Father Blum's generalate, when the Jesuits were forced to leave the country. Germany's loss in World War I and the terms of the Versailles Treaty meant that both these missions had to be abandoned by the Society. After a term in prison camps, all German SVD missionaries were expelled from Africa. Nearly a generation would intervene before another mission was opened in Africa, and this time leadership was entrusted to Americans as much as any mission is ever entrusted to any national group of

SVDs. In 1939 they began work in Ghana, then known as the British colony called "The Gold Coast."[1]

One wonders today if those missionaries were aware that the historical roots of Christian mission in Africa were even more profoundly American than efforts by American SVDs in Ghana in the 1940s. Contemporary research has brought to the fore that the first African missions to succeed on the west coast were led by American blacks who had fought for the British during the revolutionary war and were granted freedom and land in Nova Scotia in return. From among these African Nova Scotians came the first American Protestant missioners to Africa. They arrived there in 1792, and the result of their work was the first long-term success of Christians after centuries of attempting to establish communities in West Africa.[2] These efforts preceded work by Wesleyans, Baptists, Anglicans, and Catholics and, according to Sanneh, acted "as a powerful stimulus of Christianity to other parts of Africa," making it clear that only in partnership with Africans could missions be successful.[3]

THE SVD'S SECOND START IN AFRICA

The Society's second start in Africa was destined to be more enduring and successful than the first. Superior General Joseph Grendel made the announcement to the American branch of the Society in a letter written from Rome on 2 January 1939:

> Father [August] Gehring, former Africa missionary [who had worked in Togo before World War I], and Father [Alphonse] Elsbernd have been on an inspection trip to Accra to study the situation closely so as to pave the way for the preliminary measures. According to the reports of both Fathers (Father Gehring has meanwhile returned to give a personal report and talk over future plans), the new mission comprises a territory which offers great prospects and at the same time no small difficulties, for the Protestant missionaries have been active here for a long time whereas the Catholics really began only a few years ago. Precisely for these reasons, the great promise for the future and the present difficulties, the Propaganda has turned the mission over to our Society. Accepting this new mission field denotes an understanding fulfillment of will and wish of the Holy See as well as our interest in the good of the mission and our Society. We have long endeavored to obtain a field in Africa again as it is really essential for a missionary organization as ours.
>
> Recently the Propaganda, for various reasons which I need not further declare, gave orders that at least the first appointments may not be continental Europeans

---

1. For a complete history of Catholic mission in the Gold Coast, see Ralph Wiltgen, *Gold Coast Mission History, 1471–1880* (Techny, Ill.: Divine Word Publications, 1956).

2. See Lamin Sanneh, *West African Christianity: The Religious Impact* (Maryknoll, N.Y.: Orbis Books, 1983), pp. 58–68. See also Lamin Sanneh, *Abolitionist Abroad: American Blacks and the Making of Modern West Africa* (Cambridge: Harvard University Press, 2000).

3. Sanneh, *West African Christianity*, p. 106.

but expressly pointed out that besides native Britons, the Americans are best suitable and desirable. Thus the first group, at least of the Fathers, must be appointed from the Sacred Heart Province [Techny]. Would you, therefore, kindly bring this matter as soon as possible to the notice of all members of the Province and inform me at an early date who are the volunteers?[4]

Note that one of the reasons for going to Accra is the presence of Protestants. The ecumenical age was still in the future, and this was still a time of enthusiastic, even cutthroat competition. Second, to have a mission in Africa was considered a necessity "for a missionary congregation as ours." This is not surprising if one understands how large Africa loomed in the consciousness of Europeans. This continent was their "South" in a North-South relationship, and Africa was much studied by Germans. Besides the intrinsic importance of mission anywhere there were nonbelievers, an African mission would be useful both for recruitment of new missionaries and for fund raising. Knowing Father Grendel from his correspondence and from oral interviews with those who had dealings with him, it must have been very difficult for him to accept putting an American in charge in Accra. He was quintessentially German, reluctant to acknowledge that anybody other than a German could effectively head such an important enterprise. He was also very secretive, giving out as little information as he had to. Even so, it was not surprising that the Holy See insisted on native English speakers to take over the Accra mission. He seems to have needed to tell the Society's membership why Americans would be taking the leadership role. It was evident, too, that war was looming on the horizon and England and Germany would probably be on opposite sides again, while the Gold Coast was a British colony. To place Germans in charge, therefore, would run too great a risk of repeating the disaster of the SVD missions in Africa after the First World War. Again, the strengths deriving from internationalism proved essential for success. Grendel, nevertheless, interpreted "English" missionaries broadly, and would include in the definition anyone who was English speaking. Thus he sent seven young priests from the continent to England to prepare for Africa. The war began and they never got there. One need not see in this a German conspiracy, however. It reflects the predominance of Germans in the Society at the time.

Father Alphonse Elsbernd was born in Iowa in 1899 and ordained a priest in 1929. After ordination he went to Rome for graduate studies in philosophy, after which he taught in Bay St. Louis, Mississippi. Later he went to Hadzor in England to teach philosophy at St. Richard's, a recently opened seminary there. He was on temporary loan to St. Augustine's Seminary, near Bonn on the Rhine in Germany, when he was tapped to go to Africa. One day at table he happened to be seated next to a visiting priest who asked whether anyone knew of a certain Father Elsbernd, who was to accompany him to the Gold Coast to check out the new mission the Society was to take over from the Society for African Missions. And that's how Elsbernd learned of his appointment. Two days later the official letter of assignment arrived.

---

4. *Techny Chimes* (March 1939).

Gehring was the designated leader of the exploratory trip and took off on an inspection tour of the eastern region of the Gold Coast, but after two weeks he was back in Accra, a sick man. He was ordered home by the doctor. He had to be carried aboard ship on 14 December 1938. Elsbernd stayed on alone. For the next months he helped the few remaining SMA fathers still left in the eastern district that was to go to the SVD. Many Americans volunteered for Ghana in response to Father Grendel's call. The first two chosen were Fathers Harold Rigney and Adolf Noser, who was appointed superior. Father Elsbernd was the sole SVD until Father Rigney arrived in early July 1939. Rigney immediately began teaching in Achimota, where he also took over the Catholic chaplaincy. After many delays due to the outbreak of the war in Europe, Noser was finally able to reach Ghana in early December 1939; with him came the first African-American SVD missionary to go overseas, John Dauphine. Two more missionaries, Fathers Joseph Bowers (a West Indian black) and Anthony Bauer, arrived on the last day of January 1940. During 1940 four more Americans were appointed for Ghana. Father Cletus Hodapp and Brother James Doerfler arrived in January 1941, and Father Harold Lauck and Brother Lucian Orians arrived later the same month. In 1941, Fathers Alois Turbek and George Wilson (another African American) arrived. After these twelve, no more were able to go to Ghana until the war was over.

In regard to the African-American missionaries sent to Africa, the first foreign missionary fruits of Bay St. Louis and the African-American apostolate, Father Elsbernd says:

One word of appreciation I can say, on behalf of all the Black missionary confreres. The Fathers and Brothers who came to the Gold Coast from the South (and a few from the North also) helped more than they may realize: they showed to one and all that we did not draw a color line, that we did not look down on black Africans as an inferior race. That helped a lot, especially in the days when they were fighting for freedom from Colonial European rule.

The assignment of the first African Americans is said to have caused a ripple of resentment among some of the seminarians at the Bay, who expected to be assigned to work among their own after ordination. The assignment of these men to Ghana, however, made it clear that all those ordained as SVDs had to be ready and willing to go to foreign missions. After some initial grumbling the problem disappeared.

The war in Europe forced Grendel to rely on Americans to staff the mission, and he reported himself pleased with the many applications he had received. Fathers Adolph Noser and Harold Rigney were among those whose work there would be especially remembered. Noser would be the superior. Rigney, with his recent Ph.D. in hand, would go into school work.

ADOLPH NOSER, MISSIONARY OF THE "LITTLE WAY"

If any American SVD is ever to become a saint, many feel Adolph Noser will be strong in the running. Born on 4 July 1900, in Belleville, Illinois, he entered Kenrick

Seminary in St. Louis, Missouri, to prepare for the diocesan priesthood and later decided he wanted to be a missionary. He entered the SVD novitiate in 1921, and after novitiate was sent to Rome for theology. He was ordained in Steyl in 1925 and stayed in Rome for two more years of study and a graduate degree in theology. In 1927 he returned to Techny to teach in the seminary. He quickly distinguished himself in the American Society as a man whom both the Germans and Americans respected in years when the Americans yearned for superiors from their own cultural background. He became assistant novice master to Father Glorius at East Troy, Wisconsin, from 1929 to 1934, and was suggested as replacement for Father Glorius as novice master. But at this stage in the development of the SVD in the United States, the generalate was reluctant to put an American in such a sensitive position.

Noser was a prayerful, ascetical man. If Father Glorius was praised for living the life of a novice with the novices, Noser did the same, all his life long. Glorius did not want to lose him, but in 1934 Noser was appointed as rector of the minor seminary in Epworth, Iowa, and in 1937 he became both rector of the house and prefect of seminarians at St. Mary's Seminary at Techny. He held those major positions simultaneously when he volunteered to go to Africa.

When Noser was appointed to Africa in 1939, Father Markert complained bitterly to Father Grendel in a letter written on 3 April 1939. Why were they taking this American superior away from Techny? He describes the visit of the Nazi official from the German Consul's office in Chicago, checking on Techny's "cultural-political activities and Techny's position regarding the new [Third] Reich." In that context Markert complains about the appointments of three of the American SVD's brightest young Americans, noting that many at Techny felt very bad about the appointments and morale in the province was low.

> Again and again there have been complaints that this province does not have the kind of teaching staff it should. Now that we finally have good teachers at our disposal—Elsbernd, whom many recognize as a better philosophy professor than Father Esser, and Father Rigney, whose studies and teaching to date give every promise that he will become a very competent, even excellent, teacher, and Father Noser, as one who has finally cultivated an excellent spirit among the seminarians, are now taken away from us. The greatest difficulty for our seminarians has been the constant change. Some of our present seminarians have already had four prefects . . . Finally in Father Noser we finally had a man, who, in his knowledge and deep piety, in his practical way of teaching and his other wonderful characteristics as a priest, has been such a model for the seminarians that there is no comparison with his predecessors . . . The same is true of Noser as rector. Here, too, his work and influence are remarkable. Father Humel [his immediate predecessor] was a good priest, but as rector he would be "moonlight," while Noser is "sunlight," if I may use this comparison . . . He sets an example of prayer and work that affects and influences practically everybody.

Father Markert continues in this vein for another page. He has no hope that the appointment will be changed, though he does point out that Noser's health makes this appointment tantamount to a sentence of early death. This letter, with its fulsome praise of Noser and the other two appointees, does, indirectly at least, prove what was said of Grendel, that he sent the very best men to the missions. It shows, too, that the German priests were capable of recognizing solid American candidates and wanted to see them placed in key positions. The desire for American superiors was not, in other words, an American desire alone!

In the opinion of many who were there at that time, the years when Noser was rector at Techny were the golden years. Once a week he visited every brother at his place of work, to see how things were going; he would stop in the kitchen to ask the sisters what was cooking for dinner. They, the ones that so many forgot, appreciated his interest and concern immensely.

Before leaving for Ghana, Noser had to have his physical. The first doctor said he was too frail to survive in the tropics. The second one gave him six months to live if he went to Africa. Grendel insisted on a third opinion, and this one was positive. As a matter of fact, Noser thrived in the tropics, both in Africa and later in New Guinea. He looked frail because of the calm, unhurried, serene, controlled way he had of walking, working, and talking. He ate sparingly, took every opportunity to mortify his body, such as not wearing gloves in the winter as he walked outside praying his breviary. He slept on his outsized desk or on the floor rather than on a bed. He chewed rather than swallow his bitter antimalarial pills, and rumors abounded that he followed other, even harsher ascetical practices.[5] But at the same time, he definitely had great interpersonal skills.

The new missioners stepped into a situation in which the feelings of the group formerly in charge of Accra, the Society of African Missions (known as the "SMA Fathers") were somewhat hurt when Rome gave the eastern region of Ghana to the Society of the Divine Word. The reason the Holy See did so, it seems, was that the SMAs could afford to assign only two missionaries there, even though Accra was rapidly becoming the largest city in Ghana. Immigrants from other parts of West Africa were flowing into the city, a portent of the huge migrations from the countryside that would transform the colony in post-World War II years. The SMAs felt that the SVD, by promoting Ewe language prayers and songs, the language spoken in Togo, were promoting an ethnic divide in the Catholic community that the SMA was attempting to play down. The second strike against the SVD came when it sent an inexperienced man as superior to the chief city in the most important area of the Gold Coast. Noser allayed the unease these missionaries felt by approaching their bishop, William Porter, who was located at Cape Coast, and each of the other mission superiors to seek advice on what he should do and how. Once they knew him, they also readily accepted him, according to Father Kretschmer, who reports, as well, that Porter recommended splitting the diocese, making Accra a vicariate and Noser its vicar apostolic.

---

5. Some of these recollections of Noser come from Albert Kretschmer, SVD, who, at the request of his superior, wrote them in a memoir shortly after Noser died. They knew each other well, for Noser became his mentor, spiritual director, superior repeatedly, including in Africa. Kretschmer was Noser's personal secretary in Africa as well as his friend and admirer. See Albert Kretschmer, "My Personal Memories of His Grace, the Most Reverend Archbishop Adolph Alexander Noser, S.V.D, D.D.: The First Bishop of the Diocese of Accra, Africa" (Unpublished manuscript, 1981).

For Noser, the most important ingredient in missionary work was the genuineness of the missioner's interior life. The emphasis on spirituality is especially clear in letters he wrote his two sisters who had become Benedictine nuns in a convent devoted to perpetual adoration of the Blessed Sacrament. In these letters Bishop Noser talks about what is happening in his life, and as his responsibilities grew heavier, this correspondence seems to have become even more important to him. One of his sisters, named in religious life Sister Tharsilla, was put under obedience by her confessor to save all of the letters she ever received from her brother. She kept them and they were later put in the SVD generalate archives.[6] In a letter of 26 February 1941, Noser wrote:

> Now that I have been out here for more than a year, I judge pretty well the life of a missionary. It is, indeed, the life which our Blessed Lord followed, and the real missionary is one who strives to copy this Divine Model, as perfectly as possible in his union with God. This is really difficult . . . One's residence is far from being a convent, and there is no such thing as a monastic atmosphere, even at night, for the hubbub never seems to cease, especially in larger centers such as Accra. The duties are so many and great that one has little time for oneself, and when one does, one is so weary that he finds it hard to attempt anything but sleep. When one is sleepy, prayer is more than a mere struggle, especially when God seems to hide, and even flee from one.
>
> But then is the time to live by faith and hope, and renew oneself in love in spite of all absence of feeling. It is the price of immortal souls! . . . When this unsatisfied hunger for God arises, and there is no opportunity to satisfy it, I recall that it must have been much greater in the great missionaries like St. Francis Xavier, St. Peter Claver, etc., whose whole heart must have been centered on contemplation, and a desire for union with God, and who must constantly have been obliged to sacrifice that desire, and to leave God for the love of God in the service of souls. And yet, I feel that in their hearts they never did leave God, but rather that because of their constant union with Him, they were so fired with love for His image in the wretched souls for whom they so unwearyingly spent themselves. It is the ideal . . . One can hope to do but little good in the missions until one is well on the way to the perfection of the ideal.

In a letter written in 1944, he states:

> We have often heard and read that only a deeply interior man—a saint—can take on mission work without danger to himself. I can confirm that statement now from personal experience. One must be a man with something of the interior life of a Saint Peter Claver, a Saint Francis Xavier, to be a real

---

6. Several other bound volumes of letters written by Noser, especially from New Guinea, are named by Bernard Fisher (1992) "Collected Letters 1955–1972." They are preserved in archives at the Divine Word Residence at East Troy, Wisconsin. This folder comes to 494 pages. Noser was a prolific writer.

missionary. Otherwise one is just a sign-post pointing the way to others, yet remaining stationary oneself and in the end, just rotting and falling by the wayside!

In another letter written in 1945 to his sister, even more insistently he states, "To keep from being exteriorized in mission work, one must be a saint; then one carries one's solitude and recollection with him everywhere, and that is the essential for the ideal."

Noser goes on to talk about all of the distractions that militate against attaining this ideal and bemoans the fact that he is still so far from this ideal. But the importance of cultivating an intense interior life was a clear necessity, even in the midst of all kinds of distractions, to be a successful missionary. Years before he had written a brief book, *Living with God in My Heart*, in which he stressed the value of taking the teaching of the Divine Indwelling seriously and building one's spiritual life on this fact of spiritual life. Small wonder that Father Gier, the third superior general of the Society, who knew Noser well and corresponded with him over the years, esteemed Noser as being the closest replica of Blessed Arnold Janssen in his very special interior consecration and immolation to the Blessed Trinity.[7]

Noser's other intense devotion was to St. Therese of Lisieux, also called the Little Flower of Jesus. Her contribution to asceticism and spirituality was "the little way." For those who would follow it, she recommended that, however insignificant an act might seem—picking up a dust ball from the stairs was often given as an example—if done out of love for God, it became significant in the sight of God. St. Therese also said once that three minutes never went by but that she thought of God. Everything she did was offered up for missionaries and for the salvation of souls, and she was declared the Patroness of the Missions, even though she died at a young age in a small Carmelite convent in France, which she never left from the time she entered. This "way," which appealed to Noser, was the cornerstone of his own interior life. Noser also wrote a small booklet about St. Therese's spirituality, *Joy in Suffering*.

Both the practice of adverting to and adoring the indwelling Holy Spirit and the practice of the little way of St. Therese were picked up by Father Glorius and transmitted to all his novices. Then through novice masters Wilbert Wagner and John Musinsky, they made at least an indirect impact on another generation, although by Musinsky's time as novice master at Conesus in the 1960s, novices were less inclined to devotions to the saints.

The development of an intense inner life of union with God, for Noser, was the absolutely necessary requirement for a successful missionary life. The major external principle that guided his missionary work was education, not only in the building and development of elementary schools and catechumenate schools staffed by catechists, but especially in emphasizing secondary and tertiary education, including the development of a local clergy. We see this in New Guinea as well as in

---

7. This observation also comes from Kretschmer, who, as Noser's secretary, had access to his personal correspondence. Unfortunately, when Noser left Africa to go to New Guinea, he ordered Kretschmer to destroy all of his personal letters in the file.

Ghana. In this regard, Noser strongly supported and fostered the education of women as a conscious, explicit apostolate.

THE MISSION GROWS

In the first months after his arrival, Noser trekked all over the mission, meeting local chiefs and elders, identifying Catholics or Catholic sympathizers, negotiating for sites where a school or a station might be built. Schools were especially important, both to Noser and to the Ghanaians. Even if some were not interested in a church, they were always willing to help build and finance a school. And since the school could double as a church, the mission was given a way to carry on its entire evangelization task. The educational system in Ghana was British, who had stressed, developed, and paid for education for years, sometimes in cooperation with the missions. British standards were set up and applied, and the mission had to accommodate itself to them. The long-term nature of the British educational commitment meant there was a supply of available teachers, many of them highly qualified. But there were never quite enough for all the schools being built.

Some effort had gone into the development of a local clergy before the SVDs arrived, and the first priest from the eastern region that would comprise the future Diocese of Accra was ordained on 12 December 1942 in Cape Coast, by Bishop Porter, vicar apostolic for the entire Gold Coast. This priest, Bernard Sao Mensah, worked alongside the SVD from then on, as an equal.[8] As new missionaries arrived, they were assigned to develop the stations in places that had been identified as having potential. Noser continued to go on trek every three months, visiting established stations and opening new ones until an area was organized enough to hand over to the care of another missionary. There were numerous difficulties, especially during the war, but expansion continued, even though the few missionaries were stretched to the limit. Success was nothing short of phenomenal. Comparing July 1940, shortly after the SVD got started, with December 1943, this expansion becomes more clear:

	1940	1943
Residential Stations	2	5
Outstations	56	94
Schools	16	42
Pupils	1100 (510 Cath.)	2680 (850 Cath.)
Teachers	36	119
Baptized	1660 (1939 figures)	7520

---

8. The first Gold Coast African priest, Anastasius Dogli, was ordained in Cape Coast in 1922. He was a product of the SVD mission in former German Togoland, educated as a catechist in the mission's Catechist Training Center. After working as a catechist for some years, he decided to become a priest in an SVD seminary that closed at the outbreak of World War I. As soon as the Society for African Missions replaced the SVD, Dogli continued his studies with them and was ordained as a diocesan priest. See Alphonse Elsbernd, "The Story of the Catholic Church in the Diocese of Accra" (Mimeographed manuscript, ca. 1972), p. 18.

Word that the new mission had grown sufficiently to be raised to the status of a prefecture apostolic came on 19 December 1943. Father Noser became Monsignor Noser. "Above all," Alphonse Elsbernd wrote, "it was a tribute to the self-sacrificing work of Father Noser, whose zeal and energy was an example to us all."[9] In 1941 the Americans entered the war. In the Gold Coast this intervention was felt when Americans poured in and began to build a huge air facility where planes ferried from the United States were refitted for the war in North Africa. Rigney, in addition to his work on the staff of Achimota School, volunteered to act as chaplain on this military base. He was officially commissioned in 1942 and from then until 1946, he was a full-time chaplain, temporarily lost to the mission. The area he worked as chaplain included camps in North Africa, Arabia, and even Karachi in India (present-day Pakistan). He was lost to the mission of Ghana permanently, to his regret, for he hoped to return to his school work after the war. He was transferred instead to Peking to become the rector of Fu Jen, a story already told elsewhere in this history.

Noser, too, was affiliated with the United States military. He was requested by Cardinal Francis Spellman to be his vicar delegate to the U.S. armed forces in Ghana and other parts of Africa and the Near East, which meant making regular reports to the cardinal. Noser also made several long trips to military bases in other countries by military aircraft in his position as Spellman's vicar delegate.[10]

Disruption of the Ghana mission was minuscule compared with what occurred in China, New Guinea, and the Philippines. The greatest inconvenience, in fact, was not to receive new priests, brothers, or sisters. After the war the way was clear for the arrival of new missionaries. The first to arrive in 1946 was Father Leslie Hatfield, the first English-born SVD. Hatfield had a close call when the war broke out in 1939. Studying at St. Gabriel's Seminary near Vienna, Austria, he pedaled his way across Europe on a bicycle, getting over the English Channel just ahead of the German army invading the Low Countries, on board the last ship evacuating soldiers from Dunkirk.[11] Four more American SVD priests arrived after Hatfield, as well as ten Missionary Sisters of the Holy Spirit from Techny (eight Americans). Among the ten, Sister Juanita was from Argentina and Sister Virginia was from Keta in Ghana, close to what was once Togoland. When the German Holy Spirit Sisters were expelled from Togo during the First World War, she left with them. Now she was back in the Gold Coast. As everywhere else, the sisters did a marvelous job not only teaching, but as nurses and administrators. They were especially good in working with women. With the sisters and the arrival of new missionaries who had used the war years to prepare themselves during the war for work as school administrators and teachers by getting appropriate credentials, the government no longer had any excuse for refusing the SVD mission

---

9. Elsbernd, "The Catholic Church in the Diocese of Accra," p. 50. Elsbernd gives a detailed account of one of Noser's grueling treks through Ghana on pages 53–56 and 64–65.

10. Elsbernd, "The Catholic Church in the Diocese of Accra" pp. 52, 56, Kretschmer, "My Personal Memories," p. 6.

11. Elsbernd, "The Catholic Church in the Diocese of Accra," p. 62.

the authorization to build and open a teacher training college, which they proceeded to begin work on immediately. Mount Mary Training College opened in 1947 at Agomanya. Soon after the war, missionaries from countries other than America and Britain were also permitted to enter the Gold Coast, so that by the end of 1947, there were one bishop and thirteen SVD priests from the U.S., one from the West Indies, four from Holland, and one each from England and Belgium. There were still the original two SVD brothers—Lucian, the builder and James, the office manager—along with eighteen SSpS Sisters, including nine from the United States, six from Argentina, and one each from Holland, Belgium, and the Gold Coast. In addition, there were three African diocesan priests and one SMA priest, who was the education secretary. Because of its continued development, Accra was raised to the status of a vicariate apostolic, and Noser was ordained bishop at Techny on 22 August 1947 by Cardinal Samuel Stritch of Chicago. He was the first American SVD to become a bishop. He returned to Ghana in July 1948, the long interval explained by his election to the Society's 1947 general chapter as delegate from the Accra region.

The 1947 chapter was long overdue because of the Second World War. At it Noser came close to being elected the fifth superior general of the Society of the Divine Word. When the capitulars gathered, two names kept coming to the surface, Alois Grosse-Kappenberg and Adolph Noser. Father Grosse-Kappenberg did not want the job and was not in the best of health. The traditional straw ballot was taken; Noser was in the lead and would almost certainly have been elected on the first real ballot. Grendel, it seems, still the superior general, did not want Noser. The first reason is that Noser had recently been ordained a bishop, and it would be necessary to obtain a special permission for him to become superior general. But there was plenty of precedent for this in the history of other orders. Thus the second reason many gave for why Grendel did not want Noser is because he was an American. Whatever the reason, Grendel declared an eight-day break in the proceedings of the chapter, during which time he consulted with the Congregation for Religious. Grendel himself proposed the solution to the quandary that the congregation adopted. The first official ballot for superior general would be secret. Ballots would be put in boxes and sealed, then brought to the Congregation for Religious, where they would be opened and counted. This was done, and Alois Grosse-Kappenberg was declared superior general. Often Grosse-Kappenberg would remark that he had not been *elected* to the top position in the Society but *appointed*. He died in office in 1957, two years before his term would have expired, and the first American elected superior general was Father John Musinsky, who became the seventh superior general in 1967.

As new priests, brothers, and sisters poured into Ghana, opening schools and parish after parish, a building frenzy began. At the center of the whirlwind was Brother Lucian Orians, who deserves a large share of the credit for the progress of the Accra mission. Schools, clinics, convents, churches, and more, Brother Lucian built them all. He was born on 25 August 1904 in Salem in northeastern Ohio. His father died when he was nine, his mother when he was twenty-five. He finally decided he wanted to be a missionary and entered novitiate at Techny in 1936. Here his primary work was on the farm, but he also worked with Brother Fabian in the carpentry shop. He arrived in Ghana in January 1941, and began his career in construction immediately. Not only was he solid physically, he was solid spiritually. He was sent to Ghana while in temporary vows and pronounced his perpetual vows in 1944 in Ghana.

When he was given a construction job, he often had to oversee every phase of the job, from cutting the heavy tropical undergrowth away, to surveying the site, even sometimes designing the building before constructing it. Working with Africans, he picked up the language of whatever area he was working in as best he could. Lucian was sometimes isolated from contact with his confreres for weeks at a time. And although he himself was a careful worker, on at least one occasion, he was not careful enough of the work of his assistants who had put up scaffolding to build the bell tower of the church in Agomanya, with too few long nails. When Lucian began pulling up heavy timbers, the scaffold came tumbling down. Lucian suffered severe injuries to his head and back and was unconscious for some time. He recuperated enough to continue his work, but felt the effects of this fall for the rest of his life.

As he grew older, and partly as a consequence of his injuries, he had to slow down, and eventually was transferred back to the United States at the age of 60. Here he served faithfully maintaining the seminary at Miramar, where he died on 1 September 1979 after a stroke had partially paralyzed him. He was a pioneer to the mission in Ghana and a true son of Arnold Janssen in every way. He remained interested in Ghana till the day he died and was always glad when he got the chance to talk to returning Ghana missionaries. His successor in building the Ghana mission was another American, Brother Damian Bockman.

Another American brother, Cletus Lesage, one of the four Lesage brothers mentioned earlier, was also a pioneer. Brother Cletus arrived in the Gold Coast in November 1948 and the next day was busy assembling the equipment he had brought with him to start a press. He would stay at that work for ten years. Before entering the Society, Cletus had worked as a lithographer, then as a printer at Techny for eighteen years. Bishop Noser invited him to the Gold Coast to get this apostolate off the ground. Brother Cletus would boast that his was the fastest press on the Gold Coast. Catechisms, prayer books, hymn books, all this and more poured from the press in the four main languages of the country, one of which every missionary had to learn.[12] Because of growing volume, in 1963 another modern printing press had to be added. Finally, the press had to move to larger quarters, and several more modern presses were installed in 1967. It became the best press in Accra and was soon swamped with orders from many sources, including business firms.

Utilizing the buildings that Brothers Lucian and Damian built were the new missionaries arriving from Europe and America. Still further growth and expansion were made possible as more and more missionaries began to arrive. And inevitably the times were changing. The most important single event was the unraveling of the colonial empires of Britain and the rest of Europe as the winds of

---

12. These were Ga, Fante, Twi, and Krobo. There were also many Ewe-speaking people living in Ghana, some of them immigrants from Togo. This language became even more important when part of Togo was ceded to Ghana when the country became independent.

national independence began to blow across Africa. The end of the Raj in India began a train of events no one could stop. While the mission officially welcomed independence, there were also many missionaries who greeted it with ambivalence. Among other things, the British had blocked Germans from the Gold Coast mission. With the times changing so much, the British Foreign Office could no longer dictate as it used to, and in 1953 the first two SVD priests from Germany were allowed to come as missionaries. The staff by that time was already quite international. Counting both members of the SVD and SSpS, according to Father Elsbernd's records, there were now eighty-eight missionaries at work in Ghana. Their origins divided them into the following nationalities: forty-eight from the United States (among them five African-American priests), ten from Argentina, nine from Holland, three from England and Germany (who were SSpS nuns), two each from Belgium, Ireland, Switzerland, the Philippines, and one each from the West Indies, the Gold Coast, Czechoslovakia, Hungary, Brazil, Poland, and Austria.

Three years before those totals were counted, on 18 April 1950, the bishops in the Gold Coast were informed that the five vicariates apostolic would be raised to the level of dioceses, with Cape Coast the seat of the archbishop. One of the new dioceses was Accra, with Noser continuing as bishop. Starting with 1,660 Catholics in 1939 when the SVD took over, the diocese now counted almost 30,000 baptized members. On 2 December 1952, Father Bowers was chosen to become Auxiliary Bishop of Accra, thus becoming the first graduate of Bay St. Louis to become a bishop.

Why should Accra, the smallest of the five dioceses in Ghana at the time, merit an auxiliary? At least two reasons can be mentioned. The apostolic delegate had come to the Gold Coast for the Eucharistic Congress held in Kumasi shortly before. Kumasi is the center of the area where the Ashanti are located, and was the seat of one of the five dioceses. The Eucharistic Congress was the brainchild of Divine Word Father Charles Erb, who was heavily engaged in communication work and public relations of various kinds. The congress was a great success. When the apostolic delegate learned that the Anglicans were intending to consecrate an African as bishop in their church, he wanted to beat them and recommended that Father Bowers be consecrated. He beat the Anglicans' ordination of Bishop Martinson by about a year. Another reason was equally important. Bishop Noser had already been picked to resolve a deadlock on the question of who was to replace Bishop Stephen Appelhans, who had died in a plane crash in New Guinea. Bowers would succeed Noser when he gained some experience. Noser left Ghana on 18 February 1953, for the United States en route to New Guinea.

THE CHALLENGE OF INDEPENDENCE

On 6 March 1957, the Gold Coast became the first country in Africa to gain independence of its colonial master, Great Britain. It came to be known by the African name, Ghana; the old name was too reminiscent of colonial oppression. The new name harked back to an ancient kingdom of the Sudan and West Africa and was felt universally to be more fitting for an independent nation. For some years there had been agitation for independence in the Gold Coast. What most missionaries at the time were unaware of was that the Africans, and all colonized people, were accepting what made sense, rather than simply taking uncritically the words of missioners. Even after Vatican Council II, when the emphasis switched from precooked catechetical formulae to the Bible and to presenting Christ as a living person, this same translation process was underway. With no disrespect to the missionary, Africans (and Melanesians, and the Chinese and Indians, and so forth) were translating the gospel into their own categories, as the work of three distinguished historians and interpreters of African Christianity shows conclusively.[13]

Upon gaining independence, the Ghanaian populace was ecstatic. The people had high expectations that everything would soon be better when they finally ran their own affairs, made their own decisions, took their rightful place in the international community. The missions, too, were hopeful. Nkrumah was Catholic and had been educated by the mission. He had even taught for a time in a mission school. Later he studied abroad, in America and England, and most believed he was broadened by such experiences. Unfortunately, Nkrumah was also exposed to the full force of racial discrimination while he was studying at Lincoln University near Atlanta, Georgia. This experience affected him greatly and mission personnel believe it contributed greatly to his turning to Marxist socialism.

Both the general populace and the missions were destined to become quickly disillusioned with the fruits of independence. Soon after it arrived, Nkrumah and his Constitutional Peoples' Party were setting up a one-party state with Nkrumah as virtual dictator. After the passage of the Preventive Detention Act in 1958, legal rights were easily abrogated. By that act, if people were thought to be dangerous to society—which was often interpreted to mean "anybody who opposed Nkrumah"—they could be arrested. When English rule ceased, the government had a sizeable reserve of hundreds of millions of pounds sterling. By the time Nkrumah was deposed by the leaders of the Ghana armed forces, not only was the treasury empty, but the country was millions of pounds in debt. The money spent purchased a few good things, such as the Volta River Project, which still provides huge amounts of electric power to the nation, but most of it was squandered on useless projects and on developing a personality cult around Nkrumah. Members of his party and his cronies fed greedily at the public trough.[14]

Although Nkrumah never persecuted the church, neither did he assist it. Indeed, his government tried hard to take over all education in the country in order better to use the schools to promote national ideals. The church, however, felt he had other goals in mind. Recall that the Cold War was raging, and the two superpowers carried on their conflict by backing proxies in the newly emerging nations, especially in Africa where they could create a good deal of havoc at little cost. Nkrumah

---

13. See Lamin Sanneh, *Translating the Message* and *West African Christianity* (Maryknoll, N.Y.: Orbis Books, 1989 and 1983); Kwame Bediako, *Theology and Identity: The Impact of Culture upon Christian Thought in the Second Century and Modern Africa* (Oxford: Oxford Regnum Books, 1992); Andrew Walls, *The Missionary Movement in Christian History: Studies in the Transmission of Faith* (Maryknoll, N.Y.: Orbis Books, 1996).

14. See David E. Apter, *Ghana in Transition* (New York: Atheneum, 1963) for more on Ghana under Nkrumah.

and his followers were pushing a socialist ideology with help from Moscow and Beijing. The missions had little sympathy for either nation, and over time the Ghanaians themselves decided he was really benefiting himself and his cronies. The talk of nationalism came to be seen as a cover for looting the treasury. The coup that ousted him and his party from power occurred on 24 February 1960, when Nkrumah and many of his close aides and ministers were out of the country. The coup was met with great hopes. Few outside of his circle of cronies were sorry to see him go. Again there was rejoicing in the streets.

It took several years to dismantle Nkrumah's regime, and its demise was greeted with great joy by the mission community. Father Alphonse Elsbernd gives some idea of their sentiments.

> With the military and the police now in control, the coup marked the end of official alliance with communism. Within days chartered planes took off from the Accra airport filled with communist officials, Russian, Chinese and others of East European countries; their embassies closed, the "university" at Winnaba closed, as well as other schools for indoctrination. Only gradually did the nation learn the full extent of subversive activity secretly going on when hidden camps were discovered where Chinese "experts" had been training malcontents of various African nations in the art of subversion and guerilla warfare . . . in Accra. Then people realized how close to the brink the nation had come.[15]

I quote this statement verbatim and have made no attempt to verify whether its contents are historically accurate. What is unquestionably true is that Father Elsbernd mirrors the views of many in the SVD community and in it one sees what Elsbernd, a long-time resident of Ghana and an acute observer of events, thought of the direction in which Nkrumah was taking Ghana. On balance, the Catholic Church came through the struggle for independence and the corruption of the first national government relatively unscathed. Its progress continued unabated.

One consequence of independence was a hastening of the "Africanization" of the church, beginning with its hierarchy. Although Bishop Bowers was black and of African ancestry, he was neither African nor Ghanaian, and the church in Ghana and other parts of Africa by now was advanced enough to have its own hierarchy. Bishop Bowers requested a transfer to head his home diocese in the West Indies because he felt it was time to turn affairs over to an African. The resignation of Bishop Bowers was accepted, and Dominic Andoh, a priest of the Accra Diocese with varied experience, including a time as director of the regional major seminary at Pedu, was appointed. He was ordained Bishop of Accra on 3 October 1971. The appointment of indigenous bishops was made difficult by the relatively small number of available African priests, but this problem was not as difficult as discovering the way forward in creating forms of Christian life that were thoroughly African. That task goes on, and is primarily the work of native-born Africans, among whom there are now scores of SVDs from Ghana and the Congo.

---

15. Elsbernd, "The Catholic Church in the Diocese of Accra," p. 159.

We dare not leave Ghana without mentioning another American SVD who was an important figure in that mission, Father John Koster. Born in 1918 and ordained in 1944 as a classmate of the future superior general, John Musinksy, Koster taught physics and astrophysics for many years at the University of Ghana in Accra, a state-run institution, not one directed by the SVD or any other Catholic group. Having excelled in mathematics and science throughout his seminary years, Koster received a Ph.D. from the University of London in 1955 and became a key man in advancing the study of the physical sciences in Ghana. His laboratories were a testament to his ability to scrounge the basic ingredients from leftover United States Air Force materials and then to devise instruments to help his Ghanaian students grasp the principles of physics. In 1957, he gained a distinction that he sought always to shrug off with a modesty that belied his achievement. His antennae in Ghana were the first instruments in the world to detect and then identify as a true satellite the Soviet launch and successful orbiting of Sputnik, the first object that scientists put into earth orbit. Koster's life from ordination until 1979 was devoted to Ghana where his towering intellect and modest demeanor combined to show how a Christian intellectual combined faith and scholarship.

Finally, Ghana is not the only country in Africa where the SVD has been working. When the Society decided to accept a mission in the then Belgian Congo, the superior general sent Bishop Noser to check things out early in 1951. Soon SVD missionaries, mostly Europeans, were on their way to Kenge. One African American, Father Richard Winters, the first American to go to the Congo, was assigned there in 1952, where he would work until 1969, when he returned to the States because of ill health. He now lives in semiretirement in California. The mission in Kenge offers an interesting contrast between SVD mission methods and those of the Jesuits who worked there before the district was transferred to the SVD. The Jesuits concentrated their efforts in four large central stations, where everything was concentrated and where their catechumens and converts lived and worked for years, a typical example of the "gathered colony" mission method. Evangelization was intensive rather than extensive. One of the problems with this method was seen when Christians returned to their villages. There they often became indifferent, and children who had spent years away from village life found it hard to fit in. When the SVD took over, they abandoned the system of concentrating on a few large central stations. Instead, the missionaries fanned out into the villages. Their method was one of teaching people in their villages and leaving the new Christians in their villages to be yeast in the dough. In addition, they built as many schools as possible. It was the method pioneered by Freinademetz in China.[16]

Though the work of the Society in Africa has expanded to many places, the percentage of SVDs from the United States now working there has decreased. Those who remain are mostly in specialized ministries and work with African confreres as well as with other foreigners such as themselves, but today they include men from Poland, Indonesia, the Philippines, India, and South America. African SVDs work in Ghana, Congo, and Togo. Citizens of Angola, Zimbabwe, and Kenya are

---

16. Fritz Bornemann et al., *A History of the Divine Word Missionaries* (Rome: Collegio del Verbo Divino, 1981), p. 406.

preparing to take their place in the worldwide mission of the Society of the Divine Word. In a new mission opened by the Society in Madagascar, the large island off the east coast of Africa, are six Indonesian SVD missionaries, one of them the regional superior, two from Poland, one from India. The work in Africa goes on.

15

Divine Word Missionaries of North America in Transition

From the 1970s to the 1990s

This final chapter attempts to pick up and describe features of recent American SVD history that did not easily fit elsewhere. In it I bring the Society from 1970 to around 1990. In some instances, more recent events will be discussed. In this section, it is dangerous to speak of history. Rather, I know that I am dealing with current events. A balanced and complete history of these times will have to wait until the present itself becomes the more distant past. At the outset, it is good to make clear that American SVDs were sent to many missions other than the five discussed so far, although in fewer numbers. In this chapter, we will be dealing both with more recent missionary undertakings and with others in which Americans played a part, though not necessarily an important a part.

INDONESIA

We start with Indonesia, where SVD provinces are growing by leaps and bounds. In 1997, Indonesian members made up a fifth of the Society's overall membership. Indonesia was primarily and initially a mission of the Dutch branch of the Society. Long known as the Dutch East Indies, Indonesia became a colony of the Netherlands as a result of struggles by the Dutch East Indies Company dating to 1629 to gain ascendancy in the resource-rich archipelago. The Dutch took the major responsibility for bringing Christianity to the islands, and there were large numbers of Dutch missioners, both Catholic and Protestant, active there before the SVD arrived. The nation called itself Indonesia when the country declared its independence from the Dutch on 17 August 1945, two days after Japan had capitulated. After a four-year struggle with the old Dutch regime, Indonesia's independence was finally formally recognized by the Dutch government in August 1949. When the Society first took over a mission in the country in 1912, it concentrated on the Lesser Sunda Islands, namely Bali, Lombok, Sumba, Flores, and Timor.

The number of American SVDs sent to Indonesia can be counted on the fingers of two hands. Over the years more missionaries from the United States were assigned to Indonesia, but were usually refused entry visas to the predominantly Muslim land. Many, after waiting for many months, were simply reassigned elsewhere. Those few who were able to enter have done great work, in parishes, in specialized ministries, and in formation. The SVD mission in Indonesia has been so successful that the growth of Catholicism there has been nothing short of phenomenal. In 1900, the country counted fifty thousand Catholics; by 1960 that number had increased to 1.2 million, and by 1992 there were more than 5 million. As a result of this growth, the SVD in Indonesia is also shaping up as the majority group in the Society, as well as the youngest in average age. Indeed, the Society is also growing so fast in India, the Philippines, and Indonesia, with similar potential in Vietnam, to the extent that the superior general of the Society has recently begun to speak of the *Asianization of the Society*. Obviously this poses many challenges for an international Society. But true to the founder's intention, the Indonesians are pulling their missionary weight. Superior General Henry Barlage writes in the August-September 1997 issue of *Arnoldus Nota*, an internal SVD information bulletin:

It is well-known that the Indonesians have grown to be the biggest group in our congregation. With 1,234 members, Indonesia comprises 21.39% of our Society; they comprise, however, only 12.78% of all members in perpetual vows. Their average age is 33.16 years. With 425 in temporary vows, they count 41.71% of those temporarily professed. With a total of 253 (225 clerical and 28 Brother novices) they make up 62.47% of all the Society's novices.

In view of the considerable number of Indonesians working outside of their country, one can safely say that our Indonesian confreres contribute their full share to the Society's missionary endeavor. That said, we ought not to forget that our Indonesian confreres from Flores and Timor, if they work in Kalimantan or Sumatra, go beyond the boundaries of their own culture.

Furthermore, a good number of them have also made themselves available to the world mission; during these past years, we appointed 136 Indonesians to other countries. They are found in 29 of our provinces; 16 are working in PNG [Papua New Guinea], 23 in the Philippines, 22 in Brazil and 13 in Argentina. Their numbers have grown to 28 in Africa and 54 in Latin America. This July [1997] we again appointed 20 for Latin America and 8 for Africa. Since 1980, about a third of all Indonesians receiving their first assignments are working outside of their country. In 1980, only about 12.5% of all new missionaries were Indonesians; in 1996 the proportion rose to 32.52%.

Two of the first three Americans to go to Indonesia as missionaries were until very recently still active there. Both of them, William Popp and Norbert Shadeg, were born in 1921, ordained in 1949, and sent to Indonesia that same year. The third, Father Joseph Flaska, who was their classmate and was sent to Indonesia with them, died in 1977. Father Popp, who died in 1999, was active in formation work until the end. Father Shadeg worked mainly in formation, the last forty years of that work on Bali, one of Indonesia's best-known islands. In 1981 he established the Balinese Cultural Library in the village of Dalung, an example of an individual SVD who saw a need—preserving a way of life that was being threatened—and did something about it. Father Nicholas Strawn of Oelwein, Iowa, has been in Indonesia since his ordination in 1962 and remains active as a pastor and district superior. In addition, Eugene Schmitz, the last American appointed to Indonesia before the government slammed the door on new missionaries, remains at work there along with his two senior confreres, Roger Risse and Lawrence Hambach.

INDIA

In 1932, Father Peter Janser, the first rector of Techny, about whom much has already been said, went to India with another German SVD, Father Leo Krzeminski, to found the mission in Indore, India. After his ordination in 1935, the first American SVD priest, Gerard Hofstee, was assigned to India. His was a long and fruitful career as a grass-roots missionary to the poor and marginalized of India. Hofstee had a great sense of humor, fell in love with the Indians, and stayed the course for long years of productive labor for the Lord. He lived as frugally as the people to whom he ministered, spending what he could collect to expand the work of the mission. Even today, at the age of 93, blind and living in retirement at Techny, he keeps in touch with India. What little money Hofstee gets from benefactors and what he can save from the small monthly allowance he receives goes to India "for his girls," that is, to support the education of poor girls who would otherwise not be able to afford an education.

Over the years Hofstee was followed by a handful of other American SVDs, again not by choice but because of the circumstances of the times. In 1947, India threw off the colonial yoke, but retained commonwealth status. Entry visas for American missionaries were difficult to obtain, whereas Australians, Irish, and British missionaries could still claim special consideration. So SVDs from these countries were sent to India, while only a few Americans were able to enter. Most of these missionaries sent to India, as it happened, had received their theological education at Techny.

India, with a billion people, is the second most populous country in the world. Its history goes back even further than China's. India has sometimes been called the motherland of religions, having given birth to several important religions. It is still a very religious country. It is also a desperately poor country. Since this is the case and since the SVD has chosen to work by preference with the poor in India, much effort has gone into trying to improve the lives of the people while at the same time preaching the Word. One American, Father Jerome Ziliak from Indiana, who was assigned to India in 1947, was asked by his bishop in 1957 if he might be able to do something for Indore and the constant cycle of hard, hungry times that afflicted the area, and India in general. Normally a lay person would be asked to develop new patterns of farming, but the bishop had no lay people available for this, and Ziliak had the skill and background. "Since then," he writes in 1973, "I have been fully engaged—heart, head and hand—in the struggle against the triple-headed demon of hunger, thirst and disease which is still hovering over the heads of millions."[1] He has returned to Techny, where at the age of 79 he lives in semi-retirement, still hoping to be able to return to India and the many projects he has so successfully demonstrated to his beloved Indian farmers, who are putting Ziliak's methods into practice, an example of "ecotheology" long before it was popular.

As in every country where the SVD works, so, too, in India the Society early on began recruiting and educating young men for the local church, but only after the Second World War were they able to open a seminary and admit Indians for the Society of the Divine Word. This was in 1951. Here, too, as in Indonesia, the results have been remarkable. As of January 1996, forty-five years later, there are 4 Indian bishops, 425 priests, 40 brothers, 116 seminarians, and 17 clerical novices for a total of 602 Indian members of the SVD. They can be found working as missionaries not only in their own country, itself so much in need of evangelization, but in missions around the world, in New Guinea, Africa, and Latin America, holding positions of responsibility, fulfilling their promise to go wherever their superiors send them, another marvelous example of internationalism. Holding an important role in the formation of such missionaries for many years as novice master for the Indian provinces was another American, Father Felix Eckerman. In 1970, the contribution of the SVD was recognized by Cardinal Valerian Gracias, one of the prime leaders of the Indian church, when he said that the SVD had given a new dimension to the thinking of the Indian church in regard to its "catholicity."

One other American missionary to India deserves mention here. Arthur Malin is an example of a man who saw a need in his mission and set out to better a bad situation. The need in this case was providing services for the handicapped, especially retarded children and adults, whom no one seemed to care about or care for. Malin's life took a number of twists and turns before he got to India in 1947, but his true vocation began in India. In his own words, it all began with a father's visit:

> He was the father of a retarded child whom I had heard was in the neighborhood but about whom I had not till then concerned myself.
>
> Shame and misery seemed to bow this poor man who now so timidly and hesitatingly approached me. "Father, please, can you help us?" Then he poured out the sad story of his little Cyrilla, the child who turned out to be so different from his other children. "Father, do you know of any other such children? We feel so lonely and helpless." I had read of such children, but now my search began in earnest—this new vocation began to grow on me—the Forgotten Children became my prime apostolate.[2]

With this Malin began to study and read everything he could find about retardation. Taking courses in the United States, he learned all he could about techniques of caring for retarded children and then returned to India to train others in this work. Were there others like Cyrilla? If the estimate that two to three percent

---

1. Jerome Ziliak, "Next Harvest," *Word in the World* (1973): 133–34.
2. Arthur Malin, "The Forgotten," *Word in the World* (1977): 148–49.

of the population in developed countries are retarded held true for Asia as well, then there were some seventy-five million retarded persons in Asia, he estimated. Even worse, except for Japan, next to nothing was being done for these people. Malin goes on to say, "Not a single church or mission-sponsored institution for the care and rehabilitation of the retarded was to be found in India, Malaysia, Thailand, Ceylon, Singapore, Korea and the Philippines."

Malin went on to become something of an expert on retardation and how to educate retarded persons to their maximum ability. He set up schools to train teachers for the retarded, wrote and edited materials on the subject, promoted a "Day and Week for the Retarded" in India. A national Indian Federation on Retardation was started in 1965 at New Delhi and began planning for a Pan-Asian Conference on the Retarded. Because of Malin's experience in the Philippines and because he had been invited to work with the retarded in the Philippines, the first conference was held in Manila in 1973. Invited to do in the Philippines what he had been so successful in establishing in India, he was reassigned back to where he had worked as a young missionary. It was here also that he died on 17 April 1980. The schools he established for the care of retarded children, two in India and two in the Philippines, carry on his legacy. At the Fifth Asian Conference on Mental Retardation, held in Hong Kong in 1981, the president of the Malaysian Association for Retarded Children concluded his tribute to Father Malin with the following words:

> Today we honor him as one of the great leaders in the field of mental retardation in Asia to which he had given his life. The highest tribute that we can pay him is to rededicate ourselves and strive to serve the cause of mental retardation with the same faith, sincerity and singleness of purpose that he had.[3]

JAPAN

The Society's mission work in Japan was initiated during the founder's lifetime. As numbers of ordinands began to mount, Janssen began to look for another mission for his Society. South America, he knew, could absorb more missionaries, but the Society had been founded to convert non-Christians. Another mission in the tropics was also problematic, because so many sent to New Guinea and Africa had to be sent home because they took sick. The final choices for new missions were Japan or the Dutch East Indies. Father Janssen favored Japan, because he had great hopes that in Japan a solid education, including the sciences, in a Catholic institution of higher education would have a great impact on students.

In 1907 the first SVDs went to Japan. Indonesia would wait until 1913 to receive its first SVD missionaries. Still it took until 1932 for the founder's educational vision for Japan to begin to take shape in the form of a boys' high school in Nagoya. Eventually this school expanded in 1949 to include Nanzan University. Over the years, many of the American missionaries assigned to Japan

---

3. Quoted in *Word/USA* (August/September 1982): 14.

went into this educational apostolate. Here they joined an international faculty of SVDs, working with a well-trained local faculty. Over the years Nanzan University has grown into an impressive complex, not only physically, but also in terms of its reputation in Japan as an institution of higher learning, with an emphasis on internationalism.

Father Robert Riemer of Chicago served as president of Nanzan and Paul LaFarge, David Mayer, John Seland, and Richard Szippl were active in SVD education efforts in Japan. Deserving of special mention in the critical area of Buddhist-Christian dialogue and relations are Fathers James Heisig and Robert Kisala. Heisig went to Japan after doing a Ph.D. at Cambridge University and a stint teaching at Catholic Theological Union in Chicago. He mastered Japanese in record time and began working in the Nanzan Institute for Religion and Culture. The eminent scholar of Japanese religion, Joseph Kitagawa, professor of history of religions and long the dean of the University of Chicago Divinity School, once remarked that Heisig's translations of Japanese classics are unequaled, and that the work he and his colleagues carried on at the Institute was the finest Kitagawa knew for promoting dialogue and mutual understanding. Kisala, a Chicagoan ordained in 1985, has the distinction of being the first foreigner to complete a Ph.D. degree in religious studies at the University of Tokyo. His specialty in the sociology of religions came into play after the Aum Shinrikyo gas attacks on the Tokyo subway. Kisala was constantly interviewed on Japanese TV and by other media, since he was one of the few scholars with expert knowledge of the shadowy religious world out of which the Aum Shinrikyo cult had emerged.

Not all American missionaries ended up at the university. One missionary to Japan, Father Hilbert John Wiesen, was born in Dodge, Nebraska, in 1919. He was to be sent to Fu Jen University in Peking in 1947 and had begun to study Chinese. But like so many others, Wiesen had to leave China when the communists began to threaten Peking. His appointment was changed to Japan, where he arrived in 1949. Here he spent the rest of his life. For a time he taught at Nanzan University, while building Star of the Sea Church in Nagura, a suburb of Nagoya. In 1957 he was asked to go to Nagasaki where he was the founding pastor of St. Pius X Parish.

Father Wiesen made his mission and parish known far and wide by his writing and by the many pictures he took. His account of the return home to Catholicism of a family of "hidden Christians" is priceless. Because of persecutions, the Michiwaki family had kept the rudiments of the faith and prayer life of their ancestors intact since the time of their conversion in the sixteenth century. It surprised Wiesen how much of the faith had been preserved.

What surprised me from the beginning was how much the patriarch [Michiwaki] and his family knew about the faith: the Great Father of us all sent Someone to teach us and to lead us and to help us; if we live right and follow Him who was sent, we shall be forever happy in paradise.[4]

---

4. H. John Wiesen, "A Hidden Christian Returns," *Word in the World* (1974): 63.

The missionary thrust of the people of St. Pius X comes out in another brief piece written by a convert. It also describes Wiesen:

Ten years ago one of the members of St. Pius X church in the Nishimachi area of Nagasaki invited me to join. She said: "Our pastor (the Rev. H. John Wiesen, S.V.D.) is a tall, big American priest. He is a fine person. He always receives us and listens with a smile and gives kind guidance. We have no permanent church yet, so we hear Mass in Nanzan Primary School. Every Sunday the temporary chapel is filled with people. Many hymns are sung and the ardent faith of the people can be felt. You really should visit Nishimachi Church.[5]

At the age of seventy-seven, after his golden jubilee of ordination in 1996, Wiesen retired, of necessity but not willingly. Partly because of cancer of the lymph nodes he would not have to live in retirement for long. After medical treatment in the States after his jubilee celebration, he headed back to his beloved parish in Nagasaki. He landed in Japan on 7 October 1997. Before proceeding on to Nagasaki, he decided to stay overnight in Hakata, Japan. Sometime later that day or night he died of a heart attack; he was discovered dead the next morning. His obituary said, "Few Westerners ever attain the high degree of acceptance in Japanese society that Fr. Wiesen did over the forty years of his apostolate in that famous city [Nagasaki]." Cremated according to Japanese custom, his ashes are interred in Pius X Church in Nagasaki.

Another veteran American in Japan was the Chicagoan Edward Grzenia. Grzenia worked in Japan from 1947 until his death in 1996. Six weeks before his passing, Ed was summoned to Tokyo to be decorated by the Emperor with a medal of merit, "The Order of the Sacred Treasure, Gold Ray with Rosette," in recognition of his contribution to education.

LATIN AMERICA

In 1961, Pope John XXIII, because of the dire situation of the church and peoples of Latin America, called for assistance to Latin America. To make that call concrete, he requested that religious orders send ten percent of their members to Latin America as missionaries. Desperate conditions called for extreme measures. Johannes Schütte, the newly elected superior general of the Society, took this request seriously, even though twenty percent of the Society's priests (531) and thirteen percent of its brothers (169) were already at work there. He sent Father Louis Luzbetak to Mexico, Guatemala, British Honduras, El Salvador, Nicaragua, Costa Rica, Panama, Peru, Ecuador, Colombia, Venezuela, and Trinidad to do preliminary research on whether and where the Society should open new missions over and above its work already going on in Argentina, Brazil, Chile, and Paraguay, where the Society had been active since the days of the founder.[6]

---

5. Takeo Kataoka, "Why Did I Join?" *Word in the World* (1974): 129.

6. The following is taken primarily from Luzbetak's mimeographed report to the generalate in 1961 and from the *Arnoldus* 14, (1962).

Having made as many useful contacts in the United States as he could and gathered as much information as possible, Luzbetak set off on a journey that lasted from 16 June to 19 September 1961. He tried to talk to anyone who could offer insight or ideas related to establishing new branches of the Society: which bishops, for example, would be willing to accept a new congregation into their dioceses, where would be the best place to open a seminary, where might the best and most vocations be found, what would the bishops expect the Society to do by way of apostolic work? Questions regarding the political situation, family life of the people, plus many other types of information as well, were carefully researched to eventually come up with the five best possibilities. These would later be visited personally by Schütte before a final decision was made.

The five top choices of the thirteen countries Luzbetak visited were Mexico, Colombia, El Salvador, Ecuador, and Costa Rica. By 28 August 1961, the superior general was already in Colombia to visit personally the places recommended by Luzbetak. Schütte spent the longest time visiting sites in Mexico, which was recommended as the best place for the Society to begin new pastoral and vocational work. In less than three days after his return to Rome to listen to the advice and vote of his council, Father Schütte announced on 12 September 1961, that the Society would begin working immediately in Mexico, Colombia, and Ecuador. He prefaced his announcement this way:

> We would like to place the greatest emphasis on training Latin Americans for the priesthood in our Society. The only real solution for the entire Latin American problem, after all, is the creation of a sufficiently numerous local clergy. The centers, then, where we intend to begin our work, will be those which hold out the best prospects for vocations.[7]

The call for volunteers went out. Fathers Andrew Rentko and Wilbert Wagner were the first North Americans to be sent. They settled in Cuernavaca in 1962; Wagner is still active in Mexico at the age of 86. Rentko died in early 2000. The work in Mexico and in Latin America in general has expanded since then to include Nicaragua and Cuba as well as Panama and Bolivia. Mexico has also begun to fulfill the expectations held for it in terms of vocations. Of the fourteen Latin American countries where the SVD currently works, Mexico with forty-six SVDs ranks third in membership after Argentina and Brazil.

THE MOVE INTO PARISHES IN SEVERAL LOCALES

In the years since Vatican Council II, despite reservations expressed in a number of quarters, Divine Word Missionaries have increasingly taken up invitations to engage in parish work in priest-needy areas. The reader will recall that doing this on a large scale was first undertaken in the Philippines. More recently, there has been the decision to take over parishes in the West Indies. This came about when Bishop Joseph Bowers, the first alumnus of Bay St. Louis to be ordained a bishop, resigned from his position as the Bishop of Accra in 1971, in favor of a

---

7. Ralph Wiltgen, "Latin America," *Arnoldus* 14 (1962): 27.

Ghanaian bishop. At the same time he was appointed the first bishop of the newly erected Diocese of St. John's-Basseterre in the West Indies. Desperately in need of priests, he appealed to the generalate of the Society of the Divine Word. The Society agreed to support him with ten men until he retired, which he did in 1981 at the age of seventy-one. Without the SVD priests, the new bishop would have been without clergy, so they stayed on. Beautiful as they may be, these islands— Antigua, Monserrat, St. Kitts, and Jamaica-Morant Bay—are also in the direct path of ferocious hurricanes and volcanic eruptions that destroy years of work in a matter of hours. Twelve SVDs are still at work in the West Indies and will probably remain there until the bishop has enough priests of his own to staff his diocese.

Another field of parish work in a priest-poor area opened up to the Society in the Appalachian Mountains area of West Virginia in the early 1970s. The reasons for entering this apostolate were different and more complex. Before the Eastern Province had amalgamated with the Chicago Province, the high schools and other educational units for which it was responsible were gradually closing down or being transferred to the Chicago Province. The Eastern Province began to look for apostolic work for its unemployed members and a place to assign missionaries returning from overseas who were not yet ready to retire. Work in Appalachia seemed to fill the bill. It was also consonant with the Society's charism, to work among the poor who needed evangelization. And it represented a kind of cultural "crossing over," since most of those sent to work in the priestless counties of West Virginia would find themselves going to a very different culture than they were accustomed to. And so an agreement was reached with Bishop Joseph Hodges of West Virginia to staff two of the twenty-two priestless counties of that state. Prospects for building up the local church in Appalachia are not promising because of the high degree of prejudice and anti-Catholicism that exists there. With the three core parishes staffed by the SVD, each with fifty to a hundred parishioners, numbers alone would not justify holding on to the parishes. For lack of a sufficient number of diocesan priests, however, the pressure is to have religious order priests such as the SVD take over more parishes and devote more time and energy to traditional parish work.

THE SEMINARY'S OVERSEAS TRAINING PROGRAM

From the early years of the Society's existence, even during the founder's lifetime, some SVDs have done part of their studies outside their own country. In the founder's lifetime, for instance, Father Limbrock finished his theological studies in China and was ordained there. The same happened with the first two American SVDs sent abroad, Fathers King and Clark. Still, it was only after Vatican II that several events came together that made a period spent overseas in mission a usual part of SVD training. The program is called the Overseas Training Program (OTP). Johannes Schütte, the first superior general with actual field experience in mission, began to make strong recommendations that every SVD should have some missionary experience before final vows and/or ordination. The Second Vatican Council also put emphasis on a more adequate training for pastoral and missionary work. Before the council, an early entrance into practical work was considered detrimental to the religious life of the candidate. After the council, it became common to say that *apostolic* religious life was different from *monastic* life and that candidates needed to integrate spirituality with pastoral or missionary work. Finally, and not insignificantly, with the development of the jet plane, travel became easy, rapid, and relatively inexpensive to send people overseas for several years. The trigger for the SVD theologate in the United States to adopt the Overseas Training Program was the arrival of two SVD seminarians from Australia at the Catholic Theological Union at Chicago in the early 1970s to carry on theological studies prior to ordination. They had just completed two years of OTP in New Guinea. In 1975 the first five American seminarians went to New Guinea, Japan, Mexico, and Ghana. As of 1997, ninety-one seminarians had participated in OTP, and many of them were doing so for a second time, since the college at Epworth had undertaken to offer a similar OTP experience by making possible and promoting a one-year training-abroad program. Among other things, OTP experience usually afforded the seminarian a chance to learn the language of the country where he went; and as often as not, they were assigned to those countries after final vows and ordination, since the OTP gave them a head start on language and culture learning. Some seminarians opted to do their OTP in America, working in an African-American parish, for example, or among Hispanics or other minorities. The term "Overseas Training Program" became something of a misnomer for these people, so in 1993 the title was changed to Cross-Cultural Training Program (CTP). Whichever experience was chosen, the student got an experience of crossing into another culture. What he learned about himself made the decision to take final vows and/or to request ordination in a missionary society such as the SVD a good deal more realistic than that offered most SVDs during the first century of the Society's existence.

THE MEDIA APOSTOLATE

For most of the Society's first century, the means of communication (*media*) utilized for missionary purposes were almost exclusively limited to the print media such as journals, magazines, newspapers, pamphlets, books, and brochures. There were some films and other such things produced, but they were accidental and not central to the Society's media apostolates. That has changed in recent years. The interest and the attempt to use this tool, now generally referred to as "communications," have been given new and renewed emphasis in the Society's post-Vatican II constitutions.

In many countries where the SVD works, print media are still of great importance. In North America, even while Divine Word Publications was winding down its operations, there were stirrings of another kind of media work, quite different from what had gone before. In each of the three provinces, individuals initiated evangelization and outreach programs utilizing electronic and film media. The efforts of these individuals were quickly blessed and supported by the respective provinces. In the Western Province this took the form of a televangelical ministry conducted by Father Mike Manning, who has a degree in drama from the Catholic University of America. He hosts a widely syndicated television format of interviewing guests who afford Manning an opportunity to ask questions that elicit examples of creative discipleship and inspiration for viewers. His goal is to present Catholic perspectives on life's issues. More recently he has branched out into presentations called *Help the Children*, a series of television programs that aims to help abused children. Manning's work is a direct evangelization and pastoral apostolate, not one geared to promote the interests of the Society as such. Given the structure of his ministry, one regret that Manning expresses is that he cannot be as directly mission-oriented as he would like.

In the Chicago Province, Father Derek Simons initiated alternative media apostolates. Simons, a native of Wales in Great Britain, came from a background of broadcasting for the British Broadcasting Corporation before entering the Society. After working for a time with the Catholic Television Network/Chicago of the Archdiocese of Chicago and with the support of the Chicago Province, he began ECO, or Ethnic Communications Outlet. The radio and television spots produced are played primarily on African-American and Hispanic radio stations, using black and Hispanic actors. In the beginning, these spots were to empower these groups to take charge of their lives and to overcome the many obstacles that kept them from reaching their full human potential. More recently, they are geared to get all groups in North American society to work together for justice and peace. Simons's work is also in the direct apostolate and not intended to facilitate the general work of or promote the Society itself. Father Thomas Umbras followed Simons at ECO.

The Southern Province's media apostolate is directed by Father James Pawlicki. Once a month he prepares a four-page church bulletin insert called *In a Word*, because, as Pawlicki himself wrote, "Since the publication was to be brief and to the point and because Divine Word Missionaries are committed to the 'Word,' the new publication was called *In a Word*." Devoted to news about African Americans, coupled with prize-winning photos, *In a Word* was reaching thirty-five thousand people by 1993 and was subscribed to and distributed by three hundred fifty parishes, schools, and organizations throughout the U. S. and abroad. Pawlicki also produces videos of special events and filmstrip programs to help prepare persons to receive the sacraments of the church.

LAY WORKERS

A history of the SVD in North America would not be complete if it did not make note of the many lay people who did so much in so many ways for the Society and its missions. To be sure, they deserve more than a few paragraphs in this book. Simply to name them all would make a long list and still miss many whose names would be difficult, probably impossible, to retrieve.

The name of Ernie Collyer may stand for the many. Collyer's name brings a smile to all who had him as a teacher, and they were many. He began teaching for the SVD in 1928 at Miramar and went on to spend many years at Girard and Conesus. He finished his career with retirement in 1983 from Bordentown. He gave the Society a total of fifty-five years. When Father Paul Connors asked how he managed to gain the respect and confidence of his students, Collyer's answer stressed the need of a teacher to be impartial and honest, to employ a system the student could understand, and to be prompt in grading. When he retired, Collyer was presented with a medal and a certificate declaring him a Papal Knight of St. Gregory. With this he instantly became "Sir Ernie," though he preferred "Mr. SVD."

There is little question that the title "Mr. SVD of Techny" would go to Arthur (always known as "Art") Pape of the Mission Office. Pape has been involved with the Mission Office since 1946. After more than a half century, he "began" to retire—gradually. As office manager of a very complex operation, Art has been unflappable. He keeps the books, makes sure that everything is done in timely fashion, takes care of passports and visas for departing missionaries, and ensures that missionaries' trunks were packed and properly shipped. Looking at his desk, whether at the beginning, middle, or end of the day, one could only conclude that Art is either a neatness freak or extremely well organized. With no real evidence of the former, he had to be the latter. Always pleasant and ready with a genuinely welcoming smile, he gives the impression that his office existed just to take care of the latest person to come in with a problem or a need. Quiet, consistent, focused, and devoted to the SVD, Art will always hold a big place in the affections of those who ever met or worked with him. In 1996, to recognize his fifty years of dedicated missionary service, Art Pape was given the papal medal *Pro Ecclesia et Pontifice* ("For the Church and for the Pope"). That same year he was given the Verbum award by the North American SVD "for fifty years of outstanding lay leadership in the work of Divine Word Missionaries in North America." Father Kamp, who worked longest and most closely with Pape over the years, was once asked how he got along with him. He said it all when he answered, "He was my brother."

By contrast, another man, whom relatively few SVDs know, was Father Ralph Thyken's office manager for many years. Chester ("Chet") Virtue, now in his eighties as this book is written, met Father Ralph on one of Ralph's visits to Japan to check on Nanzan University's progress. Later Virtue returned to the States to manage Ralph's office. When Ralph retired in 1970 and his operation was incorporated into the Mission Office's work, Virtue, too, came to Techny to continue his work there until his retirement.

Still another person who must be mentioned is Attorney Francis Zimmermann, who died in 1996 at the age of eighty-eight. In 1948 he became Techny's principal legal adviser and remained so almost to his death. In the eulogy, Father John Donaghey, who knew him well and had much to do with him when he was provincial, commented, "Without Francis, we would not have been able to achieve the financial security we have today." Attorney Zimmermann was also elevated to the rank of Papal Knight of the Order of Pope St. Sylvester, an award reserved for outstanding lay Catholics in recognition of meritorious service to the Catholic Church.

At Miramar Joseph Walsh is "Mr. SVD." Walsh started off there as a minor seminarian in 1928, but left in his fourth year. He always kept in touch with the SVD and tried life as a candidate in the Society again for a short time in 1935. Father Joseph Ford advised him not to continue. In reality, he never really left. Since 1941 he worked at Miramar as teacher, office manager, general manager of the retreat house, and the one who took care of whatever needed to be done. You name it, Joe Walsh took care of it.

At Divine Word College at Epworth, Wilhelm Eck has been active in a dedicated fashion similar to that of the others mentioned. Eck joined the Epworth faculty in 1965 when the new facility opened its doors as a four-year college. After eight years teaching Latin, Greek, and German, he became Director of Student Financial Aid. In that position he developed a national reputation. In 1993 he assumed the position of Vice President for Finance. "I am grateful," he says, "to the SVDs who have been and continue to be a part of my life and the life of my family." And the SVD in 1999 gave Mr. Eck its second Verbum award in recognition of over thirty years of work at Epworth.

These men must stand for many more who dedicated much, even all, of their lives to the Society. In the founder's time already, in the very early days of the Society's existence, there were many of these *Kommoranten*, as they were called in German (those who "lived with" the community). They worked, in the German expression of Father Fritz Bornemann, for *Gotteslohn* (for "wages from God").[8] Their number at Steyl stood at sixty in 1881. It was small wonder that Techny also accepted the help of *Kommoranten* in its early years. Most lived at Techny and had their own dining room. Father Francis Markert served for many years as the virtual superior over as many as thirty *Kommoranten*. Not a few were relatives of members of the Society. Some eventually left and got married, others made, in effect, a lifelong commitment to the Society. They worked on the farm, in the nursery, in the offices and in the press, as painters, carpenters, or as building maintenance personnel. Some were salaried, others worked for room and board. There were also a few women who worked with the sisters in the kitchen and laundry, and who lived in a building across the road from the seminary.

One of these Techny *Kommoranten* stands out, paradoxically, because of his anonymity. He was a thin, short, slightly stooped man who spent his entire life cleaning the bathrooms and other places. Never speaking to anyone, he went about his work quietly and regularly. He was known simply as "Mr. Esser," for he reminded the community of Father Gerard Esser, the philosophy professor. Both were short, slightly stooped, and thin, but they were not relatives. "Mr. Esser" worked at Techny from at least the late 1920s to the late 1950s, perhaps longer, but as I sought to find out something concrete about him, nobody remembered his real name. Then one morning while I was showing old photos to Brother Joseph Urban, Brother Cyril Schroeder came to say that he thought the man's first name was Bernard. With that, a light of recognition came across Urban's face, as he recalled that he had been at "Mr. Esser's" funeral and knew just where he was buried in the community cemetery. Sure enough, Bernard Merten, for that was his name, was buried in the southwest corner, under the same simple cross that stood over every SVD father and brother. The inscription read: "Bernard Merten, October 4, 1886–May 14, 1956." One man remembered the circumstances of his death. Merten was dusting in one of the front parlors, where he slipped on a rug and broke a leg. When he was taken to the hospital, it turned out that he had bone cancer throughout his frail body. He died shortly after being diagnosed.

---

8. Fritz Bornemann, *Arnold Janssen der Gründer des Steyler Missionswerkes 1837–1909: Ein Lebensbild nach zeitgenössischen Quellen* (Steyl: Sekretariat Arnold Janssen, 1969), p. 116.

When Johannes Schütte became superior general in 1958, he urged that as many priests and brothers as possible be set free for the direct apostolate and that lay people be hired to do work that had been done by SVDs. As a result, the list of dedicated laity who devote their energies and talents to the SVD and its missionary work has increased dramatically. Such lay workers contribute to the work of the Society, while remaining lay, and are often drawn closely to the Society. For many, their work becomes much more than a job. They have become, in effect, dedicated coworkers with members, and this could be the beginning of a trend that will enrich the Society and the church as a whole in a new way.

THE VIETNAMESE PHENOMENON

This chapter would be woefully incomplete without mention of the influx of Vietnamese men into the North American SVD. It began in 1975 with the exodus of Vietnamese from their country after the fall of Saigon. Estimates of the number who fled Vietnam range between four and five million. Many escaped in small boats over the open sea. Some estimate that as many as one-half perished in the sea. The rest made it to places such as Hong Kong and the Philippines, and many families, especially those who had connections with the United States military, eventually made it to the United States. One such group arrived in 1975 in Ft. Chaffee, Arkansas, their temporary home until they could be relocated. Among this group was a number of Vietnamese seminarians.[9] Divine Word Father Thomas Krosnicki, working at the time for the National Conference of Catholic Bishops in their liturgy office, was informed of these seminarians and called Father Joseph Francis, then the provincial of the Southern Province, suggesting that the SVD might be able to help them as a contribution to the plight of the "boat people." Father Francis asked Father William Kelley, vocation recruiter for the Southern Province, to go to Fort Chaffee. Kelley offered to help any of the seminarians who wished to join a religious congregation or a diocese to get in touch with the appropriate people.

The action then shifted to the Divine Word College in Epworth, Iowa, where Father Louis Luzbetak was president. He turned to Brother Patrick Hogan from Fu Jen University in Taiwan, a trained linguist and teacher of English as a second language, who happened to be at Epworth at the time. The decision was quickly made to offer the facilities at Epworth to the Vietnamese seminarians to begin to teach them English so they could pursue their vocations to the priesthood and religious life. Thus Epworth, with a language program already in place, would serve as a bridge, enabling the Vietnamese seminarians to enter the seminary programs of their choice. According to Luzbetak's reasoning, the benefits of this program would be mutual. Brother Dennis Newton quotes Luzbetak as writing:

> The Vietnamese program is an idea that has come upon us unexpectedly. It offers us an opportunity to be missionaries in the truest sense of the word right here in our own backyard. It can also help the missionary spirit in our

---

9. For this story, I rely on Dennis Newton, "Fort Chaffee Calling," *Word in the World* (1995): 41–43.

community. There are risks, and they should not be minimized, but I feel the risks are worth taking.

The first class of sixteen, half major seminarians and half minor seminarians, arrived at Epworth in the fall of 1975. The language program was expanded in 1977 to offer a summer crash program in English to those Vietnamese who were already priests and religious. Thirty priests and sisters from fifteen states attended this first course. All this meant that the Vietnamese community in the United States was becoming aware of the SVD. Many of the men began to apply for admission to the Society. Their numbers have become substantial. While applicants from the SVD's traditional pool of white and black American men have greatly decreased since the mid-1970s, Vietnamese candidates have been numerous. According to the 1998 *Catalogus SVD*, the latest statistics available to me, there are sixteen Vietnamese priests in the Society. Not all entered in the United States, but the majority are in North America. Sixteen may not seem to be so many, but this is a recent phenomenon; the first SVD priest in the U.S. from Vietnam was ordained only in 1985. There are also twenty-five Vietnamese scholastics in vows and nine novices. Vietnam, though one of the last communist countries in the world, is then a source of many vocations, not just for the Society of the Divine Word but for other religious congregations as well. A group in Vietnam known as the Congregation of Saint Joseph, indeed, has amalgamated with the Society of the Divine Word *en bloc*. There is every hope that it will be successful, according to an article by Father Stanley Uroda, provincial of the Chicago Province, in the summer 1994 issue of *Divine Word Missionaries*. In addition, many Vietnamese-American SVDs have expressed a desire to return to their homeland as missionaries to their own people. The eminent Vietnamese theology professor Father Peter Phan of the Catholic University of America has said that the SVD seminarians and young priests have been extremely well trained and are one of the most important groups in the dialogue with the Vietnamese in the United States. With further education and higher degrees in theology or biblical studies, social work, or education, many possibilities for working in Vietnam and China offer themselves when these countries again open themselves to missionaries. In the meantime, the Vietnamese Americans are being sent to whatever SVD mission needs them.

THE APOSTOLATE OF THE ELDERLY

Brief mention must be made of the role that Techny has assumed in caring for the elderly of the Society, especially of the elderly whose religious lives began in the United States. In the late 1960s and early 1970s it began to become more obvious that the number of elderly members of the Society in North America was growing. It also became clear that the many missionaries sent to various places around the world were aging and that arrangements for their future would have to be made. The first step was to put everybody eligible under the United States Social Security program. This included American missionaries active in the field, and was done by a special provision in the law that allowed groups such as religious communities to assign, for bookkeeping purposes, a minimum wage as an equivalency for the services rendered by these religious and then to pay the requisite back taxes and to continue until these men retired. This ensured a minimum income for them as they got old, but more importantly it meant that they would be eligible for Medicare. Consequently, everyone eligible for Social Security, wherever they may be in the world, returns to the United States as soon as they can after they turn sixty-five to sign up for Medicare. The Society set up a special fund to handle the expenses necessary for medical care that are not paid by Medicare. We are self-insured. Under this arrangement, if anyone requires medical attention for a serious ailment, whether he works overseas or in the United States, he returns to have the required treatment. The majority of these men return to Techny, but other houses do their part by offering hospitality to men who might prefer to have their treatment in other places where they can be nearer to relatives and friends.

When several wings of the Techny seminary that Fathers Peil and Beckert built at the beginning of our story were torn down because they weren't suitable facilities for retirement or to provide nursing care, a new residence was erected as a combined residence, convalescent facility, and nursing home. The residence rooms all have their own private bathrooms, much to the surprise of many of the retirees, who had never before had such "luxuries." One wing in the new residence is reserved for those who need special nursing care. In that wing nurses are on call twenty-four hours a day, and nursing aides help with feeding and bathing those who can no longer do this themselves. Those who are mobile help those who are less so. Everyone eats cafeteria-style in the same dining room where they are joined by the rest of the community and the many visitors from around the world who pass through Techny. The entire community prays and has liturgy in common.

It has often been said that priests and brothers in religious congregations never really retire, and there is truth to this. By their patience and acceptance of whatever weakness and infirmity God sends them, or by using the strength and the abilities they still enjoy to make their contribution to the community, the priests and brothers grow in the grace and wisdom of God, continue to give good example, and call down the grace of the Holy Spirit on the apostolate to which they have dedicated their lives.

NEW USES FOR THE TECHNY PROPERTY

This final section on new uses for the Techny property completes the cycle of events at Techny. One of the first items of business for Father John Peil when it was finally decided to settle down in Shermerville was to purchase land. Whenever Peil decided to buy more land, the founder gave the permission without hesitation. At the time, the land was undeveloped and most of it was quite inexpensive. There was no idea that suburbs of Chicago would ever reach Shermerville. Nevertheless, not only did the suburbs reach Techny, they soon surrounded the property. These suburbs—Glenview, Northfield, and Northbrook—also became some of the wealthiest suburbs in the Chicago area.

For many years the land was used to support and feed the Techny community. After Vatican II, however, conditions changed. Vocations declined and isolation was no longer considered an ideal for seminary or brother training. To farm or use as flower gardens what had become highly desirable and expensive land, when it was no longer necessary or remotely profitable, made little sense. The first change in Techny's use of land came in the form of a sanitary landfill (168 acres) in the low-lying part of Techny's property. When this land use was proposed, the neighboring communities fought the idea strenuously in courts of law, but the case was finally decided in Techny's favor. The landfill became a reality, but the land itself was not sold. Rather, it was leased for this purpose. After fulfilling its purposes as a landfill, a golf course was constructed on top of the landfill. In both uses, the leasing arrangement has insured that Techny has a steady stream of money with which to pay bills and help the missions overseas and at home. In 1985 the Techny Land Committee was formed to deal with the rest of Techny's land; Father Francis Kamp has been its chairman from the beginning, insuring that a master plan for the utilization of the land was drawn up and adhered to. Under that plan, 157 acres were retained by the Society for its own use as residence areas, a cemetery, and a conference center, including some wooded and park areas. An additional 50 acres were set aside as retention ponds to control flooding. Forty-four acres were given to the Northbrook Park District for recreational purposes. While 70 acres have been sold outright, 250 acres are being leased for commercial and residential use. Over the life of the lease, the Society will be paid for the use of the land. The revenue, derived from the land so prudently purchased by Father Peil a century ago, has repeatedly been of much benefit to the Society in North America but also worldwide as the generalate taps the United States to provide financial help for projects that no other province can undertake. Four funds have been established to channel this money. seventy-five per cent of the money generated by leasing the land will go directly to Society missions; the remaining twenty-five per cent will be used for Society needs at home, which include the defraying of retirement expenses, covering medical bills of members and supporting the educational work of the Society, in particular Divine Word College at Epworth and Divine Word Theologate at Catholic Theological Union at Chicago, and assisting pastoral apostolates.

And so the story that began with the arrival of Brother Wendelin in 1895 in New York comes full circle in a little over a hundred years. With its vigorous growth in Asia, the Society of the Divine Word is one of the few major groups of male religious to grow in the past three decades. Religious orders have a long history of expansion and contraction, and those who are aware of that process are not alarmed by the present diminution of new members in Europe and North America. What counts is that—no matter how many or how few the numbers of members are—the Society be faithful to its charism and continue in the spirit of the founder, Blessed Arnold Janssen. What the SVD will look like over the long haul is impossible to predict, but its task will remain that of being true imitators and followers of Christ the Divine Word. And its objective will continue to be spreading the knowledge of Christ and him crucified and risen, fulfilling the great commission: "Go and make disciples of all nations, baptizing them in the name of the Father, and of the Son, and of the Holy Spirit" (Matthew 28:19). Following the founder's example, the society will do this under the guidance and direction of the Holy Spirit, whose light will still be what enables them to understand the gospel, to interpret the signs of the times and thus discover the will of God. And they will still be praying for the coming of the Kingdom of God. In other words, in the year 3000 the members of the Society of the Divine Word will still be following Blessed Arnold Janssen, in realizing the goals he set, that the darkness of sin and the night of unbelief might vanish before the light of the Word and the Spirit of grace.

Bibliography

Aerts, Theo, ed. *The Martyrs of Papua New Guinea: 333 Missionary Lives Lost During World War II*. Port Moresby, PNG: University of Papua New Guinea Press, 1994.

Ahner, Eugene et al. "The Relocation of the Techny Theologate: A Report on Catholic Theological Union and Washington Theological Coalition." Mimeographed report, February 1970. Techny, Ill.: SVD Archives.

———, and Flinn, Robert. "The Relocation of the Techny Theologate: Phase I, June 1969." Unpublished report. Techny Ill.: SVD Archives.

Alt, Josef. *Die Geschichte des Missionshauses St. Gabriel der Gesellschaft des Göttlichen Wortes: Das erste Jahrhundert, 1889–1989*. Rome: Collegio del Verbo Divino, 1990.

———, ed. *Arnold Janssen: Briefe in die Vereinigten Staaten von America*. No. 57 of the Studia Missiologici Societatis Verbi Divini. Nettetal, Germany: Steyler Verlag, 1994.

———, ed. *Arnold Janssen, SVD: Briefe nach Neu Guinea und Australien*. Rome: Collegio del Verbo Divino, 1996.

———, ed. *Arnold Janssen, SVD: Letters to the United States of America*. Trans. Robert Pung and Peter Spring. No. 58 of the Studia Missiologici Societatis Verbi Divini. Nettetal, Germany: Steyler Verlag, 1998.

Apter, David E. *Ghana in Transition*. New York: Atheneum, 1963.

Arens, Richard. "The Pursuit of True Humanity." *Word in the World* (1967): 58–64.

———. "Educational Activities of Our Society in the Philippines." *Verbum* 1 (1959): 228–40.

———. "Re-opening of Fu Jeu University." *Verbum* 7 (1965): 375–80.

Barlage, Henry. *Mission: Spirituality: Formation*. (Following the Word, No. 1, August 1988, 13 General Chapter, 1988) Rome: Collegio del Verbo Divino.

Barry, Colman. *The Catholic Church and German Americans*. Milwaukee: Bruce Publishing Co., 1953.

Bechtold, Paul. *Catholic Theological Union at Chicago: The Founding Years 1965–1975: History and Memoir*. Chicago: Catholic Theological Union, 1993.

Becker, Joseph M. *The Re-Formed Jesuits: A History of Changes in Jesuit Formation during the Decade 1965–1975*. Vol. 1. San Francisco: Ignatius Press, 1992.

Bediako, Kwame, *Theology and Identity: The Impact of Culture upon Christian Thought in the Second Century and Modern Africa*. Oxford: Oxford Regnum Books, 1992.

Best, Mary E. *Seventy Septembers*. Techny, Ill.: Holy Spirit Missionary Sisters, 1988.

Bonner, William. *Chronologium*. A selection of letters and other documents gathered from SVD Generalate Archives in Rome and Techny, Illinois, following events in North America day-by-day, month-by-month, and year-by-year from 1891 to 1946. Techny, Ill.: SVD Archives.

Bornemann, Fritz. *Arnold Janssen: Founder of Three Missionary Congregations 1837–1909*. Trans. John Vogelgesang. Roma: Collegio del Verbo Divino, 1975.

———. *Arnold Janssen der Gründer des Steyler Missionswerkes 1837–1909: Ein Lebensbild nach zeitgenössischen Quellen*. Steyl: Sekretariat Arnold Janssen, 1969.

———. *As Wine Poured Out: Blessed Joseph Freinademetz SVD Missionary in China*. Rome: Divine Word Missionaries, 1984.

———. *Die päpstliche Approbation der Konstitutionen SVD im Jahre 1905*. Rome: Collegio del Verbo Divino, 1966.

———. "Ehemalige Steyler als Priester in USA." *Verbum* 5 (1963): 188–98.

———. "Ferdinand Medits and Magdalena Leitner in der Geschichte des Steyler Missionswerkes," *Analecta SVD* 4 (1968).

———. *In Memoriam: Father John Schütte, 6th Superior General SVD.* Rome: Collegio del Verbo Divino, 1972.

———. *P. Wilhelm Schmidt, SVD, 1868–1954.* Rome: Collegio del Verbo Divino, 1982.

———. ed. "Remembering Arnold Janssen: A Book of Reminiscences." *Analecta SVD* 42 (1978).

———. et al. *A History of the Divine Word Missionaries.* Rome: Collegio del Verbo Divino, 1981.

Bosch, David J. *Transforming Mission: Paradigm Shifts in Theology of Mission.* Maryknoll, N.Y.: Orbis Books, 1991.

Bowers, Rodney. "The Southern Missions of the Society of the Divine Word 1904–1920." Master's thesis, Catholic Theological Union at Chicago, 1990.

Brandewie, Ernest. *When Giants Walked the Earth: The Life and Times of Wilhelm Schmidt SVD.* Fribourg: University Press, 1990.

Bray, Agnes. "Wirui Services Story." *Friends of Wewak* (June 1977): 2–5.

Brumm, Geoffrey, and Francis Mihalic. *Sent by the Word: 100 Years of Service by Divine Word Missionaries (1896–1996) on Mainland New Guinea.* Wewak, PNG: Wirui Press/Divine Word Missionaries, 1995.

Burton, Doris. *Heroic Brothers: Ten Great Religious.* Fresno, Calif. Academy Guild Press, n.d.

———. "Perils in New Guinea: Brother Eugene Frank, S.V.D. (1900–1935)." Mimeographed. Archives of Bernard Fisher, SVD, Divine Word Residence, East Troy, Wisc.

Bus, Gerard. *75 Years in New Guinea: Divine Word Missionaries 1896–1971.* Wewak, PNG: Wirui Press, 1971.

Cabey, Edwin. "Liberation and the SVD." *Word in the World* (1976): 142–47.

Camacho, Flor. "At the Foot of Mount Mayon." *Word in the World* (1965): 102–5.

Christman, Matthew. "Our Negro Missions." *Our Missions* 1 (1921): 27.

———. "Training a Colored Priesthood." *Our Missions* 5 (1925): 128–30.

Connors, Joseph M. "The Spirit and Means of Renewal." *Verbum* 8 (1966): 238–52.

———. Provincial's Letter of May 10, 1969. Techny, Ill. SVD Archives.

Daschbach, Edwin. "Country Roads, Take Me Home." *Word in the World 1994–95*: 103–4.

Davis, Cyprian. *The History of Black Catholics in the United States.* New York: Crossroad, 1990.

de la Torre, Edicio. "Letter from Prison." *Word in the World* (1979): 117–19.

Dries, Angelyn. *The Missionary Movement in American Catholic History.* Maryknoll, N.Y.: Orbis Books, 1998.

Dupuis, Jacques. *Toward a Christian Theology of Religious Pluralism,* Maryknoll, N.Y.: Orbis Books, 1997.

Eckert, Joseph. "Methods of Convert-Making Among the Negroes of Chicago," in *The White Harvest: A Symposium in Methods of Convert Making.* Ed. John A. O'Brien. New York: Longmans, Green and Co., 1927, pp. 93–109.

Eilers, Franz-Joseph. "Arnold Janssen als Publizist." *Communicatio Socialis* 8 (1975): 301–22.

Eilers, Franz Joseph, and Heinz Helf. *Arnold Janssen: 1837–1909: A Pictorial Biography. Life.* Nettetal, Germany: Steyler Verlag, 1987.

Elsbernd, Alphonse. "The Story of the Catholic Church in the Diocese of Accra." Mimeographed manuscript, c: 1972. Techny, Ill.: SVD Archives.

Engberink, Vinciana. *Memories of our Escape From New Guinea 21 May 1945.* Madang, PNG: Divine Word Institute, 1991. Also in Aerts, pp. 76–81.

Fage, John D. *Ghana: A Historical Interpretation.* Madison, Wisc.: University of Wisconsin Press, 1966.

Fisher, Bernard. *Archbishop Leo Arkfeld, SVD-PNG: The Flying Missionary Bishop.* Madang, PNG: Divine Word Institute, 1992.

———. *The Catholic Church Comes to the Central Mountains of Papua New Guinea.* Kundiawa, Simbu, PNG: Mission Procure S.V.D., n.d.

———. *Father Alphonse Schaefer, S.V.D., One of the Great Men and Women Who Built Up the Catholic Church in Papua New Guinea.* Kundiawa, PNG: Divine Word Missionaries, n.d.

———. *Father William Ross, S.V.D.* Madang, PNG: Divine Word Institute, 1991.

———. *Limbrock*. Madang, PNG: Divine Word Institute, 1992.

———. SVD Authors in PNG 1992. Madang, PNG: Divine Word Institute, 1992.

———. "Techny Highlander." *Word in The World 1994–1995*. Steyl: Steyler Verlag, 1994.

———, and John Miller, eds. *Pioneer in New Guinea: Letters of Father Alphonse Schafer, SVD*. Alexishafen, PNG: Stella Press, 1990.

Fisher, Bernard, ed. *Simbu 1937: The Beginning of the Catholic Mission in the Simbu Area, A Short History Written in German by Father Alphonse Schaefer About 1937*. Papua New Guinea: Province of Simbu, 1990.

Flinn, Robert. "The Identity of the SVD Brother: Religious and/or Lay," *Verbum* 35 (1994) 143–146.

———. "Techny's Chapel." Unpublished manuscript, 1995. Techny, Ill.: SVD Archives.

Floresca, Constante C. "A Missionary Church." *Word in the World* (1979): 91–94.

Foley, Albert S. *God's Men of Color*. New York: Farrar, Straus and Company, 1955.

Francis, Joseph. "New Directions in the Black Apostolate." *Word in the World* (1975).

———. "Selected Excerpts from Homily delivered at Bishop Harold Perry's Funeral Mass July 22, 1991." *In a Word* 9 (August 1991).

Gilkey, Langdon B. *Shantung Compound: The Story of Men and Women under Pressure*. New York: Harper Row, 1966.

Hagspiel, Bruno, and Geroch Eder. *Along the Mission Trail*. Vol. 3, *In New Guinea*. Techny, Ill.: Mission Press S.V.D., 1926.

Hagan, William. "Dorish Maru Massacre." *SVD Word PNG* 20 (February 1980): 6–8.

———. "The Hollandia Rescue." *SVD Word PNG* 21 (March 1980): 7–8.

Hamaguchi. "The Richness of the Vine." *Word in the World* (1974): 130–31.

Heick, Aloysius. "Report." *The Colored Messenger* 1 (1916): 54.

Hemesath, Caroline. "They Spread the Good News." Unpublished manuscript, 1976.

Hendrickson, Paul. *Seminary, A Search*. New York: Summit Books, 1983.

Henninghaus, Augustine. "Things Old and New from S. Shantung, China." *Our Missions* 1 (1921): 114–17.

Höltker, Georg. "Das Pidgin-English als sprachliches Missionsmittel in Neu Guinea." *Neue Zeitschrift für Missionswissenschaft*, 1 (1945): 44–63.

"House Chronicle of the Seminary at Bay St. Louis." Bay St. Louis, Miss.: SVD Archives.

Huber, Mary Taylor. *The Bishop's Progress: A Historical Ethnography of Catholic Missionary Experience on the Sepik Frontier*. Washington, D.C.: Smithsonian Institution Press, 1988.

Hunter, Robert. "Hunter's Jubilee Journal." Mimeographed, September 15, 1975, No. 2. Techny, Ill.: SVD Archives.

Janssen, Arnold. "Von den Eigenschaften eines Missionars." *Verbum* 1 (1959): 152–54.

Jaspers, Reiner. "The Unity of The Catholic Church in Papua New Guinea and the Role of Holy Spirit Seminary: A Historical Analysis of Facts, Events and Development." Papers Prepared for the Visit of John Paul II to Papua New Guinea, 1–10 May 1984, pp. 61–67.

———. "An Historical Investigation into the Foundation of the Catholic Church in Papua New Guinea and the Solomon Islands." Papers Prepared for the Visit of Pope John Paul II to Papua New Guinea, 7–10 May 1984, pp. 48–59.

Joyce, Walter. "The Changing Role of the Brother in Our Society." *Verbum* 8 (1966): 103–8.

Jungbluth, Henry. "'Bishop' and Chinese Colonel." *Word in the World* (1994/1995): 135–36.

Kamp, Francis. "Progress on TLC Master Plan." *Word/USA* (July/August, 1991).

———. "Techny Mission Lifeline." *Word in the World* (1975).

Karnow, Stanley. *In Our Image: America's Empire in the Philippines*. New York: Ballantine Books, 1989.

Kataoka, Takeo. "Why Did I Join?" *Word in the World* (1974): 129.

Kelty, Matthew. *My Song Is of Mercy: Writings of Matthew Kelty, Monk of Gethsemani*. Ed. Michael Downey. Kansas City: Sheed & Ward, 1994.

King, Clifford J. "How Chinese Win the Faith." *Our Missions* (1930): 124–26.

———. *I Remember*. Techny, Ill.: Divine Word Publications, 1968.

Koenig, Harry C., ed. "St. Elizabeth Church 1881–1981," in *A History of the Archdiocese of*

Chicago. Chicago: Catholic Archdiocese of Chicago, 1980.

Kolk, Raymond. "The Educational Contributions of the Society of the Divine Word in the Philippines." Unpublished master's thesis, DePaul University, Chicago, 1954.

Kretschmer, Albert. "My Personal Memories of His Grace, the Most Reverend Archbishop Adolph Alexander Noser, S.V.D, D.D.: The First Bishop of the Diocese of Accra, Africa." Unpublished manuscript, 1981. Techny, Ill.: SVD Archives.

Kroes, Henry. "An Honorable Exile: Where the Expelled China Missionaries Went." *Word in the World* (1981): 119.

Lannon, Maria M. *Father Francis G. Wade S.V.D. (Life of Love and Service)*. Washington, D.C.: Josephite Pastoral Center, n.d.

Leahy, Michael. *Explorations into Highland New Guinea 1930–1935*. Ed. Douglas E. Jones. Tuscaloosa, Ala.: University of Alabama Press, 1991.

———, and Maurice Crain. *The Land That Time Forgot: Adventures and Discoveries in New Guinea*. New York: Funk & Wagnalls Company, 1937.

Lenchak, Timothy. "Cross Cultural Training Makes Better Missionaries, Ministers, Religious." *Together in the Word* 4 (1997): 4.

"The Life of Bishop Harold Robert Perry." *Divine Word Messenger* 43 (No. 1, 1966).

Lonergan, Bernard. *A Second Collection*. Philadelphia: Westminster Press, 1974.

Luzbetak, Louis J. *The Church and Cultures: New Perspectives in Missiological Anthropology*. Maryknoll, N.Y.: Orbis Books, 1988.

———. "My Pilgrimage in Mission." *International Bulletin of Missionary Research* 16 (July 1992): 124–28.

———. "A Survey of the Possibilities for the Further Development of the Society in North America." Mimeographed report to the SVD Generalate, Washington, D.C., 1961.

Lyke, James P., ed. *What We Have Seen and Heard. New Pastoral Letter on Evangelization from the Black Bishops of the United States*. Cincinnati: St. Anthony Messenger Press, 1984.

Malin, Arthur. "The Forgotten." *Word in the World* (1977): 48–151.

Malin, Charles W. "Integration of the Catholic Clergy in the United States, the Divine Word Missionaries Chapter." Unpublished master's thesis, Marquette University, 1964.

Maloof, Louis J. *Adveniat Regnum Tuum: The Story of China's First Cardinal* (condensation of a longer, 1946 biography of Cardinal Tien). Techny, Ill.: SVD Archives.

Mantovani, Ennio. "Silver Jubilee of the Melanesian Institute." *Point* 19 (1994).

Markert, Francis. "God's Ways to My Priesthood. A Retrospect at his Golden Jubilee, February 6, 1960." Privately printed, 1959. Techny, Ill.: SVD Archives.

———. *Fifty Years in America: Society of the Divine Word*. Unpublished manuscript, 1959. Techny: Ill.: SVD Archives.

Markoe, William. "Catholics, the Negro, and a Native Clergy." *America* (September 24, 1921): 535–36.

———. "Negro Morality and a Colored Clergy." *America* (November 12, 1921): 79–80.

McAvoy, Thomas T. *The Great Crisis in American Catholic History 1895–1900*. Chicago: Henry Regnery Company, 1957.

McCullough, Jack. "Goodbye, Mr. SVD." *Word in the World* (1992).

McGuinn, Edward. *Call to Renewal: Ninth General Chapter, 1967–68*. Rome: Collegio del Verbo Divino, 1968.

McHenry, John P. "External and Internal Communications in the Society." *Verbum* 8 (1966): 307–10.

McHugh, Peter. *The Spirituality of Our Founder: A Theological Appreciation*. (Published for the Centennial of the Society of the Divine Word, 1875–1975). Rome: Collegio del Verbo Divino, 1975.

McMillan, Neil R. *Dark Journey: Black Mississippians in the Days of Jim Crow*. Urbana, Ill.: University of Illinois Press, 1989.

Meier, Michael. "Das Negerpriester Seminar in Bay St. Louis." *Verbum* 3 (1961): 329–408.

———. "Die Negermission SVD im Süden der USA." Ph.D. diss., Pontificia Universitas Gregoriana, 1961. Steyl: Steyler Verlag, 1961; English translation of Archbishop Meier's dissertation, "Divine Word Missionaries' Black Apostolate in Southern USA." Trans. William Bonner. Privately printed.

Mennis, Mary R. *Hagen Saga: The Story of Fr. William Ross, Pioneer American Missionary to Papua New Guinea*. Boroka, PNG: Institute of PNG Studies, 1982.

Mihalic, Francis. "The History of New Guinea Missions." Unpublished typescript, *ca.* 1995. Techny, Ill.: SVD Archives.

———. *The Jacaranda Dictionary and Grammar of Melanesian Pidgin*. Milton, Queensland, Australia: Jacaranda Press, 1971.

———. "Melanesian Pidgin English in New Guinea." *Verbum* 2 (1960): 340–44.

———. "The Medium of the Message." *Word in the World* (1995–1996): 43–48.

Müller, Manfred. "Die Gründung des Christkönigs-Missionshauses in Manila." *Analecta SVD* 45 (1979).

Murphy, Denis. "The Philippines and the U.S. Future in Asia." *America* (June 4, 1994): 10–12.

Murphy, Joseph. "Early Days of the Catholic Students' Mission Crusade." *Our Missions* 1 (1921), 123–24.

———. "The S.V.D. in the Old Capital of China," *The Christian Family and Our Missions* (January 1934): 27–31.

Murphy, Patrick. "Holy Spirit Regional Seminary: The Evolution of a Training School for an Indigenous Clergy." *Word in the World* (1969): 86–91.

Nemer, Lawrence. "A Recommendation Revisited." Unpublished paper, 1989.

Newton, Dennis. "Fort Chaffee Calling." *Word in the World* (1995): 41–43.

Nilles, John. *Bishop Francis Wolf, Divine Word Missionary*. Kundiawa, PNG: Mission Procure, 1989.

———. *They Went Out to Sow. The Beginning of the Work of the Catholic Mission in the Highlands of Papua New Guinea 1933–1934*. Rome: Collegio del Verbo Divino, 1987.

Noldin, Hieronynus. *Summa Theologiae Moralis*, 3rd edition, ed. Godefridus Heinzel, 1933.

Noser, Adolph. "The Lay Missionary Comes of Age." *Divine Word Missionaries* (Autumn 1974).

———. "Lay Mission-Helpers, Manual of the Vicariate of Alexishafen, PNG." *Verbum* 1 (1959): 355–62.

———. "Native Catholic Lay Leaders." *Verbum* 3 (1961): 234–40.

———. "Yesterday, Today and Tomorrow." *Word in the World*. Techny, Ill.: Divine Word Publications, 1969.

"Obituary of Sir Vincent Ying, K.S.G." *Bulletin Number One of the Catholic University of Peking* (1926): 29–33.

O'Brien, John A., ed. *The White Harvest: A Symposium on Methods of Convert Making*. New York: Longmans, Green & Co., 1927.

Ochs, Stephen J. "Deferred Mission: The Josephites and the Struggle for Black Catholic Priests, 1871–1960." Ph.D. diss. Ann Arbor, Mich.: UMI Dissertation Services, 1985.

———. *Desegregating the Altar: The Josephites and the Struggle for Black Priests 1871–1960*. Baton Rouge: Louisiana State University Press, 1990.

Olivier, Leonard J. "Foreign Mission Appointments of American Colored SVDs." *Verbum* 4 (1962): 198–200.

———. "The Origin and Development of Saint Augustine's Seminary." Unpublished Master's thesis, Catholic University of America, 1961.

Origin of the American Lay Retreat Movement: A Brief History of the First Decade, June 1954. Techny, Ill.: SVD Archives.

Piskaty, Kurt. "Zur Geschichte unserer Mission in Indonesien." *Verbum* 7 (1965): 57–59.

Pius XI, Pope. "Recognition of SVD Works at Bay St. Louis." *Acta Apostolicae Sedis* 15 (April 5, 1923): 216.

Posjena, Hubert. "Twenty-five Years of Brother Training in Conesus." *Verbum* 7 (1965): 275–77.

Raboteau, Albert J. *A Fire in the Bones: Reflections on African-American Religious History*. Boston: Beacon Press, 1995.

Reuter, Jakob. *Proclaiming the Word in the Power of the Spirit: A Character Delineation of Blessed Arnold Janssen*. Rome: Collegio del Verbo Divino, 1994.

Rigney, Harold W. *Four Years in a Red Hell*. Chicago: Henry Regnery Company, 1956.

———. "Report to Fumasoni-Biondi." Unpublished typescript, 3 April 1951. Rome: SVD Archives.

Rivinius, Karl Josef. *Weltlicher Schutz und Mission: Das deutsche Protektorat über die katholis-*

che Mission von Süd-Shantung (Bonner Beiträge zur Kirchengeschichte, 14) Köln: Böhlau Verlag, 1987.

Rodriquez, Alphonsus. *The Practice of Christian and Religious Perfection*, 3 vols. Trans. Joseph Rich. Chicago: Loyola University Press, 1929.

Rohner, Albert. "Coram Lumine Verbi—Das Programmgebet der Gesellschaft." *Verbum* 3 (1961): 136–54.

Ross, William A. "The American Board of Catholic Missions." *Our Missions* 1 (1921): 18–19.

Rousseve, Maurice. "History, Lest We Be Condemned to Repeat the Mistakes of the Past: Black Seminary Experiences 1920–1943." *Word/USA* (November 1976): 4.

Ruhall, Mary Elise (Ottonia). "The Fateful Yorishime Maru." in Aerts, pp. 87–95.

Ruiter, Ivo, with Bernard Fisher, *Father Ivo Ruiter, S.V.D., Missionary, Priest, Pilot: An Autobiography*. Madang, PNG: Divine Word Institute, 1992.

Sanneh, Lamin. *Abolitionists Abroad: American Blacks and the Making of Modern West Africa*. Cambridge: Harvard University Press, 2000.

———. *Translating the Message: The Missionary Impact on Culture*. Maryknoll, N.Y.: Orbis Books, 1989.

———. *West African Christianity: The Religious Impact*. Maryknoll, N.Y.: Orbis Books, 1983.

Schäfer, Alphonse. *Pioneer in New Guinea: Letters of Father Alphons Schaefer, S.V.D. 1904–1958*. Alexishafen, PNG: Bernard Fisher, 1990.

———. "Predigt mit Wiederholung." *Verbum* 3 (1961): 223–24.

Schmidlin, Joseph. *Catholic Mission Theory*. Trans. Matthias Braun. Techny Ill.: Mission Press, SVD, 1931.

Schmidlin, Joseph. *Catholic Mission History*, Trans. Matthias Braun. Techny, Ill.: Mission Press, SVD, 1933.

Schmitz, Bartley. "China's Prince of the Church." *Word in the World* (1967): 49–55.

Schütte, Johannes. "Der bestimmende Faktor in Erziehung und Ausbildung unserer Scholastiker." *Verbum* 1 (1959): 32–45.

Spitzley, Bernard. "Creating Right Relationships in Clerical Institutes." *Verbum* 35 (1994): 133–41.

Stenz, George M. "Recollections of a Beggar." *Our Missions* 5 (1925): 28.

"S.V.D. Missionaries, 25 Years in the Philippine Islands." *Christian Family and Our Missions*. (April 1934): 124.

Tschauder, John J. "Life in Prison Camps," in Aerts, pp. 82–86.

Uroda, Stanley. "Journey to Vietnam." Divine Word Missionaries, Summer 1994, 8–12.

Van Baar, Engelmund. *The Mission Years of Father Engelmund van Baar of the Society of the Divine Word: Missionary to Papua New Guinea*. Alexishafen, PNG: Stella Press, 1973.

Walls, Andrew F. *The Missionary Movement in Christian History: Studies in the Transmission of Faith*. Maryknoll, N.Y.: Orbis Books, 1996.

Weber, Anton. "Across the Strait to Taiwan." *Word in the World 1990/91*. Steyl: Steyler Verlag, 1991.

Wendel, P. J. *Our Negro Missions: A Short Historical Sketch—Present Conditions—Prospects*. Techny, Ill.: Techny Press, 1914.

Wiesen, H. John. "A Hidden Christian Returns." *Word in the World* (1974): 61–63.

Wilson, Dick. *When Tigers Fight: The Story of the Sino-Japanese War, 1937–1945*. New York: The Viking Press, 1982.

Wiltgen, Ralph. "The Death of Bishop Loerks and his Companions." Part I. *Verbum* 6 (1964): 363–97.

———. "The Death of Bishop Loerks and His Companions." Part II. *Verbum* 7 (1965): 14–44.

———. *The Founding of the Roman Catholic Church in Oceania*. Vol. 1. Canberra: Australian National University Press, 1979.

———. *Gold Coast Mission History, 1471–1880*. Techny, Ill.: Divine Word Publications, 1956.

———. "Latin America." *Arnoldus* 14 (1962).

———. "A Lesson from Togo on Expansion." *Verbum* 7 (1965): 180–82.

———. "The Plight of Central New Guinea in 1946." *Verbum* 7 (1965): 209–18.

———. *The Rhine Flows into the Tiber: A History of Vatican II*. Rockford, Ill.: Tan Books and Publishers, 1967.

Wojniak, Edward. *Atomic Apostle: The Life Story of Thomas Megan*. Techny, Ill.: Divine Word Publications, 1957.

Woodward, C. Vann. *The Strange Career of Jim Crow.* 3rd ed. New York: Oxford University Press, 1974.

Yates, Timothy. *Christian Mission in the Twentieth Century*. New York: Cambridge University Press, 1994.

Ziliak, Jerome. "The Next Harvest." *Word in the World* (1973).

Zocca, Franco. "Papua New Guinea: Land of the Unexpected." *Word in the World* (1995): 33–38.

APPENDIX

Divine Word Missionaries of North America 1895–1999

This appendix lists most Divine Word Missionaries in permanent vows who have worked or lived for a long enough time in the United States or Canada to be listed in its official catalogue.[1] The number of persons born outside the United States in this appendix bears eloquent testimony to the North American SVD role in developing the international, multinational character of the Society's philosophy of mission staffing.

In this appendix, the member's family name comes first, then his given name, followed in the case of some brothers by the italicized religious name they were given upon entrance into the Society. The numbers following names, by columns, represent:

1. year of birth (the difference between the 1800s and 1900s should be clear from the context); (when there are numbers set off in brackets after the name, this designates the year of a priest's ordination as a bishop; a second number in brackets indicates his appointment as an archbishop);
2. the year the member took first vows;
3. the year of perpetual vows in the Society;
4. the year of ordination of priest-members. In the case of brothers, two asterisks are placed in the fourth column.
5. the last column indicates where the member was born. For those born in the United States and Puerto Rico, their state of birth is indicated using standard United States Postal Service codes. For members born outside the United States, the country of origin is indicated. The legend below identifies countries of origin of men who have spent both a few years or most of a lifetime as Divine Word Missionaries of North America.

---

1. Unlike many religious communities, in which one enters a province and remains a member of that province for life, membership in a given province of the SVD is fluid. After completing initial formation, when one is assigned to a mission or province for a length of time, one becomes a full member of the new province. Many SVDs are members of several provinces in the course of a lifetime. In addition, one of the American SVD's greatest contributions over the years—reflected in this appendix—is as the place where SVDs from around the world have come for advanced degrees. This is one reason for the large number of men below who are neither Canadians nor Americans but are fully Divine Word Missionaries of North America, whose stories are integral to this book.

ANG	=	Angola	NIC	=	Nicaragua
ARG	=	Argentina	NZE	=	New Zealand
AUS	=	Australia	OES	=	Austria
BEL	=	Belgium	PAN	=	Panama
BRA	=	Brazil	PAR	=	Paraguay
CHI	=	Chile	PHI	=	Philippines
CZE	=	Czechoslovakia	POR	=	Portugal
FRA	=	France	POL	=	Poland
GER	=	Germany	RUS	=	Russia
GBR	=	Great Britain	SCO	=	Scotland
GHA	=	Ghana	SIN	=	China
HON	=	Honduras	SLO	=	Slovakia
HUN	=	Hungary	SWI	=	Switzerland
IDO	=	Indonesia	TAI	=	Taiwan
IND	=	India	TOG	=	Togo
JPN	=	Japan	VIE	=	Vietnam
KEN	=	Kenya	WIN	=	West Indies
LUX	=	Luxembourg	YUG	=	Yugoslavia
NEB	=	Netherlands/Belgium	ZAI	=	Zaire

A. BALAIAH, John	60	83	88	89	IND
ABRAHAMCZYK, Kasmierz	59	80	84	85	POL
ABRI, Julius	14	37	40	41	HUN
ADAMEK, Andrew	15	38	42	43	PA
ADAMS, William	13	40	44	45	MA
AFAGBEGEE, Edmond	59	81	85	86	GHA
AGETHEN, Bernard, *Anselm*	6	91	99	**	GER
AGGER, George	42	65	69	69	IRE
AGUILAR, M., *Deogratias*	40	63	69	**	MEX
AHNER, Eugene	36	56	62	64	PA
AI(NGA), Paulinus	25	51	54	55	SIN
AIZAWA SHUNZO, John	35	56	62	62	JPN
ALBANO, Arturo	49	69	74	74	PHI
ALBERS, Raymond, *Gregory*	30	49	55	**	IA
ALLARD, Yvon	37	58	62	64	CAN
ALLES, Clement, *Theophane*	99	29	35	**	IL
ALTENDORF, Louis	07	29	33	35	IL
AMELSE, Edward	33	53	59	61	WI
AMELSE, Gerald	31	51	57	58	WI
AMFOTIS, David Naileku	63	85	91	83	IDO
ANDRUS, Richard	55	78	83	83	OH
ANHALT, Jay	38	59	65	67	IL
ANICH, Kenneth	47	70	73	73	WI
ANJELIS, Marcelinus	63	85	91	94	IDO
ANKRAH, Francis	42	66	70	70	GHA
ANNESE, Joseph	31	54	60	62	MA
ANTHONY, M.	47	72	78	79	IND
ANTONI, Philip	04	25	29	30	GER
ANZORGE, Bogdan	55	77	81	82	CZE
APPELHANS, Stephan [+48]	05	27	31	32	KS
ARCHEY, Lawrence	10	35	39	40	MA
ARENS, Richard	12	34	38	38	GER
ARKFELD, Leo [+48-76]	12	38	42	43	NB
ARMENDARIZ, Angel	33	52	58	59	SPA
ARNOLD, Roger	33	53	59	61	PA
AROKIA, Sebastian	58	79	84	85	IND
ARTIENDA, Joseph	62	83	88	88	PHI
ARTIS, George	31	54	60	62	WV
ARTZER, James	23	43	49	50	IA
ASCHEMAN, Thomas	54	77	82	82	MN
ASSENYOH, Bernard Kwame	67	93	97	98	GHA
ATENCIO, Ricardo	47	71	81	**	PHI
AUBESPIN, Borgia	35	56	63	65	LA
AUBRY, Hugo	72	02	05	06	GER
AUER, Paul	19	40	44	45	WI
AUL, Joseph	32	52	58	60	PA
BABULIK, Joseph, *Supplicius*	02	27	33	**	SLO
BACAREZA, Hermog	30	53	59	59	PHI
BACH, Al., *Hermann J.*	07	27	33	**	GER
BACKUS, William	09	39	43	44	NY
BAECK, Gothardo	35	58	62	62	GER
BAGSIC, Victor	48	69	74	74	PHI
BAKER, Christian	05	26	30	31	PA
BALA, Kristoforus	66	89	98		IDO
BALTES, Francis	84	05	08	09	GER
BALTHAZAR, W., *James*	13	48	54	**	LA
BALZEREIT, Daniel	33	54	60	62	PA
BANCALE, Romeo	40	61	67	67	PHI
BANNERMAN, Leslie	16	49	52	53	SIN
BANTZ, Richard, *Allen*	46	68	77	**	WI

372

BAO TELUMA, Lukas	46	67	75	75	IDO
BARBIETO, Julius	22	48	50	50	PHI
BARDER, Patrick	18	44	50	51	IL
BARFUSS, Johann, *Ananias*	89	21	27	**	CZE
BARON, George	30	53	56	57	POL
BARROS, Francis	37	58	62	64	SIN
BARSALOU, Marcel	36	58	62	64	CAN
BARTHA, Charles	13	35	38	39	SLO
BARTOLOME, Virgilio	31	57	61	61	PHI
BAT MOMOLIN, Lucas	64	85	90	91	IDO
BATA, Simon	53	78	83	84	IDO
BATES, Joseph	17	40	44	44	MN
BAUCHWITZ, Eugene	36	56	62	64	IL
BAUER, Leonard, *Roman*	17	40	46	**	MO
BAUER, Anthony	12	33	38	38	OH
BAUER, Daniel	48	71	74	74	OH
BAUER, Erwin	14	36	40	41	OH
BAUER, William	05	28	32	33	IL
BAUMAN, Theodore	99	20	21	25	OH
BAUMGARTNER, F., *Gilbert*	04	30	36	**	IN
BAUR, Edward	27	48	54	55	WI
BECK, Michael	10	36	39	40	GER
BECKER, Theodore	41	61	67	**	GER
BECKERS, Wm., *Tiberius*	87	07	13	**	GER
BECKERS, P., *Theodosius*	91	09	15	**	GER
BECKERT, John	64	89	98	90	GER
BEEMSTER, Peter, *Willibrord*	98	22	28	**	WI
BEEMSTER, John	13	35	39	40	NEB
BEEMSTERBOER, Francis	24	44	50	51	IL
BEIRNE, Paul	46	68	75	76	AUS
BEKI DOREN, Ferdinandus	65	87	96	97	IDO
BELAMIDE, Paulino	23	43	49	50	PHI
BELTRAN, Octavio	51	73	78	78	PHI
BENETTI, Romeo	36	59	65	68	ITA
BENOIT, Louis	03	24	29	38	MN
BENZ, William	90	20	23	25	IN
BERGER, Ronald, *Benedict*	42	63	70	**	WI
BERGIN, James	41	64	69	69	WI
BERGIN, John	38	58	64	67	WI
BERISH, Gerard	55	78	83	83	OH
BERMAN, John	85	08	11	11	GER
BERNAL, Melchor	52	73	78	78	PHI
BERNARDING, Geo. [+59-66]	12	34	38	39	PA
BERNET, Franz, *Augustine*	91	29	35	**	GER
BERNIER, Gilles	37	59	63	65	CAN
BERRY, John	29	49	55	57	PA
BERTE, Matthias, *Matthias*	89	22	28	**	IA
BESSLER, Gary	60	83	88	89	OH
BETAN IGO, Norbertus	53	76	82	83	IDO
BETTISON, John	51	72	77	77	GBR
BEVANS, Stephen	44	66	70	71	MD
BEWERMEIER, Josef, *Theodore*	74	93	03	**	GER
BHIA WEA, Raymundus	52	75	81	82	IDO
BILIRAN, Giovanni	60	83	87	87	PHI
BILLER, Andrew	32	53	59	61	MO
BILSAK, Thomas	31	52	58	60	PA
BISHEIMER, Nicholas	15	37	41	42	KS
BISHOP, Anthony	32	60	65	66	AUS
BISKUPEK, Aloysius	84	05	08	09	POL
BISSON, Joseph	36	55	61	63	MA

BITAR, Joseph	26	45	51	52	MI
BLAIN, Edgar	30	51	56	58	AUS
BLAKE, William	44	66	74	90	CAN
BLECH, Clement	37	65	67	68	POL
BLONER, Raymond, *Berchmans*	10	32	38	**	WI
BLUME, Michael	46	69	72	72	IN
BOBERG, John	34	53	56	61	KY
BOCKMAN, Jerome, *Damian*	19	40	46	**	IA
BODNAR, Michael	13	41	45	46	PA
BOER, Peter de	08	30	34	35	NEB
BOERDING, Peter	01	24	29	30	MO
BOHLE, Henry	32	54	60	60	CHI
BOHNEN, Lawrence	17	39	43	44	MN
BOHR, Richard, *Robert*	45	66	72	**	MN
BOI-NAI, Vincent	45	70	76	77	GHA
BOLD, Albert	08	30	33	34	GER
BOLTE, Jerome, *Dismas*	45	67	73	**	IL
BONA, Bernard	14	30	33	34	POL
BONK, Bernard	90	12	15	15	GER
BONNER, Michael	37	57	63	66	IL
BONNER, William	40	62	67	67	PA
BORDAS, Richard	38	59	65	67	PA
BORKOWSKI, Edward	15	37	43	44	IL
BOTELHO, Manuel	91	21	26	27	HI
BOU, Pedro	45	70	74	74	PR
BOUCREE, Thaddeus	24	45	51	52	LA
BOURGES, Anthony	04	29	33	34	LA
BOWERS, Rodney	60	84	90	**	IA
BOWERS, Joseph [+53]	10	33	38	39	WIN
BOWMAN, John Walter	08	33	38	39	DC
BOYER, J., *Peter*	19	39	45	**	LA
BOYKINS, Charles	32	57	63	65	LA
BRABAND, James	53	77	80	80	IL
BRACKEN, Walter	45	68	71	71	CAN
BRADLEY, Vincent	12	37	41	42	MA
BRAMBRINK, William	98	21	26	27	GER
BRANDEWIE, Ernest	31	51	57	59	OH
BRAUN, J., *Ralph*	17	37	43	**	IL
BRAUN, Matthias	88	10	13	13	GER
BRENNAN, William	64	88	93	**	MA
BRENNAN, Michael	39	64	69	69	AUS
BRIGNAC, M., *Joachim*	33	62	68	**	LA
BRODERICK, Donal	39	70	73	73	IRE
BRONDER, Urban	04	27	31	32	PA
BROPHY, William Colm	51	74	78	78	IRE
BROUILLETTE, Paul	44	66	70	70	WI
BROWN, Stephan Thomas	63	86	92	93	OH
BRUCKNER, Richard	30	57	60		OES
BRUMM, Geoffrey	46	66	71	72	AUS
BRZAKOWSKI, Jerome	16	40	44	45	MI
BUBAK, Milan	56	88	93	80	SLO
BUCHCIK, Anthony	11	34	38	38	POL
BUDENHOLZER, Francis	45	66	72	72	IL
BUECKER, Franz, *Hugolinus*	82	13	19	**	GER
BUERVENIG, Max., *Germanicus*	91	11	20	**	GER
BUGNER, C., *Ignatius*	39	60	66	**	IL
BUGNER, Joseph	35	55	61	63	IL
BUIS, Simon	92	17	20	25	NEB
BUKOVSKY, John [+90]	24	45	49	50	SLO
BUNOFSKY, Walter	31	52	58	60	OH

BUNZEL, Lawrence	05	28	32	33	WI
BURBELA, Mare	52	73	77	78	POL
BURES, Francis	27	46	52	53	WI
BURGMER, Adolph	75	97	00	01	GER
BURKE, Dominic	43	64	68	69	AUS
BURKE, Henry	33	53	59	61	CHI
BURKE, Robert	39	62	66	67	IL
BURKE, Vincent	33	53	59	61	MA
BURNS, Charles	32	54	60	62	MS
BURR, Gerald [Bruno]	38	60	66	**	IA
BURRELL, Louis	36	57	63	65	PA
BURRICHTER, Paul	20	42	46	47	MO
BURROWS, William	42	65	70	71	IA
BUSCH, Bernhard, Servatius	58	91	00	**	GER
BUSCH, Henry	11	33	38	38	GER
BUSCH, Joseph	03	26	30	31	IL
BUTLER, Victor	33	55	61	64	WIN
BUTZ, Peter	19	40	44	45	IL
BUYS, John	08	28	32	33	NEB
BYRNE, Brian	36	67	71	71	AUS
CABATINGAN, Gregory	36	60	66	67	PHI
CABEY, Edwin	30	54	60	62	WIN
CAESAR, Raymond [+75]	32	53	59	61	LA
CAFFREY, William	29	51	57	59	NY
CALLAN, Dennis	55	80	86	87	PA
CALMANO, Michael	48	69	75	75	GER
CAMILLERI, Lawrence, Aaron	40	61	67	**	MI
CANAVAN, Patrick	30	57	62	63	NJ
CANNAN, Frederick, Patrick	14	43	49	**	NY
CANNULI, John	56	79	84	85	NJ

CANTWELL, Patrick	27	52	57	59	AUS
CARDOSO, Jose Maria	61	80	88	89	POR
CARDOSO, Jose	61	80	88	89	POR
CAREW, Michael	20	41	45	46	IRE
CARLIN, John, Nicholas	21	41	47	**	NY
CARLUCCI, John, Boniface	96	23	29	**	NJ
CARMO, Samuel	33	55	61	63	BRA
CARMON, Dominic [+92]	30	52	58	60	LA
CARRIER, Arthur, Michael	97	28	34	**	CAN
CASEY, Brendan	31	60	64	66	IRE
CASHMERE, Raymond	29	48	53	54	AUS
CASSABON, Paul	46	75	83	**	OH
CASSIDY, Nicholas	51	75	79	79	IRE
CASSIDY, Thomas	18	40	44	45	IL
CASTILLO, Amante	34	51	57	58	PHI
CASTILLO, Jose Alejandro	53	77	80	81	MEX
CASTONGUAY, Donald	30	50	56	58	MI
CASTRO, Emile	04	35	38	38	PHI
CASTRO, Romeo	47	68	73	73	PHI
CAVALLAR, Osvaldo	51	72	81	82	ITA
CERNAJ, Emil	23	41	50	51	SLO
CHACHERE, George	11	35	39	39	LA
CHAMBERS, Richard, De Sales	37	59	65	**	KY
CHAMPAGNE, Donald, Bernard	37	58	64	**	WI
CHARLES, Francis	30	62	66	67	WIN
CHEEKS, Monroe	27	55	61	63	MS
CHELLAMTHARA, Augustine	38	60	66	67	IND
CHENEVERT, J., Bonaventure	20	42	48	**	LA
CHENNAKUDY, Mathew	67	84	90	92	IND
CHERIPURAM, Anthony	33	57	63	63	IND

CHETANY, Joseph	40	65	71	73	IND
CHRISTIAN, Michael.. *Aloy*	88	13	20	**	HUN
CHRISTMANN, Matthew	87	09	12	12	GER
CHRZASZCZ, Anthony	86	08	11	11	POL
CLARK, Anthony Paul	44	67	73	85	DC
CLARK, Robert	95	16	19	20	NY
CLERKIN, Michael	11	32	36	38	MA
CLOOS, Herman, *Gabriel*	98	19	25	**	NY
CLOUTIER, Ronald	40	62	67	68	CAN
COADY, John	28	51	57	59	IA
COGAN, Arthur	33	53	59	62	MA
COHILL, John [+66]	07	30	34	36	NJ
COLWELL, George, *Joseph*	10	33	39	**	MI
COMMONS, Patrick	24	44	50	51	IN
COMMONS, Thomas	20	42	46	47	IN
CONEYS, Charles E., *Denis*	00	24	30	**	IL
CONLISS, John	28	57	61	63	IRE
CONNOLLY, Joseph	33	52	58	60	MA
CONNOR, Patrick	29	51	55	57	AUS
CONNORS, Joseph, *Matthew*	39	62	68	**	MA
CONNORS, Joseph	25	45	51	52	MA
CONNORS, Paul	35	55	61	63	MA
CONRAD, Fabian	62	89	94		GER
COOK, R., *Michael*	18	53	59	**	NY
COONEY, Xavier	41	62	68	83	PA
CORKILL, Albert	31	53	57	59	AUS
CORNETT, David	58	81	86	87	OH
COYLE, John	28	48	54	55	NY
COYLE, Joseph	27	48	54	55	CT
CRAWLEY, Patrick	47	73	76	77	GER

CREMASCO, Dominic	22	49	54	57	AUS
CREMERS, William	01	22	27	28	GER
CUNNINGHAM, Lloyd	53	74	81	81	IL
CZOCH, Pawel	63	86	92	94	POL
CZUJAK, Juan	60	81	86	87	POL
DA COSTA, Lawrence	42	67	75	75	IDO
DAL BIANCO, Anthony	35	55	61	64	ITA
DALY, Donal	36	56	60	62	IRE
DALZELL, James	19	43	47	49	MA
DAMOAH, Francis Kwabena	56	92	97	**	GHA
DANAHER, Philip	52	79	83	83	MO
DANG, Joseph Oanh Xuan	64	88	92	93	VIE
DANGUPON, Limmeo	61	82	87	87	PHI
DARBONNE, Sanders	41	66	70	70	LA
DASCHBACH, Edwin	38	58	64	66	PA
DASCHBACH, Richard	37	56	62	64	PA
DATIG, Edward	12	34	38	39	PA
DAUPHINE, John	10	33	38	39	LA
DAVADILLA, Patrick Joel	61	81	87	88	PHI
DAVITT, Norman	21	41	45	47	GBR
DAWAN JAGA, Joseph	53	77	83	88	IDO
DE BOLD, John	34	76	85	**	PA
DE GROOT, J., *Gonzales*	29	49	55	**	NEB
DE GROOT, Nicholas	43	63	68	69	AUS
DE GROOT, Robert	35	56	62	64	NY
DE LEON, Emmanuel	59	85	89	89	PHI
DE LOS REYES, Patricio	56	77	82	82	PHI
DE MARCO, James	40	62	67	68	PA
DE RIVERA, Cresente	54	76	81	81	PHI
DEARWORTH, Joseph	13	37	41	42	IL

DECKER, Michael	55	84	91	**	OH
DELANEY, Edward	41	63	67	68	PA
DEML, Franz	28	52	56	57	GER
DEPPE, Anthony	01	23	28	29	GER
DETIG, Joseph	35	55	61	62	NY
DI SANTO, S., *Ignatius*	01	35	41	**	NY
DICKS, Abel	33	55	62	64	TX
DIEDERICH, Allen, *Kevin*	39	62	67	**	MO
DIETSCHE, William	33	53	59	61	OH
DIETZ, Nicholas, *Gregory*	86	19	25	**	IL
DIJK, Martin van	34	57	61	62	NEB
DINGMAN, Arthur	97	19	22	24	PA
DINH, Dominic Quang Duc	61	87	91	92	VIE
DIXON, Alvin	43	65	69	69	LA
DJADOO, Maurice, *James*	31	58	66	**	TOG
D'MELLO, Vikram Peter	36	58	64	64	IND
DOCKENDORF, John, *Winandus*	72	04	10	**	GER
DOCOY, Eugenio	61	82	87	87	PHI
DOERFLER, George, *James*	01	25	31	**	PA
DOLAN, Michael	29	50	56	58	NY
DONAGHEY, Bernard	29	49	55	58	MA
DONAGHEY, John	28	47	53	54	MA
DONAHUE, Joseph	15	37	41	42	MA
DONNELLAN, Michael	31	56	60	62	IRE
DONNELLY, Eamon	45	65	69	70	IRE
DONNELLY, Timothy	59	82	87	88	OH
DOOLEY, Lester	98	20	23	26	IL
DOPKE, Mariusz Andruzej	67	87	95	96	POL
DORADE, Joseph, *Bernard*	27	56	62	**	PAN
DOROZYNSKI, Krzysztof	61	81	86	87	POL
DORSEY, Anthony, *Stephan*	23	43	49	**	DC
DOWD, Bernard Patrick	11	35	39	40	MA
DOYLE, Bernard	30	48	54	55	IL
DRESCHER, Bruno	81	06	09	10	GER
DRISCOLL, Daniel	12	33	37	38	KY
DROSTE, Allen, *Luke*	39	61	67	**	MI
DRZAIC, Francis	34	54	60	62	NB
DUAH PREMPEH, John	64	89	95	95	GHA
DUDINK, Edward	19	41	45	46	IL
DUDINK, Lawrence	13	34	38	39	IL
DUGAY, Anthony	34	54	60	62	LA
DUNN, John	17	39	43	44	OH
DUNNIGAN, J., *Patrick*	86	18	24	**	SCO
DURITZKY, Boniface	34	54	60	62	PA
DUSHECK, Leo	33	53	59	61	PA
DUSICKA, Peter	64	91	94	90	SLO
D'VALLE, Donald	33	54	60	63	PA
DZIUBA, Edmund	59	80	84	85	POL
ECIMOVICH, Francis	15	38	42	43	YUG
ECKERMAN, Felix	20	42	46	47	CO
ECKERT, Joseph	84	05	08	09	POL
EDERLE, Arnoldo	35	56	61	61	ARG
EDMONDS, Douglas	51	80	86	**	OH
EDWARDS, Edward	04	24	28	30	NY
EDZE, Yaw Peter	52	78	85	**	GHA
EGAN, Joseph	19	50	54	55	AUS
EHR, Donald	28	48	54	55	IA
ELDERS, Leon	26	47	53	53	NEB
ELSBERND, Alphonse	99	23	28	29	IA
ELSBERND, Elmer	36	56	62	65	IA

ENGEL, Clarence, *Basil*	15	35	41	**	WI
ENGELEN, Philip van	10	30	34	35	NEB
ERB, Charles	06	28	32	33	NY
ERNEST, Stephen	40	62	65	67	PAN
ERSCHENS, Anton, *Thomas*	85	22	28	**	PA
ESCHERICH, J., *Christopher*	90	23	29	**	GER
ESHMAN, Daniel, *Xavier*	37	62	68	**	OH
ESPINEDA, Cesar	57	78	84	84	PHI
ESSER, Gerard	82	02	05	06	GER
ESTEPA, Francisco	56	76	83	83	PHI
ETIENNE, Clifton	37	57	63	79	LA
FABIAN, John	35	58	61	62	GER
FAIKUS, Joseph	90	12	15	15	CZE
FARIER, Stanley	33	56	62	64	DOM
FARLEY, John	32	52	58	60	MA
FARRELL, William, *Boniface*	45	66	76	**	NY
FECHER, Vincent	24	43	49	50	IL
FECKEN, Emil, *Michael*	60	85	94	**	GER
FEEHAN, Kenneth	31	51	57	59	VT
FEELEY, John	07	32	36	38	IA
FEIFEL, Eugene	02	22	26	27	GER
FELDKAEMPER, Ludger	37	58	61	63	GER
FELDNER, William	47	70	74	74	WI
FELIX, Harold, *Raphael*	12	36	49	**	OH
FELSKI, Harry	11	33	37	38	WI
FELTEN, L., *Willibrord*	27	53	59	**	NEB
FERLEJ, Ernst	30	58	61	63	GER
FERRER, Joaquin	60	79	85	87	PHI
FERRY, Patrick	34	55	59	61	IRE
FERTAL, Joseph	31	51	57	59	PA
FIEDLER, Loyd	44	66	70	70	IA
FIGARO, Mark	21	43	48	49	LA
FIJALKOWSKI, Wlodzimierz	61	86	91	**	POL
FIMMERS, Henry	38	61	66	66	GER
FINCUTTER, John	23	43	48	50	IL
FINCUTTER, Patrick	28	48	54	55	IL
FINGER, Joseph	01	21	26	27	GER
FINKELDEY, Louis, *Linus*	65	00	06	**	GER
FINKELDEY, Hubert	08	31	34	36	GER
FINNEGAN, Lawrence	37	62	67	68	IRE
FINNEMANN, William	82	08	11	11	GER
FISCHBACHER, A., *Gosbert*	92	13	19	**	SWI
FISHER, James	54	77	83	**	IL
FISHER, Bernard	18	40	44	45	MT
FISHER, Dale	23	43	47	49	IA
FISHER, Robert	37	57	63	65	MO
FITZGERALD, J., *Kilian*	33	54	60	**	MA
FITZGERALD, Shane	37	64	68	69	IRE
FITZGIBBON, William	08	29	33	34	IN
FLANNERY, Peter	42	62	67	68	AUS
FLASKA, Joseph	21	43	47	49	RUS
FLECKENSTEIN, H., *Elzear*	71	98	06	**	GER
FLEISHAKER, Joseph	17	42	46	47	PA
FLEISSNER, Raymond	34	54	60	62	NY
FLEMING, Anthony	22	41	45	47	GBR
FLIEGER, William	31	53	57	58	GER
FLINN, Robert	29	49	55	57	PA
FLOOD, Lawrence	34	58	65	66	WI
FLORES, Antonio	57	79	85	**	PHI
FLORES, Roberto C.	62	89	95	96	ECU

FLORIAN, Albert	80	03	06	07	CZE
FLYNN, Dennis	33	54	60	61	PHI
FOERSTER, Friedrich W.	34	58	62	62	GER
FOFFEL, George	98	23	28	29	IA
FOLI-QUAYE, Andrew	56	80	84	85	GHA
FONTANA, Joseph	07	29	33	35	IL
FONVILLE, John	16	36	40	40	NEB
FORD, Joseph	03	24	29	30	NY
FOX, Frederick	22	43	48	50	WI
FRACEK, Leonard	32	54	60	62	PA
FRANCIS, Joseph [+76]	23	43	48	50	LA
FRANK, Francis, *Eugene*	00	24	30	**	IL
FRANKS, James	33	52	58	60	PA
FRATZKE, Ronald	61	85	90	**	IA
FREITAG, Augustine	89	12	15	18	GER
FRERICHS, Amos	16	45	51	52	TX
FRIEDEL, Lawrence	01	22	27	28	GER
FRITZEN, Michael	42	64	68	69	IL
FROHNAPFEL, F., *Galatius*	57	01	07	**	GER
FU, John	04	26	30	30	SIN
FUCHS, Andreas, *Peter*	75	04	10	**	GER
FUCHS, Francis Xavier	02	26	36	36	GER
FUCHS, Francis Xavier	02	31	35	35	GER
FUELLLENBACH, John	35	60	64	64	GER
FUKAE KATSUICHI, Michael	49	65	78	78	JPN
FULLER, Bernard	84	07	10	10	GER
FULLER, C. Neil	39	62	69	69	MA
GAENGER, Nicholas, *Francis*	86	11	16	**	HUN
GAGNON, Bernard, *Louis*	26	57	63	**	VT
GAIONI, Dominic	39	59	65	67	ITA

GALIZIO, Bruno	39	59	45	67	ITA
GANGGU, Alex	40	64	72	72	IDO
GANTERT, Willi	31	58	62	62	GER
GAPUZ, Teodoro	41	61	67	67	PHI
GARBACZ, Kazimierz	45	64	69	70	POL
GARRITY, Joseph	11	33	37	38	MA
GARRY, Gerald	28	54	57	59	NY
GASKA, Henryk	62	82	87	88	POL
GASPER, John	02	23	28	29	GER
GAUDREAULT, Lucien	47	83	87	88	CAN
GAWLIK, Bernard, *René*	38	59	65	**	WI
GAWLIK, Gilbert	26	47	53	54	WI
GEERS, Edwin	33	53	59	61	IA
GEHLEN, Elzear	15	39	43	44	MN
GEISSINGER, Gary, *Chanel*	41	62	67	**	MN
GENCUSKI, Theodore	33	54	60	62	WI
GENTILI, Romano	45	65	66	69	ITA
GEORGI, Willliam	13	35	38	39	GER
GERAT, Francis, *Vincent*	06	32	38	**	CZE
GERDING, John	41	63	67	68	OH
GERHARDS, Joseph	81	03	06	07	GER
GERRY, Francis	32	51	56	58	AUS
GESCH, Patrick	44	64	70	70	AUS
GESSINGER, Guenther	37	55	59	59	GER
GIALLANZA, Francis	08	28	31	32	LA
GIBBS, Philip	47	72	78	78	NZE
GILMORE, John	32	52	58	60	OH
GILMORE, Michael	33	58	63	65	GBR
GLATZEL, Joseph	32	55	59	59	POL
GLORIUS, Felix	90	13	16	16	GER

GNANAPRAKASAM, Amaldoss	46	70	76	78	IND
GODWIN, Clement	29	52	58	58	AUS
GOJAKOVICH, Franz	35	58	61	63	OES
GONZALES, Andrew	08	31	38	38	PHI
GOODLAND, Paul	41	65	70	70	AUS
GOOSSEN, Joseph, *Robert*	77	96	06	**	GER
GOOTEE, Paul	27	48	54	55	IN
GOOTEE, Stanley	17	39	43	44	IN
GORNY, Alfons	12	35	39	39	GER
GOTO FUMIO, John	29	54	60	60	JPN
GRABSKI, Andrzej Piotr	66	86	92	94	POL
GRAF, John	08	30	34	36	WI
GRAHAM, Richard	18	40	44	45	MA
GRANFIELD, Thomas, *Romuald*	30	52	58	**	MN
GRAWEY, Clarence, Titus	14	41	47	**	MI
GREBER, Joseph, *William*	08	36	45	**	GER
GREEF, Johann, *Dignus*	65	96	06	**	GER
GREVENSTETTE, H., *Clement*	08	38	46	**	POL
GRIES, Charles	09	31	35	37	IN
GRIFFIN, J., *Gerard*	29	49	55	**	LA
GRIFFIN, August	57	81	86	87	LA
GRIFFITH, Thomas	43	65	68	69	IL
GRODE, Leo	05	27	32	32	SD
GRONER, Eric	65	90	95	96	TN
GROSS, Joseph	95	22	27	28	ND
GRUBBA, John	58	81	86	87	IL
GRUENENFELDER, A., *Gallus*	94	25	31	**	SWI
GRUHN, Frederick	83	06	09	10	GER
GRUNENBERG, Richard	84	07	10	10	POL
GRZENIA, Edward	18	42	46	47	IL

GUARIN, Eduardo	55	76	82	82	PHI
GUETZLOE, Joseph	12	35	38	38	GER
GUIDRY, Joseph	26	49	55	57	LA
GUIDRY, Raymond	28	49	55	57	LA
GUILLORY, L., *De Porres*	43	65	73	**	LA
GUILLORY, Curtis [+88]	43	69	72	72	LA
GUINER, Denis	13	37	41	42	NY
GUISTO, Peter	01	28	32	33	ITA
GUMBEL, Peter, *Peregrine*	81	05	11	**	GER
GUNNING, Joseph	13	42	46	47	MA
GUSINDE, Martin	86	06	11	11	OES
GUTIERREZ, Gabriel	51	75	80	82	MEX
HAARMANN (HARMON), Joseph	82	10	13	13	GER
HAAS, Florian	95	16	19	21	IN
HACKENBERG, John, *Joachim*	61	90	98	**	GER
HADALSKI, Andrew	31	51	57	59	PA
HAEFNER, Charles	05	27	31	32	IL
HAEGELE, George, *Karl*	47	68	74	**	IL
HAFERKAMP, Hubert, *Otto*	86	12	18	**	GER
HAFNER, Walter	09	31	35	37	MN
HAGAN, William	05	31	35	37	MA
HAGELSTEIN, Edward, *Eugene*	37	58	64	**	MO
HAGEN, Hermann	83	13	21	21	GER
HAGENI, Franz, *Disibodius*	82	02	09	**	GER
HAGSPIEL, Bruno	85	06	09	10	POL
HAINES, Heinrich, *Wilfrid*	02	27	33	**	WI
HAINES, Arthur	08	31	35	37	WI
HAINES, Jerome	05	29	33	35	WI
HAYON, Alfons	42	64	72	72	IDO
HALLERAN, Thomas	07	39	43	44	CAN

HALVEY, William	28	54	60	76	IL
HAMBACH, Lawrence	33	53	59	60	OH
HAMILTON, Kenneth	54	77	82	82	IL
HANNAH, Raymond	31	52	58	68	CAN
HANNAHER, John	15	37	41	42	IA
HANNAN, Rogers	48	82	88	**	MS
HANZEL, Louis	29	49	55	57	PA
HARGARTEN, Leo	02	24	29	30	WI
HARPEL, John	17	39	43	44	MN
HART, Edward, *Arnold*	03	25	31	**	MO
HARTMAN, Robert	32	52	58	60	PA
HASULIE, Thomas	62	83	88	89	IDO
HAUBER, Joseph	99	18	21	22	GER
HAUTKAPPE, J., *Canisius*	74	93	02	**	GER
HAYON, Alfons	42	64	72	72	IDO
HEALY, John	16	38	43	43	MI
HECK, E., *Arnold*	31	54	60	**	NY
HECKEL, Frederick, *John*	31	52	58	**	KY
HECKEL, R., *Rudolph*	25	53	59	**	KY
HEEB, J., *James*	38	60	66	**	KY
HEEKS, Joseph, *Jude*	07	38	44	**	NY
HEFFELS, Gerald	81	03	06	07	GER
HEFFNER, George	26	49	55	57	CAN
HEGARTY, Patrick, *Colm*	21	47	53	**	IRE
HEGARTY, William	37	58	64	67	IRE
HEIAR, James	44	66	70	70	IA
HEICK, Aloysius	64	97	99	00	GER
HEIER, Francis	06	29	33	35	ND
HEIER, Peter	95	20	23	26	RUS
HEINTGES (MICHAEL), Peter	12	36	39	40	GER
HEISIG, James	44	65	69	69	MA
HELLEM, Gerard	22	44	50	51	KS
HEMPHILL, Anthony	31	50	56	58	PA
HENKELS, Joseph	01	22	27	28	IA
HENRY, James	31	51	57	59	NY
HENRY, Michael	36	58	63	64	AUS
HEPPELER, Joseph, *Joseph*	68	04	11	**	GER
HERBERGER, Edward	32	52	58	60	NY
HERRERA, Buenaventura E.	54	79	84	85	NIC
HERTEL, Norbert, *Roman*	07	25	31	**	WI
HERTEL, Henry	00	21	26	27	GER
HESKAMP, Charles	27	59	56	58	OH
HESSELFELD, Henry	30	54	58	58	GER
HESSLING, Norbert	40	63	67	67	GER
HILLEBRAND, Francis	88	05	08	09	GER
HILLEBRAND, C., *Wilfrid*	76	03	09	**	GER
HILT, Richard, *Peter*	37	60	66	**	WI
HIRMER, Charles	93	27	31	32	IA
HIRSCHBOEK, Albin	01	29	33	35	IL
HIRSCHMEIER, John	21	46	50	50	GER
HOBER, Raymond	32	52	58	60	PA
HODAPP, Cletus	99	22	26	27	MN
HOEFLER, Alexander	14	43	48	50	IA
HOEFLER, Leonard	18	42	46	47	IA
HOEFLINGER, Joseph	75	02	05	06	GER
HOELKEN, Joseph	87	08	11	11	GER
HOENDEROP, John	70	96	98	99	GER
HOERDEMANN, Ernest	08	29	32	33	GER
HOFBAUER, Edmund, *Agilbert*	07	31	37	**	GER
HOFF, Henry	16	39	43	44	MO

HOFFMAN, Robert	32	52	58	60	PA
HOFFMANN, Maximilian	88	10	13	13	GER
HOFSTEE, Gerard	05	29	35	35	NEB
HOGAN, F., *Anthony*	30	50	56	**	NY
HOGAN, Patrick, *Norbert*	36	57	63	**	PA
HOGAN, William	09	33	38	38	MA
HOGUTH, Aloysius	33	57	60	62	GER
HOLANDA, M. Benedito de	68	93	97	98	BRA
HOLLANDER, James de	25	47	51	51	NEB
HOLMAN, Daniel	60	83	89	**	OH
HORNE, Peter, *Alfonse*	18	47	53	**	GA
HORNEK, John, *Joseph*	17	50	57	57	SLO
HORSFALL, Liam	27	49	34	57	AUS
HORSTMAN, John	51	74	79	79	OH
HOTCHKISS, Lawrence, *André*	37	59	65	**	NY
HOTZE, Alphonse	09	31	35	37	MO
HOTZE, Clement	20	42	46	47	MO
HOTZE, Leo	16	38	42	43	MO
HOWARD, Clarence	07	31	36	37	IRE
HUANG, Joseph	18	57	60	43	SIN
HUBER, Francis	12	33	38	38	OES
HUELSEWISCHE, H., F.	79	98	06	**	GER
HUERTA, Enrique Casteneda	54	82	85	86	MEX
HUESTAEDT, Anton, *Blasius*	59	92	01	**	GER
HUGHES, Francis	21	45	51	52	MA
HUISKAMP, Gerard	19	40	44	44	NEB
HUMEL, Anthony	97	18	21	22	MI
HUMEL, Francis	99	20	23	25	MI
HUNG, John	43	69	73	73	SIN
HUNT, Joseph, *James*	25	46	52	**	PA

HUNTER, Robert	06	28	32	33	IA
HUNTER, William	14	37	41	42	IA
HUSMANN, Francis, *Bernard*	86	22	26	**	IL
HUTCHINS, Michael	49	72	75	75	IA
HUTCHINSON, Raymond	04	27		31	NB
INOUE JUN, Aloisio	60	82	87	88	JPN
IRUDAYARAN, John	61	86	92	93	IND
ISHIKAWA, Ryuzaburo	55	78	83	84	JPN
ITEN, Anton, *Fridolin*	68	94	03	**	GER
JABLONSKI, F., *Stanislaus*	30	50	56	**	NY
JACA, Antonio	63	87	90	91	ANG
JACOBI, Paul	28	47	53	54	WI
JACOBS, Anthony	82	10	13	13	GER
JACOBY, Matthew	05	26	31	32	WI
JAECKELS, Ronald	30	50	56	58	WI
JAMES, Melvin	45	66	72	75	DC
JAMES, Thomas	42	64	69	69	LA
JANKISCH, J., *Euphemius*	78	02	09	**	GER
JANKO, Johann, *Dagobert*	71	01	07	**	CZE
JANS, William	09	30	34	35	NEB
JANSEN, Charles	09	27	33	34	NEB
JANSEN, Joseph	92	19	22	24	IL
JANSER, Peter	78	99	01	02	GER
JARVIS, John	25	46	50	51	GBR
JASCHINSKI, Eckard	52	77	81	83	GER
JAWORSKI, Sylvester	20	43	47	49	IL
JAWORSKY, Anton	21	41	46	46	SLO
JAYME, Cecilio	35	60	65	67	PHI
JEBADU, Alexander	66	89	94	95	IDO
JENKINS, Alan	47	70	73	73	CA

JERONIMO, Jose	37	56	62	64	POR
JESCHKE, Richard	46	70	73	73	IA
JESSING, Ludger	35	63	67	68	GER
JEURGENS, Arnold	84	05	08	09	GER
JILEK, Robert	10	31	36	36	WI
JIMENEZ, Reynaldo	57	78	84	84	PHI
JOBIN, Gerald, *Jeremy*	47	68	77	**	IL
JOERGER, Leo	20	44	50	51	IL
JOHANNING, Edwin, *Albert*	13	36	42	**	MN
JOHNSON, Bernard	26	47	53	54	WI
JOHNSON, Robert	63	86	91	92	MI
JONES, Raymond	37	58	64	67	LA
JONES, Robert	39	59	65	68	MA
JOOREN, Cornelis	27	48	52	52	NEB
JORDAN, Phelim	49	77	81	81	IRE
JOSEPH, Herman, *Thomas*	30	56	62	**	BEL
JOSEPH, Anthony	56	81	86	87	IND
JOSEPH, M. Arul	60	82	88	89	IND
JOSEPH, Ramon	35	57	63	65	PAN
JOYCE, Michael	33	56	62	64	IRE
JOYCE, Thomas	37	57	63	66	PA
JOYCE, Walter	13	44	50	51	NY
JUNG, J., *Ludwinus*	83	03	11	**	GER
JUNGBLUTH, Henry	03	24	29	30	MO
KALAYIL, John	43	66	72	74	IND
KALINAS, John	37	57	63	65	PA
KALINOWSKI, Ryszard	47	70	73	74	POL
KALISZ, Raymond [+80]	27	47	53	54	MI
KALLANCHIRA, Joseph Babu	59	81	86	87	IND
KALWAK, Marek	68	88	96	97	POL

KAMMEYER, Henry	85	09	12	12	GER
KAMP, Francis	20	42	46	47	WI
KANE, William	20	42	46	47	MA
KASUGAI, N., *Bonaventure*	27	53	58	59	JPN
KEBAN, Bungaama Bernard	45	69	77	77	IND
KEBUNG, Konrad	54	78	83	84	IDO
KECK, James	35	56	62	64	IL
KEEFE, Michael	54	77	81	81	IL
KEHL, Balthasar	50	76	82	83	IDO
KEHRER, Harold	36	56	62	65	WI
KEHRER, Joseph	06	34	38	39	GBR
KEILEN, Ernest	15	38	43	43	MI
KELADU, Yoseph	67	89	94	95	IDO
KELCH, Edward, *Gregory*	07	34	40	**	PA
KELLEHER, James	14	35	39	40	IRE
KELLER, Alfred, *Vincent*	00	37	43	**	GER
KELLER, Bernard	28	48	54	55	PA
KELLEY, William	40	62	66	67	MA
KELLY, Austin, *Patrick*	23	50	56	**	IL
KELLY, Daniel, *Francis*	37	58	64	**	MI
KELLY, Arthur	38	68	71	71	WIN
KELLY, Richard	38	60	65	66	IRE
KELLY, Robert	56	81	85	86	IL
KELLY, William	19	43	47	49	PA
KELTY, Charles	15	41	45	46	MA
KEMPEN, Henry van	37	57	61	63	NEB
KEMPER, John	03	23	27	28	GER
KEMPINSKI, Joseph	98	20	24	26	POL
KEREKES, Steven, *Marion*	27	67	68	**	IN
KERKHOFF, L., *Bertrand*	14	34	40	**	WI

KERLIN, George	04	28	32	33	GER
KERSCHEN, G., *Francis*	25	45	51	**	KS
KERSTEN, John	15	36	40	40	NEB
KETTELER, Aloysius	14	36	39	40	GER
KIEFFER, Lawrence, *Thomas*	35	63	69	**	IA
KINDER, Conrad	91	13	21	21	POL
KING, Clifford	88	16	19	20	NY
KINTIBA, Georges	64	88	95	96	ZAI
KIRBY, Jon	45	68	71	71	CAN
KISALA, Robert	57	81	84	85	IL
KIST, John	10	32	38	39	PA
KIST, Robert	05	28	32	32	PA
KLAFFL, John	74	95	98	98	GER
KLASSEN, Winand	30	58	61	63	GER
KLEMENTA, Dieter	33	58	62	62	CZE
KLINE, Michael	61	84	91	92	CA
KLINKHAMMER, Gunther	28	60	65	66	GER
KLOESTERS, Gerard	12	33	36	38	GER
KLOSE, Dietmar	40	63	67	68	GER
KLOSE, Roland	65	83	89	90	GER
KLUNK, Wilbur	15	38	42	43	PA
KNAPPICK, Joseph, *Dominic*	04	30	36	**	PA
KNIGHT, James	36	60	65	66	AUS
KNIGHT, Michael	49	72	78	79	AUS
KNITTER, Paul	39	58	64	66	IL
KNOBLOCH, Arthur	14	36	41	42	FRA
KNOEBEL, Joseph	33	57	61	62	NY
KOCH (COOK), Albert	09	31	34	36	GER
KOCH, Martin, *Silvester*	08	36	42	**	MN
KOCH, Joseph	79	01	04	05	GER

KOEHLER, A., *Gislenus*	86	13	19	**	POL
KOEHLER, Joseph	03	26	30	31	GER
KOELLER, Theodore	95	20	23	25	NEB
KOESTER, Henry	30	52	56	57	GER
KOLATA, R., *Gabriel*	40	62	68	**	WI
KOLK, Raymond	17	40	44	45	IL
KOLKMEIER, Heinrich, *Wiho*	68	99	06	**	GER
KOLNIK, John	16	38	42	43	IL
KOLODZIEJ, Anthony	87	10	13	13	POL
KOLZEM, Karl, *Emil*	66	01	07	**	GER
KONUS, William	15	38	42	43	PA
KORATTIYIL, Thomas	53	74	81	82	IND
KORESSEL, William, *Godfry*	02	23	29	**	IN
KOSAT, Felix	54	79	84	85	IDO
KOSTER, John	18	39	43	44	IA
KOTRBA, Joseph	13	34	38	39	IL
KOWALSKI, Bernard	04	27	31	32	IL
KOWALSKI, Francis	13	37	41	42	IL
KRAEMER, Gustave	35	57	60		CZE
KRAFT, Richard	21	48	50	55	NY
KRAJCI, Anthony	18	40	44	45	IL
KRALIK, Emil	60	91	96	97	SLO
KRANEWITTER, Peter	01	23	28	30	ARG
KRAUS, William	02	23	28	29	IL
KRAUSE, John, *Stanislaus*	92	19	25	**	KY
KRAUZA, Eugeniusz	52	73	77	78	POL
KRBEZ (KRBRCZ) Jo., *William*	67	98	06	**	OES
KREINUS, Anthony, *Pascha*	40	61	67	**	NJ
KREITZ, H. J., *Egilhard*	00	26	32	**	GER
KREITZ, Lothar	38	62	66	68	GER

KRETSCHMER, Albert	20	42	46	47	WI
KREUTZ, Wilhelm	28	52	56	57	GER
KRICK, William, *Richard*	99	27	33	**	MN
KRIEG, John	37	59	65	66	SWI
KRIMM, Joseph	17	39	43	44	KY
KRISTEN, A., *Majella*	69	22	28	**	IL
KROEGER, Hermann, *Domitian*	67	00	06	**	GER
KROEHLING, Aloysius	35	57	62	65	ITA
KRONEMEYER, Francis	88	08	11	11	GER
KROSNICKI, Thomas	38	58	64	66	WI
KRUFT, Henry	95	21	26	27	GER
KUEPERS, James	37	59	62	63	NEB
KUEPPERS, John	09	33	37	37	GER
KUHL, Paul	16	42	46	47	MN
KUHN, Cireneu	59	83	87	87	BRA
KULLA, Josef, *Methodius*	02	29	35	**	POL
KULLU, Rajesh	62	89	93	**	IND
KULUEKE, Heinz	56	81	85	86	GER
KUMORDJI-EDOE, Gabriel	56	80	84	85	GHA
KUNKEL, Raymond	18	40	44	45	IN
KURKOWSKI, Robert, *Ambrose*	99	27	33	**	MN
KUSENBERG, P., *Paulinus*	84	06	12	**	GER
KUTTIKATTUKUNNEL, F.	60	82	87	88	IND
LA BAUVE, John	23	45	50	51	LA
LA CHAPELLE, James	39	57	63	65	TX
LA FORGE, Paul	30	50	56	58	MI
LA PLANTE, Lawrence	39	62	66	67	NY
LA SALLE, Byron	36	56	62	64	IA
LABBÉ, Clifton	40	64	68	89	LA
LABOR, John	15	38	42	43	PA
LAGURA, Ernest	41	63	67	69	PHI
LAKATTA, John	35	54	60	63	PA
LAMMERS, Anton F., *Felix*	16	40	46	**	MN
LAMURI, Francis Bernard	51	74	80	81	IDO
LANDTHALER, M., *Optatus*	89	10	16	**	GER
LANGAN, James	31	58	63	64	IRE
LANGE, Francis de	71	96	98	99	NEB
LANGE, Gerald	36	51	62	64	WI
LANGE, Ronald	41	63	71	71	WI
LANGENKAMP, W., *Berchmans*	22	53	59	**	OH
LANGENKAMP, Arnold	26	46	52	53	OH
LANGENKAMP, August	24	49	55	57	OH
LANKESHAFER, Heinrich	40	63	68	69	GER
LAPCZYNSKI, William	36	57	63	65	NJ
LARISH, Harold, *Bernard*	34	53	59	**	POL
LATUS, Bernard	62	81	86	87	POL
LAUCK, Harold	05	28	32	33	IL
LAUG, Francis	36	59	63	64	GER
LAVIGNE, Yvan	40	62	66	67	CAN
LAVIN, Thomas	13	36	40	41	IL
LAVIS, M., *Simplicius*	62	95	04	**	GER
LE NOUE, Albert, *Cyprian*	07	33	39	**	MN
LE, Paul Vung Van	50	81	84	85	VIE
LEBEAU, Joseph	20	43	47	49	IL
LEBRUN, Donald	31	51	57	59	NH
LEDERMANN, Karl, *Raphael*	37	57	61	**	NY
LEDOUX, Jerome	30	47	49	57	LA
LEE, Charles, *Michael*	39	60	66	**	IN
LEE, Patrick	35	61	65	67	IRE
LEEDIE, Alexander	12	36	40	41	NY

LEFERT, Joseph, *Edward*	00	41	47	**	KS
LEFROIS, Bernard	08	29	33	34	NY
LEHMEIER, Louis	27	60	63	52	GER
LEIBOLD, Thomas	13	43	47	49	OH
LEISRING, Charles	28	51	55	57	OH
LEISRING, Lawrence	97	22	27	28	KY
LEMAIRE, Guy	41	62	66	67	CAN
LENCHAK, Timothy	48	72	75	75	OH
LENGYEL, Matthew, *Paul*	23	46	52	**	HUN
LENNON, Raymond	36	56	62	64	PA
LENZEN, William	03	27	31	32	GER
LEONARD, Gerald	47	77	80	80	CA
LEONES, Felipe	39	61	67	68	PHI
LESAGE, Joseph, *Cletus*	08	31	37	**	IL
LESAGE, Alphonse	04	24	29	30	Il
LESAGE, Emil	99	21	26	26	BEL
LESAGE, Maurice	11	33	37	38	IL
LEUTHNER, Ernst, *Regis*	95	24	30	**	OH
LEWIS, Carlos [+65]	18	43	48	49	PAN
LEWIS, Gerald	24	45	51	52	PAN
LICHTENEGGER, Walter	28	54	58	59	OES
LIEBERT, William	29	49	55	57	KS
LIEBNER, James	53	74	82	85	NJ
LIM KAHLASI, Yohanes	68	91		**	IDO
LINZENBACH, Frederick	04	26	30	31	GER
LOBIANCO, Pascal	21	43	48	50	IA
LOECHTE, Augustine	80	03	06	07	GER
LOGUE, Dennis, *Joseph*	27	50	56	83	PA
LOISKANDL, Helmut	34	55	59	60	OES
LOMMEN, Henry	13	34	38	38	NEB
LOOS, Clement, *Raphael*	36	58	64	**	GER
LORBACH, Hubert	08	32	36	36	GER
LORSE, John	32	56	60	60	GER
LOVASIK, Lawrence	13	33	37	38	PA
LUBADEL, August	91	11	14	14	POL
LUIS, Edward	06	29	33	35	OK
LUIZ, Thomas	37	58	64	65	IND
LUKOVIC, Imre, *Francis*	02	31	37	**	CZE
LUNDERS, Douglas, *Damian*	42	63	69	**	IA
LUNZER, Matthias	16	40	44	45	MN
LUSI, Ujan Zacharias	61	85	91	94	IDO
LUU, Khien Mai John	58	87	91	92	VIE
LUZBETAK, Louis	18	40	44	45	IL
LYNCH, Daniel	36	57	61	63	IRE
LYNCH, John	25	46	49	50	IRE
LYNCH, Thomas	38	59	65	67	NY
LYNK, Frederick	81	02	05	06	GER
LYONS, Richard	01	20	23	26	IL
LYU, Cheng-Hsuan, Joseph	55	83	87	90	TAI
MACHALONIS, Pius	10	30	34	35	PA
MACIOLEK, F., *Simon*	35	57	63	**	MN
MACK, Lawrence	08	39	33	34	OH
MAHON, Francis	10	35	39	40	NJ
MALBOG, Renato	62	84	89	89	PHI
MALIN, Arthur	02	26	30	31	WI
MALIN, Charles	05	31	35	37	WI
MALLONEE, Robert	36	62	66	67	OH
MALONEY, Peter	25	49	52	53	IRE
MAMAWAL, Benjamin	33	52	56	58	PHI
MANION, Arthur	01	29	33	35	NY

MANNING, Michael	40	63	68	69	IN
MANSFIELD, Francis	36	55	59	61	IRE
MARCINEK, Aug., *Priscillian*	89	12	19	**	POL
MARCOLONGO, Francis	32	51	57	59	PA
MARINO, Anthony, *Victor*	29	59	65	**	NJ
MARKERT, Francis	84	06	08	10	GER
MARKS, Leon	27	47	53	54	WI
MARKS, Richard	01	22	27	28	GER
MARTENS, Cornelis	07	29	33	34	NEB
MARTIN, Leander	05	35	40	41	LA
MARTIN, Theodore	06	27	31	32	PA
MARTINS, Joao Oscar	44	67	73	74	BRA
MARUSA, Henry	06	28	32	33	OH
MARZEC, Tadeusz	54	77	81	82	POL
MASTERS, Andrew	09	29	33	34	GER
MATHIAS, Clement	11	33	37	38	GER
MAURER, Vincent, *Melchior*	32	52	58	**	GER
MAUSS, Robert, *Vincent*	48	69	74	**	IA
MAY, Anthony	02	26	30	31	NY
MAYER, David	38	58	64	66	MO
McCABE, Gregory	51	53	59	61	MN
McCARTHY, Gerard	53	84	89	89	IRE
McCAUSLAND, Mark	18	42	46	47	GBR
McCLURE, Hugo	35	59	63	65	IRE
McCORMACK, Robert	34	54	60	62	MA
McCRUDDEN, James	32	74	77	77	CA
McDERMOTT, James	31	52	58	60	MA
McDERMOTT, Joseph	25	45	51	52	IA
McDONOUGH, John	13	34	38	39	MA
McDONOUGH, Terrence	35	54	60	62	MA
McGEE, Harry	24	44	50	51	IA
McGERVEY, Richard	32	52	58	60	PA
McGRAW, Randall	50	72	79	79	IA
McGUINN, Edward	28	47	53	54	NY
McGURK, Terrence	32	52	58	60	NY
McHALE, Patrick	35	54	58	60	IRE
McHENRY, John	29	48	54	55	PA
McHUGH, Peter	40	59	64	66	GBR
McKILLIP, Dennis	21	42	46	47	WI
McKILLIP, John	23	43	48	50	WI
McLAUCHLIN, Brian	62	85	91	**	CA
McMACKIN, Thomas	35	55	61	63	NJ
McMAHON, Arnold	39	58	62	64	GBR
McMAHON, Vincent	29	49	55	57	MA
McNULTY, Matthew	11	69	74	**	IRE
McPAKE, Michael	32	52	56	58	GBR
McPARLAND, J., *Rodriguez*	37	57	63	**	NY
McSHERRY, John	33	53	59	61	NY
McVINNEY, Paul	24	43	49	50	MA
MEGAN, Thomas	99	20	23	26	IA
MELCHER, Arthur	98	22	27	28	POL
MELLERT, Gerhard Alfred	38	61	64	65	GER
MENGUTO, Emmanuel	55	76	81	81	PHI
MERTES, Robert	36	57	63	78	IL
MERTZ, James	10	30	34	36	WV
METZGER, Edward, *David*	38	59	65	**	IL
MEYER, Aloysius, *Clement*	14	34	40	**	WI
MEYER, Joseph, *Wendelin*	57	90	99	**	GER
MEYER, Clement	19	42	46	47	WI
MEYER, Cosmas	19	41	45	47	WI

MICH, Tadeusz	54	77	80	81	POL
MICHALEK, Adam	59	80	84	85	POL
MICHEL, Charles	82	04	07	08	GER
MICHOWSKI, Edward	49	69	73	74	POL
MIDOR, Adam	64	85	90	91	POL
MIHALIC, Francis	16	39	43	44	PA
MILANDER, Joseph	38	58	64	66	PA
MILDNER, Alfons	11	34	37	38	GER
MILLARD, Daryl	46	66	71	72	AUS
MILLENDORF, L., *Lawrence*	81	23	29	**	GER
MILLER, Henry	22	42	48	**	MD
MILLER, P., *Christoph*	36	60	66	**	MN
MILLER, James	21	42	46	47	GBR
MILLER, Joseph	39	59	65	68	IL
MILLER, Walter	40	62	68	69	IL
MIRSEL, Robert	63	84	89	90	IDO
MISIK, Edward	14	36	40	41	WI
MISLANG, Wilfredo	47	67	73	73	PHI
MOELLER, Charles, *Alfred*	77	97	06	**	GER
MOELLER, K., *Alfridus*	77	94	97	06	GER
MOENSTER, John	87	11	14	14	GER
MOODY, Michael	32	55	61	64	AL
MORAN, Brendan	39	63	68	69	IRE
MORGAN, John	41	63	67	68	IA
MORGAN, William	19	79	82	**	MD
MORILL, Richard	52	75	81	**	IL
MORIN, Hilarion	05	31	35	37	CAN
MORMAN, Edmund	09	31	35	37	OH
MORMAN, Wilbert	19	41	45	46	OH
MORRIS, Thomas	28	50	53	54	GBR
MORRISON, Michael	27	40	53	54	AUS
MORTON, Xavier, *Lawrence*	14	39	45	**	LA
MUA, Andreas	49	72	79	79	IDO
MUELLER, John, *Kilian*	72	25	31	**	GER
MUELLER, H., *Amalbertus*	78	99	04	**	GER
MUELLER, Hermann	20	47	51	51	GER
MUELLER, Manfred	33	62	65	56	OES
MUELLER, Thomas	32	53	59	61	WI
MUELLER, Wilhelm	36	57	61	62	GER
MULLALEY, James	13	35	39	40	IL
MULLALLY, Thomas	42	66	70	70	MI
MULLEN, James, *John*	36	56	62	**	PA
MULRENAN, Donald	32	52	58	60	MA
MUNCADA, Felipe	55	76	82	82	PHI
MURAWSKI, Casimir	14	36	40	41	PA
MURNANE, Theodore	30	51	57	58	NY
MURPHY, J., *Edmund*	31	53	59	**	MA
MURPHY, Brendan	39	63	73	73	IRE
MURPHY, Joseph	95	16	21	21	IL
MURPHY, Michael	36	64	68	69	IRE
MURPHY, Patrick	27	48	52	53	AUS
MURRIN, Donald	33	52	58	60	PA
MUSIAL, Jan	51	75	76	77	POL
MUSINSKY, John	18	39	43	44	PA
MUTTER, Henry	14	38	42	42	NEB
MYERS, Robert	17	43	47	49	IL
MYVETT, Hartfield Manuel	31	54	60	62	HON
NADICKSBERND, Elmer	37	56	62	64	KY
NADOLNY, Paul	54	84	88	89	WI
NAKANOSE, Shigeyuki	52	75	80	80	JPN

NAU, Louis	02	22	27	28	GER
NAWROT, Piotr	55	76	80	81	POL
NEMER, Lawrence	30	52	58	60	IL
NEMETH, Anthony	28	46	53	53	HUN
NEUHAUS, Francis	83	05	09	09	GER
NEWTON, Dennis	52	77	83	**	IA
NGAWAY MUTONDO, Omer	58	84	90	91	ZAI
NGUYEN, Joseph Trong	59	84	89	91	VIE
NGUYEN, Peter Sam	60	82	85	86	VIE
NGUYEN, Thanh Van	65	90	96	97	VIE
NGUYEN, Trung Dung	68	92	98		VIE
NGUYEN, Van Hiep	65	93	98		VIE
NICASIO, Lino	49	68	74	74	PHI
NIEHUSER, Paul	98	23	28	29	MN
NIESSEN, John	24	45	51	51	NEB
NIEZYCHOWSKI, Maciej	68	88	96	96	POL
NOGA, Henryk	68	90	95	96	POL
NOMO, Edmund	39	72	75	76	GHA
NOONAN, David	59	82	88	**	IA
NOORDERMEER, Henry	38	58	62	63	NEB
NOREK, Peter	15	39	43	44	IL
NORTON, Edward	19	40	44	45	MA
NOSER, Adolph [+47-66]	00	22	25	25	IL
NOSS, James	06	32	36	36	GER
NOSSEL, Francis	09	32	35	37	GER
NOWAK, Boguslaw	62	82	91	92	POL
NOWICKI, Chester	19	41	45	46	IL
NUBUASAH, Franklyn	49	76	79	80	GHA
NUNNENMACHER, Eugene	37	60	65	65	GER
NUTTMAN, J., Marian	14	34	40	**	CAN

NYTES, J., Aloysius	30	59	65	**	WI
O'DOHERTY, Gerard	38	70	74	74	IRE
O'CONNELL, Thomas	00	30	34	36	IRE
O'CONNOR, Donald	37	60	63	64	IL
O'CONNOR, James	31	51	57	58	IL
O'CONNOR, Oliver	37	57	62	64	IRE
OEHLER, Edgar	07	29	33	35	OH
OEHLERER, Anton	72	00	03	03	GER
OESER, Albert, Henry	06	31	37	**	GER
OFORI, Patrick	41	65	70	70	GHA
OHLINGER, Vincent	39	62	77	68	IA
OLAH, Albert	26	61	65	67	HUN
OLEA, Mario Roberto	55	79	87	87	ARG
O'LEARY, Malcolm	30	53	59	61	MS
O'LEARY, Robert	11	35	39	40	IL
OLESZCZAK, Jan	70	91	97	98	POL
OLIVER, William	28	50	56	58	LA
OLIVIER, Leonard [+88]	23	44	50	51	LA
O'MAHONY, John	39	61	65	68	IRE
OMMERBORN, Juergen	43	65	69	69	GER
O'NEILL, Michael	35	56	60	63	IRE
OPPENBERG, Henry	05	27	30	31	GER
OPRANDI, Anibal Luis	37	58	62	64	ARG
O'REGAN, Patrick	33	63	68	69	IRE
O'REILLY, Patrick, Joseph	15	44	50	**	IRE
O'REILLY, Brendan	27	49	52	53	IRE
O'REILLY, Michael	34	75	79	79	GBR
O'REILLY, Peter	25	48	53	54	AUS
ORIANS, Urban J., Lucian	07	38	44	**	OH
OROLIN, Joseph	23	44	49	49	CZE

OROS, Stephen, *Joachim*	12	34	40	**	CT
OSTROWSKI, Walter	37	57	63	65	PA
O'SULLIVAN, John	25	45	48	50	IRE
OSWALD, Peter	88	10	13	13	GER
O'TOOLE, John	18	39	43	44	MA
O'TOOLE, Kevin	28	50	53	54	GBR
OUBRE, John	39	59	65	67	LA
OUDENHOVEN, John van	58	98	00	01	GER
PA, Patrisius	59	82	87	88	IDO
PACANO, Thomas	09	32	36	38	PHI
PACHE, Aloysius	03	26	30	32	POL
PADLO, John	18	41	45	46	IL
PADOVANI, Martin	31	52	58	60	OH
PALANG, Mansueto	50	71	77	77	PHI
PALLAN, Berly	40	61	67	67	IND
PANIKULAM ITTOOP, George	45	68	73	75	IND
PARDON, Marek Jozef	64	85	90	91	POL
PARDY, Steven, *Lawrence*	36	58	64	**	IA
PARTSCH, John	05	31	35	37	GER
PASCOTTO, Giuseppe	42	59	65	67	ITA
PASHIA, Charles, *Gerard*	24	44	50	**	MO
PASTUSZCZAK, Jan	63	83	89	90	POL
PATIK, Anthony	14	37	41	42	IA
PATZELT, Hermann	85	06	09	10	GER
PAULSEN, Alois	13	35	38	39	GER
PAUNDER, Peter Paul	74	04	07	08	POL
PAWLICKI, James	46	69	73	73	MI
PAWLIK, Jacek	52	73	77	78	POL
PAWLOWSKI, Ladislaus	92	19	22	24	OH
PEGON, Antonio	50	72	77	77	PHI

PEIL, John	56	88	01	90	GER
PEKLO, Edward	42	64	68	69	NB
PELLEGRIN, Carlos	38	78	83	85	CHI
PERRY, Harold [+65]	16	38	43	44	LA
PERRY, James	35	58	60		GBR
PETER, Aloysius, *Amabalis*	82	01	08	**	POL
PETERS, William	37	58	62	63	NEB
PFEMETER, John	19	45	46		HUN
PHAM, Vincent Chau Minh	55	90	94	95	VIE
PHAM, Xuan Hien	56	93	98		VIE
PHELAN, Michael	32	51	54	56	IRE
PIECHOTA, Teodor	52	73	77	78	POL
PIERK, George	38	58	61	71	GER
PIMENTA, Jose	56	76	82	83	POR
PINHEIRO, Geraldo	33	51	57	58	BRA
PINS, Herbert	44	68	71	71	IA
PINTO, Charles	46	68	71	71	IND
PIOTROWSKI, Joseph, *Kostka*	16	36	42	**	MI
PITO KARANGORA, Philipus	65	88	94	95	IDO
PIWOWARCZYK, Dariusz	58	84	89	90	POL
PIZARRO, Gregory	23	45	50	50	PHI
PLUTZ, Stanley	26	46	52	53	WI
POETZ, Lawrence	17	39	43	44	IL
POLLOCK, Paul, *Radbertus*	93	12	20	**	POL
POOL, Jefferson	57	85	90	92	OH
POPP, Herman	12	34	39	39	WI
POPP, William	21	43	47	49	WI
POSCH, Frederick, *Longinus*	90	23	29	**	OES
POSJENA, Hubert	10	32	35	37	CZE
POTTS, Thomas	33	53	59	61	MO

POULIOT, Paul, *Celestine*	10	32	38	**	VT
POWELL, Elmer	19	48	54	55	KS
POWER, Francis	50	69	73	73	IRE
PRATT, Richard	17	43	47	49	MD
PRIELER, Joseph	19	40	49	49	OES
PRINCE, Henry	06	20	27	32	GER
PRINZ, William	51	72	76	**	WI
PRZYBYLSKI, Jan, *Archangel*	81	96	12	**	POL
PUGAT, Gaudencio	58	79	85	85	PHI
PUNG, Robert	16	39	43	44	MI
PUTHUMANA, Joseph	30	57	63	63	IND
PYE, Michael	42	67	67	68	GBR
PYTEL, Alexander	46	69	73	74	POL
QUETCHENBACH, Raymond	29	49	55	57	NY
QUITER, Daniel, *Fabian*	77	98	06	**	GER
RAAS, Bernard	38	60	64	65	SWI
RABE, Gerald	11	31	35	37	NY
RAEMARE, Longginus	62	85	91	92	IDO
RAHA, Andrew	07	30	34	36	OH
RAKER, John, *Gerard*	44	64	70	**	PA
RAMOS, Ponciano	46	81	84	85	PHI
RAPPERS, Gerard	77	03	06	07	GER
RASCHKE, Richard	36	55	61	63	WI
RASTALL, Robert, *Mark*	28	51	57	**	WI
RAUSCH, Dennis	52	74	80	80	MT
REBELLO, Anthony	50	69	71	76	KEN
RECKAMP, Victor, *Charles*	05	29	35	**	MO
RECKAMP, William	40	62	66	67	IL
REED, Kenneth	26	46	52	53	IN
REICHELT, Frederick	75	00	02	03	POL

REINELT, Charles	00	21	26	27	POL
REINHARDT, Eugene	35	59	63	64	GER
REISSMANN, August	75	01	04	05	GER
REITER, Johann, *Gerard*	94	17	23	**	HUN
RELLER, Wilfred	39	62	66	67	MO
REMPE, Heinrich, *Placidus*	61	91	01	**	GER
RENTKO, Andrew	20	43	47	49	PA
RESCH, Alexander, *Pius*	05	25	31	**	OES
REUBER, Anthony, *John*	89	22	28	**	IN
REYES, Alfredo	31	53	58	58	PHI
RIBEIRO, Lucio	37	57	63	66	BRA
RICHARD, James	29	49	55	57	NH
RICHARD, Walter	38	58	64	67	MA
RICHARZ, Herman	67	97	99	00	GER
RICHARZ, Stephen	74	98	00	01	GER
RIEBE, Gary	46	69	71	71	CA
RIEMER, Robert	33	52	58	60	IL
RIGNEY, Harold	00	24	29	30	IL
RISSE, Claire	18	42	46	47	IA
RISSE, James	33	53	59	61	IA
RISSE, Roger	28	47	53	54	IA
ROBINSON, Fisher	29	50	56	58	LA
ROCHFORD, Eugene	47	71	74	74	MI
RÖDLACH, Alexander	64	84	89	90	OES
RODNEY, John	31	52	58	60	IL
RODRIGUEZ, Alois	35	54	58	60	CHI
RODRIGUEZ, Luis Manuel	35	54	59	59	CHI
ROEHRHOFF, Matthias	70	02	05	06	GER
ROESSLEIN, Charles	10	34	36	36	MO
ROESSMANN, George	37	64	68	69	GER

ROINA, Ralph (Randolph)	00	29	33	35	CT
ROSARIO, Jesus del	36	59	64	65	PHI
ROSKO, Ladislaus	24	46	52	52	HUN
ROSS, William	95	17	20	22	NY
ROUSSEVE, Maurice	06	28	33	34	LA
RUANE, Martin, *Marcus*	88	25	31	**	IRE
RUANE, Patrick	28	57	62	63	IRE
RUBIT, Francis, *Philip*	36	59	65	**	LA
RUDOLPH, Frederick	28	47	53	54	PA
RUFFING, Norman	36	55	61	63	OH
RUITER, Ivo	23	43	48	50	WI
RUIZ, Miguell Antonio	69	89	94	95	ARG
RULLODA, Rafael	02	30	34	36	PHI
RUPPRECHT, R., George	89	25	31	**	WI
RUSHMAN, Lloyd	05	28	32	33	WI
RUSSELL, Charles	27	52	57	60	AUS
RYAN, James, *Walter*	12	38	44	**	PA
SAFFER, Edward	27	46	51	52	CHI
SAGAN, John, *Vincent*	08	27	35	**	POL
SAIKO, William	16	37	41	42	MN
SALOIS, Alfred, *Victor*	08	27	35	**	MI
SAMMON, Lawrence	37	58	64	66	MN
SANDERS, Raymond	14	40	44	45	IA
SANDFORTH, B., *Polycarp*	75	94	03	**	GER
SANDHAAS, Joseph	07	29	33	35	IL
SAUERBORN, Francis	04	27	31	32	GER
SCANLON, Charles	27	47	53	54	OH
SCANLON, Thomas	35	57	63	65	NY
SCHAFFHAUSER, Emil	07	29	34		IL
SCHAFFHAUSER, Louis	05	26	30	31	IL

SCHAPS, William	11	33	36	38	GER
SCHAUL, Charles	38	58	64	66	IA
SCHENKER, Arthur	07	30	34	36	IA
SCHERGER, Bernard, *Hilary*	42	67	73	**	OH
SCHERZINGER, Eugene	27	47	53	54	NY
SCHIE, John van	30	52	56	57	NEB
SCHIEL, W., *Marius*	13	37	43	**	IA
SCHILITZ, Jan	43	64	69	70	POL
SCHILLERS, Joseph, *Vitus*	70	91	01	**	GER
SCHMID, Alois, *Meinrad*	85	22	28	**	SWI
SCHMID, Maximilian, *Conrad*	11	36	42	**	GER
SCHMIDT, Paul	53	76	81	81	CA
SCHMITT, George	04	26	31	31	MI
SCHMITT, James	38	57	63	64	IL
SCHMITZ, Bernard, *Martin*	95	23	29	**	MO
SCHMITZ, Bartley	18	39	43	44	MT
SCHMITZ, Eugene	38	59	65	67	IL
SCHMUELLING, George	01	23	28	29	GER
SCHNEIDER, Charles	18	41	45	46	NY
SCHNEIDER, Cosmos	86	10	13	13	GER
SCHNEIDER, Theodore	90	12	15	15	POL
SCHNIEDERS, Hermann J.	39	61	66	66	GER
SCHNYDER, Raynard	33	53	59	61	LA
SCHODERBEK, Charles	20	42	46	47	PA
SCHOENIG, Henry	12	34	38	38	GER
SCHOLL, Ignatius	06	23	28	29	GER
SCHOUTEN, David	24	45	51	52	IL
SCHOUTEN, Francis	29	48	54	55	IL
SCHRAMM, Mark	49	72	75	75	IA
SCHREIBER, Gerard	11	33	38	38	GER

SCHREIN, Frederick, *Philip*	07	57	63	**	OH
SCHROEDER, Gerald, *Cyril*	13	33	39	**	CAN
SCHROEDER, Roger	51	72	79	79	OH
SCHUBBE, George	28	46	51	52	CHI
SCHUBERT, John	33	57	60	62	GBR
SCHULER, Norbert	99	20	23	26	NJ
SCHULER, Stephen	52	76	79	79	KS
SCHULTE, Siegfried	34	57	61	61	GER
SCHULTZ, Georg, *Tobias*	06	40	46	**	PA
SCHUMACHER, Henry	23	46	51	52	OH
SCHWAGER, F.	76	96	98	99	GER
SCHWALLIE, Nicholas	88	19	22	24	KY
SCHWARK, Marian	48	68	74	75	POL
SCHWETNER, Aug., *Andrew*	89	09	15	**	IL
SCOTT, Joseph Patrick	40	71	74	75	GBR
SCOTT, Paul	39	64	70	70	AUS
SEEWALD, Carl	41	63	67	68	PA
SEGOVIA, Pedro	41	63	70	70	PAR
SEIDEL, Francis	05	27	31	32	POL
SEIFERT, William	39	64	66	67	PA
SEIGEL, Michael	47	66	71	72	AUS
SELAND, John	38	62	67	68	PA
SELONG, Gabriel	51	55	61	63	BRA
SENG, Benedict, *Anthony*	37	63	69	**	AUS
SENGSON, Nicholas	53	77	80	80	PHI
SERMON, Wilhelm	10	31	35	35	GER
SERRAO, John	54	80	85	86	ND
SERRAO, Rock	51	75	81	82	IND
SHADEG, Norbert	21	43	47	49	MN
SHADEG, Werner	19	40	44	45	MN

SHAPKER, Clement	07	28	32	33	IN
SHAW, Douglas	49	78	80	83	PAN
SHEA, William	31	58	62	64	MA
SHEERIN, John	23	48	54	55	PA
SHELLY, Otto	14	37	40	42	IN
SHENDILL, Joseph	93	13	16	16	POL
SHERIDAN, Patrick	40	64	68	69	IRE
SHEVLIN, John	35	54	58	60	GBR
SHIGO, Francis	32	52	56	60	PA
SHUREK, Paul	92	12	20	20	POL
SHUSTER, John	51	74	79	79	PA
SIEBER, Sylvester	08	29	33	35	PA
SILVA, Jose	57	76	83	84	POR
SILVER, Lawrence	36	56	62	64	NB
SILVESTER, Edward, *Peter*	27	61	67	78	NJ
SIMON, Joseph	32	53	59	61	LA
SIMON, Peter	30	52	56	58	ARG
SIMONS, G., *Malachy*	96	27	33	**	NJ
SIMONS, Derek	37	66	70	70	GBR
SINATRA, Charles	39	59	65	67	PA
SINGLETON, Hubert	26	46	52	53	LA
SIROVIC, Francis	20	41	46	46	CZE
SKERRY, Donald	35	54	60	62	MA
SKERRY, James	28	47	53	54	MA
SKORUPKA, Joseph	17	42	46	47	NJ
SKWARA, Maximilian	07	30	34	35	POL
SKWERES, Dieter Edward	38	61	65	66	GER
SLATTERY, D., *De Porres*	41	63	73	**	NY
SLATTERY, David	33	53	59	61	WI
SMITH, Bede	42	64	69	69	MO

SMITH, Charles	59	82	87	88	IL
SMITH, Chester	59	82	87	88	IL
SMITH, Cyril	31	55	61	63	IL
SMITH, Joseph	02	24	27	30	IL
SMITH, Vincent	94	28	33	34	KY
SMITS, Peter	16	37	41	41	NEB
SMUTNY, G., *Corsinus*	05	30	36	**	CZE
SOBESKI, Donald	34	54	60	62	IL
SOKOLOWSKI, Stanislaus	58	79	83	84	POL
SOLDYGA, Anthony	27	47	53	54	POL
SOSU, Gabriel	51	80	85	86	GHA
SPECHT, Charles	32	55	58	60	GER
SPERL, Sebastian	33	56	60	61	GER
SPITKO, Michael, *Cornelius*	04	33	39	**	SLO
SPITZER, F., *Alphonsus*	76	04	10	**	GER
SPITZLEY, Bernard	54	75	81	**	MI
SPRENGER, Arnold	29	54	58	58	GER
ST. JOHN, Norman	33	54	60	62	NY
ST. PIERRE, Albert	14	42	46	47	NY
STAEBELL, Vincent	17	39	43	44	IA
STAPPEN, Henry van der	21	41	45	45	NEB
STARICEK, Andrew	13	33	39	41	PA
STAUB, Augustine	08	32	36	36	GER
STEFFEN, Arnold	29	49	55	57	IA
STEGMAN, Richard	34	55	61	63	KY
STEIB, Terry James [+83]	40	59	65	67	LA
STEIN, Joseph	82	08	11	11	GER
STEINHAUER, Julius	79	07	10	10	GER
STEINHAUSER, Wm., *Stephan*	01	24	30	**	MO
STENZ, George	69	91	09	93	GER

STEPHAN, George	06	29	33	35	NY
STEVKO, Victor	27	49	55	57	SLO
STIEG, Gerard	91	14	17	17	GER
STIER, Joseph	11	32	36	38	KY
STILLER, Joseph, *Homobonus*	66	94	03	**	CZE
STILLER, Robert	28	48	54	55	PA
STOCKER, S., *Nicolaus*	99	22	28	**	SWI
STOECKE, William	77	04	07	08	GER
STOESSEL, John	36	56	62	64	PA
STOLL, Eugene	04	24	29	30	OH
STOLL, Peter	96	22	27	28	IA
STRAWN, Nicholas	34	54	60	62	IA
STREIT, David	41	63	68	69	IL
STREVELER, Thomas	41	63	70	70	WI
STRIEWE, Hermann	77	99	02	03	GER
STRIKE, Donald	31	52	58	60	PA
STUCKART, Robert	95	20	23	26	IA
STUDENY, Robert	06	29	33	34	PA
SUCHARSKI, Michael	54	78	83	83	NY
SWIFT, William, *Thaddeus*	85	31	37	**	IA
SWIFT, Francis	15	39	43	44	IA
SWIFT, John, *Matthew*	15	38	44	75	MN
SZIPPL, Richard	51	76	80	81	OH
SZMUTKO, Stephen	17	39	43	44	NJ
SZUKALSKI, John	67	90	96	97	WI
SZYMKOWIAK, James	38	58	64	66	WI
SZYMLEKF, W., *Lawrence*	66	27	33	**	POL
SZYMLONIK, Francis, *Savio*	39	61	67	**	IL
SZYPULA, Wojciech	69	89	98		POL
TINAJERO, Francisco	59	82	88	88	CA

TAGUINOD, Delfinus	11	35	38	38	PHI
TAGURA, Pablito	62	82	88	88	PHI
TANNER, Mark, *Paul*	81	07	13	**	HUN
TAPPHORN, H., *Nicodemus*	70	00	08	**	GER
TECSON, Noel	56	77	83	**	HI
TENNANT, Edward	38	56	62	64	MA
TENNANT, Philip	40	63	67	68	MA
TENOEVER, Joseph	94	21	22	22	OH
TERENDY, Jan, *Aloysius*	14	35	41	**	CZE
TERRENAL, Quintin	21	41	45	46	PHI
TETZLAFF, Francis	83	07	10	10	GER
TEVI-BENISSAN, Pierre A.	63	91	96	97	TOG
THEIS, David	37	56	62	65	WI
THEIS, Gerald	32	52	58	60	IL
THEOBALD, Vincent	19	43	47	49	IA
THEODOR, Peter	11	35	38	39	GER
THERIAULT, Francis	28	48	54	55	MA
THERUVAPUZHA, George	53	75	82	83	IND
THIBEAU, Richard	28	49	55	57	NY
THILGES, Nichol., *Hilarion*	00	27	33	**	LUX
THILGES, John	92	21	26	27	LUX
THIRUKUDUMBAM, Xavier	58	81	86	87	IND
THORNE, Venantius (Vance)	21	46	52	53	NC
THORNTON, Lawrence	18	47	53	54	MD
THUNICH, Paul	00	22	28	29	GER
THYKEN, Ralph	99	20	24	25	WI
TIAM, Vincente	53	74	80	80	PHI
TIEN, Thomas [+39-46]	90	31	34	18	SIN
TIERNEY, N., *Theophane*	28	48	54	**	NY
TILL, Wayne, *Denis*	33	54	60	**	IA
TIMP, Frederick	45	68	71	71	MN
TOEPFER, Bernard	10	32	36	38	GER
TOOHEY, James	34	56	61	63	AUS
TOPF, Gustus, *John*	01	37	43	**	IA
TOPOL, Andrew	13	35	38	39	SLO
TRA, John	19	40	44	44	NEB
TRAN, Anthony Luc Nghi	62	90	95	96	VIE
TRAN, John Hue Dinh	62	90	95	96	VIE
TRAN, Joseph Huynh	63	87	92	93	VIE
TRAN, Joseph Thang Minh	62	85	90	91	VIE
TRAN, Thanh Tam	56	93	97	98	VIE
TRUBLOWSKI, Albin	13	39	43	44	MA
TRYBUS, Norb., *Bonaventure*	14	39	45	**	MI
TUCKER, Francis	53	83	88	89	NY
TUGADI, John	57	32	36	38	PHI
TULLY, Robert	40	62	66	67	FL
TUMAWU, John Kwame	63	89	94	94	GHA
TUOHY, Edward	29	52	56	58	NY
TURBEK, Alois	11	35	39	40	NY
TURKALJ, Michael, *Camillus*	07	34	40	**	YUG
UFER, Hermann, *Liborius*	77	95	04	**	GER
UHING, T., *Thomas*	37	58	64	**	NB
UMBRAS, Thomas	53	76	81	81	MI
URBAN, Joseph, *Donald*	36	57	63	**	LA
URODA, Stanley	48	71	74	74	MI
VALENTINE, John	19	51	54	55	GBR
VALOIS, Kenneth, *Hubert*	36	66	73	**	IL
VANDEN BERGH, R., *Lambert*	38	61	67	**	WI
VANDEN BERGH, G., *Arnold*	25	50	56	75	WI
VANDERSTAPPEN, Harrie	21	41	45	45	NEB

VARGAS, Eric	48	72	75	75	NY
VARGO, Edward	35	55	61	63	OH
VEGA, Miguel	57	80	84	85	TX
VEGA, Francis	48	73	76	76	PHI
VENZO, Mariano	40	59	65	68	ITA
VILLANUEVA, Augustine	47	74	76	76	PHI
VILLAO, Roberto	59	83	92	93	ECU
VILLENA, Peter	58	79	86	**	PHI
VO, Peter De Ta	50	83	86	87	VIE
VOELLMECKE, M., *Benedict*	95	24	30	**	IA
VOGEL, Gerhard	36	59	64	65	FRA
VOGELGESANG, John	15	37	41	42	MN
VOLK, William, *Barnabas*	37	58	64	**	GER
VORWERK, James	43	64	69	69	IA
VOS, John	01	26	30	31	GER
VU, Joseph Tri Van	53	81	84	85	VIE
VU. Joseph Tri Van	53	81	84	85	VIE
VYATHAPPAN, James	49	71	78	79	IND
WACKER, John, *Antonius*	84	17	23	**	MI
WADE, Francis	92	29	34	34	MD
WADESON, John	42	64	69	69	AUS
WAGNER, John, *Alphonsus*	98	21	27	88	OES
WAGNER, Rudolph, *Jerome*	89	21	27	**	IL
WAGNER, Lawrence	17	39	43	44	PA
WAGNER, Wilbert	12	36	39	40	PA
WAHL, Theo., *Stillfried*	09	31	37	**	GER
WAICHES, Vincent.	19	41	45	46	IL
WALACHY, Joseph	17	38	42	43	PA
WALCOT, Kevin	33	54	58	60	GBR
WALD, Edward	22	43	48	50	ND
WALD, John	15	38	42	43	ND
WALDMANN, Anthony, *Hyacinth*	04	37	43	**	RUS
WALKER, Brian	56	80	85	86	IL
WALL, Augustine John	60	87	88	91	NY
WALLER, Hubert	37	58	61	63	GER
WALSH, J., *Jeremiah*	41	61	67	**	IL
WALSH, Lawrence	06	29	33	35	IL
WARGACKI, Stanislaw	52	76	79	80	POL
WARWICK, Andrew	00	21	26	27	OH
WASHINGTON, Curtis	17	43	48	49	FL
WAWRZONEK, Jerzy	41	62	68	70	POL
WEBB, Louis, *Vincent*	08	37	43	**	OH
WEBER, Charles	36	59	62	64	GER
WEBER, Clarence	98	28	32	33	IN
WEBER, Mark	54	77	82	82	IA
WECKENBROCK, Hermann	47	69	72	72	GER
WEGO, Benignus	67	89	94	95	IDO
WEHRLE, Francis	08	28	33	34	IL
WEIGEL, Siegfried	34	62	66	67	GER
WEIGL, John	34	55	58	60	GER
WEINDL, Rupert	91	17	20	22	GER
WEISENBERGER, Raymond	12	34	38	39	WI
WEISER, Philip, *Philip*	71	09	15	**	GER
WEITZ, Joseph, *Crispian*	84	23	29	**	GER
WELLING, Louis	16	37	41	42	NB
WELLS, Orion (Francis?)	06	31	36	37	MO
WENDEL, James	81	01	05	06	GER
WENG, Leo	12	33	37	37	GBR
WENRICK, Patrick	53	76	82	82	PA
WEREZ, John	06	30	34	35	HUN

WESTERMANN, Hermann [+51]	05	27	31	32	GER
WEYLAND, Jacob, *Alphonsus*	86	17	23	**	GER
WEYLAND, Peter	95	16	19	21	IA
WHANN, Joseph	18	57	60	43	SIN
WHEATLEY, Patrick	32	52	58	60	NY
WHITE, Wilbert	32	53	59	61	LA
WIDERA, John	82	07	10	10	POL
WIESEN, Hilbert	19	41	45	46	NB
WIJTTEN, Henry	36	58	62	63	NEB
WILDENBURG, Peter	15	37	41	41	NEB
WILKINS, James	48	71	75	88	AUS
WILLCOCK, Wilfred	19	42	47	50	GBR
WILLIAMS, William	08	29	33	34	NEB
WILLIAMS, B., *Conrad*	16	37	43	**	VA
WILLIAMS, Dennis	48	69	78	**	NY
WILLIAMS, James	36	57	63	65	PA
WILLIAMS, Maxine	11	35	40	41	MS
WILSON, George	09	35	40	41	NY
WILTGEN, Ralph	21	43	48	50	IL
WINDOLPH, Charles	96	21	26	27	GER
WINTERS, Arthur	16	39	44	45	NJ
WINTERS, Richard	11	35	40	41	NJ
WIRTH, Edwin, *Urban*	11	44	50	**	WI
WISSINK, J., *Raymond*	93	33	39	**	WI
WITTWER, Dominic	98	20	25	26	POL
WOJNIAK, Edward	09	31	35	37	IL
WOLF, Charles	73	98	00	01	GBR
WOLFF, B., *Thomas*	31	53	59	**	NY
WOLFF, Richard	47	70	73	73	OH

WOLODKO, Miroslaw	65	86	94		POL
WONG, Justin	35	64	68	69	PAN
WOODS, Leo (Royal?)	07	33	38	39	IN
WROCKLAGE, Bernard	14	38	42	43	MI
WUELLNER, William	05	28	32	33	GER
WYNN, John	36	57	63	65	FL
YESCAS, Higino	57	82	86	87	MEX
YOCHIM, Michael	42	64	69	69	PA
YUNCK, B., *Daniel*	37	60	66	**	WI
ZABRANSKY, James	50	74	82	**	IL
ZALIKOWSKI, R., *Timothy*	39	61	67	**	NY
ZANDONADI, Edson	41	62	67	68	BRA
ZATKO, James	22	43	47	49	PA
ZBRUN, Reinaldo	43	64	70	72	ARG
ZEMEL, Mathew, *Roch*	43	64	70	**	NY
ZETTS, George	17	39	43	44	PA
Z'GRAGGEN, John	32	57	60	61	SWI
ZIJL, Theodore van	19	40	44	44	NEB
ZILIAK, Jerome	19	42	46	47	IN
ZIMMERMAN, Aloysius	18	42	46	47	IA
ZIMMERMAN, Anthony	17	41	45	46	IA
ZIMMERMAN, John	83	06	08	10	GER
ZIMMERMAN, Walter	36	67	71	71	GER
ZIMNY, Augusto	13	37	41	41	POL
ZOK, Joachim	56	77	81	82	POL
ZSENTKO, Chris., *Aloisius*	88	13	20	**	HUN
ZSOLDOS, Imre	31	50	59	60	HUN
ZUENTI, M., *Bellarmin*	00	25	31	**	SWI

Index

accreditation of educational programs, 92–94

Adams, William, 135

Ad gentes (Decree on Mission), 79n.7, 172

Africa, 326–27. *See also* Ghana

African Americans: apostolate to, in northern cities, 196–203; assignment of priests who were, 228–29, 232–39; background of the SVD apostolate to, 180–81; beginnings of the apostolate to, 181–85; beginnings of St. Augustine's Seminary and, 219–22; brothers who were, 231; Christman and, 232; conclusions regarding St. Augustine's and, 247–48; early attempts to establish priesthood of, 206–12; the Ghana mission and, 329; and the lasting effects of St. Augustine's, 240–47; Merigold, Mississippi, and the apostolate to, 185–89; method of the apostolate to, 193–96; 1932 statistics for, 80–81; in the 1920s, 75; opening of St. Augustine's and, 222; ordinations of, at St. Augustine's, 229–31; Pius XI and, 223; the question of an autonomous province for, 239–40; school at Greenville, Mississippi, and, 212–19; status of priests and brothers who were, 223–28; the term discussed, 179n.1; Vicksburg, Mississippi, and the apostolate to, 189–92

Ahner, Eugene, 108

airplanes, 300–303

Akikaze, the, 295–96

Albert, Brother, 166

alcohol, 37–38

Alexandria, Louisiana, 233–34, 235, 236

Alexishafen, New Guinea, 281, 296, 300

altar boys, 123–24

Amabilis, Brother, 42, 116, 161

American Board of Catholic Missions, 75–78

Americanist controversy, 27, 50, 51

Amerikanisches Familienblatt, 71, 112, 113

Amerikanisches Missionsblatt, 112

Andoh, Bishop Dominic, 340

Andrew, Brother, 44

annuities, 86

anthropology, 153, 263–64

Anton, Brother, 285

Antoniutti, Bishop Ildebrando, 96

Anzer, Bishop John Baptist, 8, 16, 129, 160, 250, 251

Apostleship of Prayer movement, 4–5

Appalachia, 351

Appelhans, Bishop Stephen, 299, 302

Archangel, Brother, 161

Arkfeld, Bishop Leo, 299, 301, 302, 303, 307

Arnold, Roger, 149

Artzer, James, 137

Asianization of the Society, 344

Aubry, Hugo, 74, 84–85, 98, 144, 236

Auer, Paul, 318

auf der Heide, Hermann, 182

Augenunger, Father, 287

Augustine, James, 206

Aum Shinrikyo, 348

Baas, Brother Anton. *See* Anton, Brother

Barlage, Henry, 344

Bates, Joseph, 271–72, 318–20

Bauer, Anthony, 329

Bauer, Daniel, 278

Bauman, Theodore, 124

Bay St. Louis, Mississippi. *See* St. Augustine's Seminary

Bechtold, Paul, 109

Becker, Joseph, 127

Beckert, John: construction and financing of Techny and, 38, 41; on establishing a

Beckert, John *(continued)*
    seminary at Techny, 35, 46; the
    Philippines mission and, 314; on the
    press, 112; at Techny, 37
Beckman, Monsignor Francis, 121
Beemster, John, 137
beer, 37–38
belated vocations, 93, 93n.5, 95
Benedict, Brother, 315
Benedict XV, Pope, 75, 113, 213, 225, 264
Benedictines, the, 20–21, 194, 264–65, 266
Benz, William, 67
Berchmans, Brother, 294
Bernarding, George, 290, 290n.12, 298, 300
Best, Mary, 187
Beutener, Klaus, 308
Bill, Peter, 129, 160
Biskupek, Aloysius, 64
Bismarck, 6, 7
blacks. *See* African Americans
Blasczyk, F. X., 68, 315
Blasius, Brother, 41
Blenk, Archbishop James, 209
Bloner, Brother Berchmans. *See*
    Berchmans, Brother
Blum, Nicolaus: on accepting Americans
    as brothers, 44; and the beginning of the
    technical school, 41, 42; cautioning Peil,
    24–25; China missions and, 69; and
    establishing the foundation at Techny,
    30, 31; on financing Techny, 40; mission
    house at Girard and, 66–67; on mission
    to the U.S., 12; New Guinea missions
    and, 282; St. Joseph's Institute and, 66;
    on U.S. markets, 11
Boberg, John, 108, 156
Bockman, Brother Damian. *See* Damian,
    Brother
Bodems, John Baptist, 38, 52, 56–57, 58,
    224
Bohnen, Lawrence, 137
Bomana, New Guinea, 307–8
Bonaparte, Joseph, 95
Bonk, Bernard, 84, 84n.4
Bonzano, Archbishop John, 216
Book of Rules for the Mission Students of
    the American Province of the Society of
    the Divine Word, 134–35
Bordentown, New Jersey, 95–96, 99
Bornemann, Fritz, 4, 21, 130, 160,
    297–98, 355
Bosco, Don, 31
Boston, 73–74

Bourges, Anthony, 229, 236, 239
Bowers, Bishop Joseph, 242, 329, 338,
    340, 350–51
Bowman, John, 188
Brambrink, William, 234
Braun, Matthias, 78, 117, 156
Breckel, Father, 24
Bremmer, David, 183, 184, 186
brothers: accepting Americans as, 43–44;
    African-American, 223–28, 231; in the
    early days at Techny, 36–38; education
    of, 106, 173; the first SVD, 7–8; forma-
    tion of, 165–66; the high school semi-
    naries and, 137–38; integration of, 240;
    Janssen and, 160–61; number of, in
    1932, 80–81; overview of roles of,
    161–65; the press at Techny and, 115;
    priests' relation to, 159–60, 175–76; role
    in building Techny, 41; the SVD press
    and, 118; the technical school and,
    41–43; Vatican II and, 166–68, 173
Bruder, Father, 18
Bruell, Wilhelm, 274, 318
Budenholzer, Frank, 275
Buecker, Theodore, 66
Burgmer, Adolf, 40–41, 67, 69, 71, 78,
    200, 212, 213
Burr, Brother Gary, 201, 324
Burrows, Bill, 308
Bürschen, Father, 68, 323
Busch, Joseph, 137

Caesar, Raymond, 306, 308
Calvin, John, 147
Camacho, Flor, 318–19
Camilleri, Brother Lawrence, 303
Canada, 96–97
Cargo Cult Movements, 309–10
Carmon, Dominic, 201
Cassidy, Thomas, 318
Catholic Church Extension Society, 57
Catholic Mission History (Schmidlin), 156
Catholic Mission Theory (Schmidlin), 156
Catholic Students' Mission Crusade,
    120–22, 154
Catholic Theological Union, 106, 108–10
celibacy, 7, 8, 106, 139
Center for Applied Research in the
    Apostolate (CARA), 104–6
centralization, 75–78, 79
Chanel College, 306
Charles, Brother, 161
Chiang Kai-shek, 257, 260

Chicago, 198–203
China: American SVDs assigned to,
253–56; appointment of Murphy
as rector at Fu Jen University, 267–69;
beginnings of mission to, 250–53; effect
on missions of war and revolution in,
259–63; expulsion of priests from, after
World War I, 68–69; financing of mis-
sions to, 71; founding of Fu Jen
University and, 264–65; mission in
Honan, 79–80; overview of mission to,
249; political events in the early
twentieth century and mission to,
256–59; two missioners sent to, in 1919,
69–70. *See also* Fu Jen University
Chinese Revolution, the, 259–63
Chou En-lai, 273
The Christian Family, 112, 113
Christman, Matthew, 191–92, 212, 216,
218, 226, 232
Christophilda, Sister, 282
Christ the King Seminary, 324
Civil Rights Movement, 193, 241, 243
Clark, Robert, 69–70, 249, 254, 351
Clement, Brother, 116
clericalism, 166
clerical novices, 72, 72n.4
clerics: term discussed, 72n.4
Clerkin, Michael, 294
Cletus, Brother, 337
Cohill, Bishop John, 306
Collyer, Ernie, 353–54
colonialism, 157–58
The Colored Messenger, 115, 213
Columbans, 121n.1
Communism, 257–58, 259–63
Communist Revolution (Chinese), 270–75
community life, 171, 174–76
Conesus, 74, 94, 98, 173
confessors, 135
Congar, Ives, 148
Congo, the, 341–42
Congregation of Saint Joseph, 357
Congregation *Propaganda Fide,* 63, 77,
78, 191
Connors, Joseph, 110, 174
Connors, Paul, 353
Conrad, Brother, 137
Considine, John, 117, 252
constitutions, 8, 166, 174, 176
Copas, Virgil, 306
Cranssen, Anthony, 285
Cross-Cultural Training Program, 352

cults, 309–10
curriculum at seminaries, 145–52
Cyprian of Carthage, 153
Cyril, Brother, 116, 355

Damian, Brother, 337
Dauphine, John, 329
Davis, Cyprian, 198, 207
Decree on Missions (*Ad gentes*), 79n.7, 172
Decree on the Appropriate Renewal of the
Religious Life (*Perfectae caritatis*), 173,
175
de Groot, Nick, 308
de Lange, Francis, 48; on the African-
American priesthood, 211; China
missions and, 71, 254; fund raising and,
79; Maryknoll and, 64–65; and the
mission house at Techny, 45; the mission
office and, 88; overview of work of,
61–62; replacing Peil, 52–53; the
Techny seminary and, 57–58, 62–63, 64
de la Torre, Edicio, 325
Deppe, Anthony, 137
Depression, the, 83–85
D'Escoto, Miguel, 118
Desmond, Bishop Daniel, 233–34, 235–36
Divine Word Airways, 302
Divine Word College, 319
Divine Word Missionaries: choice of the
name, 91–92
Divine Word Missionaries (magazine), 119
Divine Word Publications, 117–19, 352
Doerfler, Brother James. *See* James,
Brother
Dogli, Anastasius, 334n.8
dogmatic theology, 149, 151
domus formata, 171, 171n.2
Donaghey, John, 138, 148, 149, 152, 354
Dooley, Lester, 124–25, 268
Dorish Maru, the, 294, 296–98
Dorsey, John, 191, 208, 217
Douville, Bishop Arthur, 96
Doyle, Bernard, 277
Drescher, Bruno, 71, 143, 204–5, 254
Drexel, Katharine, 181–82, 185, 192
Dries, Angelyn, 51, 63
Driscoll, Daniel, 99
dropouts, 100
Dudink, Edward, 95, 135
Duxbury, Massachusetts, 73

East Troy, Wisconsin, 72–73, 98, 132, 173
Eck, Wilhelm, 355

Eckerman, Felix, 346
Eckert, Joseph, 96, 124, 200–203
Ecumenical Missionary Conference, 120
ecumenism, 108, 308–9
education: accreditation and, 92–94; curriculum at seminaries, 145–52; in the Philippines, 316–23; rationale for work in, 322–23. *See also* high school seminaries; seminaries; *and the names of specific institutions*
Ehr, Donald, 201
Eickenbrock, Bernard, 38, 131
Elder, Bishop William, 207
elderly, apostolate of the, 357–58
electronic media, 352–53
Elsbernd, Alphonse, 327, 328–29, 340
Epworth, Iowa, 94, 97–98, 132, 173, 356–57
Erb, Charles, 125, 242
Esser, Gerard, 147–49
Esser, Mr. *See* Merten, Bernard
Ethnic Communications Outlet, 353
Eugene, Brother, 286–88, 289–90
Evers, Albert, 29

Fabian, Brother, 42, 315
Faikus, Joseph, 96
Farley, Cardinal John, 64, 121
Fecken, Brother Michael. *See* Michael, Brother
Feehan, Patrick, 30
Feifel, Eugene, 269, 270
Felix, Brother, 137
film, 352–53
finances: contributions from the U.S. to the society in Europe, 70–71; the Great Depression and, 83–85; the mission office and, 87–89. *See also* fund raising
Finger, Joseph, 137–38
Fischer, Hermann, 54
Fischer, Joseph: arrival in the U.S., 22; and the controversy over chartering the SVD in Illinois, 34; the Milton interlude and, 25, 26; the move to Shermerville and, 35; overview of work of, 60; on prohibiting alcohol, 37; role in building Techny, 41
Fisher, Bernard, 287, 290–91
Fitzgibbon, William, 269–70
Fitzmaurice, Bishop John, 67
Flaska, Joseph, 344–45
Flierl, Leonhardt, 285
Flinn, Robert, 108, 164
Floresca, Constante, 324
Florian, Albert, 96

Foley, Albert, 188, 207
Ford, Joseph, 124, 354
formation: brothers and, 165–66; at high school seminaries, 132–38; Janssen and, 128–30; Medits and, 130–31; missionary life and, 152–58; the novitiate and, 138–45; overview of, 127–28; the stages and places of SVD, in North America, 131–32; at Techny, 145–52; Vatican II and, 172–76
Francis, Bishop Joseph, 232, 244–47, 356
Franciscans, 251
Franks, Jim, 304
Frederick, Brother, 161
Freedom Crusade, 274–75
freemasonry, 313
Freinademetz, Blessed Joseph, 250–53, 257, 341
Freitag, Anton, 156
Freri, Monsignor Joseph, 68–69
Frey, Gerald, 308
Friedrich, Karl, 210–11, 224–25
Froewis, Monsignor George, 70, 254
Fu Jen magazine, 114
Fu Jen University: the Communist Revolution and, 270–72; decline of, 272–75; founding of, 264–65; Murphy's appointment as rector at, 267–69; after Murphy's death, 269–70; the SVD Catholic Universities Office and, 90, 91; in Taiwan, 276–78; takeover of, 263–64, 265–67
Fumasoni-Biondi, Cardinal Pietro 233
fund raising: changing moods regarding, 89; the mission office and, 87–89; in the 1920s, 79. *See also* finances

Galatius, Brother, 42
Gehring, August, 327, 329
Gerow, Bishop Richard, 233
Gerrish, B. A., 150
Ghana: beginnings of mission to, 327–29; growth of mission to, in the 1940s and 1950s, 334–38; independence of, 338–41; Noser's work in, 329–34
Gier, Wilhelm, 48, 72; the African-American apostolate and, 195–96; China missions and, 254; Glorius and, 144; King (Clifford) and, 256; on the status of African-American priests, 225, 227, 228; St. Augustine's Seminary and, 223
Gilkey, Langdon, 270

Girard, Pennsylvania, 66–67, 87, 99, 132, 173

Glorius, Felix, 132, 139, 143, 330, 333

Glover, John, 301, 302

Gmelch, Andrew, 183, 219

Goertz, Joseph, 268, 269, 318

Gracias, Cardinal Valerian, 346

Greek (language), 133

Greenville, Mississippi, 191, 212–19, 223

Grendel, Joseph, 171; on Africa missions, 327, 328; on assigning African-American priests, 233; Fu Jen University and, 90, 265–66, 267, 268; the mission office and, 88; Noser and, 336; Philippines missions and, 324; on the status of African-American priests, 225, 228

Grosse-Kappenberg, Alois, 96, 170–71, 336

Gruhn, Fred, 69, 70

Grzenia, Edward, 349

Guetzloe, Joseph, 203–4

Guillory, Curtis, 247

Gunn, Bishop John, 192, 212, 215, 216, 219, 222, 224

Haag, Sister Martitia, 294, 297

habits (clothing), 138–39

Hagan, William, 294

Hagspiel, Bruno: on assigning African-American priests, 233, 234–35, 236; books by, 117; the Canadian missions and, 97; Catholic Students' Mission Crusade and, 120, 121–22; China missions and, 254; on decentralization, 78; on an English-language name for the order, 91–92; finances during the Depression and, 84; on first ordinations at St. Augustine's, 229–30; Fu Jen University and, 265, 268; Glorius and, 144; on King (Clifford), 255, 256; magazines and, 112, 113; Maryknoll and, 64; retreats of, 113; on the status of African-American priests, 226–27

Hambach, Lawrence, 345

Hammeke, Hubert, 23

Hammeke, Theodore, 23

Hammeke, Thomas, 181

Hannaher, John, 299

Hatfield, Leslie, 335

Healy, Alexander Sherwood, 206–7

Hecker, Isaac, 50

Heekeren, Henry, 161, 174

Heffels, Gerard, 162, 225–26, 227, 233

Heick, Aloysius: the African-American apostolate and, 184–85, 208; an African-American priesthood and, 211, 212, 213, 215; beginnings at Bay St. Louis and, 219; death of, 226; on the Greenville seminary, 219; Merigold, Mississippi, and, 185–88, 189; Vicksburg, Mississippi, and, 189, 190, 191

Heinemann, Frank, 16

Heinemann, Pauline (Sister Maria), 22

Heisig, James, 348

Henkels, Joseph, 258, 260–61, 269

Henle, Richard, 23, 257

Henninghaus, Bishop Augustine, 67–68, 69, 70, 79

Henry, Brother, 137

Hergesheimer, Michael, 68, 316

Heslin, Bishop Thomas, 183, 189

high school seminaries: CARA study and, 104–5; collapse of, 105–6; formation at, 132–38; in the 1970s, 104–5. *See also specific institutions*

Hitler, Adolf, 254

Hodapp, Cletus, 329

Hodges, Bishop Joseph, 351

Hoenderop, John, 45, 61, 191

Hoff, Henry, 155, 301, 302

Hofstee, Gerard, 345

Hogan, Brother Patrick, 278, 356

Hogan, William, 273

Holthausen, John, 44, 50

Holy Spirit Regional Seminary (New Guinea), 306–8

Homobonus, Brother: arrival of first SVD priest in the U.S. and, 22; early work in America, 18–21; first achievements of, 27–28; on funding for Techny, 39–40; the move to Shermerville and, 35; overview of work of, 59

Honan, China, 79–80, 254–55, 259, 260

Hong Kong, 250

Howard, Clarence, 236

Huber, Mary Taylor, 301

Hugh of St. Victor, 9

Hume, David, 146

Humel, Anthony, 96

Hunter, Robert, 124, 125, 198

Hunter, William, 99

Husslein, Joseph, 121

Ignatius of Loyola, St., 128, 140

inculturation, 308–9

India, 344, 345–47
Indonesia, 61–62, 343–45
integration, 193, 240
Irish, the, 56–57
Isenberg, Monsignor Anthony, 237

Jackson, Mississippi, 191
Jacobi, Paul, 135
Jakob, William, 295
James, Brother, 329, 336
Jansen, Otto, 180
Janser, Peter: an African-American broth-
    erhood and, 224; an African-American
    priesthood and, 215, 216–18, 224, 225;
    on an African-American seminary, 213;
    on the American Board of Catholic
    Missions, 76–77; booklet composed by,
    65; Boston seminary and, 73–74; China
    missions and, 69, 78, 79–80, 249; on
    finances, 71, 72, 73; Girard mission
    house and, 67; India missions and, 345;
    St. Augustine's and, 219, 220–21, 222;
    teaching load of, 64; on the Techny
    seminary, 56, 62, 66
Janssen, Arnold: the African-American
    apostolate and, 179, 182, 183, 184, 185,
    186, 187–88, 189, 191, 209–10; and the
    beginning of the technical school, 41,
    42; biographical sketch of, 3–8; brothers
    and, 43, 44, 160–61; on building a
    mission house at Techny, 44–48; China
    missions and, 250; construction and
    financing of Techny and, 38, 39, 41; and
    the controversy over chartering the SVD
    in Illinois, 34–35; decision-making
    process of, 18; and early problems at
    Techny, 36–38; and establishing the
    foundation at Techny, 30, 31–32, 33;
    fears about the American foundation,
    49–51; formation and, 128–30; the
    future and, 359–60; genesis of idea for
    American mission, 10–11, 12, 13–14;
    Japan missions and, 347; the Milton
    interlude and, 23, 24, 25, 26–27;
    missiology and, 155–56; and the move
    to Techny, 36; New Guinea missions
    and, 281; opening the Techny seminary
    and, 63; Peil and, 21–23, 52–55;
    Philippines missions and, 313–14; on
    the press, 111; on the seminary at
    Techny, 56–59; spiritual legacy of,
    8–10; statement on the opening of the
    North American mission, 36

Janssen, John, 8
Japan, 347–49
Japanese Americans, 203–4
Jeanmard, Bishop Jules, 233, 234, 235, 237
Jerome, Brother, 315–16
Jesuits, the, 128
Jeurgens, Arnold, 67
John XXIII, Pope, 147, 172, 276, 349
Joistens, Hubertus William, 13
Joseph, Brother, 137
Josephites, the, 50, 180, 185, 194, 207–9,
    218
Joyce, Walter, 316, 324
Juanita, Sister, 335
junioriate, the, 99, 99n.6, 100

Kalisz, Raymond, 306
Kamp, Francis, 88–89, 118, 354, 359
Kant, Immanuel, 146, 148
Kap, New Guinea, 306–7, 308n.33
Kaul, Anthony, 23, 24
Kelley, Francis, 75
Kelley, William, 356
Kelty, Charles, 167–68
Kilage, Ignatius, 306
King, Clifford: Catholic Students' Mission
    Crusade and, 120–22; China missions
    and, 71, 154–55, 249; Fu Jen University
    and, 267–68; fund-raising techniques of,
    254–56; kidnapping of, 258; overseas
    training of, 351; personality of, 253–54;
    recollections on being sent to China,
    69–70
King, Martin Luther, Jr., 243
Kirschbaum, Franz, 284, 285, 297, 301
Kisala, Robert, 348
Kist, John, 230, 240
Kitagawa, Joseph, 348
Koetter, Sister Adelaide, 294, 296
Kolping Society, the, 16, 18
Kommoranten, the, 355
Koster, John, 278, 341
Kotrba, Joseph, 294, 295
Kraus, Johann, 160
Krementz, Cardinal Philip, 31
Kretschmer, Albert, 326, 331, 331n.5,
    333n.7
Krick, Brother William. *See* Richard,
    Brother
Krosnicki, Thomas, 356
Krzeminski, Leo, 345
Ku Klux Klan, 188, 231
Kulturkampf, the, 7

Lafayette, Louisiana, 234, 235, 236
laity: the parish mission band and, 124–26; recent developments regarding, 353–56; retreats for, 122–24
Lake Hemlock, New York, 74
Lang, Arnold, 137
language training, 132–33
Latin America, 349–50
Latin language, 48, 132–33, 148
Lauck, Harold, 329
Laurenti, Monsignor Camillus, 224
Leahy, Dan, 286, 287–88, 297
Leahy, Mick, 286, 287–88
Lebbe, Vincent, 264
LeFrois, Bernard, 150
Leisring, Charles, 135
Leonard, Brother, 137
Leonarda, Sister, 44
Leo XIII, Pope, 51
Lesage, Alphonse, 319, 320, 321–22
Lesage, Brother Cletus. *See* Cletus, Brother
Lesage, Emil, 136–37, 136n.4
Lesage, Maurice, 155
Liebner, James, 278
Limbrock, Eberhard, 281, 282–83, 314, 351
The Little Missionary, 113, 119
Little Rock, Arkansas, 191, 192
Liturgical Press, 117
Loechte, August, 62, 84
Lonergan, Bernard, 148
Lörks, Bishop Joseph, 294, 295, 301
Lovasik, Lawrence, 124
Lucian, Brother, 329, 336–37
Luis, Edward, 124
lumina, 140
Luther, Martin, 147
Lutherans, 308
Luzbetak, Louis, 153, 349–50, 356–57
Lynk, Frederick, 112–13

MacArthur, Douglas, 295, 298
Mack, Lawrence, 92, 100–101
Madang, New Guinea, 280–81, 300
magazines: American Board of Catholic Missions and, 77; growth of Society, 112–14; purpose of the Society's, 115–16. *See also specific titles*
Malin, Arthur, 346–47
Malin, Charles, 135
Manion, Arthur, 294, 295, 296
Manning, Mike, 352–53
manualist tradition of scholasticism,

145–46, 148
Mao Tse-tung, 257, 275
Marcos, Ferdinand, 325
Marin, Philip, 229–30
Markert, Francis: on brothers at Techny, 42–43; on Brother Wendelin, 14–15; Catholic Press Month and, 114; deportations from China and, 68; on finances, 71; on the genesis of the American mission, 12; the *Kommoranten* and, 355; magazines and, 112; the media and, 113–14; on Noser, 330–31; as a source of information, 12n.1; on the Techny press, 115–17
Marschall, Albert, 16
Maryknoll: cordial relation between Techny and, 64–65; founding of, 63; in Latin America, 298; the media and, 117; Orbis Books and, 118
Mass stipends, 71, 71n.3
Maximum illud, 75, 213
May, Anthony, 88, 124
Mayer, David, 348
McDonough, John, 269–70
McGee, Harry, 302
McGovern, Thomas, 23–24, 25, 26
McGuinn, Edward, 118
McGurk, Terrence, 137
McHenry, John, 118, 135
McMahon, Vincent, 118
McMillan, Neil, 187, 187n.7
McVinney, Paul, 303
media apostolate, the, 352–53; the founder and, 11, 111–12
Medicare, 358
Medits, Ferdinand, 130–31, 141
Megan, Thomas, 259–63
Meier, Michael, 183, 185–86, 192
Meiners, Joseph, 274
Melanesia. *See* New Guinea
Melanesian Institute for Pastoral and Socio-Economic Service, 309, 310
Melcher, Arthur, 85–86, 87, 99, 264
Merigold, Mississippi, 182–89, 191
Merten, Bernard, 355
Meyer, Joseph. *See* Wendelin, Brother
Michael, Brother, 60
Michel, Charles, 151–52
Mihalic, Frank, 302, 303–5, 306
Milton, Pennsylvania, 23–28
minor seminaries. *See* high school s eminaries
Miramar, 74, 85, 94, 99, 132

missiology, 153, 155–58. *See also* mission studies
Missionaries of the Sacred Heart, 294, 296, 305–7
Missionary Congress (Chicago), 62
Missionary International Vehicular Association, 301, 301n.26
Missionary Sisters of the Holy Spirit of Perpetual Adoration, 323
Missionary Sisters Servants of the Holy Spirit, 215, 282; the African-American apostolate and, 187, 192, 194; the *Dorish Maru* tragedy and, 297; early years at Techny, 44; first member of, 22; founding of, 11; in Ghana, 335; in New Guinea, 294; number of, up to 1909, 22; in the Philippines, 314
Missionary Youth, 119
mission clubs, 154
mission houses: the purpose of, 171–72
mission office, the, 87–89
mission studies, 109–10. *See also* missiology
Modernism, 51
Mooney, Bishop Edward, 74
moral theology, 149–50
Morscheuser, Karl, 289, 290
Mundelein, Cardinal George: the African-American apostolate and, 198–200, 216; the American Board of Catholic Missions and, 76; on assigning African-American priests, 233; on centralization, 78; China missions and, 70
Murawski, Casmir, 135
Murphy, Joseph, 120, 267–69
Murphy, Patrick, 306, 307–8
Musinsky, John, xiii, xiv, 141, 173–74, 176, 333

Nanzan University, 347–48
Nationalist Chinese, 257–58, 260, 261
Nemer, Lawrence, 109–10, 156
New Guinea: the *Akikaze* incident and, 295–96; arrival of the Society in, 280–84; core cultural issues facing Catholics in, 308–11; developing the western highlands mission in, 290–94; the *Dorish Maru* tragedy and, 296–98; general and seminary education in, 303–8; opening of the highlands of, 284–88; overview of mission to, 279–80; postwar mission and, 294–95, 298–303
New Orleans, 241

Newton, Brother Dennis, 356
Nicholas, Brother, 137
Nies, Francis Xavier, 23, 257
Nilles, John, 291
Nkrumah, 339–40
Norbert, Brother, 163–64
Norton, Edward, 94, 318
Noser, Bishop Adolf: on dropouts, 100–101; and elections for superior general, 336; Ghana missions and, 329, 331–35, 338; Glorius and, 144; on high school seminaries, 105–6; New Guinea missions and, 306; at Techny, 329–31
novice masters, 143–45
novitiate, the: description of day-to-day life during, 138–47; dropouts from, in the 1950s, 101; at East Troy, Wisconsin, 72–73; locating, 93–94; in the 1950s, 100; number of participants in, in 1932, 80–81; placed after high school, 132; at Techny, 72
Nowak, Richard, 285

Ochs, Stephen, 180n.3, 181, 207, 229, 241
O'Connell, Cardinal William, 73–74, 221–22
O'Connor, V. O., 104
Oehler, Edgar, 269–70, 273, 318
O-Neh-Da Vineyard and Winery, 74
Orbis Books, 118
ordinations at St. Augustine's Seminary, 229–30
Orians, Brother Lucian. *See* Lucian, Brother
O'Toole, George Barry, 264–65
Otto, Brother, 137
Our Missions, 113, 114
Overseas Training Program, 351–52

pagan babies, 73n.5
``pagans,'' 73n.5, 156
papal infallibility, 7
Pape, Arthur, 354
parish mission band, the, 124–26
parish work, 124–26, 350–51
Pastorelli, Louis, 241
Patzelt, Herman, 88, 226, 233, 234, 236, 237
Paulinus, Brother, 113
Paulist Press, 117
Paulists, the, 50
Paulsen, Alois, 323–24
Paul VI, Pope, 243

Pawlicki, James, 353

Peil, John Baptist: on accepting Americans as brothers, 43, 44; the African-American apostolate and, 179, 182, 184, 185–86, 188–89, 190–91, 193–94; and the beginning of the technical school, 41, 42; beginnings of the African-American priesthood and, 210–11; on building a mission house at Techny, 44–48; construction and financing of Techny and, 38, 39, 40–41; the controversy over chartering the SVD in Illinois, 33–35; and early problems at Techny, 36–38; early work in the U.S., 21–28; and establishing the foundation at Techny, 29–33; and Janssen's fears about the American foundation, 49, 50; Janssen's relation with, 52–55; the move to Shermerville and, 35; and the move to Techny, 36; overview of work of, 60–61

Perfectae caritatis. See Decree on the Appropriate Renewal of the Religious Life

Perry, Bishop Harold R., 230–31, 243–44, 245–47

Perrysburg, Ohio, 97

Peser, Lewis, 265

Peter, Brother, 67

Phan, Peter, 357

Philippines, the: arrival in, 313–14; background of missions to, 312–13; educational work in, 316–23; Malin's work in, 347; overview of SVD work in, 314–15; seminary education and, 323–24; vocations from, 324–25

philosophy, 145–49

piety, 8–10

Pironio, Cardinal, 119

Pisin, Tok, 303–5

Pius IX, Pope, 7

Pius X, Pope, 51, 264

Pius XI, Pope, 113, 223, 237, 263, 266–67

Pius XII, Pope, 113, 147

Placidus, Brother, 41, 43, 67

Plantevigne, John, 208–9

Plutz, Stanley, 315

Poetz, Lawrence, 124

Popp, William, 344, 345

Powell, Elmer, 240

Practice of Christian and Religious Perfection (Rodriguez), 141

prayer, 5, 10

prefects apostolic, 135–37, 250n.1

press, the: the apostolate of the, 111–14; Divine Word Publications and, 117–19; early work of Techny, 65; growth and problems of, at Techny, 114–17. *See also* magazines

Price, Thomas, 65

procurators, 83n.3

Propaganda Fide. See Congregation *Propaganda Fide*

Protestants: in Africa, 327–28; in China, 252, 256–57; establishing the seminary at Techny and, 52; in New Guinea, 299, 308; in the Philippines, 313

Puff, Andreas, 282

Quigley, Archbishop James, 62, 183, 184

Rahmann, Rudolf, 269, 270, 318

Rahner, Karl, 148

Raimondi, Bishop Timoleone, 6, 251

recruitment: the collapse of minor seminaries and, 105; reasons for decline in, 105–6; use of magazines in, 119. *See also* vocations

Reformation, the, 147

Regis, Brother, 161

Reichart, Franz Xavier, 129, 160

Reichelt, Friedrich, 83–84

Reiner, John, Sr., 123

Reinke, Joseph, 21

Reissman, Augustus, 200

renewal chapters, 174

Rentko, Andrew, 135, 350

retreats, 113, 122–24

Reuter, Jakob, 4

Richard, Brother, 95, 161

Richarz, Herman, 48, 72, 112, 113–14, 133, 143

Richarz, Stephan, 131

Riebe, Gary, 247

Riemer, Robert, 348

Rigney, Harold, 271–75, 318, 329, 335

Risse, Roger, 345

Riverside, California, 97

Rodriguez, Alphonsus, 141

Rodriguez, Luis Manuel, 149

Ross, William: on the American Board of Catholic Missions, 76; Dooley and, 125; New Guinea missions and, 283, 284, 285, 286–88, 290–94, 298, 299

Rousseau, Jean-Jacques, 147

Rousseve, Maurice, 229, 232, 236, 238–39

Ruiter, Ivo, 303

Russell, William, 114
Ryan, Andrew, 34
Ryan, William F., 34

Sacred Heart Mission House. *See* Girard,
  Pennsylvania
Sacred Heart Retreatants' League, 123
Salesians, 31
Salois, Victor, 294, 296
San Carlos College, 317–18
Sanders, Ray, 135
San Francisco, 203–4, 205
Sanneh, Lamin, 158
Sao Mensah, Bernard, 334
Schaefer, Joseph, 16, 17, 20
Schäfer, Alphonse, 285, 286–88, 287, 288,
  289, 291, 292
Schäfers, Father, 29–30, 31
Scharper, Philip, 118
Schebesta, Paul, 153
Schilling, Bernard, 300
Schleiermacher, D. F. S., 147
Schleiermann, John, 314
Schmidlin, Joseph, 117, 155, 156–57
Schmidt, Bishop Firmin, 300
Schmidt, Wilhelm, 131, 153, 263, 267
Schmitz, Bartley, 277, 318
Schmitz, Eugene, 345
scholasticism, 146
scholastics, 80–81
Schroeder, Brother Cyril. *See* Cyril,
  Brother
Schu, Father, 252
Schütte, Johannes: on accreditation, 93;
  changes in formation and, 175–76; in
  China, 261, 276; emphasis on overseas
  training, 351; Latin American missions
  and, 349, 350; lay workers and, 356; the
  mission treasurer and, 88; overview of
  thinking of, 170–72; on the press at
  Techny, 116; Vatican II and, 79n.7,
  172–73
Schwager, Friedrich, 155
science, 263–64
seminaries: accreditation of, 92–94;
  curriculum at, 145–52; in New Guinea,
  305–8; in the Philippines, 323–24. *See
  also* high school seminaries; *and the
  names of specific seminaries*
Shadeg, Norbert, 344, 345
Shea, William, 135
Shendill, Joseph, 137
The Shepherd, 119

Sheridan, Robert, 117
Shermerville. *See* Techny (Shermerville)
Simons, Derek, 353
Slattery, John, 207–8
Smith, Vincent, 229, 236, 237
smoking, 38
Social Security, 357–58
Society for the Propagation of the Faith, 77
Society of African Missions, 331
South, the: beginnings of the apostolate in,
  181–82; method of work in, 193–96;
  work in Merigold, Mississippi, 185–89;
  work in Vicksburg, Mississippi, 189–92.
  See also Southern Province, the; *and
  specific places in the South*
Southern Province, the, 239–40. *See also*
  South, the
Spalding, Archbishop Martin, 207
Spellman, Cardinal Francis, 335
The Spiritual Exercises (Ignatius of
  Loyola), 128
spirituality: black, 244–45; Janssen's,
  8–10; Noser's, 332–34; after Vatican II,
  175–76
sports, 134, 142, 154
Stadt Gottes, 111–12
St. Augustine's Seminary: assigning
  priests from, 232–39; beginnings of,
  219–22; changes at, following Vatican
  II, 173; Christman and, 232; conclusions
  regarding, 247–48; construction of, 99;
  the division into three provinces and,
  87; effects of, 240–47; importance of,
  82n.1; length of terms of study at, 132;
  opening of, 222; ordinations at, 229–31;
  Pius XI and, 223
St. Bartholomew's Church (Little Rock),
  191, 193
Steffen, Arnold, 308
Stehle, Aurelius, 265
St. Elizabeth's (Chicago), 197, 200–203
Stenz, George, 254–55
Stephan, George, 201
Steyl: founding the seminary at, 8; printing
  at, 117; U.S. support of, after World War
  I, 71, 71n.3, 72
St. Francis Xavier Mission (San
  Francisco), 203–4
St. Francis Xavier Seminary, 74
Stiller, Brother Homobonus. *See*
  Homobonus, Brother
St. John the Apostle (minor seminary), 306
St. John the Baptist Mission House, 97

St. Joseph's Home, Industrial School for Poor Boys. *See* St. Joseph's Technical School

St. Joseph's Seminary (for belated vocations), 95

St. Joseph's Society of the Sacred Heart for Foreign Missions. *See* Josephites, the

St. Joseph's Technical School: brothers and, 41–43; closing of, 66–67; early problems with, 36–38; naming of, 49; personnel at, 66

St. Michael's Almanac, 112, 113. See also *St. Michaelskalendar*

St. Michaelskalendar, 13, 17, 27, 35, 112. See also *St. Michael's Almanac*

St. Michael's Mission House. *See* Conesus

St. Monica's (Chicago), 198–200

Stoecke, William, 203

Stoll, Eugene, 320–21

St. Peter Chanel College. *See* Chanel College

St. Pierre, Albert, 97

St. Pius X Parish (Nagasaki), 348–49

Strawn, Nicholas, 345

Stritch, Cardinal Samuel, 336

St. Rose of Lima parish, 219, 233

Student Volunteer Movement, 120

Studeny, Robert, 166

St. Vincent's (Latrobe, Pennsylvania), 241, 265

SVD Catholic Universities Office, 89–91

Swift, Francis, 306

Szippl, Richard, 348

Taiwan, 276–78

technical school at Techny. *See* St. Joseph's Technical School

Techny (Shermerville): brothers at, 161–64; changes at, following Vatican II, 173; closing the school of theology at, 106–10; construction and financing of, 38–40; controversy over chartering the SVD in Illinois and, 33–35; cost of running, in 1931–32, 70–71; curriculum at, 145–52; the division into three provinces and, 87; early problems at, 36–38; the elderly and, 357–58; establishing foundation at, 29–33; expansion of seminary at, 71–74; founding a mission home at, 44–48; Glorius and, 144; length of terms of study at, 132; mission clubs and, 154; the move to, 35–36; name change at, 49; opening of seminary

at, 41–43, 62–66; the press at, 114–17; process of approval of mission seminary at, 56–59; recent uses of property at, 358–60

Techny Chimes, 154–55

Techny Land Committee, 359

theology, 149–52

Theophane, Brother, 240

Therese of Lisieux, xii, 333

Thiele, Aloys, 30, 31–33

Third Order of St. Dominic, 130

Thomas à Kempis, 141

Thomas Aquinas, 147, 148

Thottan, Anthony, 164

Thyken, Ralph, 90–91, 264, 270–71, 354

Tien, Cardinal Thomas, 262, 277

Tolton, Augustus, 197–98, 207

Tolton House, 247

ToPaivu, Archbishop Herman, 300n.24, 305

ToVarpin, Benedict, 300, 300n.24

Tropper, William, 286, 287

Tsaohsien, China, 252–53

Tschauder, John, 295

Turbek, Alois, 329

Turner, Thomas Wyatt, 199

Umbras, Thomas, 353

Uncles, Charles Randolph, 207, 208

Upshaw, Mamie, 192

Urban, Brother Joseph, 355

Uroda, Stanley, 357

Valfre, Cardinal, 225

van Baar, Cornelius, 289, 290, 299

van Baar, Engelmundus, 299

van Baar, Monsignor William, 299

Vargo, Edward, 278

Vatican II: on brothers, 106, 164, 166–68; brothers and priests and, 175–76; the Catholic Students' Mission Crusade and, 122; closing of the school of theology at Techny and, 107; formation and, 172–75; *Missionary Youth* and, 119; the new theology and, 170; Schütte's influence at, 78–79n.7; on training for missionary work, 351–52

Vaughan, Herbert, 180

vicars apostolic: term discussed, 250n.1

Vicksburg, Mississippi, 189–92

Vietnam, 344

Vietnamese, the, 356–57

Vincent, Brother, 231

Virginia, Sister, 335

Virtue, Chester, 354

vocations: decline of, 105–6; in the 1940s, 1950s, and 1960s, 94–95, 99–103; retreats and, 123–24

Vormann, Franz, 282

votatio, the, 142

vows, 7–8

Wade, Francis, 229, 236, 237–38

Wagner, Emmanuel, 295

Wagner, Brother Jerome. *See* Jerome, Brother

Wagner, Lawrence, 114, 117

Wagner, Wilbert, 135, 144, 333, 350

Walachy, Joseph, 302

Walcot, Kevin, 304

Walsh, James Anthony, 63, 64

Walsh, Joseph, 354

Wantok (newspaper), 304–5

wantoks (persons), 306–7, 306–7n.32

Washington, D.C., 98

Washington Theological Coalition, 108–9

Webb, Louis. *See* Vincent, Brother

Wegener, Hermann, 8, 44, 48

Welbers, Lambert, 180, 181, 182, 184, 185

Wells, Francis, 236

Wendel, James, 115, 191, 210, 213, 214–15, 217

Wendelin, Brother: the African-American apostolate and, 181–82; arrival in U.S., 3, 14–16, 22; in California, 72; and the controversy over chartering the SVD in Illinois, 34; early work in America, 16–21; and establishing the foundation at Techny, 29; first achievements of, 27–28; the move to Milton, Pennsylvania, and, 23–24; the move to Shermerville, Illinois, and, 35; overview of work of, 59; preparation for American mission, 10–14; on the press, 112; role in building Techny, 41

West Indies, the, 350–51

Weyland, Peter, 283, 315

White, Theodore, 260

Wiener, Bartholomew, 164

Wiener, Carl, 164

Wiesen, Hilbert John, 318, 348–49

Wilson, George, 329

Wiltgen, Ralph, 92, 156, 295n.18

winery, the, 74

Winters, Richard, 341

Wirui Air Services, 302

Wojniak, Edward, 259, 261–62

Wolf, Bishop Francis, 283, 284, 286, 288, 294, 297, 301

World War I, 67–70, 259–63, 269–70

World War II, 82–83, 294–98

Wrockladge, Bernard, 149

Xian, China, 260

Ying, Dr. Vincent, 264–65

Ziliak, Jerome, 345–46

Zimmerman, Aloysius, 201

Zimmermann, Francis, 354